A Handbook of Sustainable Building Design and Engineering

A Handbook of Sustainable Building Design and Engineering

AN INTEGRATED APPROACH TO ENERGY,
HEALTH AND OPERATIONAL PERFORMANCE

Edited by Dejan Mumovic and Mat Santamouris

publishing for a sustainable future
London • Sterling, VA

First published by Earthscan in the UK and USA in 2009

ISBN: 978-1-84407-596-6

Typeset by Domex e-Data, India
Printed and bound in the UK by MPG Books Ltd, Bodmin
Cover design by Yvonne Booth

For a full list of publications please contact:

Earthscan
Dunstan House
14a St Cross St
London, EC1N 8XA, UK
Tel: +44 (0)20 7841 1930
Fax: +44 (0)20 7242 1474
Email: earthinfo@earthscan.co.uk
Web: **www.earthscan.co.uk**

22883 Quicksilver Drive, Sterling, VA 20166-2012, USA

Earthscan publishes in association with the International Institute for Environment and Development

A catalogue record for this book is available from the British Library

Library of Congress Cataloging-in-Publication Data

A handbook of sustainable building design and engineering : an integrated approach to energy, health, and operational performance / edited by Dejan Mumovic and Mat Santamouris.
    p. cm.
  ISBN 978-1-84407-596-6 (hardback)
  1. Sustainable buildings--Design and construction. 2. Buildings--Environmental engineering. 3. Buildings--Performance. I. Mumovic, Dejan. II. Santamouris, M. (Matheos), 1956-
  TH880.H358 2008
  721'.046--dc22
                    2008036286

The paper used for this book is FSC-certified.
FSC (the Forest Stewardship Council) is an
international network to promote responsible
management of the world's forests.

Mixed Sources
Product group from well-managed
forests and other controlled sources
www.fsc.org Cert no. SA-COC-1565
© 1996 Forest Stewardship Council

Contents

PART I – INTRODUCTION TO COMPLEX BUILT ENVIRONMENT SYSTEMS

PART II – ENERGY AND BUILDINGS

PART III – BUILDINGS AND ENVIRONMENT

PART IV – OPERATIONAL PERFORMANCE OF BUILDINGS

28 **CASE STUDY** **Impact of an Energy Refurbishment Programme in Chile:**   401
   More than Energy Savings
Eugenio Collados and Gabriela Armijo
Introduction   401
Background information   403
Design of a prioritized refurbishment programme   409
Potential programmes   418
Conclusions   422

Index   *423*

List of Figures, Tables and Boxes

Figures

Tables

Boxes

List of Contributors

Editors

Dr Dejan Mumovic
Dejan Mumovic is a Lecturer in Environmental Design and Engineering at the Bartlett School of Graduate Studies, University College London. His research interests include the interaction of ventilation, energy use and health in the built environment. Dejan is a co-founder of two specialist groups, CIBSE School Design Group and England affiliate of International Building Performance Simulation Association. He has initiated the development of an online educational database – Low Carbon Buildings Directory.

Professor Mat Santamouris
Mat Santamouris is an Associate Professor of Energy Physics at the University of Athens and Visiting Professor to the School of Architecture, Low Energy Unit at University of North London, UK. His research interests include energy performance of residential and non-domestic buildings, environmental design, passive cooling of urban buildings, bioclimatic architecture and building ventilation. Mat serves on the editorial boards of four major scientific built environment journals.

Contributors

Dr Mags Adams
Mags Adams is a Senior Research Fellow at the University of Salford. Her research interests focus on the theoretical interconnections between sustainability, urban form and individual practice. She has experience of developing and working with innovative methodologies including photo-surveys and soundwalks to highlight sensory experience and to develop research around sensory urbanism.

Hector Altamirano-Medina
Hector Altamirano is an architect with considerable expertise in social housing. He has given lectures at the Universidad Central de Chile and University College London on architectural design, sustainable architecture, and indoor mould. Currently he is working on his doctorate on the control of indoor mould in UK dwellings and on the understanding of outdoor pathogens and buildings.

Professor Gabriela Armijo
Gabriela Armijo is an architect educated at Universidad de Chile and the University of Cambridge. She is Professor and Director of Bioclimatic Laboratory at Universidad Central of Chile with research interest in bioclimatic design in architecture and urban planning. Gabriela is a partner at Ambiente Consultores, a company that provides environmental and energy consulting services to architects.

Professor Godfried Augenbroe
Godfried Augenbroe has a 25-year track record of research and teaching in building performance. He heads the Doctoral Program in Building Technology at Georgia Tech. He has advised more than 20 finished PhD theses in the field, chaired major international conferences, is associate editor of two scientific journals, and has published two books and over one hundred refereed papers.

Dr Mark Barrett
Mark Barrett is Principal Research Fellow at the Bartlett School of Graduate Studies, University College London. He has 30 years of experience in energy and environment analysis modelling as an academic and consultant. He has recently published low emission energy scenarios for 25 EU countries, and a study of emission control and the health impacts of power stations across Europe.

Dr Phillip Biddulph
Phillip Biddulph is a Senior Research Fellow at the Bartlett School of Graduate Studies, University College London. His research interests include physics, modelling, moisture transport and dust mite infestations. He is a very experienced experimental physicist with over 10 years working at the cutting edge of experimental high energy particle physics.

Professor Eugenio Collados

Eugenio Collados trained as a civil engineer at Universidad de Chile and University College London (UCL). He is Professor at Universidad de Santiago and Partner at Ambiente Consultores, a company that provides environmental and energy consulting services to architects, engineers and public bodies in Chile. His research interests include interaction between energy, environment, economics and social issues associated with buildings.

Dr Malcolm Cook

Malcolm Cook is a Reader in Building Performance Modelling at Loughborough University and works in the area of building simulation and low-energy building design. His research focuses on the use of computational fluid dynamics and dynamic thermal simulation programmes for modelling natural ventilation in large non-domestic buildings. Malcolm is secretary for the CIBSE Natural Ventilation Group and Chairman of the England affiliate of the International Building Performance Simulation Association (IBPSA).

Dr Stefano Paolo Corgnati

Stefano Paolo Corgnati is Assistant Professor at the Faculty of Architecture and Research Associate at the Department of Energy of Turin Polytechnic. He is a member of TEBE research group where he develops research activity mainly in the sectors of rational use of energy in buildings and indoor environmental quality.

Professor Vincenzo Corrado

Vincenzo Corrado is an Associate Professor in Building Physics and Building Services at the Politecnico di Torino. His research interest includes the following fields: indoor environmental engineering, building thermal physics, HVAC systems, building energy efficiency, and environmental acoustics. The main research activity focuses on the use of dynamic thermal simulation, on uncertainty and sensitivity analyses, and on the development and validation of simplified models for building energy and environment assessment.

Dr David Crowther

David Crowther is Senior Research Associate at the Martin Centre, University of Cambridge. His research interests include indoor air quality and health in buildings, with a particular focus on house dust mites and allergies. He has been an Expert Advisor and contributor to the forthcoming WHO Report on Quantifying Disease from Inadequate Housing, and to the WHO Report on Urban Pests and Health.

Professor Michael Davies

Mike Davies is Professor of Building Physics and Environment at the Bartlett, University College London (UCL). His research interests lie in the provision of healthy and comfortable environments with minimum energy use, including appropriate ventilation and indoor air quality. Mike manages the UCL components of research projects being undertaken for the UK Department of Communities and Local Government (Sustainable Buildings Division). These research projects contribute to the development of the Building Regulations (England and Wales), in particular Part F and L, which deal with ventilation and energy.

Dr Christina Diakaki

Christina Diakaki is a Research Associate of the Technical University of Crete and Adjunct Professor in the Technological Educational Institute of Crete, Greece. Her research interests include decision and data analysis, operations research, optimization, simulation, and quality control with applications in the fields of transportation and the environment.

Dr Darko Goričanec

Darko Goričanec is Assistant Professor at the Faculty of Chemistry and Chemical Engineering at the University of Maribor, Slovenia. His research interests include: energy markets, energy efficiency in buildings, renewable energy sources, heating systems and energy management systems. Darko is a member of 5 WSEAS Scientific Committees and has published over 140 refereed papers.

Dr Barbara Hart

Barbara Hart, formerly Reader in Applied Zoology and Visiting Research Fellow at the Royal Agricultural College, is an experienced acarologist, internationally recognized for her experimental work on house dust mites and mite allergens – which she has been researching for over 20 years.

Professor Hugo Hens

Hugo Hens is Professor at the Department of Civil Engineering, Catholic University of Leuven, Belgium. His research expertise includes combined heat, air and moisture transport in building elements and in buildings, performance-based design and evaluation of building elements, sustainable energy use in buildings, and low-energy buildings. He is internationally renowned as a leading authority in building physics. He is also ASHRAE Fellow.

Sung Hong

Sung Hong is a researcher at the Bartlett School of Graduate Studies, University College London. His research interest is in investigating the impact of residential energy efficient retrofit measures on indoor temperature, thermal comfort and fuel consumption.

Sung Min Hong

Sung Min is a building physicist with an interest in sustainable building design and engineering. His education included degrees in building science from Victoria University of Wellington (New Zealand) and environmental design and engineering from the Bartlett, University College London. His research interest focuses on operational performance of advanced naturally and mixed-mode ventilated buildings.

Dr David Johnston

David Johnston is a Reader in the School of the Built Environment, Leeds Metropolitan University. Work undertaken in the field of energy efficient housing has included theoretical and strategic explorations of climate change targets and their implications for the design and management of the built environment, detailed empirical work on the potential for carbon emission reductions in new and existing housing.

Miroslava Kavgic

Miroslava Kavgic is a mechanical engineer by background. She has been involved in researching indoor air quality, thermal comfort, and socio-technical issues in energy efficiency related to building stocks. Her PhD work is focusing on the development of a bottom-up energy model and optimization of carbon reduction strategies for a housing stock in Eastern Europe.

Dr Denia Kolokotsa

Denia Kolokotsa is an Assistant Professor in the Department of Natural Resources and Environment of the Technological Educational Institute of Crete. Her

research interests include distributed energy management systems, artificial intelligence (fuzzy logic, neural networks and genetic algorithms), building automation, energy efficiency in buildings, and solar energy.

Professor Djordje Kozic

Djordje Kozic is Professor of Thermodynamics and Head of the Department of Thermomechanics at the Faculty of Mechanical Engineering, University of Belgrade. Apart from theoretical thermodynamics, his research include operational performance of heat pumps, and the evolution of design through many analogies that have been made between the evolution of organisms and the human production of engineering systems components.

Professor Jurij Krope

Jurij Krope is Vice Dean of the Faculty of Chemistry and Chemical Engineering at the University of Maribor. He is Head of the Laboratory for Thermoenergetic and Power Engineering Research Group. He is an Honorary Fellow of the Hungarian Scientific Society for Buildings. Jurij has published more than 230 papers in international journals and conference proceedings.

Dr Jarek Kurnitski

Jarek Kurnitski is a REHVA- and SCANVAC-awarded scientist leading the research group at Helsinki University of Technology, Finland. Jarek has actively participated in the working groups of the European Committee for Standardization (CEN) to develop European standards for implementation of the Energy Performance in Buildings Directive, as regards indoor climate and ventilation. His list of publications includes about 180 items.

Thomas Lakkas

Thomas Lakkas is a practising architect based in London. His education included degrees in architecture from the Faculty of Architecture, Aristotle University of Thessaloniki, Greece, and environmental design and engineering from the Bartlett, University College London. His research interest focuses on sustainable cooling of city centre buildings.

Dr Susan Lee

Susan Lee is a Research Assistant in the School of Architecture, University of Sheffield. Her research interests include the environmental impact of climate change and its effects on the natural world and the urban environment. Her current research for the SCORCHIO (Sustainable Cities: Options for Responding to Climate Change Impacts and Outcomes) project focuses on the urban heat island effects of Sheffield and adaptation options for cities with a changing climate.

Professor Iro Livada

Iro Livada is an Associate Professor of Environmental Physics at the Physics Department of the University of Athens, Greece. Her scientific activities are focused on urban environment and air pollution, climatology (with emphasis on synoptic meteorology and hydrometeorology), renewable energy sources and implementation of statistic models on environmental and climatologic studies. She has much experience teaching applied physics and mathematics, and has participated in many national and international research programmes and conferences. She is the author of many university publications and scientific papers published in international scientific journals.

Dr James Milner

James Milner is a Research Fellow at the Bartlett School of Graduate Studies, University College London. His research interests include ambient and indoor air pollution, airflow modelling, the urban heat island effect and the use of remote sensing data to study urban environmental issues. His previous research at Imperial College London focused on interactions between outdoor and indoor air pollutants in urban areas.

Gemma Moore

Gemma Moore is a Research Fellow at The Bartlett School of Graduate Studies, University College London. Her research interests focus upon urban sustainability and environmental quality, particularly understanding the relationships between people, the built environment and decision-making processes.

Dr Katerina Niachou

Katerina Niachou is a Research Associate at the Department of Physics, University of Athens. Her interests include monitoring of natural, hybrid and mechanical ventilation systems in urban street canyons, and modelling of airflow within the complex configuration of urban street canyons.

Professor Tadj Oreszczyn

Tadj Oreszczyn is Professor of Energy and Environment and Head of the Bartlett School of Graduate Studies, University College London. A physicist by background he has been involved in researching energy efficient buildings since 1979. He has directed many large multidisciplinary research projects into energy and health, socio-technical issues in energy efficiency and moisture-related problems in buildings.

Dr Birgit Painter

Birgit Painter (née Krausse) is a Research Fellow at the Institute of Energy and Sustainable Development at De Montfort University, Leicester, UK. Her research interests lie in the performance analysis of low-energy buildings. She has been investigating advanced naturally ventilated buildings in terms of their thermal performance and air quality as well as building occupants' visual and thermal comfort.

John Palmer

John Palmer is Director of Building Research at Faber Maunsell. He has been researching the built environment for 30 years. His research has mainly focused on the energy and indoor environmental performance of buildings in service of the occupants' needs. John has written numerous technical papers and articles and is currently the Chairman of the CIBSE School Design Group.

Ayub Pathan

Ayub Pathan is a Research Associate at the Bartlett School of Graduate Studies, University College London. His general research interest focuses on the energy consumption in UK domestic buildings. More specifically, his research aims to understand how 'socio-technical' issues like built form, its servicing systems and human behaviour working together affect energy consumption in domestic buildings.

Professor Alan Penn

Alan Penn is Professor of Architectural and Urban Computing at the Bartlett School of Graduate Studies, University College London, and Director of the VR Centre for the Built Environment. His research focuses on understanding the way that the design of the built environment affects the patterns of social and economic behaviour of organizations and communities. Alan is a founding director of Space Syntax Ltd, a UCL knowledge transfer spin-out company.

Irini Perdikogianni

Irini Perdikogianni is a registered architect engineer with experience in practice. In the VivaCity2020 project Irini was the main UCL Research Fellow involved in developing methods to bring together quantitative analysis of spatial structure of diverse and dense urban areas with qualitative data on individuals' experience of those areas as 'places'. Irini joined Space Syntax, a UCL knowledge transfer spin-out company, in 2006 as a Research Consultant.

Dr Stephen Pretlove

Stephen Pretlove is a Reader in Architectural Science and Technology at the Faculty of Art, Design and Architecture, University of Kingston. His research interests include energy efficiency, indoor air quality and health. His research work concentrates on the hygrothermal modelling of environments in buildings and the impact that these environments have on the risk of micro-organisms, such as mites and moulds developing.

Dr Ian Ridley

Ian Ridley is a Lecturer in Environmental Design and Engineering at the Bartlett, University College London. He has a background in physics and instrumentation; his PhD investigated the performance of super-insulated low-energy social housing in the UK. Current research interests include the interaction of ventilation, moisture, energy use and health in the built environment and the application and development of building simulation tools.

Dr Glenis Scadding

Glenis Scadding is a Consultant Allergist and Rhinologist at the Royal National Throat Nose & Ear Hospital in London. She is Secretary and President-Elect of the British Society for Allergy and Clinical Immunology, and Chair of the ENT Section of the European Academy of Allergology and Clinical Immunology.

Mark Schroeder

Mark Schroeder is a Researcher in Energy and Building Science at the Bartlett School of Graduate Studies, University College London. His research interest is in the area of energy and environmental performance of residential buildings, as well as energy policy-related research. He is involved in desk and field studies evaluating the effectiveness and the efficiency of European Union Energy Policy, particularly in the UK and Germany.

Professor Emeritus Olli Seppänen

Olli Seppänen is the Secretary General of the Federation of European Heating and Air-conditioning Association (REHVA). He was Director of the Institute of Heating, Ventilating and Air Conditioning at Helsinki University of Technology, Finland, 1982–2008. His multidisciplinary research group has carried out numerous field studies with simultaneous measurements of building performance, energy use, human responses and indoor environment.

Professor Steve Sharples

Steve Sharples is Head of Environmental Design and Sustainability in the School of Architecture, University of Sheffield. His research focuses on sustainable urban environments, including the possible impacts that climate change may have on those environments. Current projects are using physical monitoring and computer modelling to investigate adaptation strategies for cities and the potential role of urban rivers in sustainable environmental design.

Professor Alan Short

Alan Short is the Professor of Architecture at Cambridge University and Principal at Short & Associates Architects. He was educated at Cambridge and Harvard Universities and was a partner in Edward Cullinan Architects on graduation for six years. He was Dean of Art and Design at De Montfort University 1998–2001, and a member of the senior executive. He continues to combine innovative practice with interdisciplinary academic research and teaching.

Professor Philip Steadman

Philip Steadman is Professor of Urban and Built Form Studies at the Bartlett, University College London (UCL). He trained as an architect, and has taught at the University of Cambridge and the Open University. Phillip has contributed to exhibitions, films and books on perspective geometry and the history of art. Vermeer's Camera is the product of 20 years' fascination with the Dutch painter.

Professor Zarko Stevanovic

Zarko Stevanovic is Professor in Research at the Institute of Nuclear Sciences – Vinca, University of Belgrade, and Visiting Professor at the Faculty of Mechanical Engineering, University of Nis, Serbia. His research interest focuses on numerical and experimental investigation of turbulent fluid flow, heat and mass transfer, applied computational fluid dynamics in the built environment, fire risk evaluation and wind power assessment.

Dr Alex Summerfield

Alex Summerfield holds an RCUK academic fellowship at the Bartlett School of Graduate Studies, University College London. He is pioneering a new area of building science described as *building epidemiology* that adopts some of the approaches and methods from public health research to investigate the dynamic interactions between occupants and buildings, or socio-technical factors that influence energy use.

Dr Marcella Ucci

Marcella Ucci is a Lecturer in Facility and Environment Management at the Bartlett School of Graduate Studies, University College London. Her research interests include facility and environment management, air quality and health within buildings, and energy efficiency. Marcella's research includes testing a combined hygrothermal population model which can predict how changes in occupant behaviour, building design and building management can impact on house dust mite infestations.

Ian Ward

Ian Ward is a Reader in the School of Architecture, University of Sheffield. His research interests lie in the field of energy efficient design of buildings, focusing on minimizing the demand for heating and cooling systems through the design of the fabric and ventilation strategies. He was the Immediate Past Chairman of the England affiliate of the International Building Performance Simulation Association (IBPSA).

Dr Pawel Wargocki

Pawel Wargocki is the Associate Research Professor at the International Centre for Indoor Environment and Energy, Technical University of Denmark and a Vice-President for Research in the International Society of Indoor Air Quality and Climate. Pawel has carried out numerous laboratory and field experiments on the effects of indoor air pollution and ventilation on prevalence of health symptoms, perceived air quality and performance of office work by adults and schoolwork by children.

Dr Pieter de Wilde

Dr de Wilde is a Lecturer with the Environmental Building Group at the School of Engineering, University of Plymouth. He specializes in building physics and building performance simulation, with an emphasis on thermal aspects. His doctoral research focused on the uptake of energy simulation tools in the building services and engineering community. Pieter is Secretary of the England affiliate of the International Building Performance Simulation Association (IBPSA).

Toby Wilkinson

Toby Wilkinson, formerly a research associate at Cambridge University and researcher at the Medical Entomology Centre, is an entomologist with extensive experience in house dust mite physiology and hygrothermal behaviours.

Oliver Wilton

Oliver Wilton is a practising architect based in Brighton who has worked on a wide range of projects including a number of award-winning low-energy designs, for practices including Studio E Architects and Foster and Partners. He has been involved in a range of research projects including major EU-funded research into passive downdraught evaporative cooling while working as an environmental consultant at Brian Ford and Associates. Oliver has taught at the University of Cambridge, University of East London and the Bartlett (UCL).

Preface

In the European Union, the issue of carbon has risen to the top of the political agenda. The current aspiration is to provide zero carbon buildings in the foreseeable future, which might prove to be more challenging then initially anticipated. Although energy is the dominant factor due to its role in tackling the most urgent sustainability issue – climate change – some of the other equally important issues concerning sustainable building design and engineering have also been addressed in this book:

- health and well-being (i.e. the provision of acceptable thermal comfort for occupants and good indoor air quality while maintaining adequate (day)lighting and indoor ambient noise levels);
- adaptability to climate change (i.e. improving the capacity of buildings to operate successfully under various climate change scenarios);
- operational performance of buildings (i.e. post-occupancy evaluation of various aspects of building design).

All of these challenges cross the boundaries of traditional disciplines and professional routes. The next generation of professionals will require an ability to work more closely with different disciplines and professionals if these challenges are to be met. The subjects covered and the depth to which they are analysed are more than sufficient to meet various syllabus requirements of undergraduate and multidisciplinary postgraduate courses in building services engineering, architecture and facility management. Furthermore, the aim of this book is to challenge the 'silo mentality' approach to building design, while promoting awareness of the technical options available to engineers and architects and their suitability for various building-related applications. As such, this book is essential reading for both young and experienced professionals looking to broaden their knowledge.

We hope that you will find this book very useful.

Dr Dejan Mumovic, University College London, UK
Dr Mat Santamouris, University of Athens, Greece
September 2008

List of Acronyms and Abbreviations

a	annum
AC	alternate current
ACH	air changes per hour
ACLCA	American Centre for Life Cycle Assessment
AHU	air handling unit
ARD	acute respiratory diseases
ASHRAE	American Society of Heating, Refrigerating and Air-Conditioning Engineers
AQCV	air quality-controlled ventilation
AQMA	air quality management area
ARD	acute respiratory diseases
BECO	German Building Energy Conservation Ordinances
BEMS	Building Energy Management System
BMS	Building Management System(s)
BRE	Building Research Establishment
BREDEM	Building Research Establishment's Domestic Energy Model
BREHOMES	Building Research Establishment's Housing Model for Energy Studies
°C	degrees Celsius
C	carbon
CAD	computer-assisted design
CAV	constant air volume
CEH	critical equilibrium humidity
CENMA	National Centre for the Environment, Chile
CFC	chlorofluorocarbon
CFD	computational fluid dynamic(s)
CFL	compact fluorescent light bulb
CHP	combined heat and power
CI	confidence interval
CIBSE	Chartered Institution of Building Services Engineers
clo	average clothing
cm	centimetre
CML	Centre of Environmental Science (Leiden University, The Netherlands)
CNE	National Energy Commission, Chile
CO	carbon monoxide
CO_2	carbon dioxide
CONAMA	National Commission of the Environment (Chile)
COP	coefficient of performance
dB(A)	decibel (A scale)
DBT	dry bulb temperature
DC	direct current
DD	degree day(s)
DECARB	Domestic Energy and Carbon Dioxide Model

Defra	UK Department for Environment, Food and Rural Affairs
DF	*Dermatophagoides farinae*
DoE	UK Department of the Environment
DP	*Dermatophagoides pteronyssinus*
DSY	design summer year
ECBCS	Energy Conservation in Buildings and Community Systems Programme
EE	energy efficiency
ELCD	European Reference Life Cycle Data System
EM	*Euroglyphus maynei*
EMPD	effective moisture penetration depth model
ENHR	European Network for Housing Research
EPA	US Environmental Protection Agency; *also* Energy Performance Assessment Project
EPBD	Energy Performance of Buildings Directive
EPSRC	Engineering and Physical Sciences Research Council
ER	escalation rate of prices, in % per year
EST	Energy Saving Trust
EU	European Union
°F	degrees Fahrenheit
g	gram
GDP	gross domestic product
GIS	geographical information system
GSHP	ground source heat pump
HDM	house dust mite(s)
HDPE	high-density polyethylene
HVAC	heating, ventilating and air conditioning
H/W	height : width ratio
IAQ	indoor air quality
IEA	International Energy Agency
IEQ	indoor environmental quality
IESD	Institute of Energy and Sustainable Development
I/O ratio	indoor : outdoor ratio
IR	infrared
ISO	International Organization for Standardization
J	joule
K	Kelvin
KPI	key performance indicator
L	litre
LCA	life cycle analysis/life cycle assessment
LCC	life cycle costing
LCI	life cycle inventory analysis
LCIA	life cycle impact assessment
LCM	life cycle management
LCS	life cycle sustainability assessment
LEB	low-energy house
LECI	London Energy and CO_2 Emission Inventory

LED	light-emitting diode
L/H	length : height ratio
LPG	liquefied propane gas
LSHTM	London School of Hygiene and Tropical Medicine
LUCID	The Development of a Local Urban Climate Model and Its Application to the Intelligent Design of Cities
LZC	low and zero carbon
m	metre
MPI	Mite Population Index
MRC	Medical Research Council
MSI	mould severity index
n	total sample population size
NGO	non-governmental organization
NH	northern hemisphere
NHBC	National House Builders Confederation
NMVOC	non-methane volatile organic compound
N_2O	nitrous oxide
NO	nitric oxide
NO_2	nitrogen dioxide
NOx	nitrogen oxide
NOKFOS	nobody knows for sure principle
NPL	neutral pressure level
NPV	net present value
O_3	ozone
OSB	oriented strand board
Pa	Pascal
PAH	polynuclear aromatic hydrocarbon
PCM	phase-change material
PDA	Environmental Pollution Abatement Programme
PEB	passive house
PI	performance index/performance indicator
PM	particulate matter
PM_{10}	particulate matter with a diameter less than or equal to 10 microns (micrometres)
PMV	predicted mean vote
POE	post-occupancy evaluation
ppb	parts per billion
PPD	predicted percentage of dissatisfied
PPEE	Programa País Eficiencia Energética
ppm	parts per million
PROBE	Post-Occupancy Review of Buildings and their Engineering
PSV	passive stack ventilation
PTEAM	Particle Total Exposure Assessment Methodology Study
PUrE Intrawise	Pollutants in the Urban Environment: An Integrated Framework for Improving Sustainability of the Indoor Environment
PV	photovoltaic(s)

PVC	polymer vinyl chloride
RCEP	Royal Commission on Environmental Pollution
R&D	research and development
REPA	resource and environmental profile analysis
RH	relative humidity
RSP	respirable suspended particulate
s	second
SAP	Standard Assessment Procedure (UK)
SARS	severe acute respiratory syndrome
SBS	sick building syndrome
SCORCHIO	Sustainable Cities: Options for Responding to Climate Change Impacts and Outcomes
SETAC	Society of Environmental Toxicology and Chemistry
SH	southern hemisphere
Sirii	Swedish Industrial Research Institutes' Initiative
SO_2	sulphur dioxide
SO_x	sulphur oxide
SOA	super output area
SPM	suspended particulate matter
SSEES	School of Slavonic and East European Studies
SUDS	sustainable urban drainage systems
SUE	Sustainable Urban Environments consortium
t	metric tonne
TABS	thermally activated building system(s)
TBP	total building performance
TC	thermal comfort
TLV	threshold limit value
TRY	test reference year
TVOC	total volatile organic compounds
UCL	University College London
UETP-EEE	University–Enterprise Training Partnership in Environmental Engineering Education
UFP	ultra-fine particle
UHI	urban heat island
UK	United Kingdom
UNEP	United Nations Environment Programme
US	United States
UV	ultraviolet
VAT	value-added tax
VAV	variable air volume
VOC	volatile organic compound
VPX	vapour pressure excess
VROM-DGM	Ministry of Housing, Spatial Planning and the Environment, The Netherlands
W	watt
WHO	World Health Organization
yr	year

SI prefixes used in this book

n	nano	$(\times 10^{-9})$
μ	micro	$(\times 10^{-6})$
m	milli	$(\times 10^{-3})$
c	centi	$(\times 10^{-2})$
k	kilo	$(\times 10^{3})$
M	mega	$(\times 10^{6})$
G	giga	$(\times 10^{9})$

Part I

INTRODUCTION TO COMPLEX BUILT ENVIRONMENT SYSTEMS

Introduction: Setting the Scene

Dejan Mumovic and Mat Santamouris

The aim of this introduction is twofold:

1   Set the scene and show that each building with its surrounding represents a complex built environment system.
2   Highlight that sustainable building design and engineering requires an integrated approach to energy, health and the operational performance of buildings.

It was Winston Churchill who once famously remarked that: 'We make our buildings, and afterwards they make us.' For example, in the case of university campuses built during the 19th century, it is absolutely conceivable that in the minds of the architects there was a link between outward expressions of grandeur and the importance of the learning that was going on within. One of the many examples could be the main University College London (UCL) building designed by William Wilkins, a leading architect of the Greek Revival in England (see Figure I.I.1). With steps leading up to an enormous Corinthian portico reminiscent of the British Museum and a dome behind, this building expressed the underlying character and value system fostered by UCL at that time.

Designing buildings in order to make some kind of statement is as important today as ever before. However, instead of grand architectural gestures, the new generation of buildings will have to show the extent to which both the client and, more importantly, the government (through standards and building regulations) take seriously the commitment to transform each of our countries into low carbon economies.

Within just a few hundred metres of the previously mentioned Wilkins building lies a relatively new addition to the UCL campus – the School of Slavonic and East European Studies (see Figure I.I.2). The client (UCL) required a low-energy, naturally ventilated and naturally lit building with low cost in use. Partially due to the reduced summer night cooling potential caused by the London urban heat island, and partially because the UK design guidelines required the use of a near-extreme weather year for the design of naturally ventilated buildings, this building designed by award-winning architects Short & Associates (Short et al, 2004) employed passive downdraught cooling operating from the top of a central well (see Chapter 20 on sustainable cooling techniques for more details). As the world's first passive downdraught-cooled public building in a city centre, theoretically speaking, it employs an extremely energy efficient way of maintaining comfort within the urban heat island. It also demonstrates the UCL commitment to reduce the carbon footprint of its own buildings.

This example indicates that clients increasingly require building professionals to provide advice on sustainability. Many large organizations, such as UCL in this case, have been developing sustainability commitments in an attempt to become 'socially responsible'. Some of the large organizations have set up objectives and targets relating to measurable environmental performance concerning issues such as waste, water consumption and carbon emission.

However, the major driver to considerable change in the construction and refurbishment of buildings is still government commitment to sustainability issues. For example, in the UK, changes are implemented through various mechanisms such as:

- *Building Regulations (England, Wales and Northern Ireland) or Building Standards (Scotland).* Part L (Energy) of the Building Regulations is concerned with the prevention of carbon emission from buildings. In the recent document on future development of the Building Regulations for England and Wales (DCLG, 2007), it has been predicted that until 2013 the standard is likely to

Figure I.I.1 *Wilkins building*

continue to be set with reference to the sources of emission, such as space heating, water heating and lighting contained in the 2006 Building Regulations Part L (Energy) with the option of adopting low and zero carbon (LZC) technologies. The step to zero carbon in 2016 is likely to include emissions from other sources (principally electrical

Figure I.I.2 *School of Slavonic and East European Studies*

appliances), which would result in the need for significant renewable generation capacity as well as other LZC systems.

- *Energy Performance of Buildings Directive.* This European Union (EU) directive requires buildings to obtain two energy ratings: an operational rating and an asset rating (EU, 2002). It also requires public buildings to display their certificates showing the energy efficiency of the building and requiring inspections for air-conditioning systems. Furthermore, the member states have to ensure that meters and systems measure customers' actual energy consumption both accurately and frequently. This might result in the increased use of smart meters that provide frequent or real-time information on actual energy consumption.

- *Climate Change Bill.* The UK has become the first country to set legally binding targets to reduce carbon emissions by 60 per cent by 2050. The bill introduces 'carbon budgets', which will be set every five years that cap emissions, and promotes greater energy efficiency with more consumers generating their own energy. Furthermore, it introduces a new statutory body, the Committee on Climate Change, to provide expert advice and guidance to government on achieving its targets.

- *Local planning policies.* In recent times, local government in London has driven a more progressive carbon agenda through its planning process than the UK government through its regulations. To stabilize the global carbon emissions at 450 parts per million (ppm) on a contraction and convergence basis means that London has to limit the total amount of carbon dioxide that Londoners produce between now and 2025 to about 600 million tonnes (Greater London Authority, 2007). This implies a target of stabilizing London and the UK's emissions at 60 per cent below 1990 levels by 2025. Achieving this reduction will be extremely challenging, realistically requiring the establishment of a carbon pricing system and further EU and UK legislation. The current *London Plan* (Greater London Authority, 2008) requires new developments to make the fullest contribution to the mitigation of, and adaptation to, climate change by incorporating energy efficiency and renewable energy measures, targeting, in particular, heating and cooling systems within developments. Developments are expected to reduce their energy needs in the first instance and then supply that energy efficiently with a proportion from renewable sources.

To complicate the issue further, the buildings are often complex bespoke systems that are difficult to control, with little feedback available on their real operation and actual performance. Evidence to date suggests the gap between 'as designed' and 'in use' performance can be very large (Bordass et al, 2001). This has considerable implications for the previously mentioned regulatory programme as the closer standards get to zero carbon the more important the gap will become. The implications of this for the required research effort over the coming years are considerable since building professionals must not only select new technology at the design stage (e.g. opting for electrically driven heat pumps instead of low-temperature water heating systems), but also ensure that a huge change in construction practices (i.e. improved airtightness, thermal bridging, etc.) takes place (DCLG, 2007). This presents a considerable challenge in the wide-ranging implications for all parts of the industry and its supply chains.

Even if the building engineering community had the answers on all technical issues, a building may be built to the most advanced sustainable standards, but if the occupants are not using it in a sustainable way, then the benefits may not be apparent. For example, it is very likely that in the next decade electrically driven heat pumps will provide the lowest carbon-emitting space heating in the UK, while also providing cooling to prevent summertime overheating. However, the increased use of comfort cooling by occupants may mean that heat pumps provide no net reduction in carbon emissions. Therefore, the time has come when we need to engage the building occupants, owners and facility managers in operating their buildings in a sustainable and more environmentally responsible way.

The importance of the facility manager in ensuring a building's services are used to their optimum cannot be overemphasized. Working on an extensive study on winter air quality, thermal comfort and acoustic performance of newly built secondary schools in England (Mumovic et al, 2008), one of the editors has attempted to provide an insight into the attitude of facility managers, teachers and pupils regarding the ventilation performance in classrooms. Almost 50 per cent of schools have been equipped with state-of-the-art Building Management Systems (BMS), providing them with an opportunity to balance energy consumption and ventilation requirements to some extent. However, in the opinions of the research team, none of the facility managers or the caretakers were fully conversant with the BMS.

This raises an important issue: training the relevant people (at least caretakers and facility managers) how to use, in this specific case, the ventilation system effectively. The teachers also did not receive any information on how to use the ventilation systems most appropriately. The information on the building services systems, including logbooks, was usually 'buried' within dozens of thick folders, and even then included no guidelines about how to get the most out of the system.

Even at this stage it is obvious that buildings are actually complex built environment systems. However, there is more. Although building occupants are not passive recipients of the indoor/outdoor thermal environment, but play an active role in creating their thermal environment by behavioural adjustments such as adjusting clothing and rescheduling activities (van Hoof, 2008), nevertheless, living in high-density urban areas, such as London, may be an important risk factor for heat-related mortality and morbidity. For example, the effects of the 2003 heat wave were greatest in London and many of the summer excess deaths that occurred during the August heat wave event may be attributable to the urban heat island effect (Greater London Authority, 2007). Furthermore, recent studies have shown that the costs of poor indoor environment for the employer, the building owner and for society as a whole are often considerably higher than the cost of the energy used in the same building. It has also been shown that good indoor environmental quality can improve overall work and learning performance, while reducing absenteeism (see Chapter 14 for more details). This has led to the development of another EU standard: pr EN 15251, Indoor Environmental Input Parameters for Design and Assessment of Energy Performance of Buildings Addressing Indoor Air Quality, Thermal Environment, Lighting and Acoustics. This standard is applicable mainly in non-industrial buildings where the criteria for indoor environment are set by human occupancy and the production or process does not have a major impact on indoor environment.

After reading this brief introduction, we hope that you are convinced that sustainable building design and engineering require an integrated approach to energy, health and the operational performance of buildings. The following chapter will attempt to answer how to actually create sustainable, healthy and viable communities with positive neighbourhood identities. Of significant importance to this book, it takes architectural and building service engineers out of their comfort zone and into the deep waters of urban planning and social geography: highly recommended.

References

Bordass, W., Cohen, R., Standeven, M. and Leaman, A. (2001) 'Assessing building performance in use 3: Energy performance of the Probe buildings', *Building Research and Information*, vol 29, no 2, pp114–128

DCLG (Department of Communities and Local Government) (2007) *Building Regulations Energy Efficient Requirements for New Dwellings – A Forward Look at What Standards May Be in 2010 and 2013*, DCLG, London

EU (European Union) (2002) *Directive 2002/91/EC Energy Performance of Buildings Directive*, European Parliament

Greater London Authority (2007) *Action Today to Protect Tomorrow: The Mayor's Climate Change Action Plan*, Greater London Authority, London

Greater London Authority (2008) *The London Plan: Consolidated with Alternation Strategies since 2004*, Greater London Authority, London

Mumovic, D., Palmer, J., Davies, M., Orme, M., Ridley, I., Oreszczyn, T., Judd, C., Medina, H. A., Pilmoor, G., Pearson, C., Critchlow, R. and Way, P. (2008) 'Winter indoor air quality, thermal comfort and acoustic performance of newly built schools in England', *Building and Environment*, in press

Short, C. A., Lomas K. J. and Woods, A. (2004) 'Design strategy for low energy ventilation and cooling within an urban heat island', *Building Research and Information*, vol 32, no 3, May–June, pp187–206

van Hoof, J. (2008) 'Forty years of Fanger's model of thermal comfort: Comfort for all', *Indoor Air*, vol 18, pp182–201

1

Building Sustainable Communities: Combining Social and Physical Perspectives

Gemma Moore, Irene Perdikogianni, Alan Penn and Mags Adams

Introduction

Sustainability has moved from a goal to a necessity in the urban environment. The recent focus of urban planning and urban regeneration practice has been to create sustainable, healthy and viable communities with positive neighbourhood identities. Visions of thriving, mixed-use, economically stable and socially inclusive cities with clean, green, safe neighbourhoods have been presented as the possible future of many urban areas. However, how to actually create such areas and communities is not entirely clear. Realistically, an answer to this question can only be reached using empirical evidence drawn from the functioning of an urban area and its dwellers' experience of everyday life within it. Understanding what makes a city sustainable therefore requires a dialogue between a huge variety of researchers. Engineers, geographers, architects, planners, designers, ecologists and sociologists all conduct research in an effort to better understand the sustainable cities and communities. Multidisciplinary research can help us to analyse how sustainability of the urban environment is framed, while disciplinary knowledges can complement each other in producing a perspective of the subject. This chapter describes both the process and outcomes of developing a conceptual and methodological framework to investigate sustainable communities within a multifarious research team: combining social and physical perspectives.

Historically the social and physical infrastructures of the city have co-evolved and are interdependent; yet we do not fully understand their interaction (see Hommels, 2000). On the other hand, earlier studies conducted by academics such as Martin (1972) or Hillier and Hanson (1984) suggested that the way in which the physical environment of a city or a neighbourhood is arranged forms new possibilities for the way in which people choose to live and work. However, to date, the focus of research has either been on individual perceptions and attitudes towards specific 'places' or on more generalized design features of urban areas. In this chapter we describe multidisciplinary research that marries these two approaches. Focusing on Clerkenwell in London, UK, as a case study of a vibrant urban community, we present a new way of thinking about contemporary urban communities. To illustrate the wide range of complex interactions between the physical, social and economic processes of the urban mechanism, our study combines quantitative analysis of Clerkenwell's street layout (incorporating information on its usage and the historical formation and transformation of the urban fabric of the area) with qualitative information on perceptions and behaviours of city centre residents.

Background: What is a sustainable community?

The concept of a sustainable community is inherently a spatial construct, focusing on place-based communities. Sustainable communities is now central to UK developmental policy; for instance, *Living Places* (ODPM, 2002), *Sustainable Communities Plan* (ODPM, 2003) and *Planning Policy Statement 1: Delivering Sustainable Development* (ODPM, 2004a) all refer to this notion, presenting an intertwining of the discourses of sustainable development and sustainable communities. The government's definition of a sustainable community clearly embodies the key principles of sustainable development; it states that sustainable communities are ones which:

> ... meet the diverse needs of existing and future residents, their children and other users, contribute to a high quality of life and provide opportunity and choice. They achieve this in ways that make effective use of natural resources, enhance the environment, promote social cohesion and inclusion, and strengthen economic prosperity. (ODPM, 2004b, p35)

Within urban spatial policy, the government promotes that a sustainable community has seven essential, balanced and integrated components (an active and cohesive community; well run in terms of governance; is environmentally sensitive; is a well-designed built environment; is well connected; has a thriving economy; and is well serviced), which should underpin planning and design processes.

The definition of a sustainable community describes a particular 'type' of neighbourhood, with a well-designed built environment, a range of employment opportunities, and a certain degree of social interaction and social cohesion that facilitates social order. Nevertheless, the formation of a neighbourhood involves a social-psychological experience with a physical space; therefore, the defined spatial area of a neighbourhood can be seen as subject to how people use and feel about the built environment. The geographer Doreen Massey has explored and strived to explain the complexities of this relationship throughout her work (see Massey, 1994). Massey argues that a person's development of place is an ongoing formation of social relations, interconnections and movements. Both Jacobs (1961) and Lynch (1960, 1984) have been instrumental in exploring spatial layouts and components that influence the prosperity of neighbourhood life (i.e. central points; clear flows in and out; places for people; a visual identity; shared open spaces; common eye on space; detailed design features). In particular, the street combined with the social activity

that takes place on its frontage emerges as one key element of analysis in this stream of research. For Jacobs (1961), Appleyard (1981) and Sennett (1994), street layout and its properties affect the possibility and form of encounters between people. In contrast Barton et al (2003) put people at the heart of creating sustainable neighbourhoods and communities. Barton suggests that while urban form can influence patterns of movement and interaction, so too can factors such as the way in which schools are designed or the existence of local associations. Barton looks at the social, economic and environmental factors that influence people's quality of life, and illustrates that to understand how sustainable communities can actually be achieved and maintained is a multifaceted, complex issue requiring an approach that is likewise multifaceted and complex.

A multidisciplinary research strategy

As multidisciplinary work thrives, innovative methods of data collection and measurement are slowly emerging within and between many disciplines. We outline an excellent example of how methodologies can be moulded and experimented with. VivaCity2020: Urban Sustainability for the 24 Hour City is a large multidisciplinary research project within the Engineering and Physical Sciences Research Council (EPSRC) Sustainable Urban Environments (SUE) consortium, aiming to develop an in-depth understanding of human behaviour in urban environments and to create new innovative tools and techniques to support sustainable design decision-making. A research strategy was developed to explore both the more experiential side of city centre living alongside the collection of quantitative data on the urban layout and form.

Example case study

An area within Clerkenwell in the London Borough of Islington, to the north-east of central London, was selected as a case study area. Clerkenwell is one of 16 wards located within the London Borough of Islington (see Figure 1.1). Parts of the ward (including Clerkenwell Green, the historical heart of the area) are designated as conservation areas by Islington Council, meaning that special planning policy applies to protect the diverse character of the ward. This area is

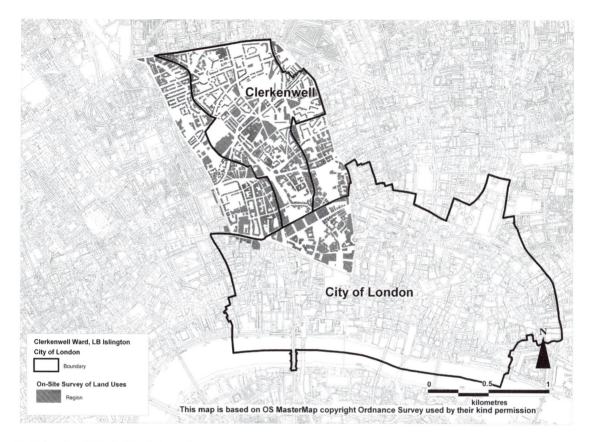

Source: based on OS Master Map, Ordnance Survey

Figure 1.1 *Map of Clerkenwell, Islington, London*[1]

residentially diverse, incorporating social housing alongside privately owned flats and houses, and is economically diverse with a variety of shops, workshops, wholesale, offices and entertainment facilities. The area was selected as an example of a diverse and viable urban neighbourhood.[2]

An examination of the way in which this area has evolved and been transformed throughout its history clearly shows that its diverse character, protected under its current status as a conservation area, is an outcome of Clerkenwell's lack of economic success. This paradox in its development could be better understood in comparison with its adjacent thriving central business district: the City of London. The latter has developed and redeveloped its buildings over the years, and in doing so has readjusted the alignment of streets, amalgamated blocks and subdivided blocks, and radically changed its structure to accommodate new economic needs. Clerkenwell's spatial

structure originated as an area of low-lying land traversed by the (now obsolete) River Fleet outside the walls of the City of London, used for the major cattle market for the city, and is broken up by a series of larger monastic properties and mansions (Pink, 2001). It prohibited its redevelopment following similar City of London urban development mechanisms. Although 19th-century road improvement programmes constructed 'bypasses' in the area, such as Farringdon Road and Clerkenwell Road, to take people and traffic through the area on larger-scale trips, Clerkenwell remained a marginal area in the larger processes of change within the city as a whole (Perdikogianni and Penn, 2005).

Methodology

Thirty-four Clerkenwell residents took part in a photo survey, a sound walk and a semi-structured one-to-one interview in order to produce data on their perceptions of their local environment. An interview date was scheduled with each participant and approximately two weeks earlier a disposable camera (27 exposure, 35mm film, 400ISO with flash), a photo survey log sheet, a return envelope and detailed instructions were sent out. Participants were asked to take photographs of their local area (incorporating both positive and negative aspects), noting the time, date, location and a short description of the photograph on the log sheet provided (the photo survey). Not wanting to be too prescriptive in telling participants what to photograph, the instructions simply stated: 'We would like you to take photos that record both the positive and negative aspects of your area.' This gave participants the freedom to take photographs of whatever they wanted at times and locations convenient to themselves. Cameras were returned to the research team after a week; the photographs were developed and catalogued according to the log sheet. At an agreed time, the researchers arrived at each participant's home. Participants were asked to complete a short questionnaire with general background information (personal data, household characteristics, residence details, local urban morphology and health details); they were also invited to identify a ten-minute walking route around their local area and to mark it on a large-scale map, centred on their home, supplied by the researchers. This map was then used as the basis for a sound walk of the local area. A sound walk is a walk around an area where the senses are directed towards the sounds that are heard, rather than the more commonplace sights that are viewed. On return to the participant's home, a semi-structured interview was conducted by one of the researchers. The interview was based upon a number of general questions about the urban environment, made specific to the resident's locality. Participants were asked to refer to their photographs and the sound walk at any stage during the interview.

This study also focused on assembling, describing, representing and analysing the multiple aspects of the physical and functional city. These were conceptualized as interdependent layers within the urban system and by using a geographical information system (GIS). An integrated spatialized database was created, bringing together primary data collected through observation-based surveys (of the use of buildings and public space) and pedestrian flow (on streets within the study area's boundaries). Physical space was considered to be the common framework for this study; hence, it was suggested that a comparative statistical analysis of this data with topological properties of the streets be made, considering the urban area as a spatial network. The land-use data gathered through on-site observation revealed the detailed activities that the buildings within the area accommodate. This enabled the investigators to identify any 'attractional inequalities' that may exist. This process was undertaken at a variety of spatial scales (the study area as whole, selected sub-areas, streets, and individual buildings or blocks) and was sensitive to temporal differences in usage. It was also acknowledged that each factor can be affected by and simultaneously have an effect on any other, both spatially and temporally.

The street morphology of the study area was analysed to identify regularities and irregularities in street layout that could account for any observed functional patterns. The analysis was enabled by a spatial model that represented all streets and public spaces as a line matrix of direct access in order to get from every location to every other possible location, following the rule of creating the longest and fewest lines (axial map)[3] (see Hillier, 1999, for details). The produced axial map was analysed in relation to its 'topological' properties by translating the line matrix into a graph and measuring the topological properties of the graph. All of the (axial) lines were differentiated or weighted in relation to their position in the global network. The measure of integration (developed during several empirical studies) quantified the syntactic properties of (axial) lines by measuring their mean topological distance (depth) from every other (axial) line considering the (urban) system as a whole[4] (see Figure 1.2).

Pedestrian flow was observed on 132 predefined locations by a group of 16 trained observers. Pedestrians passing by each location for a five-minute period were counted. The locations on main streets were observed for 2.5 minutes. Pedestrians were classified as locals working within the area and tourists based on their dress code, distinguishing between men and women. Overall, pedestrians were observed periodically in nine pre-decided time slots between 8.00 am and 8.00 pm during one weekday and one weekend day. For the land-use survey, the study area was divided into 12 sub-areas and data was collected through observation for each building and open space by a group of seven trained observers. Uses of the ground floor, first floor, the main use above first floor and the number of floors for all 3618 premises were

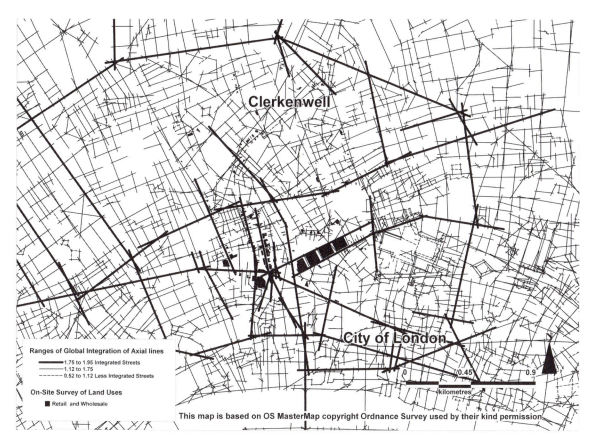

Ranges of Global Integration of Axial lines
——— 1.75 to 1.95 Integrated Streets
——— 1.12 to 1.75
------- 0.52 to 1.12 Less Integrated Streets

On-Site Survey of Land Uses
■ Retail and Wholesale

This map is based on OS MasterMap copyright Ordnance Survey used by their kind permission

Source: based on OS Master Map, Ordnance Survey

Figure 1.2 *Axial map of Clerkenwell overlaid on the surveyed retail and wholesale within study area*

recorded. Some additional information on the names and the opening hours of the retail and commercial premises was also recorded for capturing the temporal aspect of city life. The land uses were classified using an adaptation of the National Land-Use Database (NLUD) Classification.[5] Detailed multilevel land-use maps were created for the study area.

Investigating the role of space in the construction of place

We have combined physical and social perspectives in order to explore the degree that space and spatial structure affects the way in which the area is used and experienced today by people who choose to live within it.

The term spatial structure describes the way in which streets and public space are built in the overall street network. The land-use map for the ground floor use for all premises and open space revealed that there are a variety of uses within Clerkenwell, with an underlying structure in the way that these are assimilated within the overall spatial pattern. There is a clear spatial separation of residential and more mixed-use environments. There are mono-functional residential sub-areas in the north of the study area with a limited range of other uses (i.e. newsagents, local shops or pubs) often located on street corners, whereas the mixed-functional sub-areas were located in the southern sector of the case study area with a higher number of offices and retail uses. This structural separation of different uses can also be observed in a detailed examination of the area. Streets such as Exmouth Market, a thriving a semi-pedestrianized street full of restaurants, cafés and sandwich bars, is located next to Farringdon Road, dominated by housing blocks (largely rented) and commercial offices. This mix of different uses is not arbitrary; but one needs to change direction to find different spatial qualities. The axial map described in Figure 1.2 captures this by attributing different topological values for every change of direction. This framework describes that these two streets are one axial line (or step) away. In other words, residential and retail uses co-exist in Clerkenwell; however, they are located one step away (Figure 1.3).

The same pattern of spatial separation between the different land uses is reinforced by the density of pedestrian flow observed in these environments. Streets such as Exmouth Market, as emerged from the observed predefined locations, attracted a high number of pedestrians (total daily mean per hour adult flow n = 1635), while the north end of Farringdon Road attracted a smaller number of pedestrians (daily mean

per hour adult flow n = 467). The repetition of these phenomena in several empirical studies suggested that attributed topological values of streets (if we represent the street system as an axial map) have an effect on how different land and building uses are assimilated within urban systems, initiating a feedback process from land uses to the street system with the aid of pedestrian flows. Shops and restaurants occupy strategic locations that feature easy access and thus are well connected with the rest of the system (these are on streets with high global and local integration values). This is because they seek to benefit from passers-by since people tend to move on streets that are well connected to the rest of the street system (small mean distance from all other streets and, thus, a high integration value). On the other hand, residential uses benefit from privacy, so they tend to form quieter zones in more secluded areas (streets with

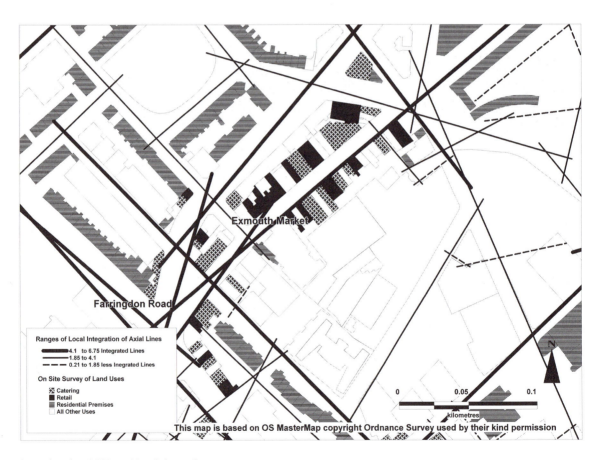

Source: based on OS Master Map, Ordnance Survey

Figure 1.3 *Around Exmouth Market: The axial map is overlaid on shops, restaurants and houses located on the ground floor*

low global or local integration values). If we think of this as an eternal dynamic feedback process, then we understand that the busy areas become busier and the quiet ones become quieter (Hillier, 1996).

Previous empirical findings have shown that a substantial proportion of people movement patterns in cities are generated by the structure of the street system itself (Hillier et al, 1993). The correlation analysis between the pedestrian flow and topological measures – namely, the local integration values of all street axial lines, suggested that instead of one entity, Clerkenwell is a structured system of smaller sub-areas. The strict localism of pedestrian movement patterns suggests that Clerkenwell is a fragmented system of six sub-areas that function as independent urban systems within the city and, as a whole, are relatively poorly related to one another (Figure 1.4). This spatial structure is, on the one

hand, at the root of Clerkenwell's failure to redevelop (remaining a marginal area in the general process of change); but at the same time it is itself a major factor since it is considered a 'well-working' diverse area that maintains its local residential, employment and leisure activities, as well as social and economic networks.

The combination of different uses (retail, commercial, residential and services) and networks within the built environment was a key element of residents' perception of their local area. The functionality of the neighbourhood was a crucial facet for residents when describing Clerkenwell. The provision of shops, restaurants, offices, doctors, pubs and transport within their wider neighbourhood was commonly referred to as a positive aspect of the area, with participants noting the convenience of having such amenities and facilities within close proximity of their home. This is illustrated

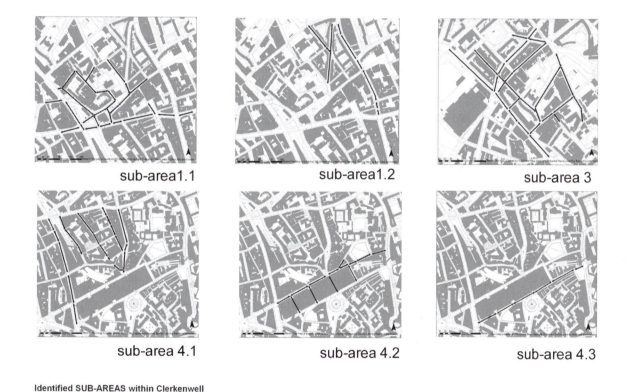

Identified SUB-AREAS within Clerkenwell

⟷ Streets that form
identified sub-area

These maps are based on OS MasterMap copyright Ordnance Survey used by their kind permission

Source: based on OS Master Map, Ordnance Survey

Figure 1.4 *The identified sub-areas within Clerkenwell's boundaries*

by quotes from one participant, Luke,[6] who used the word convenient to describe Clerkenwell and was subsequently asked to elaborate further:

It's close to work, close to transport; it means I don't have to use any tubes, trains to get to work, I can walk to work. Friends live close and that means I can get to my friends. And even if they don't live close, it's easy for them to get here. Easy for friends and family to get round. There are loads of facilities around. When they come over it's always nice; we've got hundreds of restaurants to pick [from] when we want to go and eat. We've got shops, we can go and buy something to make at home. We've got absolutely everything else that you need; so it's just convenient, that's it… It's fun. Fun, cause there's just so many things to do around here. It makes … your life easier when things are convenient and you can get people together and there's loads of things to do round here. It's just, you know if, if you're bored with one thing there's always something else to do. (Luke)

Luke's quotes illustrate the advantages that 'co-existence' can bring – multiple facilities in close proximity – raising issues such as convenience, accessibility and diversity. Alongside the benefits of having a multitude of shops and restaurants within the wider local neighbourhood, he, like many other participants, points out the degree of ease with which it is possible for people to reach the neighbourhood from other locations or for him to access elsewhere. In describing neighbourhood life, many participants took photographs of, and described in depth, specific aspects of the built environment that were significant to them. These included physical aspects (facilities, amenities, places to use, places to visit), visual aspects (things to see – i.e. views and architectural features) and social aspects (people – i.e. neighbours, groups and commuters). For instance, the quotes below from one participant, Ben, demonstrate this. In explaining the photographs he took as part of the photo survey, Ben expresses his delight at being able to have access to pubs and bars within his neighbourhood. Interestingly, like many other participants, Ben not only raises the issues of provision, but also the benefits brought about by having diversity in choice:

And then I also took pictures of nice places and, and sort of things to do, which is another thing that Clerkenwell's great for. I used to live in Bermondsey and there was nothing to do, and there were no bars really at all, sort of

All Bar One and a Brown's and one or two locals, the sort of … very soulless chain bars which just are all the same wherever you go. And what I love about Clerkenwell is its kind of diversity of … venues, and so it's got lots of kind of interesting little pubs. (Ben)

Despite the positive aspects of convenience and vibrancy brought about by the wider spatial connections, participants spoke of the disadvantages that come with living in such a mixed-use area:

They're the pluses, these are the absolute negatives, this lot here [referring to his photographs], it says itself, doesn't it? That's an incredible amount of pollution down the alleyway … there's always people throwing up everywhere around this area. (Colin)

The quote from Colin succinctly captures what many referred to: the localized, direct, negative impacts of the urban spatial system. Local door-step issues, such as rubbish, fly-tipping, anti-social behaviour, vomiting and noise, were all mentioned as aspects of urban living that residents disliked. Noise was predominately mentioned; particular sounds (such as traffic, drunken behaviour, people and sirens) became a noise nuisance to participants when they 'invaded' the participants' homes at particular times of day (i.e. late evening or early morning). The quotes below from Clive are used as an example to explain the auditory and visual experience of having non-residential neighbours 'one step away'. Clive lives very near to Exmouth Market:

CLIVE: And, the final one is early morning deliveries, which is an absolute pig.

INTERVIEWER: What time early morning?

CLIVE: It's normally between 5.30 and 6.30 in the morning and it's early morning deliveries and those kind of metal things on the front of the shops. They're sort of rolled up and make a hell of a racket.

INTERVIEWER: The shutters.

CLIVE: The shutters, and then they put the goods in and then they drive off. And invariably, I suppose once every three months, somebody leaves their van with the keys in and it gets nicked, and that happens quite regularly. You always hear: 'Oi, get out of my van', and then you hear a van go 'EEEEr' down the road and you come out half an hour later and you see there's food all over the road because it's come out of the back of the van and the thief has made off with it and it happens quite regularly in Exmouth Market. And that I, would say, is the major noise issue.

All participants spoke in depth about the interactions and conflict brought about from the differing needs of multiple uses (i.e. working times, access, services and deliveries). When the differing uses impact upon the direct locality, these are predominantly referred to as disadvantages of urban living. Despite the noted disadvantages, all participants had something positive to say about living in Clerkenwell. For most, the benefits of living in the city centre (the wider spatial issues of accessibility and proximity to neighbouring amenities) outweighed the negatives (localized problems such as crime, pollution, rubbish, etc.). Some commented upon the relationship between the benefits and disadvantages, noting that the negative aspects came hand in hand with the positives – what Healey (2006, p130) describes as the conflicts *within* ourselves. For example, when asked to describe the quality of the environment in Clerkenwell, Linda and her partner responded thus:

INTERVIEWER: How would you describe the environmental quality of the area?

LINDA: Not bad, I suppose, not bad.

LINDA'S PARTNER: I think, I think, I can see, I can see it could … be a lot worse. I don't think it's as bad as it could be, but it's not good either you know… It's what I would expect to live in an area like this; it's safe and … it's central and almost the same; the advantages contradict the disadvantages.

LINDA: So, it's noisy and polluted.

LINDA'S PARTNER: Yeah.

LINDA: So it's not good. But just … you can't have it, you can't have a lively central area with clean air and calm; it just doesn't exist. So it's one or the other.

Reflecting upon both the benefits and disadvantages of their local area enabled participants to consider the exchanges and trade-offs that they make within the urban environment. Participants commented upon compromising with the negative aspects to appreciate the benefits. The quote by another participant, Tina, clearly illustrates this: Tina spoke in detail about tolerating the negative aspects of city living (particularly the noise brought about by living next door to commercial premises), while recognizing the overall benefits brought about by the wider neighbourhood:

> But now I've actually … come to appreciate living in, sort of in London and all that it offers, you know, cause I can sort of, you know, I'm close; I like going to exhibitions and this and that, so … I'm … on the spot; I don't have to make big tube journeys or anything, and, as I say, I've … sort of learned to tolerate. It's not that I like the traffic and the, you know, various noises and stuff, and I don't like the commercial neighbours, you know I get fed up of them; but I've kind of seemed to overcome, able to tolerate it somehow. (Tina)

The participants' accounts of their experience of urban living alongside the detailed analysis of the urban form illustrate the complex interconnection and interaction between spatial scales and context for creating successful 'places' where people like to live and work. There is a clear difference between perceptions of the wider neighbourhood and the immediate locality. The relationships and interactions between these scales appear to be largely ignored, to date, in urban research; but as we have demonstrated, this has numerous implications for how we can make vibrant sustainable communities in which people choose to participate.

Reflections on processes and outcomes

Understanding and assessing certain qualities or issues within the built environment is often a difficult, intangible process. Multidisciplinary projects can give rise to exciting research opportunities, innovations in methodologies and wide-ranging analytical approaches. Within this chapter we present a project that explores sustainable communities through combining different disciplinary approaches.

The multidisciplinary and interdisciplinary turn is now well recognized across disciplines; but further debate is necessary to fully understand the impact of moving in this direction, for researchers, for knowledge transfer and for academic disciplines themselves. However, within this chapter we highlight that through combining varying approaches and accounts, a comprehensive knowledge base for certain urban issues can be constructed. Making connections between residents' perceptions of the urban environment and the physical layout assisted understandings of the trade-offs made by city residents living in urban areas. Understanding how the identity of a neighbourhood is formed is extremely important in appreciating the functioning of this area as an urban system; our evidence in the case study of Clerkenwell reinforces this suggestion. Furthermore, our findings suggest the importance of understanding the complex interconnection and interaction between spatial scales and context for creating successful 'places' where people like to live and work. For instance, a city centre resident's local environment could be the house in which they live, the surrounding neighbourhood or even the city itself. There is a complex interconnection between each of these environments – a house in an urban area does not exist in isolation. It is part of a wider neighbourhood, which is in itself part of the city network. Perceptions of each may also vary (and, in turn, influence each other). We have found that these spatial scales are particularly noticeable in people's accounts of their experiences and the trade-offs that they make in order to live in the city centre.

Considerations

This chapter has described both the processes and outcomes of developing a conceptual and methodological framework to investigate sustainable communities within a multifarious research team combining social and physical perspectives. From our experience we would like to raise a number of aspects for consideration for future research within this field:

- There is a need to understand urban communities both from a physical and social perspective (i.e. what it means to co-exist in shared mixed-use spaces and how places can be made out of such spaces).
- Building sustainable communities requires a coordinated joined approach involving a range of academics and practitioners (i.e. engineers, planners and sociologists).

- Combined disciplinary knowledge can complement each other in producing a larger perspective and richer understandings of sustainability within the built environment.
- People other than official 'experts' may have insights into research, particularly with regard to social and physical aspects. In the context of research within specific geographical areas, residents may be considered 'local experts' about aspects of their neighbourhood and its conditions.
- Putting people in groups representing different academic disciplines, professions or expertises does not necessarily guarantee interdisciplinary practices – integration of different domains of research and forms of knowledge requires thoughtful and strategic facilitation.

The ability of designers to make more sustainable decisions relies upon their having accurate and relevant information to do so. Although the social accounts outlined in this chapter are very different from the analysed physical urban form, combined together, they provide a detailed comprehensive knowledge base on the current conditions within the case study area. We urge that decision-makers take a holistic approach when exploring sustainability in the built environment, thinking about the wider relationships and connections between the physical environment and society. Effective sustainable decisions require designers to consider a range of knowledge and understandings (i.e. disciplinary, academic, professional, expert and lay) to be used at different stages of the design process. We highlight that local residents have valuable understandings of their local environment that would be beneficial to urban designers if they were listened to. However, key deliberations about building design often do not adequately involve local people. This requires the use of various targeted recruitment and public engagement practices. Recruitment is a time-consuming process; but with effort a diverse range of participants can be mobilized. We argue that using a combined qualitative (social) and quantitative (physical) methodology would give built environment designers a better understanding of a given environment or building. For instance, we have illustrated that residents' perceptions of their environment may be significantly improved by addressing door-step localized issues such as noise, rubbish and fly-tipping at the design stage by providing mechanisms for preventing or minimizing the impact of such issues.

Acknowledgements

This study forms part of the EPRSC-funded Sustainable Urban Environment Consortium Project VivaCity 2020: Urban Sustainability for the 24 Hour City (grant reference GR/518380/01). The authors acknowledge the support and contribution of all of their colleges involved in work package 2 and 4 (see www.vivacity2020.eu/).

Notes

1 This map is based on data provided through EDINA UKBORDERS with the support of the Economic and Social Research Council (ESRC) and Joint Information Systems Committee (JISC) and uses boundary material that is copyright of the Crown.
2 For further exploration of the location and wider context of the case study area, please use the search terms 'UK, London, Farringdon Road' in online maps such as Google™ Maps.
3 The axial map is based on Ordnance Survey Master Map data courtesy of Ordnance Survey for the EPSRC-funded project VivaCity2020.
4 Global integration (or radius n integration – INT R(N)) measures the mean depth (distance) of all axial lines in a plan from the line in question and then normalizes this for the number of lines that are present in the plan. Local integration (or integration radius 3, INT R (3)) accounts for the relationship between each line and all other lines restricted to two changes of direction away from it (Hiller and Hanson, 1984).
5 NLUD Classification Version 3.2.
6 The participant names quoted within this chapter are pseudonyms that were given to each participant.

References

Appleyard, D. (1981) *Livable Street*, California University Press, Berkeley, CA

Barton, H., Grant, M. and Guise, R. (2003) *Shaping Neighbourhoods for Health, Sustainability and Vitality*, E & F Spon, London and New York
Healey, P. (2006) *Collaborative Planning: Shaping Places in Fragmented Societies*, Palgrave MacMillan, London
Hillier, B. (1996) *Space is the Machine*, Cambridge University Press, Cambridge
Hillier, B. (1999) 'The hidden geometry of deformed grids: Or, why space syntax works, when it looks as though it shouldn't', *Environment & Planning B: Planning & Design*, vol 26, pp169–191
Hillier, B. and Hanson, J. (1984) *The Social Logic of Space*, Cambridge University Press, Cambridge
Hillier, B., Penn, A., Hanson, J., Grajewski, T. and Xu, J. (1993) 'Natural movement: Or configuration and attraction in urban pedestrian movement', *Environment & Planning B: Planning & Design*, vol 20, pp29–66
Hommels, A. (2000) 'Obduracy and urban sociotechnical change: Changing Plan Hoog Catharijne', *Urban Affairs Review*, vol 35, no 5, pp649–676
Jacobs, J. (1961) *The Death and Life of Great American Cities*, Penguin Books Ltd, London
Lynch, K. (1960) *The Image of the City*, MIT Press, Cambridge
Lynch K. (1984) *Good City Form*, MIT Press, Cambridge
Martin, L. (1972) *The Grid as Generator: Urban Space and Structures*, Cambridge
Massey, D. (1994) *Space, Place, and Gender*, University of Minnesota Press, Minneapolis
ODPM (Office of the Deputy Prime Minster) (2002) *Living Places: Cleaner, Safer, Greener*, ODPM, London
ODPM (2003) *Sustainable Communities Plan*, www.neighbourhood.gov.uk/page.asp?id=633, accessed March 2008
ODPM (2004a) *Planning Policy Statement 1: Delivering Sustainable Development*, ODPM, London
ODPM (2004b) *The Egan Review: Skills for Sustainable Communities*, RIBA Publishing, London
Perdikogianni, I. and Penn, A. (2005) 'Measuring diversity: A multi-variate analysis of land use and temporal patterning in Clerkenwell', 5th Space Syntax Symposium Proceedings, Delft, TU Delft
Pink, W. J. (2001) *The History of Clerkenwell*, Francis Boutle, London
Sennett, R. (1994) *Flesh and Stone: The Body and City in Western Civilization*, Faber & Faber, London

Part II

ENERGY AND BUILDINGS

Introduction: Towards Zero Carbon Buildings

Dejan Mumovic and Mat Santamouris

Chapter 2 gives an overview of building physics and highlights the importance of energy-saving houses to sustainable building engineering and design. Several forms of energy-saving buildings, such as low-energy houses, 3 litre houses, passive houses, zero-energy houses, energy self-sufficient houses and plus-energy houses have been outlined.

Chapter 3 defines various energy rating indexes (operational rating, calculated rating, design rating, asset rating and tailored rating) used for the assessment and prediction of energy use in buildings and describes both heating and cooling energy monitoring procedures. The implications of European Union (EU) Directive 2002/91/EC on the energy efficiency of buildings are discussed. For example, the introduction of the energy performance certification of buildings has resulted in the development of various methodologies (i.e. diagnostic tools) that may assist facility managers and energy monitoring professionals to detect faults or malfunctions in the energy behaviour of buildings. It is believed that energy consumption monitoring will contribute to the development of building energy performance classification and more comprehensive energy benchmarking systems.

Chapter 4 defines energy modelling as the key element of the broader discipline called building simulation, a domain that, apart from thermal aspects, also studies (day)lighting, moisture, acoustics, airflow and indoor air quality. After an overview of various aspects of energy modelling, the need for full co-disciplinary energy modelling is highlighted, allowing heating, ventilating and air-conditioning (HVAC) system experts, control system developers and architectural designers to add model components to a shared multi-domain responsive energy model during full concurrent real-time collaborative design of all systems.

Chapter 5, in a straightforward, no-nonsense way, describes various strategies in which the energy consumption of buildings can be reduced at design stage. This chapter discusses ways to reduce energy for heating (i.e. optimize the building envelope), reduce energy for cooling (i.e. optimize the use of natural climate features), reduce energy for lighting (i.e. integrate daylight with artificial light), reduce energy for equipment/processes and investigate the use of renewable and integrated energy sources.

Chapter 6 investigates the use of renewable and integrated energy sources. It clearly states that the challenge is to find renewable energy supply solutions that are socially equitable and environmentally acceptable, and that meet needs at reasonable cost. It has been argued that there is no global best renewable energy solution for cities; systems have to be designed to suit the city, regional, national and international context.

As growing environmental awareness has focused human attention on the utilization of renewable energies, Chapter 7 offers one of the possible solutions – heat pumps for urban built environments. Interestingly, the idea of using a reverse heat engine as a heat pump was proposed by James Thomson and his brother William Thomson (later to become Lord Kelvin) in the middle of the 19th century; but it was only during the 20th century that these practical devices came into common use. What does the 21st century bring to electrically driven heat pumps?

Finally, Chapter 8 explains that the life cycle of a building as well as of other systems (processes, services, etc.) is similar to the lifetime of biological organisms. In the same way that biological organisms originate, reproduce and, finally, die, buildings are constructed, used, demolished and disposed of. This chapter discusses both positive and negative aspects of the life cycle assessment (LCA) of buildings, including the most important one: LCA cannot take into account or predict future changes in current technology or demand.

Last but not least, at the end of Part II of the book we have included three case studies:

- *Chapter 9, Energy and Environmental Monitoring.* The aim of this chapter is to guide researchers along a practical methodology for energy and environmental monitoring studies to address fully the specific research questions under investigation and underpinned by benchmark methods, and to recognize the potential for wider supplementary research that can add considerable value to the original monitoring study. The topics are illustrated via a case study of 29 dwellings in Milton Keynes, UK.
- *Chapter 10, Energy Modelling.* There are two principal approaches that can be used to forecast the energy use and CO_2 emissions of a particular sector of the economy – namely, *top down* or *bottom up*. The aim of this case study is to describe in detail the development of DECARB, a physically based model of the UK housing stock that is capable of forecasting the energy use and CO_2 emissions attributable to this sector, under a range of possible futures.
- *Chapter 11, Energy Efficient Refurbishment of Buildings: A Policy Context.* The aim of this case study was to investigate the effects of German climate change policy on the reduction of carbon emissions from existing dwellings. The first part of this chapter reviews the policy landscape in Germany and the second part investigates the German CO_2 reduction programme in practice. The latter consists of a detailed calculation of the energy consumption for space heating and domestic hot water services of a building.

2

Energy Efficiency and Thermal Envelope

Jurij Krope and Darko Goričanec

Energy efficiency of buildings

Since ancient times people have dealt with the problem of constructing buildings with adequate thermal comfort. The crucial question was how to make a house warm in winter and cool in summer. Early literature in this field considers the concept of the Socratic House and provides a hypothetical description of such a building. The essence of Socrates's studies was the influence of solar motion upon the shape, material and construction of a building.

This relationship has been continuously conserved throughout the centuries. In order to realize these ideas and technical solutions, the European Union (EU) has accepted and legislated several directives on the energy efficiency of buildings. They are obligatory for EU member states.

If we review the German regulation EnEV, 2002 (Deutsche Regulative EnEV, 2002), we discover that the energy efficiency of a building depends upon total energy consumption for a building's operation (i.e. the sum consumption of energy for electricity, heating and warming clean water).

The construction of new buildings should therefore be considered from the new total building performance (TBP) point of view, which represents physiological, psychological, sociological and economic perspectives, with an emphasis upon the following aspects of building performance: visual, spatial, thermal, air quality, acoustic and building integrity (see www.ctbp.bdg.nus.edu.sg).

TBP represents the new paradigm for buildings, encompassing a systematic approach from the very beginning of construction, appropriate methodology and interdisciplinary cooperation (between architects, engineers and builders) throughout all stages of construction, which enables different demands to be met in order to achieve the desired performance of the building. The following interactions are of particular importance (Tabunchikov and Brodatch, 2005, pp33–38; Kwak Wai et al, 2006):

- choice of location;
- architecture;
- interior;
- daylighting of space;
- placement of optical bodies;
- choice of material;
- construction of façades;
- final treatment; and
- technical solutions, including choices dealing with:
  - the heat source (is it possible to use renewable energy sources?);
  - the heating system, ventilation and air conditioning; and
  - the control system.

This is the optimal way to achieve minimal energy consumption and the energy efficient construction of a building. A basic requirement of energy efficiency is to reduce heat losses through the building envelope and to exploit solar energy, which yields a real effect only if there is good thermal protection and if exploiting heat from inner sources.

When calculating gains from solar energy, the orientation and thermal characteristics of transparent surfaces, together with the possible effect of shading, the angle of incidence of sunlight and dirt on windows all have to be taken into account.

Gains from inner energy sources are due to heat released by the operation of electrical machines and devices inside the building, heat released by humans (around 100W, depending upon physical activity), the dishwasher (1kWh/person), the washing machine (0.76kWh/person) and the stove (0.20kWh/person). A fraction of inner heat gains is lost on evaporation (–25W/person) and cold water (–5W/person).

A building's heat losses are the consequence of transmission and ventilation heat losses. Transmission heat losses are caused by heat transfer through non-transparent building elements (wall, floor, ceiling, etc.) and transparent building elements (windows and special types of building envelopes), whereas ventilation heat losses are due to the heat exchange between the rooms inside the building and its surroundings. To reduce transmission heat losses, the shape factor of the building, representing the ratio between the surface area and the volume of the building, should be as small as possible. The most appropriate types of buildings are therefore square-, circle-, elipse- and octagon-shaped buildings.

Energy-saving buildings

Energy-saving buildings represent a new trend in the context of sustainable and quality architecture; besides their low consumption of energy due to their excellent thermal envelope, they provide a high level of comfort and pleasure. Today, there are several forms of energy-saving buildings:

- low-energy houses;
- 3 litre houses;
- passive houses;
- zero-energy houses;
- energy self-sufficient houses;
- plus-energy houses.

Low-energy house

Low-energy houses are buildings with annual thermal loads below 80kWh/m²a (8 litres of light fuel oil/m² of residential area/year), in line with the new European rules, determining the highest annual consumption of energy for heating (e.g. in Germany) as:

$$\frac{Q}{A} \le (26 + 13 \cdot f_0) \qquad (1)$$

Table 2.1 *Allowed heat loads*

Country	Q/A (kWh/m²a)	q (W/m²)
SLO	$45 + 40\,f_0$	$6 + 5.33\,f_0$
G	$26 + 13\,f_0$	$2.25 + 1.6\,f_0$
A	$24.55 + 81.82\,f_0$	$3.11 + 10.36\,f_0$
LEB	$13.64 + 45.45\,f_0$	$1.73 + 5.76\,f_0$
PEB	$4.1 + 13.64\,f_0$	$0.5 + 1.73\,f_0$

Notes: SLO = Slovenia; G = Germany; A = Austria; LEB = low-energy house; PEB = passive house.
Source: Novak (2005, p21)

where f_0 – the building shape factor ($f_0 = A/V_0$) – is the ratio between the outside surface area of building construction and the external volume of heated space in the building.

For some other countries the values are given in Table 2.1.

The basic requirements that allow for the construction of a low-energy building are:

- compact construction;
- adequate thermal insulation;
- controlled ventilation;
- adequate choice of heating system;
- airtight building envelope;
- thermally insulated windows;
- inclusion of active (solar collectors) or passive (glass surfaces on the southern side of the building) solar heating.

3 litre house

The annual consumption of energy for heating a 3 litre building is 30kWh/m²a, when the airtightness is $n_{50} \le 1h^{-1}$. A conventional heating system without heat bridges is the most appropriate, with a built-in ventilation system for recovering the heat of used air or a solar collector for heating clean water.

Passive house

Passive houses feature architecture where heating occurs through a heat pump together with solar collectors, and where the heat of used air from inside rooms is recovered (see Figure 2.1).

In a passive house, the heating season is usually shorter compared to a classical house: the heating season is shortened from 225 days to approximately 150 days. Additional heating is only needed for a period of 30 to 50 days; the rest of the time the gains of solar energy and inner sources are sufficient (Passiv House Institut, 2004, www.igpassivhaus.at).

The basic requirements for constructing a passive house are as follows:

- a south–north location;
- transparent glass surfaces on the southern side;
- heat transfer coefficient of glass panes with frames of $U < 0.8\text{W/m}^2\text{K}$;
- heat transfer coefficient of non-transparent elements of $U < 0.15\text{W/m}^2\text{K}$;
- construction without thermal bridges;
- appropriate ventilation $n_{50p}\text{PH} \leq 0.6\text{h}^{-1}$ and airtightness;
- ventilation system with recovery of heat from used air;
- a heating system connected with the solar system and the heat pump;
- average value of the heat transfer coefficient of the external envelope of $U \leq 0.2\text{W/m}^2\text{K}$.

The annual consumption of heat is less than $15\text{kWh/m}^2\text{a}$, which equals approximately to 1.5 'litres of light fuel oil/m²/year. Total consumption of primary energy is less than $120\text{kWh/m}^2\text{a}$, the annual consumption of electricity is $\leq 18\text{kWh/m}^2\text{a}$, and the heat losses are $\leq 10\text{W/m}^2$.

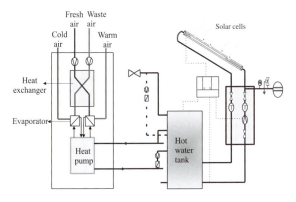

Figure 2.1 *The architecture of a passive house*

Zero-energy house

Zero-energy houses are insulated with a 40 to 60cm thick layer of thermal insulation material. There are no thermal bridges or conventional heating systems, and these houses actively and passively exploit solar energy. Zero-energy houses feature a heat depositor and are not dependent upon the public electrical grid. The heat and electrical energy needed is entirely produced through solar energy.

Energy self-sufficient house

Energy self-sufficient houses generate energy for heating, cooking, water heating and the operation of home appliances through active utilization of solar energy. These houses are not connected to the public electrical grid.

Plus-energy house

A plus-energy house has all the characteristics of a self-sufficient house but also uses all available means of energy conservation.

Currently, the comparison of different types of energy-saving buildings shows that the passive house is optimal. A passive house is a consistently built low-energy house with technical improvements in the building envelope and in the house technique. Zero-energy buildings, energy self-sufficient buildings and plus-energy buildings require additional improvements that are not economically viable considering the current prices.

Construction materials

Several building materials are eco-friendly and, due to their properties, help to conserve energy while heating. Therefore, when choosing the materials and the technology, it is worth taking into account the following:

- The chosen building technology should be standardized and tested.
- The construction should include natural and eco-friendly materials.
- The thermal building envelope should satisfy the standards of a passive house.
- The building should be airtight and diffusion permissive. Prefabrication of structural elements ensures quality and shortens the construction time.

Table 2.2 *Use of energy for producing materials*

Material	Cellulose	Cork	Coconut fibres	Mineral wool	Perlite	Wood wool	Expanded polystyrenel	Polyurethane
Energy (kWh) for $U = 0.4$W/m²K	8.3	80	12	15–85	12–24	50–70	40–90	50–60

Calculations show that when using artificial and inorganic building materials, more harmful gases are emitted to the air by the production of materials than are saved with the passive house in 30 years – and this is the time needed for the building to require renovation. In addition, use of primary energy for producing different materials differs depending upon the material's thermal insulation capability (see Table 2.2).

Wood, straw (which is compressed into bales with polypropylenic strings or wires), reedy plates (which are highly resistant to humidity, but not highly thermally insulative) and clay, from which brick-shaped products can be made that have a high capability of controlling humidity and conserving heat, are the most environment-friendly materials.

Due to their accumulation capability, massive brick, concrete or silicate brick walls are also appropriate building materials for conserving heat. However, their shortcoming is that these materials are cold to the touch, which is not always pleasant from a comfort viewpoint.

Building envelope

Heat transfer

The basis of energy-saving buildings is an efficient building envelope with all of the accompanying construction elements.

To be able to evaluate the energy effect of the building envelope, there are certain rules of heat transfer based on three basic modes: conduction, convection and radiation.

Heat flux is determined by the following equation:

$$\Phi = U \cdot A \cdot (T_n - T_0) \tag{2}$$

where:

- U = combined heat transfer coefficient (W/m²K);
- A = heat transfer surface area (m²);
- T_n = inside air temperature (K);
- T_0 = outside air temperature (K).

Next:

$$\frac{1}{U} = \frac{1}{\alpha_i} + \sum_{i=1}^{N} \frac{\Delta x_i}{\lambda_i} + \frac{1}{\alpha_0} \tag{3}$$

where:

- α_i = internal heat convection coefficient (W/m²K);
- N = number of homogeneous layers of building construction;
- Δx = thickness of a homogeneous layer (m);

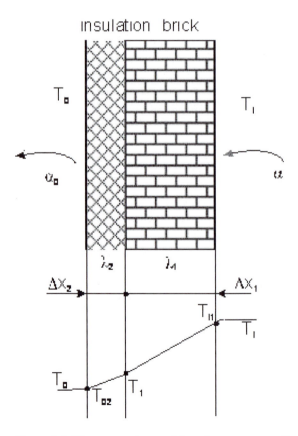

Figure 2.2 *Temperature in a multilayer homogeneous wall*

- α_0 = external heat convection coefficient (W/m²K);
- λ = thermal conductivity of the building element (W/mK).

It is important to know how to determine the temperature field within the homogeneous building construction in a steady state in order to be able to decide on the location of the melting point (0°C), and the temperatures on the internal and external surface of the building envelope (see Figure 2.2). The appropriate equation is:

$$\Phi = \alpha_i \left(T_i - T_{i1} \right) = \frac{\lambda_1}{\Delta x_1} \left(T_{i1} - T_1 \right)$$

$$= \frac{\lambda_2}{\Delta x_2} \left(T_1 - T_{02} \right) = \alpha_0 \left(T_{02} - T_0 \right). \quad (4)$$

Thermal bridges

Thermal bridges in building construction increase the heat losses of a building and the occurrence of condensation and mould. It is impossible to build a house without thermal bridges; however, with proper wall construction, their occurrence can be reduced to a minimum. In addition to the increased use of energy, the consequences of thermal bridges include deterioration of indoor air quality parameters and mould growth, as well as defects in the building itself after a certain period of time.

Special attention needs to be paid to the contact between the window jamb and the insulated wall. The in-building of the window shelf has to be made together with the insulation of the part of the brick wall below the shelf.

A thermal bridge can also occur at ferroconcrete bands in the corner, even though an insulation of appropriate thickness is later inserted from the outside. There are two possible causes for this: one is of a geometrical and the other is of a physical nature. The corner features an interior surface that is substantially smaller than the exterior surface (for receiving heat) – and this is the geometrical cause. The physical cause, on the other hand, lies in the fact that concrete has a much higher thermal conductivity than brick. To avoid unnecessary and unpleasant consequences of thermal bridges, the thermal insulation thickness has to be increased.

The temperature in non-insulated and insulated corners of two walls (the outside temperature is −10°C and inside temperature 20°C) is shown in Figure 2.3.

A ferroconcrete plate also represents a classical thermal bridge, passing over to the balcony, leading

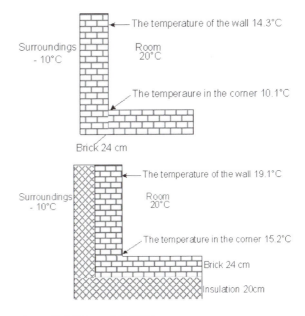

Source: Zbašnik Senegačnik (2007)

Figure 2.3 *Temperature in non-insulated and insulated corners*

away a substantial amount of heat, and almost always causing mouldiness under the ceiling. The reason for this is the large surface area of the balcony, acting as a cooling rib. The problem can be solved by a thermal separation of the balcony from the ferroconcrete plate. It can also be insulated from all sides or placed onto console holders to reduce the cooling surface.

Windows

Windows, providing natural light, ventilation and weather protection, are a very important component of office buildings, passive houses, etc.

The energy balance of a building shows that windows contribute the most to energy loss when non-transparent parts of a building are well insulated. Thus, technical solutions for windows are directed towards heat loss reduction and the search for the possibility of using solar energy (Aydin, 2006, p109). This is done through the use of insulated windows, which have the following properties:

- multilayer composition of insulation glass;
- high degree of spectral light transparency ($\tau \geq 72$ per cent);

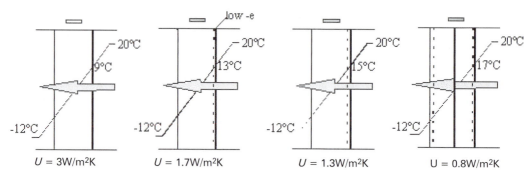

Source: Umberger et al (2006)

Figure 2.4 *Heat-insulated windows: The temperature of glass surfaces*

- neutral spectral light reflectivity (Re = 99);
- high degree of total light transparency (g ≥ 60 per cent);
- low value of heat transfer coefficient: $U \geq 1.3 \text{W/m}^2\text{K}$.

Heat transfer through an insulation glass is determined by:

- thermal radiation between glass panes;
- heat conductivity of gas between glass panes;
- convection of gas between glass panes.

On the southern side of the building, where we expect to have solar energy gains, glass surfaces are recommended to be as large as possible and, to the contrary, as small as possible on the northern side. Southern orientation enables maximum exploitation of solar energy in winter and other colder seasons, making a 40 per cent contribution to heating the building. A deviation of 10° from the building's southern orientation worsens the energy number by 0.1kWh/m²a. Therefore, the recommended deviation from the south is not more than ± 20°.

To better understand the change of U – the value of heat transfer coefficient of a two-layer glass covered by insulation – we should know that for a two-layer glass without insulation, about two-thirds of heat loss are due to heat radiation (ε ~ 0.85) and only one is the result of conduction and convection in the interspaces of the window. Covering either one of the two glass surfaces by an insulation film reduces thermal radiation practically to zero, and any further heat loss is only due to conduction and convection.

Insulation films should fulfil the following requirements:

- high degree of total light transmittance;
- natural light reflectivity;
- low value of radiation.

It is important to know that glass has optical properties that induce the greenhouse effect. Normally, glass is highly transparent at wavelengths of sunlight (0.3 < λ < 3 μm) and almost opaque for infrared (IR) waves, which are emitted by a house's interior objects.

Modern windows installed in energy-saving houses consist of two or three glass layers with inert gases (such as argon, krypton, etc.) in the interspaces, and are covered with thin layers of low emissive film on the inner surfaces to reduce the long-wave heat radiation transmission.

Low-energy houses use two-layer insulated windows with $U = 1.1$ to $1.3 \text{W/m}^2\text{K}$, while the passive houses have three-layer insulated windows with $U < 0.7 \text{W/m}^2\text{K}$. This reduces the temperature difference between the room air and the window surfaces (see Figure 2.4) and thus ensures higher comfort. Room air temperature can be lowered by several degrees. Every 1°C of room temperature reduction means 6 per cent savings in fuel consumption.

The standard for a passive house requires the surface temperature to be above 12°C at outside temperature of –10°C.

Insulation

A heated building loses its thermal energy by conduction, convection and radiation. To reduce heat losses, an appropriate thickness and type of insulation have to be chosen.

One of the basic indicators of good insulation quality is the low value of its overall heat transfer coefficient; in addition, other processes and economic restrictions have to be considered.

The process restrictions are:

- mechanical resistance;
- allowed temperature range;
- life duration;
- vapour permeability;
- acoustic insulability;
- environmental friendliness;
- possible harmful effect on health;
- ease of use; and
- resistance to chemical impacts and insects.

The economic restrictions are:

- energy savings; and
- costs.

Contrary to general knowledge, the thermal insulation of a building is most important in summer and not in winter. Bearing this in mind and the fact that we are facing global climate changes, and that newly built houses are constructed for some 100 years and that fuel prices will constantly rise, it is recommended that the building envelope be insulated with at least 30cm thick insulation.

In practice, several different types of organic or inorganic insulations can be distinguished (see Table 2.3).

The most popular and widely used insulation material is glass wool, which is vapour impermeable, non-inflammable, noise reducing, resistant to chemical influences, unharmful to health, can be used at relatively high temperature, is not water absorbing, and is environment and user friendly.

A popular insulation is polystyrene foam in the form of boards, which are light, environment friendly, easy to build in, economic, water resistant, and resistant to acids, bases and microbes.

Transparent thermal insulation materials (glass, different artificial substances, etc.) enable the heat gains of solar energy radiation.

Properties of thermal insulations

Thermal insulation should have adequate mechanical properties, be vapour permeable, durable, heat efficient and properly installed in the framework of constructing the building envelope.

In residential areas, substantial water vapour is formed by breathing, sweating, cooking and other causes. Even though, at a first glance, it appears that water vapour cannot affect the insulation and state of health in a room, the proper installation of insulation layers is of great significance for vapour permeability and the microclimate. Consequently, it is important to ensure controlled heat transfer and water vapour from the rooms to the sourroundings. This can be done in two ways:

1   the vapour-impermeable but diffusion-closed way;
2   the vapour-permeable and diffusion-open way.

In the first case we tighten the building with foils, which do not (or only slightly) let through the water vapour. The effect is similar to a windjacket, which occasionally has to be opened for the air to get inside. This is the same with the building, where we need to open the windows from time to time to let fresh air in.

Table 2.3 *Insulating materials*

Inorganic materials		Natural and organic materials	
Mineral fibres	**Foam materials**	**Plants and animal fibres**	**Foam materials**
Slag wool	Expanded glass	Coconut fibres	Polyester foam
Glass wool	Vermiculite	Cellulose fibres	Extruded polyester
Rock wool	Perlite	Wood flax	Polystyrene foam
	Expanded clay	Wool	Polyurethane foam
		Straw	Foamy formaldehyde tar
		Cotton	
		Paper	
		Cork	

In the second case, we build in vapour-permeable foils that enable water vapour, formed inside the building, to be evenly transfered throughout the building envelope, at the same time enabling a proper exchange of air and odours.

Vapour-impermeable systems prevent the diffusion of vapour through the walls and insulation from inside to outside. As a consequence, the space 'sweats'. It is therefore important to construct the vapour impermeable system in such a way as to prevent the penetration of water vapour into the insulation, which is then difficult to dry. Looking at it from the inside, the vapour blockade needs to come before the insulation.

We are familiar with the fact that when air passes from a space with a higher temperature to a space with a lower temperature, it emits moisture. To avoid this or to reduce this possibility to a minimum, the subsequent rules have to be obeyed:

•   Ensure an adequate vapour permeability of thermal insulation.
•   In a multilayer wall, ensure that each layer, counting from the inside outwards, is more vapour permeable than the previous.

This analysis is similar for the roof above a residential attic.

Insulation thickness

Good thermal protection of the building envelope contributes the most to an efficient use of energy for heating the building. In deciding on thermal protection, we take market-accessible technical solutions and the estimation of their long-term economic viability as a basis.

When constructing or renovating buildings, it is worth following the recommendations of the profession, which are based on economic calculations and contruction–physical parameters of thermal comfort in the living environment. The optimum insulation thickness depends upon climatic conditions, the location of the building and the heat loads of the house interior.

Taking into account internal heat loads, average day and average night temperatures (based on a 24-hour/365-day period) at a certain location, the optimum insulation thickness can be calculated, enabling the best protection against solar radiation during the summer and disabling heat losses in the winter.

A classically built house is, for instance, recommended to be thermally insulated in such way that the external walls attain an overall heat transfer coefficient lower than $0.4 \text{W/m}^2\text{K}$.

If we compare the non-insulated brick wall that is 29cm thick with an overall heat transfer coefficient of $1.5 \text{W/m}^2\text{K}$ with a wall insulated with 10cm thick thermal insulation, the overall heat transfer coefficient of the latter is only $0.3 \text{W/m}^2\text{K}$, meaning that the heat losses are five times less.

Considering the current prices of thermal insulation materials (e.g. glass wool), a slightly thicker thermal protection of the building envelope does not represent a much higher investment; on the other hand, the building will conform to contemporary standards regarding the use and costs of energy. Increasing the thickness of thermal protection from 5cm to 8cm on the 19cm thick fire-baked brick wall means that the original price will increase by only about 6 to 7 per cent, whereas the overall heat transfer coefficient of the wall will decrease by about 30 per cent.

Usually, we are inclined to build in a thermal insulation that is too thin, especially at the back plates facing the ventilated attics and with flat roofs above heated spaces. The insulation thickness should be between 15cm to 25cm; with flat roofs it can be somewhat thiner.

If we constrain ourselves to the passive house, we can find out that its envelope has very good thermal insulation properties: all of the building elements should have the overall heat transfer coefficient of $U \leq 0.15 \text{W/m}^2\text{K}$; often these values are even lower ($U \leq 0.1 \text{W/m}^2\text{K}$). The thermal insulation thickness depends upon the material and composition of the wall and is normally between 25cm and 40cm.

If we take glass wool thermal insulation, for example, with thermal conductivity lower than $0.04 \text{W/m}^2\text{K}$, we can calculate the overall heat transfer coefficients for different elements of the passive building envelope for recommended insulation thickness (see Table 2.4).

Advanced construction layer

Phase-change materials

The demand for the efficient use of energy encourages the construction of buildings with very low heat losses that can only be achieved with the selection of high-quality materials.

Table 2.4 *Overall heat transfer coefficients of the building envelope for recommended thickness of glass wool insulation*

Building element (construction)	Insulation thickness (cm)	Heat transfer coefficient of the building envelope U (W/m²K)
External walls	24–30	0.14–0.12
Ceiling below the non-heated attic	30–40	0.11–0.08
Roof above the heated attic	30–40	0.11–0.08
Floor above the ground	15–20	0.16–0.14

For this purpose, new materials are being developed in two ways:

1   materials based on vacuum insulation; and
2   materials that accumulate self-latent energy (phase-change materials) (see www.corporate.basf.com).

Vacuum-insulating materials do not contain any air or gas pores and significantly reduce heat leaking. If, with the use of reflective materials, we also prevent radiation and additional nano-porosity, we could reach almost zero conductivity. Phase-change materials (PCMs) are materials that accumulate energy that is released in the process of changing aggregate states from solid to liquid and vice versa.

Microgranulation materials (or 'special woof') have similar characteristics as ice. Ice changes phase when heated at 0°C and is converted to water. It absorbs a large amount of heat in the process and this results in cooling of the surroundings.

Phase-change materials have, for example, been employed in:

• the conditioning of buildings;
• heat pump systems;
• waste heat recovery;
• thermal energy storage;
• the heat depositor of passive houses;
• the construction elements of the building layer, etc.

In practice, we use PCM materials by building them in the form of micro- or nano-balls into concrete, bricks or plaster; when they change phase, they absorb a substantial amount of heat with a consequent significant rise in temperature.

When ambient temperature around a liquid material falls, the PCM solidifies, releasing its stored latent heat. Within the human comfort range of 20°C

to 30°C, some PCMs are very effective. They store 5 to 14 times more heat per unit volume than conventional storage materials such as water, masonry or rock.

A 15mm thick plaster plate with built-in micro grains of PCM is, for example, equivalent to a 12cm thick brick wall or a 9cm thick concrete wall, and it ensures that heat accumulates during the day, which is then released during the night when the temperature in the room falls (see Figure 2.5). As a result, the consumption of energy needed for heating and ventilation is minimized. During the summer season, temperature stability increases and the temperature inside the building is more pleasant. The temperature delay is much higher, as shown in Figure 2.6. With temperature stability, we mark the ability of construction to maintain stable temperatures in a room independently of outside changes. In order to achieve this, the ability of materials to accept and store heat and to release it when the temperature in the environment drops is very crucial.

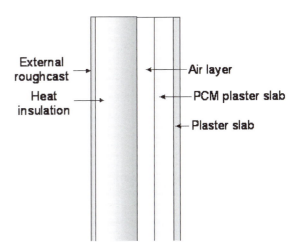

Figure 2.5 *A wall with phase-change materials*

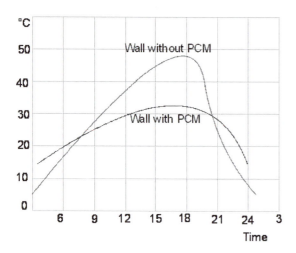

Figure 2.6 *The time profile of temperature in a wall*

Low-energy and passive buildings are becoming a reality in simple and massive construction. One of the possibilities for maximizing the heat stability of building construction is definitely through the use of phase-change materials. In the same way, we can also use latent depositors based on PCM in our heating/cooling systems.

Summary

Any building should be designed and constructed so as to increase its energy efficiency. The supply of energy to the building needs to employ innovative solutions that are technically feasible, are justified in terms of costs, are acceptable from environmental and social standpoints, and ensure a conventional level of living standard and comfort.

Engineering approaches for the economic use of energy, such as substantive insulation of buildings and the reduction of thermal bridges, has a limited influence on energy consumption. It is necessary, in addition, to apply certain active elements in housing – the exploitation of solar energy, ambient heat and wasted heat. Designing such systems requires a special approach to the problem; considering conventional energy sources as being economically and ecologically appropriate is no longer justified.

This chapter points out how important the integration of all relevant aspects within energy-saving houses is, with special emphasis on windows, which

contribute to a substantial amount of heat loss and, consequently, to environmental pollution. Therefore, it is necessary to encourage new ways of professional thinking promoted by the political directives of EU legislation, and to directly influence environmental standards, which are very important today. In the process of adopting such directives in EU member states, a crucial area is the promotion of insulated-window installation, with clear thinking about imposing a tax on CO_2 emissions per tonne or cubic metre of fossil fuel, cancelling purchase tax or value-added tax (VAT) for windows with insulated glass, and offering favourable loans and incentives for such purposes.

References

Aydin, D. (2006) 'Conjugate heat transfer analysis of double pane windows', *Building and Environment*, vol 41, p109–116

Council Directive 89/106/EEC of 21 December 1988 on the Approximation of Laws, Regulations and Administrative Provisions of the Member States Relating to Construction Products, Official Journal L40/12 of 2 November 1989

Council Directive 93/76/EEC of 13 September 1993 to Limit Carbon Dioxide Emissions by Improving Energy Efficiency (SAVE), Official Journal L237, 222/09/1993

Deutsche Regulative EnEV, 2002 (DIN V 4102 – 6 and DIN V 4701 – 10)

Directive 2002/91/EC of the European Parliament and of the Council of 16 December 2002 on the Energy Performance of Buildings, Official Journal L 001, 4 February 2003

Kwak Wai, T., Seklar, C., Eang, L. S. and Cheong, D. (2006) 'Total building performance – 9 new parading for building delivery', *KGH*, Beograd

Kyoto Protocol to the United Nations Framework Convention on Climate Change Strengthens the International Response to Climate Change (2002) May

Novak, P. (2005) 'Which way from factor 4 to 4000? Energy efficiency and IEQ are twins', *KGH*, Beograd, p21

Novaković, V. and Holst, J. N. (2006) 'Lifetime commissioning for energy efficient operation of buildings – Norwegian approach', *KGH*, Beograd, p49

Passiv Haus Institut (2004) *Passivhaus Paket*, Wolfgang Feist, Passiv Haus Institut

Tabunchikov, Y. and Brodatch, M. (2005) 'The principles of energy efficient buildings design', *KGH*, Beograd, p33

Umberger, M., Krope T. and Krope J. (2006) 'Energy economy and the protection of environment with building-in insulated windows', *WSEAS Transactions on Heat and Mass Transfer*, vol 1, no 1, pp32–38

United Nations Framework Convention on Climate Change (1992) FCCC/INFORMAL/84, United Nations

World Energy Outlook 2006 Maps Out a Cleaner, Cleverer and More Competitive Energy Future (2006) November, London

Zbašnik Senegačnik, M. (2007) *Pasive House*, University of Ljubljana, Faculty of Architecture, Ljubljana

Useful websites

National University of Singapore, Centre for Total Building Performance: www.ctbp.bdg.nus.edu.sg

IG Passivhaus Osterreich: www.igpassivhaus.at

IG Passivhaus Deutschland: www.ig-passivhaus.de

BASF: www.corporate.basf.com

BASF Micronal PCM: www.micronal.de

BAULINKS: www.baulinks.de

3

Energy Monitoring and Labelling

Stefano Paolo Corgnati and Vincenzo Corrado

Introduction

Since Directive 2002/91/EC on the energy efficiency of buildings was adopted, there has been a strong increase in the interest in rationalizing energy consumption in both new and existing buildings. The introduction of the energy performance certification of buildings has resulted in the development of various methodologies (i.e. diagnostic tools) that may assist facility managers and energy monitoring professionals to detect faults or malfunctions in the energy behaviour of buildings. Furthermore, energy consumption monitoring contributes to the development of building energy performance classification and more comprehensive energy benchmarking systems. This chapter defines various energy rating indexes used for the assessment and prediction of energy use in buildings and describes both heating and cooling energy monitoring procedures.

Energy assessment methodologies

The energy classification and the certification of buildings require an assessment methodology that can be applied without distinction to new and existing buildings. To this end, the standard *EN 15603: Energy Performance of Buildings – Overall Energy Use, CO₂ Emissions and Definition of Energy Ratings* presents several assessment methodologies enabling one to:

- obtain the same results for different data sets;
- estimate the missing data and calculate a 'standard' energy consumption for air conditioning (heating, cooling and ventilation), production of domestic hot water and lighting;

- assess the effectiveness of possible energy efficiency improvements.

EN 15603 identifies the end uses to be considered in order to evaluate the energy performance of new and existing buildings. The energy performance evaluation is based on the weighted sum of the calculated or measured consumptions by primary energy source (natural gas, oil, electric energy, etc.). According to the circumstances, we can determine the energy performance of a building through a calculation model based on the known building characteristics (*direct approach*), or assess the energy consumption through the actual consumption measurement (*inverse approach*).

In EN 15603, the following classification of energy assessments is proposed:

- *Operational rating* is obtained by measuring and summing up (after appropriate weighting) all amounts of delivered energy by each energy source (electricity, oil, natural gas, etc.).
- *Calculated rating* is obtained by measuring and summing up (after appropriate weighting) all amounts of delivered energy both by use and energy source. This assessment can be further differentiated according to the method adopted to collect the data on climate and use conditions.
- *Design rating* is based on calculations using the data derived from design results and design values estimated for a building under construction.
- *Asset rating* is the value based on calculations using the existing building data (the data is obtained from field surveys and deductive rules) and input

standard values concerning indoor/outdoor environments and occupancy.

- *Tailored rating* is based on calculations using the actual data of a building, as well as climate and occupancy data. The data concerning the building may be rectified after a comparison between calculated and measured consumptions (*validated rating*).

Asset rating represents the intrinsic potential of a building under standardized conditions of use and can be applied for energy certification. On the other side, operational rating is a measure of the in-use performance of the building, and can be useful in certifying the actual performance of the building user system. Obviously, in order to obtain an operational rating, it is essential to implement monitoring strategies that enable one to measure the actual energy consumption of the building.

EN 15603 underlines that it is impossible to compare directly the energy performance indexes obtained from an asset rating and an operational rating. However, the differences between these two ratings can be useful to evaluate the cumulative effects of the actual conditions of the building in comparison with the standard conditions. The following methods should be considered:

- Assess the compliance with technical and operational rules representative of energy targets.
- Compare the energy performances of various design alternatives for a new building.
- Set an energy performance benchmark for existing buildings.
- Evaluate the effect of possible energy-saving actions on an existing building through the analysis of the pre-intervention consumption and the estimation of the possible post-intervention savings.
- Predict the future energy requirements of a building, or a building stock, on the basis of the actual trend of energy consumptions of different buildings representative of the building stock in question.

Monitoring heating energy consumption

This section focuses on the monitoring, standardization and analysis of primary energy consumption for heating in existing buildings. In this case, the monitoring is

defined as continuous measurements during the whole heating season of those parameters that are significant in describing energy consumption for heating in a building (e.g. the amount of fuel consumed) and essential for standardizing energy consumption (e.g. total heated volume of the building).

In order to attribute a specific consumption index to the building that is able to define its energy performance, an *operational rating* procedure is applied for the following purposes of:

- continuously monitoring and controlling building energy consumption;
- setting reference consumption values for a building;
- predicting energy consumption for future heating seasons.

The attribution process of reference energy consumptions to each building is particularly important. This data can be effectively used to define costs in energy service contracts. Moreover, the attribution of such an energy index to the building is in compliance with European Directive 2002/91/EC on the energy performance of buildings. As already mentioned, it highlights the need to attribute energy performance indicators to existing buildings, even through the analysis of actual consumption.

According to each specific purpose, it may be more significant either to use energy performance indexes obtained from theoretical consumptions on the basis of the known characteristics of the building plant system (*calculated rating*), or to refer to the actual metered energy consumptions (*operational rating*). The indicators obtained from this second approach are particularly suitable to represent the consumptions of an operating building as a result of the 'building–plant–user' system dynamics.

In particular, the *operational rating* procedure is based on the estimation of an index of 'conventional specific energy consumption for heating purposes' (Corgnati et al, 2004). Essentially, this estimation procedure provides for the development of the following two phases:

1   data collection;
2   definition of the consumption index.

The first phase consists of collecting data concerning building characteristics (both typological and geometrical), local climate conditions, heating use conditions, energy consumption and, in particular:

- location of the building;
- shape and type of building;
- geometrical characteristics (gross heated floor area, useful heated surface, etc.);
- actual degree days (DD), on a yearly and, if possible, monthly basis;
- fuel type;
- actual primary energy consumption for heating (CE) on a yearly and, if possible, monthly basis;
- actual consumed energy delivered by the heat generator (QP) on a yearly and, if possible, monthly basis;
- duration of the heating period, expressed in hours, on a monthly and yearly basis;
- indoor thermo-hygrometric conditions (T and RH).

In order to analyse a sufficiently significant data sample, it is necessary to collect monitoring data representative of at least three heating seasons. The duration of the heating period is represented by the hours during which the heat generator supplies the consumed energy QP. However, other data can, in some cases, be more appropriate to evaluate the d parameter. For instance, in the case of a heating management service contract, the purchaser can consider it more significant to identify with d the number of hours during which the appropriate minimum temperature conditions must be maintained in order to ensure the occupants' comfort (i.e. 20°C during occupancy hours). In this case, the aim of the heating management company is to define a heating strategy that enables consumption to be minimized and satisfies the minimum required level of environmental quality (i.e. the above-mentioned 20°C).

The second phase consists of defining the consumption index (Corgnati et al, 2007). For example, in the case of a heating management service based on the purchase/supply of thermal energy delivered by the heat generator, the consumption index referring to the actual energy delivered by the heat generator (QP) is obtained from the following expression:

$$QP_{s,c} = \frac{QP}{V} \cdot \frac{DD_c}{DD} \cdot \frac{d_c}{d} = QP_s \cdot \frac{DD_c}{DD} \cdot \frac{d_c}{d} \qquad (1)$$

The $QP_{s,c}$ index represents the 'conventional specific energy consumption for heating purposes', given by the ratio of the delivered thermal energy (measured by heat meters) to the gross heated volume, with reference to the conventional degree days in the examined area (DD_c), and the conventional duration of the heating period (d_c). The fuel consumption, or in this case the useful delivered energy, is first of all divided by the volume in order to obtain a specific value. The mutual relation between consumption and volume is well known. The example in Figure 3.1 shows a sample of buildings heated with natural gas for the same use (therefore with approximately equal heating period duration) located in the same area (therefore with equal heating seasons and equal effective degree days).

The proposed model for the $QP_{s,c}$ index assessment provides, in accordance with the European Standard EN 15203 and former authors' works (Corrado et al, 2004), a linear dependence between the energy consumption for heating and:

- the local degree days;
- the duration of the heating period of the building.

Figure 3.2 shows an example of the monthly metered fuel consumptions in a given building (expressed in cubic metres of natural gas per cubic metre of gross heated volume) as a function of the corresponding actual monthly degree days. The regression line shows a good correlation between the data, as indicated by the R^2 value of 0.88. Moreover, the scatter of the data around the regression curve shows how consumptions are influenced by stochastic factors and deviate from perfect linearity. In particular, users' behaviour may significantly influence the size of endogenous heat supply, the ventilation rate, the incoming solar radiation, etc. Once the monitoring data have been collected, it is always convenient to make an accurate analysis, as shown in Figure 3.2, in order to assess how decisive the influence of the above-mentioned stochastic variables is on the actual consumption of an examined building.

With reference to the other parameter – that is the duration of the heating period (d) – it is important to note that its actual value is strongly related not only to the occupation time of the building, but also to the thermal dynamics of the 'building envelope plant' system (the difference between light and heavy buildings is an example).

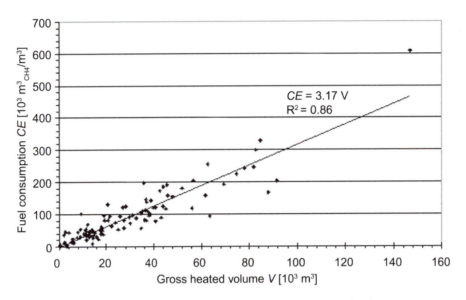

Figure 3.1 *Fuel consumption as a function of gross heated volume*

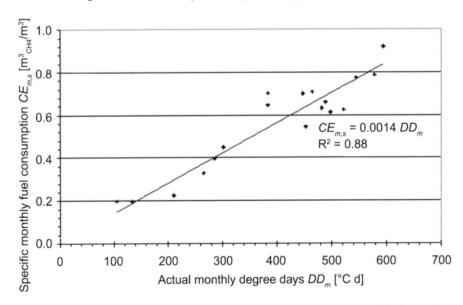

Figure 3.2 *Specific monthly fuel consumption as a function of actual monthly degree days*

While assessing the $QP_{s,c}$ index, it is important to estimate the reliability of the metered energy consumption values. The heat meters, in fact, may often give approximate values due to possible malfunctions and measurement inaccuracies. On the contrary, the metered fuel consumption values are typically more reliable. The reliability of the metered QP values is estimated by calculating, on a monthly and seasonal basis, the efficiency of the heat generator:

$$\eta_p = \frac{QP}{CE} \qquad (2)$$

The evaluation procedure for generation efficiency has been amply dealt with in a former author's publication (Corrado et al, 2004). As already mentioned, the index of conventional specific energy consumption for heating purposes $QP_{s,c}$ can be defined using monitored consumption data representative of at least three

Plant code	... ...
Building name	... ...
City	
Address	... ...

		Total	October	November	December	January	February	March	April
Duration of the heating period	[d]	183	17	30	31	31	28	31	15
Degree days	[°C d]	2628	144	389	551	600	464	358	122
Monthly average outdoor temperature	[°C]	5,6	11,5	7,0	2,2	0,6	3,4	8,4	11,8
Climatic zone	[-]	E							

Building category	E.7	School

Gross heated volume (V)	[m³]	17827
Fuel	[-]	Natural gas

Month	Conventional quantities						Measured quantities								Corrected conventional quantities		Relative deviation
	Outdoor temp.	Degree days	Duration of the heating period	Number of heating hours	Heat supply	Specific heat supply	Outdoor temp.	Degree days	Duration of the heating period	Number of heating hours	Heat supply	Specific heat supply	Fuel consumpt.	Average generation efficiency	Heat supply	Specific heat supply	[(11)-(15)] / [15]
	(1)	(2)	(3)	(4)	(5)	(6)	(7)	(8)	(9)	(10)	(11)	(12)	(13)	(14)	(15)	(16)	(17)
	[°C]	[°C d]	[d]	[h]	[MWh]	[kWh/m³]	[°C]	[°C d]	[d]	[h]	[MWh]	[kWh/m³]	[m³ o [l]]	[%]	[MWh]	[kWh/m³]	[%]
October/November	8,7	533	47	282	166	9,3	8,8	516	46	187	105	5,9	12626	86,6%	106	6,0	-1,2%
December	2,2	551	31	186	171	9,6	4,7	473	31	144	68	3,8	8105	87,7%	114	6,4	-40,2%
January	0,6	600	31	186	187	10,5	3,1	523	31	135	129	7,2	15208	88,3%	118	6,6	9,1%
February	3,4	464	28	168	144	8,1	5,3	425	29	109	102	5,7	11917	88,8%	86	4,8	18,3%
March	8,4	358	31	186	112	6,3	9,1	337	31	107	66	3,7	7852	87,8%	60	3,4	9,7%
April/May	11,8	122	15	90	38	2,1	13,1	178	26	82	32	1,8	3970	85,2%	51	2,8	-35,8%
Total	5,6	2628	183	1098	818	45,9	7,4	2452	194	764	502	28,2	59678	87,7%	535	30,0	-6,1%

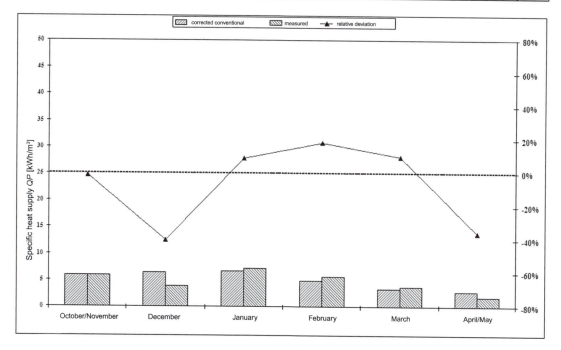

Figure 3.3 *Consumption data collection chart for a building*

heating seasons, and can be useful to define consumptions and costs for a heating management service, or simply to evaluate or predict the energy consumption of future heating seasons. The evaluation procedure presented above has been validated by the authors (see Corgnati and Corrado, 2006).

The procedure is mainly applied to compare the predicted consumption (on the basis of the specific energy consumption $QP_{s,c}$) with the actual consumption for a given heating season. An example of a data collection chart is shown in Figure 3.3.

The chart in Figure 3.3 is used to collect data concerning both the building and its consumption, as well as climate conditions. It is divided into three main sections:

1   general information;
2   monthly energy and climate data;
3   diagram of comparison between predicted and measured consumptions.

The general information includes data concerning the building (plant code, building name, city and address), climate data (average monthly outdoor temperature, monthly degree days, climatic zone and duration of the heating period), and the main characteristics of the building (category, gross heated volume and fuel type).

The monthly data section includes a table showing conventional and measured quantities. The climatic zone where the building is located is defined on the basis of the number of degree days. The time interval for the conventional duration of the heating period is identified according to the climatic zone. For instance, with reference to buildings in Italian climatic zone E (number of degree days below 3000°Cd), the heating season extends from 15 October to 15 April. The conventional daily number of hours used to calculate the conventional duration of the heating period is set on the basis of the building use (i.e. 6 hours a day for schools and offices, 14 hours a day for residential buildings).

In order to compare the measured and calculated values, it is necessary to correct the 'conventional data', according to the climate conditions and actual operating hours. To this end, the 'corrected conventional specific heat supply' can be defined as:

$$QP_{c^*} = QP_c \frac{DD_r}{DD_c} \frac{d_r}{d_c} \tag{3}$$

The comparison between measured and calculated values is fundamental in order to evaluate the accuracy of the consumption prediction, as shown by the example in Figure 3.4. The diagram represents the corrected conventional heat supply (x axis) and the measured specific heat supply (y axis) for the heating of

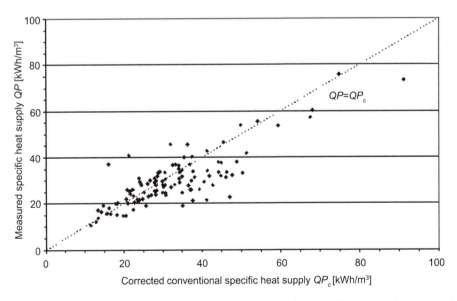

Figure 3.4 *Measured specific heat supply versus corrected conventional specific heat supply (117 school buildings)*

117 schools during one entire heating season in climatic zone E. Obviously, in the case where the predicted and measured data are perfectly coincident, the dots representing the examined sample would fall along the bisector of the first quadrant of the Cartesian coordinate system (y = x). This diagram shows that the dots, although scattered around the bisector, tend to concentrate mainly in the lower part of the quadrant, which reveals that the predictive model tends to slightly overestimate actual consumptions.

It is evident that in the case where the above-mentioned predictive model is not applied to the consumption of every single building, but to an entire sample of buildings (i.e. for heating management service in real estate), the comparison between total measured consumptions and total predicted consumptions is more significant.

The histogram in Figure 3.5 shows a comparison between metered and predicted heat supply for a mixed-use group of buildings where a heating management service is carried out. The real estate is basically composed of school buildings, representing over 95 per cent of the real estate consumptions, and some office and residential buildings covering the remaining 5 per cent of consumptions. It is evident that the total estimated consumption predicts with reasonable accuracy the total metered consumption.

The difference of 6 per cent is an acceptable value if we consider the number of stochastic factors that may interfere between predicted and actual consumptions, such as users' behaviour.

Energy labelling of heating energy consumption

The assessment methodologies for actual energy consumption can be a useful starting point to carry out diagnostic processes on real estate. In particular, the consumption analysis enables one to identify anomalies and critical issues in building (i.e. in terms of overconsumption in comparison with the average behaviour of the examined sample buildings).

The first step of the diagnostic process is the energy classification of the real estate. From the operative point of view, this means, first of all, defining the correlation between consumption and volume in order to identify any possible cases that do not reflect the statistical trend of the sample.

The frequency distribution of the specific consumption is then expressed as a basis of the energy classification (consumption class A, B, C, etc.) which may lead to planning and developing energy requalification interventions. Obviously, priority will

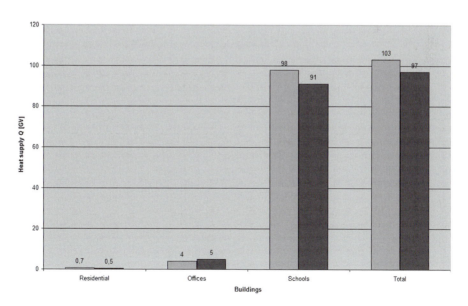

Figure 3.5 *Measured specific useful heat supply versus corrected conventional specific useful heat supply for a sample of buildings used for different purposes*

be given to high-consumption buildings (in terms of both absolute and specific values). Therefore, the aim of the analysis is to examine the distribution of both absolute and specific consumption, and to carry out an energy classification in order to identify those subgroups of the sample which present more critical issues in terms of energy.

Figure 3.6 expresses primary energy consumption for heating in a school complex.

As clearly shown in Figure 3.6, the volume of most of the buildings is below 40,000m³. However, higher volume buildings, despite their small number, have a significant impact upon total consumption. Moreover, a large number of buildings fall above the regression line (passing through the origin) representative of the sample consumption. This indicates that a number of specific consumptions are significantly higher than the sample trend.

These results must be integrated with frequency distribution and cumulated frequency of the specific consumption, expressed in kWh/m³, for the examined real estate (see Figure 3.7). About 60 per cent of the values are lower than 40kWh/m³, which is a reference value set slightly below the average specific consumption value of the sample. Moreover, it is evident that in some cases the specific consumption significantly exceeds the average: 11 per cent of the sample show consumption above 80kWh/m³ (double the sample average value), and

7 per cent show consumption above 120kWh/m³ (triple the sample average value). It is therefore necessary to deepen the diagnostic analysis on the buildings presenting such critical issues in order to identify the causes (which may be related to the building envelope, plant technology, plant management, users' behaviour, etc.) and propose corrective solutions.

A further in-depth analysis can be carried out by classifying the energy efficiency of the real estate as a function of the specific consumption value, set as an index for characterizing the consumption in existing buildings. The following methodology defining a dimensionless indicator of the actual consumption is adopted:

$$I_c = CEs / CE_{rif} \text{ (consumption index)} \qquad (4)$$

where the value of CE_{rif} (kWh/m³) (reference specific energy consumption) is obtained from the statistical analysis of the specific energy consumptions (CEs) of the sample of buildings characterized by the same use (school buildings). In this case, CE_{rif} corresponds to the average value of the examined sample of buildings. On the basis of the I_c index value, four classes are defined (see Table 3.1).

Each of the four classes depicted in Table 3.1 corresponds to an assessment of the I_c index (see Table 3.2).

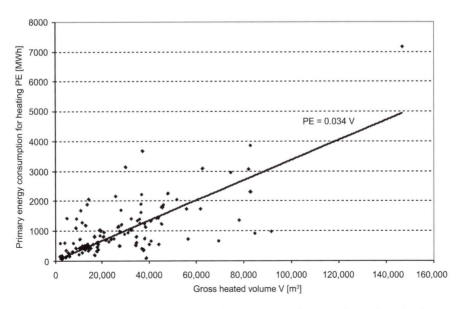

Figure 3.6 *Primary energy consumption for heating as a function of gross heated volume*

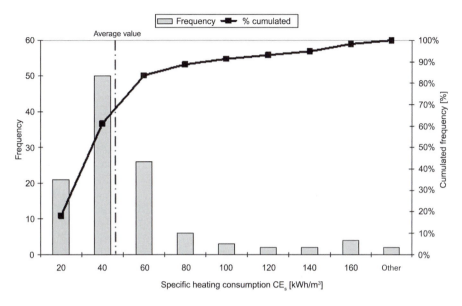

Figure 3.7 *Frequency distribution and cumulated frequency of specific heating consumption*

Table 3.1 *Variation intervals of the I_c index*

Index	Variation interval	Class	Index assessment
Consumption index	≤ 0.5	A	Excellent
I_c [−]	$0.5 < I_c ≤ 1$	B	Good
	$1 < I_c ≤ 1.5$	C	Mean
	$1.5 < I_c ≤ 2$	D	Poor
	$I_c > 2$		Non-classifiable

Table 3.2 *Assessment classes of the I_c index*

I_c	Assessment
Class A	Building consumption far below the average consumption of the reference statistical sample. No intervention is needed.
Class B	Building consumption slightly below the average consumption of the reference statistical sample. No intervention is needed.
Class C	Building consumption above the average consumption of the reference statistical sample. Intervention aimed at reducing heating consumption is recommended.
Class D	Building consumption significantly above the average consumption of the reference statistical sample. Urgent intervention aimed at reducing heating consumption is recommended.

This approach emphasizes an important aspect: it is evident that intervention priority is given to high-consumption buildings (in comparison with the average consumption of the estimated sample of buildings), although general improving interventions on the building plant system must not be excluded for classes A and B either. Therefore, the proposed diagnostic method defines the guidelines for the assignment of intervention priority within the specific examined sample of buildings. For this reason, the CE_{rif} value is not aprioristically defined on the basis of literature data, but represents a studied characteristic datum of the real estate.

Figure 3.8 shows the frequency distribution and the cumulated frequency of the specific consumption index calculated for the above-mentioned sample of buildings. The energy efficiency classification described in Table 3.2 is also shown in the diagram.

Figure 3.8 shows that it is possible to define a clear and objective subdivision of the examined real estate into energy efficiency classes. At first, the diagnostic investigation is carried out on high-consumption buildings. In this case, 10 per cent of the buildings fall into class D (= specific consumption index above 2); therefore, they are assessed as 'non-classifiable'.

These tools are useful for the energy classification of real estate, which is a preparatory activity for the diagnostic

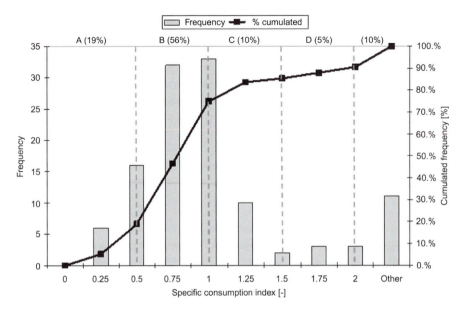

Figure 3.8 *Frequency distribution and cumulated frequency of the specific consumption index*

Table 3.3 *Annual use of electricity in dwellings with energy efficient equipment (kWh)*

Number of rooms	1	2	3	4	5	6
Number of occupants	1	1.5	2	3	4	5
Refrigerator	250	250	270	270	170	170
Freezer	0	0	0	0	200	200
Dishwasher	110	150	210	260	320	330
Oven	30	40	80	80	80	80
Washing machine	70	100	130	200	270	330
Dryer	130	200	260	390	525	660
Cooker	220	240	260	300	340	380
Other equipment	130	150	180	220	270	290
Total in kWh	940	1130	1390	1720	2175	2440
Floor area	40	60	80	110	140	170
Total in kWh/m²	24	19	17	16	16	14

investigation on high-consumption (absolute and specific) buildings. Moreover, these procedures are a particularly effective support tool for planning extraordinary maintenance activities in real estate, which implies the definition of criteria for assigning intervention priorities.

Monitoring cooling energy consumption

In order to carry out an accurate monitoring of cooling energy consumption, direct measurements on individual items of equipment (e.g. a chiller) or energy use (e.g. lighting) are preferable to overall utility energy bills. The total electricity bill, which may relate to time periods that are not ideal for monitoring purposes, combines energy consumption through numerous end uses: lighting, ventilation and small power appliances (kitchen or office equipments, home entertainment systems, etc.) and, occasionally, process loads such as air compressors, pumps, fans, etc.

Interpretation of electricity bills requires the listing of each type of electrical appliances whose consumption is included in the energy bill.

The analysis of air-conditioning performance using global energy bills will be accurate only if the share of air-conditioning energy consumption in the bill is significant. If energy consumption for cooling is submerged by that from other uses, accurate estimation will be impossible without sub-metering.

Several parameters have effects on air-conditioning energy consumption and, more generally, on all thermal energy consumption. It is possible to distinguish four types:

1   *Building parameters* are intrinsic to the construction of the building. Building envelope thermal characteristics, glazing surface, heated/cooled areas and their location belong to this category.

2   *Policy parameters* depend only upon the current building owner's decisions and his or her will to save energy. Equipment choices and investments, operational parameters such as temperature and humidity set points (if building centralized), the time of operation or maintenance, and follow-up policies are part of these parameters. The sensitivity of energy consumption to these parameters is extremely important.

3   *Behavioural parameters* depend upon the occupants' choices. Operational parameters such as temperature and humidity set points (if room localized) or the natural uneconomic behaviour of occupants fall within this category. Their influence on energy consumption can be substantial, although the duration of 'good practice' behaviour can be short.

4   *Activity parameters* depend mostly upon the use of each space. These are largely determined by the business needs of the organization. They have an important influence on energy consumption; but a building owner or energy manager cannot usually change them.

•   *Climatic data* involves obtaining external temperature and solar irradiance values from a meteorological station that is most representative of the location of the building and of the time period used for energy metering. Solar irradiance should be available for all main orientations of the building envelope that include transparent elements or elements covered with transparent insulation.

•   *Internal temperature*: the actual internal temperature should be assessed since it often differs from design temperature and has a significant influence on the energy use for cooling or heating. Possible methods involve the following:
    –   In buildings with mechanical ventilation, the air temperature in the exhaust duct upstream of the fan can give an estimate of the average temperature of the ventilated zone when the exhaust fan is on.
    –   In many large buildings, a building automation and control system controls all of the energy systems, and records the internal temperature and other energy-related characteristics at several places.
    –   The temperature can be measured or monitored (using small single-channel data loggers) at representative places during representative days (i.e. days that have

meteorological characteristics that represent the corresponding month or season).
    –   Heating or cooling systems are controlled by thermostats; their set points could be used, provided that the calibration of the thermostat is checked.

•   *Air infiltration and ventilation*: external airflow rate should be estimated as well as possible. Ways to do this include: assessments of the airflow rates of air handling units, where appropriate; and use of the tracer gas dilution method.

•   *Internal heat sources*: the occupancy (number of occupants) and occupancy time should be assessed from a survey or from the building management report. Internal sources of artificial lighting and electrical appliances are, at best, assessed from electricity bills where there are no heating or cooling systems on the same meter. EN 15193 can also be used when no field data is available for lighting.

•   *Hot water use*: where a separate meter is installed, hot water use is calculated from the difference between two readings at the beginning and end of the assessment period.

•   *Artificial lighting*: electricity bills may be useful to assess energy use for lighting, provided that there are no other systems (cooking, heating, cooling systems or other appliances) on the same meter.

Energy and microclimatic labelling

The maintenance of particular thermo-hygrometric comfort levels is linked to energy consumption and consequent energy cost (Corgnati et al, 2006a). This apparently obvious statement is, in fact, quite profound: it is useless to express energy consumption for microclimate control in a building without relating such consumption to the microclimatic quality assessed for the environment (Corgnati et al, 2008a). The aim of thorough management of the building plant system is to

Table 3.4 *Annual use of electricity for office equipment per work place in kWh and per conditioned area in kWh/m²*

	Per work place	Per m² conditioned area		
Floor area per person		10m²	15m²	20m²
With energy efficient equipment	120	12	8	6
With typical equipment	230	23	15	12

satisfy thermo-hygrometric and air quality requirements with the minimum possible consumption of non-renewable resources, and therefore to minimize the costs.

The first step is to clearly define the thermo-hygrometric quality expected and measured in the environment. In fact, it is not rare that contracts for heating management services set standard values for temperature, relative humidity and air quality with narrow tolerance intervals, often without considering that narrow thermal tolerance intervals lead to unavoidably high energy consumption. Moreover, it is often forgotten that modern theories on adaptive thermal comfort allow wider tolerance intervals, and modifications of the environment parameter values enable one to reduce energy costs.

From a normative viewpoint, the indoor environment classification in terms of microclimatic quality is dealt with in the draft standard EN 15251, which has recently been developed by the European Committee for Standardization. This draft deals in general terms with the theme of indoor environmental quality, including thermo-hygrometric, visual and acoustic comfort, and air quality. With reference to thermo-hygrometric comfort aspects and, in particular, the classification used for the thermo-hygrometric quality assessment, the draft provides for the subdivision of comfort into classes, corresponding to three different levels of environmental quality (class 1 or A is characterized by the narrowest tolerance interval and the highest thermo-hygrometric comfort; the attribution of a number or a letter to the class is being discussed). In particular, the draft standard defines the thermo-hygrometric parameters, divided according to building use, which have to be adopted at the design stage, in order to measure the building plant system during both summer and winter seasons. Figure 3.9

shows the temperature intervals with their respective classes, proposed for air-conditioned office spaces.

Figure 3.9 clearly shows that the acceptable temperature variation interval increases progressively from A to C class: the interval is of the order of 2°C for class A (both in winter and in summer), while for class C it extends to 6°C in winter and to 5°C in summer. Obviously, the extension of the interval has a direct impact, not particularly on the set-point temperature value, which must be maintained in the environment, but on the acceptable regulation bands.

Therefore, it is clear that the purpose of maintaining a certain temperature level must be supported by equipment able to achieve the objective. For instance, it is impossible to keep an office space in class A during the whole year without installing an air-conditioning system able to control the temperature within the narrow preset intervals. However, in many cases the requirement of mechanical climate control is limited to only one particular period of the year (i.e. schools just need a heating plant), or more periods of the year alternated with natural climate control periods (i.e. offices need heating in winter, cooling in summer and natural climate control in mid-season). The intervals proposed in Figure 3.9, as clearly indicated, refer to the design of fully mechanically controlled environments.

What happens when we want to examine the actual microclimatic quality of an indoor-operating environment throughout the whole year?

The *in-situ* study of microclimatic quality through long-term measurements was carried out according to a research design guide (ASHRAE RP884), focused, in particular, on the theme of thermal quality levels. The obtained results provided further impetus for a number of other *in-situ* case studies, which led to the so-called 'adaptive comfort' theory, particularly suitable for describing the thermal comfort conditions in non-fully mechanically controlled environments (de Dear and Brager, 1998).

This theory comes from the assumption that the comfort sensation can not only be explained by the thermal balance equation between the human body and the surrounding environment (as per Fanger's 1982 classic comfort model, perfectly suitable for fully mechanically controlled environments); but it must also consider other factors (behavioural, cultural, social and contextual), which may affect the thermal sensation (de Dear and Brager, 2002).

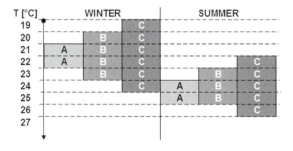

Figure 3.9 *Operating temperature intervals recommended for the design of fully mechanically controlled office spaces, during summer and winter seasons*

The impact of such factors increases in a 'naturally' controlled environment, where the microclimate is not 'artificially' created and controlled by a plant (fully mechanically controlled), but is the result of the user's direct action (even just partially, if we consider natural ventilation) (Brager and de Dear, 2000). The conducted studies have demonstrated that people have a higher tolerance for 'less narrow' microclimatic conditions (in terms of extension of the acceptable temperature intervals) in naturally ventilated environments. In fact, people can activate behavioural, physiological and psychological regulation mechanisms that lead to a wider acceptability of thermo-hygrometric conditions.

One of the main results of the ASHRAE RP884 research project is represented by the diagrams showing how the operating temperature intervals for the thermal quality classes (class A, B and C) vary according to the average monthly outdoor temperature, both in 'fully mechanically controlled' and 'naturally ventilated' environments (see Figures 3.10 and 3.11).

These figures can be opportunely used as a basis to represent the thermal monitoring results of an indoor environment (i.e. an office or a classroom), and consequently to assess thermal quality during occupancy hours.

The example in Figure 3.12 shows the results of long-term microclimate monitoring of a 'hybrid'

environment: heating by radiators and natural ventilation by opening windows during the winter season, and cooling by natural ventilation and opening windows in the mid and summer season (Ansaldi et al, 2006). For this type of environment, typical of many Italian buildings, a hypothesis of temperature intervals and microclimatic quality classes was proposed according to the above-mentioned research methods (Corgnati et al, 2008b). In particular, Figure 3.12 shows the results of a monitoring campaign, displaying indoor temperature values measured in relation to the thermal quality classes (A and B). Two parts are clearly distinguished in the figure: the left side of the diagram (mechanical climate control during the heating season) shows that values and microclimate class intervals remain constant despite varying outdoor temperature, while the right side of the diagram (no mechanical climate control) shows that values and microclimate class intervals vary according to outdoor temperature variations.

Therefore, such diagrams can be opportunely used as a basis to represent thermo-hygrometric monitoring results and, consequently, to assess the obtained environmental quality.

The thermal quality assessment of the environment can be expressed by a synthetic index called the performance index (PI) (Corgnati et al, 2006b), which

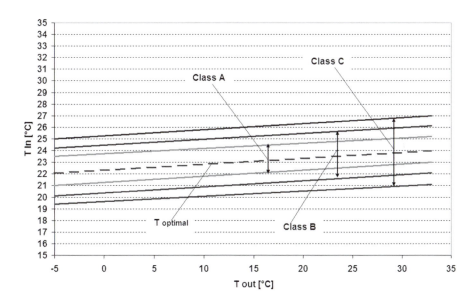

Figure 3.10 *Intervals for thermal quality classes in 'fully mechanically controlled' environments (as per ASHRAE RP884)*

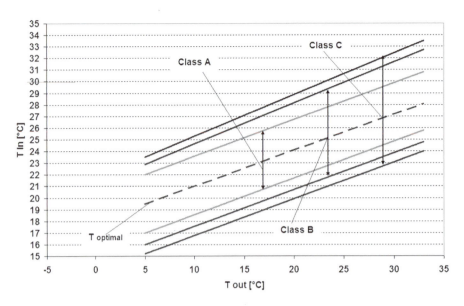

Figure 3.11 *Intervals for thermal quality classes in 'naturally ventilated' environments (as per ASHRAE RP884)*

represents the percentage of measured values falling within the acceptability interval of a given class. Therefore, this parameter indicates how often the examined environment is exposed to acceptable thermal conditions.

With reference to the measurements shown in Figure 3.12, the performance index of class A intervals is 84 per cent during the heating period, and decreases to 69 per cent if we consider the whole analysis period (from October to July). This methodology of data representation and analysis is very effective as it ensures representation clarity and easy comprehension of the thermal quality index. The microclimatic quality analysis described above can be conducted while monitoring the energy consumption for air conditioning in order to prove their correlation with the obtained thermal quality level.

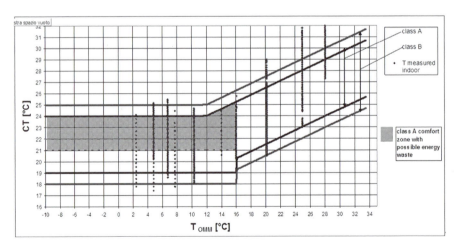

Notes: CT = operating comfort temperature; T_{OMM} = average monthly outdoor temperature.

Source: as in Corgnati et al (2008b)

Figure 3.12 *Temperature values and thermal quality classes proposed in the hypothesis of a thermal model for hybrid environments*

References

Ansaldi, R., Corgnati, S. P. and Filippi, M. (2006) 'Certification of the indoor environmental quality: Methodology and application to an office building', CLIMAMED 2006 International Conference, Lyon, France, October 2006

ASHRAE (American Society of Heating, Refrigerating and Air-Conditioning Engineers) (2005) 'Energy estimating and modelling methods', in ASHRAE (ed) *Handbook: Fundamentals*, Atlanta, Chapter 32.

Brager, G. S. and de Dear, R. (2000) 'A standard for natural ventilation', *ASHRAE Journal*, vol 42, no 10, pp21–28

CEN (2005) *Ergonomics of the Thermal Environment – Analytical Determination and Interpretation of Thermal Comfort Using Calculation of the PMV and PPD Indices and Local Thermal Comfort Criteria*, EN ISO 7730

CEN (2007a) *Indoor Environmental Parameters for Assessment of Energy Performance of Buildings, Addressing Indoor Air Quality, Thermal Environment, Lighting and Acoustics*, EN 15251

CEN (2007b) *Energy Performance of Buildings: Overall Energy Use and Definition of Ratings*, EN 15603

CEN (2007c) *Energy Performance of Buildings: Methods for Expressing Energy Performance and for Energy Certification of Buildings*, EN 15217

CEN (2007d) *Thermal Performance of Buildings: Calculation of Energy Use for Space Heating and Cooling*, EN ISO 13790

Corgnati, S. P. and Corrado, V. (2006) 'Energy assessment of heating consumption in existing school buildings: Results of a field survey', Third International Conference on Research in Building Physics IBPC 2006, Montreal, August 2006

Corgnati, S. P., Corrado, V., Filippi, M. and Maga, C. (2004) 'Energy demand for space heating in existing school buildings: Results of a field survey', in *Proceedings of the Indoor Climate of Buildings*, ISIAQ, Slovakia

Corgnati, S. P., Fabrizio, E. and Filippi, M. (2006a) 'Costs and comfort: Mutual relation between comfort conditions and energy demand in office buildings', AICARR International Conference AICARR 2006 HVAC&R: Technology, Rules and Market, Milan, March 2006

Corgnati, S. P., Filippi, M. and Perino, M. (2006b) 'A new approach for the IEQ (Indoor Environment Quality) assessment', Third International Conference on Research in Building Physics IBPC 2006, Montreal, August 2006

Corgnati, S. P., Corrado, V. and Filippi, M. (2007) 'A method for heating consumption assessment in existing buildings: A field survey concerning 120 Italian schools', *Energy and Buildings*, doi:10.1016/j.enbuild.2007.05.011

Corgnati, S. P., Filippi, M. and Fabrizio, E. (2008a) 'The impact of indoor thermal conditions, system controls and building types on the building demand', *Energy and Buildings*, vol 40, issue 4, pp627–636

Corgnati, S. P., Ansaldi, R. and Filippi, M. (2008b) 'Certification of the indoor environmental quality' ['Certificare la qualità ambientale], *CDA Journal*, March

Corrado, V., Corgnati, S. P. and Maga, C. (2004) 'A methodology for energy assessment of existing buildings using the metered energy consumption', in *Proceedings of PLEA 2004*, prEN 15203

Council Directive 93/76/EEC of 13 September 1993 To Limit Carbon Dioxide Emissions by Improving Energy Efficiency (SAVE), published on the OJ L 237 on 22 September 1993, pp28–30

de Dear, R. J. and Brager, G. S. (1998) 'Developing an adaptive model of thermal comfort and preference', *ASHRAE Transactions: Research 1998*, 4106 (RP-884)

de Dear, R. J. and Brager, G. S. (2002) 'Thermal comfort in naturally ventilated buildings: Revisions to ASHRAE Standard 55', *Energy and Buildings*, vol 34, pp549–556

Directive 2002/91/EC of the European Parliament and of the Council of 16 December 2002 on the Energy Performance of Buildings, published on the OJ L 1 of 4 January 2003, pp65–71

EN 15193 (2007) BS EN 15193: 2007, 'Energy performance of building: Energy requirements for lighting', BSI, London

4

Energy Modelling

Pieter de Wilde and Godfried Augenbroe

Introduction

Energy modelling is the discipline that models the energy flows in buildings and between a building and its (local) environment, with the aim of studying the heat and mass flow within buildings and their (sub)systems under given functional requirements that the building must satisfy. Most of the current models are computational in nature. This means that the models are implemented in the form of a computer simulation that replicates a part of physical reality in the machine. To do this efficiently, energy models idealize, quantify and simplify the behaviour of real-world systems such as buildings by describing them as a set of internal variables, distinct system boundaries and external variables. The application of physical laws leads to a set of relations between the variables of this physical model, which together constitute the mathematical model. This is then coded in some programming language and subsequently run as a computer programme (commonly named tool). In energy modelling, the area of interest is the thermal behaviour of buildings, especially in terms of energy efficiency and thermal comfort.

Energy modelling is a key element of the broader discipline called building simulation, a domain that, apart from thermal aspects, also studies (day)lighting, moisture, acoustics, airflow and indoor air quality. The discipline of building simulation first emerged during the 1960s. During this period, research efforts focused on the study of fundamental theory for building simulation, mostly for energy transfer. During the 1970s, the new field matured and expanded, driven by the energy crisis of those years. Most research was devoted to the development of algorithms for heating load, cooling load and energy transfer simulation. During the 1980s, the effects of the energy crisis waned. However, this effect was compensated for by advancements in personal computers, which made building simulation widely accessible. As a result, research efforts now concentrated on programming and testing computational tools. In the same period, natural selection set in: only tools that had active support from their makers (maintenance, updating, addition of desired new features) were able to survive. Finally, during the late 1980s and the 1990s, the field of building simulation broadened with the development of new simulation programmes that were able to deal with lighting, acoustics and airflow problems. While energy modelling is the most prominent field within building simulation, it is closely related to modelling the aspects that have a direct impact on energy use and thermal comfort. This is particularly so for the study of airflow and lighting since airflow impacts upon ventilation and infiltration losses, daylighting is coupled with solar gain, and artificial lighting contributes to internal gain and, thus, affects heating and cooling loads. Such interaction becomes especially interesting within innovative buildings such as the biomes of the Eden Project (see Figure 4.1), where a large space is subject to a mix of natural ventilation and mechanical ventilation, novel building skin elements are used, and indoor air criteria are different from normal – in this case catering for plant comfort rather than human comfort.

A good in-depth discussion of the basics of energy modelling is provided by Clarke (2001); more advanced topics in simulation are discussed by Malkawi

Figure 4.1 *Biomes at the Eden Project, Cornwall*

and Augenbroe (2004). A good and well-known treatise on heat and mass transfer in general is found in Incropera et al (2007); for more detail on building services, see the ASHRAE handbooks (e.g. ASHRAE, 2004), and for an overview of building equipment, refer to Stein and Reynolds (2006).

Energy modelling tools

There are currently many tools available for building energy modelling and analysis. Tools often featured in the literature include, amongst others, ESP-r, EnergyPlus, eQuest and IES-VE. A good overview of building energy software tools is the directory provided by the US Department of Energy (2008). This directory now lists more than 300 tools, ranging from software that is still under development to commercially available software.

Many of these tools, have over the years, fostered a community that continues to develop new components or modules that can be added to a growing library. This has produced a rich palette of component types for the major tools in the current market place. For the average user who is not interested in adding customized modules, the use of the tools is rather straightforward, but requires training and a basic level of understanding of the physical principles that underlie the simulations.

There is general consensus that the current generation of tools is mature, robust and of high fidelity (i.e. accurate enough for most applications). User interfaces are continuously improving and data transfer with other upstream and downstream applications is being automated, thus avoiding tedious preparation of

(mostly geometric) input data and cumbersome parsing of output data by hand for post-processing or design decision-making. The latter is part of providing interoperable solutions, which have a much wider scope than energy modelling software (Bazjanac, 2007).

Figure 4.2 shows an example of the typical energy modelling steps, going from (a) a design representation to (b) an idealization that is relevant to the investigation at hand to (c) a diagrammatic representation of the computational model, to (d) the output of a computation. The core part of energy modelling is choosing the right idealization (b), which then more or less automatically leads to an appropriate choice of computational model and level of resolution (c).

It is interesting to note that the current generation of closed tools 'collapses' stages (b) and (c) into one stage, as users do not (and mostly cannot) interact with the computational model; the physical idealization generates the computational model automatically. Open tools such as Matlab, on the other hand, give the user explicit access in stage (c), which obviously comes at the expense of more work and more advanced skills that are expected of the user.

In spite of the successes and growing user base of current tools, there is little reason to become complacent about the state of building energy modelling tools. Most of the current (second-generation) toolset use old-style imperative programming techniques, and their computational kernel uses quite outdated techniques. Although this software is more than adequate for routine applications, its outdated basis will eventually become a roadblock when far-reaching extensions are attempted and new application areas are entered. A future third-generation toolset will for example offer:

- functional integration of energy modelling in building design (CAD) systems; and
- full co-disciplinary energy modelling, allowing heating, ventilating and air-conditioning (HVAC) system experts, control system developers and architectural designers to add model components to a shared multi-domain responsive energy model during full concurrent real-time collaborative design of all the systems.

Several research projects over the years have set this development in motion, notably EKS (Clarke et al, 1992), SEMPER (Mahdavi et al, 1997), SPARK (Sowell and Haves, 2001), IDA (Sahlin et al, 2003) and

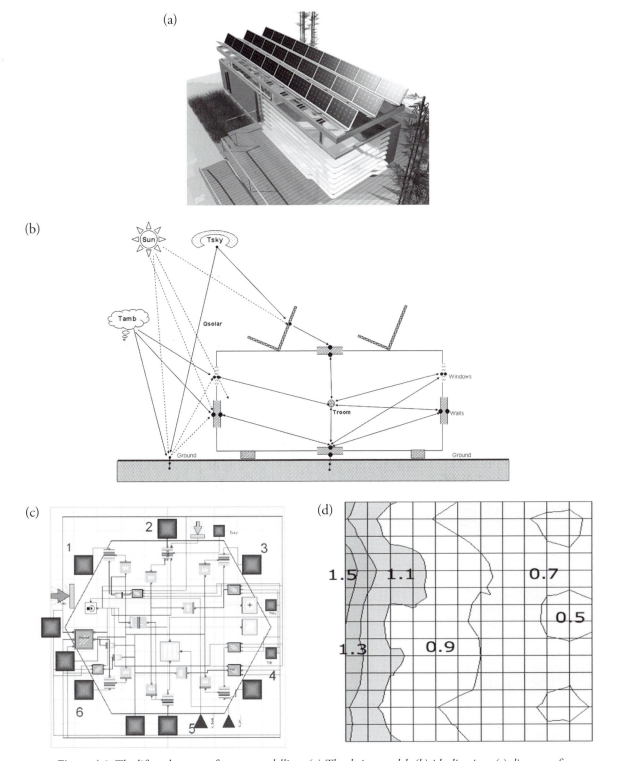

Figure 4.2 *The life cycle stages of energy modelling: (a) The design model; (b) idealization; (c) diagram of computational model; (d) generated output*

others. A breakthrough towards the third-generation tools is expected from the use of Modelica (Fritzson, 2004), which promises to deliver the generic declarative simulation language substrate on which configurable applications could be built. Early work in building simulation has been reported by Wetter and Haugstetter (2006), and the first industry strength applications can be expected in the near future.

Application in energy efficient buildings

In the engineering of sustainable buildings, energy modelling is closely integrated with the design of energy efficient buildings. Different drivers have been pushing the construction industry to make buildings more energy efficient: first the oil crisis of the 1970s, then the aim for sustainable development (WCED, 1987), and more recently the concerns about the depletion of fossil fuel reserves, peak oil (Bentley, 2002) and climate change (Stern, 2006).

As a consequence, building requirements have evolved to include increasingly stringent energy-saving demands. Recent buildings are required to meet a minimum level of overall energy performance, which can only be achieved by using holistic design approaches that minimize heating and cooling demands, integrate advanced high-efficiency building systems that utilize renewable energy sources, and make the best use of any fossil fuels through application of highly efficient energy conversion technologies. Within such buildings, all different kinds of systems interact to make buildings more energy efficient (ASHRAE, 2004). This makes ensuring the overall performance of the building a much more complex task that, rather than deferring it to the final stages of the design, needs to be undertaken during all stages of design. Designers and engineers are therefore becoming more reliant on the use of advanced dynamic building simulation tools which require special skills for the preparation of idealized or schematic models and a computational representation, as explained above. Acquiring these special skills typically takes a degree in architectural or mechanical engineering with at least two graduate courses that teach these skills. In addition, it usually requires training courses and/or a training workshop provided by the tool vendor.

The domestic state of the art in the UK is demonstrated by advanced dwellings such as the Kingspan Lighthouse, a BRE show home that is designed to meet the legislative standards anticipated to be in effect in 2016. It incorporates a complex set of interacting energy-saving measures: photovoltaic (PV) array, phase-change materials (PCMs), windcatchers for passive cooling and ventilation, passive solar windows, structural insulation panels, heat recovery for ventilation, biofuel boiler, and solar shading (Kennett, 2007), as shown in Figure 4.3. Internationally, homes built to the 'passive house' standards demonstrate the prospects of realizing extremely efficient domestic buildings with a heating requirement of less than $15kWh/m^2$ per year through a combination of passive solar design, super-insulation, advanced glazing systems, a good balance of airtightness and ventilation, energy efficient lighting, and high-efficiency heating systems such as heat pumps (Feist et al, 2001).

Commercial and public buildings, such as offices, hospitals, educational buildings, shopping centres and factories, are more complex than houses by their very nature. They use a palette of interventions that range from passive architectural features to added active systems. Many have high-tech façades and building services. In the UK, a good example of a straightforward yet sustainable office is the Home Office Headquarters in Sheffield, which utilizes solar protective glass, local ventilation and heat reclaim systems, maximal use of daylighting, occupancy sensors, and extensive monitoring of energy-use patterns (*Building Services Journal*, 2007). On the active systems side of the spectrum, an internationally acclaimed project is Council House 2 in Melbourne, Australia, the Chartered Institution of Building Services Engineers (CIBSE) 'sustainable building of the year 2007', which combines chilled ceilings, thermal night cooling, solar panels and wind turbines (World Green Building Council, 2008).

Obviously, the engineering of such buildings, whether domestic or commercial/public, requires that the design team is able to ensure that energy targets are being met, while maintaining thermal comfort in both summer and winter. Energy modelling can help this process in various ways (e.g. by supporting the evaluation of alternatives, system configuration, sizing and arrangement, and optimal system control strategies and set points). However, the process is a complex one, requiring many trade-offs and weighting of performances for subsystems. Figure 4.4 gives a high-level impression of what is involved in, for instance, the design stage of a new building complex.

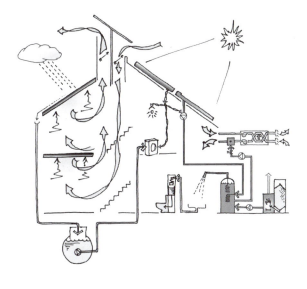

Source: Sheppard Robson, Hufton and Crow

Figure 4.3 *Kingspan Lighthouse: Concept sketch (left) and finalized building (right)*

Within the construction industry, sustainability rating methods are gaining momentum. The current voluntary schemes, such as BREEAM, GBTool and LEED, offer a quality label such as 'excellent' or 'gold', which offers status and is seen as desirable by many clients. However, it must be noted that energy use is only one of the categories considered, on average making up 10 to 20 per cent of the total score. Furthermore, energy performance is represented as improvements against a current practice base case. This makes these rating methods rather blunt when striving for high energy performance.

It is important to note that specific energy efficiency targets cannot be seen in isolation from an associated measurement principle. For managers of building portfolios (corporate owners, university campuses, etc.), targets will often be related to actual meter readings, like annual consumption (often per square metre). For buildings that are yet to be constructed, targets will be related to the performance predictions based on standardized calculation recipes. In novel design concepts, or non-routine system concepts, standard calculations will provide an estimate

of the demand; but how this demand is met by the systems, and how the systems interact with occupants and other building systems, can only be derived through advanced dynamic simulation of the building behaviour or, in short, through expert-driven building energy modelling.

Challenges in thermal building engineering

A review of earlier research efforts that focused on the uptake of simulation in building design (de Wilde, 2004) listed a number of plausible barriers to the integration of building simulation in building design. Recent publications demonstrate that many of these remain in place today. McElroy et al (2007) reiterate that the main issues facing the application of building simulation in design practice are the training of the 'simulationists', trust in the accuracy of models, (mis)interpretation of results, and the role of uncertainties. Bazjanaz (2005) reports progress in the development of data exchange (interoperability), but concedes that some of the current software is not

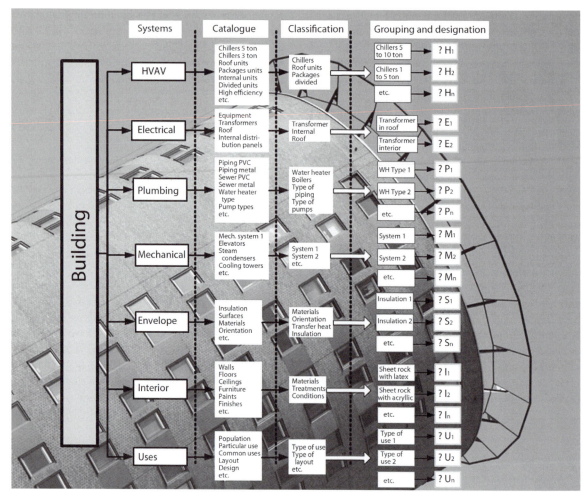

Figure 4.4 *Macro-energy modelling stage for energy code compliance*

compatible or that existing interfaces need fixing. At the same time, Schwede (2007) notes that current simulation tools still view buildings in a simplified manner and do not allow for a full 'simulative investigation'.

Yet, given the complexity of modern buildings, as described in the previous section, energy modelling needs to be a crucial instrument in the engineering of sustainable buildings. Indeed, it is already used in many projects and now plays a major role in the work of services engineers, energy systems designers and building physics consultants. The energy modelling that specialized firms provide or architectural firms do in house is diverse. It ranges from early conceptual design

support, relying mostly on the expertise and inventiveness of the energy consultant, to detailed simulations in the final stages of the design. In early design the emphasis is on creating meaningful schematic models of the proposed design concept and managing different criteria by which suggested design options can be judged. This work is not well supported by simulation tools; rather, the early stage requires deep insights and expertise supported by mostly simple calculations. In later design stages the emphasis shifts towards deep inspection of all the systems and their dynamic interactions. This requires expert skills in simulation, reflecting a shift from insight informed by simple schematics towards brute force simulations that replicate physical model behaviour as accurately as possible in the computer. The energy simulation models represent the physical behaviour of components and their dynamic interactions, recognizing all intricate phenomena in these interactions. Interpreting the outcomes and aggregating them into meaningful measures that support the dialogue with the design team becomes the crucial expert-driven after-stage of the simulation. Both types of energy modelling and their intermediate manifestations require different types of expert knowledge and, indeed, very different tools to support them. It is often stated that the early conceptual stages lack adequate tool support, which is then always declared a critical deficiency because of the far-reaching consequences of early decisions through ensuing design evolution. This raises the question of where a concerted effort to generate energy models that support conceptual design should focus. The authors of this chapter argue that true conceptual design support requires one to show which design option has a statistically high(er) chance of impacting upon the energy performance of the eventually resulting final design. Very few, if any, of the past research efforts in this area have framed the objective of their research in this way. A renewed effort is therefore needed to predict energy performance as an approximation of the probability distribution of the relevance of different design options. The underlying energy models that are needed to achieve this will be mostly normative, putting less emphasis on quantification and more on explanation. It should be stressed that the best intermediary between conceptual design decisions and an energy assessment is the trained mind of the energy modelling expert. This puts the burden of better early design support squarely on the shoulders of the educators who stand at the cradle of the emerging guild of 'energy design modellers'.

In the meantime few, if any, buildings are delivered without a detailed energy model and simulation of the energy consumption of the consumers in the building (heating, cooling, fans, pumps, hot water, lighting, appliances). Yet, at the same time, there are also many instances of buildings not living up to the expectations of the clients and design teams. Often, actual buildings require more energy to run than anticipated during the design stage (Bordass et al, 2001), and complaints about occupant discomfort persist (Karjalainen and Koistinen, 2007).

A couple of observations can be made. First of all, energy simulation models are typically based on 'idealizations' that assume that buildings are built and

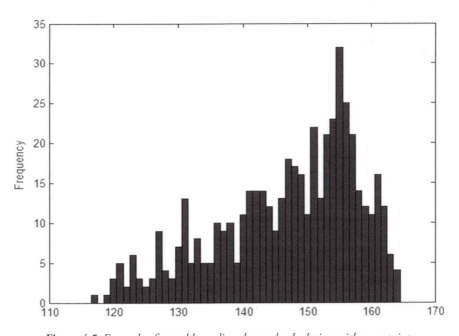

Figure 4.5 *Example of monthly cooling demand calculation with uncertainty*

operated according to specification. Moreover, they assume 'perfect knowledge' about physical properties, occupant and operator intervention, operating schedules, etc. This is hardly realistic, however, when one realizes that buildings exist in an unpredictable environment, where deteriorating systems, bad workmanship, unforeseen use and adaptations are the rule, rather than the exception.

Researchers have started to look at the role that these uncertainties play in predicting energy performance. Figure 4.5 shows an example of a small study into the effect on monthly cooling demand of a single office space (Augenbroe et al, 2008). As the figure shows, the expected mean average is around 140kWh/month; but the uncertainty ranges from 120 to 165, roughly plus or minus 20 per cent. In this case, only a subset of all uncertainties was taken into account, whereas user behaviour was not included.

Other deficiencies of current energy modelling result from the fact that our models are in some cases only abstractions of real behaviour. Advanced control strategies, for example, can look good on paper and their dynamic simulation can be carried out cleanly. However, their actual implementation is complex and plagued by all kinds of practical issues such as sensor errors, cycle times, activation delays, etc. Not surprisingly, it can take up to a year to get the building controls to perform close to expectations. In general, it is not uncommon that buildings underperform the predicted energy performance by as much as 30 per cent. The main reason is deviation from the idealized assumptions embedded in the energy model, unexpected circumstances, malfunctioning of system components and bad workmanship. Continuous commissioning is often seen as a way of restoring the energy performance of a building to its expected levels; but it should be well understood that a large part of the discrepancy may originate from too optimistic assumptions in the first place. Only the explicit modelling of uncertainties in model parameters and model assumptions will reveal the extent (probability) to which the energy model outcomes predict reality.

When looking at the role of energy modelling in building engineering, it is also important to note that the building design process is itself changing. The use of digital media is leading to new approaches to design. In these approaches, not only do designers work with new ways of representing the developing building

design, but they also develop new ways of generating forms, and they increasingly analyse the performance of their designs (Oxman, 2006). In developing new tools and design systems, it therefore is important to ensure a fit with the cognitive way in which designers work (based on design reasoning and thinking), while at the same time being aware that the design practice (tools, products and process) might change in the future (Kalay, 2006). The current – as of 2008 – status in thermal building engineering practice, as informally conveyed by numerous consultants active in the industry in the UK, is one of buoyancy. Performance requirements for energy efficiency are becoming increasingly stringent, boosting the work volume of the consultancy companies. And with events such as the 2012 London Olympics driving a multitude of construction projects, skilled modelling and simulation workers are in high demand. However, this situation leaves little room for a fundamental review of the practices in the consultancy office and for improving the state of the art from within the industry.

Recent initiatives and outlook

The work on integration of energy modelling in the building engineering process focuses on one or more of the challenges mentioned in the previous section. These efforts augment continuous work on the improvement of building performance simulation tools, in general, including work on better input data (climate files, user behaviour and system control), algorithms, data post-processing, data mining and result visualization techniques.

While the major tools are getting bigger, user friendlier and feature richer, a grassroots community is developing extensible Matlab libraries/toolboxes (Riederer, 2005). Due to the large proliferation of Matlab in the engineering curricula, this opens the door to the introduction of research-oriented energy modelling in graduate class exercises and PhD research projects. Whether this will grow out into a Matlab-based open source 'energy modelling research community' remains to be seen.

On the input side of the major energy tools, one category of research and development efforts attempts to integrate simulation with early or conceptual design by linking emerging computer-assisted design (CAD) sketching tools with energy simulation engines (see, for instance, Rizos, 2007). However, as is demonstrated by the example of the link between Sketchup and EnergyPlus, such linking depends upon inter-operability, as reported by Bazjanac (2005). A more fundamental approach, which looks at scalable and reusable spatial models, has been described by Suter and Mahdavi (2004). It is interesting to note that in the adjacent discipline of lighting modelling, simulation has already been fully integrated with CAD systems for a while: Desktop Radiance operates from within AutoCad 14, using pull-down menus (Mistrick, 2000). No similar tool has been demonstrated for energy simulation thus far.

On data post-processing and visualization, recent work at the University of Strathclyde by Morbitzer (2003) and Prazeres (2006) has focused on the presentation of simulation results by means of an integrated performance view. This tailors simulation output towards specific aims such as design exploration, analysis, representation and reporting, while providing flexibility to match individual preferences. It employs data mining and clustering techniques to filter through a range of simulation results. A related area under development is the use of uncertainty and sensitivity analysis to guide design, as previously discussed and demonstrated in Figure 4.5. Finally, it is worth mentioning the work on the coupling of energy modelling with the realm of intelligent computing. Here, advanced search and visualization techniques can be applied to the field of energy simulation, allowing one to push the boundaries of what is currently undertaken in the design office. As an example, Figure 4.6 shows two clusters, A and B, of energy efficient solutions obtained from a nine-dimensional search space using a genetic algorithm (de Wilde et al, 2008).

The Design Analysis Integration (DAI) initiative (Augenbroe et al, 2004) was aimed at addressing problems perceived in the ongoing efforts towards tool interoperability. The project built on the recognition that current solutions suffer from two major shortcomings:

1 They assume an idealistic structured data context, which allows perfect mapping between design information and analysis needs.
2 They are data driven, neglecting the process dimension of design – energy modelling interaction – where there is a clear 'analysis request'

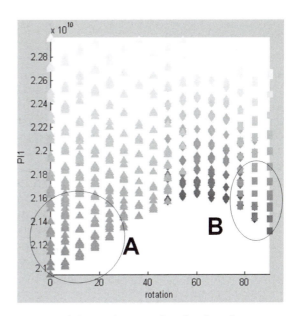

Figure 4.6 *Visualization of results of searching in a multidimensional space*

and where modelling results must be useful to the professionals who are involved in the building engineering process.

In order to overcome these issues, the DAI suggested a modular approach that starts from the premise that a set of recurring design analysis requests can be identified. These requests would represent the main questions that repeatedly are asked from modelling experts, say 80 per cent, leaving room for another 20 per cent of highly specialized requests that cannot be automated and need first-principle modelling of a specific problem from scratch. The recurring 80 per cent of requests would then allow the modelling of structured, if needed, scalable 'analysis functions', which uniquely define the quantification of specific building performance aspects in terms of performance indicators (PIs). A prototype software environment was developed and demonstrated to experts in the field; follow-up initiatives are currently under development.

Conclusions

The role of energy modelling in building engineering has co-evolved with the technology. Increasingly stringent regulations on energy efficiency, carbon emissions and more energy-conscious clients have yielded a buoyant consultancy sector that is a major factor in today's collaborative design of buildings. Yet, while energy modelling now has become an important ingredient of the engineering of sustainable buildings, a set of important challenges remain. Full integration of energy modelling and building design requires further process integration, which is a non-trivial issue due to the highly unstructured nature of the current building design process. Further investigation of how designers make decisions, and how modelling results can help to make those choices, is needed; but such research needs to take into account the fact that design practice itself is subject to change. Process integration also requires better collaboration between the actors, including improvements in data exchange, communication and the pursuit of common objectives. Furthermore, the trust in modelling outcomes, the role and impact of uncertainties, and the training of simulation experts are fields that need addressing to move the discipline forwards.

References

ASHRAE (American Society of Heating, Refrigerating and Air-Conditioning Engineers) (2004) *Handbook of HVAC Systems and Equipment*, ASHRAE, Atlanta, GA

Augenbroe, G., de Wilde, P., Moon, H. J. and Malkawi, A. (2004) 'An interoperability workbench for design analysis integration', *Energy and Buildings*, vol 36, no 8, pp737–748

Augenbroe, G., McManus, S., Zhao, F., Li, Z., Heo, Y. and Kim, S. H. (2008) 'Lessons from an advanced building simulation course', in *Proceedings of SimBuild*, Berkeley, CA

Bazjanac, V. (2005) 'Model based cost and energy performance estimation during schematic design', in *Proceedings of CIB W-79: Information Technology in Construction*, Dresden, Germany

Bazjanac, V. (2007) 'Impact of the U.S. national building information model standard (NBIMS) on building energy performance simulation', in *Proceedings of Building Simulation 2007*, Beijing, China, pp1377–1382

Bentley, R.W. (2002) 'Global oil and gas depletion: An overview', *Energy Policy*, vol 30, no 3, pp189–205

Bordass, B., Cohen, R., Standeven, M. and Leaman, A. (2001) 'Assessing building performance in use 3: Energy performance of the Probe buildings', *Building Research and Information*, vol 29, no 2, pp114–128

Building Services Journal (2007) 'Home Office goes green at new Sheffield HQ', *Building Services Journal*, November, pp41–44

Clarke, J. A. (2001) *Energy Simulation in Building Design*, Butterworth-Heinemann, Oxford

Clarke, J. A., Tang, D., James, K. and MacRandal, D. F. (1992) *Energy Kernel System, Final Report for GR/F/07880*, Engineering and Physical Science Research Council, Swindon, UK

de Wilde, P. (2004) *Computational Support for the Selection of Energy Saving Building Components*, PhD thesis, Delft University of Technology, The Netherlands

de Wilde, P., Beck, M. and Rafiq, Y. (2008) 'Visualisation of the impact of climate change on the cooling requirements of domestic buildings in the United Kingdom', in *Proceedings of Intelligent Computing in Engineering 2008*, Plymouth, UK

Feist, W., Peper S. and Görg, M. (2001) *CEPHEUS Final Technical Report*, PassivHaus Institut, Darmstadt, Germany

Fritzson, P. (2004) 'Principles of object oriented modeling and simulation with Modelica 2.1.', *IEEE*

Incropera, F. P., DeWitt, D. P., Bergman, T. L and Lavine, A. S. (2007) *Fundamentals of Heat and Mass Transfer*, John Wiley & Sons, Hoboken, NJ

Kalay, Y. (2006) 'The impact of information technology on design methods, products and practices', *Design Studies*, vol 27, no 3, pp357–380

Karjalainen, S. and Koistinen, O. (2007) 'User problems with individual temperature control in offices', *Building and Environment*, vol 42, no 8, pp2880–2887

Kennett, S. (2007) 'The UK's first carbon-neutral house', *Building Services Journal*, July, pp56–57

Mahdavi, A., Matthew, P., Kumar, S. and Wong, N. H. (1997) 'Bi-directional computational design support in the SEMPER environment', *Automation in Construction*, vol 6, no 4, pp353–373

Malkawi, A. and Augenbroe G. (eds) (2004) *Advanced Building Simulation*, Spon Press, New York, NY

McElroy, L., Cockroft, J. and Hand, J. (2007) 'Business success through process based application of simulation', in *Proceedings of Building Simulation 2007*, Beijing, China, pp1740–1746

Mistrick, R. (2000) *Desktop Radiance Overview*, Pennsylvania State University, PA

Morbitzer, C. A. (2003) *Towards the Integration of Simulation into the Building Design Process*, PhD thesis, University of Strathclyde, Glasgow, UK

Oxman, R. (2006) 'Theory and design in the first digital age', *Design Studies,* vol 27, no 3, pp229–265

Prazeres, L. (2006) *An Exploratory Study about the Benefits of Targeted Data Perceptualisation Techniques and Rules in*

Building Simulation, PhD thesis, University of Strathclyde, Glasgow, UK

Riederer, P. (2005) 'Matlab/Simulink for building and HVAC simulation – State of the art', in *Proceedings of Building Simulation 2005*, Montreal, Canada, pp1019–1026

Rizos, I. (2007) *Next Generation of Energy Simulation Tools: Coupling 3D Sketching with Energy Simulation Tools*, MSc thesis, University of Strathclyde, Glasgow, UK

Sahlin, O., Eriksson, L., Grozman, P., Johnsson, H., Shapovalov, A. and Vuolle, M. (2003) 'Will equation based building simulation make it? Experiences from the introduction of IDA indoor climate and energy', in *Proceedings of Building Simulation 2003*, Eindhoven, The Netherlands, pp1147–1154

Schwede, D. (2007) 'Towards a digital representation of physical phenomena to assess comfort in future environments', in *Proceedings of Building Simulation 2007*, Beijing, China, pp1403–1409

Sowell, E. F. and Haves, P (2001) 'Efficient solution strategies for building energy system simulation', *Energy and Buildings*, vol 33, no 4, pp309–317

Stein, B. and Reynolds, J. S. (2006) *Mechanical and Electrical Equipment of Buildings*, John Wiley & Sons, Hoboken, NJ

Stern, N. (2006) *The Economics of Climate Change – The Stern Review*, Cambridge University Press, Cambridge, UK

Suter, G. and Mahdavi, A. (2004) 'Elements of a representation framework for performance-based design', *Building and Environment*, vol 39, no 8, pp969–988

US Department of Energy (2008) *Building Energy Software Tool Directory*, www.eren.doe.gov/buildings/tools_directory/, accessed 31 March 2008

WCED (World Commission on Environment and Development) (1987) *Our Common Future*, The Brundtland report, Oxford University Press, Oxford, UK

Wetter, M. and Haugstetter, C. (2006) 'Modelica versus TRNSYS: A comparison between an equation-based and a procedural modeling language for building energy simulation', *in Proceedings of SimBuild 2006*, Cambridge, MA

World Green Building Council (2008) *CH2: Council House 2 Factsheet*, http://worldgbc.org, accessed 6 February 2008

5

Carbon Reduction in Buildings

Ian Ward

Introduction

Worldwide, almost 40 per cent of the energy used is for heating, cooling, lighting and ventilating buildings and in the UK it is almost half of the energy used. This emphasizes the fact that buildings are important in the drive to reduce both national and global consumption of resources.

The general way in which the energy consumption of buildings can be reduced is to pay attention to the following design issues.

1 Reduce energy for heating: Optimize the building envelope

The design of the building envelope can have a significant effect on the overall energy performance of the building and care should be taken in the design of the façades. Through careful design, the demand for heating can be significantly reduced:

- Compact plan reduces fabric losses.
- Exceed building regulations requirements for U values.
- Optimize glazing ratios for heat gains, daylighting and artificial lighting.
- Investigate the use of shading systems, remembering that east–west orientations will require different treatment than south elevations.
- Use thermal mass to reduce fluctuations in internal air temperatures – this can also have an influence on cooling requirements.
- Detail junctions between fabric components in order to prevent the ingress of unwanted air.

2 Reduce energy for cooling: Optimize the use of natural climatic features

The demand for cooling can be reduced by careful consideration of the climate features of the site as well as by consideration of the internal loads. Using daylight reduces the dependence upon artificial light, which reduces electrical energy used. Natural winds can be used to ventilate buildings and to provide a degree of 'free cooling'. If possible, zone the internal spaces to:

- Maximize the opportunities to use solar energy.
- Maximize the view of the sky to allow daylight to enter the building.
- Maximize the potential use of natural wind forces for natural ventilation.
- Shelter the building from strong cold winds – this reduces unwanted cold air infiltration.
- Shield windows from unwanted solar gain during hot periods of the year.
- Consider reducing the internal loads or zone areas of high loads together – this can help in minimizing the spread of cooling services throughout the building.

3 Reduce energy for lighting: Integrate daylight with artificial light

The provision of good-quality lighting not only enhances the ability of the occupants to carry out their tasks more efficiently, but can also reduce the energy demand for electric lighting. Electricity is a high-quality fuel and its production efficiency from fossil fuels is rarely more than 30 to 40 per cent:

- Maximize the amount of daylight entering the building by providing windows with a view of the sky zenith – the sky is generally three times as bright at the zenith compared to the horizon.
- Where possible, use clerestory, light pipes and roof glazing systems.
- Use light shelves to 'bounce' daylight deeper into the occupied space.
- Keep internal decorations of walls, floor and ceiling light to reflect as much light as possible.
- Plan artificial lighting switching systems to switch off lights progressively as they move further away from windows.
- Use electronic control systems to modulate light switching and levels in response to available daylight levels.
- Select glazing systems with high transmission factors for daylight.

4 Reduce energy for equipment/ processes

Boilers, chillers, fans, pumps and motors all use energy to provide the energy systems to keep the inside conditions within comfortable ranges. These systems can be designed to minimize the energy used:

- Use equipment with high efficiency ratings.
- The efficiency of particularly boilers and chillers depends upon the load imposed on them – the higher the load, the better the efficiency. To maximize the efficiency of the whole system, use modular units as they will work at full load for longer periods of time; as a result, system efficiency will be greater.
- Use heat recovery, energy storage and desiccant dehumidification to reduce heating and cooling energy usage.
- Use variable volume air systems to respond to the demands of the users – low occupancy will need less air than full occupancy; however, care should be taken to prevent air stagnation and moisture build-up.
- Use variable flow pumps and variable speed drives.
- Use zero chlorofluorocarbon (CFC)-based refrigerants.

- Use white goods with a high energy efficiency rating.

5 Investigate the use of renewable and integrated energy sources

One way of reducing the demand on fossil fuels is to use renewable or integrated energy sources which, in theory, will not run out – unlike fossil fuels:

- Look at the use of photovoltaics (PVs) to produce either electricity to be fed into the building or employed as a direct current to charge batteries – for cars, computers, emergency lights, etc.
- Investigate the use of the heat generated by PVs to supplement space heating systems in mid-season.
- Consider the use of wind generators.
- Consider the use of heat pumps – generally for every kilowatt of energy fed into a heat pump 3kW of energy are produced. If the two units are free (i.e. from groundwater, river water, air or other sources), then high efficiencies are obtained.
- Bear in mind the possibility of co-generation of heat and electricity.
- Consider the use of wood-burning stoves supplied from harvested cuttings from forests.

In order to reduce carbon emissions from buildings, it is essential that consideration is given to these issues as early on in the design process as possible. Design decisions made at concept stage are often easy to implement as the building details have not been decided upon and there are no cost implications. However, if design decisions are made late in the project, then there are likely to be costs involved and modifications could result in less of a saving compared to decisions made at concept stage.

Carbon reduction issues to be considered at the early stages of design

The main issues, which are of importance when designing an energy efficient building, are:

- site analysis;
- fabric design with respect to heat gains/losses and thermal mass;

- provision of appropriate services;
- type of control systems to be used and operational programmes.

Each of the above topics will be considered in more detail in the following sections.

Site analysis

Before carrying out a site analysis, it is necessary to establish priorities. If, for example, the site is in the middle of a city, then the scope to deal with solar access will be severely limited due to the surrounding buildings and it may not be possible to do much about it. On the other hand, on a green field site there will be more scope to maximize solar assess.

A site analysis dealing with carbon issues should take into consideration the following points:

- solar access;
- local wind environment;
- availability of daylight.

Solar access

Good solar access is important if a building is to make use of the sun's energy to help in producing a passively heated building. By keeping the south elevation free from obstructions in the northern hemisphere (NH) and the north elevation free in the southern hemisphere (SH), solar access is possible. The simple rule governing layout of buildings to maximize the benefits of sunlight can be taken as follows:

- Ensure that there are no obstructions within a 30 degree angle from the south–north elevation.
- Ensure that there is no other building obstructing the window within an elevation angle of 25 degrees.

Local wind environment

Wind shelter can be provided by several means: other buildings, natural vegetation or artificial windbreaks. Providing wind shelter may also be in conflict with the desire to provide solar access. For passive solar buildings facing south (NH) or north (SH) with planted shelter to the south and west (NH) or north and west (SH), good solar access for winter sun is maintained if the

Table 5.1 *Shelterbelts and reduction of wind speed*

Distance from belt in belt height (H)	Percentage reduction in wind speed
2	60
5	40
10	20
15	10

shelter is at least four times the height of the building distant from it for latitudes up to 55° north–south and five times the height of the building distant up to 60° north. Shelterbelts at the edge of an estate or groups of buildings should be about twice the height of the buildings away from them to protect daylight availability (although some sunlight will be sacrificed). Shelterbelts protecting open spaces will be effective at reducing wind speed by the amounts shown in the Table 5.1.

Daylight

If it important to let internal spaces be day lit, it is necessary to establish the desired daylight factor:

- Daylight factors between 2 and 5 per cent are desirable.
- If a window is to be used for providing daylight, then obstructions should not be higher than 25 degrees above the horizon.
- A room can have a day-lit appearance if the area of the glazing is at least one twenty-fifth (4 per cent) of the total room area.
- Areas of a room from which there is no direct view of the sky are likely to have a low level of daylight.
- Surfaces closer to a window than twice the height of the window head above desktop level are likely to receive adequate daylight for most of the working year.
- It is possible to establish the likely percentage of the year when daylight would be adequate for defined levels of illuminance. Normal conditions of clear or tinted glass, light interiors and working days of 9.00 am to 5.00 pm were assumed for these graphs.

A general equation that can be used to estimate the likely daylight factor is:

$$DF = \frac{\sum WT\Phi M}{A\left(1-R^2\right)} \qquad (1)$$

where:

- W = total window area (m²);
- T = transmittance of glazing system (usually 0.7 for double-glazed clear glass);
- Φ = vertical angle of the sky seen from each window;
- M = maintenance factor (usually taken as 1);
- A = total internal surface area m²;
- R = area-weighted average reflectance of surfaces.

Fabric design

Once the issues relating to the site have been established, the next issue to consider is the design of the building fabric. At the initial stages of a design, it is important to consider how the massing of the building will affect the carbon emission requirements. The following simple guidelines can help to reduce the emission rate:

- Narrow buildings use less energy in total as they can be more effectively day lit, which leads to a reduction in electrical load, which outweighs any slight increase in fabric losses due to a large façade area.
- Courtyard buildings do not perform as well as shallow buildings since they have less daylight and natural ventilation.
- Atrium buildings perform in a similar way as courtyard buildings, although the ventilation is better than in courtyards (due to stack effects). There may be a need to include mechanical ventilation in the upper floors due to the low stack pressures at higher levels.
- Buildings with very small glazing ratios will produce significantly more carbon than buildings with larger glazing ratios.
- Increasing glazing ratios much above 50 per cent will produce little extra benefit.
- The optimum glazing ratio is in the region of 30 to 50 per cent for vertical surfaces.
- The optimum glazing ratio for roof light is no more than 20 per cent.

Plan form

Plan form has a very significant role in the design for carbon efficiency. Deep plan forms will result in the building requiring a larger proportion of the floor area to be artificially lit and more reliance on mechanical cooling. It is generally accepted that a space of up to 6m deep from a window will be able to take advantage of natural lighting and natural ventilation; and if natural ventilation is a prerequisite of the design, then approximately 14m deep is regarded as the upper limit for the floor slab.

Orientation

Building orientation can play a significant role in determining the solar gains received. A building facing east or west will be more susceptible to receiving adverse low altitude sun in the morning and evening, which will contribute to the possibility of overheating these zones within the building. Low altitude sun is always more difficult to deal with than the higher altitudes during the mid-part of the day; therefore, by minimizing glazing on the east–west façades and providing solar shading of the south (NH) or north (SH), the potential adverse effects of solar penetration can be minimized.

Glazing ratios

Glazing ratios have an important role to play in the design of building façades. Windows let in light and solar heat and loose heat to the outside. The larger the window, the more daylight and solar gain will enter and the larger the losses will be. There is an optimum glazing system design, which attempts to provide a balance between these energy flows. This balance is a function of orientation, location, obstructions and user requirements. Generally between 25 and 50 per cent ratios are regarded as being optimum, depending upon the above factors.

Window design

- *Solar protection.* In order to prevent overheating, windows should always be protected from direct solar gains and external shading is recommended. Internal shading only serves to redirect the gains as they are already in the space, having passed through the glass.

- *Daylight.* The qualities of daylight are such that it should always receive serious consideration in any design analysis: there is strong evidence that occupants prefer to work in a day-lit environment. Daylight also offsets the need for artificial lighting.
- *Natural ventilation requirement.* Windows are the main source of natural ventilation and if this is required in the design, then the choice of window can significantly affect the provision of ventilation. Windows that open in such a way as to provide drafts are to be avoided. Tilting windows generally are regarded as being the best type to use. If night cooling is required, then some form of trickle ventilation is also required, and this can be provided either by devices such as perma-vents or small clerestory openings.

Thermal insulation

Building regulations require that high standards and integrity of thermal insulation are provided, and it should be normal practice to carry this out. However, with the move to even tighter thermal regulation standards, designers should be actively thinking of designing buildings with thermal insulation standards in excess of the current ones since their buildings will (it is hoped) have a lifespan of several tens of years and over that time the likelihood of the standards being improved is very strong.

Thermal mass

Thermal mass is an important aspect of design when the specification requires that the amount of mechanical cooling is minimized. Exposed thermal mass in a building is able to absorb a proportion of the heat gains produced during the working period and to remove them at night by allowing the cooler outside air to pass over the surfaces. Generally, it is accepted that by exposing the thermal mass in a building, a 2 to 4 degree drop in the inside peak internal air temperature experienced during the day can be achieved. It is important, however, to consider other factors when exposing the thermal mass, particularly the possibility of internal noise being transmitted along the space, which can be disturbing to other users of the building.

Thermal mass can be used anywhere in a building; but the most effective locations are those where it is easy to absorb heat. Exposed ceilings are perhaps the best location as warm air rises and can therefore easily be absorbed into the surface. A warm ceiling (in winter) will also help to keep the radiant temperature slightly higher, which will assist in promoting thermal comfort. The removal of heat from a ceiling can either be through passing cooler air over the surfaces (above, through or below) or by passing cooled water through the structure. There is no one solution to the position of, or removal of, heat from thermal mass – each application is specific to that building. Vertical walls can also be used; but these are frequently decorated with hangings or paintings, which will detract from their effectiveness.

In order to help determine the amount of thermal mass to include in the design, Figures 5.1 to 5.4 give an indication of the amount of heat that could be stored for a range of materials and thicknesses.

Natural ventilation

By ensuring that a building can be naturally ventilated, it is possible that the demand for air conditioning can be minimized or at least reduced in capacity. This means that the carbon footprint of a building could be lower. Accepted figures for a typical high-quality air-conditioned office block are in the region of $9.5kg/CO_2/m^2$ treated floor area, while for a naturally ventilated building the value is zero.

Services

As buildings become more energy efficient, pressure will be put on the design of the services to meet the lower requirements. Even with housing, using the current UK Building Regulations, normal radiators are becoming so small that they look out of place in a room. Figure 5.5 shows an example from a low-energy social home.

In the non-domestic sector, there are similar pressures to reduce the demand for services and to make the service systems more energy efficient. Table 5.2 indicates typical values of CO_2 emissions from the four main systems of servicing non-domestic buildings, which illustrates quite clearly that the appropriate design of the building and its services can have a significant impact upon the levels of CO_2 emitted.

The systems used to supply energy to buildings are also of importance and there is pressure not only to

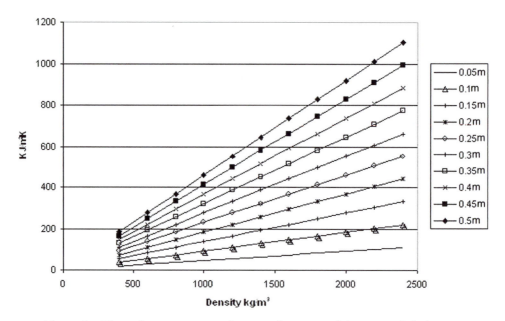

Figure 5.1 *Thermal storage capacity of concrete for a range of densities and thicknesses per degree Kelvin rise in temperature*

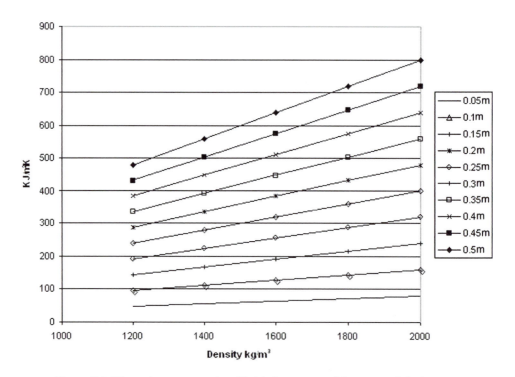

Figure 5.2 *Thermal storage capacity of brick for a range of densities and thicknesses per degree Kelvin rise in temperature*

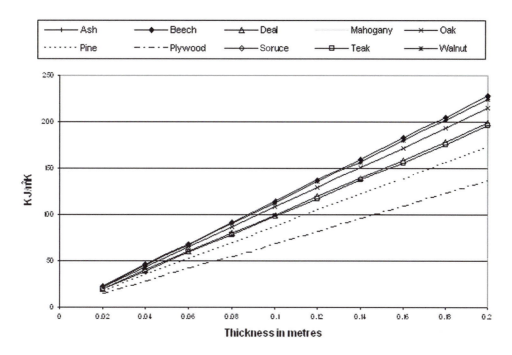

Figure 5.3 *Thermal storage capacity of a selection of timbers for a range of densities and thicknesses per degree Kelvin rise in temperature*

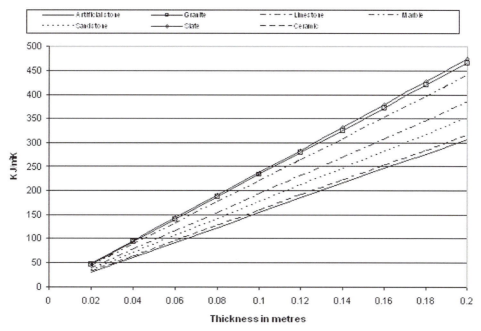

Figure 5.4 *Thermal storage capacity of a selection of stones for a range of densities and thicknesses per degree Kelvin rise in temperature*

Figure 5.5 *Radiator in a low-energy home*

improve the efficiency of these services, but also to look at new and innovative ways of providing energy.

By insulating the supply and extract ducts/pipes, it is also possible to make significant improvements in the energy losses of systems – typically these can be up to about 20 per cent of the potential losses.

Minimizing energy demands of building services

Ventilation services

Some systems are now using localized mechanical ventilation systems since it is possible to design the pressure losses in the ducts to be very low, resulting in significantly lower fan power. For example, the fan power used by such systems can be as low as 0.8W/L/s compared to the normal values of 2W/L/s.

The air velocity rate of air within ductwork is also of importance as the power required to deliver a specific amount of air increases as a cube function of velocity. To minimize this power requirement it is advisable to ensure that the air is supplied as slow as possible.

Typical duct velocities are in the region of 6m/s; but if this can be reduced, then significant energy savings can be achieved. On the negative side, by reducing the velocity, the duct area increases, which could place an extra burden on the space allocation for such services.

Heating and cooling services

Boilers and chillers are the type of equipment covered by these services. For a boiler plant to maintain maximum efficiency, it is advisable to install boilers that can operate at near their maximum output for the longest period of time. This often requires that modular boilers are installed so that as the load varies, boilers can be switched on or off as necessary. The most inefficient way of supplying heating services is to install one large boiler capable of delivering the maximum load. It is normal that in most cases the average load is around 50 per cent of the maximum; therefore, a single boiler will operate at well below its capacity (and, hence, efficiency) for a significant period of time.

A similar argument can be put forward for cooling services: being able to schedule plants on or off in order to maintain maximum output is suggested as being the best strategy to use to minimize inefficiencies.

Alternative energy supply systems

- *Micro-combined heat and power (CHP) plants.* These systems can be used to provide heat and power to either an individual home or a small community. These units produce lower values of CO_2 than traditional boiler plants, while also producing electricity. Current technologies for these systems are capable of providing the same comfort levels in a home as a traditional boiler, while at the same time reducing carbon dioxide emissions by about 1.5 tonnes per year (around

Table 5.2 *Typical range of carbon dioxide emissions from office buildings ($kgCO_2/m^2$ treated floor area)*

	Typical			Good practice		
	Heating	Cooling	Fans/pumps	Heating	Cooling	Fans/pumps
Prestige air-conditioned office	11	5.8	9.5	5.9	3	5.1
Standard air-conditioned office	9.8	4.4	8.5	5.3	2	4.3
Naturally ventilated open plan	8.3	0.3	1.1	4.3	0.1	0.6
Naturally ventilated cellular	8.3	0	0.8	4.3	0	0.3

25 per cent). Such systems produce between 1kW to 5kW of peak electricity. However, in summer periods when there is little demand for heating energy, electricity produced is at a lower efficiency, which could make such systems uneconomic.

Micro-CHP plants can be powered by a range of fuels, some of which produce little or no CO_2 (such as biofuels).

- *Biomass fuels.* Biomass fuels are often regarded as fuels that take carbon out of the atmosphere while it is growing and return it as it is burned. If it is managed on a sustainable basis, biomass is harvested as part of a constantly replenished crop. This is either during woodland or arboricultural management or coppicing, or as part of a continuous programme of replanting, with the new growth taking up CO_2 from the atmosphere at the same time as it is released through combustion of the previous harvest. This maintains a closed carbon cycle with no net increase in atmospheric CO_2 levels.

The economic realities involved in biomass fuels means that high-value material for which there is an alternative market is unlikely to become available for energy applications. However, there are large resources of residues, co-products and waste that exist worldwide that could potentially become available, in quantity, at relatively low cost, or even negative cost where there is currently a requirement to pay for disposal.

There are five basic categories of material:

1 *virgin wood*: from forestry, arboricultural activities or wood processing;
2 *energy crops*: high yield crops grown specifically for energy applications;
3 *agricultural residues*: residues from agriculture harvesting or processing;
4 *food waste*: from food and drink manufacture, preparation and processing and post-consumer waste;
5 *industrial waste and co-products*: from manufacturing and industrial processes.

- *Renewable energies – solar and wind.* Solar and wind energy have a role to play in providing renewable energy to support the demands of a building. Solar energy can be utilized in one of two ways:

1 generation of electricity;
2 generation of hot water.

Photovoltaic devices are used for the generation of electricity. There is a wide range of PV devices on the market, but all currently have efficiencies of around 10–20 per cent for the conversion of solar energy into electricity. Typical payback periods for such devices are in the region of 20 years, which can make them an unattractive option. They produce low-voltage DC electricity, which often cannot be directly used in the building and therefore has to be converted into higher-voltage AC power – this involves more equipment and there are inefficiencies associated with the conversion process.

On the other hand, the use of solar energy to produce hot water is a much better option as the initial costs are lower and the efficiencies higher. In the UK, it is conceivable that around 30 per cent of the hot water requirements of a domestic home can be supplied by solar panels. In lower latitudes, this figure can be significantly increased, which makes this type of solar collection a more attractive proposition.

Wind energy is provided by turbines and the larger the turbine, the more electricity can be produced. It is also possible to install small generators on a particular building; but often their efficiency is compromised by the local wind environment and there is evidence that such small turbines are not generating anything like their potential. The most efficient way of using wind energy is to use a large turbine located away from the building. These turbines often produce more energy than is required by the building and therefore provide the opportunity of exporting electricity to the grid.

Methods of approach to reduce carbon emissions

With the move towards low carbon-emitting buildings taking hold throughout the world, there are many ways in which this can be achieved. One methodology promoted in Europe for domestic buildings is the German *Passiv Haus* principles. These essentially involve ensuring that the following design standards are strictly adhered to:

- a design which ensures that air leakage is kept to a minimum – the standard is a leakage rate of 0.2 air

changes per hour (ACH) at a pressure test value of 50Pa;
- super-insulated structure – typically 300mm to 400mm, giving U values less than 0.15;
- good-quality windows and doors with U values in the region of 0.6 to 1.0W/m²K;
- no thermal bridges in the structure;
- use of passive solar gains, which typically supply about one third of heating requirements;
- heat-recovery whole-house ventilation with high-efficiency DC electric motors;
- ability to use hot water solar systems to supplement the demand for heating and domestic hot water;
- space heating requirements – 16kWh/m² year;
- 'A' rated domestic appliances.

Some examples of passive houses in Hannover, Germany

Example A. These homes (see Figure 5.6) use 300mm of thermal insulation on the outside walls (see Figure 5.7) and feature a grass roof with solar water heating panels. The heat recovery ventilation unit is located in the loft space (see Figure 5.8).

Example B. The design principles for this private block of flats (see Figures 5.9 and 5.10) were the same as those applied to the social housing project. The details of the construction were:

- concrete core and floors;
- external walls rendered, timber support, 300mm sheep's wool insulation, internal plasterboard and skim;

Figure 5.7 *Section of the external wall showing the thickness of the thermal insulation*

- windows – three layers of glass with low e-coatings; frames coated aluminium and timber (on inside); mechanical ventilation system giving three air changes per hour with heat recovery;
- heating supplied by preheating of ventilating air and low-level radiator in the bedroom;
- energy supply for the block by a wood-burning boiler – this also provides hot water as a backup to the solar water heating system;
- occupants say that in winter the inside temperature never drops below 22°C and in summer the flats never get warmer than 25°C (they do have external blinds).

Example C. Again this house (see Figures 5.11 and 5.12) uses the same constructional details to achieve the low heating demand.

Figure 5.6 *Social passive housing*

Figure 5.8 *Heat-recovery ventilation unit in the loft space*

Figure 5.10 *Internal view of one of the flats*

Figure 5.9 *South elevation of the block of flats*

Figure 5.11 *Private house*

Figure 5.12 *Internal view of the house*

Within the UK there has been a great deal of work carried out on the design strategies to be used to produce a house which uses 40 per cent less energy than current consumption. The main strategies to be adopted to produce such a dwelling by 2050 are:

• Electricity consumption for lights and appliances must be reduced by nearly one half to around 1600kWh per household.
• New-build homes will have close to zero heating demand.

6

Renewable Energy Sources and the City

Mark Barrett

Introduction

Facilitated by improved food supply through agriculture, the pattern of human development has been for people to concentrate into ever larger settlements – from villages to towns to cities or contiguous urban areas with tens of millions of people. Rather than nomadic people travelling to where wild plant and animal food was available, resources of food and materials were grown and collected in the hinterland and transported to settlements. As transport improved, the resource catchment areas for settlements could be extended, enabling the collection of more energy as food and fuel and other resources, thereby sustaining larger higher-density settlements. Initially, both food and fuel for direct use by people were mostly from renewable biomass. Renewable energy was then used to supplement human energy in the form of animal power, and then, beginning approximately 2000 years ago, from the increasing utilization of solar heating and lighting, and water and wind mills. About 500 years ago, coal and then other fossil fuels were increasingly exploited and the higher energy densities of these fuels and other technology developments, such as railways and electricity generation and transmission, allowed the further growth of settlements using increasingly distant energy sources.

Currently, about half of the world's people live in towns and cities, and this fraction is expected to grow towards the 80 per cent urbanization found in richer countries, although the trend may be altered by developments in energy and other resources, and by technologies. So, although this chapter is on renewable energy in cities, it should also be seen in the wider context of national energy – providing energy services in cities is a national planning problem.

All cities currently import energy to meet service needs in buildings, for heating, cooling, lighting and electrical equipment, and for transport. They import because the density of settlement in cities and their location means that most cities have small or zero fossil fuel resources within their boundaries, and the resources of renewable energy are inadequate or not fully exploited because of economic or other reasons. Although cities have to import energy, they have the potential to be more efficient in terms of energy consumption per capita than low-density rural settlements. This is because electric and public transport systems are viable, and because large buildings and energy supply systems can be made more efficient than small ones. Set against this, people in cities are generally richer than those in rural areas, and rich people have higher demands for energy services and energy-consuming technologies.

In most countries, a large and often major fraction of the energy imported to cities originates from fossil and nuclear fuels – directly as coal, oil and gas or via electricity generated with fossil and nuclear fuels. However, demand has grown and the reserves of finite fossil and nuclear fuels have depleted to the extent that over the next 50 years the availability of these fuels will decrease and the prices will rise. Figure 6.1 shows the remaining lives of finite fuels expressed as ratios of current reserves to production. These are indicative since reserves are partly determined by exploration, economic and technological parameters, and by the future levels of demand for the fuels, which will be influenced by many factors such as economic development, global warming and nuclear risks.

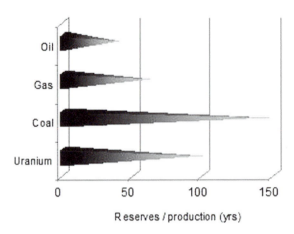

Figure 6.1 *Finite fuel reserves*

Due to the finite nature of fuel reserves, cities will have to make the transition from dependence upon fossil and nuclear fuels to renewable energy. Cities will also have to play their part in minimizing climate impacts by reducing greenhouse gas emissions, which for energy mainly concerns carbon dioxide from fossil fuels. Energy efficiency and renewable energy address the sustainability and climate challenge simultaneously. Humankind will have to return to a reliance on renewable resources as before, but with technologies benefiting from decades and centuries of development. This transition to sustainable energy services for cities will depend upon the application of energy efficiency to manage demand and of renewable energy to replace finite fuels.

Figure 6.2 depicts energy demand and renewable energy in and around cities. The top part of the diagram shows the city itself, with increasing building height and accompanying floor area per plan area leading to greater population density and its associated energy service demands. Also shown schematically are the renewable energy sources typically found with some abundance inside and outside the city, solar energy inside, and all sources outside. Apart from solar energy and environmental heat, cities do not usually have significant renewable energy resources, and a city's total exploitable renewable energy resource is generally less than its total energy demand. This is because of the density of land use and associated energy demand in a city, and because cities are generally located where resources of wind, hydro, biomass, geothermal, tidal and wave energy are small within or near the city's boundary. Cities were originally located with regard to

strategic considerations such as proximity to water, food, other settlements and navigable rivers and seas, rather than positioned with renewable energy resources in mind. There is no particular reason to require that renewable energy is generated within the city if it is not cost effective; the aim is to provide society with sustainable energy, whether it comes from the city or from remote wind turbines or hydropower.

The lower part of Figure 6.2 depicts how demand and solar supplies might vary in cross-section across the city; the flows are in watts per square metre (W/m^2), averaged over a winter's day. As population density and socio-economic activity increase towards the city's core, so, in general, do heat and electricity demands. Other demands such as transport and cooling are omitted here; but they also tend to increase towards the city's core, although transport demand depends in complex ways upon routes and technologies. Also shown in Figure 6.2 are potential solar heat and electricity production. Where heat and electricity demands are greater than the solar supply potential, other energy has to be imported from areas outside the city where there is a surplus – this is shown at the bottom of the figure by the arrows of energy imports converging on the city centre.

The energy service demands of cities and the available renewable energy resources vary due to many factors, such as building stocks, geography and climate; therefore, it is not possible to find a single best strategy suitable for all cities. To a degree, the relative proportion of energy service demands depends upon climate: cities at cold high latitudes have larger space heating and lighting loads; those at hot low latitudes have larger cooling loads. And, of course, weather and temperature variation is partially determined by solar radiation in the city's environs; the service need of space heating arises because of low solar input, and solar energy is not well suited to space heating. Conversely, space cooling or air conditioning is quite well correlated with solar radiation. This illustrates how the temporal correlation of energy service demands with renewable energy income is an important consideration. The transport demands of cities are less climate dependent and more influenced by a city's density and structure. Not only do demands and renewable supplies vary spatially, they also vary temporally because of social activity patterns and weather. Demands and renewable supplies are not always well correlated in time.

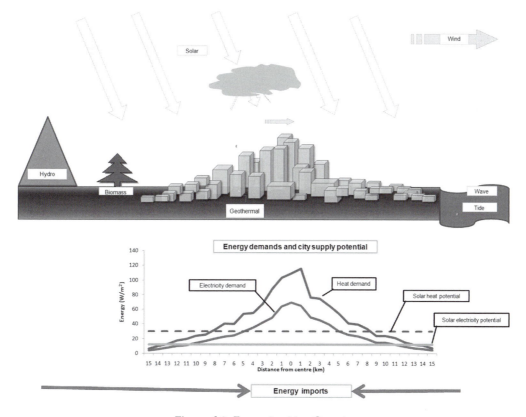

Figure 6.2 *Energy in cities: Overview*

There are many forms of renewable and other energy, and many technologies are available; these may be configured in innumerable ways. Figure 6.3 illustrates some possible connections. On the right are primary energy resources divided into income energy (renewables) driven by the sun and moon, and finite fossil and fissile energy resources. These primary resources are converted, with energy converters of different types (solar collectors, boilers, engines, etc.), into useful energy forms – food, kinetic energy, electricity, light, heat, cool air and chemical energy – that may be used to carry out personal and economic activities. All energy converters have some environmental impact; but those using fossil fuels are major emitters of carbon dioxide, a significant cause of global warming, and of air pollutants such as nitrogen and sulphur oxides. Note that food is included in the energy flows; this most vital of energy forms is a significant fraction in rich countries, but even more so in poorer countries. Food, of course, is biomass and so its supply can be in competition with others uses of biomass such as biofuels.

The renewable energy planner's challenge is to replace some finite energy with renewable energy by reconfiguring the system shown in Figure 6.3. The overarching objective is (at least in terms of cost) to provide adequate energy services to people securely in the future while meeting environmental objectives.

Planning may be accomplished through these steps:

• Analyse the demands for energy and project them over the planning period.
• Survey renewable resources and costs and the availability of finite energy resources.
• Survey the available energy technologies.
• Devise combinations of technologies and energy resources in order to meet the demands for energy.
• Consider how renewable energy may be implemented.

The following sections address these steps in varying levels of detail.

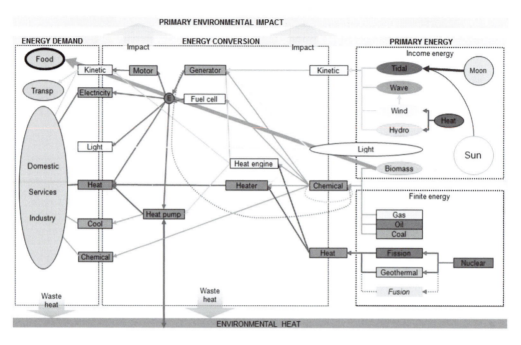

Figure 6.3 *Energy system overview*

What energy services will be required?

The starting point of any energy planning – renewable or conventional – is to thoroughly analyse energy demands: what services is the energy required for? Fundamental human needs and their associated tasks are determined by the basic physical and mental nature of human beings, and since this nature does not change except over evolutionary timescales, neither do the types of needs. But the levels of need do. The levels of needs for energy services are influenced by the prevailing cultural, social, technological and economic context. For example, in the UK, the generally accepted minimum standards of home heating and hygiene have increased enormously over the past century with increasing wealth and technological innovation. The development of relatively efficient central heating systems has occurred in parallel with the wherewithal to purchase these systems and fuels to run them. The needs of a society as a whole will be influenced by demographic change in terms of factors including total population, age structure and household size. These energy services are provided with technologies that convert fuels into services: a gas

boiler converts gas into heat for hot water; a solar collector does the same. The demands for energy can be controlled to some degree with energy efficiency. Table 6.1 summarizes human needs and energy services. Energy – in the form of gas, liquid, solid, electricity, heat – has to be input to technologies to provide the service.

The basic needs for food, water and clean air cannot be altered, whereas others can be modified to some degree. Most important is that most energy service demands and their resulting energy consumption can be reduced with measures such as insulation or more efficient boilers. This makes it easier to meet a large fraction of energy demand with renewable energy. Conversely, demands such as large televisions or air travel are culturally determined and tend to increase as wealth grows. A key part of energy planning is projecting and managing these energy demands.

Energy resources and technologies

This section summarizes renewable energy resources and technologies that can be used to meet the energy service needs outlined in Table 6.1.

Table 6.1 *Human needs and energy services*

Needs	Task	Energy form	Technologies
Food	Storage	Heat (cold)	Refrigerator
	Cooking	Heat	Cooker
Comfort	Shelter	Materials	Buildings
	Thermal	Heat	Heater
		Cool	Air conditioner
	Lighting	Light	Light bulb
			Window
Hygiene	Personal	Heat	Shower/bath
	Clothes	Heat and power	Washing machine
	Dishes	Heat and power	Dishwasher/hands
	House	Power	Vacuum cleaner
Health	Miscellaneous	Miscellaneous	Medical services
Culture	Travel	Power	Vehicles
	Telecommunications	Electricity	Telephone, internet
	Electronic media	Electricity	TV, hi-fi, etc.

Renewable energy resources

The two main primary sources of renewable energy are the sun and the moon. Sunlight – solar radiation – passes through the atmosphere where some of it is absorbed and scattered by the constituents of the atmosphere and clouds, and is finally absorbed by the Earth's land and water masses, as well as plants. The solar heating, in turn, causes evaporation, which leads to rain and hydropower resources, and to wind and, hence, to waves, from which energy may be extracted. A small fraction of the solar radiation drives photosynthesis in plants to form biomass, which contains energy. The moon and, to a lesser degree, the sun cause tides, and the motion of the water in tides can be converted into electricity with turbines at suitable locations, such as marine estuaries and straits.

Radioactive elements in the Earth heat rocks and increase their temperature to produce geothermal heat, which is generally regarded as a renewable resource, although strictly speaking it is finite. Typically, the temperature, and therefore the utility, of geothermal heat increases with depth below the ground; but the costs of extracting the heat also increase with depth. In some locations, because of geology or volcanic activity, geothermal heat is at a sufficiently high temperature and near enough the surface that it may be economically used for heating or, if at an adequately high temperature, to generate electricity.

The heating of the Earth, water and air by renewable energy, mainly solar energy, leads to 'environmental' heat, which may be regarded as renewable energy. Environmental heat is usually at a temperature that is too low to make it directly useful for heating; but with a heat pump, its temperature may be increased. Depending upon climate and resources, low-temperature environmental heat can be absorbed from the Earth or water bodies and used for cooling.

The availability of these renewable energy sources varies spatially and temporally because of geographical factors, the world's weather and tidal systems, and diurnal and seasonal variations brought about by the Earth's rotation and position in its orbit.

The city itself can modify renewable energy resources:

- Buildings in a city exert a drag on the wind, so that the wind speed is generally lower in cities than outside.
- Air pollution from activities in a city can reduce the amount of solar energy reaching ground level, although such pollution is generally diminishing because of environmental policies and the expansion of renewable energy, which generally emits less pollution than fossil energy, though with exceptions such as biomass combustion.

Renewable energy technologies

Renewable energy technologies collect renewable energy and transform it into a form that will, ultimately, meet energy service demands. Some of the leading renewable technologies and typical city resources are summarized in Table 6.2.

Table 6.2 *Summary of renewable energy for cities*

Source	Typical city resource	Technology	Environmental impacts	Output	Cost
Solar	Large	Photovoltaic	Small	Electricity	High
	Large	Solar thermal	Small	Heat	Low
Environmental heat	Large	Heat pump	Small	Heat	Low
Geothermal	Small		Small	Heat	Low
Biomass	Small	Boiler	Various	Heat	Medium
		Combined heat and power	Various	Heat	Low
			Various	Electricity	Low
Wind	Small	Wind turbine	Small	Electricity	Low
Wave	Small/zero	Wave machine	Small	Electricity	Medium
Tide	Small/zero	Tidal flow	Small	Electricity	Medium
	Small/zero	Tidal barrage	Large	Electricity	Medium

More detail is given below on technologies that exploit the most commonly available renewable energy in cities. For more detail, there are many publications available – for example, *A Review of Microgeneration and Renewable Energy Technologies* (BRE, 2008) and *Renewable Energy* (Boyle, 2004).

Solar energy

Solar energy is generally the most available renewable energy source in cities because it provides food, and cities usually originally developed near food supplies; in addition, solar energy ensures that the climate is not too cold or gloomy – all conducive to a viable human settlement. Solar energy can be utilized via a range of technological pathways to provide electricity, light and heat (see Figure 6.4).

Solar energy is absorbed by surfaces and heats them up. The fraction of solar energy absorbed by surfaces can be maximized by making the surfaces black and using special coatings. Buildings can make some use of this solar heating directly by orienting buildings to absorb solar energy through walls and windows; this is called passive solar heating. The problem is that the less solar energy there is, the greater the need for space heating because solar energy heats the local environment. There are few cities located where there is a simultaneous demand for space heating and plentiful solar energy as this is generally at high altitude where temperatures are lower but skies are clear. It is difficult to make windows that gain much more solar energy

than is lost as heat through conduction and convection; windows lose five or ten times as much heat as an insulated wall per square metre for a given temperature difference.

Since buildings were first developed, solar energy has been used to provide interior light, and in modern times this has replaced electric lighting. However, windows create a heating problem, losing more heat than walls – and the contribution of windows to lighting is least when heat losses are greatest, during the winter. Furthermore, without careful design, the use of passive solar heating and lighting makes buildings more likely to overheat in the summer. Passive solar heating requires significant areas of walls and windows to face the sun and not be over-shaded.

Active solar heating is where solar energy is absorbed by a collector through which water (usually) is pumped and is heated up; this heat is passed to a storage tank for later use, usually with further heating, to meet hot water and, sometimes, space heat demands. Photovoltaic solar collectors convert solar energy directly into electricity, which can be conditioned to be compatible with grid electricity.

Optimal solar collection requires surfaces directed towards the main incidence of solar energy – south in the northern hemisphere. Active solar heating and photovoltaic panels requires surfaces – usually roofs – facing close to (within perhaps a 30 degree angle) the predominant direction of the sun (south in the northern hemisphere) in order to capture the maximum solar energy per square metre of collector. There may be

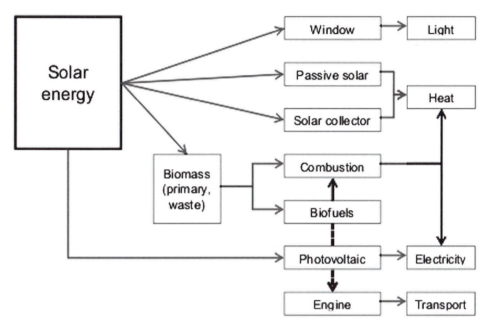

Figure 6.4 *Solar energy pathways*

problems in avoiding over-shading and achieving the correct orientation in a crowded city laid out without renewable energy in mind. Buildings are usually high rise in cities, and so the roof and total envelope area per energy demand is less than in low-rise buildings outside the city, making it difficult to achieve high fractions of renewable energy supply using city resources. Generally, solar collection is cheaper when integrated within building envelopes; but this places constraints on building design.

Heat pumps

Heat pumps lower the temperature of heat in one place and increase it in another. A refrigerator heat pump takes heat from inside the refrigerator, decreases the temperature of the air inside the refrigerator and increases it outside (you can feel warm air from the back of the refrigerator). To use a heat pump for heating water or rooms, we take low-temperature heat from the environment, from the ground, or from water or air, and use the heat pump to raise its temperature and heat the building or the water. Typically, electric heat pumps will raise one or two units of environmental heat to useable temperature for every unit of electricity consumed by the pump (note that

these pumps can also be powered with gas or oil engines, though this is less common). In this way, a unit of renewable electricity, from a wind turbine, for example, can be used to deliver two or three units of useful heat. Since the environmental heat originates from solar energy, it may be argued that heat pumps are partially renewable energy systems.

Biomass

Plants use solar energy to form biomass (wood, seeds, stems, leaves, etc.), which is used for food and fuels. Biomass can come from waste (e.g. sawdust) or from purpose-grown energy crops. The problem with energy crops is that they require additional land, competing with food production, as well as inputs such as fertilizers and fossil fuels. Energy crops can increase the emissions of greenhouse gases such as nitrous oxide to the degree that some energy crops are currently thought not to reduce global warming overall.

Biomass – wood, straw, dung, etc. – was first used in open and later in simple enclosed fires that were inefficient and produced copious health-damaging air pollutants; in poorer parts of the world, such fires are still used. Technologies have improved biomass combustion such that efficiency has increased and pollution has been reduced, and biomass can be used in boilers from the domestic to the industrial scale. One advantage of biomass is that it can be stored at low cost and can therefore provide energy when needed, although providing storage space for biomass can be problematic in high-density cities and dwellings. Biomass can supply heat and electricity at any time because the energy is in a stored form, unlike other renewables.

For cities, biomass for combustion has a number of drawbacks. From a strategic perspective, biomass should be used as near as possible to where it is produced since the transport of biomass usually requires premium liquid fuels. Cities do produce waste biomass in the form of sewage, municipal waste (paper, etc.), waste biomass from park maintenance, and so on; but the quantities, though useful, are relatively small. In general, the optimum use for biomass combustion is probably in combined heat and power (CHP) plants near to the source of biomass. The potential output of CHP depends upon the availability of biomass and appropriate low-temperature heat demands (e.g. on farms, rural factories or at the peripheries of settlements). CHP converts fuel into heat, which is then used to produce steam and electricity, and the waste heat meets heating demands. CHP plants efficiently utilize about 85 per cent of the energy in biomass and produce high-grade electricity as well as heat. The amount of electricity that may be generated from this in CHP plant may be calculated using an efficiency to electricity of about 25 per cent. As a result, CHP uses about two-thirds as much fuel as required in the generation of electricity, with CO_2 emissions reduced accordingly.

Biomass may be transformed into a secondary fuel. Sewage, municipal landfill sites and agricultural wastes can be used to fabricate solid fuels or to generate biogas that may be used like natural gas in boilers or power stations. Biomass can also be converted into liquid fuels of a sufficient quality, replacing diesel and gasoline; but the efficiency of doing this is generally low.

Economics

Cost and performance figures for renewable technologies vary with installation. For most renewable technologies, future cost reductions are to be expected because of technological development and mass production. However, these are uncertain, particularly for photovoltaics, where there may be step changes in technological improvement, and for wave and tidal power, for which there is little commercial experience. Renewable resources outside the city – the bulk of resources – depend, in part, upon the availability and cost of competing fuels: the greater the cost of other fuels, the greater the 'economic' renewable resource. This is particularly so for wind and wave, which have large offshore resources. There are, however, narrower technical limits to some renewable sources, most notably hydro and waste biomass. Boyle (2004) and Barrett (2007) give some information on the technical and economic potential of renewable energy.

Most energy technologies show significant economies of scale in terms of cost and performance going from individual dwelling size to large building or neighbourhood size. Small may be beautiful, but it is often inefficient and expensive! There is, however, a point at which further increases in size are counterproductive. Large machines are generally more efficient than small ones; and as size increases, capital and operational costs decrease per unit of energy produced. For example:

- A large CHP plant might have an electrical efficiency of 30 per cent and be capable of using biomass and other fuels with low emissions, whereas a dwelling-scale CHP unit might be 5 to 10 per cent efficient, incapable of using biomass and cost five or ten times as much.
- A remote 3MW wind turbine might produce electricity at less than 10 per cent of the cost of an urban 3kW turbine.

These economies even apply to building-scale heat and electricity technologies such as solar photovoltaic panels and solar water heaters, although to a lesser degree. A large solar installation on a hotel or hospital will deliver energy more cheaply than an installation for an individual dwelling. However, an individual dwelling solar water heater may deliver heat at a cost competitive with CHP and district heating. Figure 6.5 illustrates the effect of scale on the costs of energy production from different-sized renewable energy installations. This is for illustration only; the actual costs will vary widely depending upon the particular conditions.

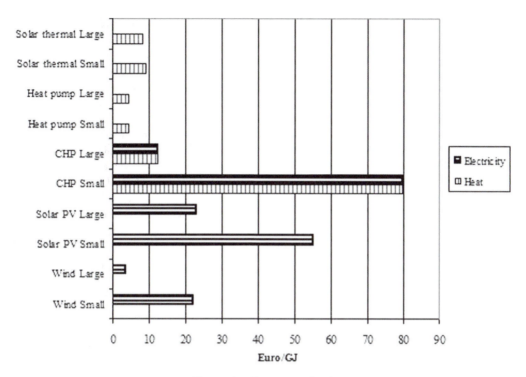

Figure 6.5 *Economies of scale*

Renewable energy transport and multi-fuelling

Renewable and other energy has to be transported within the city and its buildings, and be imported from outside. Energy can be transported in various forms and by different means:

- electricity in cables;
- heat by pipe;
- chemical energy;
- solids such as biomass by surface transport (road, rail and water);
- liquids such as biofuels by surface transport or pipe;
- gases such as biogas or natural gas by surface transport or pipe.

Electricity and heat can be transported in cables and pipes, respectively, and configured into transmission grids. These grids have the advantage that multiple renewable and conventional energy sources can then be used. Once in place, these grids can change the mix of energy inputs without requiring changes for the consumer. For example, the UK predominantly uses natural gas, which will have to be replaced with renewable energy sources. A district heating or heat grid consisting of hot water delivered through pipes can be developed. Over the next decades, this could use gas CHP to input the heat to the grid; a transition could then be made to a multi-renewable sourced system, with heat inputs from a mix of biomass CHP, solar, heat pumps and so on. The grid facilitates flexibility. Such systems have already been developed in Scandinavia.

Planning and implementation

The planning and implementation of the transition from finite to renewable energy requires the application of many disciplines – engineering, planning, architecture, finance, law, environmental science – and the better these are integrated, the smoother and less costly the transition will be. These disciplines need to be applied at all scales, from national to city, to neighbourhood and to individual buildings and energy systems. The planning has to ensure that there is consistency across all scales: for example, there is no point in many individual developers designing new developments, assuming a large fraction of renewable energy is biomass, if there is insufficient biomass in total to meet the demands in that city and elsewhere. Accordingly, in general, planning should proceed from the large to the small scale. When planning renewable and conventional energy supplies, it is necessary to look 20, 30 and more years into the future since implementing energy efficiency and new supplies is a slow process.

The best mix of renewable energy technologies is that which provides the required amounts of energy at least cost, while meeting other constraints such as air pollution emission and air quality. It is not possible to generalize about the best mix because the demands for energy and renewable resources vary greatly between cities located in different parts of the world. For an example of city planning including renewables, see the Greater London Authority's (2007) report *London CO₂: Action Today to Protect Tomorrow – The Mayor's Climate Change Action Plan*.

Renewable energy systems design

When designing and implementing renewable energy technologies, a systems approach is needed, whether the system is for providing hot water in a house or renewable electricity to a city. Energy has to be delivered at the right time to the location where energy services occur. In general, renewable energy is not closely correlated with demands. The designer needs to consider the following:

- What are the spatial and temporal patterns of future energy demands, and of renewable resources?
- How much transmission, storage and backup supplies from biomass or fossil fuels will be needed?

For small systems supplying individual energy consumers, standard system designs have been developed. In most countries, solar water heating and photovoltaic and heat pump systems are available and may be sized and installed with little advanced technical knowledge. For example, a domestic solar water heating system consisting of $4m^2$ of collector, a 200 litre pre-heat tank, and ancillary pumps and controls could be installed in most buildings with an appropriately oriented roof and sufficient internal space for the

system. However, at times the renewable energy collected and stored from these individual 'in-house' systems is insufficient to meet demand and some other energy input is required, such as electricity or gas. This must come from public supplies; therefore, the utility or city authority has to design large-scale systems to provide this. For example, the mass installation of solar water heating in a UK city will reduce the amount of gas or electricity required for water heating substantially in the summer, but not in the winter; and the city gas or electricity system has to meet this shortfall.

When designing larger-scale systems utilizing renewable energy, sophisticated design methods are required that include the technical and economic modelling of energy systems – demand and supply. An example of this applied to renewable electricity is found in Barrett (2007).

Illustration of energy planning, including renewable energy

This section illustrates some aspects of renewable energy planning for a fictitious UK city of 5 million people with some 1.9 million households in 1990 growing to 2.8 million in 2050. Other demands (non-domestic buildings, transport) are excluded (the illustration is based on a simple dwelling stock model of the author and is just that, an illustration). Energy efficiency and renewable energy can be introduced into dwellings at rates that depend upon how fast new houses are built, and how fast existing dwellings are refurbished and have conventional energy systems replaced or supplemented with renewable energy systems.

Figure 6.6 shows the number of dwellings built before 1990 (labelled 'pre-1990 orig') and then refurbished after 2010 (labelled 'pre-1990 refurbished'), allowing for loss of these due to demolition. It then shows in subsequent layers the number of new houses built in each five-period from 1990 to 1994, 1995 to 1999 and so on.

First, energy efficiency is applied to reduce space heat demand, both through refurbishing pre-1990 dwellings and by efficiency regulations applied to the construction of new dwellings. This is depicted in Figure 6.7. The lowest band represents dwellings existing in 1990, and then later refurbished, and the upper bands those dwellings built in the periods of

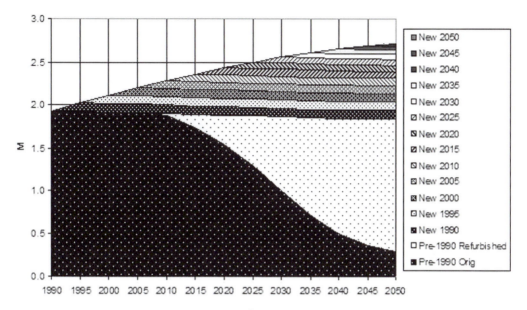

Figure 6.6 *City-dwelling stock population*

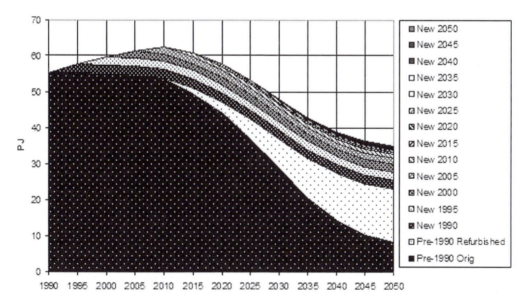

Figure 6.7 *City dwellings: Space heat demand*

1990 to 1995, 1995 to 2000 and so on. It should be noted that the slow turnover of the stock means that existing dwellings still predominate in 2050, emphasizing the importance of energy efficient refurbishment and the retrofitting of renewable energy technologies, such as solar water heaters. This also emphasizes that there are two approaches to

increasing the fraction of renewable energy supply: first, reduce demand and, second, increase renewable supply.

Growth in population and number of households results in water heat increasing to about half of heat demand, as shown in the Figure 6.8. Solar water heating is one of the more practical options in the

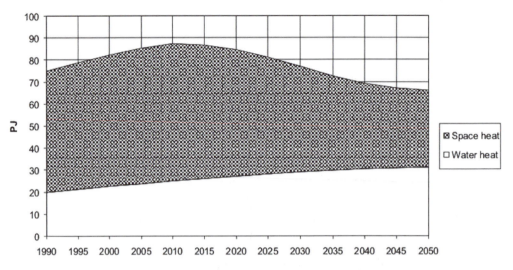

Figure 6.8 *City dwellings: Space and water heat demand*

UK – typically, a dwelling system will provide about half of hot water demand – and so it can meet an increasing fraction of total heat demand.

The changes in space heat efficiency and water demand will change the monthly and hourly patterns of heat demand, as shown in Figures 6.9 and 6.10. Figure 6.9 depicts monthly variation in space heat demand that arises because of a lack of solar energy; this underlines the

difficulty of meeting this demand with solar heating – the peak demand is in winter when there is least sun. However, energy efficiency means that space heat demand does decline. Also, lower temperatures in the winter make heat pumps less efficient.

Heat demand for dwellings, without any heat storage varies throughout the winter, as depicted in Figure 6.10. For active solar and heat pump systems, this diurnal

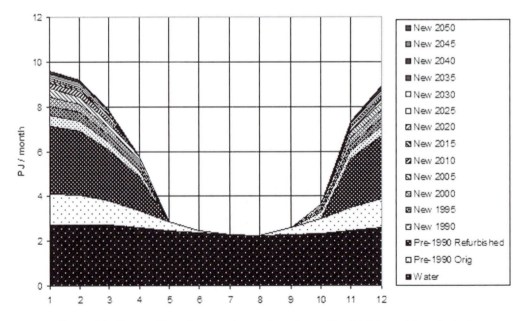

Figure 6.9 *City dwellings: Space and water heat demand in 2050 (monthly variation)*

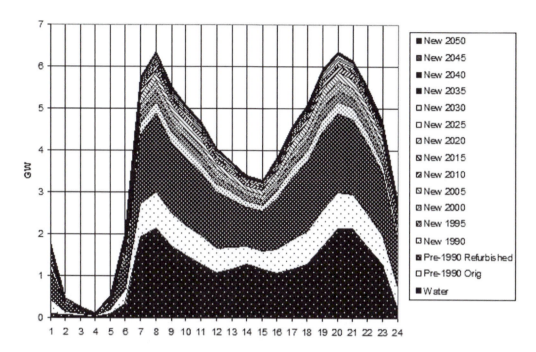

Figure 6.10 *City dwellings: Space and water heat demand in 2050 (hourly variation)*

variation can be accommodated with heat storage, such as hot water tanks. For passive solar heating, it is more difficult to store heat from day to night.

Heat demands may then be added to other demands, such as cooking and appliances, to arrive at the total energy demands of the city's dwellings. These demands are then met with solid, liquid, gas fuels, solar and CHP heat, and electricity, as illustrated in Figure 6.11. An increasing fraction of the CHP heat and electricity would come from renewable sources. This shows how the demand for fossil fuels might gradually be reduced through energy efficiency and renewable energy supply outside and inside the city.

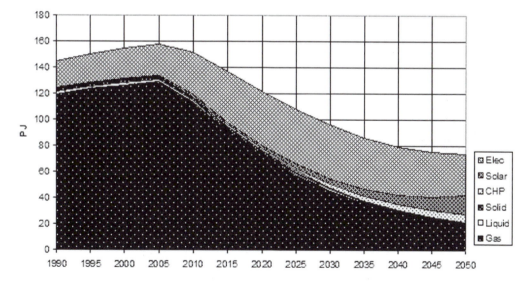

Figure 6.11 *City dwellings: Energy supply*

Table 6.3 *Examples of instruments to implement renewable energy*

	Regulation/planning	Market	Public investment
Local/city	Renewable energy requirement on new developments	Taxation related to energy	Renewable energy on public buildings
National	New building regulations Sectoral targets for renewable energy	Subsidy/tax relief/feed-in tariffs for renewables	Renewable energy on public buildings
International	Technology performance standards (buildings, appliances, vehicles) National targets for renewable energy	Renewable certificate trading	

In this particular illustrative example for dwellings, there is some renewable supply in the city; but the major portion would be imported as renewable electricity from wind turbines and so on. A similar picture would result if the city energy scenario were extended to cover non-residential sectors – commercial and services buildings, transport and industry.

Implementation

Having used technological and economic analysis to devise what may be close to an optimal least-cost plan for energy efficiency and renewable energy in a city (as illustrated above), the problem, then, is to implement the plan. Renewable energy may be implemented using a range of instruments: planning, regulation, market, public investment and information. These instruments need to be tailored to account for the technologies involved for different contexts of buildings, ownership and so forth. It is particularly important to ascertain whether renewable energy planning is to be used for new urban areas or buildings, or for retrofitting existing built environments. Some instruments can be applied by local government; others are controlled by national government or international bodies such as the European Union. Table 6.3 provides some examples of instruments. The reader is encouraged to consult other examples of how cities are developing plans for sustainable energy futures with low environmental impacts (e.g. Greater London Authority, 2007).

Conclusions

People are congregating in cities of ever-increasing size and growing wealth, and the adoption of Western lifestyles is leading to the concentration of energy service demands into small geographical areas. At the same time, fossil fuel use – particularly oil and gas – will decline because of reserve depletion and efforts to combat global warming. This poses the problem of meeting energy service needs in cities with renewable energy resources that are diffuse, and geographically and temporally variable. There is no problem with the absolute availability of renewable energy as resources are more than adequate for all people to enjoy the lifestyles of the rich today. The challenge, however, is to find renewable energy supply solutions that are socially equitable and environmentally acceptable, and that meet needs at reasonable cost. There is no global best renewable energy solution for cities; systems have to be designed to suit the city, regional, national and international context.

The great advantage of renewable energy systems is that they are generally safe and stable economically, whereas the availability of finite fossil and nuclear fuels will diminish and their prices will escalate unpredictably. Renewable energy development must go hand in hand with cost-effective demand management and energy efficiency. Exercising these options will ensure a secure and sustainable future with a high quality of life for people living in cities.

References

Barrett, M. (2007) 'A renewable electricity system for the UK', in Boyle, G. (ed) *Renewable Energy and the Grid: The Challenge of Variability*, Earthscan, London

Boyle, G. (ed) (2004), *Renewable Energy*, second edition, Oxford University Press, Oxford

BRE (2008) *A Review of Microgeneration and Renewable Energy Technologies*, NF 7, IHS BRE Press on behalf of NHBC Foundation,

Greater London Authority (2007) *London CO_2: Action Today to Protect Tomorrow – The Mayor's Climate Change Action Plan*, Greater London Authority, February, www.london.gov.uk

7

Heat Pumps in City Centre Buildings

Djordje Kozic and Darko Goričanec

Introduction

A heat pump is any device that extracts heat from a source at low temperature and gives off this heat at a higher temperature. The basic objective of heat pumping is exactly the same as the objective of refrigeration: the heat is removed at a low temperature and rejected at a higher temperature. The difference between these two systems is that a refrigeration system generally transfers heat from a low-temperature object to the ambient, whereas a heat pump transfers heat from the ambient to a higher-temperature object – for example, from a low-temperature heat source (e.g. air, water or ground) to a higher temperature heat sink (e.g. air or water).

The idea of using a reverse heat engine as a heat pump was proposed by James Thomson and his brother William Thomson (later to become Lord Kelvin) in the middle of the 19th century; but it was only during the 20th century that these practical devices came into common use.

Growing environmental awareness has focused human attention on the utilization of renewable energies. Fossil fuels, such as gas and oil, are finite. We have become increasingly aware of this fact – and it is this awareness that spurs us on to utilize renewable forms of energy to provide us with heat. There is now also a stronger political drive to use fossil fuels with greater consideration of their impact on the environment. Apart from the finite nature of fuel reserves, climate protection plays an important role. The reduction of CO_2 emissions and those of other climate-affecting gases cannot wait if the threat of climate change is to be averted. All of these arguments support the use of renewable energies. Heat pumps provide a particularly energy efficient and environmentally friendly solution to the demand for central heating.

Heat pumps utilize renewable energies from the environment. Solar energy stored underground, in groundwater and in the air, is converted into convenient heating energy using electricity. Heat pumps are efficient enough to be usable as a sole heating source – all year round.

As a consequence, heat pumps have experienced a renaissance. They have the advantage of being combustion free, and thus there is no possibility of generating indoor pollutants such as carbon monoxide. Initial technical shortcomings, which brought a rapid end to their first boom in the 1980s, have now been remedied. Today, heat pumps provide a reliable, cost-effective heating system, which operates with particular environmental responsibility.

They are suitable for providing heat in any type of building, such as detached houses and apartment blocks, hotels, hospitals, schools, office buildings and industrial structures, in newly built and modernization projects alike. Trying to meet all of the requirements specified for energy efficient houses almost inevitably induces the need for a heat pump.

There is a saying that a heat pump is 'a unique device which enables man to outwit nature in order to get more then invested'. Basically, as is well known, it is a well-conceived organization of energy flows and processes: a smaller amount of exergy (available energy) is added to a greater amount of anergy (unavailable energy), which together increases the exergy of the working fluid (process medium) (see Figure 7.1).

According to the definition of efficiency (the use of which, in this case, represents an incorrect approach to

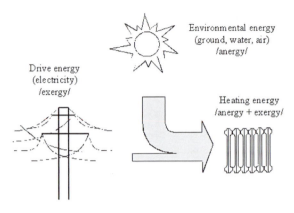

Figure 7.1 *Heat pump principle*

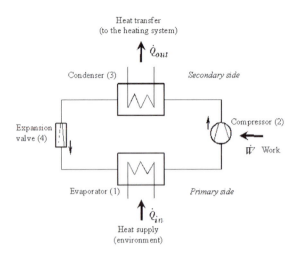

Figure 7.2 *Schematic of a heat pump operation*

the problem), its value would turn out to be well beyond 100 per cent. Of course, this is not acceptable, and for quality evaluation of energy transformation a coefficient of performance (COP) has been introduced, with its value always greater than 1. Basically, this matter cannot be solved unless the quality of energy and the fact that only exergy (but not energy itself) can produce work are taken into account.

Heat pump installations have been widely used in many developed countries of the world, mostly for the purpose of saving more expensive fuels as well as alleviating the harmful environmental effects of energy plants. It is estimated that the total number of operating heat pumps is approaching the 20 million figure, while the load interval ranges from 0.1kW to 10MW or more.

Experts from many countries share the same view that, in the near future, heat pumps are not only going to be widespread, they will also take the dominant role in heat-providing systems.

Thermodynamics of the heat pump

A heat pump is a significant thermodynamic invention. It belongs to devices that operate in a cycle. Numerous heat pump cycles and systems are available, in practice, including vapour compression, absorption, thermoelectric, metal hydride and others. Figure 7.2 shows a schematic diagram of a compressor heat pump, which is the most widely used type of heat pump.

When heat is captured from the surroundings, liquid working fluid (refrigerant) is at low pressure on

the primary side (cold side) inside the evaporator (see 1 in Figure 7.2). The external temperature level is higher than the boiling temperature of the working fluid, which is subject to pressure. This results in the evaporation of the working fluid, which leads to heat being extracted from the ambient. Therefore, the temperature level can certainly lie below 0°C. The compressor (see 2 in Figure 7.2) sucks the evaporated working fluid from the evaporator and compresses it. This raises the vapour pressure and temperature (similar to a bicycle pump when blowing up a tire). From the compressor, the working fluid flows to the condenser (see 3 in Figure 7.2) on the secondary side (hot side – heating system) in the form of vapour. Heating water surrounds the evaporator (heat exchanger). The heating water temperature is lower than the condensation temperature of the working fluid, so the vapour cools down and transforms back into liquid form. The heat captured by the evaporator plus the additional heat generated during the compression process are then transferred together to the heating water. The working fluid is subsequently returned via an expansion valve (see 4 in Figure 7.2) into the evaporator. In the process, it is expanded from the high condenser pressure to the lower pressure of the evaporator and cools down. The cycle is complete.

The objective of this cycle is to deliver the heat transfer $\dot{Q}_{out}$ to the warm region, which is the space to be heated. In a steady state, the rate at which energy is supplied to the warm region by heat transfer is the sum of the energy supplied to the working fluid (refrigerant) from the cold region, $\dot{Q}_{in}$, and the net rate of work input to the cycle, $\dot{W}$:

$$\dot{Q}_{out} = \dot{Q}_{in} + \dot{W}. \tag{1}$$

The COP of a heat pump cycle is defined as the ratio of the heating effect to the net work required to achieve that effect:

$$\mathrm{COP} = \frac{\dot{Q}_{out}}{\dot{W}}. \tag{2}$$

The COP of the idealized Carnot heat pump cycle (plotted in Figure 7.3), with $\dot{m}$ as the flow rate of working fluid is:

$$\mathrm{COP_{Carnot}} = \frac{\dot{Q}_{out}/\dot{m}}{\dot{W}/\dot{m}} = \frac{area\ 2\ a\ b\ 3\ 2}{area\ 1\ 2\ 3\ 4\ 1} \tag{3}$$
$$= \frac{T_H(s_a - s_b)}{(T_H - T_C)(s_a - s_b)} = \frac{T_H}{T_H - T_C}.$$

Equation 3 represents the maximum theoretical coefficient of performance for any heat pump cycle operation between two regions at temperatures T_C (in a real cycle this is the temperature of working fluid evaporation) and T_H (temperature of working fluid condensation). Actual heat pump systems have coefficients of performance that are lower than would be calculated from Equation 3.

A study of Equation 3 shows that as the temperature T_C of the cold region decreases, the coefficient of performance of the Carnot heat pump decreases. This trait is also exhibited by actual heat pump systems and suggests why heat pumps in which the role of the cold region is played by the local atmosphere (air-source heat pumps) normally require backup systems to provide heating on days when the ambient temperature becomes very low. If sources such as well water or the ground itself are used, relatively high coefficients of performance can be achieved despite low ambient air temperatures, and backup systems may not be required.

Modern electric heat pumps obtain approximately three-quarters of the heat required for heating from the environment; the remaining quarter is drawn as electrical power for driving the compressor. Since this electrical power will also finally be converted into heat, it, too, can be utilized for heating purposes.

Temperatures and pressures in the circuit of a real process are commonly illustrated in a *p-h* diagram (where *p* = pressure [Pa] and *h* = enthalpy [J/kg]) for a particular working fluid. For the basic heat pump process, individual stages – evaporation (4 to 1), compression (1 to 2), condensation (2 to 3) and expansion (3 to 4) – can be read off as distances (enthalpy differences). In addition, the COP can be determined: it represents the ratio between released heat and compressor electricity consumption. The predominant part of heat transfer to the heating system occurs in the working fluid wet vapour range.

As one can see, the coefficient of performance describes the relationship between the heating output and compressor electricity consumption. In other words, COP = 4 means that the heat produced is four times more than the electrical energy consumed. It is a value determined from measurements under fixed operating conditions (operating point). The following applies universally to all heat pumps: the lower the temperature difference between the heating water and

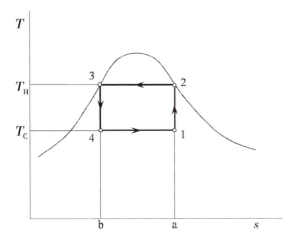

Figure 7.3 *Carnot heat pump cycle*

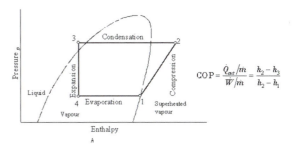

Figure 7.4 *Principal features of the heat pump cycle in a* p-h *diagram*

the energy source, the higher the performance factor and, consequently, the efficiency. For this reason, heat pumps are best suited to heating systems operating at low temperatures (i.e. floor, wall or ceiling heating systems). Modern electrical heat pumps can achieve – subject to the selected energy source and heating system temperature – a COP between 3.5 and 5.5. In other words, this means that for every kilowatt hour (kWh) power consumed, 3.5kWh to 5.5kWh heating energy can be created. This does more than compensate for the energy production disadvantage arising from the use of electrical power (power station efficiency today is approximately 34 per cent).

Heat pumps enable the total heat release to be generated from renewable energy sources, which is financially motivated by the power supply companies. In such cases, heat pumps represent the sole heating system beside the solar technology, which enables heat to be generated with zero CO_2 emissions.

Beside COP, another important factor for electrically driven compressor heat pumps is the annual performance factor. The seasonal performance factor is a value determined for an entire heat pump system over a 12-month period. It expresses the relationship between the usable heat and the power consumed, including the power required to drive the circulation pumps, electronic control units, etc.

Today, modern electric heat pumps represent compact units that cannot be compared – either visually or technically – with the heat pumps produced during the 1980s. The heart of the heat pump is its compressor, which raises the temperature level from the cold side (energy source) to the hot side (heating circuit). Modern hermetically sealed scroll compressors for electric heat pumps are different from piston compressors, which used to be employed in heat pumps, in that they offer a longer service life and much quieter operation. Compared to conventional piston compressors, sound emission is reduced by approximately 6dB(A), which represents a reduction by one quarter of discernible noise development. Generally today, R 407C, R 410A, R 404A and R 134a are used as working fluids (refrigerants) inside the process circuit. These are chlorofluorocarbon (CFC)-free, non-toxic, biologically degradable and non-combustible. Each refrigerant has its own *p-h* diagram and the value of COP depends strongly upon the referring enthalpy values.

In heat pumps, stainless steel plate heat exchangers are primarily utilized for evaporators (exception: air/water heat pumps) and condensers. In contrast to pipe bundle heat exchangers, stainless steel plate heat exchangers provide a turbulent and not a laminar flow pattern. This results in improved heat transfer characteristics. The arrangement can also be more compact, making the design more space efficient.

Most heat pumps are designed to be used for cooling, as well as heating, and it is in this form that the heat pump is the most efficient. These heat pumps have a reversing valve that allows them to cool as well as to heat the space. This valve changes the fluid flow direction so that the indoor coil becomes an evaporator and the outdoor coil becomes a condenser.

Ground source heat pumps in city centre buildings

For heating and cooling of buildings in city centres (i.e. commercial and institutional buildings, offices, stores, hospitals, hotels, apartment buildings, schools, restaurants, etc.), the highest proportion of newly installed systems gain energy from the ground as the energy source.

During the winter, it is much easier to capture heat from the soil at a moderate temperature (e.g. 10°C) than from the atmosphere when the air temperature is below zero. This is also why heat pumps that use ground or groundwater as a heat supply from the environment encounter no difficulty blowing comfortably warm air through the ventilation system, even when the outdoor air temperature is extremely cold. Conversely, in summer, the relatively cool ground absorbs a building's waste heat more readily than the warm outdoor air. Roughly 70 per cent of the energy used in a heating and cooling system is the renewable energy from the ground. The remainder is clean, electrical energy, which is employed to collect the low-temperature heat from the ground and transport it from one location to another.

Ground source heat pumps (GSHPs), coupled with certain types of low-temperature distribution system, have been identified as the most efficient and environmentally friendly heating and cooling technology for many climates. These systems are very efficient and use the relatively constant temperature of the ground to obtain heat during the winter and provide cooling during the summer.

For a heating regime, the pipe fluid absorbs heat from the Earth. The fluid passes through a heat exchanger (acting as an evaporator), where it transfers

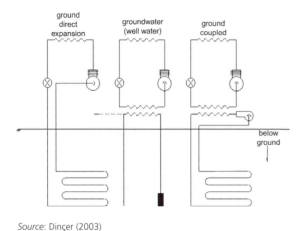

Source: Dinçer (2003)

Figure 7.5 *Main categories of ground source heat pumps, schematically*

heat to the working fluid. In the summer, the cycle reverses to remove heat from the house. Some of the heat is used for hot water; the remainder is dumped into the Earth via the ground loop.

There are three GSHP categories (see Figure 7.5): direct expansion, groundwater and ground coupled. For direct-expansion systems, a working fluid is circulated in a buried heating exchanger and evaporates in the ground without an intermediate heat transport fluid. In the other two, water is used or water mixed with antifreeze.

When using geothermal heat pumps, horizontally embedded or vertically installed heat absorbers are utilized to ensure heat exchange with the ground. Horizontal flat or trench collectors as closed-loop heat absorbers of GSHPs are not suitable for city centres because the land area is limited. Most GSHPs that are used for these purposes include vertical U-pipe heat exchangers (see Figure 7.6) placed in boreholes (50m to 200m depth) to ensure heat exchange with the ground. Water is used as the heat carrier in systems operating at $T > 0°C$, while for winter modes in cold regions, at sub-zero temperatures, antifreeze must be added.

GSHPs are preferred by many people and many institutions because they are, indeed, an environmentally benign technology, with no emissions or harmful exhaust. This is again favourable for city centres where there is chronic lack of fresh and clean air. Although most GSHP units require electricity to operate the components, a high COP means that GSHP systems provide significant reductions in levels of CO_2, SO_2 and NO_x emissions (all related to greenhouse gas emissions and global warming).

Vertical closed-loop systems are surely the most expensive but also the most efficient configuration due to the fact that the subsoil level of temperature increases and stabilizes with depth, as can be seen in Figure 7.7.

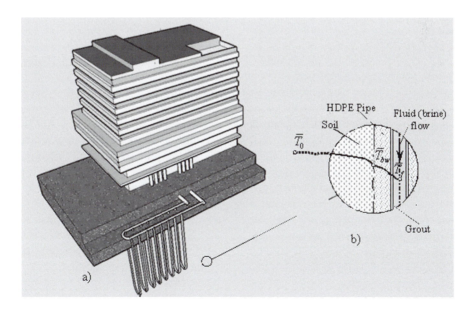

Figure 7.6 *Building heating based on the GSHP system with a vertical heat exchanger and pipe detail*

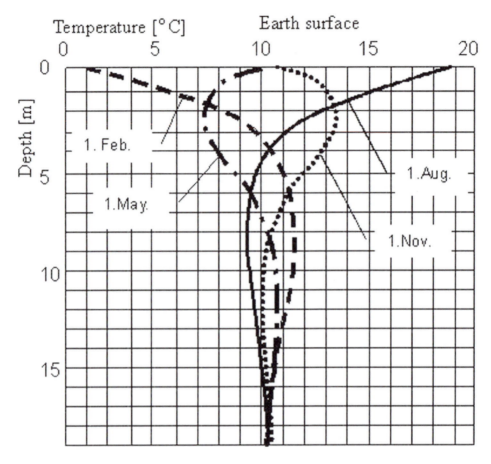

Source: VIESSMAN (2006)

Figure 7.7 *Annual underground temperature distribution*

GSHP systems are inherently more expensive to install than gas, oil or electric heating units, but they do compete with any type of combined heating/cooling system. Installing ground probes, however, can be accomplished in only a few hours using modern drilling equipment. For ground probe systems, determining the layout and drilling depth are of crucial importance. This is done by geologists and drilling contractors who have the relevant knowledge and software to size and optimize such installations. Extract warranties (e.g. over ten years) can be contractually arranged with such specialist companies. In many countries, such systems require a permit from local water boards. These are responsible for drillings down to depths of 100m. Deeper drillings require the additional agreement of local mining authorities. A prefabricated probe is inserted into these boreholes, following which the annular gap between the probe tube and the bored hole is filled with tamped-down backfill. In most cases, four pipes are installed in parallel (dual U-shaped pipe probe).

The hot side of the heat pump is determined by the type of low-temperature panel heating system (floor, wall or ceiling), air heating or low-temperature radiators and convectors (designed for a typical operational temperature of 30°C to 45°C). Depending upon the quality of building thermal insulation to the required building thermal load, Q_{out} is calculated, and based on the heating system type, the mean thermodynamic temperature of the heating fluid (water) is defined.

However, the cold side of the heat pump, related to the coupling of the heat pump evaporator to the heat exchanger in the energy extraction borehole, requires detailed analysis from which the optimal value of brine mean temperature $\bar{T}_f$ should emerge. As can be seen from the following discussion, this can result in the second important measure: the optimal borehole depth Z. When designing a ground source heat pump system, determining the borehole depth is one of the most important tasks.

As can be seen from a GSHP system example (see Figure 7.6), the vertical heat exchanger consists of three main components: the pipe, the grout (filling) material around a pipe and the soil around the grout. The vertical borehole is a drilled cylindrical hole that can vary in diameter and depth. The pipe material is high-density polyethylene (HDPE) that forms a U-shaped pipe, with a U-bend at the bottom of the borehole. The grout plays an important role in heat transfer between the soil and the fluid flowing within the pipe. It is preferable for the grout to have a high thermal conductivity. The uncertainty of the soil thermal properties is often the most significant problem facing a GSHP system. Designers of ground-loop heat exchangers have a difficult job when estimating the soil thermal conductivity k and the soil volumetric heat capacity (pcp). Both soil thermal properties are generally required when the designer is sizing the ground-loop heat exchanger depth and number of boreholes. The heat capacity of a borehole system is critically dependent upon thermal resistance between the surrounding soil and the heat carrier. A lower thermal resistance means that a smaller temperature difference is required between the soil and the heat carrier for a given heat power.

The longer the amount of piping used in an outdoor loop, the more heat can be extracted from the ground (or water) and transferred into the house. Installing less loop than specified by the manufacturer will result in a lower indoor temperature, and more strain on the system as it operates longer to compensate for reduced heat exchange. However, excessive piping can also create different sets of problems as well as the additional costs. Each manufacturer provides specifications for the amount of pipes required. The greater the distances between buried loops, the higher is the efficiency. It is suggested that there should be 3m between sections of buried loop in order to allow the pipe to collect heat from the surrounding soil without interference from the neighbouring loop.

It is interesting to determine this parameter from a thermodynamic point of view. Since the fluid (brine) temperature difference between the inlet and outlet of the borehole is usually small (about 2 degrees), it is possible to use the arithmetic mean temperature:

$$\bar{T}_f = \frac{T_{f1} + T_{f2}}{2}.\tag{4}$$

Referring to Figure 7.7, the specific heat extraction from ground q, given per unit length of a borehole (W/m), in steady-state conditions, can be determined from:

$$\dot{q} = \frac{\bar{T}_{o_1} + \bar{T}_{f_2}}{R_{gf}}\tag{5}$$

where T_o is an appropriate local average temperature known as the natural undisturbed ground temperature.

In Equation 5, R_{gf} – (mK)/W – refers to the overall thermal resistance associated with different thermal resistances. We will not enter the problems of R_{gf} determination because it will exceed the scope of this chapter; but, only as a comment, we can say that there are special thermal response test measurements (*in situ*) of the heat transfer capacity of energy extraction (Saljnikov at al, 2006).

Even when the performance of a heat exchanger and soil parameters are correctly determined, there is an obvious problem of finding out the optimal parameters of the GSHP system concerning the coupling of a borehole exchanger with a heat pump. With the use of an ideal thermodynamic model of the reverse Carnot cycle (see Figure 7.3), the basic idea about the possibility of obtaining optimal values $\bar{T}_f$ can be observed. A higher temperature of the heat pump's heat source (in essence, higher evaporation temperature) is more favourable from the aspect of heat pump efficiency, but less favourable from the cost aspect of an energy extraction borehole. In that case, substantially more heat must be extracted, which, in given conditions, would account for a much greater borehole depth.

On the other hand, lower evaporation temperature would be less favourable from the heat pump perspective, but would, at the same time, mean the reduction of Z, which would reduce the initial cost of the project.

In essence, the classical problem is obvious: the correct balance between capital cost and operating cost has to be found in order to minimize the total annual cost of produced heat.

Based upon the Equations 1, 2 and 4, one obtains:

$$\dot{Q}_{out} = \dot{Q}_{in}\left(1 - \frac{1}{COP}\right) \qquad (6)$$

and:

$$\dot{Q}_{in} = \dot{q}Z = \frac{\bar{T}_0 - \bar{T}_f}{R_{gf}} Z. \qquad (7)$$

Total borehole depth can be expressed from Equations 6 and 7 as:

$$Z = \frac{\dot{Q}_W \cdot R_{gf}}{\bar{T}_0 - \bar{T}_f}\left(1 - \frac{1}{COP}\right). \qquad (8)$$

This is exactly the total length of the ground heat exchanger. The length of one borehole probe is obtained through dividing Z by the number of boreholes (see Figure 7.5).

The above result is obtained by thermodynamic analysis. The optimal values of $\bar{T}_{f,\,opt}$ and Z_{opt} are the subject of thermo-economic analysis (Kozic, 2001) and are out of the scope of this text.

Costs for creating one borehole, including the probe, can lie, subject to ground conditions, between 30 and 50 Euros per metre. For a borehole depth of approximately 100m, drilling costs are about 3000 Euros to 5000 Euros. Design and installation require a sound knowledge of ground conditions, the order of ground layers, the ground resistance and the presence of, groundwater or stratum water, including determining the water levels and flow direction. Table 7.1 provides some approximate values for the extraction by ground probes.

Under standard hydrologic conditions, an average probe capacity of 50W/m probe length can be assumed for ground probes. GSHP units do not need to meet 100 per cent of the calculated heat loss of a building as long as they have an auxiliary electric heating source for backup and for emergencies. Almost 90 per cent of a house heat load can be met by a GSHP unit that is sized to 70 per cent of the heat loss, with the remaining 10 per cent of load supplied by the auxiliary plenum heater. GSHP technology relies on a stable underground temperature to function efficiently. In most cases, the deeper a loop is buried, the more efficient it will be. A vertical borehole is the most efficient configuration; but this type of digging can be very expensive.

Care must be taken to ensure that the vertical borehole is drilled in accordance with local regulations. The main advantages of vertical closed-loop systems are high efficiency with less property space requirement, and greater security from accidental post-installation damage. The main disadvantages of vertical closed-loop systems are that it is usually the highest-cost option and that it could cause environmental damage to the ground if not mounted properly.

The savings attainable with a heat pump will reflect the size of the building and its quality of construction (particularly the level of insulation); the building's heat loss and sizing; the COP of the GSHP unit; local

Table 7.1 *Expected specific extraction for dual ground U-pipe probes*

Substrate	Specific heat extraction
General guide values	
Poor substrate (dry sediment) ($\lambda < 1.5$ W/(m·K))	20W/m
Standard solid rock substrate with water-saturated sediment ($\lambda < 1.5 - 3.0$W/(m·K))	50W/m
Solid rock with high heat conductivity ($\lambda > 3.0$ W/(m·K))	70W/m
Loose rock	
Gravel, sand, dry	< 20W/m
Gravel, sand, with waterways	55–65W/m
Clay, loam, moist	30–40W/m
Limestone (solid)	45–60W/m
Sandstone	55–65W/m
Acidic magmatite (e.g. granite)	55–70W/m
Basic magmatite (e.g. basalt)	35–55W/m
Gneiss	60–70W/m

Source: VIESSMAN (2006)

Note: λ = thermal conductivity.

climate and energy costs; the occupier's lifestyle habits; efficiency of alternative heating systems; the configuration of the loop; interior temperature; ductwork required on a retrofit; site accessibility for equipment; and the vast quantity of various additional options selected.

Generally, a GSHP can produce heat with average savings of 10 to 15 per cent over natural gas, 40 per cent savings over oil, and 50 per cent savings over propane; air-conditioning savings average 40 to 60 per cent over conventional systems. High efficiencies of GSHP systems allow commercial users to save up to 70 per cent in operating costs compared to electric resistance heating, then up to 50 per cent over air-source heat pumps, and finally up to 45 per cent over fossil fuel-combusting furnaces (GHPC, 2001).

These cited combined cost savings associated with GSHP typically provide a significant return on investment for any business or institutional organization that is mainly located in city centres. Although the initial installation cost of a GSHP system may be higher, the systems typically pay for themselves in less than five years (often in less than two years). Another advantage is their extraordinarily low operating costs. Recently developed new drilling techniques have brought down the costs of installing the loops and, hence, the initial costs of GSHP systems.

There are a number of factors that have a major influence on the installation and performance of a GSHP system. Therefore, it is important to understand the following issues clearly and to base the design on a thorough knowledge of these factors.

The most important first step in the design of a GSHP installation is to find out how much heat is required to satisfy one's comfort level. This method requires knowledge of the insulation levels of all walls and windows, the number of occupants, geographic location and soil type, and many other factors in order to determine the total annual heat loss in kilowatt hours (kWh). It is also important to calculate cooling loads for the summer (units can provide sufficient cooling if a unit is large enough to provide sufficient heat) and for hot water heating, if included. With this final heat loss satisfied, the installed unit will match the total demand.

During the last decade, the use of geothermal energy through suitable systems integrated with Earth-coupled structures has become more and more frequent. These structures are the deep foundations of buildings, such as piles, diaphragm walls, base slabs and other forms of reinforcement – that can reach depths with constant Earth temperature. Heat-absorbing pipes in the form of coils are included in the concrete units. For example, in energy piles, vertical heat exchangers (HDPE pipes) are attached to the reinforcement cage of the pile. The cage is inserted into a prepared borehole and grouted with concrete.

Ideal structures for geothermal energy utilization are bored or cut (and covered) tunnels like, for example, subway lines. Large inner surfaces that are in contact with the ground, at constant temperature because of depth, serve as an excellent energy source (sink) for GSHPs in adjacent buildings. There are many possibilities for energy extraction in the form of piles, diaphragm walls or anchors.

Figure 7.8 provides an example of extracting energy for GSHPs and neighbouring buildings from municipal wastewater. The lower part of the moistened perimeter of a circular-type sewer is equipped with absorber pipes embedded in concrete.

These systems are an innovation in sustainable development and feature numerous benefits. First, they provide ecological benefits as a non-polluting and environmentally friendly technique and support compliance with international obligations (such as the Kyoto Protocol), contributing to the reduction of fossil fuels and CO_2 emissions. Other benefits are savings on investments due to the 'double use' of units (building foundations, bored tunnels, systems of municipal wastewater, etc.), low operation cost using low-temperature applications, a self-regeneration energy source and long service life.

For investors, these renewable energy foundations are particularly important because additional costs for these systems are, in many cases, paid back within a short period.

The most significant merits of GSHP systems in city centre buildings are as follows:

- Efficient heating and cooling: when measured against other existing systems, this type of heat pump provides a higher COP.
- Durability that induces low maintenance costs – GSHPs require 30 to 50 per cent less maintenance than a fossil fuel-based heating and cooling

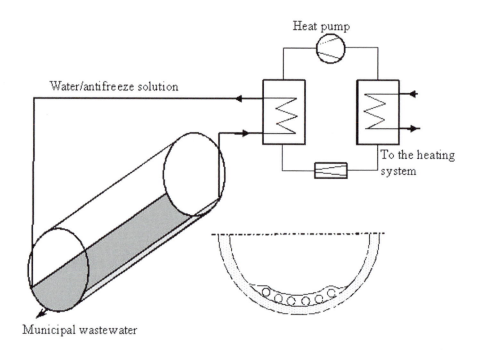

Figure 7.8 *Energy from municipal wastewater*

system; in addition, most geothermal systems can run without any repair maintenance for over 20 years.

The key benefits of GSHP systems can thus be expressed in terms of cost savings with regard to enhanced comfort and appearance and an improved environment. GSHPs are ideally suited to public and commercial places that are located in city centres due to the following advantages: allowed simultaneous heating or cooling of different zones; reduced possible damage from severe weather conditions; lower mechanical space requirements and fewer costs; quiet operation; high reliability; and easy air conditioning.

References

Dinçer, I. (2003) *Refrigeration Systems and Applications*, John Wiley & Sons

GHPC (2001) *Geothermal Heat Pumps*, Geothermal Heat Pump Consortium, Washington, DC, www.ghpc.org

Kozic, D. (2001) 'Thermoeconomic optimization of the ground source heat pump system', in *Proceedings of the Second International Conference on Energy Efficiency and Cooling*, Santiago de Cuba

Saljnikov, A., Goričanec, D., Kozic, D., Krope, J. and Stipic, R. (2006) 'Design of an experimental test set-up for thermal response tests to be used in Serbia', *WSEAS Transactions on Heat and Mass Transfer*, vol 1, no 4, pp481–487

VIESSMAN (2006) *Heat Pump*, Technical Series

8

Life Cycle Assessment of Buildings

Christina Diakaki and Denia Kolokotsa

Introduction

The life cycle of a building as well as of other systems (processes, services, etc.) is similar to the lifetime of biological organisms. In the same way that biological organisms grow, reproduce and, finally, die, buildings are constructed, used and, finally, demolished and disposed of.

At each stage of their life cycle, building systems interact with other systems; thus, their life cycle is actually an open cycle. Their construction, demolition and disposal interact with the wider natural, economic and social environment since raw materials and energy, labour, technology and capital are required. The developed relations and interactions are dynamic; in some cases, they may even become competitive. For example, the construction of a green building usually requires an increase of the related cost. Therefore, in order to achieve globally acceptable solutions, all of the factors involved during the life cycle of a building should be studied. To this end, several methods and tools may be used, such as life cycle assessment (LCA) (IEA, 2004).

LCA refers to the study of the environmental impacts of stage of a system's life cycle. It generally constitutes a set of systematic procedures that quantify the inflows and outflows of energy and other resources throughout its total life cycle. Based on this quantification, LCA then evaluates and identifies any potential environmental impacts, aiming to determine appropriate improvements.

LCA is not the only approach for analysing the environmental impacts of a system; it is probably, however, the most comprehensive one (IEA, 2004). When applied to the building sector, LCA may focus

on building materials and component combinations, single buildings, building stocks (i.e. groups of buildings), specific aspects of a building system (e.g. the air-conditioning system), or specific stages of a building's life cycle (e.g. the construction stage) (Kotaji et al, 2003; IEA, 2004). This chapter aims to present the main characteristics of the LCA approach with particular emphasis on its application to the building sector.

The chapter starts with a short review of the evolution of LCA from its roots, dating back in the decades of the 1960s and 1970s, until today, discussing also the efforts of different international organizations to standardize the overall procedure. Then, the goal and scope of the approach is followed by a description of the LCA procedures. The chapter concludes with a few final remarks and a discussion of its main topics.

The evolution and standardization of the life cycle assessment method

LCA has a life history of almost 40 years. The roots of the method lie in the early studies of the 1960s and 1970s that became known as resource and environmental profile analyses (REPAs) in the US and Ecobalance in Europe (Ciambrone, 1997). During these decades, several studies were conducted by research institutes and consulting firms addressing issues mainly concerning the private sector (Assies, 1993; Tan and Culaba, 2002).

As their title indicates, the early LCA studies placed emphasis on energy and raw materials demand, as well as on waste production. The oil crises of 1973 and 1979 further advanced the conducting of such studies, focusing on fuels and energy-related issues and analyses (Boustead and Hancock, 1979; Sørensen, 2004).

At the end of the 1980s, the production and disposal of packaging with negative environmental impacts began to be acknowledged as an issue of major importance, and a recycling trend spread throughout the world, a further advancement emerges for LCA in that it is now recognized as one of the most important methods for analysing environmental impacts (Ciambrone, 1997).

The modern LCA methodology is based on the standards developed during the 1990s. More specifically, in 1991, the Society of Environmental Toxicology and Chemistry (SETAC) published a guide for the conduct of LCA studies (SETAC, 1991). A few years later, the International Organization for Standardization (ISO) released the standard series ISO 14040 on LCA as a supplement and expansion of the ISO standard series 14000 on environmental management. The new version of the ISO 14040 series has been recently released (ISO 14040, 2006; ISO 14044, 2006).

Although the ISO 14040 series standards are quite similar to the SETAC guide, they have superseded the SETAC guidelines due to the dominant position of ISO in the development of international standards.

Goal and scope of life cycle assessment

Life cycle is a concept underlining several environmentally oriented approaches. These approaches, also called the 'cradle to grave' way of thinking about products, services or processes, can generally be split into analytical and practical elements (UNEP, 2005). Independently of the category where they belong, all life cycle-based approaches are steered by concepts such as sustainable development, ecology and eco-efficiency, which are guiding principles on how to achieve a life cycle economy. Moreover, their application is based on the availability of data and information such as databases with specifications on resources' use, emissions and toxic substances, or demographic data.

The analytical approaches are used to assess, in a scientifically sound way, the effects of planned actions and decisions, while the practical approaches aim to put the results of the analytical approaches into practice. The LCA approach addressed here is an

analytical life cycle approach (UNEP, 2005) that may contribute to the following (Tan and Culaba, 2002; Kotaji et al, 2003; ISO 14040, 2006; Nebel, 2006):

- formulation of environmental laws;
- decision-making by the industry, as well as by governmental or non-governmental organizations (NGOs);
- development of business strategies, including investment plans;
- identification of opportunities for improving the products' environmental aspects at several points during their life cycle;
- selection of indicators for surveillance, evaluation and/or measurement processes;
- marketing, including ecological labelling and improvement of corporate image;
- benchmarking;
- purchasing decisions.

The wide range of possible applications also points to the wide range of stakeholders who may use and benefit from LCA results (Nebel, 2006):

- industry and other commercial enterprises;
- governmental and regulatory bodies;
- consumer organizations and environmental groups;
- consumers.

When applied to buildings, LCA aims to assess environmental loadings and impacts throughout their entire life cycle, which includes the following main stages (see Figure 8.1):

1   design;
2   materials and components production;
3   construction;
4   use and maintenance;
5   demolition.

A process that should also be considered within all of the aforementioned stages of a building's life cycle is transportation. Usually, the loadings from transportation are considered separately from the other processes due to several difficulties that may arise. The most significant difficulty is the attempt to account for transportation during the use stage of a building's life cycle (IEA, 2004). At this particular stage, it is necessary to predict the building occupants' behaviour and to formulate transportation scenarios, performing tasks that are not at

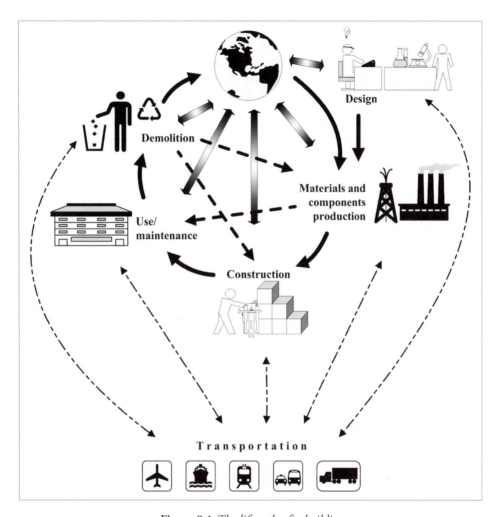

Figure 8.1 *The life cycle of a building*

all trivial and that depend upon several factors which cannot be anticipated during the design and construction stage (e.g. the future development of the site and transportation infrastructures).

The LCA method recognizes that all of the aforementioned stages of a building's life cycle have environmental impacts that need to be identified, quantified, analysed and improved. Areas of concern usually include resource use, human health and ecological consequences (SETAC, 1991). Depending upon the goals of each particular study, a building may be viewed in many different ways (IEA, 2004): as a product that is manufactured, used/maintained and finally disposed of. It may also be viewed as a process intended, through its operation, to provide a number of services to users, as well as appropriate conditions for living, working, studying, etc. Finally, it may be viewed as a place in which to live, thus placing the emphasis on the comfort and health of its users. Therefore, LCA must be customized accordingly in order to include or exclude specific life cycle stages, or specific loadings and impacts.

Generally, the environmental loadings of a building include the input of resources (e.g. energy) and the output of substances (e.g. liquid effluents), while its environmental impacts include resource depletion, global warming, ozone depletion, etc., as well as their associated impacts upon the ecosystem (see Figure 8.2). The self-evident advantage of LCA application is that it enables potentially significant though well-hidden environmental effects to be revealed. However, buildings are very distinctive systems with characteristics that may complicate or frustrate the application of the method (Kotaji et al, 2003; IEA, 2004):

- The life time of a building is long and unknown – often more than 50 years. During this lifespan, the building may undergo many changes, even more significant than the original construction, which cannot be predicted accurately.
- The location of a building is specific. As a consequence, many of its impacts are at the local level, in contrast to the global effects considered by LCA.
- Buildings are complex systems comprising several distinctive subsystems and products. As a consequence, numerous data are needed in order to perform an LCA study that may also differ from one location to another. This means that the LCA results for a building located in a specific area are, usually, substantially different from the LCA results obtained by placing the same building in another area.

- The environmental impacts of a building are substantially affected by the behaviour of its users, services' operators and other third parties.
- Indoor environmental quality improvement that is expressed in terms of comfort and health usually has significant impacts upon its external environment.
- Buildings are closely integrated with various elements of their external environment, such as roads, pipes, grids, etc., that formulate the urban infrastructure. As a consequence, if the LCA of buildings is isolated from these elements, the analysis may provide misleading results.

Despite these problems, however, many applications of LCA may be found in the related bibliography covering different issues and aspects. Table 8.1 provides an indicative list of such applications, along with their particular characteristics.

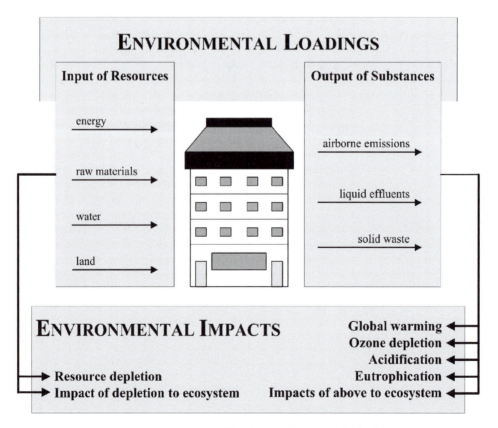

Figure 8.2 *Environmental loadings and impacts of a building*

Table 8.1 *Indicative building-related LCA studies*

Goal and scope	Functional unit	System boundaries	Considered impacts	Source
Study of a residential home to determine total life cycle energy consumption of materials' fabrication, construction, use and demolition.	A whole home building with its auxiliary areas (i.e. garage, etc.) of specific structural characteristics and functions, with four occupants and 50-year lifespan.	Extraction of raw materials and production of engineered materials; manufacturing of building components; transportation of materials from extraction to fabrication and from fabrication to the construction site; on-site building construction, including site earthwork; energy consumption during use stage; embodied energy of maintenance and improvement materials; demolition and transportation of demolished materials to recycling centres or landfills.	Primary energy Global warming potential Other impacts such as life cycle cost	Blanchard and Reppe (1998)
Comparison of three houses: the current construction standard in France (reference), a solar and a wooden frame house.	A whole building, built in a given site and planned for a specified use (dwelling, office, etc.), generally occupied and assumed comfortable and healthy (a unit of living area 1m² can be used as a functional unit under the same conditions).	Direct fluxes caused by external processes such as energy use for transportation of building materials from the source to the construction site were taken into account. Note that the energy used to build the infrastructure used for transportation of the building materials was neglected. However, the energy used for building infrastructure for so-called internal processes, such as hot water preparation, was taken into account.	Energy consumption Water consumption Depletion of abiotic resources Waste creation Radioactive waste creation Global warming potential Depletion of the ozone layer potential Acidification potential Eutrophication potential Aquatic eco-toxicity potential Human toxicity potential Photochemical oxidant formation potential Malodorous air potential	Peuportier (2001)
The energy and environmental implications of applying different conservation technologies in school buildings in arid Andean regions of Mendoza-Argentina.	The environmental impact of implementing a given technology in the school building (together with all of the additional materials required), including the reduction of heat losses over its operative lifetime.	Only locally available technologies were taken into consideration; environmental aspects included in the study accounted only for external effects. Construction and operation stages were considered, but with the exception of some factors such as people transportation during the operation phase, etc.	Global warming potential Acid rain potential Photochemical smog Resource consumption Eutrophication potential Toxicity	Arena and de Rosa (2003)

Table 8.1 *Indicative building-related LCA studies* (cont'd)

Goal and scope	Functional unit	System boundaries	Considered impacts	Source
Assess the environmental impacts of residential ventilation units over a 50-year life cycle in an area of Finland of 120m² to 150m² or a typical three-bedroom house in Canada.	Providing an outdoor ventilation airflow of 50L/s, corresponding to the recommended ventilation rate of 0.5ACH in Finland for a one-floor house.	Production of materials and use of the ventilation unit in a single family house in Helsinki, Finland, for a life cycle of 50 years (the ventilation unit was assumed to operate 24 hours per day, 365 days per year).	Global warming potential Acidification potential Potential for the photochemical formation of oxidants (smog)	Nymana and Simonson (2005)
Analysis (concerning energy and environmental performance) and comparison of different types of fuel intended either for direct use (e.g. domestic boiler combustion) or indirect use (production of electricity that will be consumed) in order to satisfy the energy requirements of a typical apartment building in Thessaloniki, Greece.	A whole apartment building, built in a given site (city) and equipped to provide specific comforts and facilities (a unit of living area 1m² can be used as a functional unit under the same conditions).	Emissions of light heating-oil refining, transportation and combustion for natural gas, transportation and combustion in the building's boiler and other domestic appliances.	Energy consumption Light heating oil Natural gas Electricity Global warming potential Acidification potential Eutrophication potential Winter smog potential Heavy metals potential	Theodosiou et al (2005, 2007)
Environmental, economic and social analysis of materials for doors and windows based on their use in school buildings.	The area of doors that is required to provide access and the area of windows that is required to provide sufficient light and ventilation for a 20 foot long and 20 foot wide room that is located in a single-storey school building for 50 years.	All processes in the life cycle of timber and aluminium doors and windows, from extraction of raw materials to disposal.	Embodied energy Global warming potential Acidification potential Nutrification potential Other impacts such as economic viability and social concerns (thermal comfort, good interior aesthetics, ability to construct fast, strength, durability)	Abeysundra et al (2007)
Evaluate in terms of energy usage and air emissions the wood- and steel-reinforced	1kg of emission per year per m² during the design life of a house.	All stages of the life cycle.	Global warming potential Acidification potential Eutrophication potential Human toxicity	Gerilla et al (2007)

Goal	Functional unit	System boundaries	Impact categories	Reference
concrete for housing construction. Identify key issues associated with the life cycle of brick produced and used in Greece.	A brick of dimensions 17cm × 14cm × 28cm weighing 5.945kg after the baking process.	Raw material acquisition, industrial production, packaging and transportation.	Greenhouse emissions Acidification potential Eutrophication potential Winter smog Summer smog Solid waste	Koroneos and Dompros (2007)
Model selected energy systems that provide space heating and cooling, electricity for lighting and equipment, and domestic hot water in commercial buildings to assess the potential life cycle environmental impacts that might result from the production and use of energy.	1kWh of energy consumption.	Extraction of raw materials and energy resources, transportation, production, combustion/ conversion and use.	Global warming potential Acidification potential Tropospheric ozone precursor potential Primary energy consumption	Osman and Ries (2007)
Define the energy and environmental profile of an insulation product based on a natural fibre composite material.	The mass (kg) of insulating board that involves a thermal resistance R of $1m^2K/W$ during the insulation lifetime.	Cultivation and kenaf crop; transport in all phases; kenaf fibre refining; manufacturing of insulation board; use (installation and maintenance impacts were neglected); incineration during disposal stage.	Global energy requirement Global warming potential Acidification potential Nutrification potential Photochemical ozone creation potential Ozone depletion potential Water consumption Waste generation	Ardente et al (2008)
Evaluate the environmental impact of a borehole-based system, taking into account its entire life cycle.	An air-conditioning system that conditions and distributes a variable airflow volume of a maximum $5m^3/s$, including the cooling and the air distribution systems.	Production of materials; energy use for the operation of systems; removal and air distribution system in the building.	Acidification potential Eutrophication potential Global warming potential Photochemical ozone creation potential	Heikkilä (2008)

The methodology of life cycle assessment

The application of the LCA methodology (see Figure 8.3) follows four phases (Ciambrone, 1997; Guinée et al, 2001; Sørensen, 2004; ISO 14040, 2006):

1   *Goal and scope definition.* This phase is responsible for determining the system to be studied and the desired/required depth of analysis.
2   *Life cycle inventory analysis (LCI).* This phase is responsible for identifying and quantifying the environmental loadings (inflows and outflows) of the system under study during its entire life cycle.
3   *Life cycle impact assessment (LCIA).* This phase is responsible for analysing and assessing the environmental impacts of the system under study.
4   *Interpretation (according to ISO 14040) or improvement assessment (according to SETAC).* This final phase is responsible for the analysis, assessment and synthesis of the results of all previous LCA phases with the aim of identifying

any potential actions and policies that support the reduction of identified environmental impacts of the system under study.

The following sections describe in more detail the goals, methodology and contribution of each one of the aforementioned phases of the LCA methodology. Moreover, Table 8.2 provides a list of software packages that may support the application of LCA in buildings. More information on LCA-related software may be found in Jönbrink et al (2000), Kotaji et al (2003), IEA (2004), as well as at the European Platform on Life Cycle Assessment (see http://lca.jrc.ec.europa.eu/lcainfohub/toolList.vm).

Goal and scope definition

The first phase of LCA is responsible for defining the goal and scope of the study. This includes determining the system's space and time boundaries, as well as its purpose and life cycle. In addition, under this phase, the pursued results and the methodology for conducting, reviewing and reporting the study are specified. The data and information necessary for achieving the subsequent phases are also identified and located in order to be compatible with the general aspirations of the study.

LCA also requires, especially for comparative purposes, the definition of a common reference base called a functional unit or comparison basis. The functional unit refers to one or more of the functions of the system to be assessed, and to the duration of its utilization. When referring to buildings, this choice is not a trivial task since, due to their multifunctional nature, a unit that is suitable for one function may be unsuitable for the others (Kotaji et al, 2003; IEA, 2004).

To obtain true functional equivalence when comparing buildings, the whole structure over its entire life cycle, defined according to a series of pre-established performance characteristics such as conformity, location, indoor conditions, adaptability, safety, comfort, etc., should be considered (Kotaji et al, 2003). Other bases of comparisons may include criteria such as the square metre or cubic metre of the building area over a typical year, or the number of occupants or households (IEA, 2004). It might also be useful, occasionally, to analyse a building in terms of rooms or services provided (IEA, 2004). On the other hand,

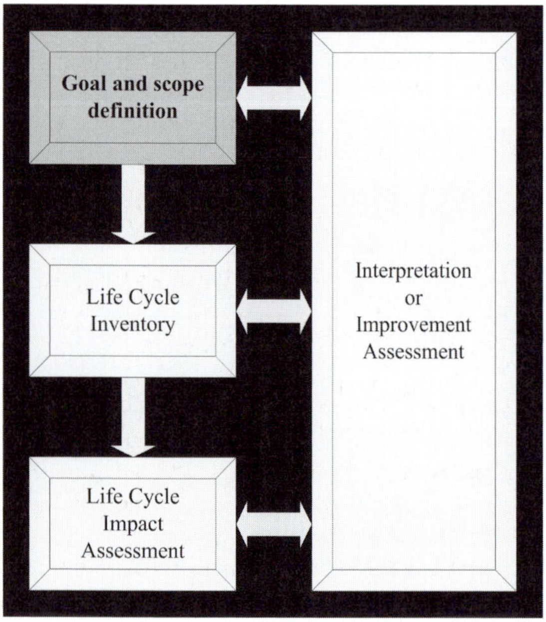

Figure 8.3 *The application phases of the LCA methodology*

Table 8.2 *Building-related LCA software*

Name	General Information	Inventory data	Impact indicators	Available at
ATHENA	Covers material manufacturing (resource extraction and recycled content), related transportation, on-site construction and regional variation in energy use. Building type and assumed lifespan. Maintenance, repair and replacement effects. Demolition and disposal. Operating energy emissions and pre-combustion effects.	Natural resources, energy and water inputs to processes; emissions to air, water and land for the manufacture, transportation and use of all of the individual building products.	Embodied primary energy use Global warming potential Solid waste emissions Pollutants to air Pollutants to water Weighted resource use	www.athenasmi.ca/
BEES	Focuses on environmental performance of building products by using the environmental life cycle assessment approach specified in ISO 14040 standards. All stages in the life of a product are analysed: raw material acquisition, manufacture, transportation, installation, use, and recycling and waste management.	230 building products across a range of functional applications.	Life cycle environmental and economic performance scores for various building product alternatives Physical flow quantities for each environmental impact (CO_2 for the global warming impact), embodied energy, and first and future costs	www.bfrl.nist.gov/oae/bees.html
BREEAM Tools	Focus on different stages of the construction process: manufacturing of building materials (i.e. life cycle analysis of materials in *BREEAM Specification: The Green Guide*), design stage (i.e. *BREEAM Envest* and *BREEAM Buildings*), construction stage (i.e. *BREEAM Smartwaste*) and post-construction (i.e. *BREEAM Buildings*). *BREEAM Building* assesses the operational and the embodied environmental impacts of individual buildings.	Available with each tool.	Energy: operational energy and CO_2 emissions Transport: location issues related to transport Pollution: air and water pollution (excluding CO_2) Materials: environmental implications of materials selection, recyclable materials Water: consumption issues Ecology and land use: ecological value of the site, green-field and brown-field issues Health and well-being: internal and external issues relating to health and comfort	www.bre.co.uk
ECO-BAT	Focuses on environmental impacts produced during the building lifespan, from its construction to its demolition, including fabrication, replacement, waste management and transport. The impacts are evaluated	Ecoinvent database (www.ecoinvent.ch).	Non-renewable energy, global warming potential, acidification potential and photochemical ozone creation	http://ecobat.heig-vd.ch

Table 8.2 *Indicative building-related LCA studies* (cont'd)

Name	General Information	Inventory data	Impact indicators	Available at
EQUER	at different levels: materials, elements and the whole building. Evaluates environmental impacts during the different phases (fabrication of materials, construction, utilization, renovation and demolition). Combines life cycle analysis and energy calculations. The functional unit considered is the whole building over a certain duration.	Building model.	Primary energy consumption, water consumption, acidification, eutrophication, global warming over 100 years, non-radioactive waste, radioactive waste, aquatic eco-toxicity of polluted water, human toxicity, photochemical ozone (smog)	www.cenerg.ensmp.fr/english/themes/cycle/index.html
GABI	Focuses on design for environment, life cycle assessment (LCA), life cycle costing (LCC), life cycle impact assessment (LCIA), life cycle inventory (LCI), life cycle management (LCM), life cycle sustainability assessment (LCS), supply chain management, substance/material flow analysis.	Comprehensive database including 110 European Reference Life Cycle Data System (ELCD) and life cycle cost information.	All environmental impact indicators such as: Primary energy demand Global warming potential (100 years) Eco-indicator score Waste generation Water consumption	www.gabi-software.com/
LEGEP	Focuses on design, construction, surveying and evaluation of new or existing buildings or building products. Covers all life cycle phases from construction to maintenance, operation, refurbishment and demolition.	Ecoinvent database (www.ecoinvent.ch).	Cost, energy, mass flow, global warming potential over 100 years, acidification, photochemical ozone creation potential, ozone depletion potential, eutrophication potential, primary energy consumption, renewable and non-renewable energy	www.legep.de/
LISA	Focuses on identifying key environmental issues in construction and design that are based on whole life cycle of buildings.	Data for buildings are entered by the user.	Resource energy use, tonnes of equivalent CO_2, suspended particulate matter (SPM), non-methane volatile organic compound (NMVOC), water, NO_x, and SO_x	www.lisa.au.com

when comparing building materials and component combinations, the functional unit used should be a part of a functional unit that corresponds to the whole building (e.g. per tonne unit for a material such as mortar per installed unit such as 1m^2 wall with thermal resistance 2.5m^{2}K/W) (Kotaji et al, 2003).

The choices for the functional unit are many, involving trade-offs that should be carefully considered, and the final decision should only depend upon the particular processes, products, activities, services and geographical scale defined for the building to be analysed (Kotaji et al, 2003; IEA, 2004). Examples of functional units used in building-related LCAs can be found in Table 8.1.

Another issue that arises during this stage is the pinpointing of the hypotheses and limitations that should be taken into account while performing the study. In the case of long-lived products such as buildings, several assumptions or estimates are necessary for (Kotaji et al, 2003; IEA, 2004):

- their service lifetime, as well as the service lifetime of their constituent components that determine the number of repairs and replacements;
- their use and maintenance scenarios;
- their major refurbishment or renovation scenarios;
- their adaptation to changing expectations, users and technologies (many buildings are vacated or demolished long before their useful life due to lack of adaptability); and
- the demolition and recycling scenarios (i.e. the end-of-life scenarios that divide waste streams into streams sent to landfill, incineration or recovery).

All of these assumptions and estimates may significantly affect the LCA results.

This phase is potentially the most important. It provides a guide for conducting the entire study. It also ensures that the obtained results will be compatible with the goal and scope of the study. It should be noted, however, that this guide is not static. LCA is an iterative procedure. It starts with some initial choices and requirements that may be revised and adapted later in the light of new evidence from the analyses. Such revisions and adaptations, however, should be made only after serious and careful consideration.

Life cycle inventory analysis

The second LCA phase is perhaps the most demanding (Goedkoop and Oele, 2007). It concerns all of the activities/processes that are involved in the system under study and includes the direct and/or indirect use of energy and/or mass.

Inventory analysis is the phase where the system under study must be specified in detail. This includes (Guinée et al, 2001):

- the refinement of system boundaries (i.e. the definition of its precise boundaries in relation to the natural environment and other systems);
- the development of a building model, including all processes and sub-processes that will be considered; and
- the collection, quantification, recording and validation of all relevant data based on the developed building model.

The building comprises a set of processes, interconnected via energy and/or mass exchange, which perform a specific task. The building is also separated from the rest of the world, which constitutes its environment via existing or virtual boundaries. There are three types of such boundaries (Guinée et al, 2001; UNEP, 2005): boundaries separating the system under study from the natural environment; boundaries defining the sub-processes relevant to the system (allocation); and boundaries separating the system from irrelevant processes (cut-off).

The first type of boundary defines the kind of environmental and financial processes that are considered or excluded from the study and that directly affect the LCA results. The second type of boundary concerns the way in which several environmental impacts resulting from a multifunctional process (i.e. a process that produces more than one product) are allocated in its several sub-processes. Consider, for example, the total energy required in a factory that produces metal products for the automotive and building industries, where records exist to discriminate the amounts of energy required for each type of product. There are several ways to allocate energy (e.g. according to the product weight) with a single objective in order to ensure that each product will receive its fair share of environmental interventions originating from the shared processes (Kotaji et al, 2003; IEA, 2004). Similar problems and careful allocation procedures are also needed in the case of using recycled products.

Finally, the third type of boundary determines which particular processes of the system under study will be excluded from the LCA for reasons of simplicity or lack of relevant data. Obviously, the impacts of the excluded processes should comprise a negligible part of the total impacts of the system.

Setting system boundaries for buildings is critical in achieving valid and comparable results. Comparative studies implementing different LCA tools have shown that the majority of the variations observed in the results come from differences in the considered system boundaries (IEA, 2004). Unfortunately, boundaries can be established in all areas (life cycle stages, geographical scale, resources, concerned groups, impacts of concerns, etc.), and there are no specific rules on where to draw them beyond the fact that they should generally reflect the type of LCA that is to be conducted and its intended use. For example, the comparison of two different buildings may require more inclusive boundaries than the comparison of alternative technologies for the same building project. Examples of system boundaries set for building-related LCAs can be found in Table 8.1.

The output of the inventory analysis phase is an inventory table that includes all of the quantitative data collected with respect to the inflows and outflows of the system under study. It should be noted, however, that in parallel to the quantitative data, several other types of qualitative data and information may be collected that cannot be quantified but that, nevertheless, may be particularly useful and necessary during the last LCA phase (i.e. during interpretation). For this reason, any qualitative data and information potentially collected should also be reported in order to be available during analysis of the results (Sørensen, 2004).

Life cycle impact assessment

The third LCA phase aims to evaluate the environmental impacts of the system under study based on the inventory results in relation to the goal and scope of the study. To this end, the inventory results are further processed with respect to the pre-established environmental impacts and social preferences (Guinée et al, 2001).

The impact assessment is a quantitative and/or qualitative process that is used to characterize and interpret the negative consequences of the environmental impacts identified during the inventory phase. Five steps are followed for the impact assessment: classification; characterization; normalization; grouping; and weighting (Guinée et al, 2001; ISO 14040, 2006; Goedkoop and Oele, 2007). The last three steps are optional but are frequently followed as their results facilitate the interpretation of the results of the entire analysis during the fourth LCA phase.

During the classification, the impact categories are refined and finalized, taking into account the degree of required detail that has been specified during the first LCA phase. The inventory data is then assigned to the defined impact categories. During this process, it is possible that some data is allocated to more than one impact category. The impact categories that are usually taken into account concern degradation of the ecosystem, waste of natural resources, degradation of the quality of human life and consequences to human health (see Figure 8.2). Examples of impact categories considered in building-related LCAs can be found in Table 8.1.

In the special case of building-related LCAs where site-specific environmental impacts are also involved, the following site-specific impacts may also be considered (Kotaji et al, 2003; IEA, 2004):

- neighbourhood impacts (e.g. microclimate, glare and solar access);
- indoor environment (e.g. indoor air quality and thermal comfort);
- local ecology (e.g. land surface occupation and ecologically sensitive areas);
- local infrastructure (e.g. water supply and transport systems).

Moreover, during the construction stage, several types of substances can affect the health of workers (Kotaji et al, 2003). Traditional LCA aggregates all of the loadings and calculates impacts at the regional or global scale – local impacts that are connected to a building, such as those mentioned above, are not addressed. In order, therefore, to apply LCA to buildings, either the site-specific impacts are excluded from the assessment by appropriately setting the system boundaries, or they are inventoried and classified separately (Kotaji et al,

2003; IEA, 2004). In the second case, a more extensive data collection is needed at the LCIA stage, when a more balanced view of building performance is obtained. Unfortunately, current LCA models and tools are not able to account for the majority of site-specific impacts, and the best available alternative is to combine LCA with more passive and qualitative evaluation tools in order to obtain a generic and balanced view of building performance (Kotaji et al, 2003; IEA, 2004; Blom, 2006).

During the second step of impact assessment (i.e. characterization), the inventory data is quantified and summarized within each impact category. To this end, appropriate characterization methods are specified in order to assess the inventory data's contribution to the impact category or categories to which it has been assigned. There are several methods that may be employed (e.g. the eco-indicator method) (Goedkoop and Spriensma, 2001; Goedkoop and Oele, 2007). However, since the results of this phase are particularly important for the overall outcome of the LCA study, it is essential that the characterization method selected for each impact category is explicitly reported and analysed.

Specification of the characterization method is followed by a calculation of the category indicators based on the inventory data that is quantified and aggregated through the use of appropriate characterization factors that reflect the relative contribution of the LCI results into a single result for each impact category. This result, called the category indicator result, expresses the contribution of the specific impact category in terms of equivalent amount of an emitted reference substance (e.g. the global warming potential impact indicator result is expressed in terms of emitted kilograms of CO_2 equivalents). The set of all category indicator results comprises the environmental profile of the system under study.

Normalization (i.e. the third step of impact assessment) is used to assess the magnitude of the effect that a particular impact category has upon the wider environmental problem. According to ISO 14040 (2006), normalization is the calculation of the category indicator results in relation to a base case. The base case may refer to a particular geographical area (e.g. Greece, Europe, etc.), a person (e.g. Greek citizen, European citizen, etc.), or another system for a given time period. Additionally, other types of information may be taken

into account, such as a future desirable state. The main aim of normalizing the category indicator results is to better understand the relative importance, as well as the magnitude, of the results as far as the system under study is concerned. Normalization is also used for the compatibility check of the results and the preparation of data for the next phases. The outcome of this step is an alternative environmental profile for the system under study called the normalized environmental profile.

During the grouping step of the impact assessment, the different impact categories are aggregated into one or more sets. Grouping may be based either on the classification of the impact category indicators according to a nominal scale (e.g. specific emissions) or on the sorting of the impact category indicators according to an ordinal scale (e.g. high, medium and low priority).

Finally, during the last step of impact assessment (i.e. weighting), specific weights are defined for the impact category indicators' results that have been assessed during normalization. The weights reflect the relative importance of each category indicator's result according to some given social values and preferences. The category indicator results are then multiplied by their weights and aggregated, resulting in a new alternative profile for the system under study called the weighted environmental profile.

Weighting is especially helpful when attempting to reduce LCA to a single score, as far as the environmental impact is concerned, and when making comparisons between alternative buildings or designs. Such a reduction is certainly useful when someone does not have the time or interest to delve into the details. However, aggregation can suffer from a lack of detail. Moreover, weighting is not allowed across impact categories for public comparisons between products, according to ISO 14040 (2006), due to the fact that the weights are largely based on subjective views.

Interpretation

This particular LCA phase is not specific for buildings (Kotaji et al, 2003), nor does it present any particularities when applied in this field. Moreover, it is very difficult to be standardized in the sense that there are no strict and rigorous rules applicable to each case.

Generally, during interpretation, the results of all previous analyses are interpreted and used as a basis for decision-making regarding actions that are expected to improve both the system under study, as well as the environment and human welfare. Moreover, the results of all previous analyses, all choices that were made and all hypotheses assumed are assessed through sensitivity analyses to ensure consistency, completeness, soundness and robustness (Guinée et al, 2001).

Based on the analyses and assessments discussed in this chapter, conclusions are drawn and recommendations are made for decision-making regarding the system under study.

Conclusions

LCA was not originally conceived as a tool for analysing buildings or other complex and long-lived products or processes. Nevertheless, its applicability in this sector is accelerating rapidly, and is currently considered as one of the major tools supporting the efforts towards achieving sustainable buildings (Kotaji et al, 2003; IEA, 2004). Moreover, although LCA has a significant contribution to make with regard to environmental concerns, it has, at the same time, several limitations due to its complexity.

In order to perform a detailed LCA of a system, all of the related processes and environmental impacts should be identified and analysed. This results in an extremely complex and time-consuming procedure, with increased data and specialized knowledge requirements.

Other problems result from the fact that LCA cannot take into account or predict future changes in current technology or demand. This limits the validity of LCA results over time. Moreover, it does not take into account the effects caused by possible changes in methodological choices or decisions regarding the boundaries set or the specific system. As a result, LCA is limited to the analysis of impacts that are known and that can be quantified, and, in practice, it must be combined with sensitivity analyses and/or other approaches to account for the effects of the choices and assumptions considered.

Generally, the application of LCA may be limited by a lack of (UNEP, 2005):

• appropriate acknowledgement of its necessity/utility;
• specialized knowledge;
• a necessary budget;
• appropriate data and methods.

In addition, when applied in buildings, adaptation is needed for LCA to account for the long lifespan; local impacts; wide boundaries; maintenance, renovation and replacement needs; adaptation to changing expectations, users and technologies; occupants' behaviour; and diverse interests of the building's involved stakeholders.

However, if a clear justification is provided for adopting this particular assessment method, if the principles of the method are adopted consciously in building applications, if the way in which the analysed results are to be communicated both internally and externally is clearly defined, and if a reasonable budget is available, then LCA may become a powerful tool towards developing sustainable buildings, leading to a more environmentally friendly building sector.

References

Abeysundra, Y., Babel, S., Gheewala, S. and Sharp, A. (2007) 'Environmental, economic and social analysis of materials for doors and windows in Sri Lanka', *Building and Environment*, vol 42, pp2141–2149

Ardente, F., Beccali, M., Cellura, M. and Mistretta, M. (2008) 'Building energy performance: A LCA case study of kenaf-fibres insulation board', *Energy and Buildings*, vol 40, pp1–10

Arena, A. P. and de Rosa, C. (2003) 'Life cycle assessment of energy and environmental implications of the implementation of conservation technologies in school buildings in Mendoza-Argentina', *Building and Environment*, vol 38, pp359–368

Assies, J. A. (1993) 'Life cycle assessment in a historical perspective', in Pedersen, B. (ed) *Environmental Assessment of Products: A Course on Life Cycle Assessment*, University-Enterprise Training Partnership in Environmental Engineering Education (UETP-EEE), Helsinki, Finland

Blanchard, S. and Reppe, S. (1998) *Life Cycle Analysis of a Residential Home in Michigan*, MSc thesis, University of Michigan, School of Natural Resources and Environment, Ann Arbor, Michigan, US

Blom, I. (2006) 'Environmental assessment of buildings: Bottlenecks in current practice', *European Network for Housing Research (ENHR) International Conference in Housing in an Expanding Europe: Theory, Policy, Participation and Implementation*, Ljubljana, Slovenia, 2–5 July, http://enhr2006-ljubljana.uirs.si/publish/W13_Blom.pdf, accessed 4 March 2008

Boustead, I. and Hancock, G. F. (1979) *Handbook of Industrial Energy Analysis*, Ellis Horwood, Chichester, UK

Ciambrone, D. F. (1997) *Environmental Life Cycle Analysis*, Lewis Publishers, Boca Raton, Florida, US

Gerilla, G. P., Teknomo, K. and Hokao, K. (2007) 'An environmental assessment of wood and steel reinforced concrete housing construction', *Building and Environment*, vol 42, pp2778–2784

Goedkoop, M. and Oele, M. (2007) *SimaPro 7 – Introduction to LCA with SimaPro 7*, Pré Consultants, Amersffort, The Netherlands

Goedkoop, M. and Spriensma, R. (2001) *The Eco-indicator 99: A Damage Oriented Method for Life Cycle Impact Assessment*, Methodology Report, Pré Consultants, Amersffort, The Netherlands

Guinée, J. B., Gorrée, M., Heijungs, R., Huppes, G., Kleijn, R., De Koning, A., Van Oers, L., Sleeswijk, A. W., Suh, S., Udo de Haes, H. A., De Bruijn, H., Van Duin, R. and Huijbregts, M. A. J. (2001) *Life Cycle Assessment: An Operational Guide to the ISO Standards*, Final report, Ministry of Housing, Spatial Planning and the Environment (VROM-DGM) and Centre of Environmental Science, Leiden University (CML), The Netherlands

Heikkilä, K. (2008) 'Environmental evaluation of an air-conditioning system supplied by cooling energy from a bore-hole based heat pump system', *Building and Environment*, vol 43, pp51–61

IEA (International Energy Agency) (2004) *Annex 31 Energy-Related Environmental Impact of Buildings*, Report of IEA Energy Conservation in Buildings and Community Systems Programme (ECBCS), Canada Mortgage and Housing Corporation, FaberMaunsell Ltd, Birmingham, UK, www.annex31.org, accessed 4 March 2008

ISO 14040 (2006) *Environmental Management – Life Cycle Assessment – Principles and Framework*, International Organization for Standardization, Geneva, Switzerland

ISO 14044 (2006) *Environmental Management – Life Cycle Assessment – Requirements and Guidelines*, International Organization for Standardization, Geneva, Switzerland

Jönbrink, A. K., Wolf-Wats, C., Erixon, M., Olsson, P. and Wallén, E. (2000) *LCA Software Survey, IVL Report No B 1390*, SIK research publication SR 672, IVF research publication 00824, Swedish Industrial Research Institutes' Initiative (Sirii) SPINE Project Report Summary, Stockholm, Sweden, www.ivl.se/rapporter/pdf/ B1390.pdf, accessed 4 March 2008

Koroneos, C. and Dompros, A. (2007) 'Environmental assessment of brick production in Greece', *Building and Environment*, vol 42, pp2114–2123

Kotaji, S., Schuurmans, A. and Edwards, S. (2003). *Life-Cycle Assessment in Building and Construction: A State of the Art Report*, Society of Environmental Toxicology and Chemistry (SETAC), Pensacola, Florida, US

Nebel, B. (2006) *White Paper: Life Cycle Assessment and the Building and Construction Industry*, Beacon Pathway Ltd, Auckland, New Zealand, www.nzgbcservices.org.nz/ resources/events/LCA2006/LCA%20White%20paper .pdf, accessed 4 March 2008

Nymana, M. and Simonson, C. J. (2005) 'Life cycle assessment of residential ventilation units in a cold climate', *Building and Environment*, vol 40, pp15–27

Osman, A. and Ries, R. (2007) 'Life cycle assessment of electrical and thermal energy systems for commercial buildings', *International Journal of Life Cycle Assessment*, vol 12, no 5, pp308–316

Peuportier, B. L. P. (2001) 'Life cycle assessment applied to the comparative evaluation of single family houses in the French context', *Energy and Buildings*, vol 33, pp443–450

SETAC (1991) *A Technical Framework for Life Cycle Assessments*, Society of Environmental Toxicology and Chemistry, Washington, DC, US

Sørensen, B. (2004) *Renewable Energy*, Elsevier Science, Amsterdam, New York, San Diego, Oxford, Edinburgh, Madrid, Philadelphia, St. Louis, London, Shannon, Rio de Janeiro, Paris

Tan, R. R. and Culaba, A. B. (2002) *Environmental Life-Cycle Assessment: A Tool for Public and Corporate Policy Development*, American Center for Life Cycle Assessment (ACLCA), www.lcacenter.org/library/pdf/PSME2002a. pdf, accessed 4 March 2008

Theodosiou, G., Koroneos, C. and Moussiopoulos, N. (2005) 'Alternative scenarios analysis concerning different types of fuels used for the coverage of the energy requirements of a typical apartment building in Thessaloniki, Greece. Part II: Life cycle analysis', *Building and Environment*, vol 40, pp1602–1610

Theodosiou, G., Koroneos, C. and Moussiopoulos, N. (2007) 'Alternative scenarios analysis concerning different types of fuels used for the coverage of the energy requirements of a typical apartment building in Thessaloniki, Greece. Part I: Fuel consumption and emissions', *Building and Environment*, vol 42, pp1522–1530

UNEP (United Nations Environment Programme) (2005) *Life Cycle Approaches*, UNEP, Paris, France, http:// lcinitiative.unep.fr/default.asp?site=lcinit&page_id=A9F7 7540-6A84-4D7D-8F1C-7ED9276EEDE3, accessed 4 March 2008

9

Energy and Environmental Monitoring

Alex Summerfield, Hector Altamirano-Medina and Dejan Mumovic

Introduction

Building research, particularly with respect to energy performance, appears to be undergoing a transformation not seen since the first oil crisis. Governments have begun to recognize the scale and urgency of the challenge presented by climate change and that buildings can make a substantial contribution to reducing national carbon emissions (DTI, 2007). Thus, building research is likely to focus increasingly on climate change mitigation and adaptation strategies across the built stock. In research terms, this translates into a rapid shift from more familiar small-scale projects, such as exemplar or prototype buildings of design and academic interest, to field studies that generate the kind and scale of empirical evidence that can inform energy policies at the national level.

The dynamic interactions between people and their built environment form a complex system that renders research of any detail or duration in this area a major challenge. These are not clinical trials, laboratory bench studies or just occupant questionnaires, but involve extensive environmental monitoring, detailed building and social surveys, and sometimes require major interventions in people's homes, such as replacing heating systems or refurbishment. So, apart from dealing with participant recruitment, ethical issues and the often intrusive nature of the work, the sheer logistics and organization of such studies represent a major undertaking within typical resource and financial constraints. On the other hand, it is people living and working in buildings that essentially make this fieldwork interesting; they can highlight the limitations and confound the predictions of purely technical or physical models. They are essentially why we still need to do this type of research.

The aim of this chapter is to guide researchers along a practical methodology for these studies both to address fully the specific research questions under investigation and underpinned by benchmark methods, and to recognize the potential for wider supplementary research that can add considerable value to the original study. There are numerous related issues, such as statistical methods of recruitment to obtain representative samples or detailed energy analysis, that have been dealt with elsewhere and moreover would require a volume in their own right (BRE, 2005; Fowler, 2008). Hence, this chapter focuses on the underlying principles and techniques that guide the selection and implementation of methods to undertake this type of research.

The topics are illustrated via a case study of 29 dwellings in Milton Keynes, situated about 75km north-west of London, that were originally monitored for hourly energy and temperature from 1989 to 1991. The dwellings essentially follow conventional UK housing design but were constructed to higher standards of energy performance than required by building regulations at that time. They incorporated energy efficiency features, such as increased floor and wall insulation, double-glazing and condensing boilers, so that they broadly complied with building standards of a decade later (Edwards, 1990). During 2005 to 2006, a follow-up study was undertaken in 14 of the gas centrally heated homes from the original study to determine if internal temperature or energy consumption had changed over the intervening years. The original and follow-up studies are referred to as MK0 and MK1, respectively (Summerfield et al, 2007).

The chapter comprises three main parts. First, we describe the process of planning a research project in translating precise research questions into protocols for monitoring temperature and energy; as well as using building and occupant surveys. Second, we discuss issues of analysis and communication of results. This is illustrated by the approach taken to analyse the MK0–MK1 comparison. The last section illustrates supplementary research, not necessarily considered as part of the original research agenda, but that can greatly enhance its scientific value. The work uses the MK0 and MK1 data to investigate the environmental conditions that lead to mould growth.

Research methodology

The renewed focus on building research has been accompanied by rapid technological developments that greatly facilitate monitoring and data collection – for instance, via wireless remote loggers – and at a far more practical and cost-effective level than previously. Thus, it is now possible to consider studies that would have been almost inconceivable only a few years ago. However, recruitment and ongoing contact with households for what may amount to a major intervention and monitoring spell, such as installing and monitoring new technology, remains a considerable barrier. For this reason energy studies may be conducted conjointly with other projects that focus on issues from disparate fields, such as issues of sociology or epidemiology across households (Hong et al, 2006). There is considerable incentive to seek out opportunities for collaboration where recruitment has already been incorporated within the logistics, since for minimal additional cost the value of a project may be extended greatly by including the energy research component. If this is the case, then it is all the more important that the methodology is well thought through so that the work is not unwittingly compromised by the priority of other research agendas.

Study planning

It is not unlikely for researchers in the built environment to find themselves in ambitious collaborative projects with tight budgets and timelines, and multiple or even conflicting objectives. Therefore, it is imperative that considerable effort is invested in precisely determining a set of core research questions that may be augmented later, but here serve as a basis around which the study can be designed. These should remain a central focus during the inevitable compromises and adjustments that take place during the planning and implementation phase of the project. Research questions have typically moved on from being merely descriptive (such as finding the level of roof insulation in the building stock) to relational investigations (or determining the effect of this insulation on energy usage for different building types). Studies may be used to evaluate the potential of a particular technology or efficiency improvement and to identify the relationship between various operational parameters that affect performance or its impact on the environment. Studies often take the form of determining the changes across time within the same dwelling or household, such as before and after the installation of efficiency improvements.

Relational studies therefore implicitly involve a series of comparisons and the critical point to planning the study is to determine as precisely as possible upon what basis the comparison is drawn so that any effects are not confounded by other factors that may have also changed. As well as defining the research questions or hypotheses, it is worthwhile writing a hypothetical sentence about the results as if each hypothesis were affirmed. Thus, an initial and broad hypothesis with respect to the MK1 study was that *household energy consumption has increased since 1990 (due to building fabric deterioration, more appliances and higher internal temperatures)*. This might be translated into a hypothetical result along the lines of:

> In a sample of 'low-energy' homes in Milton Keynes (under standardized daily external temperature conditions), it was found that gas/electricity consumption has increased by Y per cent to ZkWh/m² since 1990, even after allowing increases in floor area due to extensions. This is consistent with trends seen in national statistics on UK dwellings and may be due to increased internal temperatures.

Regardless of whether this is found after analysis to be the case, the detailed nature of hypothetical results helps to clarify the content required of the study. Specifically, the study must obtain data on:

- composition and attributes of the sample (e.g. the dwelling type, location and construction);
- external conditions included in the monitoring period (over the heating season);
- internal temperature (and placement of loggers and frequency of readings);
- energy usage by fuel (and frequency of readings);
- measurements that permit comparison with other studies and national statistics.

Thus, there are two main sets of criteria driving the research agenda within the resource constraints: those aspects prescribed by the primary research objectives and then the underlying need to fit into existing methods and collect 'benchmark' parameters, such as dwelling type or number of occupants. This will allow the results to be placed in a wider scientific context – for instance, by comparison with previous studies – so that their significance can be properly gauged. In terms of providing guidance for models or policies, this often means knowing to what extent these dwellings/occupants are typical of those in the stock/population or, if not typical, what proportion they might represent. So data needs to be gathered on all the main aspects that define representativeness, from dwelling type to socio-economic level of the occupant, and done so in a standard way. This debate between what is required to meet project specifics and the standard measurements needs to be engaged fully as the planning of equipment and logistics are developed. Resource constraints mean that limitations in the ambitions of research projects are inevitable, particularly so when investigating complex systems that exist in the built environment; but these limitations should be understood and acknowledged early on, rather than arising as an unexpected consequence of omissions in the methodology.

If budgetary and time issues appear to be the most obvious constraint on the scope and scale of monitoring, it should be noted that these largely reflect the time costs of installation and data retrieval (due to arranging appointments and visiting houses), rather than of the physical equipment itself. But there is a further consideration of good survey protocol in not disturbing the occupants too frequently to reset equipment and possibly alter their behaviour. In the end, such decisions also reflect cultural norms and the exact situation of each dwelling (e.g. if energy meters are located outside, it may not be necessary to disturb occupants). A different level of acceptability may apply for private homes with working families, whereby access inside may be largely restricted to a brief appointment at the weekend than, say, for social housing for the elderly, where not only is someone at home and available at most times, but they may welcome the social contact of a regular visitor. There is also a role for *quid pro quo*, so if the project provides a free heating system, then it might be negotiated that this is in exchange for the opportunity to monitor performance – so long as the implications are clearly stated at the outset. Remote logging, where data may be retrieved wirelessly or via the household internet connection, can reduce costs and disturbance of the occupants, while providing an early alert of problems. Whatever the approach chosen, ethical considerations regarding the occupants and good survey practice should remain paramount.

Monitoring temperature

The purpose of monitoring is to collect sufficient data to provide information to address the research objectives (and beyond a minimum required by standard methods). But this statement of the obvious often belies the numerous issues raised when we consider a protocol for implementation across many sites. The general point is well illustrated by quantifying internal temperature in the dwelling, an essential part of most energy surveys. The difference between internal and external temperature is fundamental to parameterize the fabric heat loss and to understand any heating or cooling demand in terms of meeting occupant comfort. So the task is to identify the most appropriate spatial and temporal arrangement for monitoring that captures this effective internal temperature across the whole dwelling in a way that is applicable and consistent across the entire sample and where little knowledge may be available beforehand.

Temperature and relative humidity (RH) data loggers are compact devices usually about the size of a pack of cards that can be programmed in various ways in terms of start time and frequency of reading. The unit illustrated in Figure 9.1 has four channels: temperature, relative humidity, illuminance and a spare channel to take the input from other detectors, such as for CO_2 levels. The readings are instantaneous measures rather than cumulative, which would be needed for energy usage. The capacity of this unit is 43,000 readings, or about 150 days for ten-minute

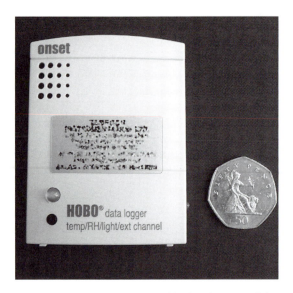

Figure 9.1 *Example of a portable data logger used for measuring temperature and relative humidity*

readings in two channels. The logger takes about 1 minute to download via USB cable to computer and to relaunch. The ability to check battery status is an essential feature to ensure at the outset that sufficient charge remains to last over any proposed monitoring period. It may well be used more than once in any study. Each should be labelled with a unique code and a return address. It is crucial to have adequate systems in place to download, reprogramme and administer the hundreds of loggers that may well be required.

For quantifying space heating demand, the effective internal temperature will be a weighted combination of average temperatures from each heating zone in the dwelling – where these are defined by the design of the home, heating system and by occupant living patterns. Typically, this means that the living area is defined as zone 1, where the main thermostat or room controller is located. Note that separate lounges may not be part of the living space, especially if they are reserved just for certain activities, such as formal socializing. Zone 2 is usually represented by occupied bedrooms, which may have a substantially different daily heating profile than the living space, corresponding to differences in the occupancy patterns. If necessary, zone 3 can describe indirectly heated areas and mostly unoccupied spaces such as hallways and other circulation spaces, spare bedrooms and so on. There

may be specific rooms worth monitoring, such as studies with large amounts of electrical equipment; utility rooms where the boiler or heating system is located; and sunspaces or conservatories, where these may assist with understanding the indirect and solar gains. This is also the kind of detail that might be useful for validating any dynamic computer modelling of temperature.

The overall design of the dwelling also has a bearing on the monitoring required – for instance, a two- or three-storey house may exhibit a considerable temperature gradient, with the higher temperatures at the top leading to greater heat losses through the roof space than might be anticipated from the average overall temperature. In contrast, well-insulated homes are likely to have far more uniform temperatures across the dwelling – reducing the difference between zones and potentially the number of loggers required. Given the complexity of deciding and administering all of this on a dwelling-by-dwelling basis with limited prior information, a generic protocol may be adopted:

- Over part of the heating season at least, monitor every room in the dwelling.
- If resources are tightly constrained (and given that for space heating, summer months are less critical), this could be reduced at other times to three monitoring points, one for each zone: living room, main bedroom and hallway.
- Include one or two extra loggers for rooms of special interest, such as sunspaces or conservatories.

There remains the issue of locating each logger within each space to obtain a representative reading of temperature and RH on a daily basis. In MK1 we positioned loggers according to the following protocol:

- on a shelf or ledge, between 1m and 2m high away from direct sunlight;
- if possible, out of sight, such as behind ornamental objects, so that loggers had less chance of being moved and any light-emitting diode (LED) flashes from the logger will not disturb the occupants (an important issue in bedrooms);
- away from potential heat sources, such as mantle pieces (over fireplaces) and bookcase lamps and electronic equipment;
- additional loggers to be placed in large open-plan spaces.

Regarding the frequency of reading programmed in each logger, for meaningful analysis most studies – including MK1 – require at least average daily temperature. Typically, this is achieved with hourly measurements to calculate average temperature with a minimum of 24 samples. But if the researcher wishes to detect finer grain changes as a result of occupant activity, such as opening a window, then the interval between measurements should be a least half the expected length of the activity period for the change to be detected with two measurements – otherwise the change can occur between measurements or just appear as a spike (so an event may be detected but there is no indication of the length of change). The instrumentation of the loggers also imposes constraints since its response to rapid change in conditions (say 5 degrees) may mean that it takes several minutes to stabilize. Logger data storage capacity will limit the frequency of sampling if site visits for replacement (or data downloads) are kept to a minimum. In MK1 sites, we initially logged at 10-minute intervals for the first month and thereafter at half hourly readings with replacement of the logger every three months.

To address more involved research questions, additional temperature loggers may be placed next to radiators as a means of indirectly identifying heating system operation or even on specific appliances of interest. But the overall benefits of using a generic protocol as a benchmark methodology and as a minimum standard are that it can be applied across a range of dwelling types and across studies. With rapidly advancing technology, in the medium term the benchmark for new developments may be to incorporate monitoring devices as part of their Building Management Systems, installed prior to occupancy.

External temperature is a critical data stream as it serves to standardize the environmental conditions and permit comparison across studies. Not only is there considerable variation from years to year, but the UK, like many countries, has had a generally warmer climate over recent years, leading to redefinitions in standard year weather conditions. If energy consumption were compared without correcting for differences in external conditions, then simply due to warmer winters in the UK we would expect dwellings to use less energy than in 1990, with no need to ascribe the reductions as resulting from improvements in building performance.

Monitoring external temperature and RH can be done on site if equipment is located away from the dwelling – for instance, in its garden – by placing a logger in a Stephenson Screen: a vented container that shields instruments from direct radiation and precipitation but permits air circulation. For studies where all dwellings are located in the same neighbourhood, this can be achieved with a single measurement location. If the dwellings are geographically dispersed, then finding reliable places for each site and having sufficient Stephenson Screens may become problematic. An alternative is to use official metrological data, which depends both upon the location of weather stations and the availability of data. Universities and other such institutions often monitor weather conditions as part of other scientific research and may be willing to provide accurate and reliable data. In MK1, local monitoring was conducted, as well as using data from the UK Meteorological Office for the nearby city of Bedford. This hourly data set provided a single source of measurement that spans the MK0 and MK1 studies from the 1980s onwards.

Monitoring energy

With the decline in the use of solid fuels in the UK domestic sector, monitoring for energy usage has been simplified in most urban settings by having just two sources of energy: gas and electricity. Monitoring usage of other fuels poses considerable difficulties. Oil use for central heating may at least be read from storage tank levels or, more accurately, by installing flow meters; but to quantify biomass and other solid fuel usage in a reliable manner is highly problematic. The energy content of such materials varies greatly, from waste wood and pellets to coal, as does the efficiency of stoves and fireplaces in which they are burned. These monitoring issues would need to be resolved on a case-by-case basis. Fortunately, the MK1 sample comprised gas centrally heated homes.

Gas and electricity are frequently metered externally for ease of access by the utility companies. Unfortunately, in the UK, numerous types of meters remain in use and these differ in age, technology and method of reading. Electricity usage in kilowatt hours (kWh) requires two readings if the occupant has *Economy 7* tariff, where there is a peak and off-peak or night rate. Gas readings are provided in cubic metres or cubic feet and converted to energy using calorific values provided in the UK on a monthly and regional basis by the national gas grid. Calorific value may also appear on utility bills. Staff resources permitting, anything from monthly to weekly (or even daily) manual meter readings on site are probably the most straightforward and robust method. It should be noted that some occupants may have more than one meter, and sometimes a single meter serves more than one household. For the MK1 study, gas and electricity meters were read manually on a semi-regular basis, varying from weekly to monthly, according to external conditions and with more frequent winter readings in order quantify space heating.

Alternatively, high-resolution monitoring of electricity usage can be obtained by a current clamp placed around the live wire and data logger and combining this with meter readings. Another option is for an optical sensor to count revolutions of the spinning meter disc. Since gas suppliers usually object to the presence of any electrical devices within the meter box, such optical devices may need to be placed outside, strapped to the glass window of the meter box. For detailed research on appliance usage, individual circuits can be monitored and sophisticated equipment can be installed which identifies specific appliance types based on the 'signature' that they leave in the demand profile. Such systems are sufficiently complex and expensive to remain an unlikely option for medium or large-scale studies. With the potential roll-out of *Smart* meters across the UK domestic sector by utility companies, where relatively high-resolution data can be provided to both the occupants and suppliers, many current monitoring issues may be resolved so long as researchers can reach a cooperative agreement between all parties to obtain and analyse the data.

Dwelling and occupant surveys

Key dwelling characteristics are necessary in order to make sense of energy usage data. The study must consider the detail and scope of information, as well as the method of collection. This includes generic characteristics such as type, size and age, as well as specific attributes such as construction and glazing types, boiler age and model, type of control systems being used, and set-point temperatures (that is the room thermostat setting). All of this data is gathered primarily to estimate the thermal performance or U values of the building fabric (including windows), the efficiency of the heating systems, and ventilation rates. Often, as part

of logger installation or replacement, skilled researchers can conduct a building survey regarding the key building attributes. Occupants may also provide useful information about the dwelling and, particularly, regarding any extensions or renovations.

Ideally, such data should comply with a standard or accepted classification system to avoid the proliferation of incompatible data across studies. Remaining consistent with the inputs to national benchmarks provides researchers with the means of comparing results across standard categories and typologies, and, hence, of judging the relevance of their sample to the national stock or to the results of other studies. For instance, where other information is lacking, building age can often be used to help infer construction type and, hence, U values; this may not be identified as a specific year of construction but by an age band, such as '1985 to 2000'. The question is: what age bands would be best to choose? Another point is the definition of floor area of the dwelling, from the external to internal dimensions or to considering heated areas only or including all enclosed areas. Such differences can amount to a variation of more than 20 per cent of the area. The best policy is to seek out definitions that are used as part of a national standard. One starting place in the European Union is the data behind the Energy Performance Certificate that is increasingly mandatory across the building stock. For the domestic sector in the UK, the Standard Assessment Procedure (SAP) lies at the heart of carbon emission calculations used to comply with building regulations (BRE, 2005; ODPM, 2006a, b). The reduced SAP uses a simpler set of items, combined with typical assumptions, to estimate the SAP and annual energy usage. In MK1, we were fortunate in already having construction details and plans from MK0, so it was relatively straightforward for MK1 to note changes to the layout or the heating system.

These methods are sufficient but by no means comprehensive. They can always be augmented or refined so long as this is not done in a way that leads to incompatibilities. In SAP calculations, while conservatories or sunspaces are noted, they are only considered integral to the heated space as an addition to the dwelling: In reality, they have a substantial impact by increasing floor area and affecting average U values (otherwise they simply serve to reduce the exposed wall area). Yet, previous surveys have indicated that it is not uncommon in the UK for occupants to leave internal doors to conservatories open, or to occupy and heat conservatories through winter (Oreszczyn, 1993). Similarly, variations in appliance ownership and usage, which largely determine electricity consumption, are not noted on a dwelling-by-dwelling basis. Yet, for researchers, it might be precisely this area that is of most interest. Standard occupant surveys that capture such issues are still being researched (Leaman, 2008) and currently none have been sufficiently validated to warrant recommendation. However, it should be noted that for basic socio-demographic variables in the UK, a series of harmonized questions are available from the Office of National Statistics (ONS, 2004). In the MK1 survey, we used a combination of questions taken from the original survey (to maintain compatibility) and standard questions from the ONS and the *English House Condition Survey* (ODPM, 2003).

Energy analysis

Describing the full range of statistical analyses possible with energy and temperature data is beyond the scope of this chapter and would entail a volume in its own

right. Calculating conventional annual performance statistics often poses problems for research due to attrition of occupants over the period for reasons such as moving house, as well as insufficient monitoring data. Annualized results also contain such variability in seasonal weather and occupancy patterns (key underlying factors for energy consumption) so that unravelling usage patterns from such aggregated indicators is difficult. Standardized weather on an annual basis is usually achieved via a comparison of the number of degree days experienced by each dwelling to that of a nominated standard year. For many outside the field of energy analysis, degree days are an unfamiliar concept that creates a further disadvantage in communicating results to policy-makers.

Instead, we illustrate this energy analysis with an alternative strategy adopted for the MK1 project that is both easily understood and requires minimal winter data (Summerfield et al, 2007). By normalizing energy usage under daily external conditions of $T_{ex} = 5°C$, close to average temperatures over the heating season in the UK are obtained. Such conditions are immediately familiar to people living in temperate climates such as the UK, and daily usage is easier to comprehend in terms of scale

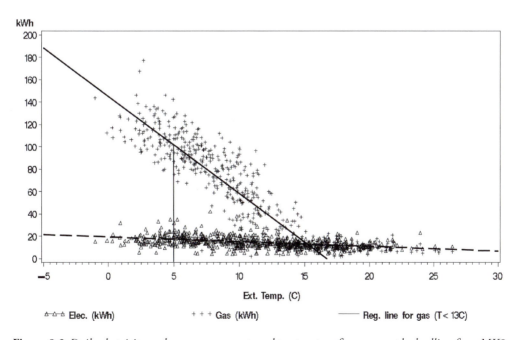

Figure 9.2 *Daily electricity and gas use versus external temperature for an example dwelling from MK0*

than annual data. For MK0 we used daily data; but weekly data can also be used to allow for occupant variability in usage from weekdays to weekends and other patterns, such as shift work. Simple linear regression models were fitted for each dwelling, with mean daily external temperature as a predictor of gas and electricity usage (see Figure 9.2). The regression model was fitted when $T_{ex} < 13°C$ for gas usage, with parameter estimates, defined by slope and intercept, used to obtain values for both gas and electricity usage under the standardized conditions of $T_{ex} = 5°C$. A similar process was carried out for the MK1 data, except using mean T_{ex} over intervals corresponding to the meter readings of usually between two weeks to one month.

Since the distribution of energy consumption was found to be highly skewed, dwellings were then grouped into thirds based on their total energy consumption in the 1990 study, and referred to as the low (n = 5), mid (n = 5) and high (n = 4) energy groups. Once a dwelling had been classified according to its energy consumption in 1990, it remained in the same group throughout the subsequent analysis to simplify interpretation of the results. Thus, any change detected

in a group has occurred to the same group of dwellings from baseline to follow-up studies. This classification process could have been done separately by gas and electricity; however, it was found that essentially the same groups were formed in all cases (in other words, high gas usage was likely to be accompanied by high electricity consumption). As previously, regression models were then used to obtain estimated energy consumption of each group (see Figures 9.3 and 9.4) when $T_{ex} = 5°C$. The process was repeated for MK1 data. The regression data output from SAS 9.1 provides confidence intervals for these estimates – hence a test for whether statistically significant change has occurred.

A key part of analysis is the communication of results. With these estimates of energy usage under specific conditions, it was possible to generate a series of charts that succinctly summarize the key point about differences in energy consumption between baseline and follow-up studies. A consistent pattern emerged where high energy users accounted for almost all of the increases only weakly apparent in the overall statistics. From Figure 9.5a, there was only weak evidence that across all dwellings the gas use rose by 10 per cent to

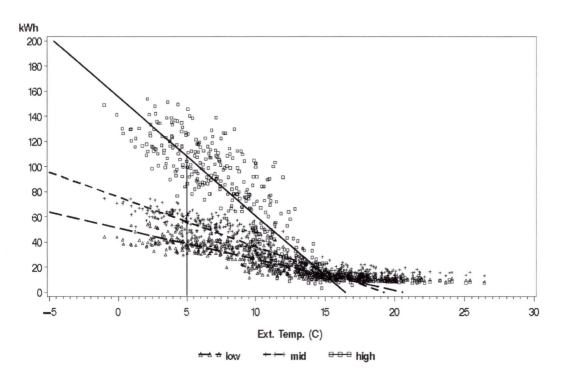

Figure 9.3 *Daily gas use versus external temperature in MK0 for each energy usage group*

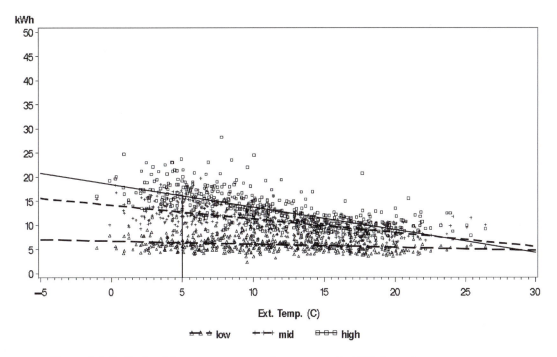

Figure 9.4 *Daily electricity use versus external temperature in MK0 for each energy usage group*

71kWh/day (95 per cent confidence interval (CI): 63 to 80), whereas for the high energy group alone the increase was 20 per cent to 130kWh (95 per cent CI: 110 to 150). When gas consumption is normalized for floor space (see Figure 9.5b), the change is no longer statistically significant, giving no indication of deterioration in the building performance for any group. The rise in space heating in the high group is, instead, accounted for by increased floor area or extensions to these dwellings (9 per cent), which had not occurred in other groups.

Overall, electricity usage was 30 per cent higher at 15kWh/day (95 per cent CI: 13.5 to 16.5). But compared to the other groups, electricity usage has jumped in the high group by 75 per cent to 28 kWh (95 per cent CI: 25 to 31). This high energy group not only accounts for more than half (57 per cent) of the total energy used in 2005, but this is three times more than the low group (47kWh/day, 95 per cent CI: 42 to 52) and double that of the middle group (68kWh/day, 95 per cent CI: 64 to 73) (Summerfield et al, 2007). Although not necessarily representative of changes in dwellings across the UK building stock, these findings highlight issues regarding the importance of effective

targeting of energy conservation measures both to where consumption is greatest and where it is increasing most rapidly.

Supplementary research: Indoor environment and mould

The MK1 data sets have also provided an invaluable opportunity to undertake supplementary research on the occurrence of indoor mould. It is well established that indoor environments contaminated with mould can adversely affect the health of occupants, and individuals with respiratory problems and asthma are amongst those most likely to be affected (Bush et al, 2006; Mazur et al, 2006; Burr et al, 2007). The prevalence of respiratory symptoms and asthma in the UK is one of the highest in the world (Janson et al, 2001), with more than 1500 deaths reported annually from asthma alone (Denning et al, 2006). Moreover, a high proportion of UK homes affected by mould, condensation and damp had been reported during the last 20 years (Sanders and Cornish, 1982a, 1982b; Sanders, 1989; DETR, 1991, 1996; RSHA, 2001).

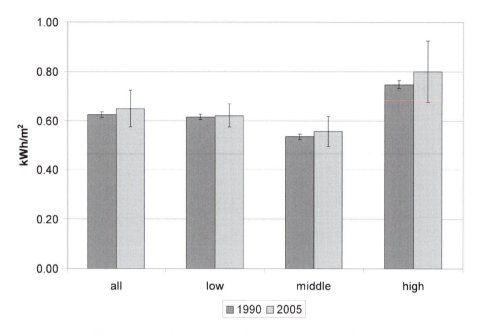

Figure 9.5 *Daily gas per unit floor area for 1990 and 2005 by energy group (at T_{ex} = 5°C)*

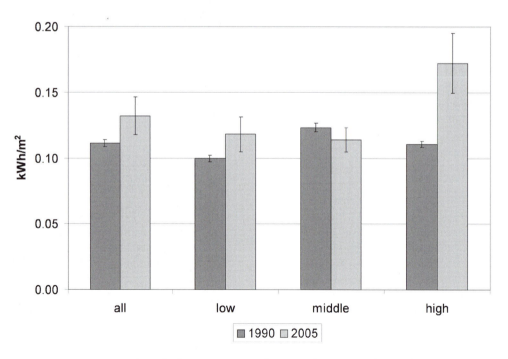

Figure 9.6 *Daily electricity per unit floor area for 1990 and 2005 by energy group (at T_{ex} = 5°C)*

Primarily based on laboratory measurements, it has been shown that mould growth occurs when wall surface relative humidity (RH) is above 80 per cent for a period of several weeks, or even for some species when relative humidity is as low as 70 per cent. These results have led to a number of guidelines being proposed to avoid the occurrence of mould. However RH is continually fluctuating in buildings due to changes in internal temperature, moisture generation, external vapour pressure, ventilation (natural and occupant controlled), and moisture transport through the building envelope. Mould growth in the indoor environment is a complex problem and even though it has been studied for many years, analysis of the details remains unclear. Therefore, these guidelines need further verification and, possibly, amendment depending upon the results of laboratory work and field data.

Data requirements

This supplementary research aimed to investigate the relationship of various indoor parameters, such as airtightness of the house and household moisture production, with the development of indoor mould. Ideally, the information specifically related to mould should include the following:

- physical condition related to the environment where mould is present (building materials, building age, etc.);
- temperature and RH: hourly measurement of indoor and external conditions (in view of the time required for mould spores to germinate and *Mycelium* to grow, these parameters should be for at least four to six months, or a complete season);
- occupancy behaviour and indoor moisture production via a questionnaire;
- visible mould occurrence: a simple index can be used where two or three categorization levels can be employed (e.g. no visible mould, small spots, hand size patches, and large patches);
- indoor air quality, ventilation and airtightness;
- identification of potential thermal bridges and damp problems via visual inspection and measurement.

For the MK1 study, this information took the form of:

- airtightness of the house calculated with fan pressurization tests;

- information on occupancy, moisture production and mould occurrence from a questionnaire survey;
- thermal bridges and damp problems identified through infrared (IR) images and visual inspection;
- hourly measurement of temperature and RH (indoor and outdoor conditions).

Derived parameters

Temperature factor

The standard BS EN ISO 13788:2002 details a method for assessing the thermal quality of each building envelope element. The thermal quality is characterized by the temperature factor at the internal surface:

$$f_{Rsi} = \frac{\theta_{si} - \theta_e}{\theta_i - \theta_e}$$

Figure 9.7 *Electric blower door for fan pressurization tests*

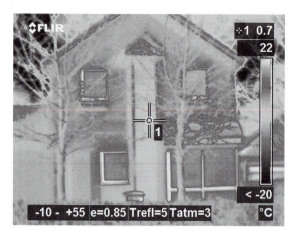

Figure 9.8 *IR image of MK1 dwelling; note signs of thermal bridging around the window frames*

where θ_{si}, θ_i, θ_e represent temperatures at the internal wall surface, for internal air temperature and for external air temperature, respectively. The internal surface temperature will depend upon the nature of the structure, especially in the presence of thermal bridges causing multidimensional heat flow, and the value of internal surface resistance. The temperature factor, f_{Rsi}, calculated for all MK1 properties fluctuated between 0.69 to 0.73. Note that it should be close to 1 for well-insulated buildings; however, to avoid mould growth, a temperature factor of 0.75 and higher is considered sufficient.

Vapour pressure excess (VPX)

The standard BS5250 (BSI, 2002) gives details of typical moisture production rates as a function of occupant numbers and behaviour. The occupancy is defined as dry (up to 300Pa) where there is proper use of ventilation and it includes those buildings unoccupied during the day. Where internal humidity is above normal, possibly a family with children who do not ventilate the dwelling sufficiently, the occupancy is defined as moist. If VPX exceeds 600Pa, the occupancy is defined as wet. For each dwelling, regression of indoor VPX with outdoor temperature was used to obtain estimates of daily indoor VPX under standardized conditions (T_{ex} = 5°C and RH = 80 per cent).

Mould severity index (MSI)

Since each dwelling was assessed for the occurrence and extent of mould on windows, walls and ceilings, we

assigned it a value according to the mould severity index (MSI), as developed for the *English House Condition Survey* (DETR, 1996).

Modelling

Transient thermal modelling

The steady state method of calculation defined in BS EN ISO 13788:2002 was used to obtain the surface temperatures of the selected 'as designed' construction details for the identified thermal bridges in MK1 dwellings. The modelled results have then been compared with surface temperature readings obtained from the thermal images for the same boundary conditions. In order to achieve the similar severity of the thermal bridges identified, the effect of the build quality had to be taken into account, which led to deterioration of thermal performance of the 'as designed' construction details; this iterative process of progressively adjusting the 'as built' construction details was carried out until comparable results were obtained.

Boundary condition for mould growth

The modelled surface temperatures were then used to obtain boundary conditions for the mould growth assessment model – WUFI Bio. This model is based on WUFI, a validated advanced model that is able to predict moisture balance under realistic transient boundary conditions.

The monitoring and modelling results used to analyse the causes of mould growth were divided into three categories:

1 boundary conditions (external temperature and RH);
2 occupant behaviour (inside temperature, moisture generation and ventilation);
3 building construction and design (building form/layout, thermal performance of building envelope, moisture buffer capacity, presence of preferential condensation surfaces, and type of finish).

Results

Factors for mould

Mould was identified in 4 out of 12 houses studied. In all cases, the reasons for mould growth are the result of the combination of one or more previously mentioned

(a)

(b)

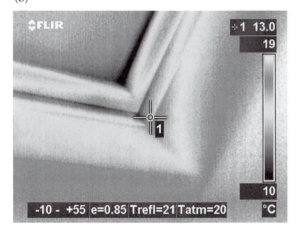

Figure 9.9 *Detail of mould growth by window frame (a) and IR image of the same area (b) indicating thermal bridging in the same area*

Table 9.1 *Four dwellings with mould and the presence of factors for mould growth*

Influencing Parameters	Dwelling A	Dwelling B	Dwelling C	Dwelling D
Internal temperature	–	Yes	–	–
Thermal bridging	Yes	Yes	Yes	Yes
Moisture generation	Yes	Yes	–	Yes
Building form	–	Yes	–	–
Ventilation	Yes	–	–	Yes

factors. However, the main factors that seem to have an effect on the development of mould are:

- thermal bridging – poor thermal performance of building envelope (in four out of four cases where the mould was identified, the thermal bridging was of significant importance for mould growth);
- moisture generation – high vapour release at source (in four out of four cases, the mould grew either in the bathrooms or in the adjacent bedrooms);
- insufficient ventilation – reduced adventitious ventilation (in two out of four cases);
- building form/layout – rooms with more than one external surface and located near high moisture-generation sources, such as en-suite bathrooms (in one out of four cases).

Thermal bridges

It was evident that the association of mould with thermal bridges was usually located either on external corners of the room or around the windows. The most severe thermal bridges are located at room corners where the minimum temperature factor calculated was 0.68. In addition, it was possible to identify three types of external bridges:

1. detailing around roof lights;
2. detailing at wall/ceiling intersection;
3. gaps in roof insulation.

Water vapour

Water vapour is usually generated locally within a house in wet processes areas such as kitchens and bathrooms. The dominant mechanism for transporting this water vapour to other drier and usually colder areas is the airflow to the building. This is the case for MK1 as the mould grew either in bathrooms or in bedrooms with en-suite bathrooms.

Insulation and ventilation

Although mould growth is usually associated with non-insulated houses, this study has shown that mould can also occur in well-insulated modern dwellings. However, this is usually due to the combined effect of a few factors, most notably thermal bridging coupled with high moisture generation and/or insufficient ventilation. It is significant that thermal bridging is usually coupled with insufficient ventilation and that higher moisture generation is the most likely reason for mould contamination in the studied Milton Keynes houses.

Although not all of the main observations required of a mould study were available from MK1, it has still been possible to develop a new methodology that includes the calculation and simulation of new parameters. This accounts for the deficiency of the building envelope in localized areas (i.e. the accurate modelling of fluctuating temperature conditions at the 'deficient' building surfaces), which significantly increases the likelihood of mould growth. This detailed case study analysis based on the monitored data in real dwellings, the physical surveys and the consequent modelling work has provided insight into identifying the parameters of most importance for mould growth in buildings. Alongside the results of other studies, it will help to inform guidelines for avoiding mould in well-insulated UK dwellings.

Discussion

More than just a case study, the MK0 study has been a highly invaluable sample to select for follow-up research. This specific group of dwellings represented best practice in the UK domestic sector for the symbolically important year – in Kyoto Protocol terms – of 1990 and which were roughly a decade ahead of their time with respect to building regulation standards. As a result, they also provide an indication of what might be expected a decade from then, from dwellings of an equivalent standard. Our results found no evidence for any decline in the building fabric that has significantly affected building energy performance, though there was evidence of construction issues and thermal bridging in places, particularly around window frames – leading in some dwellings to mould growth. The general increase in gas use for space heating was accounted for by the increased floor space in the MK1 sample, but specifically in the top third of energy users in 1990. These tended to be larger dwellings and were where extensions had been added. This high group also had a substantial rise in electricity usage, and by 2005 they used more energy than the other two groups combined. Although not representative of the UK dwelling stock, this work has pointed to the need for further research to help policy-makers refocus specifically on where energy is used and where change is occurring the most.

With the supplementary research, the MK1 study has also proven its usefulness for research on mould growth on UK dwellings. A methodology that combined modelling with detailed data of temperatures and RH has clarified the role of four factors, including thermal bridging and moisture production. This information will contribute to the analysis and results for other studies and, ultimately, improve guidelines for avoiding mould. It is also the case that with some minor additions and improvements on the initial data collection methodology for MK1, it would have been possible to investigate mould growth with an even more sophisticated and informative analysis.

In summary, the MK0 and MK1 studies provide a useful illustration for some of the issues and possibilities of energy and environmental research in the domestic sector. We have outlined the various considerations that need to inform the planning process for the study, while ensuring that the primary research objectives are met and being aware of the potential that good research methods have in enabling supplementary work to add value to the original data set. We have also highlighted the importance of referring to existing standard methodologies of data collection and classification to maintain compatibility and permit the results to be set within an appropriate scientific context. By describing in some detail the range of options associated with even the basic objectives, such as monitoring temperature and RH, we have endeavoured to portray the numerous considerations to be addressed, from maximizing reliability and accuracy to minimizing costs and occupant disturbance. Complex or even chaotic it may be on a large scale, but worthwhile research in this field must cope with the unpredictable and messy world of people and buildings as they are, rather than just how we imagine things should be in a laboratory or computer simulation.

Acknowledgements

We would like to acknowledge the support provided by Les Shorrock at the Building Research Establishment (BRE), who provided access to the original 1990 data set from Milton Keynes Energy Park, and to the residents who participated in the follow-up study.

References

BRE (Building Research Establishment) (2005) *The Government's Standard Assessment Procedure for Energy Rating of Dwellings*, 2005 edition, BRE, Watford, UK

BSI (2002) *BS EN ISO 13788:2002: Hygrothermal Performance of Building Components and Building Elements*, BSI, London

Burr, M. L., Matthews, I. P., Arthur, R. A., Watson, H. L., Gregory, C. J., Dunstan, F. D. J. and Palmer, S. R. (2007) 'Effects on patients with asthma of eradicating visible mould: A randomised controlled trial', *Thorax*, vol 62, pp766–771

Bush, R. K., Portnoy, J. M., Saxon, A., Terr, A. I. and Wood, R. W. (2006) 'The medical effects of mould exposure', Environmental and Occupational Respiratory Disorders, *Journal of Allergy and Clinical Immunology*, vol 117, no 2, February, pp 326–332

Denning, D. W., O'Driscoll, B. R., Hogaboam, C. M., Bowyer, P. and Niven, R. M. (2006) 'The link between fungi and severe asthma: Summary of the evidence', *European Respiratory Journal*, vol 27, no 3, pp615–626

DETR (Department of Environment, Transport and the Regions) (1991) *English House Condition Survey 1991 Energy Report*, DETR, London

DETR (1996) *English House Condition Survey 1996 Energy Report*, DETR, London

DTI (Department of Trade and Industry) (2007) *Meeting the Energy Challenge: A White Paper on Energy*, DTI, Government Stationery Office, London

Edwards, J. (1990) 'Low energy dwellings in the Milton Keynes Energy Park', *Energy Management*, vol 26, pp32–33

Fowler, F. J. (2008) *Survey Research Methods*, fourth edition, Sage Publications, Thousand Oaks, CA

Hong, S. H., Oreszczyn, T., Ridley, I. and the Warm Front Team (2006) 'The impact of energy efficient refurbishment on the space heating fuel consumption in English dwellings', *Energy and Buildings*, vol 38, pp1171–1181

Janson, C., Anto, J., Burney, P., Chinn, S., de Marco, R., Heinrich, J., Jarvis, D., Kuenzli, N., Leynaert, B., Luczynska, C., Neukirch, F., Svanes, C., Sunyer, J. and Wjst, M. (2001) 'The European Community Respiratory Health Survey: What are the main results so far?' *European Respiratory Journal*, vol 18, pp598–611

Leaman, A. (2008) 'Building performance: Research methods' *Monitoring: Proving Carbon Reductions and Informing the Path to a Low Carbon Future*, Good Homes Alliance

Workshop April 2008, London, www.goodhomes. org.uk/library_files/43, accessed May 2008

Mazur, L. J., Kim, J. and the Committee on Environmental Health (2006), 'Spectrum of non-infectious health effects from moulds', *Journal of the Academy of Paediatrics*, vol 118, pp1909–1926

ODPM (Office of the Deputy Prime Minister) (2003) *English House Condition Survey 2001*, ODPM, London

ODPM (2006a) The Building Regulations, Approved Document F1 – Means of Ventilation: 2006, OPDM, NBS, London, UK

ODPM (2006b) The Building Regulations, Approved Document L1a – Conservation of Fuel and Power in New Dwellings: 2006, OPDM, NBS, London, UK

ONS (Office of National Statistics) (2004) *Harmonised Concepts and Questions for Social Data Sources Primary Standards*, ONS, www.statistics.gov.uk/about/data/harmonisation, May 2008

Oreszczyn, T. (1993), 'The energy duality of conservatory use', in *Proceedings of the 3rd European Conference of Architecture: Solar Energy in Architecture and Planning*, Florence, Italy, pp522–525

RSHA (Regional Strategic Housing Authority) (2001) *Northern Ireland House Condition Survey 2001 Final Report*, RSHA, UK

Sanders, C. H. (1989) 'Dampness data in the 1986 English House Condition Survey', *International Energy Agency – Annex XIV: Report* UK-T7-35/1989, Building Research Establishment Scottish Laboratory, East Kilbride, Glasgow, Scotland

Sanders, C. H. and Cornish, J. P. (1982a) 'Dampness: One week's complaints in five local authorities in England and Wales', *Building Research Establishment Report*, HMSO, London

Sanders, C. H. and Cornish, J. P. (1982b) 'Dampness complaints', *Building Research Establishment News*, vol 58, pp2–3

Summerfield, A. J., Lowe, R. J., Bruhns, H. R., Caeiro, J. A., Steadman, J. P. and Oreszczyn, T. (2007) 'Milton Keynes Energy Park revisited: Changes in internal temperatures and energy usage', *Energy and Buildings*, vol 39, pp783–791

10

Energy Modelling

David Johnston

Introduction

The aim of this case study is to describe in detail the development of the Domestic Energy and Carbon Dioxide Model (DECARB), a physically based model of the UK housing stock that is capable of forecasting the energy use and CO_2 emissions attributable to this sector under a range of possible futures. This model has been used to develop a number of illustrative scenarios for the UK housing stock in order to explore the technical feasibility of achieving CO_2 emission reductions in excess of 60 per cent within this sector by the middle of this century. Reductions of this order are likely to be required across industrialized countries in order to stabilize the atmospheric CO_2 concentration and mitigate the effects of climate change.

Forecasting energy use and CO_2 emissions

In recent years, a variety of models have emerged that are capable of analysing and developing various strategies that are designed to achieve the long-term goals associated with climate stabilization. These models have the ability to model the complex interactions that occur between the energy use and the CO_2 emissions associated with a particular sector of the economy, to examine the effect of various CO_2 abatement strategies and policies, and to suggest the possible impact that these strategies and policies may have on future energy use and CO_2 emissions. Consequently, these models are required in order to help us understand which strategies and policies are important, when such strategies and policies should be implemented, and the potential effects of their implementation.

There are two principal approaches that can be used to forecast the energy use and CO_2 emissions of a particular sector of the economy – namely: *top down* or *bottom up*. Top-down methods tend to start with aggregate data and then disaggregate this data as far as they can. They focus on the interaction between the energy sector and the economy at large, using econometric equations to model the relationships that exist between the energy sector and economic output. They also rely on aggregate economic behaviour (which is based on past energy–economy interactions) to predict future changes in energy use and CO_2 emissions (IEA, 1998). Data input into these models largely comprises econometrically based data, such as gross domestic product (GDP), fuel prices and income. Various other factors that can have an important influence on energy use can also be incorporated within top-down models – for instance, technological progress, saturation effects and structural change.

The use of econometrically based data within top-down models means that these techniques are capable of modelling the interactions that occur between various economic variables and energy demand, ensuring that macroeconomic factors are taken into consideration and are not ignored, and providing feedback from the economy. Thus, top-down models are particularly appropriate for modelling the societal cost-benefit impacts of various energy and emissions policies and scenarios (MIT, 1997). However, their reliance on past energy–economy interactions to predict future changes in demand makes it difficult to use top-down methods for predictions that incorporate structural change or novel technologies, unless of course they adhere to past energy–economy interactions. They also tend to lack technological detail, so are inappropriate for adequately identifying differences in the energy efficiency of various end-use technologies, or taking into account technological changes to end-use systems or changes to the energy efficiency of such systems.

Bottom-up methods, on the other hand, tend to start with disaggregated data and then aggregate this data as far as they can. They focus on the energy sector alone, using highly disaggregated physically based engineering-type models to model in detail the energy demand and supply sectors. Data input into these models largely comprises quantitative data on physically measurable variables, such as the energy consumption of a refrigerator, and this data is used to describe in detail the past, present and future stocks of energy-using technologies within particular sectors of the economy. The use of such data acknowledges the fact that, over time, the current stocks of energy-using technologies will be replaced with new ones as their useful lifetime is reached. The physically measurable data, along with other relevant information on factors such as usage patterns, saturation effects, appliance replacement cycles and alternative technological options, is then used to determine the demand for energy within various sectors of the economy. The use of detailed physically measurable data enables bottom-up models to

adequately take into account technological changes to end-use systems or changes to the energy efficiency of such systems, to identify and include the complex interactions that exist between the different end uses of energy, and to incorporate changes in ownership, substitution effects and saturation effects. Thus, bottom-up models are particularly appropriate for suggesting the likely outcome of policies or to identify a range of technological measures that are intended to improve end-use efficiencies (Shorrock, 1994).

Domestic Energy and Carbon Dioxide Model (DECARB)

Bottom-up modelling techniques have been used to develop DECARB, a physically based bottom-up energy and CO_2 emission model of the UK housing stock that is capable of exploring the technological feasibility of achieving CO_2 emission reductions in excess of 60 per cent from the UK housing stock by the middle of this century. DECARB has been developed from work previously undertaken in this area by Shorrock et al (2001) using the Building Research Establishment's Housing Model for Energy Studies (BREHOMES). The structure and form of DECARB is illustrated in Figure 10.1.

As Figure 10.1 indicates, DECARB has been constructed around two separate but interrelated components: a data module and a calculation module.

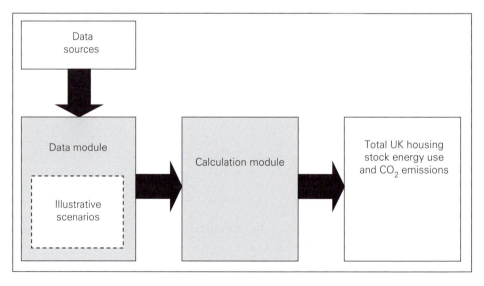

Figure 10.1 *Structure and form of DECARB*

The data module contains internally and externally generated data on a wide range of factors that are likely to influence the energy use and CO_2 emissions of the UK housing stock, such as population projections, mean household size data, levels of insulation, and the ownership and usage of various appliances. Where possible, this information has been obtained from relatively uncontentious external data sources. In addition, a number of logistic functions (s-curves) devised by the Building Research Establishment (BRE) have been used to determine the likely uptake rate and ownership of various insulation measures (see Shorrock et al, 2001). Other information, which is required as input into the data module, has been generated internally, either by manipulating the existing data sets or by deriving the data based upon the results of other modelling studies or practical case studies. For instance, information contained within the *English House Condition Survey* (DETR, 1996) has been taken as being representative of the UK, and the experience gained from a number of exemplar case study dwellings has been used to determine the sorts of technological measures that can be implemented into the UK housing stock.

Since it would be impractical to attempt to obtain or generate all of the relevant data for all of the existing dwelling types in the UK, transparency within DECARB has been preserved by adopting a parsimonious approach to detail. Thus, a selectively disaggregated approach has been adopted when constructing the model. This approach has enabled the model structure and the data collection to be biased towards those sectors that dominate domestic energy use and CO_2 emissions and those sectors where energy efficiency measures are likely to be implemented. For instance, space heating not only dominates domestic energy use and CO_2 emissions, but there are also a large number of energy efficiency measures that could be applied to this sector to reduce its energy use and CO_2 emissions. Therefore, space heating has been disaggregated down to a level where different types of building envelope construction are capable of being described (cavity walls and solid walls). This has enabled a variety of measures, such as retrofitting existing un-insulated cavity walls with blown fibre insulation or externally insulating solid walls, to be incorporated within the model. Such an approach has resulted in the main emphasis of DECARB being concentrated upon the demand side of the domestic sector.

One of the major features of adopting a selectively disaggregated approach has been the incorporation of just two 'notional' dwelling types[1] within the data module of DECARB. The physical properties of these 'notional' dwellings are based upon an average of the currently available fully disaggregated data, and take into account the likely effects of new-build rates, demolition rates, refurbishment cycles, heating system and appliance replacement cycles, and so on. A two-dwelling approach is justified on two accounts. First, data on, and projected trends in, insulation ownership, the use of lights and appliances, and stock replacement cycles can only be identified at the level of the whole housing stock (see, for example, Shorrock and Dunster, 1997). Second, at the whole stock level, the impact of dwelling type on energy use and CO_2 emissions is very small in comparison with the impact of the thermal characteristics of the building fabric and system efficiencies. Therefore, in the long term, what is important is the average performance of a wall, a roof, a space heating system and a lighting system across the stock, rather than the individual differences in geometry, thermal performance and energy use of the various individual dwelling types.

The two 'notional' dwelling types have been deemed to be representative of pre- and post-1996 construction, respectively. The distinction between pre- and post-1996 dwellings was undertaken for a number of reasons. First of all, 1996 is the base case year used within DECARB. This year was chosen since it is the most recent year where a fairly comprehensive breakdown of the various factors that are likely to influence UK housing stock energy use and CO_2 emissions is available. Therefore, the ability to be able to distinguish between pre- and post-1996 construction gives a convenient way to look at new (post-1996) and existing (pre-1996) construction. Second, the distinction between new and existing construction is important because of the distinct differences in the average performance of these two separate categories of dwellings, apart from at the margin, and the limitations they impose on the application of various technological measures. For instance, the average external wall U value of a new dwelling will, no doubt, be much lower than the average external wall U value of an existing dwelling. Consequently, various strategies and technologies that are aimed at improving the performance of one particular category of dwelling may not always be appropriate for the other. Third, such a distinction represents an absolute minimum categorization of the stock in terms of their age-related structure.

The information that is contained within the data module is then used, along with a number of assumptions, to formulate a number of detailed illustrative scenarios for the UK housing stock for each 'notional' dwelling type. Relevant scenario-specific information relating to each of the scenarios on factors such as the number of households, dwelling size, thermal and ventilation characteristics of the building envelope, type and seasonal efficiency of the space and hot water heating systems, information on lights, appliances and cooking, occupancy details, and the effects of global warming is then fed into the calculation module. The calculation module is based upon a modified worksheet version of the Building Research Establishment's Domestic Energy Model (BREDEM) Version 9.60 (DETR, 1998). Various modifications were made to BREDEM 9.60 in order to simplify the model, where applicable, to reduce the required input data, and to enable the model to utilize additional disaggregated data from the illustrative scenarios. For instance, BREDEM 9.60 has been modified to include detailed disaggregated information on the internal heat gains associated with lights, appliances and cooking. This data replaces the existing algorithm contained within BREDEM 9.60, which assumes that these heat gains are a function of the dwelling's total floor area. In addition, BREDEM 9.60 has also been modified to incorporate a very simple energy supply-side model. The supply-side model is based around just two fuels, natural gas and electricity, with the carbon intensities of these fuels being used to describe the performance of this sector. A BREDEM-based energy and CO_2 emission model was used for a number of reasons. First of all, BREDEM is capable of taking into consideration the complex interactions that take place both between and within the different end uses of energy within dwellings. Second, utilizing a model that predominantly models space heating energy use has been undertaken because space heating is currently the largest energy demand and CO_2 emission category within the domestic sector, and the potential for reducing the space heating energy requirement of dwellings is extremely large. Furthermore, since the fabric of the UK housing stock is the most important determinant of space heating energy use and has a very long physical life, it is also one of the most difficult

areas to change. Finally, BREDEM is not only the most widely used approach to modelling the space heating energy requirement of dwellings in the UK: it has also been extensively validated against monitored data (see Shorrock et al, 1991, and Dickson et al, 1996).

The scenario-specific information that is contained within the calculation module is then used to calculate the delivered energy use and CO_2 emissions attributable to each 'notional' dwelling type for the particular year in question. This process is undertaken from the base case year 1996 to 2050 inclusive. The year 2050 was chosen because this year is commonly referred to in climate stabilization calculations. Furthermore, undertaking detailed projections of the UK housing stock over this sort of timescale (almost 60 years) has a number of important advantages. First of all, 60 years corresponds to a timescale over which long-term policies can be expected to operate. Second, many energy-using devices in the domestic sector, such as boilers and electrical appliances, will be replaced at least once, if not several times, over a 60-year time period. Third, the lifetime of many electricity generation systems is around 30 to 50 years; so undertaking projections over this sort of timescale should see at least one complete replacement cycle within the electricity generation sector. Finally, information on the total number of 'notional' dwellings available in each year is then combined with information on the performance of these dwellings in order to scale the delivered energy use and CO_2 emissions up to the level of the whole UK housing stock.

The illustrative scenarios

So far, DECARB has been used to develop and evaluate three illustrative scenarios for the UK housing stock. These scenarios have been constructed to explore the technical feasibility of achieving CO_2 emission reductions in excess of 60 per cent within the UK housing stock by the middle of this century. Reductions of this order are likely to be required across industrialized countries in order to stabilize the atmospheric CO_2 concentration and mitigate the effects of climate change. The remainder of this case study presents a broad overview of the results of these scenarios. A much more detailed discussion of the results and the insights gained from the scenarios can be found within Johnston (2003).

The three developed scenarios are exploratory in nature and assume the application of currently available technology only. They have been termed the 'business as usual', 'demand side' and 'integrated' scenarios. The 'business as usual' scenario represents a continuation of current trends in fabric, end-use efficiency and carbon intensity trends for electricity generation. The 'demand side' scenario represents what may happen if the uptake

Table 10.1 *Description of some of the assumptions incorporated within the illustrative scenarios*

	Scenario		
	Business as usual	**Demand side**	**Integrated**
Building fabric	80% of pre-1996 cavity walls insulated by 2050. 10% of uninsulated pre-1996 solid walls insulated by 2050. All pre-1996 glazing replaced at least once by 2050. 10% of pre-1996 dwellings undergo post-construction airtightness work by 2050. Building regulations wall U values fall to 0.25W/m²K by 2009, to 0.23W/m²K by 2015, to 0.20W/m²K by 2020 and to 0.15W/m²K by 2025. Building regulations window U values fall to 1.8W/m²K by 2009, to 1.5W/m²K by 2015, to 1.3W/m²K by 2020 and to 1.0W/m²K by 2025. Air leakage rates are introduced into the building regulations in 2005 at 10ACH per 50Pa and fall to 5.0ACH by 2015, to 3.0ACH by 2020 and to 1.0ACH by 2025.	All pre-1996 cavity walls insulated by 2050. All pre-1996 uninsulated solid walls insulated by 2050. All pre-1996 glazing replaced at least once by 2050. 30% of pre-1996 dwellings undergo post-construction airtightness work by 2050. Building regulations wall U values fall to 0.25W/m²K by 2005 and to 0.15W/m²K by 2010. Building regulations window U values fall to 1.5W/m²K by 2005 and to 1.0W/m²K by 2010. Air leakage rates are introduced into the building regulations in 2005 at 10ACH per 50Pa and fall to 5.0ACH by 2007 and to 1.0ACH by 2010.	As demand side scenario.
Mean internal temperature	Pre- and post-1996 dwellings saturate at 21°C by 2040 and 2020, respectively.	Pre- and post-1996 dwellings saturate at 21°C by 2040 and 2020, respectively.	As demand side scenario.
Space and water heating systems	All dwellings have a central heating system installed with an average seasonal efficiency of 88% by 2050.	All dwellings have a central heating system installed which is fuelled by a gas-fired condensing boiler (seasonal efficiency of 91%) or an electrically driven heat pump (seasonal efficiency of 230%).	As demand side scenario.
Lights, appliances and cooking	Ownership of the majority of lights, electrical appliances and cooking appliances saturate around 2020. Appliance efficiencies rise over the period of 1996 to 2050.	Ownership of the majority of lights, electrical appliances and cooking appliances saturate around 2020. Appliance efficiencies rise over the period of 1996 to 2050, resulting in higher efficiencies than experienced within the business as usual scenario.	As demand side scenario.
Carbon intensity of natural gas	Remains constant at 51kgCO₂/GJ over the period 1996 to 2050.	Remains constant at 51kgCO₂/GJ over the period 1996 to 2050.	Remains constant at 51kgCO₂/GJ over the period of 1996 to 2050.
Carbon intensity of electricity	Reduces to 92kgCO₂/GJ by 2050.	Reduces to 92kgCO₂/GJ by 2050.	Reduces to 51kgCO₂/GJ by 2050.

of energy efficiency measures within the demand side of the domestic sector were to be increased. Finally, the 'integrated' scenario shares the same demand-side assumptions as the 'demand side' scenario, but represents what may happen if the carbon intensity of electricity generation were to fall even further.

In addition to internally and externally generated data, a wide range of assumptions have also been used to develop the 'business as usual', the 'demand side' and the 'integrated' scenarios. Unfortunately, it is not possible to present all of these assumptions here. However, a brief description of some of the assumptions that have been incorporated within each of the illustrative scenarios can be found within Table 10.1. Further details concerning the various assumptions that have been used to develop each of the illustrative scenarios can be found within Johnston (2003).

Results of the illustrative scenarios

Figures 10.2 and 10.3 illustrate the delivered energy use and CO_2 emissions attributable to the UK housing stock under each of the scenarios. The results show that by the year 2050, considerable reductions in delivered energy use and CO_2 emissions are expected to occur

within all of the scenarios. All of these reductions are expected to occur despite a number of opposing trends. These trends include a substantial increase in the total number of UK households; an increase in thermal comfort standards; and a substantial increase in the ownership and usage of central heating systems and various electrical appliances.

The scale of the projected reductions in delivered energy use and CO_2 emissions varies between each of the scenarios (see Figures 10.2 and 10.3). Under the business as usual scenario, which assumes a continuation of current trends, building fabric improvements, increases in end-use efficiency and a continued reduction in the carbon intensity of electricity generation result in a 21 per cent and a 33 per cent reduction in delivered energy use and CO_2 emissions, respectively, by the middle of this century. These reductions in delivered energy use and CO_2 emissions could be reduced by a further 29 and 25 percentage points, respectively, if the current rate at which fabric and end-use efficiency measures are being implemented in the demand side of the UK housing stock are increased to the levels that have been identified within the demand side scenario. Figure 10.3 also illustrates that a further 7 percentage point

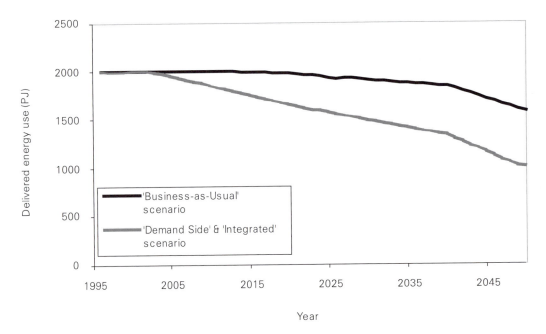

Figure 10.2 *Total delivered energy use attributable to the developed scenarios over the period of 1996 to 2050*

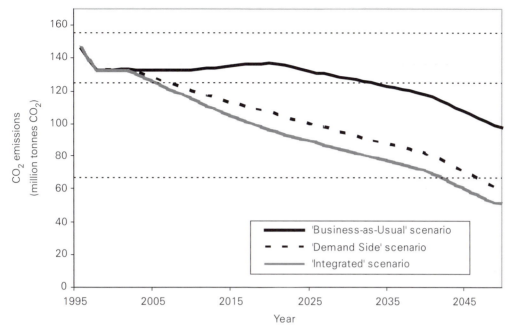

Figure 10.3 *CO_2 emissions attributable to the developed scenarios over the period of 1996 to 2050*

reduction in CO_2 emissions could be achieved if various measures are also applied to the electricity generation side of the energy supply sector.

The CO_2 emission trajectories of all three illustrative scenarios have also been compared against the UK's Kyoto Protocol target of a 12.5 per cent reduction in CO_2 emissions between 2008 and 2012, the UK government's domestic target of a 20 per cent reduction in CO_2 emissions by 2010 (DETR, 2000), and the UK government's Energy White Paper target of a 60 per cent reduction in CO_2 emissions by 2050 (DTI, 2003). Relative to the 1990 baseline,[2] Figure 10.3 indicates that although all of the scenarios are likely to achieve the UK's Kyoto target, only the demand side and the integrated scenario are likely to achieve the UK government's domestic target. More importantly, the results also suggest that the Royal Commission on Environmental Pollution (RCEP) target of a 60 per cent reduction in CO_2 emissions by the year 2050 could be achieved under both the demand side and the integrated scenarios. However, achieving these sorts of emission reductions will require a considerable increase in the current uptake rate of efficiency measures within both the demand side and the supply side of the UK housing stock.

Conclusions

This case study has described the development of DECARB, a selectively disaggregated physically based bottom-up energy and CO_2 emission model of the UK housing stock and illustrates how this model has been used to explore the technical feasibility of achieving CO_2 emission reductions in excess of 60 per cent within the UK housing stock by the middle of this century. This has been achieved by constructing and evaluating three illustrative scenarios for this sector – namely, a 'business as usual' scenario, which represents a continuation of current trends in fabric, end-use efficiency and carbon intensity trends for electricity generation; a 'demand side' scenario, which represents what may happen if the current rate of uptake of fabric and end-use efficiency measures were to be increased; and an 'integrated' scenario, which shares the same demand-side assumptions as the 'demand side' scenario, but represents what may happen if the carbon intensity of electricity generation were to fall even further.

The scenario results indicate that it is technically feasible, using currently available technology, to achieve the sorts of CO_2 emission reductions that are likely to be required to stabilize atmospheric CO_2 concentrations and to mitigate the effects of climate change under the demand side and integrated scenarios. These reductions appear feasible despite a substantial increase in the total number of UK households, an increase in thermal comfort standards and a significant increase in the standards of service that occupants are likely to expect. However, achieving these sorts of emission reductions will be technically demanding and will require a considerable increase in the current rate of uptake of energy efficiency measures within both the demand side and the supply side of the UK housing stock.

Notes

1   In this context, dwelling types refer to a very broad range of dwellings, rather than to dwellings of a particular size, form, tenure or age-related category.
2   The year 1990 has been used as a baseline as it is commonly referred to in climate change scenarios.

References

DETR (Department of Environment, Transport and the Regions) (1996) *English House Condition Survey 1996 Energy Report*, DETR, London

DETR (1998) *The Government's Standard Assessment Procedure for the Energy Rating of Dwellings*, DETR, London

DETR (2000) *Climate Change: The UK Programme – Summary*, DETR, London

Dickson, C. M., Dunster, J. E., Lafferty, S. Z. and Shorrock, L. D. (1996) 'BREDEM: Testing monthly and seasonal versions against measurements and against detailed simulation models', *Building Services Engineering Research and Technology*, vol 17, no 3, pp135–140

DTI (Department of Trade and Industry) (2003) *Energy White Paper: Our Energy Future – Creating a Low Carbon Economy*, DTI, HMSO, London

IEA (International Energy Agency) (1998) *Mapping the Energy Future: Energy Modelling and Climate Change Policy*, Energy and Environment Policy Analysis Series, IEA/OECD, Paris, France

Johnston, D. (2003) *A Physically-Based Energy and Carbon Dioxide Emission Model of the UK Housing Stock*, PhD thesis, Leeds Metropolitan University, UK

MIT (Massachusetts Institute of Technology) (1997) *Energy Technology Availability: Review of Longer Term Scenarios for Development and Deployment of Climate-Friendly Technologies*, MIT Energy Laboratory, Cambridge, Massachusetts, US

Shorrock, L. D. (1994) *Future Energy Use and Carbon Dioxide Emissions for UK Housing: A Scenario*, BRE Information Paper IP9/94, Building Research Establishment, Garston, Watford, UK

Shorrock, L. D. and Dunster, J. E. (1997) 'The physically-based model BREHOMES and its use in deriving scenarios for the energy use and carbon dioxide emissions of the UK housing stock', *Energy Policy*, vol 25, no 12, pp1027–1037

Shorrock, L. D., Macmillan, S., Clark, J. and Moore, G. (1991) 'BREDEM 8: A monthly calculation method for energy use in dwellings: Testing and development', in *Building Environmental Performance 1991*, University of Kent, Canterbury, 10–11 April 1991, BEPAC, London

Shorrock, L. D., Henderson, J., Utley, J. L. and Walters, G. A. (2001) *Carbon Emission Reductions from Energy Efficiency Improvements to the UK Housing Stock*, BRE Report 435, Building Research Establishment, Garston, Watford, UK

11

Energy Efficient Refurbishment of Dwellings: A Policy Context

Mark Schroeder

Introduction

The challenge that building stock poses in the face of climate change urges building professionals in many countries across the globe to renovate existing stock with sustainability and energy efficiency in mind. Around 30 to 40 per cent of worldwide primary energy is used in buildings (UNEP, 2007) and space heating and domestic hot water services are taking up a considerable share of almost 75 per cent (WWF, 2008). It is expected that an existing home requires four times as much energy for heat as does a new home (DTI, 2007). One of the few industrialized countries in which CO_2 emissions have been reduced since 1990 is Germany. A considerable share of savings made in Germany in recent years can be attributed to the national climate protection programme under which credit programmes were launched in October 2000 for renovating existing buildings. Along with other policies, these programmes will allow Germany to meet a 54 per cent reduction in CO_2 emissions of 1990 levels by the year 2030. The overall aim is to reduce the CO_2 emissions from 1990 to 2050 by 80 per cent. The KfW CO_2 Building Rehabilitation Programme proved to be Germany's most effective element of the national climate protection programme for existing housing stock. The two most effective components within this programme are (UBA, 2008):

1   retrofitted external insulation of existing buildings;
2   replacement of boilers with new high-efficiency heating systems.

These findings were confirmed by recent research in the UK (Lowe, 2007). However, relevant incentives or programmes to deal with these issues have yet to be introduced in most countries of the European Union. As of today, the trend in the UK, for example, is towards higher energy consumption, the energy delivered to UK dwellings, for example, has increased by 30 per cent over the last 30 years (Oreszczyn and Lowe, 2005).

The aim of this case study is therefore to investigate the effects of German climate change policy on the reduction of carbon emissions from existing dwellings. Most countries urgently need efficient 'tried and tested' policy tools to tackle the effects of climate change. The first part of this case study reviews the policy landscape in Germany, and the second part investigates the German CO_2 reduction programme in practice. The latter consists of a detailed calculation of the energy consumption for space heating and domestic hot water services of a building. The trends of the change in energy demand and the associated carbon emissions indicate the effectiveness of technical interventions and the efficiency of relevant policy instruments.

The German policy landscape

In line with most European countries after World War II, Germany consumed fossil fuels as if they were available in unrestricted quantities. Most energy policies, therefore, focused solely on supply. Until the first oil crisis in 1973, one of the few criteria in building design was to provide adequate heating (Poeschk, 2007), and this often led to oversized building services equipment. However, when the oil crisis resulted in a steep increase in oil prices, this attitude changed radically and awareness of the uncertainty of future fossil fuels supplies rose. As a result, the Energy Conservation Act came into power in 1976. Today, this act still functions as the legal basis for the relevant German Building Energy Conservation Ordinances (BECO). The first ordinance's ultimate aim in 1977 was to reduce the energy demand for space heating through increased insulation for new buildings. Through this first step, energy demand was cut by one third from 250 to 350kWh/(m² a). In the following 30 years, efforts were increased to tighten building standards. As a result of this, ordinances were changed five times, and every six years, on average, so that the annual energy demand for space heating was reduced by a factor of five (Forschungszentrum Juelich, 2000).

Despite these efforts, no real cut in CO_2 emissions from the domestic building stock was observed between the years of 1990 and 2000. Emitted CO_2 varied between 130 to 140MtCO$_2$ and at the same time showed no clear downward or upward trend. The reasons for this development can be seen, first, in the added new-built floor area between 1990 and 2000, where 5 per cent of floor area was added to the stock based on 1990 levels; and, second, in the lack of attention to existing stock, where energy efficiency measures were not implemented to meet targets. The main reason for this is a lack of relevant policies and incentives. It is important to bear in mind that the existing stock carries the potential to save 35 to 75 per cent in energy consumed for space heating and hot water. Due to individual restrictions in practice, this potential can be exploited by around 50 per cent, on average (Forschungszentrum Juelich, 2004), still giving a considerable savings potential.

In order to achieve a sustained drop in CO_2 emissions from the residential building stock, the political effort has to eventually focus on existing buildings. So far, this seems to be one of the most challenging tasks.

Efforts concerning existing stock in Germany became more serious than in previous years when the German government launched the Climate Protection Programme (*Klimaschutzprogramm*) in the year 2000. The ultimate aim of this programme was to fulfil the Kyoto Protocol and to initiate the required cut in carbon dioxide emissions. Previous German governments had also committed to ambitious carbon reduction targets;

but the Climate Protection Programme 2000 also aimed to close the gap between the Kyoto agreement and the actual savings. Germany had agreed to reduce its carbon dioxide emissions from 1990 to 2005 by 25 per cent. However, in 1998 the projected savings were only as high as 15 to 17 per cent. This is why, in 2000, a catalogue of new measures was introduced in order to achieve the proposed savings. One of these measures was the KfW CO_2 Building Rehabilitation Programme, which hands out low-interest loans via the government-owned KfW Bank. The aim of this programme was to explore the carbon reduction potential in the existing building stock. Because of the high potential to reduce carbon emissions, the focus was on improved thermal insulation and reduced losses for domestic hot water services (BMU, 2000).

The KfW CO_2 Building Rehabilitation Programme

Established in 1996, this programme finances technical interventions to existing buildings aimed at reducing carbon dioxide emissions. Usually these measures consist of already set packages given the numbers 0 to 3. These packages require various combinations of the following technical interventions:

* upgrade the roof insulation;
* upgrade the insulation on the exterior walls;
* upgrade the insulation of the basement ceiling;
* replace existing windows; and
* replace the existing heating boiler.

A combination of these measures was possible if the overall reduction in annual carbon dioxide emissions reached a minimum of 40kg per square metre of treated floor area. The beneficiaries of this programme were the people responsible for the buildings (e.g. private landlords, investors, housing associations, housing co-operatives, municipalities, districts, etc.). Applicants received a fixed interest rate and a long-term and low-interest loan for all expenses of up to 250 Euros per square metre of living space. The length of the loan is limited to 20 years. These programmes were adjusted to changing market conditions and technical restrictions; up-to-date terms and conditions for this programme can be obtained from the KfW Bank website directly. In recent years, the requirements for qualifying for the programme were tightened. Today, the energy performance of retrofitted buildings has to match current BECO standards for new built.

Since the year 2001, the government has invested 200 million Euros per year. However, the total credit volume of the programme amounted to 5 billion Euros. Until the end of the year 2004, around 4 billion Euros were handed out to improve 16.3 million square metres of living space in existing houses, reducing nationwide carbon dioxide emissions by 0.5Mt (Fraunhofer ISI, 2006).

In the following years, the German government decided to continue this programme and handed out an increased credit volume for the years 2005 and 2006 of 1.1 billion Euros and 3.4 billion Euros, respectively. This money was used on 225,000 dwellings, for which the annual carbon dioxide emissions per square metre of living space were brought down from $97kgCO_2$ pre-intervention to $38kgCO_2$ post-intervention. With an accuracy of 10 per cent, it is thought that following these two years, nationwide carbon dioxide emissions were reduced by over 1Mt (Bremer Energie Institut, 2007). It is also worth noting that climate protection was not the only objective of the programme. Two other objectives were to strengthen the weak-performing building sector and to renew the existing building stock in a sustainable way.

With the increased effort in recent years, the KfW CO_2 Building Rehabilitation Programme has become the single most effective policy instrument in the residential sector, producing a saving of 5.3Mt CO_2 by the year 2030. Further possibilities for improving these savings are seen in the increased realization of the carbon reduction potential that lies in plant efficiency, thermal insulation, increased use of renewable energies, and an improvement in public relations, consultancy and training. It is thought that within the residential building stock sector, the use of fossil fuels can be reduced by 44 per cent from 2005 to 2030, corresponding to around 23 per cent of the total German consumption of natural gas and fuel oil. The resulting drop of CO_2 emissions will, accordingly, be 44 per cent (UBA, 2008). Various German think tanks and practitioners are reducing energy demand even further by using Passivhaus components when refurbishing existing buildings. Passivhaus projects use building materials that have previously only been used on new buildings. However, employing these materials as a retrofit option can deliver substantial savings of energy consumption of about 75 to 90 per cent.

Case study: Modernization of dwellings in north Germany

This study evaluates the modernization of dwellings in north Germany. The property selected is a multi-storey building from the period of 1962 to 1967. BECO 2002 differentiates between two possibilities for the energy analysis of existing buildings:

1   examination of the energy quality of the outer components;
2   annual primary energy analysis.

The following sections show the annual primary energy analysis and the energy-saving effects of these measures in a 'before and after' analysis, using the literature of Jagnow (Jagnow et al, 2002). Furthermore, all modernization measures are evaluated for kilograms of CO_2 reduction.

Background

As mentioned above, the dwellings are in a multi-storey building constructed in a fashion typical for 1962 to 1967 that have since not been subject to any modernization. The buildings are owned by a housing co-operative and located in Schleswig-Holstein in north Germany. The chosen reference object is detailed in Figure 11.1.

The whole area is supplied by local district heating by the Municipal Electricity and Water Works, thus ensuring that the buildings are heated and supplied with drinking and hot water. As illustrated in Figure 11.2,

Figure 11.1 *Front view of case study dwellings in Schleswig-Holstein, north Germany (one third of the building)*

Figure 11.2 *Garden view of monitored building*

the building has a complete (wall-to-wall) cellar and three upper floors. The internal height of the rooms is 2.75m in the living space and the cellar has an internal height of 2.3m. The area below the pitched roof has a height of 3.5m, but is not occupied or in use. The house is constructed in separate three blocks (see Figures 11.1 and 11.2) and consists of three entrances and three stairwells.

In some areas, the components of the technical facilities have been maintained (e.g. circulation pumps) and comply with today's technical standards. All windows were renewed some years ago and show a thermal heat exchange co-efficient of U (W/m²K) = 2.6.

The condition of the dwellings and the features of the supply systems are given in detail in the following section.

Calculating energy performance

Following Jagnow et al (2002), the energy condition of the buildings is determined by means of an energy demand calculation. Definitions of the sizes to be calculated are taken from the German standard DIN V 4701–10 (DIN V 4701, 2001). The relevant parameters of energy performance were measured from the drawings according to DIN standard so that the reference parameters were determined as follows: the energy-relevant floor area AEB = 1005.6m², the outer surface area AH = 1929m²; the outer volume of the building Ve = 3210.3m³; and the sum of the window surface area AFe = 201.8m². This results in the following characteristics for this building:

- AH/Ve ratio: AH/Ve = 1929m²/3210.3m³ = 0.6m⁻¹;
- degree of compactness: AH/AEB = 1929m²/1005.6m² = 1.9;
- window surface ratio: AFe/AH = 201.8m²/1929m² = 0.11.

Based on the determined values, this building can be designated as a multiple family dwelling or, rather, an apartment building.

Climatic conditions

The observed building shows an internal room temperature of 20°C for the used parts of the building and 16°C for unused areas, such as hallways and storage closets. The surface ratio is approximately two-thirds used and one third unused, thus producing an average internal temperature of ϑ_i = 18.7°C. A night-time heating reduction is not carried out during the heating period, resulting in a factor for night-time reduction of f_{ABS} = 1.0 (i.e. the rooms have individual temperature regulators in the form of thermostatic valves); the factor for the temperature regulation is thus f_{REG} = 1.03. The mean internal temperature can be equated as follows:

$$\vartheta_{im} = f_{ABS} \times f_{REG} \times \vartheta_i = 1.0 \times 1.03 \times 18.7°C$$
$$= 19.26°C \qquad (1)$$

The heat temperature limit is initially adopted at ϑ_{HG} = 18.0°C; it represents the temperature above which room heating by district heating is no longer necessary. Using local weather data, there is a heating period of t_{HP} = 306.7days/a (i.e. 306.7days/a × 24h/day = 7360h/a). The mean outside temperature is taken from the different VDI 3808 annual data sets and calculated from this:

- 1 September–31 May: $\varnothing\vartheta A$ = 5.3°C (9 months = 270 days);
- 1 June–31 August: $\varnothing\vartheta A$ = 13.4°C (3 months = 90 days).

For the heating period of 306.7 days, 270 days are calculated with a mean outside temperature of 5.3°C. For the remaining 36.7 days, the mean outside temperature is 13.4°C:

$$\vartheta_{am} = (270/306.7) \times 5.3°C + (36.7/306.7) \times$$
$$13.4°C = 4.666°C + 1.603°C = 6.3°C \qquad (2)$$

Thus, the mean outside temperature during the heating period is given as $\vartheta_{am} = 6.3°C$.

Heat loss due to transmission

Heat loss due to transmission q_T is calculated as follows based on Equation 3 and using given heat exchange coefficients U for the individual components as well as the individual surface area A and the reduction factor f_{MIN}:

$$q_T = \sum (A_{component} \cdot U_{component} \cdot f_{MIN})$$
$$\cdot \frac{(\vartheta_{im} - \vartheta_{am})}{A_{EB}} \cdot t_{HP}. \qquad (3)$$

$$q_T = 3333.3 \frac{W}{K} \cdot \frac{(19.2 - 6.3)K}{1005.6m^2}$$
$$\cdot 7360 \frac{h}{a} = 314.7 \frac{kWh}{m^2 \cdot K}. \qquad (4)$$

Heat loss due to ventilation

Heat loss due to ventilation q_V is heavily dependent upon the air exchange rate n, as well as upon the mean internal temperature ϑ_{im} and the average temperature of the external air entering the building ϑ_{am}. The following approach is valid for buildings without mechanical ventilation systems, according to which the natural air exchange rate n_{nat} and the air exchange rate according to building type Δn are calculated as follows:

$$n = n_{nat} + \Delta n = 0.6h^{-1} + 0.2h^{-1}$$
$$= 0.8h^{-1} \qquad (5)$$
$$n_{nat} = 0.6$$
$$\Delta n = 0.2.$$

The heat loss due to ventilation is calculated using the average room height h_R and the term Wh/m³K = 0.34 for the physical properties of air:

$$q_V = n \cdot h_R \cdot 0.34 \frac{Wh}{m^3K}$$
$$\cdot (\vartheta_{im} - \vartheta_{am}) \cdot t_{HP} \qquad (6)$$

$$= 0.8h^{-1} \cdot 2.75m \cdot 0.34 \frac{Wh}{m^3K}$$
$$\cdot (19.2 - 6.3)K \cdot 7360 \frac{h}{a}$$
$$= 71 \frac{kWh}{m^2 a}. \qquad (6)$$

Solar heat gains

The solar heat gain q_S is caused by radiant heat gain, which is passed into the inside of the building through the existing windows. Since global radiation G_m depends upon the orientation of the building, North (N), South (S), East (E), and West (W), a differentiation with regard to the compass points must be taken into account. Furthermore, a reduction factor r_m for overshadowing, or dirt on the glass panes, etc., must be taken into account, as well as the g value g_m as a measure of the rate of solar heat gain through a window. The energy gain from solar radiation thus is:

$$q_S = g_m \cdot r_m \cdot G_m \cdot \frac{A_{Fe}}{A_{EB}}$$
$$N = 210 \frac{kWh}{m^2 a} \cdot 0.5 \cdot 0.86 \cdot 4.32m^2$$
$$= 8325.7 \frac{kWh}{a}$$
$$E = 375 \frac{kWh}{m^2 a} \cdot 0.5 \cdot 0.86 \cdot 97.7m^2$$
$$= 14947.9 \frac{kWh}{a}$$
$$S = 560 \frac{kWh}{m^2 a} \cdot 0.5 \cdot 0.86 \cdot 4.32m^2 \qquad (7)$$
$$= 1040.3 \frac{kWh}{a}$$
$$W = 375 \frac{kWh}{m^2 a} \cdot 0.5 \cdot 0.86 \cdot 100.4m^2$$
$$= 16189.5 \frac{kWh}{a}$$
$$q_S = 40.3 \frac{kWh}{a}.$$

Internal heat gain

All internal heat gained from people, devices, appliances or lighting is determined by the following

Table 11.1 *Heat loss due to transmission*

–	A (m²)	U (W/(m²K))	f_{MIN} (–)	A * U * f_{MIN} (W/K)
Roof	437.2	1.53	0.8	534.8
Walls	1053.0	1.49	1.0	1564.8
Windows	201.8	2.60	1.0	524.6
Basement	437.2	2.32	0.7	709.1
Sum				3333.3

equation. An approach for multiple family dwellings is given in Jagnow et al (2002). The internal remote heating gains q_{IG} are developed from this according to the following:

$$q_{IG} = 3.5 \frac{W}{m^2}$$

$$q_{IG} = 3.5 \frac{W}{m^2} \cdot 7360 \frac{h}{a}$$

$$= 25.8 \frac{kWh}{m^2 a}. \tag{8}$$

Utilizing remote energy

The extent to which the generated internal remote energy gain can be used is heavily dependent upon the performance of the regulation circuit present. Very slow-acting regulatory circuits contribute to a relatively small use of internal heat gain. In the case under observation, thermostatic valves are used, resulting in an evaluation factor for remote energy usage f_η of 0.7. Furthermore, the gain–loss ratio γ has to be determined from the already evaluated energy balance:

$$\eta = f_\eta \cdot (1 - 0.3 \cdot \gamma)$$

$$f_\eta = 0.7$$

$$\gamma = \frac{q_I + q_S}{q_T + q_V} = \frac{25.8 + 40.3}{314.7 + 71} \tag{9}$$

$$= \frac{66.1}{385.7} = 0.171$$

$$\eta = 0.7(1 - 0.3 \cdot 0.171) = 0.663.$$

Remote energy usage is 66.3 per cent (i.e. approximately two-thirds of the internal energy gain generated can be used for the building's heating system).

Checking the heating temperature limit

The initially set heating temperature limit ϑ_{HG} should now be checked using the dimensions determined above. The correct choice of the heating temperature limit is essential for the success of this calculation and represents an iterative process. A number of calculations have been used up to this section for its exact determination:

$$\vartheta_{HG} = \vartheta_{im} - \eta \cdot \gamma \cdot (\vartheta_{im} - \vartheta_{am})$$

$$= 19.2 \cdot 0.663 \cdot 0.176$$

$$\cdot (19.2 - 6.3) K \tag{10}$$

$$\vartheta_{HG} = 17.7°C$$

assumed 18°C.

Losses of the services system

According to Jagnow et al (2002):

… during an analysis of heat loss of distribution pipes, [one should] take into account that not all pipes and storage heaters are continually supplied… Connections to radiators are, for example, only supplied when the thermostatic valves are open. If they are closed, the heating water in these pipes cools down.

The term defined for this is the influence of operation factor f_{BH}. For the case study, the whole piping system was divided into different sections: continual supply ($f_{BH} = 1$) and non-continual supply ($f_{BH} = 0.5$). The following list of calculations is based on a specific heat loss in pipes q_L of 34.7W/m obtained for an uncontrolled, continuous 90/70 heating system (adapted from Jagnow et al, 2002, Table 6.21). The term L equals the length of the relevant pipework leading to the heat loss of the relevant section q_d.

Radiator connections

$L = 180\text{m}$

$A_{EB} = 1005.6\text{m}^2$

$\dfrac{L}{A_{EB}} 0.179$

$\dot{q}_L = 34.7\dfrac{\text{W}}{\text{m}}$ 　　　　　　　　　(11)

$\dfrac{3}{3} = $ not constantly open $f = 0.5$

$q_d = \dfrac{L}{A_{EB}} \cdot f_{BH} \cdot \dot{q}_L$

$= \dfrac{3}{3}\left(\dfrac{180}{1005.6} \cdot 0.5 \cdot 34.7\right)$

$q_d = 3.1\dfrac{\text{W}}{\text{m}^2}$ for connection pipes.

The performance loss at pipe connections to radiators is thus 3.1W/m². For the stairwell and the cellar pipes, the loss is determined as follows, using heat losses of the relevant pipework q_L from Jagnow et al (2002).

Rising mains

$L = 366\text{m}$

$\dfrac{L}{A} = 0.364\dfrac{\text{m}}{\text{m}^2}$

$\dfrac{50}{50} = \begin{matrix} f = 1 \\ f = 0.5 \end{matrix}$

$q_L = 39.3\dfrac{\text{W}}{\text{m}}$ 　　　　　　　　　(12)

$q_d = \dfrac{1}{2}(0.364 \cdot 1 \cdot 39.3) +$

$\dfrac{1}{2}(0.364 \cdot 0.5 \cdot 39.3)$

$= \dfrac{1}{2} \cdot 14.3 + \dfrac{1}{2} \cdot 7.152$

$q_d = 10.7\dfrac{\text{W}}{\text{m}^2}$ for risers.

Cellar distribution pipes

$L = 260\text{m}$

$\dfrac{L}{A} = 0.259\dfrac{\text{m}}{\text{m}^2}$ 　　　　　　　(13)

$q_L = 27.7\dfrac{\text{W}}{\text{m}}$

$f_{BH} = 1 \rightarrow \dfrac{2}{3} = 4.783$

$f_{BH} = 0.5 \rightarrow \dfrac{1}{3} = 1.196$ 　　　　(13)

$q_d = \dfrac{2}{3}(0.259 \cdot 27.7 \cdot 1) +$

$\dfrac{1}{3}(0.259 \cdot 27.7 \cdot 0.5)$

$= 6\dfrac{\text{W}}{\text{m}^2}$ for basement.

The specific heat loss in the piping system in W/m in this calculation reflects the current insulation standard of pipes and also the condition of the pipe insulation. The overall performance loss is calculated as follows:

$$q_{d,H} = \Sigma\left(f_{BH} \cdot \dot{q}_L \cdot \dfrac{L}{A_{EB}}\right) \cdot t_{HP}$$

$$q_{d,H} = (3.1 + 10.7 + 6)\dfrac{\text{W}}{\text{m}^2} \quad (14)$$

$$\cdot 7360\dfrac{\text{h}}{\text{a}} = 145\dfrac{\text{kWh}}{\text{m}^2\text{a}}.$$

This value appears to be relatively high measured against overall consumption; however, it was confirmed at this level by viewing the object. All parts of the room with water pipes show a considerably higher room temperature than neighbouring rooms without the piping system. In addition, the insulation is damaged in areas and stop taps are seldom insulated (see Figures 11.3 and 11.4).

Use of hot water

The use of hot water could not be determined using the available consumption calculation and is thus based on an area-related unit. According to Jagnow et al (2002, Table 6.28), the heat loss from hot water usage q_W is adapted from the following assumption:

$$q_W = 15\dfrac{\text{kWh}}{\text{m}^2\text{a}}. \quad (15)$$

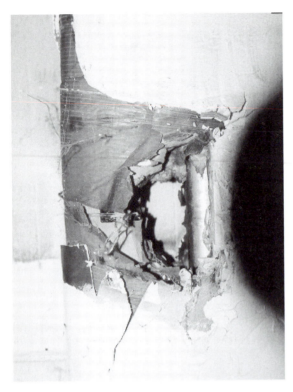

Figure 11.3 *Defective insulation of the distribution pipe*

Figure 11.4 *Uninsulated isolation valves*

Regulation of calorifiers

A loss factor for the building heating system, which consists of the same components, must also be determined for hot water preparation, similar as for the control factor. The storage tank is operated without a timer and thus the reduction factor is 1:

$$f_{BW} = 1 \qquad (16)$$

Heat loss in the distribution system q_L

An analysis of the distribution of hot water was also carried out to establish which parts of the pipes were under permanent circulation and which sections had standstill periods. Circulation pipes in heated rooms:

$$L = 36.6\text{m}$$

$$\dot{q}_L = 8.6 \frac{\text{W}}{\text{m}} \qquad (17)$$

$$q_L = \frac{36.6}{1005.6} \cdot 1 \cdot 8.6 = 0.313 \frac{\text{W}}{\text{m}^2}.$$

Circulation pipes in unheated rooms (e.g. the cellar):

$$L = 89\text{m}$$

$$\dot{q}_L = 12.3 \frac{\text{W}}{\text{m}} \qquad (18)$$

$$q_L = \frac{89}{1005.6} \cdot 1 \cdot 12.3 = 1.089 \frac{\text{W}}{\text{m}^2}.$$

Hot water pipes in heated rooms:

$$L = 216.6\text{m}$$

$$\dot{q}_L = 14.9 \frac{\text{W}}{\text{m}} \qquad (19)$$

$$q_L = \frac{216.6}{1005.6} \cdot 1 \cdot 14.9 = 3.209 \frac{\text{W}}{\text{m}^2}.$$

Hot water pipes in unheated rooms:

$$L = 89\text{m}$$

$$\dot{q}_L = 8.8 \frac{\text{W}}{\text{m}} \qquad (20)$$

$$q_L = \frac{89}{1005.6} \cdot 1 \cdot 8.8 = 0.779 \frac{\text{W}}{\text{m}^2}.$$

Finally, the overall loss of all drinking water distribution pipes is represented as follows:

$$q_{d,W} = \Sigma \left(f_{BW} \cdot \dot{q}_L \cdot \frac{L}{A_{EB}} \right) \cdot t_y \qquad (21)$$

Figure 11.5 *Hot water storage tank*

$$q_{d,W} = \sum (0.313 + 1.089 + 3.209 + 0.779) \cdot$$
$$8760 \frac{h}{a} = 47.2 \frac{kWh}{m^2 a}. \tag{21}$$

Heat loss in the hot water storage tanks

The loss of the hot water storage tank is determined by the condition as shown in Figure 11.5. The water storage tank opening is not insulated; the contents are 2000 litres at approximately 60°C and the insulation is damaged on the body of the tank.

The calculation of the loss $q_{S,W}$ is presented as follows:

$$V_S = 2000L$$
$$q_{SP} = 0.41 \frac{W}{L} \tag{22}$$
$$q_{S,W} = \frac{2000}{1005.6} \cdot 1 \cdot 0.41 \cdot 8760 = 7.14 \frac{kWh}{m^2 a}.$$

Heat generation for hot water

The calorifiers are supplied, as mentioned above, by district heating. The generated efficiency factor for domestic hot water heating has been determined as follows.

$$e_{g,W} = 1.1 \tag{23}$$

Analysis of auxiliary energy

To complete the primary energy analysis, the electrical devices (pumps, etc.) must also be evaluated. The annual consumption is determined using Jagnow et al (2002, Table 6.36).

For circulation pumps:

$$q_{EI} = 0.4 \frac{W}{m^2} \cdot 8760 \frac{h}{a} = 3.5 \frac{kWh}{m^2 a}. \tag{24}$$

For heating pumps:

$$q_{EI} = 0.7 \frac{W}{m^2} \cdot 8760 \frac{h}{a} = 6.1 \frac{kWh}{m^2 a}. \tag{25}$$

For the whole:

$$\dot{q}_{EI} = 9.6 \frac{kWh}{m^2 a}. \tag{26}$$

Overall energy analysis inventory

An overview of the overall energy, which forms the general analysis, can now be created from the evaluated dimensions of the previous sections. First, the specific useful heat q_h, which is determined by the transmission heat loss, air heating loss and the heat gain, must be calculated:

$$q_h = [q_T + q_V - \eta \cdot (q_I + q_S)]$$
$$= 314.7 + 71 - 0.663(25.8 + 40.3)$$
$$= 314.7 + 71 - 44 = 341.7 \frac{kWh}{m^2 a}. \tag{27}$$

The annual final energy balance q_H of the entire heating system can only be determined when the useful heat, the heat loss of the distribution pipes, the efficiency and the storage are taken into account, considering the efficiency of the system $e_{g,H}$ as well as the number of systems in place a:

$$q_H = [q_h + q_{d,H} + q_{s,H}] \cdot \sum (a \cdot e_{g,H})$$
$$q_H = 341.7 + 145 + 0 = 486.7 \frac{kWh}{m^2 a}. \tag{28}$$

The annual consumption for the drinking water storage q_W must also be calculated as follows and contains all of the distribution and storage losses:

$$q_W = [q_w + q_{d,W} + q_{s,W}] \cdot \sum (a \cdot e_{g,W})$$
$$= [15 + 47.2 + 7] \cdot 1.11 = 76.8 \frac{kWh}{m^2 a}. \tag{29}$$

All energy sources are thus finally considered in the following equation and at the same time represent the completion of the inventory:

$$q = q_H + q_W$$

$$q = 486.7 + 77 = 563.7 \, \frac{\text{kWh}}{\text{m}^2\text{a}}. \tag{30}$$

Degree days

In order to be able to compare the determined energy values with other references, the climatic influences in the observation were compared to a defined standard year.

District heating supply

The annual final energy determined up to this point does not contain a factor for the primary energy conversion in the municipal power plant. The essential features of the public analysis are, however, the emissions, measured by the CO_2 emissions. During an ecology audit for the municipal works, this factor with $f = 0.318 \text{kg } CO_2/\text{kWh}$ was used as a basis. All subsequent water sanitation measures can thus be evaluated in kilograms of CO_2 emissions. This fulfils an essential part of this assessment.

Energy performance assessment of modernization

In the following sections, the modernization measures planned in the modernization package are to be evaluated. The following modernization measures are planned:

- insulation of the outer façade;
- insulation of the roof;
- renewal of windows;
- insulation of heating pipes;
- insulation of drinking/hot water pipes;
- renewal of district heating transfer station;
- renewal of thermostat valves;
- hydraulic balance.

These measures bring about a change in the calculation parameters of our initial calculation for the inventory building. After their completion, one must expect the heating temperature reductions to be approximately $\theta_{HG} = 12°C$ due to the better insulation and controls,

where the heating period will also be shorter than previously:

$$\text{New HG} \rightarrow \vartheta_{HG} = 12°C$$
$$\rightarrow \vartheta_{am} = 5.3°C \tag{31}$$
$$\text{Degree days} \left[\frac{\text{d}}{\text{a}}\right] = 225 = 5400 \, \frac{\text{h}}{\text{a}}.$$

Interventions applied to thermal envelope

The entire heat-conducting outer façade will be cladded with insulation, which can produce an essentially better U value for the heat exchanging surfaces. The comparison is primarily based on the calculations and terms described in previous sections since the physical base calculations do not change.

Retrofitted insulation of façade

$$q_{TF} = U_{new} \cdot (\vartheta_{im} - \vartheta_{am}) \cdot \frac{A_H}{A_{EB}} \cdot t_{HP}$$

$$U_{new} = 0.21 \frac{\text{W}}{\text{m}^2\text{K}}$$

$$q_{TF\,new} = 0.21 \cdot (19.2 - 5.3) \cdot \frac{1053}{1005.6} \tag{32}$$

$$\cdot 5400 \frac{\text{h}}{\text{a}} = 16.5 \frac{\text{kWh}}{\text{m}^2\text{a}}.$$

Renewal of windows:

$$q_{TF} = U_{new} \cdot (\vartheta_{im} - \vartheta_{am}) \cdot \frac{A_H}{A_{EB}} \cdot t_{HP}$$

$$U_{new} = 2.5 \frac{\text{W}}{\text{m}^2\text{K}}$$

$$q_{TF\,new} = 2.5 \cdot (19.2 - 5.3) \cdot \frac{201.8}{1005.6} \tag{33}$$

$$\cdot 5400 \frac{\text{h}}{\text{a}} = 37.6 \frac{\text{kWh}}{\text{m}^2\text{a}}.$$

Retrofitted insulation of top floor ceilings:

$$q_{TF} = U_{new} \cdot (\vartheta_{im} - \vartheta_{am}) \cdot \frac{A_H}{A_{EB}} \cdot t_{HP}$$

$$U_{new} = 0.280 \frac{\text{W}}{\text{m}^2\text{K}}$$

$$q_{TF\,new} = 0.28 \cdot (19.2 - 5.3) \cdot \frac{437.2}{1005.6} \tag{34}$$

$$\cdot 5400 \frac{\text{h}}{\text{a}} = 9.1 \frac{\text{kWh}}{\text{m}^2\text{a}}.$$

Retrofitted insulation on cellar ceilings:

$$q_{TF} = U_{new} \cdot (\vartheta_{im} - \vartheta_{am}) \cdot \frac{A_H}{A_{EB}} \cdot t_{HP}$$

$$U_{new} = 0.40 \frac{W}{m^2 K}$$

$$q_{TF\,new} = 0.4 \cdot (19.2 - 5.3) \cdot \frac{437.2}{1005.6} \qquad (35)$$

$$\cdot 5400 \frac{h}{a} = 13.1 \frac{kWh}{m^2 a}.$$

Summary of thermal measures applied to envelope

The newly reduced energy performance is calculated by adding the energy values evaluated above. The reduced emissions ΔCO_2 for this measure are the difference in energy demand multiplied by the emission factor f:

$$\Delta CO_2 = \Delta q \cdot f$$
$$\Delta CO_2 = (314.7 - (16.5 + 37.6 + 9.1$$
$$+ 13.1)) \frac{kWh}{m^2 a} \cdot 0.318 \frac{kgCO_2}{kWh} \qquad (36)$$
$$\Delta CO_2 = (314.7 - 76.3) \cdot 0.318$$
$$= 75.8 \frac{kgCO_2}{m^2 a}.$$

The building envelope shows a reduced heat loss at 76.3kWh/(m²a) post-intervention, thus reducing this value by 238.4kWh/m²a.

Increasing building tightness

Carrying out the refurbishment will also increase the building's airtightness, thus producing less ventilation heat loss:

$$\Delta q_V = \Delta n \cdot h_R \cdot 0.34 \frac{Wh}{m^3 K}$$
$$\cdot (\vartheta_{im} - \vartheta_{am}) \cdot t_{HP}$$
$$\Delta q_V = 0.2 \frac{1}{h} \cdot 2.75m \cdot 0.34 \frac{Wh}{m^3 K} \qquad (37)$$
$$\cdot (19.2 - 5.3) K \cdot 5400 \frac{h}{a} = 14 \frac{kWh}{m^2 a}.$$

The reduced emissions for this measure are:

$$\Delta CO_2 = (71 - 14) \cdot 0.318 = 18.1 \frac{kgCO_2}{m^2 a}. \qquad (38)$$

Insulating the piping system

The entire heating installation, as well as the circulation and hot water pipes are to be reinsulated. This measure will be effective as follows.

For the rising mains:

$$\dot{q}_{Lnew} = 6.2 \frac{W}{m^2}$$

$$\frac{50}{50} = \frac{f_{BH} = 0.5}{f_{BH} = 1}$$

$$L = 366m$$

$$\frac{L}{A_{EB}} = 0.364 \frac{m}{m^2} \qquad (39)$$

$$q_{d,H} = \left(f_{BH} \cdot q_L \cdot \frac{L}{A_{EB}} \right) t_{HP}$$

$$= \frac{1}{2} \left(0.5 \cdot 6.2 \frac{W}{m} \cdot 0.364 \frac{m}{m^2} \right)$$

$$\cdot 5400 \frac{h}{a} + \frac{1}{2} (1 \cdot 6.2 \cdot 0.364) \cdot 5400$$

$$= 3.0 \frac{kWh}{m^2 a} + 6.1 \frac{kWh}{m^2 a} = 9.1 \frac{kWh}{m^2 a}.$$

For the cellar pipes:

$$\dot{q}_{L,new} = 7.8 \frac{W}{m}$$

$$f_{BH} = 1 \rightarrow \frac{2}{3}$$

$$f_{FH} = 0.5 \rightarrow \frac{1}{3}$$

$$L = 260m$$

$$\frac{L}{A_{EB}} = 0.259 \frac{m}{m^2} \qquad (40)$$

$$q_{d,H} = \left(f_{BH} \cdot q_L \cdot \frac{L}{A_{EB}} \right) \cdot t_{HD}$$

$$= \frac{1}{3} (0.5 \cdot 0.78 \cdot 0.59) \cdot 5400 +$$

$$\frac{2}{3} (1 \cdot 7.8 \cdot 0.259) \cdot 5400$$

$$= 1.8 \frac{kWh}{m^2 a} + 7.3 \frac{kWh}{m^2 a} = 9.1 \frac{kWh}{m^2 a}.$$

For the radiator connections:

$$\dot{q}_{L,new} = 5.0\frac{W}{m}$$

$$f_{BH} = 0.5$$

$$L = 180m$$

$$\frac{L}{A_{EB}} 0.179\frac{m}{m^2} \tag{41}$$

$$A_{EB} = 1005.6m^2$$

$$q_{d,H} = \left(f_{BH}\cdot\dot{q}_L\cdot\frac{L}{A_{EB}}\right)\cdot t_{HD}$$

$$= (0.5\cdot5\cdot0.179)\cdot5400\frac{h}{a} = 2.4\frac{kWh}{m^2a}.$$

This measure will affect the heating pipes as follows:

$$q_{d,H} = \sum\left(q_{d,H}\right)$$

$$= 2.4 + 9.1 + 7.3 = 18.8\frac{kWh}{m^2a}$$

$$\Delta q_{d,H} = q_{d,H(pre)} - q_{d,H(new)}$$

$$= 145 - 18.8 = 126.2\frac{kWh}{m^2a} \tag{42}$$

$$\Delta CO_2 = 126.2\frac{kWh}{m^2a}\cdot0.318\frac{kgCO_2}{kWh}$$

$$= 40.1\frac{kgCO_2}{m^2a}.$$

Furthermore, the circulation pipes will be insulated in heated rooms as follows:

$$\dot{q}_{L,neu} = 6.1\frac{W}{m}$$

$$L = 36.6m$$

$$\frac{L}{A_{EB}} 0.313\frac{m}{m^2} \tag{43}$$

$$q_{d,H} = \left(\dot{q}_L\cdot\frac{L}{A_{EB}}\right)\cdot t_{HD}$$

$$= (6.1\cdot0.313)\cdot8760\frac{h}{a} = 16.7\frac{kWh}{m^2a}$$

and in unheated rooms as follows:

$$\dot{q}_{L,neu} = 8.8\frac{W}{m}$$

$$L = 89m$$

$$\frac{L}{A_{EB}} = \frac{89}{1005.6} = 0.088\frac{m}{m^2}$$

$$q_{d,W} = \left(\dot{q}_L\cdot\frac{L}{A_{EB}}\right)\cdot t_{HD} \tag{44}$$

$$= \left(8.8\frac{W}{m}\cdot0.088\frac{m}{m^2}\right)\cdot8760\frac{h}{a}$$

$$= 6.8\frac{kWh}{m^2a}.$$

Drinking/hot water in heated rooms:

$$\dot{q}_L = 7.5\frac{W}{m}$$

$$L = 216.6m$$

$$A_{EB} = 1005.6$$

$$\frac{L}{A_{EB}} = 0.215\frac{m}{m^2} \tag{45}$$

$$q_{d,W} = 2.5\cdot0.215\cdot8760$$

$$= 4.7\frac{kWh}{m^2a}.$$

Drinking/hot water in unheated rooms:

$$\dot{q}_L = 4.6\frac{W}{m}$$

$$L = 89m$$

$$q_{d,W} = 4.6\frac{W}{m}\cdot0.088\frac{m}{m^2}\cdot8750\frac{h}{a} \tag{46}$$

$$= 3.6\frac{kWh}{m^2a}.$$

This measure will affect the drinking/hot water pipes as follows:

$$q_{d,W} = \sum\left(q_{d,W}\right) = 16.7 + 6.8 + 9.7 + 3.6$$

$$= 31.8\frac{kWh}{m^2a}$$

$$f_{BW} = 0.9 \tag{47}$$

$$q_{d,Wnew} = q_{d,W}\cdot f_{BW} = 31.8\cdot0.9$$

$$= 28.6\frac{kWh}{m^2a}$$

$$\Delta q_{d,W} = 47.2 - 28.6 = 18.6 \frac{kWh}{m^2 a}$$

$$\Delta CO_2 = 18.6 \cdot 0.318 = 5.9 \frac{kgCO_2}{m^2 a}. \tag{47}$$

Renewing the hot water storage tanks

The current tank with a volume of 2000 litres and partly missing insulation will be exchanged for a new 1000 litre tank. This measure will be effective as follows:

$$V_S = 1000L$$

$$q_{SP} = 0.2 \frac{W}{L}$$

$$q_{S,W} = \left(f_{BW} \cdot q_{SP} \cdot \frac{\dot{V}_S}{A_{EB}} \right) \cdot t_y$$

$$= 0.9 * 0.2 \frac{W}{L} \cdot 1 \tag{48}$$

$$= 0.18 \frac{W}{m^2} \cong 0 \frac{kWh}{m^2 a}$$

$$\Delta CO_2 = 0.96 - 0 = 0.96 \cdot 0.318$$

$$= 0.3 \frac{kgCO_2}{m^2 a}.$$

Auxiliary energy

A relatively high saving is expected due to the use of efficient pumps, which will bring about an additional energy-saving effect:

$$q_{el,new} = \dot{q}_{El} \cdot t_{El}$$

Circulation pump $0.1 \frac{W}{m^2} \cdot 7300 \frac{h}{a} = 0.7 \frac{kWh}{m^2 a}$

Boiler pump $0.2 \frac{W}{m^2} \cdot 5000 \frac{h}{a} = 1 \frac{kWh}{m^2 a}$

Control FW $0.1 \cdot 9760 = 0.9 \frac{kWh}{m^2 a}$

$$q_{el,new} = 2.6 \frac{kWh}{m^2 a} \tag{49}$$

$$\Delta q_{el} = q_{el,pre} - q_{el,new} = 9.6 - 2.6 = 7 \frac{kWh}{m^2 a}$$

$$\Delta CO_2 = 7 \frac{kWh}{m^2 a} \cdot 0.318 \frac{kgCO_2}{kWh} = 2.2 \frac{kgCO_2}{m^2 a}$$

Review of modernization

The individual sums thus form the entire savings for the planned modernization measures as follows:

$$CO_{2\ reduction} = \sum \Delta CO_2 = 75.8 + 18.1 +$$
$$40.1 + 5.9 + 0.3 + 2.2 \tag{50}$$
$$= 142.4 \frac{kgCO_2}{m^2 a}.$$

Conclusions

The results of this refurbishment, which was triggered by German energy policies, lie well within the government's objective of achieving a sustained drop of carbon emissions from the existing building stock. The examined case shows a substantial drop in carbon emissions of 75 per cent. This is due to the fact that one of the credit programme's requirements is the set minimum for the reduction of carbon dioxide emissions of 40kg per square metre of energy-relevant floor area. As a result, a thorough high-efficiency refurbishment is carried out with a detailed look into areas previously untouched in building refurbishment (i.e. insulation of the basement ceiling).

This particular housing co-operative has so far refurbished 188,000m² of living area, thus reducing the overall carbon emissions of their homes by around 40 per cent. The reduced annual fuel consumption equals 944,000 litres of oil equivalent.

References

BMU (Bundesministerium für Umwelt) (2000) *Umwelt, Sonderteil Nationales Klimaschutzprogramm*, no 11/2000, BMU, Naturschutz und Reaktorsicherheit Referat Öffentlichkeitsarbeit, Berlin

Bremer Energie Institut (2007) *Effekte des KfW CO₂ Gebaeudesanierungsprogramms 2005 und 2006*, Bremer Energie Institut, Bremen

DIN V 4701 Part 10 (2001) *Energetische Bewertung heiz- und raumlufttechnischer Anlagen; Heizung, Trinkwassererwärmung, Lüftung*, Beuth Verlag GmbH, Berlin

DTI (Department of Trade and Industry) (2007) *Meeting the Energy Challenge: A White Paper on Energy*, The Stationery Office, London

Forschungszentrum Juelich (2000) *Die Entwicklung des Waermemarktes für den Gebaeudesektor bis 2050*, Forschungszentrum Juelich GmbH, Juelich

Forschungszentrum Juelich (2004) *Klimaschutz durch energetische Sanierung von Gebaeuden – Band 1*, Forschungszentrum Juelich GmbH, Juelich

Fraunhofer ISI (2006) *Energy Efficiency Policies and Measures in Germany 2006*, Fraunhofer Institute for Systems and Innovation Research, Karslruhe

House of Commons (2008) *Existing Housing and Climate Change – Seventh Report Session 2007–2008*, HMSO, London

IPCC (Intergovernmental Panel on Climate Change) (2007) *Summary for Policymakers: Contribution of Working Group I to the Fourth Assessment Report of the Intergovernmental Panel on Climate Change. Climate Change 2007*, IPCC, The Physical Science Basis, Geneva

Jagnow, K., Horschler, S. et al (2002*) Die neue Energieeins parverordnung 2002*, Deutscher Wirtschaftsdienst, Köln

Lowe, R. (2007) 'Technical options and strategies for decarbonizing UK housing', *Building Research and Information*, vol 35, no 4, pp412–425

Oreszczyn, T. and Lowe, R. (2005) *Evidence to the House of Lords Select Committee on Science and Technology: Energy Efficient Buildings*, The Authority of the House of Lords, London, pp70–74

Poeschk (2007) *Energieeffizienz in Gebaeuden – Jahrbuch 2007*, Vme Verlag und Medienservice Energie Juergen Poeschk, Berlin

Sustainable Development Commission (2006) '*Stock Take': Delivering Improvements in Existing Housing*, Sustainable Development Commission, London

UBA (2008) *Politikszenarien für den Klimaschutz IV – Szenairen bis 2030*, Umweltbundesamt, Dessau

UNEP (United Nations Environment Programme) (2007) *Buildings and Climate Change: Status, Challenges and Opportunities*, UNEP, Paris

VDI 3808 (1993) *Energiewirtschaftliche Beurteilungskriterien für heiztechnische Anlagen*, Beuth Verlag GmbH, Berlin

WWF (World Wide Fund for Nature) (2008) *How Low? Achieving Optimal Carbon Savings from the UK's Existing Housing Stock*, WWF-UK, Godalming

Part III

BUILDINGS AND ENVIRONMENT

Introduction: Emerging Design Challenges of the 21st Century

Dejan Mumovic and Mat Santamouris

Adapting to and ameliorating the effects of urban heat islands on energy use, comfort and health will require appropriate policies for urban planning, housing and transport. However, before these policies can be developed, quantitative tools are required to identify and quantify the *net* effectiveness of mitigation and adaptation strategies. Chapter 12 advocates that the wider picture should be considered. The authors explain that, in summer, urban heat islands in the UK will tend to result in an increased cooling load and an increased number of excess deaths due to overheating. Conversely, in winter urban heat islands will tend to result in reduced heating loads and a reduced number of cold-related excess deaths. This chapter therefore explains that the *net* effects of these impacts must be borne in mind when considering large-scale urban modifications.

Taking into account the growing concerns related to the exposure of urban dwellers to air pollution, Chapter 13 aims to summarize airflow and air pollution patterns in urban environments, and to discuss possible implications for building design. The authors address the fundamental principles related to urban indoor/outdoor air quality modelling and monitoring, which are of importance to both building design and urban planning professionals.

Chapter 14 takes us indoors: humans in developed parts of the world spend 85 to 95 per cent of their time indoors (at home, work, school or when commuting). This chapter describes how indoor environment quality can affect humans without discussing the energy consequences for creating high-quality indoor environments (energy-related issues are explained in Part II of this book). Emphasis is placed on the thermal environment and air quality, and their effects on health, comfort and performance. This is followed by a detailed discussion of state-of-the-art indoor air quality and ventilation modelling tools that are available to building design and academic communities (see Chapter 15).

Moisture is responsible for 70 to 80 per cent of all damage in buildings. Thus, correct moisture control is a prerequisite for achieving sustainable buildings. Chapter 16 explains that adequate control is only possible if we know how moisture is transferred to and moves in building assemblies, and how assemblies degrade when staying moist over prolonged periods of time.

Chapter 17 gives an overview of natural ventilation in non-domestic buildings and describes more advanced natural ventilation strategies and technologies available to optimize the performance of naturally ventilated systems. Special attention is paid to urban areas as lower wind speeds, the existence of heat islands, and the potentially high ambient noise and air pollution levels represent a serious challenge to designers of naturally ventilated buildings. Since natural ventilation is based on pressure differences created by temperature differences and wind, in some conditions it will not be possible to maintain the adequate temperature and/or to provide ventilation at the rates predicted at the design stage. Therefore, it is crucially important to familiarize ourselves with the state-of-the-art mechanical and mixed-mode ventilation systems for city centre buildings. Due to supply and exhaust air fans, these ventilation systems are more flexible with respect to building design, and often more energy efficient than other systems if heat recovery means are used. These issues are covered in Chapter 18.

While Chapter 12 focuses on the impact of urban climate on energy use, health and comfort, Chapter 19 discusses the potential impacts of climate change (temperature, precipitation, wind and subsidence) on buildings and offers options for changing building design to make buildings more resilient to future climates. Both chapters are based around two large Engineering and Physical Sciences Research Council (EPSRC) projects that have begun to investigate these issues, with a particular focus on the UK LUCID (The Development of a Local Urban Climate Model and Its Application to the Intelligent Design of Cities) and SCORCHIO (Sustainable Cities: Options for Responding to Climate Change Impacts and Outcomes) projects. To highlight possible building service solutions for changing climate, Chapter 20 provides an overview of sustainable cooling strategies for urban buildings.

Last but not least, at the end of Part III we have included three case studies:

1   *Chapter 21, Indoor Air Quality in City Centre Buildings.* This case study focuses on the experimental investigation of the impact of the urban environment on the effectiveness of natural and hybrid ventilation since the efficient design of these ventilation systems is the determinant for thermal comfort, indoor air quality and energy savings.

2   *Chapter 22, Indoor Air Quality and Health.* This case study describes a number of measures for allergen (pet and mite) removal and avoidance, including tailored advice aimed at reducing mite population growth via changes in moisture production, heating and ventilation habits.

3   *Chapter 23, Indoor Air Quality and Ventilation Modelling.* This case study provides a general guide to the use of computational fluid dynamics (CFD) for assessing thermal comfort and air quality in and around buildings. Within this framework, relevant experimental and theoretical problems are also briefly discussed. The examples include:

- urban air-quality modelling for regulatory purposes in Glasgow, Scotland;
- assessment of the impact of a new building on airflow and pollution distribution in a district of Copenhagen, Denmark; and
- assessment of indoor air quality and thermal comfort in a typical medium-sized mechanically ventilated theatre.

12

Urban Climate: Impacts on Energy Use, Comfort and Health

Michael Davies, Philip Steadman and Tadj Oreszczyn

Introduction

One of the best-known effects of urbanization on the local climate is urban warming – this phenomenon is commonly referred to as the urban heat island (UHI). A range of factors vary between rural and urban areas and contribute to the UHI – for example, the thermal properties of materials, the height and spacing of buildings and air pollution levels. These factors result in more of the sun's energy being captured, absorbed and stored in urban surfaces compared to rural surfaces during the day and a slower loss of this energy at night, thus resulting in comparatively higher air temperatures. In addition, less evaporation (with the consequent reduction in associated cooling) takes place in the typically drier urban areas. Finally, urban areas also have greater inputs of heat as a result of the high density of energy use in cities. All of this energy (used in buildings and for transport) ultimately ends up as heat. Strategic planning is therefore required that takes account of the above factors, particularly in the context of climate change.

The value of the UHI in any city will have significant spatial and temporal variations; the maximum intensity is typically reached several hours after sunset (Oke, 1987). With regard to the UK, in London during the August 2003 heat wave, the maximum temperature difference between urban and adjacent rural locations reached 9°C on occasions (Greater London Authority, 2006b). Watkins et al (2002) reported on an extensive series of measurements made in London during the period of 1999 to 2000, which demonstrate in detail the behaviour of London's UHI.

It should be noted that for certain cities a 'negative' UHI can, instead, be dominant. In arid regions, cities with large amounts of irrigated green space may actually be *cooler* than the surrounding dry areas (Grimmond, 2007). UK cities, however, appear to exhibit features of a 'conventional' UHI (as would be expected) and it is such cities that this chapter focuses on.

The concept of the 'urban heat island' is now well established. However, the *distribution* of local temperatures within the urban environment and their relation to land use and building form is much less well understood. These variations in temperatures are important for several reasons. First, populations typically display an optimum temperature range at which the (daily or weekly) death rate is lowest. Mortality rates rise at temperatures outside this optimal zone. The temperature–mortality relation varies greatly by latitude and climatic zone. People living in urban environments are at greater risk than those in non-urban regions (McMichael et al, 2006). Adapting to and ameliorating such dangerous conditions, whose effects have recently been experienced, for instance, in Chicago in 1995 (Klinenberg, 2002), in Greece in 2001 and in France in 2003 will require appropriate policies for urban planning, housing and transport (Hunt, 2005). But before these policies can be developed, quantitative tools are required to identify

Source: University College London

Figure 12.1 *London*

and quantify the *net* effectiveness of mitigation and adaptation strategies. For example, while the lowering of urban temperatures in summer is likely to reduce rates of heat-related mortality, the number of cold-related deaths is far higher in the UK than the death toll due to excessive summer heat. This should be borne in mind before any major intervention in a city is contemplated.

Increased mortality represents an extreme consequence of rising temperatures. However, it is clear that the proportion of the time that people will feel 'uncomfortable' has the potential to increase. This raises the possibility of a large increase in the use of mechanical cooling systems and a consequent rise in energy use, particularly in urban areas.

The urban environment, then, has an impact on energy use, comfort and health. It is possible to modify this environment in an attempt to address these issues. The next section describes some options that are available.

Modifying factors

A range of physical scales applies to the strategies that may be used in an attempt to modify the urban climate. The UHI is a city-scale effect and research is currently

being undertaken to examine modification strategies that can be implemented at levels ranging from street to city wide. At a local scale, these include the modification of surface properties ('cool roofs', 'green roofs' and 'cool pavements'), planting trees and vegetation, and the creation of green spaces.

The geometry of the built environment and anthropogenic (man-made) heat emissions are also issues to consider. A useful guidance document is

Source: istock

Figure 12.2 *Green space*

available that provides further details of these issues with a specific focus on London (Greater London Authority, 2006a). A brief discussion of all of these factors follows – anthropogenic heat emissions are reviewed initially.

Several studies have shown the effect of anthropogenic heat emissions on the urban climate (see Klysik, 1996; Taha, 1997; Ichinose et al, 1999; and Coutts et al, 2007). The Ichinose et al (1999) study of Tokyo quantified the increase in temperatures within the urban environment, on the basis of a detailed survey of energy consumed, to be up to 1.5°C within areas of high anthropogenic heat emission. The influence was strongest during winter months and weakest during summer as the short-wave radiation varied along with seasonal daily temperature profiles. The Taha (1997) analysis of several American, Canadian and European cities indicated that anthropogenic heat emission was strongest in cold-climate city centres, but was nearly negligible in suburban areas. The study suggested that an increase of 2°C to 3°C could be seen due to the impacts of anthropogenic heat.

A recent study (Hamilton et al, 2008) estimated the anthropogenic heat emission from buildings in London at a range of spatial and temporal scales – an example of the data is shown in Figure 12.3 and refers to the emissions per square metre of *ground* area. A wide spread of annual average heat emissions was identified, with 50 per cent of London emitting less than 10W/m², 25 per cent emitting between 10 to 18W/m², 20 per cent emitting between 18 to 30W/m², and 5 per cent emitting above 30W/m². The annual average building-related heat emission for the *whole* of London is estimated at approximately 9W/m². In comparison, the London Energy and CO_2 Emission Inventory (LECI) database (Greater London Authority, 2006a) estimates the annual average energy delivered for transport in London as approximately 2W/m².

The highest levels of annual heat emission from buildings in London are concentrated in central London, although there a few isolated pockets of high emitting areas in outer London. The pattern follows the concentration of domestic and non-domestic buildings, their clustering, and the density of the development.

The study also compared the anthropogenic heat emissions and total incident net short-wave solar radiation balance of four representative London sites. In those urban areas with deep canyons and high

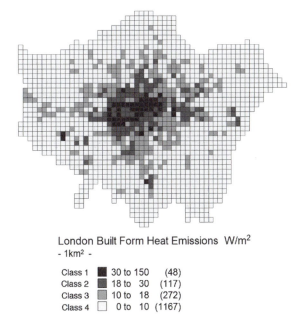

London Built Form Heat Emissions W/m²
- 1km² -

Class		W/m²	(n)
Class 1	■	30 to 150	(48)
Class 2	■	18 to 30	(117)
Class 3	▨	10 to 18	(272)
Class 4	□	0 to 10	(1167)

Source: authors' own work and Hamilton et al (2008)

Figure 12.3 *Annual average anthropogenic heat emission from buildings in London*

densities, the anthropogenic energy constitutes a significant portion of the total energy input. A study of London's UHI phenomenon indicated that the centre of the island sits above the Old Street and Farringdon Road area within the City of London (Watkins et al, 2002). This location is also where the anthropogenic heat emission is greatest. It indicates that the reduction of energy use within such areas may be particularly relevant with regard to the UHI.

In the future, it is likely that not only will our use of energy reduce, but that the sources from which this energy is supplied will alter due to the pressures of meeting our climate change obligations and to maintain security of supply. This may involve the decentralized distribution of energy as greater use is made of combined heat and power and local authorities increasingly demand that new buildings generate a percentage of their energy locally (e.g. the Merton Rule: a policy adopted in 2003 by the London Borough of Merton that stated: 'All new non-residential developments above a threshold of 1000 square metres will be expected to incorporate renewable energy production equipment to provide at least 10 per cent of predicted energy requirements').

These changes may have an impact on anthropogenic heat emissions. If conventional power stations were moved into cities, then this would clearly have an impact in raising the local emission of heat; but if the power stations were instead used for combined heat and power generation then the effect on heat emissions may be negligible. Notice that the future move to decarbonized electricity in its own right is unlikely to make a major change since it does not matter how power is generated. The energy, whether low carbon or high carbon, all ends up as heat at the place of use. However, it is worth considering the implications resulting from a widespread move to solar heating because of the potential impact that this will have on the reflectance of roofs.

The reflectance (albedo) of a roof surface will have a significant impact on the resultant temperature of that surface. Modifications to the albedo will then impact upon the resultant energy flows, both directly to the building and indirectly to the nearby environment. Green roofs will have a similar impact, but with the additional potential benefit of associated evaporative cooling (assuming appropriate access to water). Large-scale urban solar collection of energy may make it difficult to reduce the impacts of future climate change upon urban areas – there may be a potential conflict between solar panels and the desire for highly reflecting roofs to mitigate the UHI.

Just as a modification to the albedo of roofs will affect the energy balance of that surface and the surrounding environment, the same issues apply to other urban surfaces such as pavements and parking areas. If this modification to the albedo is also combined with improved water permeability, then evaporative cooling will also be enhanced. Highly reflective roads and pavements may also be advantageous for night-time street lighting.

Other options for modification strategies can make use of the fact that air temperatures in and around green spaces can be several degrees lower than their surroundings (e.g. Spronken-Smith and Oke, 1998). Trees and vegetation are good modifiers of climate as they not only provide shade, but offer enhanced evaporative cooling – assuming appropriate water availability. Gill et al (2007) demonstrate the potential of green space using Manchester as a case study.

Finally, a key factor that differentiates the energy balance of rural and urban areas is the ability of the urban area to reduce the emission of long-wave radiation at night. This is due to the reduced view of the sky of the urban surfaces. The orientation of streets will also impact upon local wind velocities. Issues of sky view and orientation could be considered and addressed at the planning stage. However, clear evidence needs to be provided of the potential impact.

Energy use

There has been much work in this area and, hence, only a brief summary is provided in this chapter.

Energy impacts of the UHI

In general, the UHI would be expected to result in an increased cooling energy demand in summer and a reduced energy demand during the heating season – the literature supports this view. With regard to the UK, measured air temperature data have been used (Kolokotroni et al, 2007) as inputs to a building energy simulation computer programme to assess the heating and cooling load of a typical air-conditioned office building positioned at 24 different locations within the London UHI. It was found that the urban cooling load is up to 25 per cent higher than the rural load over the year, and the annual heating load is reduced by 22 per cent. For this particular building and set of assumptions, the absolute gains due to the heating load reductions were outweighed by the increased cooling loads. For non-air-conditioned buildings, the UHI as

Source: istock

Figure 12.4 *Solar panels*

described by this data set would tend to result in net energy savings, albeit coupled with higher summer temperatures.

Elsewhere, Landsberg (1981) compared heating and cooling degree days for several American cities and at airports outside of them. A modified table was published by Taha (1997) – see Table 12.1. The relevant data for London has also been added to the table for the purposes of this chapter. The heating and cooling degree days are both calculated to a base of 18.3°C.

The data for London in Table 12.1 comprises the average heating and cooling degree days (1993 to 2006) for the London Weather Centre (central London) and Northolt (near to and at a similar radial distance from the centre of London as Heathrow Airport). Theoretically, the heating and cooling energy used should be a linear function of the number of cooling and heating degree days provided that the correct base temperature is used. Although the percentage change is much greater for cooling degree days than heating, the absolute change in heating degree days is greater for heating than cooling in most of the locations in Table 12.1 and the difference becomes greater the further north the location.

Energy impacts of modifications to the urban environment

Strategies for the intentional *modification* of the urban climate can be effective and, hence, can have a significant impact upon the energy used by buildings. The effect on energy use may be usefully split into two components – *direct* (i.e. modifying the energy use of an individual building via the application of a cool roof for example) and *indirect* (i.e. modifying the energy use of all buildings via the impact that the methods outlined earlier – if applied on a large scale – may have on the ambient conditions).

One study (Synnefa et al, 2007) looked specifically at the direct impact upon an individual building from using cool roof coatings on the cooling and heating loads and the indoor thermal comfort conditions of residential buildings for various climatic conditions. For the locations studied (27 cities worldwide), the heating penalty (0.2 to 17kWh/m² year) was less important than the cooling load reduction (9 to 48kWh/m² year).

Akbari and Konopacki (2005) developed summary tables for approximately 240 locations in the US, sorted by heating and cooling degree days, based on simulations to quantify the effect of a range of strategies (i.e. solar-reflective roofs, shade trees, reflective pavements and urban vegetation).

The tables provide estimates of savings for both the direct and indirect effects for three building types: residences, offices and retail stores. The study found significant energy savings. For all building types, over 75 per cent of the total savings were from *direct* effects of cool roofs and shade trees.

Both the UHI and relevant modifications to the urban environment have the potential to significantly affect energy use. However, more analysis is required into what happens in practice. Research is currently being undertaken at University College London (UCL)

Table 12.1 *Heating and cooling degree days*

Location	Heating degree days			Cooling degree days		
	Urban	Airport	Δ	Urban	Airport	Δ
Los Angeles	384	562	–178	368	191	+177
Washington, DC	1300	1370	–70	440	361	+79
St Louis	1384	1466	–82	510	459	+51
New York	1496	1600	–104	333	268	+65
Baltimore	1266	1459	–193	464	344	+120
London	2419	2779	–360	248	207	+41
Seattle	2493	2881	–388	111	72	+39
Detroit	3460	3556	–96	416	366	+50
Chicago	3371	3609	–238	463	372	+91
Denver	3058	3342	–284	416	350	+66

Source: data from US cities adapted from Taha (1997) and authors' own work

Source: istock

Figure 12.5 *Shading trees*

to examine the impact of climate change on energy use, and analysis of monitored energy use with external temperature suggests that the effect is more complex than previously thought. For example, as temperatures rise, the benefits of warmer external conditions are not always taken as reduced energy use, but as higher internal temperature and increased levels of ventilation. Energy use in cities is highly complex. For instance, the requirement for air conditioning in cities is often driven more by traffic noise and pollution than the UHI. New feedback mechanisms could also be foreseen in the future. For example, lightweight electric cars could be quiet and less polluting while contributing less heat to the urban heat island, and this could encourage the use of natural ventilation instead of energy-intensive air conditioning.

Health and comfort

With regard to the UHI, issues of health and comfort are inevitably linked. Higher summer temperatures will result in increased discomfort; but prolonged elevated temperatures cause significant increases in mortality rates. In the summer of 2003, much of Europe experienced a persistent heat wave. In England, there were 2091 excess deaths (17 per cent increase) during the heat wave. The impact was greatest in the southern half of England, particularly in London, where deaths increased by 42 per cent (Johnson et al, 2005).

The elderly (over 75s) are most vulnerable to heat-related mortality, particularly those living alone. However, other groups are also at risk: children and sick adults (e.g. those with chronic cardio-respiratory disease).

The design of dwellings can also play a critical part in modifying the risk of death. A recent study that considered the impact of the August 2003 heat wave in France (Salagnac, 2007) noted that:

> ... thermal insulation plays a considerable role as a risk reduction factor: the odds ratio is decreased by a factor of 5 between non-insulated and insulated dwellings. A bedroom under the roof leads to an increase by a factor of 4 or more the risk of death. Surroundings with a high vegetation index also considerably reduce the risk.

As well as temperatures, pollutant concentrations are an important factor during heat waves in England. Ozone has been linked with increased hospital admissions for respiratory diseases (Anderson et al, 1996). In the 2003 heat wave, excess exposure to ozone and PM10 were recorded for all regions in England, most notably in London and the south-east. A significant proportion of the excess deaths in the 2003 heat wave could be attributed to ozone and PM10 (Stedman, 2004), although this study assumed no interaction between high temperatures and high pollutant exposures.

Work is under way via the Engineering and Physical Sciences Research Council (EPSRC)-funded LUCID (The Development of a Local Urban Climate Model and Its Application to the Intelligent Design of Cities) project to assess vulnerability to the health impacts of heat waves in the London setting and to address any synergistic effect of pollutants and temperature. An element of the project, led by the London School of Hygiene and Tropical Medicine (LSHTM) initially aims to quantify the degree to which micro-variations in the temperature and pollution have influenced mortality during past heat waves, and then apply this evidence to models of future heat waves under a range of assumptions about climate change and urban development. This work will extend research currently being undertaken as part of a range of other projects on heat-related mortality in the UK funded by the Medical Research Council (MRC) and the European Commission. It will entail linkage of four principal data sets:

1   modelled micro-variations in temperature and airborne pollutants (principally PM10, ozone) for past heat wave periods;
2   daily mortality data for London, geo-referenced using the full postcode of residence;
3   small-area socio-demographic characteristics derived from the 2001 census at super output area (SOA) level, including population age structure and an index of socio-economic deprivation;
4   data on the characteristics of domestic properties combined with new relationships being developed by UCL to predict summertime overheating in dwellings based on both field data and modelling.

The project will then specify a number of illustrative policies relating to urban planning and for each one will use the LUCID urban climate model to predict temperatures and pollution levels under future climate change scenarios. With these urban policy scenario combinations, the work will apply the evidence derived from analysis of past temperature–mortality patterns in London to estimate the future numbers of heat-attributable deaths in London.

While increased mortality represents an extreme impact of overheating, the issue of discomfort is also a critical one. A full treatment of comfort issues is given elsewhere in this book (see Chapter 14), so discussion of the relevant factors will be limited here to a short summary. A recent paper (Watkins et al, 2007) also provides a detailed treatment of this issue, with a focus on London.

For the purposes of this chapter, it is sufficient to note that many factors (air temperature, clothing, activity level, relative humidity, radiant exchange and air speed) are involved in the perception of comfort. It is certainly possible, in principle, for societies to adapt to elevated temperatures; indeed, the future temperature projections for London are currently the norm for some lower latitude countries. The greater challenge for urban societies may be in dealing with the adaptation to the mitigation strategies relating to the reduction of CO_2 emissions. An element of the EPSRC-funded PUrE Intrawise (Pollutants in the Urban Environment: An Integrated Framework for Improving Sustainability of the Indoor Environment) project that the authors are part of will consider such issues. In an attempt to reduce the energy use of buildings and, hence, the associated heat emissions, the impacts of increased insulation and reduced air change rates may – in poorly designed buildings – lead to overheating and poor indoor air quality. The associated health risks need to be borne in mind.

The issue of discomfort is closely linked to that of increased energy use for cooling. Two recent projects (Orme and Palmer, 2003; Hacker et al, 2005) have demonstrated via computer modelling the effect that ventilation could play in reducing the take-up of air conditioning. Higher temperatures associated with the urban heat island are expected to make the challenge more difficult. In particular, one strategy for passive cooling of buildings is through storing heat within the building fabric during the day and cooling through ventilation at night. But this method relies on the night-time temperatures being sufficiently low. The UHI is typically most pronounced at night, and so it is important to know whether or not this method remains viable. In general, strategies that may have served historic buildings well may no longer be appropriate. Buildings both respond to and contribute to the local microclimate. Effective building design requires a knowledge of, and ways of dealing with, this microclimate.

Conclusions

The local character of the built environment can have a strong influence and generate a localized microclimate, which leads to variation in the strength of the urban heat island across a city. We have seen, for example, how green space interspersed into the urban landscape can substantially reduce undesirable impacts of buildings upon the microclimate. In this and other ways, intelligent master planning of large-scale development can alleviate overheating in urban areas. However, at present there are no suitable quantitative tools available to architects, planners and designers to analyse the impact of urban development on the microclimate – and, hence, health, comfort and energy use – across this range of scales. What is needed is a robust and appropriate model that can reliably predict localized urban temperatures – a 'weather forecast' model for the urban environment. This would mean a move away from 'traditional' generic weather files that are currently utilized within building engineering towards 'tailored' predictions specific to the local environment. To address each of the concerns requires *local* environmental prediction – on scales from whole-city scale down to hundreds of metres. In the UK, for example, there are no established practical methods or tools for assessing the impact of local planning decisions (land use; building layout, orientation and design; size of open spaces or parks) on the fine details of the local climate. Widespread and immediate modification of the relevant properties of the urban environment in order to affect the UHI is not feasible for UK cities on a large scale. However, the collective effect of many smaller changes may be significant at a variety of scales.

A number of recent projects have begun to investigate these issues, with a particular focus on the UK – in particular, two EPSRC-funded projects: Sustainable Cities: Options for Responding to Climate Change Impacts and Outcomes (SCORCHIO) and, as noted earlier, LUCID. The authors of this chapter are involved in the LUCID project that will develop, test and apply state-of-the-art methods for calculating *local* temperature and air quality in the urban environment. The impact on energy use and the consequences for health of changes to the urban climate will then be explored. The implications for urban planning will be considered in detail. Such methods applied to urban areas would contribute greatly to the generation of guidance in the planning process; indeed, modelling is seen as essential to estimate and predict the transition from the current unsuitable practices to more sustainable communities.

There is much current interest in attempting to ameliorate potential summer overheating (i.e. a focus on the consequences of heat waves). However, the wider picture should also be considered. During the summer, in the UK, the UHI will tend to result in an increased cooling load and an increased number of excess deaths due to overheating. Conversely, in winter, the UHI will tend to result in reduced heating loads and a reduced number of cold-related excess deaths. As noted earlier, the *net* effects of these impacts must be borne in mind in the consideration of large-scale urban modifications.

In the UK, it would be possible to hypothesize that the UHI may actually have a net positive energy, health and comfort effect over the year. The research challenge is to test this hypothesis both for the present day and also for the future, taking into account climate and other social and technical changes. Detailed studies of these issues with regard to the UK are now under way and the results of this research should be fully understood before any major changes to the urban infrastructure are undertaken that may impact upon the UHI.

Acknowledgements

The authors gratefully acknowledge UK Engineering and Physical Sciences Research Council (EPSRC) funding of the LUCID project that informs this chapter and also the EPSRC Platform Grant that supports the work of the Complex Built Environment Systems Group at UCL.

References

Akbari, H. and Konopacki, S. (2005) 'Calculating energy-saving potentials of heat island reduction strategies', *Energy Policy*, vol 33, no 6, pp721–756

Anderson, H. R., Ponce de Leon, A., Bland, M. J., Bower, S. J. and Strachan, D. P. (1996) 'Air pollution and daily mortality in London: 1987–1992', *British Medical Journal*, vol 312, pp665–669

Coutts, A. M., Beringer, J. and Tapper, N. J. (2007) 'Impact of increasing urban density on local climate: Spatial and temporal variations in the surface energy balance in Melbourne, Australia', *Journal of Applied Meteorology*, vol 46, pp477–493

Gill, S. E., Handley, J. F., Ennos, A. R. and Pauleit, S. (2007) 'Adapting cities for climate change: The role of the green infrastructure', *Built Environment*, vol 33, no 1, pp115–133

Greater London Authority (2006a) *London Energy and CO₂ Emissions Inventory 2003: Methodology Manual*, Greater London Authority, London

Greater London Authority (2006b) *London's Urban Heat Island: A Summary for Decision Makers*, Greater London Authority, London

Grimmond, S. (2007) 'Urbanization and global environmental change: Local effects of urban warming', *Geographical Journal*, vol 173, pp83–88

Hacker, J. N., Belcher, S. E. and Connell, R. K. (2005) *Beating the Heat: Keeping UK Buildings Cool in a Warming Climate*, UKCIP, Oxford

Hamilton, I. G., Davies, M., Steadman, J. P., Stone, A., Ridley, I. and Evans, S. (2008) 'Significance of London's anthropogenic heat emissions: A comparison against captured shortwave solar radiation', *Building and Environment*, in press

Hunt, J. C. R. (ed) (2005) *London's Environment: Prospects for a Sustainable World City*, World Scientific Publishing Co, NJ

Ichinose, T., Shimodozono, K. and Hanaki, K. (1999) 'Impact of anthropogenic heat on urban climate in Tokyo', *Atmospheric Environment*, vol 33, pp3897–3909

Johnson, H., Kovats, R. S., McGregor, G., Stedman, J., Gibbs, M., Walton, H., Cook, L. and Black, E. (2005) 'The impact of the 2003 heat wave on mortality and hospital admissions in England', *Health Statistics Quarterly*, no 25

Klinenberg, E. (2002) *Heat Wave: A Social Autopsy of Disaster in Chicago*, University of Chicago Press, Chicago

Klysik, K. (1996) 'Spatial and seasonal distribution of anthropogenic heat emissions in Lodz, Poland', *Atmospheric Environment*, vol 30, pp3397–3404

Kolokotroni, M., Zhang, Y. and Watkins, R. (2007) 'The London heat island and building cooling design', *Solar Energy*, vol 81, pp102–110

Landsberg, H. (1981) (ed) *The Urban Climate*, Academic Press, New York, NY

McMichael, A. J., Woodruff, R. E. and Hales, S. (2006) 'Climate change and human health: Present and future risks', *The Lancet*, vol 367, 11 March, pp859–869

Oke, T. R. (1987) *Boundary Layer Climates*, second edition, Methuen, London

Orme, M. and Palmer, J. (2003) *Control of Overheating in Future Housing: Design Guidance for Low Energy Strategies*, FaberMaunsell, UK

Salagnac, J (2007) 'Lessons from the 2003 heat wave: A French perspective', *Building Research and Information*, vol 35, no 4, July

Spronken-Smith, R. A. and Oke, T. R. (1998) 'The thermal regime of urban parks in two cities with different summer climates', *International Journal of Remote Sensing*, vol 19, no 11, pp2085–2104

Stedman, J. (2004) 'The predicted number of air pollution related deaths in the UK during the August 2003 heatwave', *Atmospheric Environment*, vol 38, no 8, pp1087–1090

Synnefa, A., Santamouris, M. and Akbari, H. (2007) 'Estimating the effect of using cool coatings on energy loads and thermal comfort in residential buildings in various climatic conditions', *Energy and Buildings*, vol 39, no 11, pp1167–1174

Taha, H. (1997) 'Urban climates and heat islands: Albedo, evapotranspiration, and anthropogenic heat', *Energy and Buildings*, vol 25, pp99–103

Watkins, R., Palmer, J., Kolokotroni, M. and Littlefair, P. (2002) 'The London heat island: Results from summertime monitoring', *Building Service Engineering Research and Technology*, vol 23, no 2, pp97–106

Watkins, R., Palmer, J. and Kolokotroni, M. (2007) 'Increased temperature and intensification of the urban heat island: Implications for human comfort and urban design', *Built Environment*, vol 33, no 1, pp85–96

13

Air Pollution and the Urban Built Environment

Dejan Mumovic and James Milner

Introduction

Breaches of prescribed air quality standards in cities are frequently associated with the need to travel from residential suburban areas to city centres for business, shopping, entertainment and leisure facilities, universities and historical heritage sites. Although most European cities have a well-developed rail network, most commuter traffic is by motor vehicles, which concentrate pollutant emissions as they converge on, or diverge from, the city centre. Recently, the local authorities in the UK have started supporting the creation of new multi-storey residential developments within city centres, which will inevitably lead to the creation of deeper street canyons and a reduction of natural ventilation. The inhabitants of these new residences are likely to be subjected to higher pollutant concentrations, and for longer periods than the commuters, who spend more time in less-polluted suburbs.

Taking into account the growing concerns related to exposure of urban dwellers to air pollution, this chapter aims to:

* define basic outdoor air-quality modelling practices used to identify locations where health-based air-quality standards might be exceeded;
* classify air-quality sampling locations according to characteristics of the urban micro-environment;
* analyse siting considerations for permanent stationary air-quality monitoring stations;

* summarize airflow and air pollution patterns in complex built environments and discuss possible implications for building design;
* highlight the main factors influencing penetration of outdoor air pollutants into buildings;
* highlight the pros and cons associated with using multi-zonal and computational fluid dynamic (CFD) modelling in assessing outdoor–indoor air-quality relationships in urban environments.

Note that this chapter aims to address the fundamental principles related to urban indoor–outdoor air-quality modelling and monitoring. Specific details of ever-changing air-quality standards and regulations can be found elsewhere. The UK National Air Quality Archive is recommended as an excellent source of information.

Urban air-quality management areas

Local authorities in the UK and throughout the European Union (EU) are required by law to review and assess air quality in their areas and to identify locations where health-based air-quality standards are likely to be exceeded. These relatively recent responsibilities have been introduced as a consequence of policy developments during the late 1990s, notably:

* the EU Framework Directive on Ambient Air Quality Assessment and Management (96/32/EC),

which defined the general legislative structure, supplemented by four related daughter directives (1999/30/EC, 2000/69/EC, 2002/3/EC, 2004/107/EC) which define standard air-quality thresholds and prescribe minimum requirements for the assessment of air quality levels in urban areas;

• the 1995 UK Environment Act, which required the development of a National Air Quality Strategy that was published, after consultation, in 1997 (revised in 2000, 2002 and 2007), setting challenging health-based targets for eight main air pollutants and laying the foundations of local air-quality management.

Local air-quality management plays a key practical part in the strategy to achieve air quality objectives in urban areas. Following the first review and assessment of air quality in the UK, almost 130 local authorities have declared air quality management areas (AQMAs) (Woodfield et al, 2006). The designation of an AQMA is a statutory requirement and local authorities are required to identify all areas where the standard air-quality thresholds are likely to be exceeded (see Table 13.1). Note that the objectives defined in the strategy apply at locations outside buildings or other natural or man-made structures, above or below ground and where

members of the public are regularly present and might reasonably be expected to be exposed over the relevant averaging period (Longhurst et al, 2006). The assessment of public exposure to air pollution would ideally follow a cohort of representative individuals throughout their day, integrating exposure to chosen pollutants. This should include exposure within the home and place of work or recreation and during travel, as well as any exposure within an AQMA. Those at work or in shops within an AQMA will be subject to ventilation with outdoor air and the position of the air intake will have a strong influence on its quality. Those passing through the AQMA on foot or in a vehicle will follow a trajectory in space and time with exposure to a highly variable concentration field. Direct monitoring of individuals using exposure meters is a possibility; but this would be costly and impractical. The alternative is to use an exposure model, which predicts pollutant concentrations in space–time and which could be used to calculate exposure for individuals and cohorts. Many of the large local authorities with considerable air-quality problems, such as Glasgow City Council, have adopted this balanced approach, combining air quality monitoring and modelling. It should also be noted that measured concentrations are only available at points in the AQMA, whereas modelled values are available throughout the AQMA.

Table 13.1 *Air quality objectives for protection of human health in England and Wales, 2007*

Pollutant	Concentration	Measured as
Benzene	5.00μg m⁻³	Annual mean
1,3-butadiene	2.25μg m⁻³	Running annual mean
Carbon monoxide	10.0μg m⁻³	Maximum daily running eight-hour mean
Lead	0.25μg m⁻³	Annual mean
Nitrogen dioxide	200μg m⁻³, not to be exceeded more than 18 times a year	One-hour mean
Particles (PM10) (gravimetric)	50μg m⁻³, not to be exceeded more than 35 times a year	24-hour mean
Particles (PM2.5) (gravimetric)*	25μg m⁻³ (target)	Annual mean
Sulphur dioxide	266μg m⁻³, not to be exceeded more than 35 times a year	15-minute mean
Polynuclear aromatic hydrocarbons (PAHs)*	0.25μg m⁻³	Annual mean
Ozone*	100μg m⁻³, not to be exceeded more than 10 times a year	Daily maximum of running eight-hour mean

Note: * not included in regulations at present.

Source: UK National Air Quality Archive

Air pollution modelling practices: Regulatory and research approaches

The most widely used approach to regulatory air quality modelling in urban areas includes the modelling screening tool DMRB and more complex commercially available packages, such as ADMS-Urban, AEOLIUS and OSPM (Woodfield, 2003). All of these models take into account three different factors:

1 the contribution from the pollutant flow from the source to the receptor (a plume model);
2 the recirculation component due to vortex formation within an urban street (a simple box model);
3 the urban background contribution.

Although quite advanced, all of these models use a number of predetermined parameters in relation to the size of the wind vortex within the street, the rate of exchange of pollutants across the boundaries of the recirculation zone and the wind profile above and within the urban canopy. However, all three models ignore the effects of junctions and non-flat roofs, leading to the conclusion that they are incapable of describing the microenvironment in urban street canyons.

In the UK, a Technical Guidance Note, LAQM TG (03) was introduced to provide local authorities with advice on air quality management in built areas; but both computational fluid dynamics and wind tunnel modelling were disregarded as too complex to use, except in very contentious cases. However, this advice is overly pessimistic in our view and throughout this chapter we set out to demonstrate that modelling can be a very useful addition to the monitoring and management of urban air quality. In the highly complex geometry of city centres, the wind flows are characterized by a multitude of recirculation regions, overlapping with complex wake structures. The fluid motion governing the dispersion process is highly turbulent and influenced by meteorological conditions and local scale effects, and these issues could be better addressed using CFD. In the short term, further development of existing advanced Gaussian-based models is worth pursuing. However, in the medium to longer term, there is no doubt that these simpler models will be superseded by CFD models, with their much superior fundamental basis, aided by further developments in computing power.

Air pollution monitoring practices

The current monitoring programmes are usually based on two main systems:

1 a relatively small number of continuous monitors at fixed sites, located away from the roadside, which give instantaneous background values and can identify pollution episodes;
2 a rather larger number of diffusion tube samplers that give a crude average exposure.

However, intensive kerbside research studies have shown that the pollution levels experienced by pedestrians might be two to three times greater than background concentrations and that the pollution climate varies enormously in space and time and with meteorological conditions (Hassan and Crowther, 1998). Therefore, the questions of network design and the location of monitoring stations are very important due to the cost as well as the representativeness of the

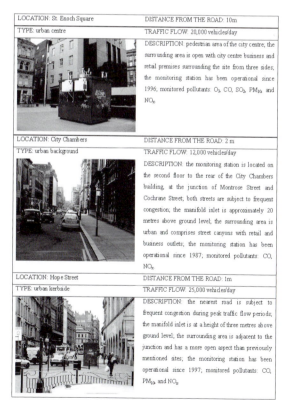

LOCATION: St. Enoch Square	DISTANCE FROM THE ROAD: 10m
TYPE: urban centre	TRAFFIC FLOW: 20,000 vehicles/day
	DESCRIPTION: pedestrian area of the city centre, the surrounding area is open with city centre business and retail premises surrounding the site from three sides; the monitoring station has been operational since 1996; monitored pollutants: O_3, CO, SO_2, PM_{10} and NO_x
LOCATION: City Chambers	DISTANCE FROM THE ROAD: 2 m
TYPE: urban background	TRAFFIC FLOW: 12,000 vehicles/day
	DESCRIPTION: the monitoring station is located on the second floor to the rear of the City Chambers building, at the junction of Montrose Street and Cochrane Street; both streets are subject to frequent congestion; the manifold inlet is approximately 20 metres above ground level; the surrounding area is urban and comprises street canyons with retail and business outlets; the monitoring station has been operational since 1987; monitored pollutants: CO, NO_x
LOCATION: Hope Street	DISTANCE FROM THE ROAD: 1m
TYPE: urban kerbside	TRAFFIC FLOW: 25,000 vehicles/day
	DESCRIPTION: the nearest road is subject to frequent congestion during peak traffic flow periods; the manifold inlet is at a height of three metres above ground level; the surrounding area is adjacent to the junction and has a more open aspect than previously mentioned sites; the monitoring station has been operational since 1997; monitored pollutants: CO, PM_{10} and NO_x

Figure 13.1 *Summary of the main characteristic of permanent air-quality monitoring stations*

chosen location. General guidance for monitoring network design is given by the European Commission, and for an AQMA like Glasgow, three sampling points for continuous measurement are required to assess compliance with limit values for the protection of human health (see Figure 13.1).

In general, the following types of air-quality sampling locations are characteristic of urban microenvironments:

- urban kerbside (sites with sample inlets within 1m of the edge of a busy road and sampling heights between 2m and 3m);
- urban centre (non-kerbside sites located in an area representative of typical population exposure in town or city centre areas – for example, pedestrian precincts and shopping areas – with sampling heights typically between 2m and 3m);
- urban background (urban locations distanced from sources and broadly representative of city-wide background concentrations – for example, elevated locations, parks and urban residential areas).

Taking into account the large size of the designated air quality management area in cities such as Glasgow, an additional monitoring campaign could be carried out using an environmental monitoring trailer (see Figure 13.2). The trailer used by one of the authors of this chapter was equipped, for example, with instruments for the continuous monitoring of carbon monoxide (Gas Filter Correlation CO Analyser, API model 300), oxides of nitrogen (API Model 200A chemi-luminescent $NO/NO_2/NO_x$ analyser) and PM_{10} (TEOM Series 1400a, Rupprecht and Patashnick Co). In addition to air-quality monitoring equipment, the trailer was equipped with an anemometer providing an indication of wind speeds within the street canyons. In these cases, 24-hourly samples are usually collected daily during the four-week period at each of the chosen monitoring sites. The locations should be carefully chosen according to traffic flow data in order to give more detailed information on local pollution-level differences within street canyons in a designated AQMA.

Different siting considerations for permanent air-quality monitoring stations

Taking into account the capital and operating costs of permanent air-quality monitoring stations, it is of paramount importance to determine their best

Figure 13.2 *Mobile air pollution station*

location. The different siting considerations for the permanent air-quality monitoring stations were discussed in two comprehensive monitoring studies carried out in central areas of London and Paris. The first study was carried out at the Bartlett (Croxford and Penn, 1998) and provided an insight into both temporal and spatial variations of carbon monoxide distribution in the Bloomsbury area of central London. The area was largely homogeneous in terms of building height, with most streets having a canyon-type profile with an aspect ratio (height to width) ranging from 0.7 to 1.7. All of the measurement points were at the same height (2m) and as far from any street junction as possible. Radical variations were observed between monitors located at sites within a few metres of one another, prompting a simple protocol on positioning of air-quality monitoring equipment within urban areas. The second study (Vardoulakis et al, 2005) detected the strong spatial and temporal variability of traffic-related air pollution in the vicinity of a permanent monitoring station in central Paris. Diffusive BTX samplers were exposed to ambient air for 28 consecutive seven-day periods, placed at 2.6m intervals at the ten roadside locations (horizontally and vertically). Comparing with additional data from the permanent air-quality monitoring station, it was concluded that the measurements from this site do not give a representative picture of air quality in the surrounding area and are, therefore, inappropriate for population exposure studies.

Using both monitoring and modelling it has been shown (Mumovic et al, 2009) that the dispersion of air pollutants within street canyons is controlled primarily by the micro-meteorological effects of urban geometry. Therefore, when discussing different siting considerations for the permanent air-quality monitoring stations, one should address the issue of local concentration gradients within urban street canyons. Although not a perfect tool, this study has certainly shown that CFD may help to resolve a number of questions related to local concentration gradients in complex built environments. The study concluded with a call for the use of CFD in decisions relating to the positioning of permanent air-quality monitoring stations within urban areas. Where the costs justify the approach advocated, practicality and local turbulence also have to be considered when deciding if a location is suitable for air quality monitoring. By satisfying the

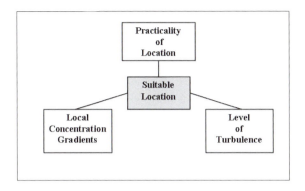

Figure 13.3 *Different factors that have to be included when positioning air-quality monitoring equipment in urban street canyons*

following requirements, one can determine an appropriate location for positioning of air monitoring equipment (see Figure 13.3):

- analysis of local concentration gradients;
- practicality of the location in the real physical domain;
- turbulence intensity at the chosen location.

Siting monitoring equipment in this way will allow a more meaningful comparison between different sites in AQMAs and between modelled and measured concentrations. The adoption of this approach will tend to avoid pollution hot spots, which are often close to areas of high concentration gradient. However, the exposure of individuals moving through an AQMA will be averaged over position and time, yielding a value between urban background and the hot spot values. When comparing the numerical modelling results and field measurements in urban street canyons, it has to be recognized that the controlled approach flow conditions assumed in that study and, to some extent, simplified geometry tend to provide modelled flows with strong wind speed and concentration gradients. However, the wind flow disturbances in a real complex configuration of street canyons, caused by observed large variation of instantaneous wind direction and speed, might have a smoothing effect on the flow irregularities. Therefore, a smaller spatial variability of mean flow, turbulence field and, consequently, of pollutant concentration may be observed if measured within a real urban built environment.

Airflow and concentration patterns in complex built environments

To address this issue, the distribution of air pollutants has been analysed using the developed integrated air-quality model of Glasgow's AQMA (Mumovic et al, 2006). Figure 13.4 illustrates the distribution of carbon monoxide within the designated AQMA in the city centre of Glasgow. The results are obtained at the height of 1.75m, assuming that the prevailing wind is a westerly, blowing at 6m/s. For the purpose of this study, the numerical modelling was done for two prevailing wind directions, and four different wind speeds, as follows:

- wind speed: 2m/s, 5m/s, 6m/s, 11m/s;
- wind direction: westerly and south westerly.

The wind velocity vectors are representative of the meteorological patterns observed in the area. The aspect ratio of street canyons in the computational domain varies from 0.8 to 1.1. Note that the results of the analysis of local concentration gradients have been generalized.

Qualitatively, the results are very similar to those obtained in wind tunnel experiments:

- lower concentration at the windward-facing side of street canyons that are almost perpendicular to the wind direction;

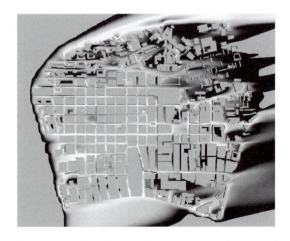

Figure 13.4 *Distribution of carbon monoxide in the air quality management area (Glasgow city centre)*

- higher concentration at the leeward-facing side of street canyons that are almost perpendicular to the wind direction;
- wash-out and accumulation effects along those canyons whose axes are parallel to the wind direction.

In addition, comparison of the distribution of the pollutant for the same wind direction, but different wind speeds (2m/s, 5m/s and 11m/s) shows that considerable differences can be observed in concentration values:

- During low wind periods the convective transport of the pollutant is greatly reduced, causing higher concentration at the very lower levels of street canyons.
- During periods of very high wind speed, the wash-out effect increases significantly, generally lowering the concentration levels within the city centre.

Analysing the flow field patterns, it has been shown that flow within streets is the vector sum of a channelling and recirculation vortex and that a relatively short distance from an intersection the flow seems to be characterized by the main large-scale features – along-street channelling and an across-street recirculation vortex. This is in agreement with comprehensive flow field measurements carried out in the proximity of an urban intersection in London (Dobre et al, 2005). Furthermore, the model observations show that centrally located vortices are not formed when the wind is incident obliquely to the street canyon axis (south-westerly wind) and the wind speed is lower than 6m/s. However, due to elevated kinetic energy, when the wind speed is set to 11 m/s, the expected centrally located vortex has been formed. As in the previous cases, it has been shown that increased levels of pollution occur near the leeward-facing side; but when the wind speed is very low and the wind direction is oblique to the axis, it can be observed that the large local concentration gradients exist only at the bottom of the street canyon. Furthermore, it is observed that for low wind speeds, the change of vertical concentration gradients tends to be very small, preventing the pollutant from dispersing all over the cross-section of street canyon. In contrast to this, the very high wind speed of 11m/s increases the natural ventilation, especially in the case of the oblique

Table 13.2 *Assessment of local concentration gradients*

Wind incident	Local concentration gradients	
	Small	Large/medium
Perpendicular	Upper leeward side	Lower windward side (large)
	Vortex centre	Bottom of the canyon (large)
	Lower leeward side	
Oblique	Upper leeward side	Lower leeward side (medium)
	Vortex centre	Bottom of the canyon (medium)
	Lower windward side	

wind direction. In relatively long canyons without connecting streets, field measurements have shown that maximum street-level concentrations are more likely to occur when the synoptic wind is parallel to the street axis. The summary of the results is given in Table 13.2.

Finally, an analysis of local concentration gradients with street canyons will be described, assuming that the observed cross-sections are located away from crossroads and that the height of buildings on both sides of the analysed canyons is the same. Note that this problem has been thoroughly researched over the last ten years, but never before using a realistic CFD model of an actual AQMA. A number of street canyons have been analysed and a typical distribution of carbon monoxide within a canyon is shown in Figure 13.5.

Figure 13.5 *A typical distribution of carbon monoxide within Glasgow's street canyons for perpendicular wind incidents*

It seems that very steep concentration gradients exist at the leeward lower corner of the street canyon. Consequently, small differences in monitoring station positioning may yield significant variations of measured mean concentration due to large values of horizontal, $\partial C/\partial x$, and vertical, $\partial C/\partial y$, local concentration gradients. These results have significant implications for positioning monitoring equipment, not just in street canyons, but probably in wind tunnel experiments as well. Generally speaking, it suggests that monitoring stations should not be positioned at the lower leeward-facing side of a street canyon. By contrast, one can observe relatively smooth concentration gradients at the windward-facing side, at the upper leeward side of the street canyon, and possibly in the central part of a vertical cross-section of the street canyon. These figures clearly show the formation of three regions of relatively smooth concentration gradients, as was observed in the previous sections:

- in the vicinity of the vortex centre;
- in the lower corner of the windward-facing wall;
- in the upper part of the leeward-facing wall.

The effect of crossroads on horizontal local concentration gradients is shown in Figure 13.6. Note that the source of pollution was placed at the leeward side of the studied street canyon. This was done in order to compare the modelling results with available experimental results (Crowther and Mumovic, 2003). However, the formation of the vortices and, consequently, the prediction of pollutant concentrations in street canyons are subject to considerable uncertainty. It has to be stressed that the mentioned local wind field within the canyon is unlikely to occur if the wind direction changes rapidly in time. Note that the developed integrated air-quality model does not take into account differential across-road traffic count.

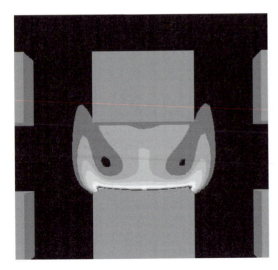

Figure 13.6 *Examining the effect of crossroads: The source was placed at the leeward side of the studied street canyon*

Relationships between outdoor and indoor air pollution

In the absence of indoor sources, indoor air pollutant concentrations are generally lower than outdoors due to attenuation by the building. However, in the presence of indoor sources, indoor concentrations may well exceed the local outdoor levels. People who live and work close to busy streets in urban areas may experience a large part of their total exposure to air pollution while indoors. As such, it is vitally important that this contribution to overall exposure is properly understood. Unfortunately, most research on urban air pollution has focused only on outdoor air, with far less work considering exposure in the indoor environment.

Penetration of pollutants into urban buildings

In urban areas, a significant proportion of indoor air pollution can be due to penetration through the building façade of pollutants generated outdoors. Pollutant levels within a building, resulting from outdoor sources, depend upon:

- complex dispersion processes around the building (as discussed earlier in this chapter);

- the ventilation strategy of the building (i.e. natural or mechanical);
- the locations of air intakes (for mechanically ventilated buildings);
- the airtightness of the building (affecting the rate of infiltration);
- the specific pollutant and its physical and chemical properties.

Other environmental parameters, such as the local meteorology, also play important roles in influencing indoor pollution concentrations in indirect ways. Once indoors, the concentration may be decreased by indoor chemical reactions, by deposition onto indoor surfaces and through ventilation back to the outdoors (see Figure 13.7). Although indoor sources (especially cooking and smoking activity) should be taken into account, these are out of the scope of this chapter.

A key distinction is between long-range and short-range sources of air pollution. For far-off releases (say, more than 500m away), the concentration in the envelope surrounding the building may be assumed to be relatively constant due to vertical and lateral spreading of the plume. However, for closer releases (less than 500m), the outdoor concentration close to the building may not be assumed to be constant. For such sources, concentrations are usually high at short ranges and vary considerably over the surface of the building, fluctuating over time periods as short as seconds.

Peak penetration of pollutants into buildings occurs at points of both high pressure and high contaminant concentration, the patterns of both of which can become extremely complex in urban areas due to the close proximity and configuration of surrounding

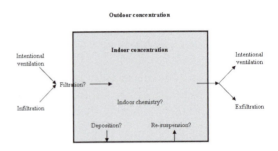

Figure 13.7 *Factors determining indoor air pollution concentrations*

buildings (Kukadia et al, 1999). It is, thus, also true that internal concentrations in an urban building close to busy roads can be highly spatially and temporally variable. Both indoor and outdoor concentrations measured at single fixed locations may not be sufficiently representative of the overall distribution of concentrations and the actual exposure experienced by the occupants of the building (Milner et al, 2006b).

Simultaneous indoor and outdoor measurements

The relationship between the indoor (I) and outdoor (O) air pollution level for a building at a given time is usually expressed in terms of the I/O ratio. The I/O ratio gives an indication of the protective effect of a building for a given pollutant. However, I/O ratios are affected by many factors, such as ventilation rates and the local meteorology. In fact, I/O ratios have been shown to vary greatly, even for an individual building.

Since monitoring work can be technically difficult and expensive, it is often not practical to sample in multiple locations. For single or relatively few sampling locations, it is therefore important to give careful consideration to the siting of equipment. The aim is to find a location that is as representative of the exposure of building occupants as possible. Depending upon the situation, this is likely to be in the centre of the room, at head height of a seated adult and away from internal pollution sources (unless the source is of particular interest). In reality, it is often necessary to compromise when choosing a suitable location.

Ideally, multiple measurement locations will give a clearer picture. An example of this is provided by Milner et al (2006a), who monitored carbon monoxide (CO) concentrations in different locations within an office building in central London and at an external location close to the building. The building was flanked by two heavily trafficked streets and two quiet streets. In general, the data suggested that:

- Indoor CO concentrations were greater on the lower floors of the building (see Figure 13.8).
- Indoor CO concentrations on the same floors were greater closer to the busier roads.
- Correlation between the outdoor and indoor data decreased within the building with distance from the outdoor site and was found to improve with the introduction of a time lag.

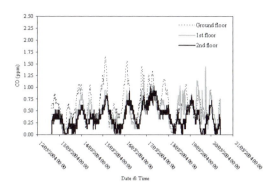

Figure 13.8 *Fifteen-minute average carbon monoxide concentrations on different floors of an office building in central London*

These findings imply that the protection offered by the building shell may be increased further away from the busiest roads. For this particular building, the highest I/O ratios were observed for north-westerly winds, although the highest internal and external concentrations were for south-easterly winds. This suggests that a higher rate of penetration of low ambient concentrations occurred during north-westerly winds and demonstrates how complex the situation may be in an urban setting.

Differences in I/O ratios for a particular building will also occur depending upon the type of pollutant. The I/O ratios of three of the most common indoor pollutants resulting for outdoor sources will now be discussed in more detail: particulate matter (PM_{10} and $PM_{2.5}$), nitrogen dioxide (NO_2) and carbon monoxide (CO). Recently, these pollutants (among others) were considered for guideline limits in indoor air by the UK Department of Health (COMEAP, 2004). However, the committee decided it was not currently feasible to define a satisfactory guideline for indoor particle concentrations. The guidelines for NO_2 and CO are shown in Table 13.3.

Particulate matter

The results of a US Environmental Protection Agency project, the Particle Total Exposure Assessment Methodology Study (PTEAM) (e.g. Özkaynak et al, 1996), suggest that transport from outdoors to indoors is the primary source of particles in the indoor environment. In general, most studies find that, under normal ventilation conditions and in the absence of

Table 13.3 *COMEAP recommended indoor air quality guidelines for NO$_2$ and CO*

Pollutant	Averaging period				
	Annual	8 hour	1 hour	30 minutes	15 minutes
NO$_2$	20ppb (40µg/m³)		150ppb (300µg/m³)		
CO		90ppm (100mg/m³)	50ppm (60mg/m³)	25ppm (30mg/m³)	90ppm (100mg/m³)

indoor sources, indoor particle concentrations closely follow the concentrations outdoors, with indoor levels lower than outdoors. However, great variations in I/O ratios for particulate matter are reported in the literature. For particles, predicting indoor levels based on observed outdoor concentrations is complicated by the sizes of the particles since the penetration and deposition rates of smaller and larger particles will vary.

Nitrogen dioxide

Indoor NO$_2$ is more greatly influenced by indoor sources than either CO or particulate matter. Sources of NO$_2$, such as gas cookers, lead to considerably raised indoors levels, as well as to increased variation in these levels. However, when no internal sources are present, indoor NO$_2$ is usually below ambient levels due to chemical reactions and deposition on internal surfaces. Due to the importance of internal sources on indoor levels, contributions from outdoor sources will clearly be relatively less important for NO$_2$.

Carbon monoxide

As a non-reactive pollutant, of which more than 85 per cent in the atmosphere is traffic related, indoor CO concentrations have been shown to follow outdoor levels closely, especially near busy roads (see, for instance, Chaloulakou et al, 2003). Theoretically, pollutants that are non-reactive with little or no filtration and negligible deposition, such as CO, should have an I/O ratio close to 1 in the absence of indoor sources. The only occasion in which indoor concentrations of CO may become higher than outdoors is following a concentration peak since the indoor gas is enclosed and, hence, has a longer residence time. However, indoor sources (such as faulty gas appliances) can lead to potentially dangerous levels of CO in buildings.

Modelling air pollution in urban buildings

Both monitoring work and physical (wind tunnel) modelling may be difficult, costly and time consuming. Furthermore, the results may only be valid for the specific conditions in which the experiment was carried out. Therefore, monitoring studies report a wide range of indoor concentrations and I/O ratios due to the complexity of indoor–outdoor transport, indoor sources and the wide range of variable parameters that may have an effect.

As such, there are two modelling techniques that are commonly used for predicting indoor air pollution concentrations from outdoor sources: mass balance modelling and CFD modelling. The former is relatively simple to apply, but has the important disadvantage that it assumes spatially uniform external and internal concentrations, while the latter is highly complex and is used primarily as a research tool.

Mass balance models

Mass balance models, which may be subdivided into micro-environmental models and more complex multi-zone models, are used to simulate average indoor air pollutant concentrations as a function of outdoor concentrations, building and pollutant characteristics, and indoor sources. These models consider transport of air pollutants between outdoors and indoors, as well as between indoor compartments, which are assumed to be instantaneously well mixed. They are widely used due to the simplicity of the mathematics involved. The concentration within a compartment at steady state C is usually written as an ordinary differential equation, such as:

$$\frac{dC}{dt} = S - LC \qquad (1)$$

where S is the sum of all sources and L is the sum of all sinks in the compartment.

Equation 1 may include further parameters, such as a deposition loss rate (if the pollutant readily deposits), a filtration factor (to account for losses in the building shell) or a mixing factor (to approximate the proportion of the indoor space that is well mixed). For an example of mass balance modelling, see Dimitroulopoulou et al (2006), who describe the application of the INDAIR model to studying indoor air pollution in UK homes.

The main strength of these models is the simulation of air pollutant concentrations that may be compared with results from experimental measurements. Mass balance models can be used to identify the key building factors that influence indoor concentrations of air pollutants and to estimate the relative importance of different pollutant sources. In this way, mass balance models, in conjunction with exposure models, can relatively quickly evaluate the potential benefits of measures to reduce indoor air pollutant levels and the implications of policy decisions on population exposure.

Mass balance models also have some significant limitations, the most important of which are the assumption of a spatially uniform concentration outside the building and the internal well-mixed assumption. As discussed previously, the concentration in the envelope surrounding an urban building may be extremely variable, especially due to sources close to the building. Using a single value to represent the outdoor concentration at a given time may lead to serious inaccuracies in the results produced. The use of internal well-mixed zones is only generally appropriate for average-sized residential buildings since intra-room mixing is usually orders of magnitude faster than inter-room exchange and physical walls act as partitions. However, in very large rooms with localized ventilation and/or many internal source locations, a significant spatial concentration gradient may persist and a single well-mixed compartment may be inappropriate to represent the room.

CFD models

CFD modelling takes a microscopic view by simulating the detailed airflows and concentration distributions within a room or between rooms. Although these

techniques have been used in this context since the 1970s (e.g. Nielsen, 1973), most whole-building analysis currently relies on multi-zone mass balance modelling. Despite this, the rapid development of computational speed and power over recent years has led to growing popularity of CFD methods.

CFD models have been applied extensively to simulate pollutant dispersion in urban areas and in indoor spaces. Given the highly variable nature of urban air pollution, in order to accurately model indoor air pollution due to external sources it is important, first, to model the external concentration pattern. As discussed earlier in this chapter, CFD is well suited for this, while operational street canyon models such as those described earlier have considerable limitations (e.g. see Vardoulakis et al, 2007) and cannot sufficiently account for variability in external air pollution close to buildings.

Source: adapted from Milner et al (2005)

Figure 13.9 *Example visualizations of combined indoor and outdoor CFD modelling: Shown are flow vectors (top), pressure distribution (middle) and plan view of constant pollution concentration 'iso-surface' (bottom)*

However, most CFD studies of indoor airflow and pollutant transport concentrate only on the indoor environment and not on the transport of pollutants from outdoors to indoors. Much further research is needed in the area of combining indoor and outdoor CFD modelling (see Figure 13.9). Combined indoor and outdoor CFD modelling has rarely been performed and only then for natural ventilation modelling rather than contaminant transport. In one of the few published examples, Jiang et al (2003) compared CFD simulations with wind tunnel data for three ventilation strategies and found that the numerical results were in good agreement with the experimental data.

In contrast to mass balance models, CFD simulations are highly specific and complex to use, requiring powerful computers and lengthy run times. As such, the method is currently used primarily as a research tool. Although the complexity of CFD models can be problematic, the technique allows the model user control of far more parameters and variables, as well as providing a quantitative description of the situation that the user may visualize. As computational power increases, CFD has the potential to become a viable alternative to wind tunnel methods for modelling both outdoor and indoor air pollution.

References

Chaloulakou, A., Mavroidis, I. and Duci, A. (2003) 'Indoor and outdoor carbon monoxide concentration relationships at different microenvironments in the Athens area', *Chemosphere*, vol 52, pp1007–1019

COMEAP (Committee On the Medical Effects of Air Pollution Report) (2004) *Guidance on the Effects on Health of Indoor Air*, COMEAP, UK Department of Health, HMSO, London, UK

Crowther, J. M. and Mumovic, D. (2003) '3-dimensional numerical modelling of dispersion of air pollutants in a complex configuration of street canyons'. Fourth International Conference on Urban Air Quality: Measurements, Modelling and Management, Charles University, Prague, March

Croxford, B. and Penn, A. (1998) 'Siting considerations for urban pollution monitors', *Atmospheric Environment*, vol 32, no 6, pp1049–1057

Dimitroulopoulou, C., Ashmore, M. R., Hill, M. T. R., Byrne, M. A. and Kinnersley, R. (2006) 'INDAIR: A probabilistic model of indoor air pollution in UK homes', *Atmospheric Environment*, vol 40, pp6362–6379

Dobre, A., Arnold, S. J., Smalley, R. J., Boddy, J. W. D., Barlow, J. F., Tomlin, A. S. and Belcher, S. E. (2005) 'Flow field measurements in the proximity of an urban intersection in London, UK', *Atmospheric Environment*, vol 39, pp4647–4657

Hassan, A. A. and Crowther, J. M. (1998) 'Modelling of fluid flow and pollutant dispersion in a street canyon', *Environmental Monitoring and Assessment*, vol 52, pp281–297

Jiang, Y., Alexander, D., Jenkins, H., Arthur, R. and Chen, Q. (2003) 'Natural ventilation in buildings: Measurement in a wind tunnel and numerical simulation with large-eddy simulation', *Journal of Wind Engineering and Industrial Aerodynamics*, vol 91, pp331–353

Kukadia, V., Hall, D. J. and Sharples, H. (1999) *Ventilation of Urban Buildings in Relation to External Pollution: A Review*, Building Research Establishment (BRE) Report CR 524/99, CRC Ltd., London, UK

Longhurst, J. W. S., Beattie, C. I., Chatterton, T. J., Hayes, E. T., Leksmono, N. S. and Woodfield, N. K. (2006) 'Local air quality management as a risk management process: Assessing, managing and remediating the risk of exceeding an air quality objective in Great Britain', *Environment International*, vol 32, pp934–947

Milner, J. T., ApSimon, H. M., Pain and C. C. (2005) 'Modelling the transport of air pollutants into buildings in urban areas', in *Proceedings of the 5th International Conference on Urban Air Quality*, Valencia, Spain, 29–31 March 2005

Milner, J. T., ApSimon, H. M. and Croxford, B. (2006a) 'Spatial variation of CO in an office building and outdoor influences', *Atmospheric Environment*, vol 40, pp6338–6348

Milner, J. T., Dimitroulopoulou, C. and ApSimon, H. M. (2006b) 'Indoor concentrations in buildings from sources outdoors', *Atmospheric Dispersion Modelling Liaison Committee Annual Report 2004-2005*, ADMLC/2004/02 (Annex B)

Mumovic, D., Crowther, J. and Stevanovic, Z. (2006) 'Integrated air quality modelling for a designated air quality management area in Glasgow', *Building and Environment*, vol 41, issue 12, pp1703–1712

Mumovic, D., Crowther, J. and Stevanovic, Z. (2009) 'Analysis of local concentration gradients in complex built environment: Implications for air quality management areas', *The International Journal of Environment and Waste Management*, vol 3, no 2

Nielsen, P. V. (1973) 'Berechung der luftbewegung in einem zwangsbelufteten raum', *Gesundheitsingenieur*, vol 94, p299

Özkaynak, H., Xue, J., Spengler, J. D., Wallace, L. A., Pellizzari, E. D. and Jenkins, P. (1996) 'Personal exposure to airborne particles and metals: Results from a particle

TEAM study in Riverside, CA', *Journal of Exposure Analysis and Environmental Epidemiology*, vol 6, pp57–78

Vardoulakis, S., Gonzales-Flesca, N., Fisher, B. and Pericleous, K. (2005) 'Spatial variability of air pollution in the vicinity of a permanent monitoring station in central Paris', *Atmospheric Environment*, vol 39, pp2725–2736

Vardoulakis, S., Valiantis, M., Milner, J. and ApSimon, H. (2007) 'Operational air pollution modelling in the UK: Street canyon applications and challenges', *Atmospheric Environment*, vol 41, pp4622–4637

Woodfield, N. K., Longhurst, J. W. S., Beattie, C. I. and Laxen, D. P. H. (2003) 'Critical evaluation of the role of scientific analysis in UK local authority AQMA decision making: Method development and preliminary results', *The Science of Total Environment*, vol 311, pp1–18

Woodfield, N. K., Longhurst, J. W. S., Beattie, C. I., Chatterton, T. and Laxen, D. P. H. (2006) 'Regional collaborative urban air quality management: Case studies across Great Britain', *Environmental Modelling and Software*, vol 21, pp595–599

14

Ventilation, Thermal Comfort, Health and Productivity

Pawel Wargocki

Introduction

Indoor environmental quality (IEQ) plays an important role for human health, comfort and performance. One of the main reasons is that humans in developed parts of the world spend 85 to 95 per cent of their time indoors (at home, at work, at school or when commuting). Indoor environmental issues received much attention in the mid-19th century and a renaissance of indoor environmental sciences was observed after the energy crisis during the 1970s when the tightening of buildings, use of new building materials and dramatic reductions of energy use resulted in numerous complaints from occupants of indoor spaces. A similar situation is likely to occur in the 2000s as the issue of climate change is reflected in the trend to, again, reduce energy used to create indoor environments, since it constitutes 30 to 40 per cent of the total energy use in buildings. To overcome this threat, emphasis is placed on maintaining IEQ as high as possible when energy reductions have been implemented (EPBD, 2002). This chapter will describe how IEQ can affect humans, without discussing the energy consequences of creating high-quality indoor environments. Emphasis will be placed on the thermal environment and air quality and their effects on health, comfort and performance. Although light and noise are also important constituents of IEQ, they will not be discussed here. Health is understood very broadly, reflecting the basic definition of the World Health Organization (WHO, 1948), which states that health is a state of complete physical, mental and social well-being and not merely absence of disease or infirmity. Comfort expresses satisfaction with the environment. Performance is related to the ability of an individual to perform different mentally and physically demanding tasks. Often the term productivity is used instead of performance; however, it is a wider economic term, including a volume measure of output (e.g. performance of several individuals) in relation to input (e.g. the costs relating to the work of these individuals). Health, comfort and performance (productivity) can be influenced by physiological, behavioural and psychological factors, while performance (productivity) can also be influenced by personal, social and organizational variables. The impact of these factors is not discussed in this chapter, which deals solely with the effects of IEQ.

Thermal environment

Thermal comfort

The most important variables that affect thermal comfort are air temperature, mean radiant temperature, relative air velocity, water vapour pressure in ambient air, activity level (heat production in the body) and the thermal resistance of the clothing (clo-value). These six variables are included in the comfort model developed by Fanger (1970) based on extensive American and European experiments involving over 1000 subjects exposed to well-controlled environments. The premise of the comfort model is that the body must be in thermal balance so that the rate of heat loss to the environment is equal to the rate of heat production in the body; that the mean skin temperature should be at the appropriate level of comfort; and that there is a preferred rate of sweating related to metabolic rate. Based on the model and its assumptions, two thermal comfort indices were created to describe the effects of the thermal environment on humans, the predicted mean vote (PMV), which predicts the mean vote of a large group of individuals on the seven-point scale (see Figure 14.1), and the predicted percentage of dissatisfied (PPD), providing the percentage of persons dissatisfied with the thermal environment. The relation between PMV and PPD is illustrated in Figure 14.2

and forms the basis of many international standards (e.g. ISO Standard 7730, 1994).

The PMV model predicts well the thermal response when the individual is not experiencing unwanted heating or cooling of a particular part of the body. This issue should be considered separately; therefore, parameters describing local thermal discomfort have been introduced. They include draught risk, asymmetric thermal radiation, vertical air temperature difference and contact with warm or cold floors. Draught is an unwanted local cooling of the body caused by air movement. Dissatisfaction due to draught is caused by air velocity and turbulence intensity; thus, cooling is caused not only by air velocity, but also by fluctuation in the air stream. For people in thermal neutrality, the draught risk model was developed predicting the percentage of individuals dissatisfied due to draught (Fanger et al, 1988). An example of the practical application of the model is shown in Figure 14.3, indicating the combination of air temperature, turbulence intensity and air velocity that will cause

3 — Hot	CLEARLY ACCEPTABLE ⌐ 1
2 — Warm	
1 — Slightly warm	
0 — Neutral	JUST ACCEPTABLE ⌐ 0
	JUST NOT ACCEPTABLE ⌐ 0
-1 — Slightly cool	
-2 — Cool	
-3 — Cold	CLEARLY NOT ACCEPTABLE ⌐ -1

Source: Fanger (1970): thermal comfort; Gunnarsen and Fanger (1992) and Clausen (2000): continuous acceptability scale

Figure 14.1 *The seven-point scale for thermal comfort and the continuous acceptability scale*

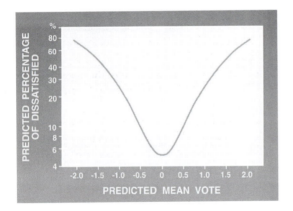

Source: Fanger (1970)

Figure 14.2 *Predicted percentage dissatisfied (PPD) as a function of the predicted mean vote (PMV)*

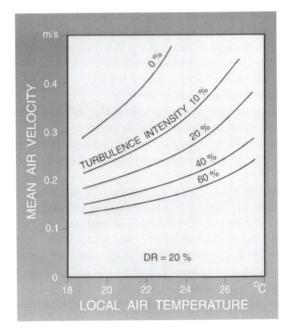

Source: ISO Standard 7730 (1994)

Figure 14.3 *The combination of air temperature, turbulence intensity and air velocity causing 20 per cent of people to be dissatisfied with draught*

20 per cent of people to be dissatisfied with draught. The model is used in international standards (e.g. ISO Standard 7730, 1994).

Asymmetric thermal radiation can be caused by cold/hot surfaces such as windows, exterior walls, ceilings, etc. It is defined as the difference between the plane radiant temperatures of the two opposite sides of small plane elements. Based on the work reported by Olesen (1985), the limits for radiant asymmetry were established. Environments are expected to cause less than 5 per cent dissatisfied people due to asymmetric radiation if the difference between the plane radiant temperature is below 10K for vertical surfaces and below 5K for heated ceilings (ISO Standard 7730, 1994). Stratification of indoor air can result in vertical temperature gradients that can contribute to local thermal discomfort. The work by Olesen et al (1979) indicates that the percentage dissatisfied with the vertical temperature difference will be below 5 per cent if the temperature difference between ankles (0.1m above the floor) and the head (1.1m above the floor for a seated person) is below 3K. Floor temperature can also result in local thermal discomfort, especially in winter, causing cold feet. The general requirement is that floor temperatures should be between 19°C and 26°C for light, mainly sedentary, activity in winter and a floor heating system design temperature of 29°C.

While the PMV model predicts thermal sensation well in buildings with heating, ventilating and air-conditioning (HVAC) systems, field studies in warm climates in buildings without air conditioning have shown that it predicts a warmer thermal sensation than the occupants actually feel (Brager and de Dear, 1998). The reason for this discrepancy could be that thermal perception is affected not only by heat balance of the body, but also by other factors such as behavioural adjustments and physiological and psychological adaptation. Since the PMV model was developed on the basis of studies in climate chambers, these influences could have been overlooked. The impact of these other factors on thermal response form the premise of the adaptive model of thermal comfort, which relates the neutral temperature indoors (temperature at which people are thermally neutral according to the seven-point scale; see Figure 14.1) to the monthly average temperature outdoors (de Dear and Brager, 2001). Figure 14.4 shows the application of the model suggested by EN 15251 (2006). The basic

assumption of this model is that building occupants are not passive recipients of the thermal environment, but play an active role in creating their thermal environment by behavioural adjustments, such as adjusting clothing, opening windows or rescheduling activities. Furthermore, their thermal responses are modified by acclimatization, habituation and expectation. Fanger and Toftum (2002) proposed an extension to the PMV model including an expectancy factor (e) that should be multiplied by the PMV. The expectancy factor depends upon whether the non-air-conditioned building is located in regions where air conditioning is common (e = 0.9–1.0) or where there are few air-conditioned buildings (e = 0.5–0.7). With this adjustment, the PMV seems to provide a reasonable estimation of thermal comfort in non-air-conditioned buildings.

The existing thermal comfort models refer to steady-state conditions. There have been numerous efforts to describe transient effects of thermal sensation and comfort (e.g. de Dear et al, 1989, 1993; Goto et al, 2003, 2006); but there is a need for further data on this issue. For example, Goto et al (2003) investigated transient effects on the human thermal response of clothing adjustments, the most common behavioural thermoregulatory action. They showed that, independently of the activity level, the thermal sensation votes respond immediately (within 5 minutes) after up-step or down-step of the adjustments of clothing insulation. The effect of metabolic step changes on thermal sensation was investigated by Goto et al (2006). They suggested weighting factors to estimate a representative average metabolic rate with varying activity levels using steady-state comfort models: 65 per cent to weight the activity during the most recent 5 minutes; 25 per cent during the prior 10 to 5 minutes; and 10 per cent during the prior 20 to 10 minutes.

Thermal conditions also affect the perception of air quality, as discussed later in this chapter.

Thermal environment and health

Thermal conditions affect health. This is best illustrated by the rates of mortality in nursing homes (Marmor, 1978) and ordinary households (Rogot et al, 1992) during hot weather. When thermal conditions are less extreme, elevated temperatures have been associated

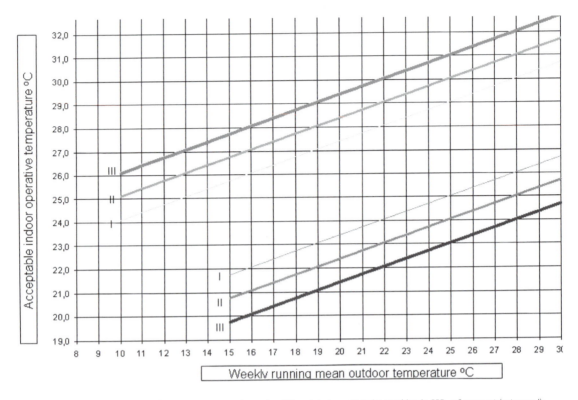

Note: Upper and lower limits of the operative temperature are shown for different design categories resulting in PPD < 6 per cent (category I); PPD < 10 per cent (category II); and PPD < 15 per cent (category III).

Source: adapted from EN 15251 (2006)

Figure 14.4 *Indoor operative temperature as a function of the outdoor temperature*

with increased prevalence of symptoms typical of sick building syndrome (SBS), non-specific building-related symptoms of headache, chest tightness, difficulty in breathing, fatigue, and irritation of eyes and mucous membranes, which are alleviated when the individual leaves the building (WHO, 1983). The survey by Burge et al (1990) in six office buildings showed that the occupants in buildings with lower dry bulb air temperature experienced fewer SBS symptoms. An intervention study by Burt (1996) showed that reducing the temperature from 22°C to 20.4°C reduced SBS symptoms. High air temperatures were found to be a risk factor for work-related general symptoms (headaches and difficulty in concentration) in 14 office buildings studied by Skov et al (1990). In an intervention study by Krogstad et al (1991) virtually all

SBS symptoms increased with temperature from a minimum of 20°C to 21°C, up to 24°C among office workers performing computerized work; the prevalence of headaches and fatigue increased from 10 to 60 per cent and effects of similar magnitude were observed for other symptoms. These field data are supported by experiments in chambers. Fang et al (2004) observed that the intensity of headaches and difficulty in thinking clearly increased when thermal conditions were increased from 20°C/40 per cent relative humidity (RH) to 26°C/60 per cent RH. Similarly, Willem (2006) observed that a temperature of 26°C tended to elevate neuro-behavioural symptoms among subjects in tropical regions compared to 20°C. These studies indicate that it is beneficial to keep the temperatures in buildings at the lower level of thermal comfort.

Thermal environment and performance

Thermal conditions can affect the performance of work through several mechanisms (Wyon and Wargocki, 2006a):

- thermal discomfort distracts attention and generates complaints that increase maintenance costs;
- warmth lowers arousal (the state of activation of an individual) (Willem, 2006), exacerbates SBS symptoms and has a negative effect on mental work;
- cold conditions lower finger temperatures and thus have a negative effect on manual dexterity;
- rapid temperature swings have the same effects on office work as slightly raised room temperatures, while slow temperature swings merely cause discomfort; and
- vertical thermal gradients reduce perceived air quality or lead to a reduction in room temperature that then causes complaints of cold at floor level.

The evidence obtained so far shows that thermal conditions within the thermal comfort zone can reduce performance by 5 to 15 per cent (Wyon, 1996). Based on the results from 24 studies investigating the effects of temperature on performance of office work,

Seppänen et al (2006a) created the relationship between temperature and work performance (see Figure 14.5), suggesting a reduction of performance by about 1 per cent for every 1°C change.

The data points presented in Figure 14.5 were obtained mainly in laboratory experiments with human subjects; however, three recent studies in buildings with normal office employees provide quantitative estimates similar to the magnitude of effects observed in the laboratory. Niemelä et al (2002) showed that the operator performance was better (average talk time was 5 to 7 per cent lower) when temperatures remained below 25°C in a telecommunication call centre. Federspiel et al (2002) showed that qualified nurses providing medical advice in a call centre worked 16 per cent more slowly when writing up their reports after the call was over when temperatures were above 25.4° C. Tham et al (2003) showed that the average talk time of the call-centre operators in the tropics was reduced by 4.9 per cent (performance improved) when the air temperature was decreased by 2°C from 24.5°C. Moderately elevated temperatures also affect the performance of schoolwork by 10- to 12-year-old children. Reducing the temperature by 1°C in the range from 24°C to 25° C to 20°C would improve the performance of language-based and numerical tasks typical of schoolwork by 2 to 4 per cent (Wargocki and Wyon, 2006). It should be noted that the data

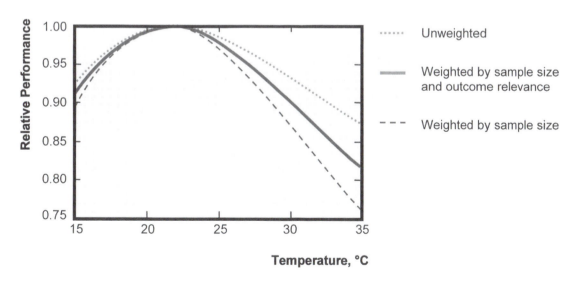

Source: adapted from REHVA (2006)

Figure 14.5 *Relative performance as a function of temperature*

presented in Figure 14.5 does not include the results from studies in which people were asked to judge themselves whether the thermal conditions affect their work (so-called self-estimated performance). The studies of Preller et al (1990) and Raw et al (1990) in office buildings indicate that self-estimated performance is higher when individuals can control their own thermal climate.

An attempt to relate thermal discomfort to performance was made by Roelofsen (2001), who correlated Fanger's PMV model (Fanger, 1970) with Gagge's two-layer model (Gagge et al, 1986). No verification of the model has been obtained so far; but studies in which subjects were clothed for comfort under different thermal conditions indicate no effect on performance (Wyon et al, 1975; Fang et al, 2004).

Indoor air quality

The quality of indoor air can be defined as the level of the contaminants/pollutants in indoor air. These pollutants comprise organic species such as volatile organic compounds; inorganic species such as particles, fibres and allergens; radioactive gases such as radon; or species of microbiological origin such as moulds or fungi. The contaminants can originate from outdoor sources (e.g. urban traffic and combustion) or from indoor sources (e.g. people, their activities, tobacco smoke, building and furnishing materials, as well as electronic equipment, cleaning products or HVAC systems). The criteria for acceptable levels of these pollutants can be set based on the effects on health and performance as well as sensory effects on humans. To mitigate the air quality problems, the following methods are usually applied: filtration, air cleaning, avoidance/reduction of sources of pollution, or ventilation. Often, indoor air quality is closely associated with ventilation, considering that ventilation is the process of exchanging indoor (polluted) air with outdoor (presumably fresh and clean) air. Thus, ventilation is considered as a surrogate or proxy of the indoor air quality, and many studies have expressed the effects of indoor air quality on health, comfort and performance in relation to ventilation. The use of proxies for indoor air quality is necessitated by the fact that indoor climates are multi-factorial environments, and often it is not known which of the pollutants indoors are responsible for the effects observed.

Perceived air quality

The quality of the air indoors may be expressed as the extent to which human requirements are met. There are, however, substantial differences between the requirements of individuals. Some people are rather sensitive to an environmental parameter and are difficult to satisfy, whereas others are less sensitive and are easier to please. To cope with these individual differences, environmental quality can be expressed by the percentage of people who find an environmental parameter unacceptable (= percentage dissatisfied). If there are few dissatisfied, the quality of the environment is high. If there are many dissatisfied, the quality is low. Prediction of the percentage dissatisfied is used to establish ventilation requirements for reaching a certain level of air quality. This approach is illustrated in Figure 14.6, showing the relationship between ventilation rate per standard person and the percentage dissatisfied with air quality. Three different categories of indoor air quality are presented causing 15, 20 and 30 per cent dissatisfied (CEN, 1998). The relationship presented in Figure 14.6 is used by many ventilation standards and is based on the experiments in which human subjects assessed the air quality immediately upon entering the rooms polluted mainly by the emissions from humans (bio-effluents) (Fanger and Berg-Munch, 1983; Berg-Munch et al, 1986). These studies were carried out in Europe; but similar experiments in Japan (Iwashita et al, 1990) and in the US (Cain et al, 1983) showed very similar results.

The percentage of persons dissatisfied with air quality cannot yet be measured directly with an instrument, although there are attempts to create such instruments (Wenger et al, 1993; Müller at al, 2007). Panels of subjects judging air quality are the only feasible way at present. The subjects render a judgement of indoor air quality immediately upon exposure (within 15 seconds, unadapted vote) independently of other observers. Usually an untrained panel of at least 20 impartial subjects is used. The subjects judge whether the air quality is acceptable or not (ASHRAE Standard 62, 2007) generally using a continuous acceptability scale (Gunnarsen and Fanger, 1992; Clausen, 2000); based on the assessments, the percentage dissatisfied with the air quality is estimated. A panel of 10 to 15 trained judges is sometimes used (Bluyssen et al, 1989) judging the degree of annoyance

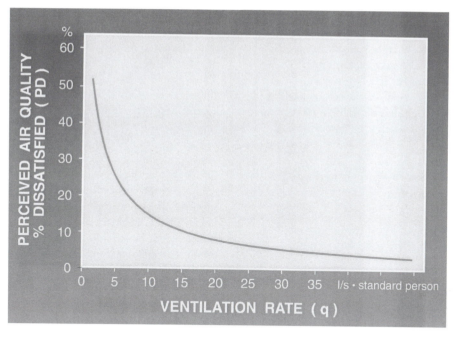

Source: Fanger (1988)

Figure 14.6 *Percentage dissatisfied with air quality as a function of ventilation rate per standard person*

with the air quality due to perceived odour and irritation, compared to well-defined reference exposures of 2 propanone.

The assessment of indoor air quality is influenced by stimulation of the olfactory sense (sensitive to >0.5 million odorants) and the general chemical sense (sensitive to >100,000 irritants). Studies by Berglund and Cain (1989), Fang et al (1998a, 1998b) and Toftum et al (1998) show that the perception of air quality is also influenced by the humidity and temperature of the inhaled air even when the chemical composition of the air is constant and the thermal sensation for the entire body is kept neutral. Keeping the air dry and cool reduces the percentage dissatisfied with the air quality (Figure 14.7) and causes the air to be perceived as fresh and pleasant. This effect is probably due to stimulation of the thermal sense as a result of convective and evaporative cooling of the

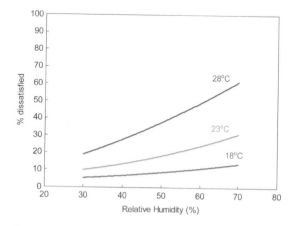

Source: Fang et al (1998b)

Figure 14.7 *Percentage dissatisfied with air quality as a function of temperature and relative humidity of inhaled air*

respiratory tract if only the temperature is different from the mucosal temperature, which is approximately 30°C to 32°C.

It should be noted that some harmful pollutants are not sensed by humans at all (e.g. radon or carbon monoxide, which have negative effects on health). This means that any health risk should be considered separately from the sensory effects. Although some harmful pollutants cannot be sensed, the sensory effects may in many cases also provide a first indication of a possible health risk since human senses have an important warning function against danger in the environment.

Indoor air quality and health

Health effects of indoor air quality include allergies, irritation of mucous membranes, SBS symptoms, toxic reactions, infections, inflammation, cancer and mutagenic effects. In the case of industrial environments, these hazardous effects are handled by defining maximum acceptable concentrations or threshold limit values (TLVs) for individual substances. In the case of non-industrial environments, the situation is more complicated as the pollutants are at concentrations much lower than TLV levels and the effects can be caused by interactions and mixtures of pollutants. One of the most comprehensive discussions on the effects of the indoor environment on health was proposed by NORDWORKS (EUROWORKS) (Sundell and Bornehag, 1999). They created an interdisciplinary consensus on the state of the art of air quality effects on health by reviewing scientific peer-reviewed literature within specific areas. The review was carried out by an invited multidisciplinary team of scientists – experts in different disciplines related to indoor air research. The reviews, in general, showed no association between total concentration of volatile organic compounds, microbially produced matter and indoor particulate matter and health effects (Anderson et al, 1997; Bornehag et al, 2001; Schneider et al, 2003). The lack of effects of particulate matter is worth noting as it was observed in spite of the reliable epidemiological evidence showing that the particles found in outdoor air do have negative health effects for both adults and children (e.g, Ward and Ayres, 2004; Dominici et al, 2006). Nevertheless, recent studies in schools tend to confirm the absence of effects of

particles indoors (Mattson and Hygge, 2005; Wargocki et al, in press). The NORDWORKS (EUROWORKS) reviews showed a clear relation between working in a damp building, ventilation and health. Working in a damp building was associated with cough, wheeze, allergies and asthma, and there are indications that general SBS symptoms such as fatigue and headache and airway infections are also associated with dampness (Bornehag et al, 2001). The relative risk of experiencing health problems when staying in a damp building is 40 to 120 per cent higher compared to a building with no dampness problems. In spite of this high risk, it is still unclear which pollutants/agents are responsible for the health effects observed in damp buildings. Ventilation was found to be strongly associated with health: SBS symptoms, inflammation, infections, asthma, allergies and short-term sick leave (Wargocki et al, 2002a). The scientific evidence indicates that outdoor air supply rates below 25L/s per person increase the risk of SBS symptoms and increase short-term sick leave, while ventilation rates below $0.5h^{-1}$ in homes increase infestation of house dust mites in Nordic countries and may increase the risk of allergies. These conclusions correspond with other literature reviews on the effects of ventilation on health, showing that the ventilation rates at or below 10L/s per person can significantly aggravate SBS symptoms (Mendell, 1993; Godish and Spengler, 1996; Menzies and Bourbeau, 1997; Seppänen et al, 1999) and that there is an indication that increasing the ventilation rate from 10L/s to 20L/s per person may further reduce SBS symptoms (Seppänen et al, 1999). A recent study on the relationship between indoor air quality and asthma supports the conclusions obtained in a review (Bornehag et al, 2004). By comparing air quality in 200 homes with asthmatic children and 200 homes with healthy children in Sweden it was found that lowering the ventilation rate (in a range from $0.62h^{-1}$ to $0.17h^{-1}$) increased the risk of allergic symptoms; the risk was also increased by the presence of phthalates emitted from polyvinyl chloride, including plasticizers in children's rooms. Similar results were observed in a repetition of the study in Bulgaria (Kolarik et al, 2008).

When discussing the effects of ventilation on health it is worth mentioning that the literature indicates that occupants of many buildings with air-conditioning systems may be subject to an increased risk of SBS symptoms compared with occupants in naturally or mechanically ventilated buildings (Seppänen and Fisk, 2002; Wargocki et al, 2002a). Potential causes of adverse health effects due to HVAC systems comprise poor maintenance; poor hygiene of HVAC systems; intermittent operation of HVAC systems; lack of moisture control; and lack of control of HVAC system materials and used filters. Other causes may include recirculation, draught, noise and fibres; but there is little information on these issues in the scientific peer-reviewed literature (Wargocki et al, 2002b).

Li et al (2007) reviewed the literature on the role of ventilation in airborne transmission of infectious agents, similar to the work performed by NORDWORKS (EUROWORKS) described above, and concluded that there is strong and sufficient evidence that ventilation and air movement in buildings are associated with the spread and transmission of infectious diseases such as measles, tuberculosis, chickenpox, influenza, smallpox and severe acute respiratory syndrome (SARS). These results emphasize the importance of indoor air quality and ventilation for health, especially considering the risk of an avian influenza pandemic.

Indoor air quality and performance

The mechanisms by which indoor air quality affects performance are not well understood; but it seems reasonable to assume that people who do not feel very well and experience SBS symptoms, such as headaches and difficulty concentrating and thinking clearly when air quality is poor, will not work very well. Other possible mechanisms for an effect of poor air quality on performance include distraction by odour, sensory irritation, allergic reactions or direct toxicological effects. Studies of adult subjects performing simulated office work (Bakó-Biró et al, 2005) provide further information on the effects of indoor air quality on performance. They showed that increased air pollution caused by gaseous emissions from typical building materials, furnishing and office equipment caused subjects to exhale less carbon dioxide. This must either be a consequence of reduced metabolic rate due to reduced motivation to perform work in polluted air, or a consequence of physiological changes leading to inefficient gas exchange in the lungs when polluted air is breathed. The latter mechanism would lead to an increased CO_2 concentration in the blood, which is known to cause headaches.

There are fewer studies showing the effects of indoor air quality on performance than for the effects of thermal environment on performance (Wyon and Wargocki, 2006a, 2006b). In the study by Wargocki et al (1999), text-typing performance improved as typing speed improved by 6.5 per cent and the error rate was reduced by 18 per cent when the proportion dissatisfied with air quality was reduced from 70 to 25 per cent by removing a 20-year-old carpet. A repetition of this study with the same carpet showed that text-typing performance improved by 1.5 per cent and errors were reduced by 15 per cent when the proportion dissatisfied with air quality was reduced from 60 to 40 per cent (Lagercrantz et al, 2000). In the study by Bakó-Biró et al (2004), text-processing performance improved by 9 per cent when the proportion dissatisfied with air quality was reduced from 40 to 10 per cent by removing personal computers. In the study by Wargocki et al (2000a), text-typing performance improved by about 1 per cent for every twofold increase in outdoor air supply rate in the range between 3L/s and 30L/s per person, causing the proportion dissatisfied with air quality to be reduced from 60 to 30 per cent. The laboratory experiments described above were summarized by Wargocki et al (2000b, 2000c), who showed that the performance of office tasks improves linearly following the reduced proportion dissatisfied with air quality upon entering a space: a 10 per cent reduction in the percentage dissatisfied with air quality corresponds to about a 1 per cent increase in the performance of office work (see Figure 14.8).

No field measurements were carried out in which the performance of office work was quantified; at the same time, air quality was measured by quantifying the proportion dissatisfied. In one study performed in the field by Wargocki et al (2004), replacing the used bag ventilation filter with a new one improved the performance of call-centre operators by 10 per cent because the pollution load in a space was reduced, similar to the interventions made in the laboratory studies described above; consequently, air quality was improved. However, the percentage dissatisfied with air quality was not measured.

There are few studies in which the ventilation rate was modified and the performance of office work was measured. Considering that increasing the ventilation rate improves perceived air quality (Seppänen et al,

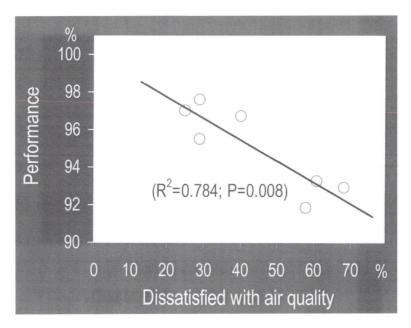

Source: Wargocki et al (2000c)

Figure 14.8 *Performance of simulated office work as a function of the percentage dissatisfied with air quality*

1999; Wargocki et al, 2002a), it is reasonable to assume that the effects on performance due to altering the ventilation rate observed in field experiments are due to improved indoor air quality. Wargocki et al (2004) showed that the performance of call centre operators improved by 6 per cent when outdoor air supply rate was increased from 2.5L/s to 25L/s per person, but only when new ventilation bag filters were installed; with used bag filters the increase of the ventilation rate reduced the performance by 8 per cent. In a study by Federspiel et al (2004), the performance of operators improved by 2 per cent when the ventilation rate was increased from 8L/s to 94L/s per person; but an increase to 20L/s and 53L/s per person reduced the performance, probably because used bag filters were installed, similar to the observation by Wargocki et al

(2004). Tham et al (2003) showed that the performance of call-centre operators improved by 9 per cent when the ventilation rate was increased from 10L/s to 23L/s per person in an office building with no bag filters (electrostatic filters were used instead). In a study by Milton et al (2000), short-term sick leave was 35 per cent lower in office buildings ventilated with an outdoor air supply rate at 24L/s per person compared with buildings ventilated at 12L/s per person.

Based on the results of the studies investigating the effects of ventilation on performance of office work, Seppänen et al (2006b) suggested the quantitative relationship of office work and ventilation rate (see Figure 14.9) showing that work performance will, on average, increase by approximately 1.5 per cent for each doubling of the outdoor air supply rate.

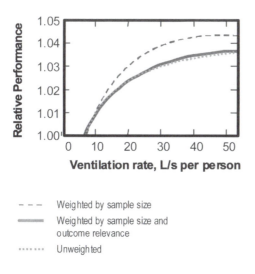

– – – Weighted by sample size

—— Weighted by sample size and
     outcome relevance

········ Unweighted

Source: adapted from REHVA (2006)

Figure 14.9 *Performance as a function of ventilation rate relative to the performance at a ventilation rate of 6.5L/s/person*

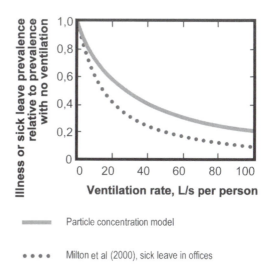

▬▬▬ Particle concentration model

●●●● Milton et al (2000), sick leave in offices

Source: adapted from REHVA (2006)

Figure 14.10 *Predicted trends in illness or sick leave as a function of ventilation rate*

It should be noted that when developing the relationship presented in Figure 14.9, no data on the effects of ventilation on self-estimated performance was included. The data also suggests the benefits of increased ventilation on performance as, for example, in a study by Kaczmarczyk et al (2004), providing a personalized ventilation system that increased the amount of unpolluted air supplied to the breathing zone of people. The relationship in Figure 14.9 is based on studies in which the performance of office work was measured. Studies in schools suggest that increasing the outdoor air supply rate in classrooms will also be beneficial for the schoolwork of 10- to 12-year-old children, including language-based and numerical tasks – doubling the ventilation rate (in a range from 3L/s to 9.5L/s per person) would improve the performance of school tasks by 8 to 14 per cent (Wargocki and Wyon, 2006).

Since ventilation seems to affect short-term absenteeism, Fisk et al (2003) attempted to create the relationship between sick leave and ventilation rate (see Figure 14.10). This relationship was estimated on the basis of studies using sick leave or short-term illness as outcomes. The analysis suggests a 10 per cent reduction in illness or sick leave when doubling the outdoor air supply rate.

Economic implications

There are enormous potential benefits from improving the thermal environment and air quality in relation to the investments required, considering that worker salaries in offices typically exceed building energy and maintenance costs by a factor of approximately 100 and that they exceed annual amortized cost of construction or rental by almost as much (Woods, 1989). Even a 1 per cent increase in performance (productivity) will justify the expenditure. The results presented in previous sections show that the effects of improved IEQ can be much higher than 1 per cent. Crude estimates of benefits from improving indoor environments for the US suggest that potential annual savings and productivity gains can be from US$29 billion to US$168 billion (Fisk and Rosenfeld, 1997). Implementing all improvements to indoor air quality in US buildings that do not meet ASHRAE 62 and ASHRAE 55 standards (ASHRAE, 2005, 2007) results in an annual benefit of US$62.7 billion due to improved health and productivity and a simple payback time of 1.4 years for investments (Dorgan et al, 1998). Seppänen (1999) estimated that the value of improved productivity in Finnish offices resulting from a reduction in the prevalence of SBS symptoms is annually approximately 330 Euros per worker. The reduction in absenteeism due to improved ventilation would produce net savings of US$400 per employee per year (Milton et al, 2000).

In spite of the above benefits, it must be emphasized that indoor environments should be improved in a way that accepts the principles of sustainable design while decreasing energy consumption. New and energy efficient technologies are required for this purpose and their development may require an understanding of the mechanisms by which IEQ affects humans.

Acknowledgements

The work for this chapter was supported by the International Centre for Indoor Environment and Energy established at the Technical University of Denmark.

References

Anderson, K., Bakke, J. V., Björseth, O., Bornehag, C.-G., Clausen, G., Hongslo, J. K., Kjellman, M., Kjærgaard, S., Levy, F., Mølhave, L., Skervfing, S. and Sundell, J. (1997) 'TVOC and health in non–industrial indoor environments', *Indoor Air*, vol 7, pp78–91

ASHRAE (American Society of Heating and Air-Conditioning Engineers) (2005) *ASHRAE Standard 55: Thermal Environment Conditions for Human Occupancy*, ASHRAE, Atlanta, GA

ASHRAE (2007) *ANSI/ASHRAE Standard 62.1–2007: Ventilation for Acceptable Indoor Air Quality*, ASHRAE, Atlanta, GA

Bakó-Biró, Z., Wargocki, P., Weschler, C. and Fanger, P. O. (2004) 'Effects of pollution from personal computers on perceived air quality, SBS symptoms and productivity in offices', *Indoor Air*, vol 14, pp178–187

Bakó-Biró, Z., Wargocki, P., Wyon, D. P. and Fanger, P. O. (2005) 'Indoor air quality effects on CO_2 levels in exhaled air during office work', in *Proceedings of Indoor Air 2005: The 10th International Conference on Indoor Air Quality and Climate*, Beijing, China, vol I, no 1, pp76–80

Berglund, L. and Cain, W. S. (1989) 'Perceived air quality and the thermal environment', in *Proceedings of IAQ '89: The Human Equation – Health and Comfort*, San Diego, CA, pp93–99

Berg-Munch, B., Clausen, G. and Fanger, P. O. (1986) 'Ventilation requirements for the control of body odor in spaces occupied by women', *Environment International*, vol 12, pp195–199

Bluyssen, P. M., Kondo, H., Pejtersen, J., Gunnarsen, L., Clausen, G. and Fanger, P. O. (1989) 'A trained panel to evaluate perceived air quality', in *Proceedings of CLIMA 2000*, Yugoslav Committee of Heating, Refrigerating and Air Conditioning, Sarajevo, Yugoslavia, vol 3, pp25–30

Bornehag, C.-G., Blomquist, G., Gyntelberg, F., Järvholm, B., Malmberg, P., Nielsen, A., Pershagen, G. and Sundell, J. (2001) 'NORDDAMP: Dampness in buildings and health', *Indoor Air*, vol 11, pp72–86

Bornehag, C.-G., Sundell, J. and Weschler, C. J. (2004) 'The association between asthma and allergic symptoms in children and phthalates in house dust: a nested case-control study', *Environmental Health Perspectives*, vol 112, pp1393–1397

Brager, G. S. and de Dear, R. J. (1998) 'Thermal adaptation in the built environment: A literature review', *Energy and Buildings*, vol 27, pp83–96

Burge, P. S., Jones, P. and Robertson, A. S. (1990) 'Sick building syndrome: Environmental comparisons of sick and healthy buildings', in *Proceedings of Indoor Air '90*, Toronto, Canada, vol 1, pp479–483

Burt, T. (1996) 'Sick building syndrome: The thermal environment', in *Proceedings of Indoor Air '96*, Nagoya, Japan, vol 1, pp1037–1042

Cain, W. S., Leaderer, B. P., Isseroff, R., Berglund, L. G., Huey, R. J., Lipsitt, E. D. and Perlman, D. (1983) 'Ventilation requirements in buildings – I. Control of occupancy odour and tobacco smoke odour', *Atmospheric Environment*, vol 17, no 6, pp1183–1197

CEN (1998) *Technical Report CR 1752: Ventilation for Buildings: Design Criteria for the Indoor Environment*, European Committee for Standardization, Brussels, Belgium

Clausen, G. (2000) 'Sensory evaluation of emissions and indoor air quality', in *Proceedings of Healthy Buildings 2000*, Espoo, Finland, vol 1, pp53–62

de Dear, R. J. and Brager, G. S. (2001) 'The adaptive model of thermal comfort and energy conservation in the built environment', *International Journal of Biometeorology*, vol 45, pp100–108

de Dear, R. J., Knudsen, H. N. and Fanger, P. O. (1989) 'Impact of air humidity on thermal comfort during step-changes', *ASHRAE Transactions*, vol 95, part 2, pp336–350

de Dear, R. J., Ring, J. W. and Fanger, P. O. (1993) 'Thermal sensations resulting from sudden ambient temperature changes', *Indoor Air*, vol 3, pp181–192

Dominici, F., Peng, R. D., Bell, M. L., Pham, M. S., McDermott, A., Zeger, S. L. and Samet, J. M. (2006) 'Fine particulate air pollution and hospital admission for cardiovascular and respiratory diseases', *Journal of American Medical Association*, vol 295, no 10, pp1127–1134

Dorgan, C. B., Dorgan, C. E., Kanarek, M. S. and Willman, A. J. (1998) 'Health and productivity benefits of improved indoor air quality', *ASHRAE Transactions*, vol 104, part 1A, pp658–666

EN 15251 (2006) *Indoor Environmental Input Parameters for Design and Assessment of Energy Performance of Buildings – Addressing Indoor Air Quality, Thermal Environment, Lighting and Acoustics*, European Committee for Standardization, Brussels, Belgium

EPBD (2002) *Directive 2002/91/EC of the European Parliament and of the Council of 16 December 2002 on the Energy Performance of Buildings*, Brussels, Belgium

Fang, L., Clausen, G. and Fanger, P. O. (1998a) 'Impact of temperature and humidity on the perception of indoor air quality', *Indoor Air*, vol 8, pp80–90

Fang, L., Clausen, G. and Fanger, P. O. (1998b) 'Impact of temperature and humidity on perception of indoor air quality during immediate and longer whole-body exposures', *Indoor Air*, vol 8, pp276–284

Fang, L., Wyon, D. P., Clausen, G. and Fanger, P. O. (2004) 'Impact of indoor air temperature and humidity in an office on perceived air quality, SBS symptoms and performance', *Indoor Air*, vol 14, supplement 7, pp74–81

Fanger, P. O. (1970) *Thermal Comfort: Analysis and Applications in Environmental Engineering*, McGraw Hill, New York, NY

Fanger, P. O. (1988) 'Introduction of the olf and the decipol units to quantify air pollution perceived by humans indoors and outdoors', *Energy and Buildings*, vol 12, pp1–6

Fanger, P. O. and Berg-Munch, B. (1983) 'Ventilation and body odor', in *Proceedings of an Engineering Foundation Conference on Management of Atmospheres in Tightly Enclosed Spaces*, ASHRAE, Atlanta, GA, pp45–50

Fanger, P. O. and Toftum, J. (2002) 'Extension of the PMV model to non-air-conditioned buildings in warm climates', *Energy and Buildings*, vol 34, pp533–536

Fanger P. O., Melikov, A. K., Hanzawa, H. and Ring, J. (1988) 'Air turbulence and sensation of draught', *Energy and Buildings*, vol 12, pp21–39

Federspiel, C. C., Liu, G., Lahiff, M., Faulkner, D., Dibartolomeo, D. L., Fisk, W. J, Price, P. N. and Sullivan, D. P. (2002) 'Worker performance and ventilation: Analyses of individual data for call-center workers', in Levin, H. (ed) *Proceedings of Indoor Air 2002: The 9th International Conference on Indoor Air Quality and Climate*, Santa Cruz, CA, vol 1, pp796–801

Federspiel, C. C., Fisk, W. J., Price, P. N., Liu, G., Faulkner, D., Dibartolomeo, D. L., Sullivan, D. P. and Lahiff, M. (2004) 'Worker performance and ventilation in a call-center: Analyses of work performance data for registered nurses', *Indoor Air*, vol 14, supplement 8, pp41–50

Fisk, W. J. and Rosenfeld, A. H. (1997) 'Estimates of improved productivity and health from better indoor environments', *Indoor Air*, vol 7, pp158–172

Fisk, W. J., Seppänen, O., Faulkner, D. and Huang, J. (2003) 'Cost benefit analysis of ventilation control strategies in an office building', in *Proceedings of Healthy Buildings 2003*, Singapore, vol 3, pp361–366

Gagge, A. P., Fobelets, A. P. and Berglund, L. G. (1986) 'A standard predictive index of human response to the thermal environment', *ASHRAE Transactions*, vol 92, part 2, pp709–731

Godish, T. and Spengler, J. D. (1996) 'Relationships between ventilation and indoor air quality: A review', *Indoor Air*, vol 6, pp135–145

Goto, T., Toftum, J., Fanger, P. O. and Yoshino, H. (2003) 'Transient thermal sensation and comfort resulting from adjustments of clothing insulation', in *Proceedings of Healthy Buildings 2003*, Singapore, vol 1, pp835–840

Goto, T., Toftum, J., de Dear, R. J. and Fanger, P. O. (2006) 'Thermal sensation and thermophysiological responses to metabolic step-changes', *International Journal of Biometeorology*, vol 50, no 5, pp323–332

Gunnarsen, L. and Fanger, P. O. (1992) 'Adaptation to indoor air pollution', *Energy and Buildings*, vol 18, pp43–54

ISO Standard 7730 (1994) *Moderate Thermal Environments – Determination of the PMV and PPD Indices and Specification of the Conditions for Thermal Comfort*

Iwashita, G., Kimura, K., Tanabe, S., Yoshizawa, S. and Ikeda, K. (1990) 'Indoor air quality assessment based on human olfactory sensation', *Journal of Architecture, Planning and Environmental Engineering*, vol 410, pp9–19

Kaczmarczyk, J., Melikov, A. and Fanger, P. O. (2004) 'Human response to personalized ventilation and mixing ventilation', *Indoor Air*, vol 14, supplement 8, pp17–29

Kolarik, B., Naydenov, K., Larsson, M., Bornehag, C.-G. and Sundell, J. (2008) 'The association between phthalates in dust and allergic diseases among Bulgarian children', *Environmental Health Perspectives*, vol 116, pp98–103

Krogstad, A. L., Swanbeck, G., Barregård, L., Hagberg, S., Rynell, K. B. and Ran, A. (1991) *A Prospective Study of Indoor Climate Problems at Different Temperatures in Offices* (in Swedish), Volvo Truck Corp, Göteborg

Lagercrantz, L., Wistrand, M., Willén, U., Wargocki, P., Witterseh, T. and Sundell, J. (2000) 'Negative impact of air pollution on productivity: Previous Danish findings repeated in new Swedish test room', in *Proceeding of Healthy Buildings 2000*, Espoo, vol 1, pp653–658

Li, Y., Leung, G. M., Tang, J. W., Yang, X., Chao, C. Y. H., Lin, J. Z., Lu, J. W., Nielsen, P. V., Niu, J., Qian, H., Sleigh, A. C., Su, H.-J. J., Sundell, J., Wong, T. W. and Yuen, P. L. (2007) 'Role of ventilation in airborne transmission of infectious agents in the built environment: A multidisciplinary systematic review', *Indoor Air*, vol 17, pp2–18

Marmor, M. (1978) 'Heat wave mortality in nursing homes', *Environmental Research*, vol 17, pp102–115

Mattsson, M. and Hygge, S. (2005) 'Effect of articulate air cleaning on perceived health and cognitive performance in school children during pollen season', in *Proceedings of Indoor Air 2005*, Tsinghua University Press, Beijing, China, vol I, no 2, pp1111–1115

Mendell, M. J. (1993) 'Non-specific symptoms in office workers: A review and summary of the epidemiologic literature', *Indoor Air*, vol 3, pp227–236

Menzies, D. and Bourbeau, J. (1997) 'Building-related illnesses', *The New England Journal of Medicine*, vol 337, pp1524–1531

Milton, D., Glencross, P. and Walters, M. (2000) 'Risk of sick-leave associated with outdoor air supply rate, humidification and occupants complaints', *Indoor Air*, vol 10, pp212–221

Müller, B., Müller, D., Knudsen, H. N., Wargocki, P., Berglund, B. and Ramalho, O. (2007) 'A European project SysPAQ', in *Proceedings of CLIMA 2007*, Finland, CD-ROM

Niemelä, R., Hannula, M., Rautio, S., Reijula, K. and Railio, J. (2002) 'The effect of air temperature on labour productivity in call centres: A case study', *Energy and Buildings*, vol 34, pp759–764

Olesen, B. W. (1985) 'Local thermal discomfort', *Brüel & Kjær Technical Review*, no 1

Olesen, B. W., Schøler, M. and Fanger, P. O. (1979) 'Discomfort caused by vertical air temperature differences', in Fanger, P. O. and Valbjørn, O. (eds) *Indoor Climate*, Danish Building Research Institute, Copenhagen, Denmark, pp561–579

Preller, L., Zweers, T., Brunekreef, B. and Boleij, J. S. M. (1990) 'Sick leave due to work-related health complaints among office workers in the Netherlands', in *Proceedings of Indoor Air '90: The 5th International Conference on Indoor Air Quality and Climate*, Canada Mortgage and Housing Corporation, Ottawa, Canada, vol 1, pp227–230

Raw, G. J., Roys, M. S. and Leaman, A. (1990) 'Further findings from the office environment survey: Productivity', in *Proceedings of Indoor Air '90: The 5th International Conference on Indoor Air Quality and Climate*, Canada Mortgage and Housing Corporation, Ottawa, Canada, vol 1, pp231–236

REHVA (2006) *REHVA Guidebook 6: Indoor Climate and Productivity in Offices: How to Integrate Productivity in Life Cycle Costs Analysis of Building Services*, Wargocki, P. and Seppänen, O. (eds), Federation of European Heating and Air-Conditioning Associations, REHVA, Brussels

Roelofsen, P. (2001) 'The design of the workplace as a strategy for productivity enhancement', in *Proceedings of CLIMA 2001*, Napoli, Italy, CD-ROM

Rogot, E., Sorlie, P. D. and Backlund, E. (1992) 'Air-conditioning and mortality in hot weather', *American Journal of Epidemiology*, vol 136, pp106–116

Schneider, T., Sundell, J., Bischof, W., Bohgard, M., Cherrie, J. W., Clausen, P. A., Dreborg, S., Kildesø, J., Kjærgaard, S. K., Løvik, M., Pasanen, P. and Skyberg, K. (2003) 'EUROPART: Airborne particles in the indoor environment – a European interdisciplinary review of scientific evidence on associations between exposure to particles in buildings and health effects', *Indoor Air*, vol 13, pp38–48

Seppänen, O. (1999) 'Estimated cost of indoor climate in Finnish buildings' in *Proceedings of the 8th International Conference on Indoor Air Quality and Climate – Indoor Air '99*, vol 4, pp13–18

Seppänen, O. and Fisk, W. (2002) 'Association of ventilation system type with SBS symptoms in office workers', *Indoor Air*, vol 12, pp98–112

Seppänen, O. A., Fisk, W. J. and Mendell, M. J. (1999) 'Association of ventilation rates and CO_2-concentrations with health and other responses in commercial and institutional buildings', *Indoor Air*, vol 9, pp226–252

Seppänen, O., Fisk, W. and Lei, Q. H. (2006a) 'Effect of temperature on task performance in office environment', in *Proceedings of Cold Climate HVAC Conference*, Moscow, CD-ROM

Seppänen, O., Fisk, W. and Lei, Q. H. (2006b) 'Ventilation and performance in office work', *Indoor Air*, vol 16, pp28–35

Skov, P., Valbjørn, O., Pedersen, B. V. and the Danish Indoor Climate Study Group (1990) 'Influence of indoor climate in sick building syndrome in a office environment', *Scandinavian Journal of Work, Environment and Health*, vol 16, pp363–371

Sundell, J. and Bornehag, C.-G. (1999) 'Nordic interdisciplinary reviews of the scientific literature concerning the relationship between indoor environmental factors and health, NORDWORKS', in Raw, G., Aizlewood, C. and Warren, P. (eds) *Proceedings of Indoor Air '99, Eighth International Conference on Indoor Air Quality and Climate*, Edinburgh, Scotland, vol 1, pp177–182

Tham, K. W., Willem, H. C., Sekhar, S. C., Wyon, D. P., Wargocki, P. and Fanger, P. O. (2003) 'Temperature and ventilation effects on the work performance of office workers (study of a call center in the tropics)', in Tham, K. W., Sekhar, S. C. and Cheong, D. (eds) *Proceedings of Healthy Buildings 2003*, Stallion Press, Singapore, vol 3, pp280–286

Toftum, J., Jørgensen, A. S. and Fanger, P. O. (1998) 'Upper limits of air humidity for preventing warm respiratory discomfort', *Energy and Buildings*, vol 28, pp15–23

Ward, D. J. and Ayres, J. G. (2004) 'Particulate air pollution and panel studies in children: a systematic review', *Occupational and Environmental Medicine*, vol 61, (electronic paper: oem.2003.007088)

Wargocki, P. and Wyon, D. P. (2006) 'Effects of HVAC on student performance', *ASHRAE Journal*, October, pp22–28

Wargocki, P., Wyon, D. P., Baik, Y. K., Clausen, G. and Fanger, P. O. (1999) 'Perceived air quality, sick building syndrome (SBS) symptoms and productivity in an office with two different pollution loads', *Indoor Air*, vol 9, pp165–179

Wargocki, P., Wyon, D. P., Sundell, J., Clausen, G. and Fanger P. O. (2000a) 'The effects of outdoor air supply rate in an office on perceived air quality, sick building syndrome (SBS) symptoms and productivity', *Indoor Air*, vol 10, pp222–236

Wargocki, P., Wyon, D. P. and Fanger, P. O. (2000b) 'Productivity is affected by the air quality in offices', in *Proceedings of Healthy Buildings 2000*, Espoo, vol 1, pp635–640

Wargocki, P., Wyon, D. P. and Fanger, P. O. (2000c) 'Pollution source control and ventilation improve health, comfort and productivity', in *Proceedings of Cold Climate HVAC 2000*, Sapporo, pp445–450

Wargocki, P., Sundell, J., Bischof, W., Brundrett, G., Fanger, P. O., Gyntelberg, F., Hanssen, S. O., Harrison, P., Pickering, A., Seppänen, O. and Wouters, P. (2002a) 'Ventilation and health in nonindustrial indoor environments: Report from a European multidisciplinary scientific consensus meeting', *Indoor Air*, vol 12, pp113–128

Wargocki, P., Sundell, J., Bischof, W., Brundrett, G., Fanger, P. O., Gyntelberg, F., Hanssen, S. O., Harrison, P., Pickering, A., Seppänen, O. and Wouters, P. (2002b) 'The role of ventilation in nonindustrial indoor environments: Report from a European multidisciplinary scientific consensus meeting', in *Proceedings of Indoor Air 2002, The 9th International Conference on Indoor Air Quality and Climate*, Monterey, US, vol 5, pp33–38

Wargocki, P., Wyon, D. P. and Fanger, P. O. (2004) 'The performance and subjective responses of call-centre operators with new and used supply air filters at two outdoor air supply rates', *Indoor Air*, vol 14, supplement 8, pp7–16

Wargocki, P., Wyon, D. P., Jensen, K. and Bornehag, C. G. (in press) 'The effects of electrostatic filtration and supply air filter condition in classrooms on the performance of schoolwork by children', *HVAC&R Research*

Wenger, J. D., Miller, R. C. and Quistgaard, D. (1993) 'A gas sensor array for measurement of indoor air pollution: Preliminary results', in *Proceedings of Indoor Air '93*, Helsinki, Finland, vol 5, pp27–32

WHO (World Health Organization) (1948) *The Constitution of the World Health Organization*, WHO

WHO (1983) *Indoor Air Pollutants: Exposures and Health Effects*, EURO Reports and Studies 78, WHO Regional Office for Europe, Copenhagen, Denmark

Willem, H. C. (2006) *Thermal and Indoor Air Quality Effects on Physiological Responses, Perception and Performance of Tropically Acclimatized People*, PhD thesis, National University of Singapore, Singapore

Woods, J. E. (1989) 'Cost avoidance and productivity in owning and operating buildings', *Journal of Occupational Medicine*, vol 4, pp753–770

Wyon, D. P. (1996) 'Indoor environmental effects on productivity', in *Proceedings of IAQ '96 Paths to Better Building Environments*, ASHRAE, US, pp5–15

Wyon, D. P. and Wargocki, P. (2006a) 'Room temperature effects on office work', in Clements-Croome, D. (ed) *Creating the Productive Workplace*, second edition, Taylor & Francis, London, pp181–192

Wyon, D. P. and Wargocki, P. (2006b) 'Indoor air quality effects on office work', in Clements-Croome, D. (ed) *Creating the Productive Workplace*, second edition, Taylor & Francis, London, pp193–205

Wyon, D. P., Fanger, P. O., Olesen, B. W. and Pedersen, C. J. K. (1975) 'The mental performance of subjects clothed for comfort at two different air temperatures', *Ergonomics*, vol 18, pp359–374

15

Indoor Air Quality and Ventilation Modelling

Ian Ridley

Introduction

Over the last 30 years two interrelated themes have become of increasing interest to those designing, commissioning and, indeed, using buildings: the need for energy efficiency and the provision of adequate indoor air quality. Both are intrinsically linked together via the ventilation regime of the building. The energy used to supply and condition fresh air to a building can be a significant contribution to the carbon footprint of a building, while the resultant ventilation rate along with the strength of pollutant sources will determine the level of indoor air quality (IAQ).

The ability to be able to predict building ventilation rates and the subsequent impact on both energy use and IAQ is therefore highly desirable. Computer-based simulation tools provide a suitable methodology of calculating airflows in both naturally and mechanically ventilated buildings and their impact on pollutant concentrations, allowing the adequacy of designs and strategies to be assessed in terms of the energy and IAQ performance.

This chapter is intended to be a brief introduction to the use of such models, raising some issues that the novice practitioner should be aware of. For further information readers should refer to Liddament (1986); Feustel (1998); Persily (1998); Persily and Martin (2000); Musser (2000) and Persily and Ivy (2001).

Types of application

Building regulations and design briefs often demand that specific performance criteria are met by a building in terms of energy consumption and IAQ. Ventilation rates, temperatures, relative humidity and pollutant concentration targets may all need to be met. In naturally ventilated buildings, the ventilation rate will be driven by factors such as external and internal temperature, wind speed and direction, and area of ventilation opening, all of which are subject to transient variation. As a result, buildings will have a distribution of performance, with ventilation rates and IAQ levels varying throughout the year. As an example (modelled by the author), the distribution of predicted heating season air change rate in an airtight, naturally ventilated house with a background air permeability of $3m^3/m^2h$ at 50Pa, located in the UK is given in Figure 15.1.

If performance-based standards are to be used to assess the success of a building, design simulation can be used to predict how the building will perform under different weather conditions and with varying occupant use, both in terms of pollutant loads and interaction of the occupant with the ventilation system. The exposure of occupants to different pollutants under different scenarios of pollutant source strength and profiles, and in conjunction with varied patterns of available ventilation, can be estimated and compared to recognized guidelines and recommended limits.

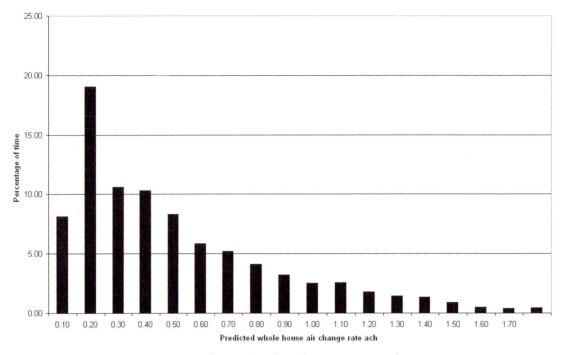

Figure 15.1 *Distribution of predicted heating season air change rate*

Similarly, the risk of condensation and likelihood of mould growth or house dust mite infestation can be examined by predicting the relative humidity as a result of moisture production and achieved ventilation rate.

Demand-controlled ventilation, which aims to reduce energy consumption by matching the ventilation rate to the actual need, by its very definition assumes that ventilation rates will vary according to the conditions within a building at a specific time. The need for simulation tools to include elements of control and feedback is therefore apparent.

Types of models

There are typically four types of models that can be considered to be of use in this area:

1   In their simplest form, thermal and energy simulation models will predict the consequences of a predefined or specified ventilation rate on temperature and energy consumption. Pollutant prediction will often be limited only to a consideration of moisture.

2   Airflow and contaminant models will predict airflows and subsequent pollutant concentrations within zones, but will not predict energy consumption. Zone temperatures will often need to be user defined.

3   Integrated airflow and thermal models have greater capabilities to model the effects of temperature on ventilation rates and vice versa, allowing the energy consumption in naturally ventilated systems to be more accurately measured; however, their contaminant modelling capabilities are not as advanced as type 2 models.

4   Finally, zonal models have the ability to model pollutant concentrations and temperature distributions within zones, predicting airflows in great detail at a high spatial and temporal resolution. In terms of complexity, zonal models can be considered to lie between single node airflow and full computational fluid dynamic (CFD) models, producing distributions of temperature and contaminants without the time penalty of full CFD treatment. The room, or zone, is subdivided into a number of small cells, to which

the equations of conservation of heat and mass are applied.

Each type has advantages and disadvantages. For some applications, where both energy and pollution concentrations are required, a combination of different approaches may be necessary. In this chapter we will focus on the use of airflow and contaminant models, as well as integrated thermal and airflow models. Examples of such models are CONTAMW (NIST, 2008), and Energy Plus (EERE, 2008). A comprehensive list of building energy and ventilation tolls can be found in the Building Energy Software Tools Directory (BESTD, 2008).

Multi-zone indoor air quality and ventilation tools are typically designed to predict:

- whole building infiltration and ventilation rates due to mechanical systems, wind pressure and stack effects, and airflow between zones;
- the concentration of pollutants from both internal and external sources in each zone, as well as the transport of pollutants between zones (the predicted concentrations may then be used to estimate occupant and artefact exposure to these contaminants).

Validation and testing

As with all simulation models, it is important that testing and validation studies are carried out to inform potential users of the confidence they can place on the results of such models and to identify and solve possible sources of error. Multi-zone airflow and contaminant models have been subject to some validation and comparison exercises (Fiirbringer et al, 1996). It should be noted that the level of effort and instrumentation required to produce experimental data of sufficient quality to test ventilation models is a challenge even in highly controlled and monitored environmental chambers.

It is, however, important to note the need for further validation work under a wider range of weather conditions and for a varied range of both systems and applications. Analytical tests, comparing simulation results with exact analytical solutions, are possible; however, they are limited to only the most simple of

multi-zone buildings. A series of inter-model comparisons between a number of software tools have been undertaken to allow the relative consistency between models to be assessed. Empirical validation against experimental data has also been carried out for a small number of cases (Emmerich, 2001). Such studies conclude that a knowledgeable user can make reasonable predictions of air change rates and contaminant concentrations for residential-scale buildings.

Creating the model

As with all simulation tools, the reliability of the output of ventilation and contaminant models is intrinsically governed by the quality of input data used. The input required in order to model the airflow and subsequent contaminant concentrations in a building can be broken down into the following subgroups.

Building dimensions and orientation

The volume and floor area of each zone to be modelled are required, as are the heights of each floor and the orientation of each façade.

Weather file

The simulation is driven by a steady-state or transient weather file, usually with hourly resolution. This file includes external temperature and relative humidity, wind speed and direction, and external pollutant concentration. As with weather files used to drive thermal and energy building-simulation tools, test reference years for particular locations may be employed. Historical hourly external pollution data from networks of automatic monitoring sites can now be readily downloaded to create external pollution concentration input files.

Openings and flow elements

Details must be given of the cracks, openings and ventilation through and for which the airflow will be calculated. Openings and cracks may be defined in terms of an opening area and discharge coefficient or by a flow exponent and flow coefficient.

Zonal infiltration models are based on an empirical (power law) relationship between the flow and the pressure difference across a crack or opening in the building envelope. If the flow characteristics, the flow coefficient and exponent of a building element are known, either from experiment or from tabulated values, the air infiltration due to the element may be calculated as a function of pressure difference:

$$Q = C\{\Delta P\}^n \tag{1}$$

where:

- Q = flow (m³/s);
- C = flow coefficient;
- ΔP = pressure difference (Pa);
- n = flow exponent.

The flow exponent should consist of a value of between 0.5 and 1.0, with larger openings commonly having a value of 0.5, and small gaps and cracks being given a value closer to 0.65. Similarly, if the flow element is defined in terms of its opening area and flow characteristic, the flow may be expressed by the following equation, where the discharge coefficient for openings with sharp edges is typically 0.6:

$$Q = C_d A \{2\, \Delta P / \rho\}^{0.5} \tag{2}$$

where:

- Q = flow (m³/s);
- C_d = discharge coefficient;
- ΔP = pressure difference (Pa);
- ρ = air density (kg/m³).

Simple mechanical systems such as extract fans can be defined in terms of a constant flow rate or in terms of performance curves. The height of the flow element in a zone must be provided.

A simple method of incorporating the gaps and cracks in a building that contribute to the background air permeability is to distribute them equally around the building façade. The results of a fan pressurization test or a target air permeability value may be used. The permeability can be distributed between zones according to the proportionate façade area. It is common practice to insert permeability at high and low levels within each zone.

As an example, the flow characteristics of domestic ventilation devices such as background trickle ventilators are measured by a protocol outlined in CEN Standard CEN/TC 156, *Ventilation for Buildings*; more specifically, EN 13141-1 refers to 'The performance characteristics of the components/products for residential ventilation'. The flow exponent, flow coefficient and equivalent opening areas of such products are freely available from manufacture specification sheets.

Wind pressure coefficients

One of the aims of using zonal airflow models is to predict the airflow through cracks and openings in the building and, hence, the ventilation rate due to the action of wind. The wind pressure exerted on the façade of a building can be approximated using Equation 3 by employing the wind speed in the weather file, modified by the local terrain, and wind pressure coefficients related to the form of the building (ASHRAE, 2001):

$$P_w = \frac{\rho V_{met}^2}{2} A_o^2 \left(\frac{H}{H_{ref}}\right)^{2a} f(\theta) \tag{3}$$

where:

- P_w = wind pressure (Pa);
- ρ = air density (kg/m³);
- V_{met} = reference wind speed (m/s);
- A_o = terrain coefficient;
- a = terrain exponent;
- H = wall height (m);
- H_{ref} = reference wind speed height (m);
- $f(\theta)$ = wind pressure profile;
- θ = relative wind angle.

Wind pressure coefficients are dimensionless and vary as a function of wind direction. For real buildings, wind pressure coefficients can be measured on site by correlating the output of pressure sensors on the building façade with locally measured wind speed and direction. Alternatively, wind tunnel studies of scale models may be used. In most simulation applications, a 'standard' set of wind pressure coefficients for standard building formats will be taken from databases and tables (ASHRAE, 2001)

Zone temperature

The temperature of each zone is another important determinant of the airflow in the building and, as such, needs to be defined by the user. The stack pressure exerted by cold air entering at low level rising and exiting at high level can be approximated using the following equation:

$$P_s(T_o,h) = \rho g(H_{NPL} - h)\frac{T_i - T_o}{T_i} \qquad (4)$$

where:

- P_s = stack pressure (Pa);
- g = acceleration due to gravity (ms^{-2});
- h = height (m);
- H_{NPL} = neutral pressure level (m);
- T_i = internal temperature (°C);
- T_o = external temperature (°C).

The main advantage of using integrated airflow and thermal models, such as Energy Plus, is precisely that the internal temperatures will be calculated as part of the simulation. Such software will, of course, require further input at a level of details required to perform a full thermal and energy simulation. Therefore, the thermal properties of the fabric – both opaque and transparent – will be required, along with details of any heating or cooling equipment. Similarly, a more detailed weather file, including solar radiation data, will be required to run such a simulation. When using airflow and contaminant models, such as CONTAM, which do not have an integrated thermal modelling capability, internal temperatures can be user defined, or the output of building simulation can be used as input.

Contaminants

Sources of individual contaminants can be defined in each zone. These may have a constant emission rate or a variable rate that is controlled by a release schedule. Contaminants could come from the building occupants, the fabric and fittings or from appliances.

The most commonly considered contaminants from occupants are carbon dioxide, bio-effluents and moisture. The building fabric and its fixtures and fittings can be a source of volatile organic compounds. Combustion appliances such a gas cookers and boilers are sources of carbon monoxide and nitrous oxides, whereas appliances such as photocopiers and laser printers can be sources of ozone.

A large literature exists on the measurement of pollutant source strengths from building materials, often made in environmental chambers. In certain specific modelling tasks, a user may wish to enter user-defined schedules based on a specific scenario. Often, however, a modeller may wish to assess the effectiveness or adequacy of a proposed building or ventilation design when challenged by a standardized contaminant emission rate. It should be recognized that the task of simulating and then assessing IAQ would be greatly aided if there was a consistent and recognized database or library of common pollutant source rates and schedules. As an example of how to approach the construction of a contaminant source schedule for a dwelling, the following examines the creation of a moisture production schedule for a three-bedroom house occupied by two adults and two children.

Moisture production schedule

Tables 15.1 to 15.6 present the results of an extensive literature review of published academic papers and national standards, designed to gather information on moisture production rates from domestic activities. The sources of moisture were split into the following household activities:

- occupant breathing and sweating (Table 15.1);
- cooking (Table 15.2);
- clothes washing (Table 15.3);
- washing of floors and surfaces (Table 15.4);
- washing dishes (Table 15.5);
- drying clothes (Table 15.6);
- bathing;
- indoor plants.

It can be seen that, although consistent, the moisture production rates within each category reflect a large range, dependent upon occupant activity and, more fundamentally, upon the intensity of moisture production. When designing the schedule, the user must consider if an average or extreme scenario should be considered. After gathering data on production rates associated with different household activities, the next step is to assign specific activities for the most relevant room or zone at a specific time. An example production schedule in a dwelling that produces a relatively high daily moisture load of 9kg is presented by source in Table 15.7 and by room in Table 15.8.

Table 15.1 *Moisture production due to occupant breathing and sweating*

Author	Moisture production rate per person
BS5250	Asleep (40g/h) Awake (55g/h)
Annex 27	Adult asleep (30g/h) Adult awake (55g/h) Child asleep (12.5g/h) Child awake (40g/h)
HMSO (1970)	0.625kg/day
Finbow (1982)	0.752kg/day
BRE (1985)	Person asleep (0.25–0.5kg/day) Person active (0.75–1.5kg/day)
CIBSE (1986)	0.96–2.4kg/day
CIBSE (1999)	40–100g/h
Boyd et al (1988)	0.7475kg/day
Angell and Olsen (1988)	1.26kg/day
Stum (1992)	1.44kg/day
Lstiburek (1993)	65g/h
Hanson (2002)	180g/h
Treschel (2001)	Light activity (30–120g/h) Medium (120–200g/h) Heavy activity (200–300g/h)
Rousseau (1984)	50g/h
Yik et al (2004)	40–100g/h
Pretlove (2000)	Asleep (40g/h) Awake (55g/h)

Table 15.2 *Moisture due to cooking*

Author	Moisture production rate per person
BS5250	Gas (3 kg/day) Electricity (2 kg/day)
Annex 27 (includes dishwashing)	Breakfast (50g/h) Lunch (150g/h) Dinner (300g/h)
HMSO (1970)	0.525kg/day
Finbow (1982)	0.6kg/day
BRE (1985)	0.5–1kg/day
CIBSE (1986, 1999)	0.9–3 kg/day
Boyd et al (1988)	Gas (3kg/day) Electricity (2kg/day)
Angell and Olsen (1988)	Gas (1.35kg/day) Electricity (1.0kg/day)
Lstiburek (1993)	Breakfast gas/electricity (520/200g/day) Lunch gas/electricity (300/680g/day) Dinner gas/electricity (700/1600g/day)
Hanson (2002)	0.920kg/day
Treschel (2001)	1.5kg/day
Rousseau (1984)	950kg/day
Pretlove (2000)	Gas (0.55kg per person per day) Electricity (0.38kg per person per day)

Table 15.3 *Moisture due to washing clothes*

Author	Moisture production rate per dwelling
BS5250	0.5kg/day
Annex 27	0.2kg/day
HMSO (1970)	2.0kg/day
Finbow (1982)	1.0kg/day
BRE (1985)	0.5–1.0kg/day
CIBSE (1986, 1999)	0.5–1.8kg/day
Meyringer (1985)	0.15kg/day
Boyd et al (1988)	0.5kg/day
Stum (1992)	0.63kg/day
Hanson (2002)	1.96kg/day
Pretlove (2000)	0.5kg/day

Table 15.4 *Moisture from washing floors/surfaces*

Author	Moisture production rate per dwelling
BS5250	–
Annex 27	–
HMSO (1970)	1.1kg/day
CIBSE (1986, 1999)	1.0–15kg/day
Angell and Olsen (1988)	0.15kg/m^2 cleaned
Stum (1992)	0.14kg/day
Lstiburek (1993)	0.18kg/m^2 cleaned
Hanson (2002)	0.15kg/m^2 cleaned
Treschel (2001)	0.12kg/m^2 cleaned
Rousseau (1984)	0.13kg/m^2 cleaned
Yik et al (2004)	0.05kg/m^2 cleaned
Pretlove (2000)	0.22kg per person per day

Table 15.5 *Moisture due to washing dishes*

Author	Moisture production rate per dwelling
BS5250	0.4kg/day
Annex 27	– (Included in cooking)
HMSO (1970)	0.5kg/day
Burberry (1994)	0.4kg/day
CIBSE (1986, 1999)	0.15–0.45kg/day
Boyd et al (1988)	0.4kg/day
Lstiburek (1993)	0.15kg/day
Hanson (2002)	0.45kg/day
Rousseau (1984)	0.5kg/day
Yik et al (2004)	0.08kg/day
Pretlove (2000)	0.113kg per person per day

Table 15.6 *Moisture due to drying clothes*

Author	Moisture production rate per dwelling
BS5250	1.5kg/day per person
Annex 27	2 kg/day
CIBSE (1986, 1999)	5–14kg/day
Stum (1992)	1.5kg/day per person
Lstiburek (1993)	2.5–3.4kg/load
Hanson (2002)	11.9kg/day
Treschel (2001)	2.2–2.9kg/load
Rousseau (1984)	1.74kg/day
IEA (1991)	0.05–0.2kg/h spin dried 0.1–0.5kg/hour dripping wet
HMSO (1970)	12kg/day
BRE (1985)	3–7.5kg/day
Yik et al (2004)	16kg/day
Pretlove (2000)	2.5kg per load

Table 15.7 *Moisture production by source*

Time	0	1	2	3	4	5	6	7	8	9	10	11	12	13	14	15	16	17	18	19	20	21	22	23
Number of people	3	3	3	3	3	3	3	3	3	1	1	1	1	1	1	1	2	2	2	3	3	3	3	3
Moisture gen. rate/person	40	40	40	40	40	40	40	40	40	55	55	55	55	55	55	55	55	55	55	55	55	55	40	40
Tot. moisture – people	120	120	120	120	120	120	120	120	120	55	55	55	55	55	55	55	110	110	110	165	165	165	120	120
Cooking								400						600					1000	1000				
Bathing									600												200			
Dishwashing									200					200							200			
Washing clothes											250	250	250											
Drying clothes indoors															150	100	100	100	100	100	100	100	100	100
Plants	10	10	10	10	10	10	10	10	10	10	10	10	10	10	10	10	10	10	10	10	10	10	10	10
Tot. moisture(g)	130	130	130	130	130	130	130	530	930	65	315	315	315	865	215	165	220	220	1220	1275	675	275	230	230

Table 15.8 *Moisture production by room*

Time	0	1	2	3	4	5	6	7	8	9	10	11	12	13	14	15	16	17	18	19	20	21	22	23
Bed 1	80	80	80	80	80	80	80																80	80
Bed 2	40	40	40	40	40	40	40																40	40
Bathroom								83	883				83	67	50	33	33	33	33	33	233	33	33	33
Living room	10	10	10	10	10	10	10	93	93	38	38	38	121	104	88	71	98	98	98	126	126	136	43	43
Kitc								400		28	278	278	111	694	78	61	88	88	1088	1116	316	116	33	33
Tot. moisture (g)	130	130	130	130	130	130	130	575	975	65	315	315	315	865	215	165	220	220	1220	1275	675	275	230	230

Table 15.9 *Comparison of recommended domestic ventilation rates*

Country standard reference	Whole building ventilation rates	Living room	Bedroom	Kitchen	Bathroom and toilet	Toilet only
Belgium (NBM D50-001, 1991)	1L/s/m² of floor area with specific values for kitchen, toilets and bathrooms	Supply 1L/s/m² Perhaps limited to 150m³/h	Supply 1L/s/m² Perhaps limited to 36m³/h	Exhaust 1L/s/m² Perhaps limited to 75m³/h	Exhaust 1L/s/m² Perhaps limited to 75m³/h	Exhaust 25m³/hr
Canada (NBC, 2005) based on F326,1-M1989	>0.3 ACH 5L/s/person		Prescribed principal exhaust 'solutions' at rates based on number of bedrooms (like ASHRAE 62.2, 2004)	Exhaust 50L/s intermittent; 30L/s continuous	Exhaust 50L/s intermittent; 30L/s continuous	
Denmark (BR, 2005)	0.5 ACH	Clear opening of minimum 30cm² per 25m² floor area		Exhaust 20L/s	Exhaust 15L/s	Exhaust 10L/s
Finland (Finland NBC-D2, 2003)	Exhaust airflows can be reduced when spaces are not in use provided that the whole dwelling is greater than 0.4 ACH and minimum airflow rates in bedrooms and living rooms are met	0.5L/s/m²	6.0L/s/person or 0.35L/s/m² floor area	Exhaust 10L/s (continuous); 15L/s (boost)	Exhaust 7L/s (continuous); 10L/s (boost)	
France				Continuous: 20–45m³/h Intermittent: 75–135m³/h	15–30m³/h	15–30m³/h
Netherlands Building Decree (NB dm³/s– L/s)		0.9dm³/s/m² floor area	0.9dm³/s/m² floor area	21dm³/s	14dm³/s	7dm³/s
New Zealand (ASRAE 62, 1999)	0.35 ACH; minimum 7.5L/s/person			Continuous: 12L/s Intermittent: 50L/s or openable window	Continuous: 10L/s Intermittent: 25L/s or openable window	

Table 15.9 Comparison of recommended domestic ventilation rates (cont'd)

Country standard reference	Whole building ventilation rates	Living room	Bedroom	Kitchen and toilet	Bathroom	Toilet only
Sweden (BFS, 1988:00) Update 2006	Requirements: rooms will have continual 0.35L/s/m² floor area when in use		Recommendation: <4L/s/bedroom	Recommendation: extract 10L/s	10L/s with openable window or 10L/s with high speed rate up 30L/s or 15L/s without openable window	
Switzerland (SIA 180:00) England and Wales (ADF, 2006)	15m³/h/person (non-smoking) 13L/s – 1 bedroom 17L/s – 2 bedrooms 21L/s – 3 bedrooms 25L/s – 4 bedrooms 29L/s – 5 bedrooms Minimum ventilation rate not less than 0.3L/s per m² of floor area	Rapid vent: 1/20th of floor area Background vent: 8000mm²	Rapid vent: 1/20th of floor area Background vent: 8000mm²	Rapid vent: opening window Background vent: 4000mm² Extract vent rates: 30L/s adjacent to hob or 60L/s elsewhere, or passive stack ventilation (PSV)	Rapid vent: opening window Background vent: 4000mm² Extract vent rates 15L/s or PSV	Rapid vent: opening window Background vent: 4000mm² Extract vent rates: 15L/s or PSV
US (ASHRAE 62-99, amended 2005)	0.35 ACH; minimum 7.5L/s/person	Continuous: 12L/s Intermittent: 50L/s or openable window	Continuous: 10L/s Intermittent: 25L/s or openable window			
German passive house	Recommend a supply flow rate of 30m³/h/ person (8.5L/s/person) and the system should also allow for a minimum air supply setting for times with no occupancy, with a corresponding airflow rate of 0.2h⁻¹					
Swedish passive house	0.5 ACH					

In a similar manner, schedules can be built up for gaseous pollutants from cooking or combustion appliances. First, the user goes to published databases on the relevant emission rates, and then a time-specific schedule is produced.

As well as the sources of contaminants, the user should also be aware of contaminant sinks, which can remove pollution from buildings. For example, the fabric and furnishings within a building will act as a buffer, absorbing and releasing moisture. This effect should be taken into account when modelling indoor relative humidity. CONTAM includes a boundary layer diffusion model, which may be used to take moisture buffering into account. The issue of moisture buffering in buildings has been covered in depth by *Annex 41, Whole Building Heat, Air and Moisture Response* (Woloszyn and Rode, 2008). Energy Plus incorporates an effective moisture penetration depth model (EMPD) to account for moisture buffering (Crawley et al, 2001)

Output and analysis

Having run the simulation, the output data must be analysed using a suitable set of metrics and criteria in order to assess if adequate ventilation and IAQ performance is being achieved. The output of the models may well be substantial in both size and temporal resolution. Typically, the user will be able to export the transient airflows predicted for each ventilation element and the transient pollutant concentration in each zone. The airflows may be converted into zonal or whole building air change rates, which can be plotted as a frequency distribution, showing the expected range of ventilation availability achieved in a building on an annual or heating seasonal basis. Such a distribution can be used to assess what percentage of time the building is under- or over-ventilated. If an integrated thermal and airflow model is being used that does not have the ability to model pollutant concentrations, the predicted ventilation rate will be the basis of analysis. In dwellings, the hourly air change rates can be compared against recommended domestic ventilation rates of between 0.5 to 1.0 air changes per hour (ACH) as described in BS5250 (BSI, 2002) and CIBSE (2006).

Ventilation rates achieved, represented by air change rates or litres/person, may be compared to those recommended by local standards or targets. Some recommended ventilation rates are summarized in Table 15.9.

Another useful predictor of IAQ is indoor relative humidity (RH), which will be commonly available as an output of integrated thermal and airflow models. Several criteria exist to predict the risk of mould as a result of indoor RH. The Building Regulations for England and Wales state that:

> … the moisture criterion will be met if the relative humidity (RH) in a room does not exceed 70 per cent for more than 2 hours in any 12-hour period, and does not exceed 90 per cent for more than 1 hour in any 12-hour period during the heating season.

IEA Annex 14 is an extensive body of work that looks in detail at the issue of mould growth in buildings. It suggests a 'long-term' (monthly) limit to average air RH of 70 per cent in line with BS5250. The condition under which mould germinates and grows may be represented by a series of isopleths (Sedlbauer, 2001). The predicted RH may be compared to these isopleths and used as input to mould prediction models such as WUFI-bio, (WUFI, 2005). Such an approach has been used to examine mould growth in UK dwellings (Altamirano Medina et al, 2008).

The concentrations of other pollutants, such as formaldehyde and carbon monoxide, should be compared against the recommended World Health Organization (WHO) acceptable level of concentrations within dwellings (WHO, 2000). The predicted level of carbon dioxide is often used as a proxy measure for the adequacy of IAQ; indoor levels of CO_2 >1000ppm suggest inadequate ventilation rates within an occupied space (Mansson, 1995)

Conclusions

Ventilation modelling provides a valuable theoretical method for assessing the performance of domestic ventilation systems, both in terms of ventilation rates achieved and the resultant indoor air quality. In order for these models to become more widely used and accepted as a reliable method of assessing IAQ and ventilation rates in buildings, there is a need for continued testing and validation. The production of benchmarks and common exercises, which could be employed as tutorials and learning material for novice modellers, would be very welcome. The creation of common methodologies, accepted best practice and competent schemes for individuals should also be promoted, especially if such tools are to be used in the future as possible compliance methods to assess performance-based building and ventilation regulations.

References

Altamirano Medina, H., Davies M., Ridley, I., Mumovic, D. and Oreszczyn, T. (2008) in *Proceedings of the 8th Nordic Building Physics Symposium*, Copenhagen, Denmark, 16–18 June 2008, p1205

Angell, W. J. and Olson, W. W. (1988) *Moisture Sources Associated with Potential Damage in Cold Climate Housing*, Cold Climate Housing Information Centre, St Paul, US

Annex 27 (2003) *Evaluation and Demonstration of Domestic Ventilation Systems*, ECBCS, Sweden

ASHRAE (American Society of Heating, Refrigerating and Air-Conditioning Engineers) (2001) *ASHRAE Handbook – 2001 Fundamentals*, ASHRAE, Atlanta, GA, Chapter 16

BESTD (Building Energy Software Tools Directory) (2008) *Building Energy Software Tools Directory*, www.eere.energy .gov/buildings/tools_directory/, accessed June 2008

Boyd, D., Cooper, P. and Oreszczyn, T. (1988) 'Condensation risk prediction: Addition of a condensation model to BREDEM', *Build. Serv. Eng. Res Tech*, vol 9, no 3, pp117–125

BRE (Building Research Establishment) (1985) *Surface Condensation and Mould Growth in Traditionally Built Dwellings*, BRE Digest 297, BRE, UK

BRE (2003) *BRE IP2/03 Background Ventilators for Dwellings*, Ross D., Stephen R. and Pierce J. (eds) BRE, UK

BS5250 (2002) *Code of Practice for Control of Condensation in Buildings*, BSI, London

Burberry, P. (1994) *Environment and Services*, seventh edition, Longmans, UK

CEN/TC 156 (2002) *Ventilation for Buildings – Performance Testing of Components/Products for Residential Ventilation – Part 1: Externally and Internally Mounted Air Transfer Devices*, prEN 13141-1(e), CEN

CIBSE (Chartered Institution of Building Services Engineers) (1986) *Guide A: Environmental Design (1986 edition)*, Chartered Institution of Building Services Engineers

CIBSE (1999) *Guide A: Environmental Design (1999 edition)*, Chartered Institution of Building Services Engineers

CIBSE (2006) *Environmental Guide A*, CIBSE Publications, CIBSE, Norwich, Norfolk, pp4–18

Crawley, D. B., Lawrie, L. K., Pedersen, C. O., Strand, R., Liesen, R. J., Winkelmann, F. C., Buhl, W. F., Huang, Y. J., Erdem, A., Fisher, D. E., Witte, M. J. and Glazer, J. (2001) 'EnergyPlus: Creating a new generation building energy simulation program', *Energy and Buildings*, vol 33, issue 4, April, pp319–331

EERE (2008) www1.eere.energy.gov/buildings/about.html, accessed June 2008

Emmerich, S. J. (2001) 'Validation of multizone IAQ modeling of residential-scale buildings: A review', *ASHRAE Transactions*, vol 107, part 2

Feustel, H. E. (1998) *COMIS: An International Multizone Air Flow and Contaminant Transport Model*, August, LBNL-42182

Fürbringer, J. M., Roulet, C. A. and Borchiellini, R. (1996) *Energy Conservation in Buildings and Community Systems Programme Annex 23: Multizone Air Flow Modelling*, Final report, IEA

Finbow, M. (1982) 'Avoiding condensation and mould growth in existing housing with the minimum of energy input', *ASHRAE Transactions*, vol 24, pp1030–1034

Hanson, A. T. (2002) 'Moisture problems in houses', *Canadian Building Digest*, CBD231, http://irc.nrc-cnrc.gc.ca/pubs/cbd/cbd231_e.html

HMSO (1970) *Measurement of Humidity*, HMSO, London

IEA (1991) *Sourcebook, Report Annex XIV*, volume 1, International Energy Agency, Leuven, Belgium

Liddament, M. W. (1986) *Air Infiltration Calculation Techniques: An Application Guide*, AIVC, UK

Lstiburek, J. W. (1993) *Moisture Control Handbook: Principles and Practices for Residential and Small Commercial Buildings*, Van Nostrand Reinhold

Mansson, L. (1995) *Evaluation and Demonstration of Domestic Ventilation Systems – IEA ECBCS*, Annex 27 Report A12:1995, Swedish Council for Building Research, Stockholm, Sweden

Meyringer, V. (1985) 'Ventilation requirements to prevent surface condensation: Case study for a three person dwelling', *Refrigerating Engineering*, vol 31, no 6, pp345–350

Musser, A. (2000) 'Multizone modeling as an indoor air quality design tool', in *Proceedings of Healthy Buildings 2000*, Espoo, Finland.

NIST (2008) www.bfrl.nist.gov/IAQanalysis/index.htm, accessed June 2008

Persily, A. K. (1998) *A Modeling Study of Ventilation, IAQ and Energy Impacts of Residential Mechanical Ventilation*, National Institute of Standards and Technology. NISTIR 6162

Persily, A. K. and Ivy, E. M. (2001) *Input Data for Multizone Airflow and IAQ Analysis*, Building Environment Division, Building and Fire Research Laboratory, National Institute of Standards and Technology, NISTIR 6585

Persily, A. K. and Martin, S. R. (2000) *A Modeling Study of Ventilation in Manufactured Houses*, National Institute of Standards and Technology, NISTIR 6455

Pretlove, S. E. C. (2000) *Predicting Relative Humidity in UK Dwellings*, PhD thesis, University of London, London, March

Rousseau, M. Z. (1984) 'Source of moisture and its migration through the building enclosure', *ASTM Standardization News*, November, pp35–37

Sedlbauer, K. (2001) *Prediction of Mould Fungus Formation on the Surface of and Inside Building Components*, Dissertation, Universität Stuttgart, Germany

Stum, K. R. (1992) 'Winter steady state relative humidity and moisture load prediction in dwellings', *ASHRAE Transactions*, vol 98, no 1

Trechsel, H. R. (2001) 'Moisture analysis and condensation control in building envelopes', *ASTM Manual Series: MNL 40*

Van Den Bossche, N., Steeman, M., Willems, L. and Janssens, A. (2006) *Performance Evaluation of Humidity Controlled Ventilation Strategies in Residential Buildings*, Working Meeting, IEA Annex 41, Whole Building Heat, Air and Moisture Response (MOIST-EN), Lyon, October 2006

WHO (World Health Organization) (2000) *Air Quality Guidelines for Europe*, second edition, WHO Regional Office for Europe, Copenhagen, Denmark

Woloszyn, M. and Rode, C. (2008) *Final Report Subtask 1, Annex 41, Whole Building Heat, Air and Moisture Response*, International Energy Agency, Energy Conservation in Buildings and Community Systems Programme (ECBCS), April 2008

WUFI (2005) *WUFI Bio*, www.wufi.de/index_e.html

Yik, F., Sat, P. and Niu J. (2004) 'Moisture generation through Chinese household activities', *Indoor Built Environment*, vol 13, pp115–131

16

Moisture Control in Buildings

Hugo L. S. C. Hens

Introduction

Moisture is responsible for 70 to 80 per cent of all damage in buildings. Thus, correct moisture control is a prerequisite for achieving sustainable buildings. True control, however, is only possible if we know how moisture is transferred to, and moves in, building assemblies and how assemblies degrade when staying moist.

Why is water so aggresive? The reason is its asymmetric molecular structure, with the one oxygen atom and the two hydrogen atoms forming a very active dipole. This turns water into an effective solvent and explains why it adheres easily to surfaces. Water, furthermore, has its triple point at 0°C, which means that freezing starts there, a phase change causing 10 per cent volumetric expansion. The equilibrium between solid, liquid and vapour also causes condensation to appear at normal environmental temperatures.

Terminology

Before expanding on sources, transfer, damage and design, some terminology is first clarified (Hens, 2007).

The term 'density' is used for weight per cubic metre of dry material. The many microscopic small voids in a material fix its 'porosity'. Only part of these voids may be accessable for water molecules, quantifying the 'open porosity'.

The word 'moisture' relates to water in its three states (vapour, liquid and solid) with inclusion of all substances, such as salts, dissolved in it. Moisture in vapour form is present in all materials with open pores

wider than 0.23 Angstrom. Liquid moisture demands larger open pores. In fact, water molecules form chains in the liquid phase with a larger effective diameter.

To describe the presence of moisture in open porous materials, different moisture parameters have to be defined (see Table 16.1).

Although indicating the same thing, numerical values may be quite different. Take a brick, for example, with a density of 1800kg/m³ and a moisture content of 200kg/m³. The moisture ratio than is 100 * 200/1800 = 11.1% kg/kg, while for the volumetric moisture ratio, one gets: 100 * (200/1000) = 20% m³/m³. 11.1 is a smaller number than 20 and 200. As a rule of thumb the lower figures mean fewer moisture-related problems for materials with a density below 1000 kg/m³, volumetric moisture ratio gives the smaller number and is favoured. To avoid such confusion, apply the following rules:

- For open, porous, stony materials, use moisture content.
- For timber-based materials, use moisture ratio in percentage kg/kg.
- For extremely porous materials, use volumetric moisture ratio in percentage m³/m³.

Water vapour in the air

Dry air and water vapour both behave more or less as ideal gases:

For air: $p_a V = 287 m_a T$

For water vapour: $p V = 462 m_v T$ (1)

Table 16.1 *Definitions of moisture parameters*

Moisture content	kg/m³	The mass of moisture per cubic metre of material
Moisture ratio	Percentage kg/kg	The mass of moisture per unit mass of dry material
Volumetric moisture ratio	Percentage m³/m³	Cubic metre of moisture per cubic metre of material
Saturation degree	Percentage	Ratio between moisture content and moisture content at saturation

with V the volume considered (in cubic metres); m_a mass of air and m_v mass of water vapour in that volume (in kilograms); T temperature (in Kelvin); p_a partial dry air pressure (in Pa); and p partial water vapour pressure (in Pa), also called vapour pressure.

Since humid air is a mixture of ideal gases, total pressure obeys Dalton's law: equal to the sum of both partial pressures. Under atmospheric conditions, the mixture is exactly defined when two state variables are known – for example, temperature in °C and vapour pressure in Pa. As air is hardly soluble in water, the mixture is characterized by the same vapour saturation pressure as in a vacuum (see Figure 16.1). Vapour pressure cannot attain a higher value in humid air at a given temperature. Adding more water vapour than saturation allows will cause condensation to occur.

Equation 2 defines the widely concept of relative humidity: the ratio between the actual vapour pressure in the air and the vapour saturation pressure at the air's temperature:

$$\phi = \frac{p}{p_{sat}\left(\theta_a\right)} \tag{2}$$

A relative humidity 1 or 100 per cent means saturation. The value may shift between 0 and 100 per cent. In Figure 16.1, for example, the 50 per cent line is drawn.

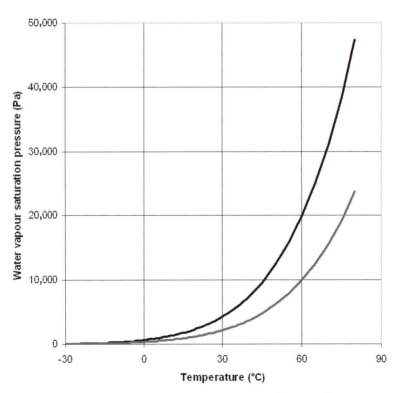

Figure 16.1 *Water vapour saturation pressure as a function of temperature*

Two very specific changes of state could initiate condensation:

1 *Adding vapour to the air volume at constant air temperature.* The starting point in Figure 16.1 then moves parallel to the pressure axis. At a given release, the saturation line is reached and condensation starts, while vapour pressure remains at saturation value. Such isothermal change of state more or less occurs in a bathroom during showering, when the mirror becomes misty.
2 *Keeping the amount of vapour in the air constant and lowering temperature.* Crossing the saturation line, then, occurs at a certain temperature. That temperature is called the dew point, a word that reflects grass moistened during clear summer nights.

Of course, in infinite number of other changes of state will cause condensation. Adiabatic humidification, for example, is used to measure humidity in the air as it forces the air temperature to drop to a value called wet bulb temperature (θ_{wb}). A psychrometer measures this quantity plus the air temperature. Transposition to vapour pressure yields:

$$p = p_{sat}\left(\theta_{wb}\right) - 66.71\left(\theta_{db} - \theta_{wb}\right). \tag{3}$$

Air and moisture scale

As mentioned earlier, pores in building materials may be open or closed. Empty open pores are filled with humid air. Starting from dry, pores become filled stepwise, with their moisture saturation degree (S_m) crossing typical intervals and values, coupled with a changing air saturation degree (S_a) (see Table 16.2).

In capillary-porous materials, the equation is:. $0 < S_{m,H} < S_{m,cr} < S_{m,c} < S_{m,cr,fr} < 1$. In materials with wide pores only, critical moisture saturation degree moves to

Table 16.2 *The moisture and air saturation degree scale*

S_m (percentage)	S_a (percentage)	Meaning
0	1	**Dry material** Complete drying is physically impossible. Dry always means nearly dry.
$0 \leq S_m \leq S_{m,H}$	–	**Hygroscopic interval** Porous materials see their moisture saturation degree crossing that interval when in contact with humid air. Resulting moistening appears as sketched in Figure 16.2, with a hysteresis between sorption and desorption. Two phenomena shape the curve: molecular adsorption against all pore walls at low relative humidity and capillary condensation at higher relative humidity.
$S_{m,cr}$	–	**Critical moisture saturation degree** This marks the border between moisture in the pores transported as vapour only and moisture transported in liquid form. The critical moisture saturation degree limits the moisture saturation degree in a porous material by interstitial condensation and helps to explain the transition from surface drying to drying from inside the material.
$S_{m,c}$	$S_{a,cr}$	**Capillary moisture saturation degree** This stands for the moisture saturation degree that a porous material attains when remaining in contact with a water surface. Once capillary saturated, the escape routes for all air pockets left are closed, shutting off outflow. The air saturation degree is therefore called critical.
$S_{m,c} \leq S_m \leq 1$		**Beyond capillary** This interval is reached when a material remains in contact with water without any possibility of drying or when submersed in water. In fact, as time goes on, the air pockets left slowly dissolve in the sucked water. The critical moisture saturation degree for frost damage ($S_{m,cr,fr}$) sits somewhere in that interval. Below this, frost damage is unlikely; above, its probability turns to 1.
$S_m = 1$	$S_a = 0$	**Saturation** Arriving at saturation is only possible through special treatment, such as vacuum saturation process or boiling it in water. Once saturated (i.e. once all open pores fill with liquid), the air saturation degree is definitely zero.

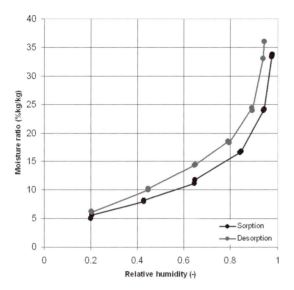

Figure 16.2 *Hygroscopic curve*

saturation until gravity starts draining the porous system. If the pores are too fine for capillary action, the same happens, although without gravity drainage.

Moisture sources

There is a substantial difference between liquid and vapour (see Table 16.3).

Moisture damage

Open pores in building materials that are filled with humid air are not harmful. Only when the air moves while experiencing temperature differences can problems arise. The fact that some layers in a building assembly turn wet is not even a disadvantage by definition. Veneer walls, for example, are used as rain buffer. Their wetness should not be of concern in cold and cool climates, except if non-frost-resistant bricks or mortars are used. The same holds for surface condensation against single glass. True: it is annoying; but it does no damage unless so much condensate is deposited that runoff attacks the timber casings. Although many examples of tolerance can be given, moisture is one of the main causes of damage. Invisible or hardly visible degradation includes an increase in thermal conductivity, more latent heat transfer, a decrease in strength and stiffness, and swelling and shrinking as moisture varies. For certain wood-based materials, a decrease in strength and stiffness, as well as volume change, may be quite extreme.

Visible damage is as follows.

Wood-based materials:

* Hydrolysis of the resin in particle board, plywood, strawboard and oriented strand board (OSB).
* Bacterial rot, mould attack and fungal attack. Fungi are damaging as they convert cellulose into water; in this way, timber looses its integrity, which may lead to collapses as shown in Figure 16.3.

Stony materials

* Mould, algae, moss and certain types of vegetation are more of an aesthetic problem, although the roots of plants may destroy joints and organic acids may attack lime-based materials.

Table 16.3 *Moisture sources*

Liquid	
Accidental	Dripping pipes, leaky joints around a shower pan, etc.
Rising damp	Moisture sucked up from the bottom of a wall. Could be groundwater, below-grade capillary water, rain runoff or splashing rain.
(Wind-driven) rain	In many climates, this is the most important moisture source.
Water and air pressure heads	Present above and below the phreatic surface; wind induced.
Built-in moisture	All moisture present in the building fabric at the moment of decommissioning.
Vapour form	
Humidity in the air	Many materials adsorb or desorb vapour in equilibrium with the relative humidity in the surrounding air.
Surface condensation	Stands for water vapour condensing on wall surfaces. Its presence indoors is seen as a problem; its presence outdoors is not, although surface condensation by under-cooling may generate as much moisture as wind-driven rain.
Interstitial condensation	Points to water vapour condensing inside a building. Interstitial condensation may stay invisible for quite some time.

Figure 16.3 *Swimming pool: Wooden roof girder collapsed by fungal attack*

- Salt crystallization and hydration: surface drying stages yield efflorescence, drying from inside the porous system. This, alongside hydration and dehydration, induces tensile stress in building material, which sometimes ends in complete pulverization of the salt-attacked parts.
- Frost damage: this occurs in very wet, open porous materials and during temperatures that oscillate around zero. The result may be spalling and pulverization.

Metals:

- Corrosion is the most feared of all types of damage. In many cases, the corroding volume expands, which is the reason why older reinforced concrete starts to spall around the bars.

Plastic materials:

- Hydration may plasticize material, ending in loss of structural integrity.
- Plastic foams can show substantial irreversible expansion under thermal loads once the cells are partially filled with water.

Moisture displacement

Several driving forces cause moisture to move in and throughout open porous materials. With regard to the vapour phase, two forces intervene: diffusion and bulk transport. Diffusion develops each time differences in vapour concentration exist in the humid air that surrounds the material and fills its pores. For simplicity, resulting moisture movement is considered to be Fickian, with the gradient in vapour pressure as the driving force:

$$g_v = -\partial\,grad\left(p\right) \tag{4}$$

where ∂ is the vapour permeability of the open porous material in kg/(m².s.Pa). The Fickian model, of course, simplifies things. In fact, many phenomena intervene. In extremely fine pores, Knudsen diffusion governs movement. With capillary condensation occuring, vapour moves between water islands with condensation/evaporation at each island. Above a certain relative humidity, surface flow develops in the adsorbed water layers between the water islands, etc.

Bulk flow reigns each time that humid air infiltrates, exfiltrates and loops in and through assemblies:

$$g_v = -0.621\,10^{-6}\,p\,g_a \tag{5}$$

with g_a the air flux in kg/(m².s). The amounts of water vapour transferred that way are greater than those driven by diffusion, the reason why bulk flow is the main player behind damage, something that was recognized decades ago. In any event, many practitioners and experts still overlook it when detailing highly insulated envelope assembles or when explaining damage.

Turning to the liquid phase, three main forces act together: suction, gravity and pressure differences. Suction is a direct consequence of capillarity: the fact that hydrophilic materials pick up water each time that they contact a water surface. Capillary force is inversely proportional to the equivalent pore diameter or crack width and is proportional to the surface tension of water multiplied by the cosine of the contact angle between water and material:

$$s = -\frac{4\sigma cos\left(\vartheta\right)}{d} \tag{6}$$

The smaller a pore is and the closer the contact angle is to zero (i.e. the more hydrophilic an open porous material is), the stronger it sucks. Displacement, however, is largely refrained in smaller pores, resulting in a bulk liquid flow proportional to the third power of the equivalent diameter or width. Materials with very small open pores hardly allow suction flow to develop. It is important to know that suction can never end in water outflow! A basement wall, for example, may turn wet by suction. However, when leakage is observed, the cause is gravity or flow driven by external pressure differences. Hydrophobic materials, instead, expel water with a force identical to capillary force.

Gravity is only active vertically. It takes over from suction as soon as the weight of a water column in an open porous system exceeds capillary suction. The result is water displacement and outflow. External pressure differences do the same, although they mobilize all flow directions.

Moisture modelling

Moisture modelling is never an solated activity. Since temperature and air pressure differences act as driving forces, one always has to combine hygrothermal modelling with heat and air transport. All models start from the axioms of mass and energy conservation and combine these with the transport equations and equations of state. As shown earlier, the first link moisture (vapour and liquid), heat and air fluxes to the driving forces (temperature, partial water vapour pressure, air pressure, suction, gravity and external pressures), while the second describe all thermodynamic equilibriums involved, such as enthalpy versus temperature, vapour saturation pressure versus temperature, and moisture content versus relative humidity.

Solving a combined heat, air and moisture problem demands knowledge of the exact geometry of a building assembly, together with the starting conditions, the exterior and interior boundary conditions, and the contact conditions between material layers. The exterior boundary conditions include temperature, relative humidity, wind, solar radiation, under-cooling, precipitation and wind-driven rain. Each is influenced by the environment around the building, the building form, building orientation and envelope detailing. Temperature, vapour pressure and air pressure, in turn, shape the interior boundary conditions. Contacts between materials may be diffusion only, capillary only or a mixture of capillarity and diffusion. Contact surfaces may also have properties that are different from both materials in contact.

One simple model has been standardized: Glaser's scheme. The assumptions behind this model are far reaching: building materials should behave as a one-dimensional assembly; air may not intervene as a carrier for water vapour; the assembly must be dry enough for vapour diffusion to be the only transport mechanism; no material is hygroscopic; and capillary, heat and water vapour flows are steady state, and surface and interstitial condensation are the only moisture responses considered. Calculations start during the coldest month. Vapour and vapour saturation pressures are calculated across the assembly. If both intersect, interstitial condensation occurs. Correct vapour pressure is then found by constructing the tangents to the saturation line through the vapour pressure value inside and the one outside, and linking the contact points with intermediate tangents if necessary (see Figure 16.4). The condensate per time and surface unit in each contact point is then given by the difference in slope between ingoing and outgoing tangent. With interstitial condensation a fact, the points where moisture is deposited remain on saturation pressure until complete drying occurs (Glaser, 1959).

Since Glaser published his method (which was conceived in order to evaluate cold storage room envelopes), several upgrades have been proposed, extending the method to assemblies with wet layers, allowing limit-state analysis and introducing bulk water vapour flow as an additional vapour drive (with far-reaching consequences for moisture-tolerant design) (see Vos and Coelman, 1967; Hens, 1978, 2007).

From the 1980s on, full models were developed, first at the part-building level and recently at the whole-building level. These models calculate transient heat, air and moisture response with inclusion of latent to sensible heat conversion, sorption/desorption, bulk vapour flow and liquid transport by suction. Moisture sources were extended to include rain, built-in moisture and rising damp. Most models, however, still struggle with gravity and pressure flows (Philip and De Vries, 1957; Luikov, 1966; Van der Kooi, 1971; Nielsen, 1974; Kießl, 1983; Kohonen, 1984; Pedersen, 1990; Künzel, 1994; Descamps, 1997; Küntz and van Mier, 1997; ASHRAE, 2005; Rode and Woloszyn, 2008).

Since then, achievements have included coupling with stress/strain calculations and the probability of crack formation (Carmeliet, 1992). Salt transport with

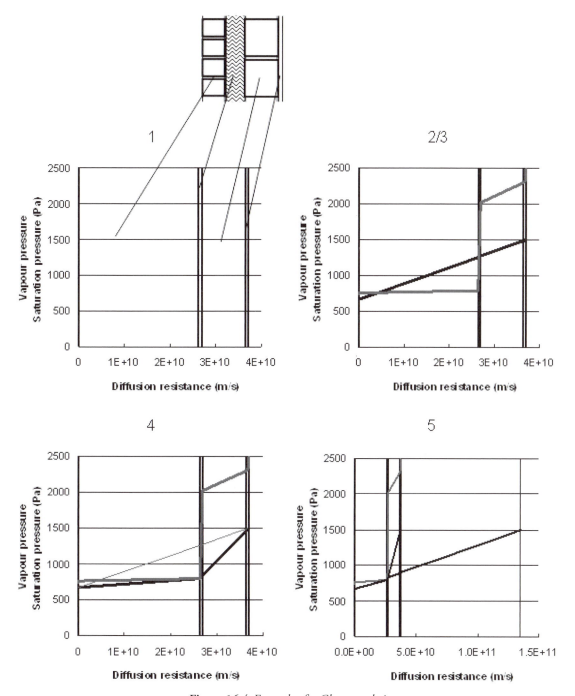

Figure 16.4 *Example of a Glaser analysis*

Note: Successive steps involve:

1   Redress the wall as a diffusion resistance versus vapour pressure image.
2, 3   Trace vapour (p) and saturation pressure (p_{sat}). If they intersect, interstitial condensation occurs.
4   Vapour pressure is replaced by the tangents.
5   Diffusion resistance is added at the warm side of the insulation in order to prevent interstitial condensation.

crystallization and hydration, as well as volatile organic compound (VOC) emissions have been added, turning combined heat, air and moisture modelling into damage and indoor air quality (IAQ) prediction tools (Grunewald et al, 2007; Nicolai et al, 2007). Risk, however, should be added as the ultimate refinement, facilitating well-balanced decision-making on acceptability.

Moisture-resilient design

Building component level

The starting point is the set of moisture sources, mentioned above and discussed in detail in Trechsel (2001) and Rose (2005).

Groundwater and seeping water pressure heads

Both act below grade. Leakage avoidance and thermal quality are the main performances to be guaranteed. If seeping water is the only factor to be considered, tolerance is gained by drainage around the basement in combination with a moisture-barring layer against the basement walls and floor. If a moderate groundwater head has to be turned around, the basement could be constructed in watertight concrete with the insertion of special profiles and adding injection tubes at all construction joints in order to inject curing resin if needed. In case large water heads have to be turned around, outside or inside water tightening should be applied. Inside, floors and walls are typically rendered with a watertight mortar or covered with a PVC membrane, which is stabilized by reinforced cast concrete walls and floor. Outside, a concrete floor 0.5m larger than the basement is cast first and covered with a multilayer watertight felt with very high tensile strength. Then, the actual basement floor is cast together with the walls. These are lined up at the outside with the same watertight felt, which is joined together with the horizontal felt. Finishing includes watertight perimeter insulation and extra mechanical protection.

Sloping terraces away from the building and adding a drain at the terraces' head are additional aids in keeping the basement dry.

Rising damp

The performance criterion is straightforward: avoid rising damp. How to do this is simple in new construction: insert watertight membranes in all walls above grade and respect continuity. As shown in Figure 16.5, however, things can still go wrong: if rain penetrates the ground floor the walls will suck up the water.

Floors on a grade demand special care. Research has shown that the ground below acts as a substrate on 100 per cent relative humidity. If the contact temperature between slab and ground surpasses the temperature inside and non-water-resistant glue fixes the vapour-retarding floor finish, it will slowly get moist and, finally, detach.

(Wind-driven) rain

Rain should neither moisten the thermal insulation or the layers behind. On low-slope surfaces, the only remedy is to avoid coverage with a watertight roofing felt as rain may pond and create water pressure heads in this way. Such a solution is called a one-stage system.

On sloped surfaces, coverage with overlapping elements such as tiles or slates may create rain-tightness, with rain flowing down from one element to the other. Watertightness, however, is not achieved in this way. High wind velocities may press runoff into the overlaps, causing leakage. For this reason, redundancy is sought by adding a second line of defence: the underlay. Roof elements and the underlay must drain into the gutters, which, in turn, transport the water to the downspouts.

Figure 16.5 *Rising damp*

In vertical wall assemblies, the layers catching the wind-driven rain may act as a drainage plane, buffer volume or transmission route. Their combination results in three systems of rain protection (Straube and Burnett, 1999):

1   Usage of massive walls with such high buffer capacity that even the longest rain spell does not wet half of the wall thickness: old masonry buildings are constructed in this way.
2   The one-stage system: walls are finished outside with a material acting as a drainage plane. The layer hardly buffers rain and should not transmit it to the layers behind. Stuccoed buildings follow this road, although their effectiveness may be destroyed by cracking.
3   The two-stage system: in such cases the airtight inside leaf with thermal insulation is protected by an external veneer with an air cavity behind. This veneer functions as an outside drainage plane and buffer layer. It also transports rain across cracks and voids to the inside, where the veneer's surface acts again as a drainage plane, with the air cavity behind functioning as a capillary break. This prevents rain from jumping to the inside leaf. Some non-capillary fibrous insulation materials may contact the veneer without causing leakage (see Figure 16.6).

The three systems are not equivalent in terms of overall performance. Buffering only results in a loss of thermal quality since wet materials conduct heat better than dry ones. At the same time, rain runoff is very unlikely to happen, which means that moisture load on joints – for example, those between masonry and windows – remains modest.

A one-stage system keeps the wall behind dry, but produces much more runoff with heavier moisture loads on joints and a higher probability of leakage.

The two-stage system is the most efficient: the wall keeps dry while runoff is minimal. However, the rain drained at the veneers inside should be redirected to outside. This necessitates cavity trays at the right spots with weep holes above. Even then, a problem remains: summer condensation. Veneers become wet by rain. When sunny weather follows, the moist veneer will heat up to 50–55°C. This produces very high vapour saturation pressures in the masonry, much higher than the vapour pressure inside, inducing a vapour drive to

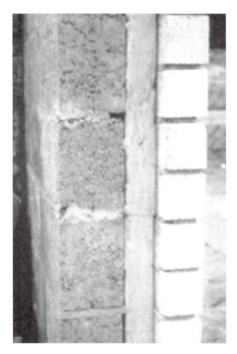

Figure 16.6 *Example of two-stage rain protection: Cavity wall with water-repellent fibrous insulation touching the veneer; the inside leaf is still lacking its air-retarding plaster finish*

the inside with, occasionally, interstitial condensation against (and in layers inside of) the thermal insulation. Timber-framed walls, in particular, suffer from this.

Built-in moisture

The only performance requirement here is that wet construction must dry without harming thermal quality and durability. Drying may proceed to the inside as well as to the outside. If necessary, the insulation should be sandwiched between two air and vapour barriers in order to avoid becoming wet from a vapour drive emanating from the wet layers. This, for example, is done in low-slope roofs, where the insulation is mounted on an air and vapour retarder and is covered by felt.

Hygroscopic moisture

The cause of hygroscopic behaviour is relative humidity in the air, which depends upon local temperature.

When humidity is much lower than the value inside, a higher relative humidity will be measured than inside. If surpassing 80 per cent for long periods of time, the likelihood for mould to germinate increases to 1. Mould is more an aesthetic than a medical problem. Only sensitive people respond negatively. Cleaning does not help and since mould spots look dirty, people generally believe that they have moisture problems, etc. In cold and cool climates, mould is easily avoided by insulating properly, excluding thermal bridging when insulating, heating enough in winter, and ventilating with an eye on healthy indoor conditions. In hot and humid climates, air drying is the only effective measure (Anon, 1990; Adan, 1994; Sedlbauer, 2001).

In museums, churches and monumental buildings with rich wooden ornaments, a too low and too rapid fluctuation in relative humidity is frequently a problem as timber will crack and paint will resemble alligator skin. In cold climates, air humidification may be necessary, while in cool climates, moderate heating already offers part of the solution.

Surface condensation

The performance requirement is simple: avoid or, at least, keep the risk below 5 per cent. Surface condensation happens each time the relative humidity at a surface reaches 100 per cent. Capillary surfaces suck the condensate. On non-porous surfaces, tiny water droplets appear that, once big enough, will run off. Avoidance in cool climates, cold climates and hot and humid climates demands the same measures as for mould.

Interstitial condensation

Here, long-lasting moisture build-up must be avoided, while annual winter moisture may be tolerated unless thermal performance degrades too much, durability is compromised or water drips out.

Tolerance against interstitial condensation demands excellent airtightness against infiltration and exfiltration and a correct balance between the vapour resistances at both sides of the thermal insulation. In cool and cold climates, the highest vapour resistance should be found inside. In hot and humid climates, where cooling is required, the highest vapour resistance should occur outside. In mixed climates, where the vapour drive

changes direction, it is best to use airtight mounted vapour-retarding thermal insulation (Janssens, 1998).

Building level

When analysing wind-driven rain patterns on buildings, the highest floors are typically affected more intensely than lower ones, with the upper corners the most exposed parts. Overhangs may protect the envelope efficiently. Inclined surfaces are extremely critical: they are not only wetted by wind-driven rain, but also by precipitation.

Inside, temperature is a controlled comfort parameter. In many buildings, relative humidity is not. Its value depends upon the instantaneous balance between ventilation flows; airflows among rooms; water vapour produced by building users and wet construction assemblies or removed by the heating, ventilating and air-conditioning (HVAC) system; the sorption/desorption behaviour of finishes, furniture and furnishing; and air buffering. Yet, the average relative humidity over longer periods depends upon average vapour pressure outside (p_e in Pa); average water vapour production or removal inside ($G_{v,P}$ in kg/h); average ventilation ($\dot{V}_a$ in m³/h); inside temperature (θ_i); and, sometimes, surface condensation, which helps in removing water vapour:

$$\phi_i = \frac{1}{p_{sat}(\Theta_i)}\left[p_e + \frac{462(273.15+\Theta_i)\left[G_{v,P} - max\left[O, \beta A_{cond}\left[\phi_i p_{sat}(\Theta_{s,cond})\right]\right]\right]}{\dot{V}_a}\right] \quad (7)$$

with θ surface film coefficient for water vapour diffusion in s/m, A_{cond} area affected by surface condensation in m² and $p_{sat}(\beta_{s,cond})$ saturation pressure on that surface in Pa. Peaks and valleys in inside relative humidity are dampened by sorption/desorption and air buffering. In extreme cases, such as libraries with numerous shelves filled with books, relative humidity may become very stable, even without air conditioning.

Airflows among rooms and between the building and outdoors are driven by stack, wind and fans. Airflows carrying water vapour produced inside can traverse air-permeable envelope parts, occasionally causing severe interstitial condensation problems. Flows infiltrating through rain-buffering layers, in turn, transport extra water vapour to the inside (Rode and Woloszyn, 2008).

Case studies

Building with inclined walls

A university building had to accommodate a very diverse programme: underground parking, lecture theatres, library, smaller seminar rooms and individual office rooms. For this purpose, the design team proposed a building that narrowed from the basement to the top. The lecture theatres were situated just above the parking and the library was positioned in between these theatres and the seminar rooms and offices, which filled the top floors. The result was a building with oblique cavity walls composed of masonry veneer, partially filled cavity and reinforced concrete inside leaf with brick finish inside (see Figure 16.7).

Once in use, complaints about large moisture spots and rain penetration along the window sills surfaced (see Figure 16.8).

The diagnosis included calculation of the catch ratio patterns on the building envelope for wind-driven rain coming from the south-west. This confirmed the high degree of rain exposure. Observation of the runoff showed that the oblique façades functioned as active drainage planes with a concentration at the edges, something no model could predict. Since the veneer had received a water-repellent treatment, runoff primarily loaded the small cracks between bricks and mortar joints, causing leakage into the cavity. There, the leaking water dripped on the insulation, ran off, penetrated the joints between the boards and wetted the concrete inside leaf, where shrinkage cracks directed the water to the brick finish inside. The sills, in turn, lacked step-ups below the window frames, causing direct rain penetration.

To solve the problem, the contractor first replaced one of the oblique veneer walls through a stepwise regressing veneer. This was not a success as the view was not pleasant and the solution created thermal bridges, which lifted the U value of the wall from $0.49W/(m^2.K)$ to $0.64W/(m^2.K)$. Trays were also forgotten, leaving room for continued leakage. The final solution involved exchanging the brick veneers for a watertight zinc veneer on timber lathing. This also solved the sill problem.

Summer condensation

A new office building with five floors was built. Soon after, complaints about water running down the inside face of the windows on the highest floor surfaced (see Figure 16.9). Dripping became so annoying that the top floor could not be leased any more.

Figure 16.7 *Building with rain penetration*

Figure 16.8 *Rainwater runoff and missing sill step below the window frames*

The contractor thought surface condensation was the cause, which, of course, was unlikely since runoff always occurred during warm weather. An in-depth study revealed that the highest floor was heavily hit by wind-driven rain (see Figure 16.10). That is, the calculated catch ratio (the flux of rain on the building walls divided by the flux of rain on the ground) was very high for various rainfall rates R_h (mm/h). The envelope was conceived as a cavity wall with a veneer, constructed of dense bricks, a cavity filled with mineral fibre and an inside leaf in very dense, hardly capillary, pre-cast concrete. The trays above windows were point-wise fixed to the concrete, leaving open joints in between, while the windows themselves were mounted in the veneer, ahead of the filled cavity.

Each rain spell filled the joints in the veneer with water, providing cavity-side runoff that slowly moistened

the bricks. When the sun shined, the moisture evaporated. The vapour traversed the mineral fibre fill and condensed against the concrete inside leaf, where it was not sucked, but ran down, passed the joint between the tray and the concrete, and dripped down along the windows.

Three solutions were offered, from most risky to very safe:

1   Treat the bricks with a water-repellent agent.
2   Take down the veneer on the fifth floor, glue the tray correctly against the concrete leaf and rebuild the veneer.
3   Stucco the whole building with a water-repellent lime-based mortar.

Although solutions 2 or 3 were advised as being the least risky, the contractor decided for the most risky, but cheapest, first solution.

Figure 16.9 *Dripping water and runoff along the inside face of the windows*

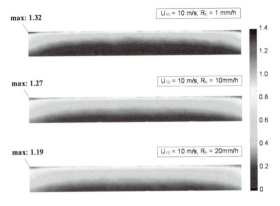

Figure 16.10 *Wind-driven rain, calculated catch ratio*

References

Adan, O. (1994) *On the Fungal Defacement of Interior Finishes*, PhD thesis, Eindhoven University of Technology, Netherlands

Anon (1990) *Guidelines and Practice*, Final report of IEA ECBCS Annex 14, Condensation and Energy, ACCO, Leuven

ASHRAE (American Society of Heating, Refrigerating and Air-Conditioning Engineers) (2005) *Handbook of Fundamentals*, ASHRAE, Atlanta, GA

Carmeliet, J. (1992) *Durability of Fabric-Reinforced Stucco for Outside Insulation: A Probabilistic Approach Based on Non-Local Continuous Damage Mechanics*, PhD thesis, University of Leuven, Leuven (in Dutch)

Descamps, F. (1997) *Continuum and Discrete Modelling of Isothermal Water and Air Transport in Porous Media*, PhD thesis, University of Leuven, Leuven

Glaser, H. (1959) 'Grafisches verfahren zur Untersuchung von Diffusionvorgänge', *Kältetechnik*, vol 10, pp345–349

Grunewald, J., Nicolai, A., Li, H. and Zhang, J. S. (2007) 'Modelling of coupled numerical HAM and pollutant simulation-implementation of VOC storage and transport equations', in *Proceedings of the 12th Symposium on Building Physics*, Technische Universität Dresden, Dresden, 29–31 March, pp792–799

Hens, H. (1978) 'Condensation in concrete flat roofs', *Building Research and Practice*, October, pp292–309

Hens, H. (2007) *Building Physics: Heat, Air and Moisture, Fundamentals and Engineering Methods with Examples and Exercises*, Ernst & Sohn (A Wiley Company), Berlin, Germany

Janssens, A. (1998) *Reliable Control of Interstitial Condensation in Lightweight Roof Systems*, PhD thesis, University of Leuven, Leuven

Kießl, K. (1983) *Kapillarer und dampfförmiger Feuchtetransport in mehrschichtigen Bauteilen*, PhD thesis, Universität Gesamthochschule Essen, Germany

Kohonen R. (1984) *A Method to Analyse the Transient Hygrothermal Behaviour of Building Materials and Components*, Technical Research Centre of Finland (VTT), Publication 21, Finland

Küntz, M. and van Mier, J. G. M. (1997) 'Field evidences and theoretical analysis of the gravity-driven wetting front instability of water runoffs on concrete structures', *Heron*, vol 42, no 4, pp231–244

Künzel, H. M. (1994) *Verfahren zur ein- und zweidimensionalen Berechnung des gekoppelten Wärme- und Feuchtetransports in Bauteilen mit einfachen kennwerten*, PhD thesis, University of Stuttgart, Germany

Luikov, A. V. (1966) *Heat and Mass Transfer in Capillary-Porous Bodies*, Pergamon Press, Oxford

Nicolai, A., Grunewald, J. and Zhang, J. S. (2007) 'Salt transport and phase transitions: Modelling and numerical solution in the simulation code Delphin 5/Champ-bes', in *Proceedings of the 12th Symposium on Building Physics*, Technische Universität Dresden, Germany, 29–31 March, pp877–884

Nielsen, A. F. (1974) *Moisture Distribution in Cellular Concrete during Heat and Moisture Transfer*, PhD thesis, Thermal Insulation laboratory, Technical University of Denmark, Denmark

Pedersen, R. C. (1990) *Combined Heat and Moisture Transfer in Building Constructions*, PhD Thesis, Thermal Insulation laboratory, Technical University of Denmark, Report 214, Denmark

Philip, J. R. and De Vries, D. A. (1957) 'Moisture movement in porous materials under temperature gradient', *Transactions of the American Geophysical Union*, vol 38, no 2

Rode, C. and Woloszyn, M. (2008) *Whole Building Heat, Air and Moisture Transfer: Modelling Principles*, Final Report IEA-RCBCS Annex 41, ACCO, Leuven

Rose, W. B. (2005) *Water in Buildings*, John Wiley and Sons, New York, NY

Sedlbauer, K. (2001) *Vorhersage von Schimmelpilzbildung auf und in Bauteilen*, Thesis, Universität Stuttgart, Stuttgart, Germany

Straube, J. and Burnett, E. (1999) 'Rain control and design strategies', *Thermal Envelope and Building Science*, vol 23, pp41–56

Trechsel, H. (ed) (2001) *Moisture Control in Buildings*, ASTM Manual Series: MNL 18

Van der Kooi, J. (1971) *Moisture Transport in Cellular Concrete Roofs*, PhD thesis, University of Delft, Uitgeverij Waltman

Vos, B. H. and Coelman, E. J. W. (1967) *Condensation in Structures*, Report no BI-67-33/23, TNO-IBBC

17

Natural Ventilation in City Centre Buildings

Dejan Mumovic, Oliver Wilton and Sung Min Hong

Introduction

Natural ventilation can serve a range of purposes in buildings, from delivering fresh air in order to maintain air quality to ventilative cooling to limit temperatures during the summertime. It is also known as passive ventilation since no energy is used to drive airflow. Designs utilizing natural ventilation range in complexity from simple arrangements controlled by manually opened windows to complex automated Building Energy Management System (BEMS)-linked mixed-mode systems, and those involving induced airflow via techniques such as passive downdraught evaporative cooling.

A major motive for the use of natural ventilation and ventilative cooling is the potential for low operational energy use and associated low CO_2 emissions and operational costs. The UK PROBE study (Bordass et al, 2001) has revealed that nine out of the ten highest CO_2 emitters were air-conditioned and mixed-mode buildings. The study showed that in the air-conditioned and mechanically ventilated buildings, the CO_2 emissions resulting from the fans and pumps required to move conditioned air accounted for up to 50 per cent of the emissions associated with space heating and cooling. Furthermore, since the air-conditioned buildings tend to be a deep plan, the CO_2 emissions associated with artificial lighting are substantial. These facts have caused a reappraisal of the natural means of ventilation and a surge of interest in advanced natural ventilation technologies.

There is a range of further motives for utilizing natural ventilation techniques. A number of research projects have shown that naturally ventilated buildings tend to be more desirable to occupants than mechanically ventilated or air-conditioned buildings. Usually, the occupants of the naturally ventilated buildings report lower sick building symptom prevalence in comparison to the mechanically and air-conditioned buildings. In addition to the health-related benefits, carefully designed naturally ventilated buildings can cost less to construct and maintain than more heavily mechanically serviced equivalents. Maintenance is generally required infrequently and is of a relatively simple and unspecialized nature when it is required.

This chapter gives an overview of natural ventilation in non-domestic buildings and describes more advanced natural ventilation strategies and technologies available to optimize the performance of naturally ventilated systems. Special attention is paid to urban areas as the lower wind speeds, the existence of heat islands and the potentially high ambient noise and air pollution levels represent a serious challenge to designers of naturally ventilated buildings.

It is important to note that in successful naturally ventilated buildings, natural ventilation strategy is integrated within the wider building environmental and architectural design strategy during a process of synthesis that occurs as the design develops.

Theoretical background

The magnitude and pattern of natural air movement through a building depends upon the pressure difference acting across the ventilation path and the resistance of that flow path. The pressure difference driving the airflow is a function of two driving forces: wind and buoyancy.

Figure 17.1 shows the airflow around an isolated pitched roof building located in a low-density suburban environment with no built or natural elements that can obstruct the flow: plan view (top) side view (bottom). The wind-induced pressure fluctuation on the building surfaces varies in time and space. The approaching flow separates in front of the cube (A) and forms the front stagnation point (B) at about three-fifths of the height of building. The flow goes down towards the ground, where it has more kinetic energy than the approaching flow, rolls up and forms a primary separation vortex (C). The main so-called 'horse-shoe vortex' (D) is formed around the base of the property forming the wake (E) and has a typical converging behaviour. A large separation region (F) develops behind the property, ending with the reattachment point (G). The results of turbulence modelling suggest the existence of two strong three-dimensional coherent vortices (H). A region of very low pressure is generally observed on the roof surface (I). Note that flow at a certain distance from the roof should be unaffected by obstacles (J).

As can be seen, wind pressures are generally positive on the windward side of a building and negative on the leeward side. The occurrence and change of wind pressures on building surfaces depend upon wind speed and wind direction relative to the building, the location and surrounding environment of the building, and the shape of the building.

When air movement is due to temperature difference between indoors and outdoors, the flow of air is in the vertical direction and is along the path of least resistance. The temperature difference causes density differentials and, therefore, pressure differences, that drive the air to move. This is known as the stack effect. When buoyancy force acts alone, a *neutral pressure level* (NPL) exists, where the interior and exterior pressures are equal (see Figure 17.2 a). At all other levels, the

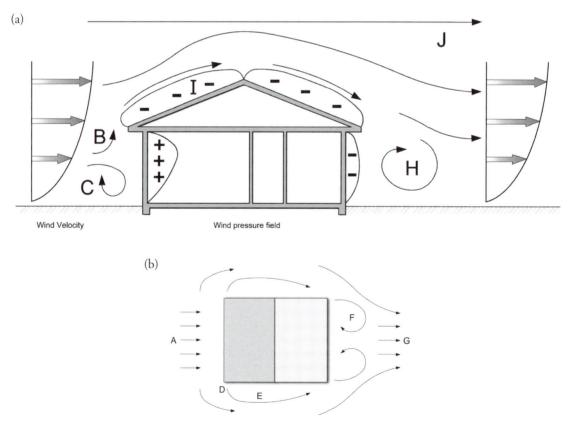

Figure 17.1 *Wind pressures acting on an isolated building: (a) elevation; (b) plan*

pressure difference between the interior and exterior depends upon the distance from the neutral pressure level and the difference between the densities of inside and outside air. Note that the length of the horizontal arrows represents the magnitude of the resulting pressure difference across each opening. Figure 17.2 b shows the variation in wind surface pressure with height.

However, even the lowest wind speeds will induce pressure distribution on the building envelope that will also act to drive airflow. Therefore, the pressure patterns for actual buildings will continually change with the relative magnitude of buoyancy and wind forces. Figure 17.2 c shows the combined effect of buoyancy and wind forces. The pressures due to each effect are added together to determine the total pressure difference across the building envelope. To achieve the shown flow patterns in practice (inflow at the lower three openings and exhaust via the top), one has to adjust the internal pressure by judicious sizing of the ventilation openings. In this context, assuming that the same ventilation rate is required at each occupied level, the sum of all the inflows has to balance the single high-level outflow. Detailed analysis of driving forces for natural ventilation can be found elsewhere (CIBSE, 2005; Santamouris and Wouters, 2006).

Design requirements and site analysis

Client brief and design requirements

Building designs are developed in response to the client brief, to site-specific conditions and constraints, and to further statutory and technical requirements. These factors set out parameters within which designs develop, with some cases where there is significant delimitation to the range of viable design responses and others where there is less so.

The client brief will set out the basics of building type (residential, offices, educational, auditoria, etc.) and specific accommodation requirements, and will go on to deal with a range of further matters at a level of detail that can vary greatly. Environmental performance requirements (temperature targets, lighting levels, etc.) will generally be set out. The nature and structuring of these requirements are of key importance as they effectively determine the viability of natural ventilation as a response. For example, single figure summertime temperature targets are not deliverable via the use of pure natural ventilative cooling as this tends to deliver a temperature range relative to outside temperature rather

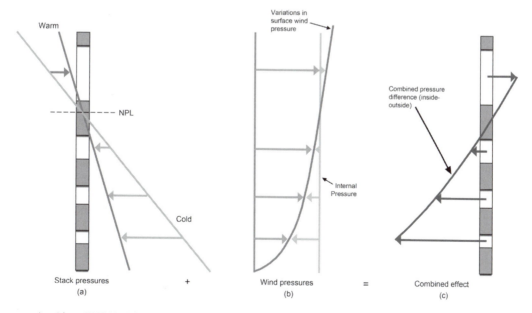

Source: reproduced from CIBSE AM10 (CIBSE, 2005) by permission of the Chartered Institution of Building Services Engineers

Figure 17.2 *Combined buoyancy and wind-driven ventilation: (a) Stack pressures; (b) wind pressures; (c) combined effect*

than an absolute temperature regardless of the weather. Temperature targets set out as ranges with associated frequencies of occurrence are becoming increasingly common (for examples, those set out in BB101 for school design) and these can lead to the delivery of comfortable environments without precluding the use of natural ventilation.

Further briefing matters having a bearing on the application of natural ventilation include the level of compartmentalization of internal spaces, acoustic compartmentalization requirements between spaces, occupancy patterns and densities, and internal heat gains.

It is of key importance that, wherever possible, the design team collaborates in the development of the final client brief. This is in order to ensure that client needs and ambitions are reflected in performance requirements, while also aiming not to preclude the development of the most elegant and efficient design response – which, in many cases, may involve a level of natural ventilation.

Further 'givens' when developing designs include the site-specific conditions and constraints. These include the physical nature of the site itself (whether it is land and/or existing buildings) and its surroundings (urban fabric or otherwise), local microclimate and related factors, and constraints exerted via the development control or planning system. The planning system exerts constraints on building form and fabric, as does the use of natural ventilation – and these can conflict. In most cases, design solutions delivering natural ventilation will sit comfortably within planning parameters and may well be actively encouraged. However, in certain cases, such as projects involving listed buildings or sited within conservation areas, planning constraints may conflict with and therefore constrain natural ventilation solutions. A simple example of this would be the application of external shading on a listed building,

which may be necessary to bring gains down within levels where natural ventilative cooling can be used but may well be of an unacceptable appearance to gain planning (and listed building) approval.

The points addressed above together largely determine the design requirements for a project, these being the requirements against which the success of a building design can be measured. A design is then developed as a process of synthesis in response to these requirements. When considering the use of natural ventilation, it is important at an early stage of the design process to ascertain what it could achieve given the particular constraints and requirements. In particular, the technical viability of natural ventilation to deliver the following should be assessed:

- provide an appropriate level of indoor air quality by removing and diluting airborne contaminants;
- reduce overheating in the building (particularly during summer months);
- integrate with all other aspect of the building design, such as the daylighting and acoustics design.

Microclimate and weather data

The microclimate of a building site can have a strong influence on the effectiveness of natural ventilation systems. In the urban environment, the mean velocity of wind is reduced significantly and wind direction might be changed. As a consequence, the wind-induced pressure on a building envelope is lower (see Figure 17.3).

It is very difficult to offer specific guidance on the design of naturally ventilated buildings within urban street canyons. However, as a starting point, one should take into account the following rules of thumb (Santamouris and Wouters, 2006):

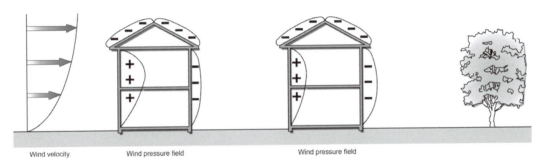

Figure 17.3 *Wind pressures acting on an urban building*

- The potential for natural ventilation is greatly reduced if the height-to-width ratio of the street canyon is higher than unity.
- When the wind is perpendicular to the street canyon axis, the airflow inside of the canyon is nearly vertical and parallel to the window; as a consequence, the pressure coefficients inside a building are lower than the pressure coefficients calculated from the ambient wind speed directions. In this case, the horizontal pivot, top-hung or louvred windows should be used to direct flow towards occupants for daytime ventilation.
- When the wind is parallel to the street canyon axis, the flow inside of the canyon is nearly horizontal and parallel to the window; as a consequence, the pressure coefficients inside a building are lower than the pressure coefficients calculated from the ambient wind speed directions. In this case, the vertical pivot and side-hung (casement) windows should be used to provide either a positive or negative wing wall effect in response to the prevailing wind.
- When the wind is oblique to the street canyon axis, the pressure coefficients inside a building are still lower than the pressure coefficients calculated from the ambient wind speed directions, but higher then the pressure coefficients calculated when the ambient flow is either parallel or perpendicular to the street canyon axis.

Solar radiation absorbed by urban surfaces results in a temperature increase that is important to take into account as it will limit the cooling potential of natural ventilation. In less dense urban areas, this might be only a local phenomenon for intakes located on south-facing walls, while in dense urban areas it might result in a general increase of outdoor temperatures compared to rural areas. This effect, known as the heat island effect, is addressed in the Chapter 12. A detailed analysis of the effect of the London urban heat island on building summer cooling demand and night ventilation strategies can be found elsewhere (Kolokotroni et al, 2006).

In order to assess the internal temperatures likely to occur in naturally ventilated buildings and to establish the required ventilation rates, the Chartered Institution of Building Services Engineers (CIBSE) has produced two weather years for 14 UK locations:

- design summer year (DSY);
- test reference year (TRY).

DSY is an actual year containing fairly extreme temperatures for the six months between April and September and should be used to assess whether or not there is an acceptably low risk of summertime overheating in naturally ventilated buildings. For example, to create the DSY for London Heathrow, the average dry bulb temperature was calculated for each year from 1976 to 1995. These were ranked in order of magnitude and the third ranked was selected as the DSY. This particular year, 1989, has 267 hours with a dry bulb temperature in excess of 25.8° C and an absolute peak temperature of 33.7° C.

TRY is a synthesized typical weather year and should be used to analyse energy use and overall environmental performance of buildings. The TRY for London Heathrow consists of successive typical months that have been extracted from 20 different years. However, when assessing a building to be sited in the middle of London, the effects of both the heat island and the CIBSE design conditions must be considered. This is because Heathrow, the source of the CIBSE London data, is outside the heat island. Preliminary research has indicated that when these factors are considered, some form of cooling must be used to maintain comfort in buildings sited in central London. A detailed investigation of the impact of newly published CIBSE weather data on natural ventilation design is given elsewhere (Ren et al, 2003).

Air pollution

A second important issue in designing naturally ventilated buildings in urban areas is the impact of outdoor air quality. While inadequate outdoor air quality affects both naturally and mechanically ventilated buildings, there are three reasons why the naturally ventilated designs are more sensitive to elevated levels of outdoor air pollution:

1 typical ventilation systems do not incorporate particle filtration;
2 natural ventilation systems may introduce far greater quantities of outdoor air into the building to reduce overheating, particularly in summer months;
3 due to low natural driving forces, the positioning of the air inlets is more limited and inlets at high level (where levels of certain pollutants are generally lower) are often not a viable option.

Chapter 13 provides a detailed analysis of the distribution of air pollutants in urban areas and their effect on air quality within buildings. In summary, when designing natural ventilation systems for urban buildings, one has to take into account the following rules of thumbs (see Figure 17.4):

- lower concentrations at the windward side of street canyons that are almost perpendicular to the wind direction;
- higher concentrations at the leeward side of street canyons that are almost perpendicular to the wind direction;
- a negative correlation between concentration and wind speed;
- wash-out and accumulation effects along those canyons whose axes are parallel to the wind direction.

Note that with different wind speed values, considerable differences would be observed in concentration values obtained (Mumovic et al, in press). Generally, during low wind periods the convective transport of the pollutant would be greatly reduced, causing higher concentration at the very lower levels of street canyons. In contrast, during periods of very high wind speed, the washing-out effect increases significantly, generally lowering the concentration levels within the city centre. As has been seen, the flow patterns that develop around buildings govern the pressure distribution and, consequently, concentration distribution in a built

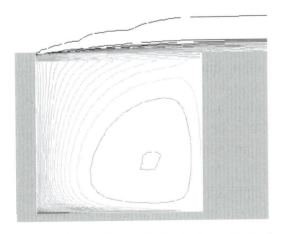

Figure 17.4 *Air pollution distribution in an idealized street canyon*

environment. Although these rules of thumb are useful when designing natural ventilation for urban buildings, be aware that in a more complex built environment, the superimposition and interaction of flow patterns associated with adjacent buildings dominate the airflow and dispersion of air pollutants. Accordingly, the concentration distribution function becomes much more complex, taking into account the additional parameters (Mumovic et al, 2006):

> Concentration distribution = f (street width, height, length, orientation, wind speed, building geometry, upwind building configuration, intersection location and geometry).

Obviously, the local pollution concentration variation indicates that natural ventilation may still be a viable option for buildings within urban air quality management areas. In this case, the designers should employ modelling tools such as computational fluid dynamics (CFD) to predict indoor pollutant concentrations resulting from various case scenarios of different ventilation rates and outdoor air pollution concentration levels (see Chapter 13). A detailed analysis of local concentration gradients in complex built environments is given elsewhere (Mumovic et al, in press).

Noise

A third important issue in designing natural ventilation in buildings in urban areas is noise, whether it comes from outdoor or from other rooms in the same building. The noise is attenuated by the physical boundaries of the room, such as the building envelope, internal partitions, doors and windows. Furthermore, the room acoustics (geometry and acoustic reflectivity of surfaces) controls whatever noise is transmitted into the room. In urban areas, traffic noise can be of particular concern. There are two main solutions to this problem:

1 positioning of ventilation inlets on the sides of the building away from the noise source;
2 use of sound-attenuating ventilation openings – for example, those incorporating noise-reducing baffles or acoustic labyrinths.

Note that the noise-reducing mechanisms usually involve significant resistance to airflow and a careful balance between the two opposing effects must be sought. Absorbing internally generated noise in spaces with large areas of hard surface (usually associated with thermally massive buildings) is another important acoustic issue that can be resolved either by using absorbent partitions and hangings or by using carefully profiled ceilings. A detailed analysis of various noise-control strategies for naturally ventilated buildings is given elsewhere (De Salis, et al, 2002).

Developing a ventilation design strategy

The variety and diversity of purpose-provided natural ventilation systems that have been proposed in recent years is staggering, especially in Europe. Often, mechanical devices are added to enhance ventilation system performance and control, adding to the complexity. Nevertheless, these systems are invariably conceived as variants of the basic forms of ventilation strategies. In this section, these basic forms of ventilation strategy are defined and related to the form and layout of the building for which they are typically best suited. General terms used are as follows: vents are ventilation openings through which air flows into or out of a space; an inlet is a vent through which air flows into a space; and an outlet is a vent through which air flows out (these often reverse in naturally ventilated buildings).

Single-sided ventilation

Single-sided ventilation typically serves single rooms and relies on vents on one side only of the enclosure. It is closely approximated in many multi-room buildings with opening windows on one side of the room and a closed internal door on the other side. Figure 17.5 shows a schematic of two variants of this basic ventilation form:

1   *Single-sided ventilation with single opening* (Figure 17.5 a). Relative to the other strategies, this one offers the least attractive natural ventilation solution and is characterized by lower ventilation rates and the ventilating air penetrating a smaller distance into the space. As a rule of thumb, the limiting depth for effective ventilation is about twice the floor to ceiling height, typically 4m to 6m in depth. In summer, it relies upon wind turbulence

to generate reversing flows in and out of the room. In the winter when greater temperature difference exists, it is possible to obtain buoyancy-driven exchanges if the single opening is reasonably tall.

2   *Single-sided ventilation with double opening* (Figure 17.5 b). Driving forces in this case are enhanced by room-scale stack effects. The stack-induced flow increases with the vertical separation of the openings and with the temperature difference between inside and outside. Furthermore, wind-induced ventilation is slightly improved due to the increased probability of pressure differences occurring between two openings. In order to prevent cold draughts from the lower-level openings in winter, special attention has to be paid to the positioning of the inlets within the room. As a rule of thumb, the limiting depth for effective ventilation is about 2.5 times the floor to ceiling height, typically 7m to 8m.

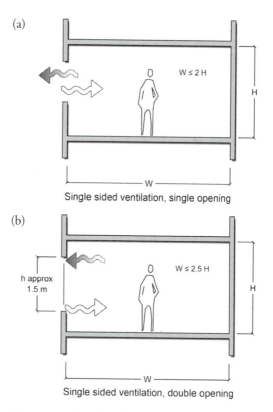

Single sided ventilation, single opening

Single sided ventilation, double opening

Figure 17.5 *Single-sided ventilation: (a) single opening; (b) double opening*

Cross-ventilation

Cross-ventilation is usually driven by wind-generated pressure differences inducing positive (inward-acting) pressures on windward surfaces and negative (outward-acting) pressures on leeward surfaces. The floor depth in the direction of ventilation has to be limited to effectively prevent heat and pollutant build-up from the space during ventilation due to typical driving forces. As a rule of thumb, the limiting depth for effective ventilation is about five times the floor to ceiling height, typically up to 15m (see Figure 17.6). This implies a relatively narrow plan depth for the building that is usually achieved by adopting either a linear built form or an open courtyard form. Note that in the latter case the significant differences in wind pressure between the inlet and outlet opening will be more difficult to achieve because the courtyard and the leeward side of the building will be at similar pressures.

The ventilation principles of wind-driven natural ventilation systems utilizing roof-mounted ventilators are illustrated in Figure 17.7. Using compartmentalized vertical vents, the pressure difference across the segment facing the wind drives the air into a space, while the suction created by the negative pressure on the leeward segments draws air out of the space. Combined inlet and outlet static roof-mounted natural ventilation systems are typically made up of a louvred terminal, a base and damper assemblies that allow the user or an automated control system to adjust the ventilation.

Buildings that are particularly suited to roof-mounted ventilation include educational buildings,

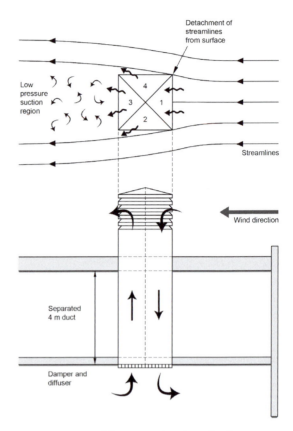

Figure 17.7 *Flow around and inside of a square roof-mounted ventilator*

libraries, and health and community centres (all of which require low operational and maintenance costs). Figure 17.8 shows the temperature and airflow distribution within a space ventilated by means of two roof-mounted ventilators manufactured by Monodraught™. The optimum performance of this well-established system at a given speed and orientation is only possible if the ventilator is located in a free air stream, undisturbed by any obstructions. Other parameters affecting the performance include the shape of the louvres, the resistance of dampers, the height of the louvres above roof level, the size of the louvred area and the temperature difference between the indoor and outdoor temperature. When installed in areas of heavy local traffic, consideration should be given to providing an acoustic internal lining which might affect the operational performance of the system. Detailed design, sizing and testing methodologies are given elsewhere (BSRIA, 2005).

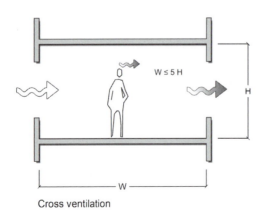

Cross ventilation

Figure 17.6 *Cross-ventilation*

(a)

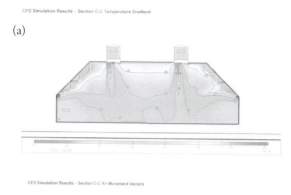

(b)

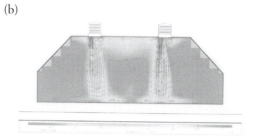

Source: Monodraught™

Figure 17.8 *CFD simulation results: (a) temperature gradients; (b) air velocity vectors*

Stack ventilation

A number of designers are achieving deeper floor plans than described above by providing stack ventilation within the building. This may occur via purpose-built vertical ducts (also known as stacks or chimneys) or via an internal atrium or other type of vertical spatial continuity within the building. Stack ventilation is buoyancy driven and relies on density differences to draw cooler, denser outdoor air into a building via low-level vents and to exhaust warmer, less dense indoor air via high-level vents. Should the air inside of the building at any time be cooler than that outside, then the airflow direction will reverse. For any time where indoor air temperature is higher that outdoors (generally the case in the UK, other than for the hottest summer days in thermally massive buildings), the following stack effect occurs (see Figure 17.9):

• The warmer air in the building rises up as the indoor air temperature is higher than that outdoors.
• The upward air movement produces a negative indoor pressure at the bottom and a positive indoor pressure on the top.

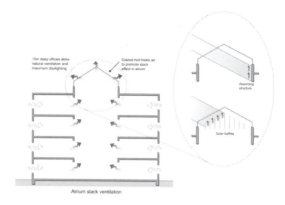

Source: reproduced from *CIBSE Guide B2* by permission of the Chartered Institution of Building Services Engineers

Figure 17.9 *Atrium stack ventilation*

To promote natural ventilation, the elevated temperature should be maintained over a reasonable height within the atrium or solar chimney. However, if the atrium is open to surrounding spaces, this may result in unacceptable temperatures at occupied levels. This could be prevented by absorbing solar gains at high levels using the elements of the structure or solar baffles. Note that the roof vents must always be positioned in a negative pressure zone with regard to wind-induced pressure. This could be achieved by adopting one of the following design strategies (CIBSE, 2005):

• designing the roof profile so that the outlet is in a negative pressure zone for all wind directions (possibly utilizing the Venturi effect);
• installing an automatically controlled multi-vent system which would open and close outlets to ensure that the opened ones are always in a negative pressure zone (or using a single vent system that turns to face away from the wind).

Stack-ventilated buildings can be divided into four main types according to implemented stack ventilation strategies (Lomas, 2007; see Figure 17.10):

• the edge in, centre out (E–C);
• the edge in, edge out (E–E);
• the centre in, edge out (C–E);
• the centre in, centre out (C–C).

Edge-in strategies are susceptible to the noise, pollution and security concerns associated with natural

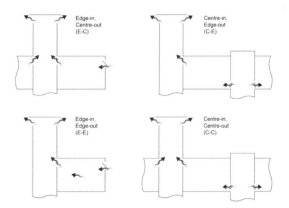

Figure 17.10 *Stack ventilation strategies*

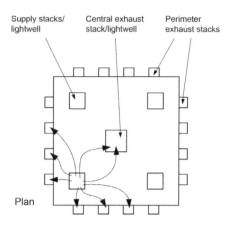

Figure 17.11 *The centre-in, edge-out strategy (Lanchester Library)*

ventilation design in urban areas. During the winter, perimeter heating elements could be used to preheat the outside air, while in the summer the operable windows could be used to enhance air movement throughout the building without disrupting the basic airflow strategy. The edge-in, centre-out strategy (E–C) allows for a deep-plan naturally ventilated building design and has been widely exploited in recent years.

The centre-in strategies enable the external façade to be sealed; therefore, airflow is not susceptible to localized air pollution, noise and security concerns. Apart from being the air supply route, the central stack can introduce daylight into a deep-plan building. The exhaust stacks are located at the perimeter of the building allowing more flexible internal space planning. Figure 17.11 shows the simplified C–E strategy implemented in the Lanchester Library. Note that the centre-in natural ventilation strategies, if necessary, could be easily converted to the contingency or complementary mixed-mode ventilation design by adding mechanically assisted ventilation. Detailed discussion on the architectural design of an advanced naturally ventilated building form is given in Lomas (2007).

Mechanically assisted ventilation

As promising as these advanced natural ventilation systems are, the purely natural ventilation systems will fail when the natural driving forces are simply not available (no wind for wind-driven systems, no internal/external temperature difference for stack-driven systems). As a consequence, recent trends have favoured mechanically assisted ventilation. For

example, in stack-driven systems, extract fans are often installed in chimneys and/or high-level atriums and can pull air through the building as a means of providing adequate ventilation on very hot and still days. Note that in the natural ventilation mode the installed fan can provide a significant resistance to the airflow.

The inclusion of mechanical reinforcement of natural ventilation is the first step in the mixed-mode direction. The physical mixed-mode strategies are classified as (CIBSE, 2000):

*   *Contingency design*: usually naturally ventilated buildings in which the mechanical ventilation or cooling could be easily added or subtracted if necessary.
*   *Complementary design*: both natural and mechanical ventilation systems are present and designed to avoid clashes and wasteful and inefficient operation.
*   *Zoned design*: here different ventilation strategies service different parts of the building.

For complementary systems, the operational strategies fall into two categories (CIBSE, 2000):

1   *Concurrent operation*: an intrinsically efficient mechanical ventilation system (with or without cooling) operates in parallel with natural ventilation systems.
2   *Changeover operation*: natural and mechanical ventilation systems are available and operate as alternatives according to need, but they do not

necessarily operate at the same time; some examples include seasonal changeover (winter, summer and mid-season modes), mechanically assisted night ventilation, top-up cooling (mechanical refrigeration provided when free cooling options are insufficient) and local changeover (if a window is opened the mechanical cooling is switched off automatically).

CIBSE Application Manual 13 (CIBSE, 2000) identifies desirable features and discusses the issues involved throughout the process from inception and briefing to handover and operation of mixed-mode ventilation systems.

Mixed-mode systems tend to be inherently more complex than pure natural ventilation systems. They also tend to expend more energy during operation, although there are exceptions to this. An example would be the use of natural ventilation in summer and mechanical ventilation with heat recovery in winter for a building located in Northern Europe, where energy used for mechanical ventilation in winter is more than offset by the heating energy saved via the heat recovery system. Mechanical ventilation with heat recovery for the winter season is becoming increasingly widespread in Northern Europe, particularly for high-occupancy buildings such as schools where heat loss can occur predominantly through ventilation.

Further refinements

The systems outlined in previous sections have the potential to work very well under a range of conditions (both external and operational). Outside of these conditions, the options are to develop a mechanically assisted or fully mixed-mode system and/or to exploit a number of further refinements in natural ventilation strategies. These further refinements are generally implemented when external temperatures and/or internal heat gains are too high to enable the limiting of internal air temperatures during occupied hours within comfortable limits. They can be categorized as those that:

- thermally temper the building fabric via airflow outside of occupied hours;
- thermally temper incoming air prior to introduction into the space.

The most commonly utilized refinement is that of night ventilation cooling, which falls under the first category

above. Here, the intention is to offset daytime internal gains by cooling the building's thermal mass with outdoor air during the previous night assuming that the outdoor temperature drops below the upper comfort limit temperatures (see Figure 17.12). Depending upon the technique used to transfer heat between the thermal mass and the conditioned space, night ventilation systems can be classified as either direct or indirect systems.

In direct systems the thermal mass of the building has to be exposed to the circulating cool air, which could be driven either by natural or mechanical ventilation. In indirect systems, cool air circulates through a thermal storage medium, which is usually a concrete slab covered either by a false ceiling or a raised floor. During the day, the incoming air, with a temperature generally higher than the corresponding temperature of the thermal storage medium, is circulated by means of mechanical ventilation. A further development here is the use of phase-change materials. Although still in its infancy, this technology has the potential to improve the effectiveness of night ventilation cooling. The efficiency of these systems depends upon the phase-change temperature of the material, the night ambient air temperature and the airflow rate.

Night ventilation affects indoor conditions during the next day by reducing peak air temperatures, reducing air temperatures in the morning and creating a time lag between the occurrence of external and internal maximum temperatures. The effectiveness of night cooling ventilation depends upon three main parameters (Santamouris and Wouters, 2006):

1 the temperature and the flux of the ambient air circulated in the building during the night period;
2 the thermal capacity of the storage medium;
3 the quality of the heat transfer between the circulated air and the thermal mass.

A number of other refinements are in use that fall within the second category at the start of this section, tempering external air prior to movement into the space. These refinements include the use of thermal labyrinths and ground pipes, as well as the use of passive downdraught evaporative cooling. Ground pipes involve the routing of air into a space via a duct under the ground in order to pre-cool the air prior to introduction into the space. This arrangement can be utilized with purely natural ventilation drivers. Thermal labyrinths are similar to ground pipes but involve airflow into a space being

(a)

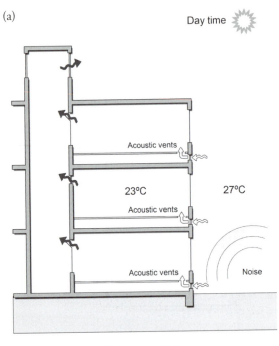

Minimum ventilation

(b)

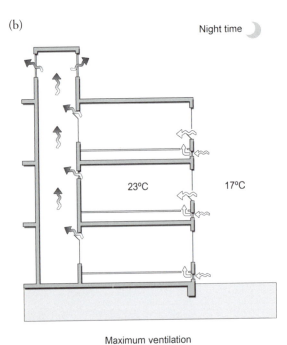

Maximum ventilation

Figure 17.12 *Night ventilation strategy: (a) day time; (b) night time*

directed via a tortuous route through an area of high thermal mass in order to precipitate significant heat transfer. Resistance to airflow is typically high and mechanical assistance is usually required. Passive downdraught evaporative cooling can work where external air conditions are hotter and drier than target conditions inside. It involves introducing a water source (typically a fine water spray) into the incoming air at high level within a space. This then evaporates, causing a rise in relative humidity and an associated drop in air temperature, and induces a downdraught through the space (functioning as a stack ventilation system with high-level inlets and low-level outlets). This type of cooling can function as a part of a conventional stack-driven system, operating only during the hottest summer months.

Integration of basic strategies

The previously described basic strategies are commonly used concurrently in a building to handle a variety of ventilation requirements (see Figure 17.13). For example, single-sided ventilation with a double opening might be adopted for a number of cellular shallow spaces (room A). However, a local stack ventilation system might be used to provide adequate ventilation in deeper spaces (room B). Additionally, to temper the incoming air and to provide a greater control of air distribution across the building, the use of in-slab fresh air distribution could be adopted (room C). This type of

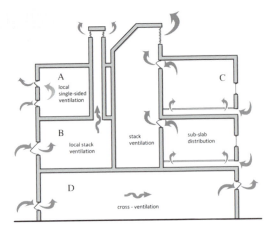

Section - Different types of ventilation

Figure 17.13 *Integration of basic ventilation strategies*

fresh air distribution is similar to displacement ventilation, most commonly implemented mechanically, and similarly relies on thermal plumes generated by equipment and by occupants to assist airflow and improve air quality in the ventilated enclosure. Finally, for deeper high occupant-density spaces (room D), the cooling potential of natural ventilation might not be sufficient to prevent overheating, and an additional mechanically assisted strategy might be necessary.

An example of such an approach is Portcullis House in London, designed in 2000 by Michael Hopkins and Partners (see Figure 17.14). Visually, the exterior of the building takes its references both from Charles Barry's 1860 Palace of Westminster and from Norman Shaw's neighbouring 1890 New Scotland Yard building on Victoria Embankment. This seven-storey high building has a simple rectangular courtyard plan. The courtyard is covered by a glass roof at the second-floor level and is surrounded by a two-storey cloister. The building is cellular in nature and the construction is thermally heavyweight, with partitions and soffits being exposed concrete. Each office has a triple-glazed window with an adjustable dark inter-pane blind aimed at providing adequate thermal comfort in winter and summer. Fresh air is provided via the floor void and extracted via the window and directly from the room. The fresh air is drawn in via openings at the base of roof turrets and the vitiated air is exhausted via openings at the top of the turrets. Prior to discharge, the air passes through a thermal wheel providing preheating to the incoming fresh air. The system operates at night to provide a night-cooling mode. Additional cooling is provided through the use of the borehole groundwater drawn at around 42° C from the chalk 150m below and is discharged to the river after being used in the grey water system. Heating is provided by a conventional gas-fired condensing boiler operating on a 70°C/50°C temperature regime. A detailed description of this building can be found elsewhere in Dix (2000).

Design performance evaluation

In order to ensure that the developed natural ventilation system performs adequately, it is important that sound engineering-based methods are employed. This will include evaluating the design under various weather conditions and heat loads and determining potential situations where design goals might not be met. Depending upon design requirements, the analysis of the

Figure 17.14 *Portcullis House, London*

natural ventilation systems will require consideration of energy consumption (and associated CO_2 emission), airflow (due to wind, density differences and mechanical forces in the case of mixed-mode ventilation systems), and air pollutants distribution. The complex interaction between building envelopes and their indoor and outdoor environment make it difficult to address all of these issues using one tool only. This has led to the development of a wide range of different analysis tools and they typically fall into two broad categories:

1 mathematical models;
2 physical models.

Mathematical models

Mathematical models used to design natural ventilation systems fall typically into three basic categories:

1 single-zone models;
2 multi-zone models;
3 computational fluid dynamics (CFD).

Single-zone models consider the entire building to consist of a single volume of well-mixed air with no internal partitions. Some methods also account for thermal characteristics of the building envelope. In general, they solve the equations that govern the flow of air through openings in the building envelope:

$$\sum q_i = 0 \tag{1}$$

$$q_i = C_{di} A_i S_i \sqrt{\frac{2|\Delta p_i|}{\rho_0}} \tag{2}$$

$$\Delta p_i = \Delta p_i - \Delta \rho_0 g z_i + 0.5 \rho_0 U^2 C_{pi} \tag{3}$$

where i identifies the opening, q_i is the flow rate through the opening (m³/s); C_{di} is the discharge coefficient (–); A_i is the area of opening (m²); Δp_i is the pressure difference (Pa); $\Delta \rho_0$ is the air density difference (kg/m³); g is the gravitational acceleration (m/s²); z_i is the height of opening above ground level (m); sign of the pressure difference (+1 for flow entering the space; –1 for flow leaving the space); U is the wind speed (m/s), and C_{pi} is the wind pressure coefficient.

Equation 1 represents conservation of mass for the building envelope (i.e. the net mass flow into the building is equal to zero). Equation 2 defines the relationship between the flow rate through an opening and a pressure difference across it by means of the discharge coefficient and a specified geometric area. Finally, Equation 3 defines the pressure difference across an opening whose inlet or outlet is situated in the external flow. Note that the single-zone models ignore internal resistances to airflow and are generally considered useful for the initial calculations only. A spreadsheet may be downloaded for free from the CIBSE website (see www.cibse.org/venttool). More detailed descriptions of the single-zone models can be found in Chapter 15.

Multi-zone models are based on an idealized physical representation of building systems and can be used to describe a building as a set of zones that are interconnected by airflow paths. It is assumed that the zones are typically well mixed (i.e. the pressure, temperature and pollutant concentration is the same throughout the zone). Nowadays, more advanced multi-zone design tools have been able to simulate airflow through openings in combination with the thermal

response of a building. Using these features, one can perform simulations to investigate the differences in airflow rates obtained by varying different building features and weather conditions, including the size and placement of ventilation openings in the building envelope, the orientation of the building in relation to the prevailing wind, the outdoor temperature, and the size and location of ventilation stacks. Furthermore, some of the more advanced design tools can be used to determine the microscopic airflow and temperature fields within a given zone. More detailed descriptions of the multi-zone models can be found in Chapter 15.

CFD modelling is the process of representing a fluid flow problem by mathematical equations based on the fundamental laws of physics, and solving these equations to predict the variation of the calculated parameters within and around buildings. The applications of CFD to the design of naturally ventilated buildings include, but are not limited to, the following:

- calculation of velocity, temperature and air pollutants distributions in single- and multi-cell buildings;
- prediction of the external wind flow around a building and the resulting pressure field from which the pressure coefficient, C_{pi}(–), can be calculated;
- calculation of internal flow patterns through ventilation components.

Chapter 23 describes the main principles and concepts associated with CFD modelling. Furthermore, it highlights the fundamental problems of the micro-scale CFD models, which lie in the physical difficulties of modelling the effect of turbulence, as well as the accuracy of the spatial discretization of complex building geometries, the numerical procedures applied, the boundary conditions and the physical property selected.

Physical models

Although the mathematical models are more cost effective, the physical models are still used by both research and building design communities as they offer relatively high accuracy. These include:

- wind tunnel modelling;
- salt bath modelling.

Wind tunnel testing is generally used to determine wind pressure coefficients for individual building designs. A physical model of a building and its surroundings can be constructed and placed in a wind tunnel where it is subject to a controlled wind flow. A boundary layer wind profile should be comparable to that appropriate for the site and can be induced in the wind tunnel by means of blockages. Determination of wind speed for evaluating wind pressure coefficients is carried out using the following formula:

$$U = U_{met}kz^a \qquad (4)$$

where U is the wind speed at height (m/s), z is the height above ground (m) and k and a are the coefficients determined by the terrain in which the building lies. Values for the terrain coefficients are given in Table 17.1. Most building application wind tunnels operate at scales of 1:100 to 1:500. As long as the Reynolds number is kept high through high wind tunnel air speeds, the turbulent regime is ensured and scaled, and real flows will match. The results of measurements are available as design data for generic building forms.

Wind tunnels can also be used for flow visualization by introducing smoke or other tracers in the wind tunnel and observing the flow characteristics. For example, by introducing a fine grain in the wind tunnel one can observe airflow characteristics and assess the impact of a new development on pedestrian comfort in urban areas (the grain will be cleared from more windy areas, indicating wind exposure). Lately, wind tunnels can also be used for directly measuring the ventilation rate of a building providing that the volume of the envelope at model scales allows tracer gas measurements inside the model. However, this is subject to certain limitations (i.e. full-scale ventilation openings have to be sufficiently large to be accurately modelled). Therefore, if possible, wind tunnel testing offers relatively high accuracy in determining

ventilation rates due to wind because the effect of wind turbulence is inherent in measurements.

The salt bath method is a relatively recent development and is primarily used for testing buoyancy-driven ventilation strategies. Figure 17.15 shows a small-scale model of a building envelope that is immersed in a transparent bath containing saline solutions of different concentrations that simulate the density (temperature) differences. This is for airflow between rooms that are interconnected through several openings, enabling air to move between rooms through different paths. The water in the experiment is coloured with dye and flows in at the bottom right, and can flow out of the tank at the top right only. Note that when using the salt bath method, it is not possible to realistically simulate boundary conditions, such as solar patching on the floor of an atrium.

Detailed design

Ventilation components

Primary vent sizing in natural ventilation systems tends to be determined by airflow rates needed to deliver ventilative summertime cooling. The issue of overheating in the summer is one of the main technical barriers related to natural ventilation systems. To avoid overheating, the airflow will commonly need to exceed that required solely to satisfy the minimum required for indoor air quality and health. As a result, sizes of openings are at least an order of magnitude larger than that used for winter ventilation.

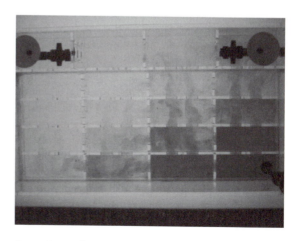

Source: Liora Malki-Epshtein, University College London

Figure 17.15 *The salt bath test*

Table 17.1 *Terrain coefficients*

Terrain	k	a
Open flat country	0.68	0.17
Country with scattered windbreaks	0.52	0.2
Urban	0.35	0.25
City	0.21	0.33

Source: CIBSE (2005)

Windows remain the most commonly used vents in natural ventilation systems. Different types of windows create different indoor airflow patterns and provide different options for controlling the direction and level of volumetric flow. The main windows types can be classified in four groups (see Table 17.2).

Sliding (sash) windows

This group of windows includes horizontal and vertical sash windows. These windows do not really affect airflow distribution around the openings. Although the direction of the flow path cannot be influenced by projecting sashes, this design allows for the control of the airflow path within the interior place by height (vertical sash windows) and width (horizontal sash windows). These windows have a fairly high ventilation capacity, and the effective area is a maximum 50 per cent of the structural opening.

Horizontal-vane opening windows

This group of windows includes horizontal pivot, top-hung, bottom-hung and louvred windows. The windows affect the airflow path mainly in a vertical direction either upward (e.g. bottom-hung inward-opening windows) or downward (e.g. top-hung inward-opening windows). The horizontal pivot and louvred windows can be designed to direct the airflow in either direction according to the position of sashes. The horizontal pivot windows have a high ventilation capacity and the geometry promotes good air distribution. However, due to security and health and safety reasons, the length of throw of stays is usually restricted, which might affect the ventilation capability of these windows. Unlike the horizontal pivot windows the louvred windows can be made secure and still having a high ventilation capacity. A less satisfactory seal and, consequently, increased ventilation loss in winter is the major disadvantage of this particular design (see Figure 17.16). If located adjacent to the ceiling, bottom-hung inward-opening windows are suitable for night ventilation cooling.

Vertical-vane opening windows

This group of windows includes vertical pivot and side-hung (casement) windows. The windows affect airflow path mainly in a horizontal direction. The most common window of this type in Europe is the double-sided hinged

Table 17.2 *Classification of windows*

Sliding (sash) windows	Horizontal-vane opening windows	Vertical-vane opening windows	Tilt and turn windows
Vertical sash	Horizontal pivot	Vertical pivot	Tilt and turn
Horizontal sash	Top/Bottom hung	Side hung	
	Louvred		

inward-opening casement window, which has great versatility with regard to airflow control. However, ventilation characteristics are strongly influenced by wind speed and direction. Vertical pivot windows have a high ventilation capacity and will provide either a positive or negative wing-wall effect. The vulnerability of vertical vane-opening windows to driving rain limits their popularity in the UK.

Tilt and turn windows

Note that these windows have been designed for manual operation and cannot be linked to an actuator, which limits their application in automatically controlled naturally ventilated buildings. If well designed and properly used by occupants, this type of window can offer great versatility with regard to airflow control as they provide two different opening geometries in a single unit.

Vents are controlled either manually or mechanically via actuators. An actuator responds to the output signal from a controller and provides the mechanical action to operate the vent (such as a window or damper). The choice of vent type and its integration with different actuator options requires special attention, particularly when using windows, as these have generally been originally designed for manual operation. Windows used for automatic control may require adaptation to accommodate a motorized actuator and strengthening to take into account a number of forces imposed on an actuator, such as ventilator weight, external forces (wind and snow), actuator position and speed operation (high-speed operation causes greater stresses and shock loadings

at each end of its travel). If automatic control is required, the horizontal-pivot top- and bottom-hung windows are usually used with linear and chain actuators. The louvred windows are generally coupled either with rotary or linear actuators. More detailed analysis of actuators suitable for natural ventilation can be found in CIBSE (2005).

For winter ventilation, trickle ventilators are commonly used and are generally able to provide the necessary background ventilation to satisfy the minimum ventilation requirements. To minimize cold draughts, the trickle ventilators should be at high level (typically 1.75m above floor level) and designed to promote rapid mixing within the room. The possible benefits of automatic ventilation control of trickle ventilators in dwellings have been investigated at the Bartlett (Ridley et al, 2007). Such ventilators could offer an improvement in performance over fixed ventilators due to their ability to adjust to environmental conditions without occupant interaction, thus providing adequate indoor air quality while decreasing ventilative heat losses and, thus, improving energy efficiency. Field tests in a highly instrumented test house were carried out on three types of trickle ventilator: fixed, pressure controlled and relative humidity controlled. A computer model of the performance of these types of trickle ventilators was developed and the results of the simulations set out the potential for pressure ventilators to reduce the occurrence of over-ventilation in dwellings, and for humidity-controlled ventilators to reduce the incidence of excess humidity without significantly increasing ventilation heat loss.

Background ventilation can also be provided via more sophisticated methods that can deliver energy-saving benefits. The most common example is mechanical ventilation with heat recovery. A less commonly utilized option is natural ventilation with heat recovery.

Whenever the air has to pass through more than one room on its way from the inlet opening to the outlet, it encounters additional resistance, which depends upon the size of interior openings. As well as providing a resistance to airflow, changes in direction, contraction and expansion of air streams create turbulence and further reduce the airflow rate. Therefore, special attention has to be taken to ensure that the ventilation path is not obstructed. For example, if cellular office space is required, transfer grilles will be needed to allow the air to move across the building.

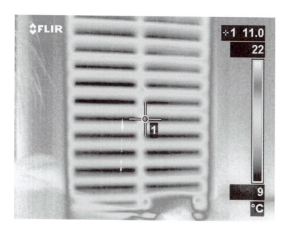

Figure 17.16 *Louvred window: An infrared image*

Control systems

The need to maintain ventilation rates reliably using natural ventilation forces is a major challenge for the development of advanced natural ventilation systems. Wind and buoyancy forces are stochastic in their nature, making control more difficult. As a result of poor controllability of natural ventilation systems, the ventilated enclosures may be:

- under-ventilated, resulting in deterioration of air quality and overheating;
- over-ventilated, resulting in higher heat ventilation losses; or
- may not provide acceptable air distribution resulting in local thermal discomfort (cold draughts or insufficient cooling) or local air quality problems (pockets of stagnant air).

An automatic control system for a naturally ventilated building is composed of one or more sensors measuring the parameters required for implementing any control strategy. In most cases, one or more temperature sensors are normally positioned in the room to achieve an average reading. This is the simplest method of automatic control and is suitable for most applications. For example, the dampers are normally set to commence opening at 16°C during summer months and open 20 per cent for every 1°C rise in internal room temperature. Seasonal switching enables the temperature set points to be increased in the winter setting in order to prevent heat loss during this period. In atriums and other buffer spaces, the coarse on/off method is most commonly used as the close control of comfort conditions is not essential. In the case of a building's densely populated areas, such as classrooms or conference theatres, CO_2 sensors may be used in conjunction with the temperature sensors. A key control problem is to provide sufficient but not excessive background ventilation while avoiding draughts. The preferred location for the CO_2 sensor may be around seated head height and away from direct draught. In addition to the temperature and CO_2 sensors, automatic control for a naturally ventilated building could comprise room occupancy, humidity, rain detection, outside air temperature, wind speed and wind direction sensors. Generally, these parameters can be recorded, but are usually used for performance assessment purposes.

Sensible integration of user and automated controls is therefore critical to the success of natural ventilation. In the case of the user control, the resulting control strategy is based on purely subjective criteria (i.e. perceived indoor air quality and thermal comfort). In the control of their indoor environment, occupants are usually willing to accept wider comfort bands, even if they are not ideal. They will rarely act in anticipation of becoming uncomfortable. However, if uncomfortable, occupants will take action to alleviate their discomfort and in this case rapid response is essential. Note that automated control must not usurp control too rapidly after user intervention.

Installation, commissioning and post-occupancy evaluation

Installation and commissioning is a four-stage process (CIBSE, 2005):

1   *Installation.* Achieving successful automatically controlled natural ventilation systems depends critically upon the installation and integration of ventilation components. It is important that all involved take ownership of the agreed strategy, including the quantity surveyors. Elements that are fundamental to the ventilation strategy cannot subsequently be regarded as insignificant in cost-cutting exercises. The installer and commissioning specialist should establish systematic site-control procedures to assist the progressive monitoring of the standard of the installation practices maintained on site.

2   *Static completion.* This is a term that indicates that an installation is ready for commissioning. Briefly, it means that all components have been installed in accordance with the manufacturers' specifications, have been subject to final inspection, have been tested for air leakage, and have been cleaned, made safe and ready to work.

3   *Practical completion.* This should take into account all local conditions and consider the use and occupancy patterns within the space. In order to allow for adjustments in the controls to suit the range of different activities that may take place in the building, initial monitoring may be required.

4   *Fine-tuning.* After practical application, fine-tuning should be carried out in the year following

handover. It should focus on problems reported by the occupants and the analysis of the operational performance of the installed ventilation system. This process should be repeated for each of the ventilation modes (i.e. winter, summer and mid-season ventilation modes).

Post-occupancy evaluation of buildings is defined as 'an activity which originates out of an interest in how a building performs once it is built' (FFC, 2003). A detailed algorithm for post-occupancy evaluation of buildings can be found in Chapter 24. Post-occupancy evaluation is increasingly being identified as an indispensable part of the building design, construction and occupation process. The key benefits include feedback of the success of the hypothesis set out during the design development process, with lessons learned fed into subsequent design work, as well as the opportunity to identify elements of the project that are operating outside of their intended parameters – possibly to the detriment of the entire project – so that they can be rectified post-occupancy.

Acknowledgements

This chapter is based on an accepted postgraduate dissertation by Sung Min Hong entitled 'Design and Operational Performance of Advanced Naturally Ventilated Buildings', in partial fulfilment of the requirements for the degree of MSc in Environmental Design and Engineering at the Bartlett, University College London (2008).

References

Bordass, W., Cohen, R., Standeven, M. and Leaman, A. (2001) 'Assessing building performance in use 3: Energy performance of the Probe buildings', *Building Research and Information*, vol 29, no 2, pp114–128

BSRIA (2005) *Wind-Driven Natural Ventilation Systems*, BG 2/2005, BSRIA, Bracknell, UK

CIBSE (Chartered Institution of Building Services Engineers) (2000) *CIBSE Application Manual 13: Mixed Mode Ventilation*, CIBSE, London

CIBSE (2005) *CIBSE Application Manual 10: Natural Ventilation in Non-Domestic Buildings*, CIBSE, London

De Salis, M., Oldham, D. and Sharples, S. (2002) 'Noise control strategies for naturally ventilated buildings', *Building and Environment*, vol 37, pp471–484

Dix, T. (2000) 'An engineering approach to ventilation system design', *Indoor and Built Environment*, vol 9, pp75–96

FFC (Federal Facilities Council) (2003) *Learning from Our Buildings: State of the Practice*, National Academies Press, Washington, DC

Kolokotroni, M., Giannitsaris, I. and Watkins, R. (2006) 'The effect of the London urban heat island on building summer cooling demand and night ventilation strategies', *Solar Energy*, vol 80, pp383–392

Lomas, K. (2007) 'Architectural design of an advanced naturally ventilated building form', *Energy and Buildings*, vol 39, pp166–181

Mumovic, D., Crowther, J. and Stevanovic, Z. (2006) 'Integrated air quality modelling for a designated air quality management area in Glasgow', *Building and Environment*, vol 41, issue 12, pp1703–1712

Mumovic, D., Crowther, J. and Stevanovic, Z. (in press) 'Analysis of local concentration gradients in complex built environment: Implications for air quality management areas', *International Journal of Environment and Waste Management*, vol 3, no 2, in press

Ren, M., Levermore, G. and Doylend, N. (2003) 'The impact of new CIBSE weather data on natural ventilation design', *Building Service Engineering Research and Technology*, vol 24, no 2, pp83–91

Ridley, I., Davies, M., Booth, W., Judd, C., Oreszczyn, T. and Mumovic, D. (2007) 'Automatic ventilation control of trickle ventilators', *International Journal of Ventilation*, vol 5, no 4

Santamouris, M. and Wouters, P. (2006) *Building Ventilation: The State of the Art*, Earthscan, London

18

Mechanical and Mixed-Mode Ventilation in City Centre Buildings

Jarek Kurnitski and Olli Seppänen

Principles of mechanical and mixed-mode ventilation

Buildings with mechanical ventilation use fans to supply air to, and exhaust air from, the rooms. Depending upon demand, the supply air may be heated, cooled, humidified or dehumidified. The ventilation system may be equipped to recover heat from the exhaust air. The system may also recirculate extract air. Windows may be sealed or operable.

Mixed-mode ventilation combines mechanical ventilation with the use of natural driving forces. When stack effect or wind pressure differences are available, fans are no longer operated. Mixed-mode systems are either low-pressure fan-assisted mechanical systems or two-mode ventilation systems operating mechanical ventilation or natural ventilation, depending upon conditions.

During the last decade, major developments have taken place or been further refined, such as various kinds of demand-controlled ventilation, systems with improved airflow characteristics at room level (e.g. displacement ventilation), heat recovery systems with efficiencies of up to 90 per cent, major developments in fan characteristics (e.g. direct current and inverter drive variable speed fans), low-pressure air distribution systems, etc. In mechanically ventilated buildings, the ventilation air may also be conditioned before it is supplied to the rooms via duct systems. Because of supply and exhaust air fans, the system is more flexible with respect to building design and more energy efficient than other systems if heat recovery means are used. However, mechanical ventilation systems may also deteriorate indoor air quality if not properly operated and maintained as a dirty air-handling system may itself be a source of pollution, and moisture in air-handling systems can cause mould growth. These issues have to be solved in order to achieve good indoor air quality.

Airflows in ventilation systems have different names depending upon in which part of the building or the system the flows occur (see Figure 18.1). The function of the airflow is described as follows:

- Outdoor air is used for ventilation. Usually the term ventilation rate refers to the outdoor airflow taken outside the building and therefore not previously circulated through the ventilation system (single-room outdoor air).
- Supply air to the room can be conditioned (heated, cleaned, cooled, humidified or dehumidified). It can be 100 per cent outdoor air or a mixture of recirculation air and outdoor air depending upon the system. The supply air may not only be used for ventilation but also for temperature and humidity control of the room. Usually the airflow required for thermal control of the room is greater than that for ventilation (outdoor airflow) (single-room supply air).
- Indoor air is the air in the ventilated space. In mixing air distribution systems, indoor air quality is uniform in the space. In displacement

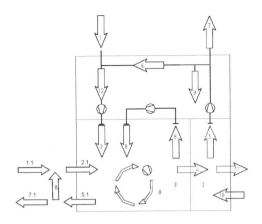

Source: EN 13779 (2007b)

Figure 18.1 *Various airflows in a ventilation system*

ventilation systems, gradients of concentrations and temperature are intentionally created.

- Transfer air is the air moving between adjacent rooms in the building. This airflow can be used to prevent pollutants from spreading from rooms with low air quality to rooms with better air quality, such as tobacco smoke from smoking areas to non-smoking areas.
- Extract air is the air extracted from the room. Extract air should be taken from the location in the room where the air has the lowest quality (single-room extract air).
- Recirculation air is a part of extract air (clean air) that is not exhausted from the building.
- Exhaust air is extract air that is exhausted from the building and is not recirculated (single-room exhaust air).
- Secondary air is the air that is circulated within one space (extracted and supplied); usually it is treated during circulation. Secondary air can be used, for example, for heating a room or can be circulated through an air cleaner. Secondary air handling units can be located outside the room or in the room.
- Leakage: if the duct and air handling system is not airtight, air will leak from, or into, the system depending upon the pressure in the system, and reduce the air delivery efficiency of the system.
- Infiltration is the air flowing through the building envelope into the building. The infiltration

depends upon pressure difference over the structure and the flow paths. This may bring harmful pollutants into the building.
- Exfiltration is the air flowing through the building envelope from inside to outside due to the pressure difference. In cold climates, this may cause moisture damage in the construction due to condensation of moist indoor air in the structure.
- Mixed air is the mixture of outdoor air and recirculation air. The amount of outdoor air is based on ventilation requirements of the space. Total supply air rate flow is based on the cooling or heating requirements of a space.

Ventilation systems for residential buildings

Why mechanical ventilation?

The idea of a mechanical ventilation system is that the required ventilation rate can be maintained in all weather conditions without the influence of a building's occupants. When ventilation is provided with a mechanical system, the building envelope can be made airtight; in this way, the energy losses due to infiltration and exfiltration are reduced. A tight building envelope also improves sound insulation and reduces the transfer of external noise into the building. The energy efficiency of ventilation can be further improved with heat recovery from exhaust air and demand-controlled ventilation by occupancy, moisture or air quality. Ventilation air can be cleaned of outdoor air pollutants. Heating and cooling can easily be combined with mechanical ventilation systems. Mechanical ventilation systems may also control the pressure differences over the building envelope and prevent moisture damage in the building's structures. Figure 18.2 illustrates some of the problems related to a natural ventilation system. Since natural ventilation is based on pressure differences created by temperature differences and wind, in some conditions pressure differences will reverse airflows, and the exhaust air stacks, which may be contaminated, then become air supply routes, spreading pollutants into the living room. The use of a cooker hood fan may also overcome the pressure differences of natural forces and reverse the flows (see Figure 18.3).

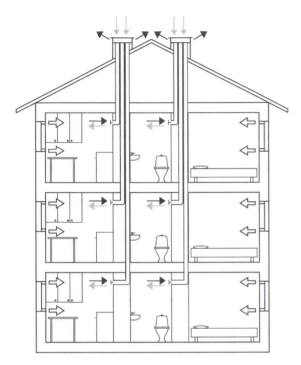

Figure 18.2 *In some weather conditions the flow in the stack may be reversed (light grey arrows) in natural ventilation systems, which rely on temperature difference as a driving force for ventilation*

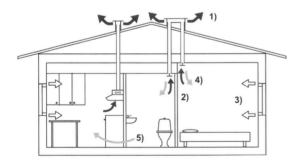

Notes: 1 Exhaust air in normal operation.
2 Extract air in normal operation.
3 Ventilation air in normal operation.
4 Reversed airflow.
5 Transfer air due to operation of cooker hood fan

Figure 18.3 *Use of the cooker hood fan may reverse the airflows (dark grey arrows) in the shafts for natural ventilation*

Mechanical exhaust ventilation

In mechanical exhaust ventilation systems, air is exhausted from the rooms with higher pollutant generation and lower air quality. Air infiltration through the building envelope or special air intakes brings outdoor air for ventilation into the building. In apartment buildings, exhaust from the different floors can be connected to the same duct (see Figure 18.4) if the pressure drop in the exhaust grille is high enough to prevent airflow from floor to floor. A central fan serves all apartments. Room airflows can be controlled with adjustable grilles by humidity or CO_2 concentration or other pollutants, or by occupancy sensors.

The advantages of the mechanical exhaust system are as follows:

- a constant ventilation rate;
- small negative pressure in the building prevents moisture penetration into the construction of external walls and prevents condensation and, consequently, mould growth.

The drawbacks of the mechanical exhaust system comprise the following:

- Air infiltration through the building envelope creates draughts during winter in cold climates.
- Typical air intakes have low sound attenuation for outdoor noise.
- Heat recovery from the exhaust air is not easy to implement – recovered heat cannot be used to heat ventilation air. It can, however, be used to preheat domestic hot water (using a heat pump).
- Since the exhaust is usually from kitchens, bathrooms and toilets, ventilation supply airflow is not evenly distributed in bedrooms and living rooms.
- Distribution of outdoor air for ventilation depends upon leakage in the building envelope.

These problems are illustrated in the Figure 18.5, which shows that air may flow directly from the location of infiltration to the exhausts (airflow where the building envelope is less airtight, such as in the kitchen window and entrance door). If the building envelope is airtight in bedrooms and living rooms, the outdoor air does not ventilate those rooms but flows

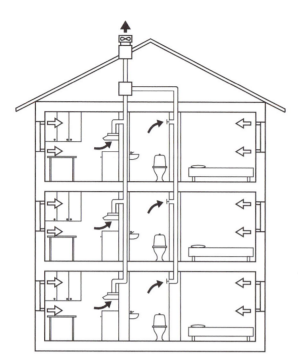

Figure 18.4 *A mechanical exhaust ventilation system may serve one or several apartments*

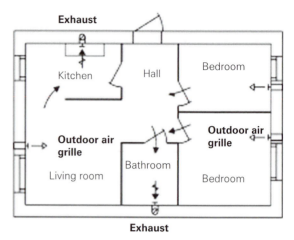

Figure 18.6 *Outdoor air grilles in the bedrooms and living room guarantee that the ventilation air flows to the bedrooms and living room before entering the exhausts*

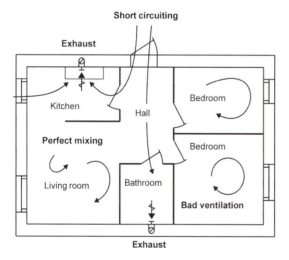

Figure 18.5 *Example of the short-circuiting ventilation in an apartment with mechanical exhaust ventilation*

directly to extract air openings in the kitchen and bathroom. This kind of short-circuiting of airflow reduces the efficiency of ventilation and should be avoided. Ventilation may be very low and air quality

unhealthy particularly at night when bedroom doors are closed. This short-circuiting can be avoided by arranging supply air grilles into each bedroom and living room, as illustrated in Figure 18.6.

Mechanical supply and exhaust ventilation

In mechanical supply and exhaust systems, the air is supplied via ducts and fans to bedrooms and living rooms, and typically exhausted from the kitchen, bathroom and bedrooms (see Figure 18.7). Usually the exhaust air flows through a heat exchanger before it is discharged outdoors. In a heat exchanger, a major part of the heat content of the exhaust air is recovered and used to heat the outdoor air for ventilation. Thus, mechanical supply and exhaust systems are free of draught and outdoor noise problems typical of mechanical exhaust or natural ventilation systems. Use of recovered heat for heating ventilation air is usually the most economical method as the need for heating is synonymous with available heat. Another alternative for using heat is heating domestic hot water.

Mechanical supply and exhaust ventilation provides effective filtering of outdoor air. This is important in urban areas with high traffic or industrial combustion loads. It has been demonstrated that mechanically ventilated buildings protect occupants from outdoor air

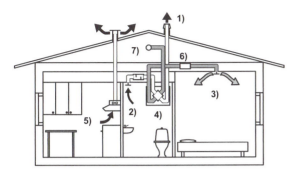

Notes: 1 Exhaust air.
2 Extract air.
3 Supply air to the bedroom.
4 Heat recovery exchanger.
5 Kitchen exhaust.
6 Sound attenuator.
7 Outdoor air intake for ventilation.

Figure 18.7 *Principle of mechanical exhaust and supply systems in a house*

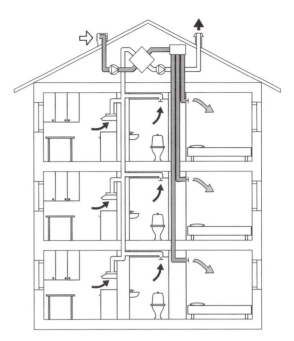

Figure 18.8 *Centralized mechanical supply and exhaust system with heat recovery in an apartment building*

pollutants. A probabilistic exposure-modelling exercise has demonstrated that reducing particulate matter ($PM_{2.5}$ – particles smaller than 2.5 micrometres) infiltration in all buildings in Helsinki to the level of office buildings built after 1990 would reduce population exposure to $PM_{2.5}$ from ambient origin, as well as lower adverse health effects by 27 per cent – in fact, almost as much as total elimination of all traffic sources from within the metropolitan area limits (Hänninen et al, 2005). Effective ways of preventing outdoor pollution from entering indoors are through tightening the building envelope and filtering the air intake.

In an apartment building, the mechanical supply and exhaust system can be centralized (see Figure 18.8) or decentralized (similar to Figure 18.7). Typically, the centralized systems have better heat recovery efficiency; but the control is more complex than in decentralized systems. For heat recovery to be beneficial, the heat recovered has to exceed the additional energy expended by the fans. Where carbon is the base comparator and where the unit of embodied carbon is higher for electricity than for the primary heating fuel source (e.g. natural gas), it may be difficult to justify in moderate climates (without careful design of the ductwork system) an efficient heat exchanger and energy efficient fans and motors. In decentralized systems, the number of components requiring maintenance is higher and more spread out; on the other hand, ventilation is easier to control by demand.

Ventilation systems for non-residential buildings

Ventilation rates and requirements are usually higher in commercial rather than residential buildings. This is due to higher occupant density and generally higher expectations. Ventilation systems are often made more complex by floor plans that require provision of mechanical ventilation to all rooms. Usually, outdoor air is treated in an air handling unit and supplied to the rooms via ductwork. Conditioning of the air may include cleaning, heating, cooling, humidification and dehumidification.

Constant air volume (CAV) system

The most common system for mechanical ventilation is illustrated in Figure 18.9, where outdoor air is filtered and heated in an air handling unit and supplied to rooms. Ventilation air is partially heated with heat recovered from extract air and district heating. Rooms are heated with hot water radiators. The water is heated by district heating, and flow is controlled with thermostatic radiator valves. The airflow is continuous to all rooms. The system in Figure 18.9 does not have air conditioning – only air cleaning and heating. The system illustrated in Figure 18.10 also has a cooling coil for air cooling and dehumidification, if necessary. Today, the purpose of supply air is not only to ventilate for air quality but also to cool the rooms. Heating can occur with supply air; but in cold climates, radiators are more common (see Figure 18.10). Cooling is achieved through direct expansion cooling coils or through water chillers with a storage capacity as illustrated in Figure 18.10. The system does not feature any recirculated air. Its energy-saving function is replaced with heat recovery.

CAV systems may be easily combined with natural ventilation through openings, resulting in a mixed-mode ventilation system. This combines the best features of natural and mechanical ventilation at different times of the day or season. In such systems, mechanical and natural forces are combined in a two-mode system. The operating mode varies according to the season and within individual days; thus, the current mode reflects the external environment and takes maximum advantage of ambient conditions at any point in time. Mixed-mode systems will switch automatically between natural and mechanical modes in order to minimize energy consumption and to maintain a satisfactory indoor environment. The aim of the strategy is to reduce energy, costs and the environmental side effects of year-round air conditioning while optimizing indoor air quality and thermal comfort by combining the two modes of

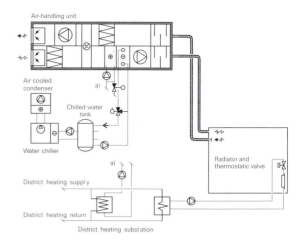

Notes: Air is conditioned in an air handling unit before it is supplied via duct systems to the rooms. Ventilation air can be heated or cooled. The air handling unit is equipped with filters and a heat recovery heat exchanger. The rooms are heated with radiators. Heat supply can be district heating, as here, an individual fuel-fired boiler or a heat pump.

Figure 18.10 *Air handling unit with air conditioning*

ventilation. The operating mode performs according to the seasons and depends upon external ambient conditions. Figure 18.11 shows the combination of a balanced ventilation system with natural ventilation. When the ambient conditions allow it, the atrium is

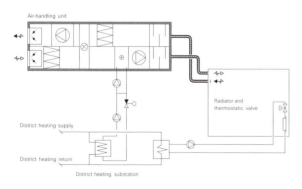

Notes: Air is heated and filtered in an air handling unit before it is supplied via duct systems to the rooms. The air handling unit is equipped with filters and a heat recovery heat exchanger. The rooms are heated with radiators. Heat supply can be district heating, as here, an individual fuel-fired boiler or a heat pump.

Figure 18.9 *Air handling unit for heating only*

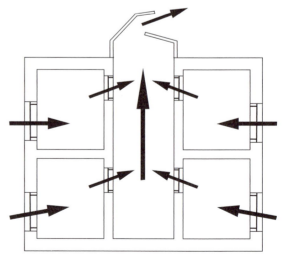

Figure 18.11 *Utilization of mixed-mode ventilation in a building with an atrium (a mechanical ventilation system is not shown; see Figure 18.9)*

naturally ventilated. Even the office rooms can, in principle, be naturally ventilated. During unfavourable weather conditions, natural ventilation is first shut down in offices with stricter requirements and in extreme conditions in the atrium; the mode is then switched in two steps to mechanical ventilation.

Variable air volume (VAV) system

The flow of supply air to the rooms can be controlled by a room temperature sensor for heating or cooling purposes. The cooling demand of the room typically leads to higher design airflow in VAV systems than is required for ventilation. In the operation, it is possible that the airflow is too low for ventilation if the control of the airflow is by room temperature only – the minimum supply air should be guaranteed to all rooms. Due to variable airflow, the energy for conditioning and transferring the air is lower than with CAV systems.

The pressure in the duct work is kept constant by controlling the fan speed and dampers. A pressure sensor in the duct work is used to control the fan speed and, consequently, the supply airflow (see Figure 18.12). In advanced systems, the fan speed is minimized so that at least one damper is always completely open. Since the average flow of air is less, and the fan has a speed control, the energy use of the system is lower than in a constant flow system.

Ventilation in fan coil system

As the cooling or heating demand of rooms usually leads to higher design airflow than needed for ventilation, commercial buildings are often equipped with specific room units for cooling. This avoids high design airflows and large size ductworks typical to VAV systems.

In fan coil systems, air is circulated via a coil that is heated or cooled with warm or chilled water (see Figure 18.13). Fan coils can also operate as stand-alone units. In this case, it may draw in the outdoor air for ventilation. Fan coils can be placed in the ceiling or below the window on the floor. Ventilation is usually separated from fan coils, but may also be integrated within fan coils (see Figure 18.14).

Fan coils can provide effective dehumidification of supply and indoor air, as well as very high cooling capacity if needed. Dehumidification is achieved by condensation of water vapour in the cooling coil; but

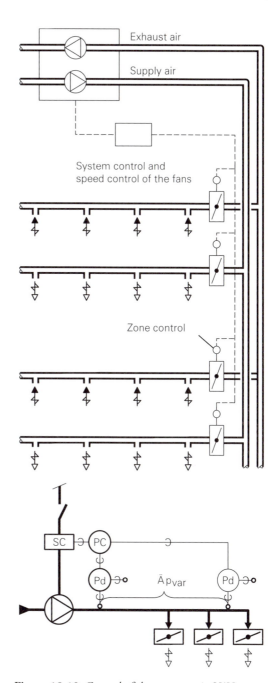

Figure 18.12 *Control of duct pressure in VAV systems reduces fan energy use*

when higher water temperatures are used, non-condensing dimensioning with lower cooling capacity is also possible. For fan coil systems, somewhat higher air velocities and noise levels compared to chilled beam

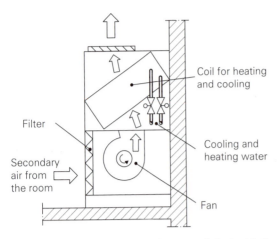

Figure 18.13 *Cooling can also be accomplished with fan coils, where the room air is circulated via a coil that is heated or cooled with warm or chilled water*

systems are typical. Other drawbacks are the maintenance requirements (replacing filters) and electricity use of fans.

Ventilation in chilled beam and cooled ceiling systems

Chilled beams are induction-type room conditioning units installed in the ceiling and controlled by room temperature sensors (see Figures 18.15 and 18.16). There are no fans in chilled beams. In active chilled beams, supply air ducted to the beam induces room airflow through the cooling coil. In passive chilled beams, only temperature differences cause the airflow through cooling coils and the cooling capacity is therefore lower.

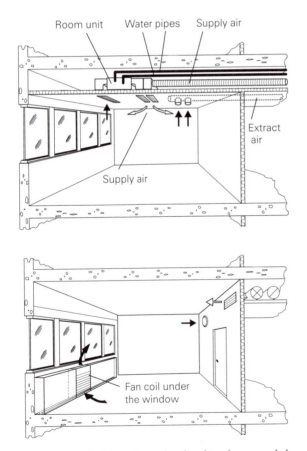

Figure 18.14 *Fan coils can be placed in the suspended ceiling (top) or under the window (bottom)*

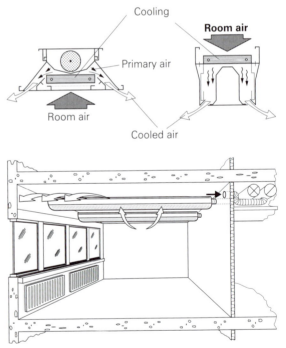

Figure 18.15 *Chilled beams may be used in free installation in the ceiling as shown in the figure or in the suspended ceiling installation: Cross-sections (top left) illustrate an active chilled beam where the supply air (ventilation air) is integrated within the beam to improve the heat transfer in the cooling coil and in the (right) passive chilled beam*

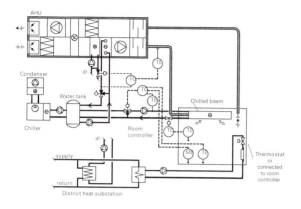

Notes: TE = temperature sensor; ME = moisture sensor;
TC = temperature controller.

Figure 18.16 *Ventilation and air-conditioning system with active chilled beams: Chilled beams are installed in the ceiling and controlled by room temperature sensors*

A chilled water system serves both the air handling unit and the chilled beams. Supply airflow is selected based on ventilation requirements, but is heated or cooled depending upon the requirements of the room. The major part of cooling and heating is still supplied by the water systems (beams and radiators, respectively).

In passive chilled beam systems, supply air is not connected to the beam but provided by supply air diffusers. This is similar to cooled ceiling systems where

large water-cooled panels are installed in the ceiling and ventilation is provided by supply air diffusers. In these systems, non-condensing dimensioning is always needed and supply air can be dehumidified only in an air handling unit.

Chilled beam and cooled ceiling systems are most suitable for moderate cooling loads up to 80W per square metre of floor area. In such conditions, high indoor climate standards with low air velocities not exceeding 0.2m/s, as well as silent operation, can be easily achieved (Virta, 2004). These systems have outstanding energy performance since room units do not include fans, and relatively high cooling water temperatures are used due to non-condensing dimensioning and large heat transfer surface areas.

Control of ventilation by air quality (demand-controlled ventilation)

Typically, ventilation runs with constant outdoor airflows through all operational hours, and these airflows are not altered with changes in the use of a room. Usually, the ventilation loads of the interior spaces vary with time, and the ventilation rates should be adjusted to the loads. Air quality-controlled ventilation (AQCV) is a ventilation system where room airflows are controlled according to the contaminant loads or concentrations (see Figure 18.17) – term *G* in Equation 1. The use of

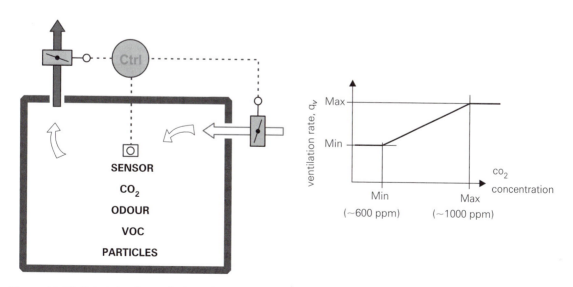

Figure 18.17 *Principle of control of ventilation by air quality (air quality-controlled ventilation, or AQCV) and an example of the control curve of ventilation rate by CO₂ concentration*

AQCV is based on temporarily varying contaminant sources and the actual needs of ventilation when the system of constant airflow ventilation wastes energy, whereas a system with varying airflows saves energy but does not compromise on indoor air quality.

The simplest way to do this is to adapt the ventilation according to demand. Contaminants originate from building and decorative materials, furniture, people and their activities, and intake air. For AQCV, proper air-quality sensors are needed. A room sensor can be one of the following: CO_2, mixed gas, occupancy, combined CO_2/mixed gas, combined occupancy CO_2/ temperature or combined CO_2/CO. At present, CO_2 and temperature sensors are generally used for AQCV in normal spaces due to the cost and unreliability of other types of sensors. CO sensors are used in special cases, such as large garages.

Practical experience shows that adapting the ventilation to the actual requirement can frequently substantially reduce the energy use of a ventilation system. Annual savings of up to 50 per cent have been reported.

Ventilation system components

Duct systems

The purpose of a duct system is to transfer the air to and from rooms in an energy efficient and hygienic way. The energy losses in ducts should be kept at reasonable levels with proper layout and the selection of duct dimensions, good design and installation practice of the duct system, and airtight construction. Figure 18.18 illustrates a duct system where an air handling unit on the roof is connected to room via ducts. The duct system is built from straight ducts (either round or rectangular), connection fittings (bends, T-pieces, etc.), dampers for flow control, terminal devices, inspection doors, measuring devices and sound attenuators (see Figure 18.19).

The cross-section of the ducts may be large in big buildings, which is often a limiting factor for the free placement of the ducts. The horizontal ducts are often installed above a corridor's false ceiling (see Figure 18.20). The room supply and exhaust are connected to the main ducts. The open-plan offices and other large spaces usually have suspended ceilings that form a plenum for air ducts and other installations.

Figure 18.21 illustrates two basic principles for the layout of ducts in an office building. The advantage of

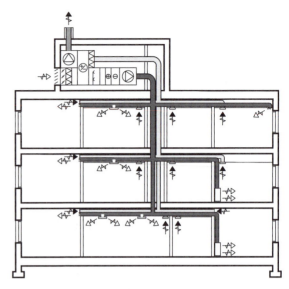

Figure 18.18 *Air handling unit on the roof: Ducts drop first in the vertical shafts and are then running horizontally through the building*

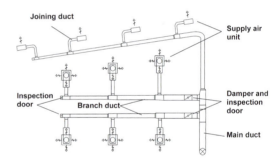

Figure 18.19 *Duct work consists of ducts, fittings, air terminal devices, dampers and openings for inspection*

the upper layout is having fewer vertical shafts but more space for vertical ducts. The advantage of the lower layout is having less space for vertical ducts but more vertical shafts. The space required for the vertical shafts can be estimated with the help of Figure 18.22.

Air handling units

The air handling unit (AHU) consists of several components. The number and selection of components depends upon the requirements for the treatment of air. The cross-section in the air handling unit is usually constant (see Figure 18.23). As the pressure drop in the air handing unit depends upon the average velocity, it is

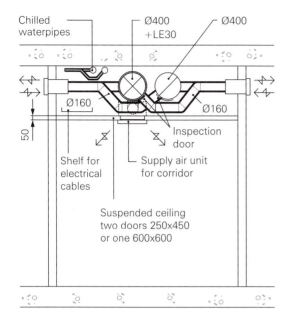

Figure 18.20 *Ducts often run above the suspended ceiling of corridors in office buildings*

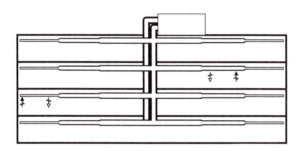

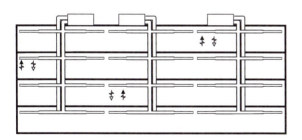

Figure 18.21 *Two alternative principles of duct systems: (top) One air handling unit with large vertical and horizontal ducts; (below) three air handling units with smaller ducts*

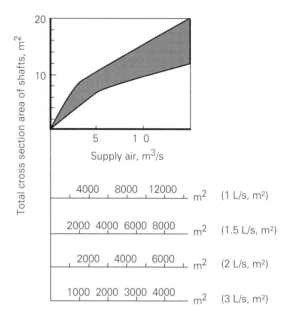

Figure 18.22 *Space required for vertical shafts in office buildings depending upon floor area and design supply airflow rate (L/s, m^2)*

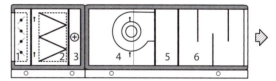

Figure 18.23 *The components of a small air handing unit: Components included: (1) air damper; (2) filter; (3) heating coil; (4) fan; (5) connection component; and (6) noise attenuator*

may have a lower initial cost. The air handling unit may also include heat recovery, as illustrated in Figure 18.24.

Air handling units are often placed in a common mechanical plant room. The required floor area and height for such a room can be estimated from Figure 18.25. It is important that the plant room has enough spare floor area to perform the necessary maintenance operations, such as changing the filters.

Filters

Most relevant urban air particles associated with adverse health effects are fine particulate matter $PM_{2.5}$ (particle mass smaller than 2.5 microns). These particles largely originate from traffic and combustion

important that the velocity is not too high – usually a unit with a larger cross-section is more economical in life cycle costs than a unit with a smaller cross-section area that

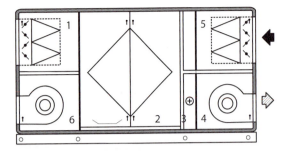

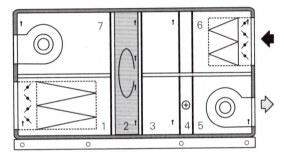

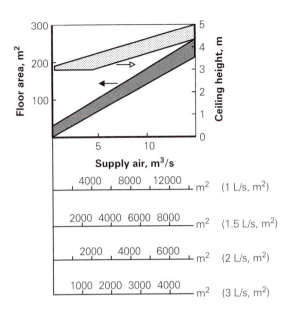

Figure 18.25 *The floor area and required height for a mechanical room depending upon the conditioned floor area and supply airflow per floor area*

Figure 18.24 *A heat recovery system can be an integrated part of an air handling unit: (top) AHU with plate-type heat exchanger comprising the following parts: (1) filter; (2) cross-flow plate-type heat exchanger; (3) heating coil; (4) supply air fan; (5) filter; (6) exhaust air fan; (below) AHU with wheel-type regenerative heat exchanger comprising the following parts: (1) filter; (2) regenerative heat exchanger; (3) space for future use; (4) heating coil; (5) supply air fan; (6) filter; (7) exhaust air fan*

• Exposure of occupants to harmful outdoor particles (e.g. from traffic, energy production, combustion, industry, pollen, spores, etc.) will be reduced.
• The air handling equipment will stay clean and perform better (e.g. better performance of heat exchangers and fans, and lower pressure drop in ducts).
• Cleaner supply air due to filtration also helps to keep the room surfaces clean and reduces the cleaning cost of the building.

processes, such as fireplaces and energy production plants. Particles in indoor air are described by indoor–outdoor ratio and size distribution, both highly affected by filtration and the airtightness of the building envelope.

Based on ambient air measurements and mortality records, epidemiologists have estimated that fine particulate matter ($PM_{2.5}$) exposures cause hundreds of thousands of excess deaths in the developed world (Pope et al, 2002). It has been demonstrated that health effects are caused by the levels of PM of ambient origin and not by exposure to indoor-generated particles (Wilson et al, 2000).

The purpose of air filtration is to prevent harmful particles in the outdoor air from entering the building via the ventilation system. The benefits of air cleaning are as follows:

Particles are usually removed from the outdoor air with fibre filters; the removal efficiency of these particles depends upon filter media (fibre dimensions and type, type of filter media, pressure drop, velocity through the media, etc.). Fine filters (filter class F8 or higher) remove most of fine particulate matter ($PM_{2.5}$), as shown in Figure 18.26.

As the pressure drop of a filter increases due to the accumulated dust in the filter, the airflow through the filter will decrease. The filters will have to be changed when the pressure drop has risen above the preset value. The filter media of fine filters cannot be cleaned, but have to be replaced regularly depending upon the amount of accumulated dust in the filter and the dust-holding capacity of the filter.

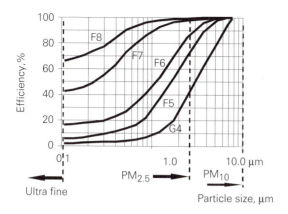

Notes: Exact efficiencies show some variation within the filter class depending upon the product. Filter class G4 refers to coarse filters capturing only large-sized particles and dust. The main filter of outdoor air should be a fine filter with filter class F7 or higher.

Figure 18.26 *Typical efficiency of common fibre filters versus particle size*

The filters described above are particle filters that only remove solid substances from the air. Gas filters, based on adsorption, can be used to remove odours and other gaseous pollutants from the air. This is necessary in highly polluted areas such as highly industrialized regions, near airports, etc. and in the case of special clean environments such as operation theatres or industrial clean rooms. A common type of filter contains activated carbon made from crushed coconut shells.

For short time/peak gas concentrations, particle filters covered with a thin adsorptive media layer may be used. Such filters effectively remove odours from exhaust gases, etc. and have a low pressure drop similar to common particle filters.

Basic design principles of ventilation

Air balance, direction of airflows and air quality

The relative pressures of the building, different spaces and the ventilation system should be designed so that spreading of odours and impurities in harmful amounts or concentrations is prevented. No significant changes to pressure conditions are allowed due to fluctuations in weather conditions. The airtightness of the building envelope, floors and partition walls, which affect pressure conditions, should be studied and defined in the design stage, taking account of both temperature and wind conditions.

The most important principle in designing for good indoor air quality is to try to avoid unnecessary pollutant generation and the spread of pollutants in or between rooms. To achieve this:

- Low pollution products and materials should be used whenever possible.
- The escape of pollutants to room air should be prevented by sealing production processes as much as possible.
- The processes causing pollution will be equipped with local exhaust systems.
- Pollution-generating processes should be located in separate rooms whenever possible in order to minimize the spread of pollutants to other rooms.
- The air balance (difference between supply and exhaust airflows) of the rooms should be so that air flows from less polluted rooms to more polluted rooms.
- Supply air jets should be directed so that they do not increase the spread of pollutants but decrease it.

The air balance principle of ventilation means that air always flows from rooms with higher air quality to rooms with lower air quality and higher pollution generation. This means that clean air is supplied in the cleaner rooms and exhausted from the polluted rooms, and air is transferred from 'clean' to 'dirty' rooms. In residential buildings, this means that outdoor air is supplied to bedrooms and living rooms and exhausted from kitchens, bathrooms and toilets, etc.

In commercial buildings, air is supplied to the occupied zones and exhausted from rooms with pollution generation so that air balance is positive in the occupied rooms and negative in rooms with higher pollution generation. The following principles, as outlined in Figure 18.27, should be applied.

Air distribution

The airflow pattern in a ventilated room depends upon the selection and location of supply air devices, whereas extract air devices have only a small effect on it. This is due to the high momentum (air jet) of supply air

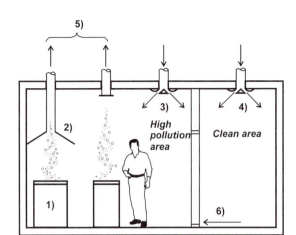

Figure 18.27 *Principles to control air quality in a mechanical ventilation system*

Notes: 1 Pollution-generation processes are equipped with local exhaust.
2 Exhaust air grilles and openings are located above warm pollution-generation sources.
3 Air is supplied in the occupied zone in rooms with high pollution generation in order to reduce exposure of the occupants to pollutants.
4 Clean air is supplied to rooms with no specific pollution generation.
5 Total exhaust airflow is larger than the supply air in rooms with high pollution generation.
6 Air is transferred from cleaner areas to more polluted areas through the openings in walls or doors.

compared to almost zero velocity near the suction point of extract air. There are two main types of airflow pattern:

1   mixing (dilution) ventilation; and
2   displacement ventilation.

Mixing ventilation is used in rooms with normal height (most homes and offices) and can be provided with supply air diffusers, fan coils or chilled beams (see Figures 18.18, 18.14 and 18.15). In mixing ventilation (see Figure 18.28) the air is supplied in such a way that the room air is fully mixed, and the pollutant concentration, diluted by ventilation, is equally distributed throughout the room. If the supply air is not fully mixed with the room air, a part of it may flow directly to an extract air opening. This short-circuiting reduces the efficiency of ventilation (term ε in Equation 1) and should be avoided (Mundt, 2003).

Especially in high rooms such as concert halls, auditoria, etc., it is more efficient to bring fresh supply

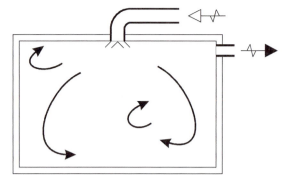

Mixing flow pattern

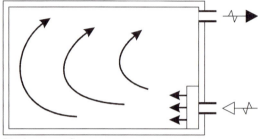

Displacement flow pattern

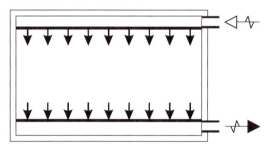

Laminar piston flow pattern

Figure 18.28 *Mixing, displacement and laminar flow patterns: The upper diagram illustrates complete mixing with a uniform concentration of contaminants in the room*

air directly to the breathing zone. This can be done by displacement ventilation, where a stratified flow is created using supply air that is a few degrees lower than room temperature. Displacement ventilation creates a cleaner and cooler lower zone and a more polluted and warmer upper zone (Skistad, 2002). The air quality in the occupied zone is, thus, better than for mixing ventilation at the same ventilation rate due to higher ventilation effectiveness.

The opposite of a mixing flow pattern is piston flow, where airflow is laminar and the room air is not mixed at all with the supply air. This flow pattern, with maximum possible ventilation effectiveness, is used in special cases, such as operating theatres and other rooms demanding high hygiene.

Performance criteria for ventilation

Ventilation (outdoor airflow) has to be adequate to remove and dilute indoor-generated pollutants and humidity, and to provide an acceptable level of contaminants in indoor air. Control of pollutant sources, however, should be considered as the first alternative to improving indoor air quality. Ventilation should be energy efficient and introduced so that it does not deteriorate indoor air quality and climate, and does not cause any harm to the occupants or to the building. Ventilation rates should be based on the pollution loads and use of the building.

The concentration of indoor air pollutants can be used to calculate the ventilation rate needed for the dilution or removal of pollutants. The source of the pollutants can come from a variety of internal sources, from the metabolic pollutants of the occupants (CO_2) to pollutants from processes taking place in the building. The dilution ventilation flow rate for a known emission rate and a known pollution concentration level within the building can be calculated from pollutant mass balance (see Figure 18.29) by Equation 1:

$$q_v = \frac{G}{C_{in} - C_o} \frac{1}{\varepsilon} \qquad (1)$$

where:

- q_v = the volume flow rate of supply air in m³/s;
- G = the net mass flow rate of emission to the room air in mg/s;
- C_{in} = the allowed concentration in the room in mg/m³;
- C_o = the concentration in the supply air in mg/m³;
- ε = the ventilation efficiency (ε = 1 for complete mixing to ε = 2 for ideal piston flow).

Equation 1 does not take into account the removal of the pollutant indoors by factors other than ventilation, including deposition on surfaces, filtration of indoor

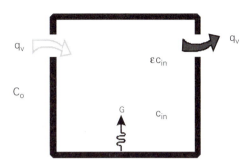

Figure 18.29 *Airflow and pollutant emission in the room: Symbols are given in Equation 1*

air, chemical reactions, etc., which may reduce the emission term. In complete mixing of the air (typical for most common air distribution schemes, as discussed above), ventilation efficiency ε = 1 (i.e. the pollutant concentration in the occupied zone is equal to the pollutant concentration in the extract air). Short-circuiting of the supply air will decrease ventilation efficiency below 1 and higher airflow rate is needed for the same concentration. Displacement ventilation improves ventilation efficiency typically to ε = 1.2 to 1.5, and lower airflow rate is needed for the same concentration.

The same type of mass balance equation also applies for the humidity balance of air. Removal of indoor-generated humidity can be calculated by Equation 2:

$$q_v = \frac{G_h}{v_{in} - v_o} \qquad (2)$$

where:

- q_v = the volume flow rate of supply air in m³/s;
- G_h = the indoor humidity generation in the room in g/s;
- v_{in} = the humidity by volume of the indoor air in the room in g/m³;
- v_o = the humidity by volume of the supply (outdoor) air in g/m³.

Ventilation removes the humidity at a flow rate of $G_h(v_{in} - v_o)$. Since the outdoor humidity is not constant, humidity removal is higher (ventilation is more effective) at low outdoor air humidity. In hot climates, the outdoor humidity may be higher than indoor humidity. In this case, ventilation brings in humidity and humidity is usually removed by air conditioning (condensation on the cooling coil).

In the case of different pollutants, it is necessary to check all relevant pollutants in order to determine the most critical one. As a rule, source control is preferable to ventilation. Equation 1 is valid for a steady-state situation (default situation) with a long-lasting constant emission. It also assumes that all pollution generated in a room is carried out with the airflow – no other sinks are assumed to be in the room. When the emission period is short, it may not be possible to achieve a stationary equilibrium concentration, or the airflow may be reduced for a given maximum concentration level. The time dependence of the concentration level in the room is given by Equation 3 (supply air rate = extract air rate):

$$C_{in}(t) - C_o = C_{in}(0) + \frac{G}{q_v}\left(1 - e^{-\frac{q_v}{V} \cdot t}\right) \quad (3)$$

where:

- $C_{in}(t)$ = the concentration in the room at time t in mg/m³;
- C_o = the concentration in the supply air in mg/m³;
- $C_{in}(0)$ = the concentration in the room at the beginning (t = 0) in mg/m³;
- q_v = the volume flow rate of supply air in m³/s;
- G = the mass flow rate of emissions in the room in mg/s;
- V = the volume of air in the room in m³;
- t = the time in seconds.

There is no common standard index for indoor air quality that will allow using Equations 1 to 3 for determining the required ventilation rate. Indoor air quality may be expressed as the required level of ventilation or carbon dioxide (CO_2) concentration. CO_2 concentration can be used as a surrogate of ventilation rates; but its use in measuring ventilation is uncertain as its concentration in buildings seldom reaches a steady-state condition due to variations in occupancy, ventilation rates and outdoor air concentration. Steady-state values of carbon dioxide concentration can be calculated from CO_2 generation of 0.00567L/s per occupant in office buildings.

It is generally accepted that indoor air quality is influenced by emissions from people and their activities (bio-effluent, smoking, etc.), and from buildings, furnishings, and ventilation and air-conditioning systems themselves (i.e. building components). Required ventilation is based on health and comfort criteria. In most cases, health criteria will also be met by the required ventilation for comfort. Health effects may be attributed to specific components of emissions, and if the concentration of one source is reduced, the concentration of others is also lowered. Comfort is more related to perceived air quality (odour and irritation). In this case, different sources of emissions may have an odour component that adds to odour level. There is, however, no general agreement on how different sources of emissions should be added together. In the latest standards (EN 15251, and ASHRAE 62.1 and 62.2) the criteria are expressed as the addition of people (smoking, non-smoking) and building components. The total ventilation rate for a room is calculated from the following formula:

$$q_{tot} = n \cdot q_p + A \cdot q_B \quad (4)$$

where:

- q_{tot} = total ventilation rate of the room (L/s);
- n = design value for the number of people in the room (–);
- q_p = ventilation rate for occupancy per person (L/s, pers);
- A = room floor area (m²);
- q_B = ventilation rate for emissions from buildings (L/s, m²).

The ventilation rates for occupants (q_p) only depend upon indoor climate category (EN 15251, 2007a):

- category I (high) (10L/s, pers);
- category II (medium) (7L/s, pers);
- category III (basic) (4L/s, pers).

Ventilation rates (q_B) for building emissions are shown in Table 18.1. An example of how ventilation rates are specified by pollution load with Equation 4 is given in the Table 18.2.

If ventilation rates are reduced, energy is saved; at the same time, indoor air quality deteriorates. The minimum ventilation rate is 10 to 15L/s per person, which is approximately 1L/s per square metre in office buildings with normal occupant density. For better IAQ and productivity, a doubled airflow rate of 2L/s per square metre is recommended for typical landscape and cellular offices. This is supported by the latest research of Seppänen and Fisk (2004) and Fisk and Seppänen (2007), who summarize the effect of ventilation with regard to health and productivity as follows:

- Ventilation rates below 10L/s per person are associated with a significantly higher prevalence of health or perceived air quality outcomes.
- Increases in ventilation rates above 10L/s per person, up to approximately 20L/s per person, are associated with a significant decrease in the prevalence of sick building syndrome (SBS) symptoms or with improvements in perceived air quality and task performance and productivity.
- Relative to natural ventilation, air conditioning is often associated with a statistically significant increase in the prevalence of one or more SBS symptoms.

For residential buildings, ventilation rates below 0.5 air change per hour (ACH) have been documented as a health risk in Nordic residential buildings (Wargocki et al, 2002; Sundell and Levin, 2007).

Energy efficient equipment

Moving the air in and out of the building requires energy in mechanically ventilated buildings; typically, however, this is usually much lower that the energy used to condition the air either in the air handling system or in the building. The use of electric energy by fans can be reduced by decreasing the pressure drop in the system and by selecting high efficiency equipment. The specific fan power (see Equation 5) is used to define the overall air-moving efficiency of each fan. When the specific fan power is defined for the air handling unit, the input power term P comprises the input powers of the supply and exhaust fans:

$$P_{SFP} = \frac{P}{q_v} = \frac{\Delta p}{\eta_{tot}} \qquad (5)$$

where:

- P_{SFP} = the specific fan power (Wm^{3}s^1);
- P = the input power of the motor for the fan (W);
- q_v = the nominal airflow through the fan in (m^3/s);
- Δp = the total pressure difference across the fan (Pa);
- η_{tot} = the total efficiency of the fan, motor and drive.

Ventilation air can also be used for air conditioning. If air conditioning is used, high efficiency equipment

Table 18.1 *Ventilation rates (q_B) for building emissions*

Category	Very low-polluting building (L/s, m²)	Low-polluting building (L/s, m²)	Non-low-polluting building (L/s, m²)
I (high)	0.5	1.0	2.0
II (medium)	0.35	0.7	1.4
III (basic)	0.3	0.4	0.8

Source: EN 15251 (2007a)

Table 18.2 *An example of ventilation rates for offices depending upon the pollution load in three categories*

Category	Occupants only (L/s, m²)	Low-polluting building (L/s, m²)	Non-low-polluting building (L/s, m²)
I (high)	1.0	2.0	3.0
II (medium)	0.7	1.4	2.1
III (basic)	0.4	0.8	1.2

Source: EN 15251 (2007a)

should be selected. For example, the selection of the best class A chiller instead of worst class F air-cooled chiller will reduce the use of electricity by a factor of over 2.5 (Eurovent: see www.euroventcertification.com).

The heating energy of supply air can be substantially reduced by using effective heat-recovery equipment (a heat exchanger transfers heat from extract air to supply air). Good heat recovery efficiency of 80 per cent will decrease heating energy by a factor of 5: only 20 per cent of heating needs should be covered by a heating coil since the remainder is recovered from extract air.

References

ASHRAE 62.1 (2007a) *ANSI/ASHRAE Standard 62.1-2007: Ventilation for Acceptable Indoor Air Quality*, American Society of Heating Refrigerating and Air-Conditioning Engineers, Atlanta, GA

ASHRAE 62.2 (2007b) *ANSI/ASHRAE Standard 62.2-2007: Ventilation and Acceptable Indoor Air Quality in Low-Rise Residential Buildings*, American Society of Heating Refrigerating and Air-Conditioning Engineers, Atlanta, GA

EN 15251 (2007a) *European Standard: Criteria for the Indoor Environment, Including Thermal, Indoor Air Quality, Light and Noise*

EN 13779 (2007b) *European Standard: Ventilation for Non-Residential Buildings – Performance Requirements for Ventilation and Room Conditioning Systems*

Eurovent (undated) *Classification of Chillers*, www.eurovent certification.com/

Fisk, W. and Seppänen, O. (2007) 'Providing better indoor environmental quality brings economic benefits: Keynote lecture', in *Proceedings of 9th REHVA World Congress Climate 2007*, www.rehva.eu

Hänninen, O., Palonen, J., Tuomisto, J. T., Yli-Tuomi, T. et al (2005) 'Reduction potential of urban $PM_{2.5}$ mortality risk using modern ventilation systems in buildings', *Indoor Air*, vol 15, pp246–256

Mundt, E. (ed) (2003) *Ventilation Effectiveness: REHVA Guidebook No 2*, European Federation of Heating and Air-Conditioning Associations, www.rehva.eu

Pope, C. A., Burnett, R. T., Thun, M. J., Calle, E. E., Krewski, D., Ito, K. and Thurston, G. D. (2002) 'Lung cancer, cardiopulmonary mortality, and long-term exposure to fine particulate air pollution', *Journal of the American Medical Association*, vol 287, no 9, pp1132–1141

Seppänen, O. and Fisk, W. J. (2004) 'Summary of human responses to ventilation', *International Journal of Indoor Air Quality and Climate 2004*, vol 14, supplement 7, pp102–118

Skistad Håkon (ed) (2002) *Displacement Ventilation: REHVA Guidebook No 1*, European Federation of Heating and Air-Conditioning Associations, www.rehva.eu

Sundell, J. and Levin, H. (2007) *Ventilation Rates and Health: Report of an Interdisciplinary Review of the Scientific Literature*, Final report submitted to American Society of Heating, Refrigerating and Air-Conditioning Engineers

Virta, M. (ed) (2004) *Chilled Beam Application Guidebook: REHVA Guidebook No 5*, European Federation of Heating and Air-Conditioning Associations, www.rehva.eu.

Wargocki, W., Sundell, J., Bischof, W., Brundrett, G., Fanger, O., Gyntelberg, F., Hanssen, S. O., Harrison, P., Pickering, A., Seppänen, O. and Wouters, P. (2002) 'Ventilation and health in non-industrial indoor environments: Report from a European multidisciplinary scientific consensus meeting', *International Journal of Indoor Environment and Health*, vol 12, pp113–128

Wilson, W. E., Mage, D. T. and Grant, L. D. (2000) 'Estimating separately personal exposure to ambient and non-ambient particulate matter for epidemiology and risk assessment: Why and how', *Journal of the Air and Waste Management Association*, vol 50, pp1167–1183

19

Climate Change and Building Design

Steve Sharples and Susan Lee

Introduction

Predicting the impact of climate change on manufactured and natural systems is, given the complexities of the systems and the uncertainties in the modelling, a difficult and contentious area of research. However, it is a fact based upon reliable thermometer measurements taken over the last 150 years that global temperatures have risen. There is also a general scientific consensus that climate change arising from global warming is the result of increased greenhouse gas emissions from human activity. Envisaged future changes to weather patterns, based on various emission scenarios, have geographical variations, but the major foreseen changes include warmer and drier summers, milder and wetter winters and rising sea levels. In addition, extreme events may include an increased number of very hot days, more intense periods of rain and a greater frequency of storms. Most of the current building stock will still be in use in 50 years' time and historical weather data will have been used to calculate building performance and needs. However, it is not clear how relevant these calculations will be 50 years from now for what may be a very different prevailing climate. In this chapter the potential impacts of climate change on buildings will be discussed and the options for changes to building design to make buildings more resilient to future climates will be considered (see also Sanders and Phillipson, 2003; TCPA, 2007; Wilby, 2007).

Climate change and temperature

Impacts

Global average temperatures are expected to rise by 1°C to 6°C during the coming century, with the greatest warming taking place at high latitudes. In urban areas, this warming will add to the already higher temperatures experienced in cities due to the urban heat island (UHI) effect (Watkins et al, 2007). The impact of hotter summer days and much warmer summer nights will include thermal discomfort and difficulty sleeping. There are suggestions that night-time temperatures may be more significant then maximum daytime temperatures in terms of health impacts upon people (Department of Health, 2008). Warmer temperatures are associated with several serious diseases, such as malaria, and an increase in food poisoning, air pollution and water contamination. However, the most serious thermal climate change impact upon people is the predicted increase in the frequency of heat waves. There is a direct relationship between very hot conditions and human illness and mortality. The European heat wave of August 2003 is estimated to have been responsible for around 35,000 excess deaths, with the elderly and the ill being most affected (Confalonieri et al, 2007). In France, 91 per cent of victims were over 61 years old (Salagnac, 2007). Figure 19.1 shows the total daily deaths in London during 2003 for people aged over 75, with a marked peak occurring during the August heat wave. It is believed that the European temperatures experienced during the summer of 2003 heat wave will become 'typical' by the 2040s and could be considered 'cool' by the 2080s (Stott et al, 2004).

Responses

The first stage of managing higher future internal temperatures in buildings is to attempt to make the external air as cool as possible. Within the built

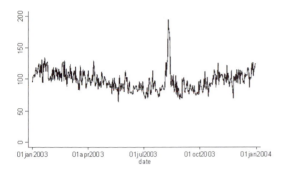

Source: Greater London Authority (2006)

Figure 19.1 *Total daily deaths of people over 75 in London, 2003*

environment, this involves enhancing the green and blue infrastructure of parks, trees, open spaces, open water and water features. Parks and other open green spaces can be beneficial through their cooling effects in summer through shading and transpiration (Yu and Hien, 2006; Gill et al, 2007) and improved access for natural wind-driven ventilation. In addition, water, plants and trees contribute to microclimate cooling and are an important source of moisture within the mostly arid urban environment (Robitu et al, 2006). Urban surfaces should be cool or reflective to limit solar gain. Pavements, car parks and roads can be constructed with lighter finishes and have more porous structures. There is a growing interest in the use of rooftop gardens, green walls and green roofs for their cooling effect (Liu and Baskaran, 2003). Building surfaces, particularly roofs, should also have a high reflectance (or albedo) to solar radiation in order to minimize solar gain in the opaque fabric. This is a common practice in southern Europe, but currently rare in cooler climates. Figure 19.2 shows typical roof albedos for different roof materials, while Figure 19.3 shows the results of a theoretical analysis that examined the midday air temperature on the third day of a sunny period for a range of urban albedo values.

The key building fabric responses to climate change will involve solar shading, thermal mass, ventilation and insulation. The main building services considerations will include heating and cooling systems.

Solar gain through windows and opaque elements will typically represent one of the largest heat gains in a building and, therefore, is one of the most important

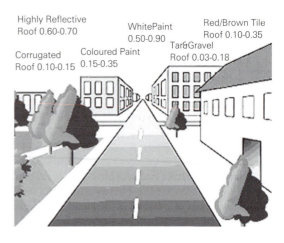

Source: EPA (2007)

Figure 19.2 *Typical albedo values for roof materials*

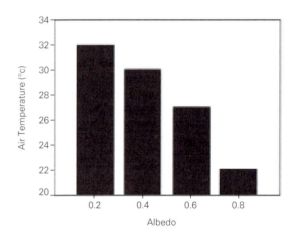

Source: Greater London Authority (2006)

Figure 19.3 *Theoretical impact of changing albedo on noon air temperature*

parameters to control in a warming climate. Shading devices can take several forms (e.g. louvres, blinds and shutters); but they should all, ideally, be light coloured, porous, external and moveable. Roofs should be shaded at latitudes where the sun reaches a high altitude in its path across the sky. In climates that are already hot, building form and layout are also used to provide shade – for example, by placing buildings close together or by forming courtyards. A detailed discussion of solar shading control is given in the CIBSE publication TM37 (CIBSE, 2006).

Thermal mass is related to how much heat a material can absorb and how quickly that heat is transmitted through the material. Concrete and stone are high thermal mass materials and the interiors of caves and cathedrals demonstrate how effective mass can be in keeping spaces cool even on very hot days. This is obviously a very useful feature in a warming climate, but has the disadvantage that the heat is still stored within the building fabric at night, when the UHI has its greatest impact. Night ventilation (by opening secure vents and windows) can be used to purge some of the heat out of the building mass, leaving the building a few degrees Celsius cooler by the start of the next day. Figure 19.4 shows a typical temperature profile for an office with and without night ventilation.

In addition to night cooling, ventilation is obviously also important in buildings for providing fresh air, removing stale air, controlling relative humidity and offering daytime cooling in summer. Natural ventilation strategies involve wind-driven forces (determined by wind speed and direction) and stack or buoyancy forces driven by the height between inlet and outlet ventilation openings and the indoor–outdoor temperature difference. Future wind speed and direction scenarios are currently poorly understood; but it is clear that in a warming environment, the potential of summertime natural ventilation to cool building interiors is greatly diminished. This implies that the demand for active or mechanical systems to cool buildings will increase, with consequences for energy demand and possible waste heat injection into an already warm urban environment.

Thermal insulation is used in building envelopes to reduce heat losses in winter, minimize energy use and maintain thermal comfort. During the summer, insulation can have two impacts: it can reduce and retard external solar heat gains being transmitted through the fabric to internal rooms; but insulation can also impede heat generated within a room (such as solar gains through windows or casual gains from activity) from leaving the space. In a warming climate, it becomes less clear how conventional insulation should be used in a future building design. As an alternative, for example, green roofs offer good winter insulation but also provide summer cooling, biodiversity and longer roof life.

Heating systems are likely to require much smaller capacities in the future to meet reduced winter heating loads. The efficiency of a boiler is highest when it is running close to full output; so the required maximum output of a boiler sized using historical weather data will need to be revised each time the boiler is replaced (say, every ten years). For buildings constructed to a very high insulation and airtightness standard, a warming climate may remove the need for a central heating system altogether and enable a space to achieve thermal comfort using just passive solar gains and casual internal gains from people and electrical equipment.

It is very probable that the traditional passive means of cooling buildings (natural ventilation, thermal mass and evaporation) will not be able to ensure summer thermal comfort for future climate scenarios, especially in heat waves. Current active cooling systems are normally refrigerant-based air-conditioning units that have high electrical energy consumption and use ambient air as a heat sink. There are alternative, more energy efficient, cooling systems, which include the use of chilled beams, groundwater, evaporative cooling and ground-coupled cooling (see GPG, 2001). Although there is little doubt that mechanical cooling systems will become more widely used to combat climate warming, they should always be the final step after all other passive cooling strategies have been designed into the building.

The Chartered Institution of Building Services Engineers (CIBSE, 2005) has analysed how effective

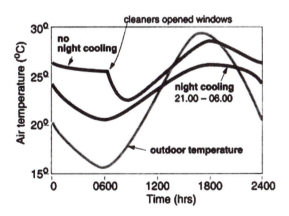

Source: Rennie and Parand (1998)

Figure 19.4 *Impact of night ventilation on indoor air temperature*

some of the above passive adaptive measures might be in combating climate change. They modelled the performance (space heating, risk of summer overheating, need for comfort cooling, and performance of mechanical air-conditioning systems) of a variety of building types for a current design hot weather year and future weather scenarios. For a newly built detached house, the adaptive measures examined included mass, solar shading, a reduction of ventilation during the warm part of the day and an increase in ventilation at night. Discomfort temperature levels were taken as 28°C in the living room and 25°C in the bedroom. Figure 19.5 shows the impact of mass on overheating in a living room for an unadapted house in London for a period stretching from the 1980s to the 2080s, expressed as the number of days in a year when indoor temperatures exceeded 28°C. The high-mass house performs significantly better than the equivalent lightweight house. However, a similar analysis for an upstairs bedroom showed only a marginal difference in performance.

Figure 19.6 shows the equivalent living room results, but includes the influence of the adaptation measures.

The adapted high mass is seen to perform significantly better and to provide a good level of thermal comfort in the living room up to the 2080s. The same is not true for the bedroom analysis, where even the high-mass adapted house displayed overheating problems by the 2020s. This type of finding is persuading some house designers to suggest that, in the future, bedrooms should be located on ground floors with living areas at first-floor level.

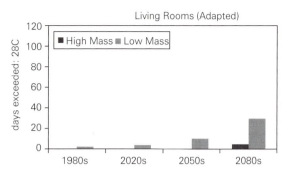

Source: CIBSE (2005)

Figure 19.6 *Impact of mass and adaptation on living room air temperature*

Climate change and precipitation

Impacts

The expected climate change patterns for precipitation are, typically, drier summers, wetter winters and a greater incidence of heavy rainstorms. More frequent and intense rainfall will lead to river flooding and the failure of urban drainage systems. Such flooding creates many problems, including building damage, disruption to transport, interference to water supplies and potential health risks (Ahern et al, 2005). Rising sea levels will add to flood risk for both coastal locations and low-level cities on or near rivers.

Responses

Urban development and pressure on land use have meant that more buildings have been, and continue to be, constructed on what were traditional sacrificial floodplains. This has had the effect of distorting and damaging natural drainage systems, and the consequences are increasingly evident, with large-scale flooding becoming more common. The impact of climate change will probably be to make these flooding events more severe and more frequent. At the urban scale, flood risk management can use sustainable urban drainage systems (SUDS), which attempt to control and slow down the runoff of surface water following heavy rain. This approach includes the use of vegetated gently sloping landscape elements, soakaways to allow the rain to get directly back into the ground, permeable and porous pavements and car parks, and sacrificial

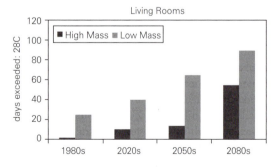

Source: CIBSE (2005)

Figure 19.5 *Impact of mass on living room air temperature*

areas, such as fields and ponds, to store the floodwater. A detailed description of SUDS is given by CIRIA (2008).

For an individual building, the aims of flood risk management are to minimize the risk of flooding and to reduce the damage caused by flooding. Apart from creating physical barriers between floodwater and the building, other risk-reduction approaches include reducing the runoff of rain through harvesting of rainwater, providing permeable and/or drained ground surfaces and the use of green roofs (these suggestions are also part of a SUDS strategy). Green roofs, in particular, are seen as a potentially very powerful tool in adapting buildings to reduce climate change urban flood risk (Carter and Jackson, 2007). In order to minimize flood damage to buildings from present and future events, there are a series of steps that can be implemented. Floodwater will penetrate not just through obvious openings in walls, but also through cracks, defects, service penetrations and other openings; therefore, general maintenance and repair of the structural envelope is important, particularly for buildings in known flood-risk areas. All utility services, such as supply meters, electrical fittings and boilers, should be at least 1m above ground-floor level, with pipes and cables dropping from the first-floor level. Drainage and sewer pipes should have one-way valves fitted to prevent the backflow of contaminated floodwater entering the building.

A FEMA publication in the US (FEMA, 1999) provides a very detailed discussion of protecting building utilities from flood damage. Flood-resistant finishes, such as plastics, vinyl, concrete, ceramic tiles and pressure-treated timber, should be used in place of carpets, chipboard, soft woods and fabric, and gypsum plaster should be replaced with a more water-resistant material, such as lime plaster or cement render. To reduce the amount of repair after flooding, it is helpful to fix plasterboards horizontally on timber-framed walls rather than vertically and to replace mineral insulation within internal partition walls with closed cell insulation. Some of the most advanced ideas for making buildings flood resilient can be found in Holland, a country that is, even before climate change, 6m below sea level. One architectural solution is floating buildings that rise and fall with water levels. Examples of this approach are described by H$_2$OLLAND (2006).

Climate change and wind
Impacts

The major interactions of wind and buildings are in structural loading, wind speeds at pedestrian level and as a driving force for natural ventilation and cooling. There is a great deal of uncertainty about future patterns of wind speed and direction, and climate models are not robust or consistent in their predictions. However, it is believed that there will be an increase in the number and severity of storms.

Responses

The most important wind feature is the once in 50-year design wind speed used in structural loading calculations. Given that buildings might stand for up to 100 years, it could be argued that structural building codes will need to review the design wind speeds and frequency of events to factor in safety margins in response to future climate change. Roofs suffer the greatest amount of destruction in high winds, mainly due to a failure to tie the roof securely to its supporting walls or supports. Low-pitch roofs are very susceptible to wind damage and a better choice might be a mansard roof, which has two slopes on each side, with the lower slope being almost vertical and the upper slope being almost horizontal. Other design features, such as buildings having a more aerodynamic form or minimum roof overhangs, may appear beneficial but would need to be tested to ensure that other problems are not created – for example, small overhangs might exacerbate flooding problems.

Climate change and subsidence
Impacts

Paradoxically, under predicted climate change scenarios, some regions of the world may be concerned with increased flood risk while others will be suffering from very dry seasons, water shortages and the risk of soils drying out. Reduced soil moisture levels have impacts on agriculture, flood control and buildings, where subsidence damage will become an increasing problem. UKCIP (2002) suggested that for different scenarios, soil moisture will fall by between 20 and 40 per cent by the 2080s.

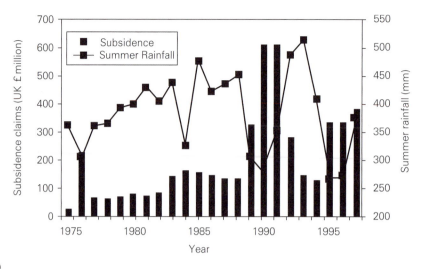

Source: IPCC (2001)

Figure 19.7 *Relationship between rainfall and subsidence*

Responses

Subsidence is already a significant cause of building damage, and climate change is only likely to make things worse. Figure 19.7 shows the cost and scale of subsidence claims in the UK for a 20-year period and the relationship with summer rainfall.

For existing buildings, it is not viable to underpin original foundations in a way that will make them climate change resilient, and so the incidence of subsidence damage to buildings will increase during the coming decades. To make new and future buildings climate change resilient, it will be necessary to change the design of foundations to make them stronger, stiffer and deeper in order to resist movement. New foundation technologies, such as pile-and-beam foundations, are described in a National House Builders Confederation publication (NHBC, 2007), which also highlights the importance of careful tree planting management to avoid soil shrinkage and foundation damage by roots.

Conclusions

The mechanical servicing of buildings is a relatively recent phenomenon, with its origins only beginning at the start of the 20th century. For thousands of years

before then, buildings had to modify the prevailing climate using only passive or low-energy systems. It is not surprising that many of the building design issues relating to climate change resonate with elements found in the vernacular architecture and urban layouts of other countries. Features such as courtyards, wind catchers, narrow streets, green roofs, water features and houses raised on stilts all reflect a response to the contemporary local climate. It is too simplistic to say that since temperatures in London may one day resemble those already existing in, say, Lisbon, then a linear design extrapolation can be implemented. The most obvious climatic difference is the different range of solar altitudes resulting from differences in latitude; but there are also cultural and historical traditions to respect. However, it is also true that there are lessons relevant to climate change to be learned from vernacular architecture as it offers an historical perspective on how, globally, built environments evolved to deal with the challenges of changing climates.

References

Ahern, M., Kovats, R. S., Wilkinson, P., Few, R. and Matthies, F. (2005) 'Global health impacts of floods: Epidemiologic evidence', *Epidemiologic Reviews*, vol 27, pp36–46

Carter, T. and Jackson, C. R. (2007) 'Vegetated roofs for stormwater management at multiple spatial scales', *Landscape and Urban Planning*, vol 80, pp84–94

CIBSE (2005) 'Climate change and the indoor environment: Impacts and adaptations', *CIBSE Technical Memorandum TM36*, CIBSE, London

CIBSE (2006) 'Design for improved solar shading control', *CIBSE Technical Memorandum TM37*, CIBSE, London

CIRIA (2008) www.ciria.org.uk/suds, accessed 1 May 2008

Confalonieri, U., Menne, B., Akhtar, R., Ebi, K. L., Hauengue, M., Kovats, R. S., Revich, B. and Woodward, A. (2007), 'Human health', in *Climate Change 2007: Impacts, Adaptation and Vulnerability: Contribution of Working Group II to the Fourth Assessment Report of the Intergovernmental Panel on Climate Change*, Cambridge University Press, Cambridge, UK, Chapter 8, pp391–431, www.gtp89.dial.pipex.com/chpt.htm, accessed 1 May 2008

Department of Health (2008) *Heat Wave Plan: 2008*, UK government publication, www.dh.gov.uk/en/Publications andstatistics/Publications/PublicationsPolicyAndGuidance /DH_084670, accessed 1 May 2008

EPA (2007) www.epa.gov/heatisld/strategies/coolroofs.html, accessed 1 May 2008

FEMA (1999) *Protecting Building Utilities from Flood Damage*, FEMA Report 348, www.fema.gov/hazard/ flood/pubs/pbuffd.shtm, accessed 1 May 2008

Gill, S. E., Handley, J. F., Ennos, A. R. and Pauleit, S. (2007) 'Adapting cities for climate change: The role of the green infrastructure', *Built Environment*, vol 33, no 1, pp115–133

Greater London Authority (2006) *London's Urban Heat Island: A Summary for Decision Makers*, Greater London Authority, www.london.gov.uk/mayor/environment/climate-change/uhi.jsp, accessed 1 May 2008

GPG (2001), *Ventilation and Cooling Option Appraisal: A Client's Guide*, Good Practice Guide 290, BRECSU, Watford, www.carbontrust.co.uk, accessed 1 May 2008

H₂OLLAND (2006) 'Architecture with wet feet', www.h2olland.nl/, accessed 1 May 2008

IPCC (Intergovernmental Panel on Climate Change) (2001) 'Insurance and other financial services', *Working Group II Report: Impacts, Adaptation and Vulnerability*, Chapter 8, www.ipcc.ch/ipccreports/tar/wg2/321.htm, accessed 1 May 2008

Liu, K. and Baskaran, B. (2003) *Thermal Performance of Green Roofs through Field Evaluation*, National Research Council of Canada Report NRCC-46412, Ottawa, Canada

NHBC (National House Builders Confederation) (2007) *NHBC Standards, Part 4 – Foundations*, NHBC, Milton Keynes, UK

Rennie, D. and Parand, F. (1998) *Environmental Design Guide for Naturally Ventilated and Daylit Offices*, BRE report BR 345, Construction Research Communications Ltd, London

Robitu, M., Musy, M., Inard, C. and Groleau, D. (2006) 'Modeling the influence of vegetation and water pond on urban microclimate', *Solar Energy*, vol 80, pp435–447

Salagnac, J. (2007) 'Lessons from the 2003 heat wave: A French perspective', *Building Research & Information*, vol 35, no 4, pp450–457

Sanders, C. H. and Phillipson, M. C. (2003) 'UK adaptation strategy and technical measures: The impact of climate change on buildings', *Building Research & Information*, vol 31, no 3–4, pp210–221

Stott, P. A., Stone, D. A. and Allen, M. R. (2004) 'Human contribution to the European heat wave of 2003', *Nature*, vol 432, pp610–614

TCPA (2007) *Climate Change Adaptation by Design*, TCPA, London, www.TCPA.org/publications.asp

UKCIP (2002) 'Future changes in UK seasonal climate', in *Climate Change Scenarios for the United Kingdom: The UKCIP02 Scientific Report*, Tyndall Centre, Norwich, Chapter 4, pp51–52, www.ukcip.org.uk/index.php? option=com_content&task=view&id=353&Itemid=408

Watkins, R., Palmer, J. and Kolokotroni, M. (2007) 'Increased temperature and intensification of the urban heat island: Implications for human comfort and urban design', *Built Environment*, vol 33, no 1, pp85–96

Wilby, R. L. (2007) 'A review of climate change impacts on the built environment', *Built Environment*, vol 33, no 1, pp31–45

Yu, C. and Hien, W. N. (2006) 'Thermal benefits of city parks', *Energy and Buildings*, vol 38, no 2, pp105–120

20

Sustainable Cooling Strategies

Thomas Lakkas and Dejan Mumovic

Introduction

The aim of this chapter is to provide an overview of sustainable cooling strategy options and to highlight the main design characteristics and requirements. Sustainable low-energy cooling strategies have the capability to minimize mechanical cooling loads in buildings while reducing the occurrence of summertime thermal discomfort and overheating. Increased interest in sustainable cooling strategies has been underpinned by the fact that almost half of global energy consumption originates from buildings and 16 per cent of this energy represents the energy consumed by air conditioning (Ortiz, 2006). Furthermore, due to climate change, growing internal heat loads in buildings and the inappropriateness of building construction, cooling energy demand in Europe is continuously rising (see Figure 20.1).

With changing climate it is probable that average temperatures in the UK will increase by 4°C to 6°C over the next 50 to 80 years, resulting in a higher frequency of summertime temperatures in the range of 30°C to 36°C (CIBSE TM 36, 2005). Temperatures within free-running buildings are always closely linked to those outside, meaning that the future will offer greater challenges to the designers of low-energy buildings. However, in line with the Latin saying that times are changing and we are changing with them (*'Tempora mutantur, nos et mutamur in illis'*), one has to take into account another variable – occupant behaviour. It should be noted that in the future, comfort expectations are likely to change and people will either adapt to higher temperatures or, with increasing disposable income, will have higher summertime thermal comfort

expectations than are currently typically experienced in naturally ventilated buildings. In all cases, the integration of sustainable low-energy cooling strategies in building design seems a sound way forward.

Developing the sustainable cooling strategy

A sound sustainable cooling strategy should consider the following five steps (see Figure 20.2):

1 reduction and modulation of heat gains;
2 use of direct and indirect ventilative cooling;
3 cooling energy from renewable sources;
4 analysis of free cooling options;
5 implementation of sustainable distribution systems.

The key issues that need to be considered as part of developing a successful sustainable cooling design include the following:

* Sustainable energy cooling must not be considered an independent part of the building, but needs to be integrated within the building design.
* The process of designing sustainable cooling systems is essentially *iterative* and *progressive*; this requires close collaboration between architects and building service engineers, and ideally should take into account the views of a number of stakeholders, including end users (if known) and facility managers.

The following sections briefly summarize the main design requirements for each of the five steps.

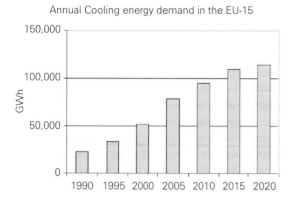

Annual Cooling energy demand in the EU-15

Source: Keep Cool Project (2005)

Figure 20.1 *Annual cooling energy demand in the European Union*

Reduction and modulation of heat gains

Reduction and modulation of heat gains is perhaps one of the critical steps in developing a sustainable cooling design. In most cases, achieving acceptable summer conditions requires two main features in the design:

1   *Effective solar control.* The principal function of the advanced building envelope in summer is to control solar gain. The main objective of the effective solar control is to achieve a balance between controlling solar gain, admitting sufficient daylight and providing occupant views, while ensuring the architectural appeal of the building envelope.

2   *Control of internal heat gains.* The parameters that should be taken into consideration concern the envelope's insulation, the façade's solar shading and the air infiltration (CIBSE TM29, 2005). Furthermore, energy efficient equipment and lighting can reduce significantly internal heat gains. However, heat gains from people are difficult to cope with, especially in spaces with high occupancy patterns. A good way of modulating heat emitted by occupants is to spread the heat gains within the internal spaces in order to avoid peaks. This can be achieved at the design stage, while designing the spaces and deciding upon the occupancy patterns, together with the target temperatures for the different uses of the internal spaces.

Direct and indirect ventilative cooling

Ventilative cooling techniques contribute to reducing cooling-related carbon emissions by removing the higher indoor temperature and replacing it with fresh low-temperature ambient air. Selection of a sustainable ventilative cooling strategy is affected by location, plan depth, heat gains, internal layout, internal and external sources of pollution, cost effectiveness and energy consumption. Figure 20.3 illustrates a typical decision-making process for selecting the ventilation strategy.

Natural ventilation

The cooling capacity of natural ventilation is not very high and depends mainly upon the temperature of the outside air. Therefore, in most cases, it cannot cope with the internal heat gains, especially in non-domestic buildings situated in the urban heat island, where outside temperatures are higher than in rural areas. The most important key aspect in natural ventilation is the building layout, which can enhance airflow. The airflow path defines the different ventilation modes, which are illustrated in Figure 20.4: single-sided ventilation, cross-ventilation, stack ventilation and sub-slab distribution. More details concerning natural ventilation are given in Chapter 17.

Night ventilation (natural or mechanical)

Night ventilation strategies take advantage of night temperatures, which are lower than daytime ones and usually below thermal comfort in cool climates. The concept of this strategy is based on cooling the structure of the building with the use of either natural or mechanical ventilation during the night. Figure 20.5 illustrates how the strategy works: during the daytime, the exposed thermal mass, usually slab, provides radiant cooling by absorbing internal heat gains. When night comes, the absorbed heat gains are spread out of the building by cooling the exposed thermal mass using ventilation. The following day, the thermal mass is able to absorb more heat than it would otherwise, significantly reducing the need for mechanical cooling. The key factor in night-time ventilation is the thermal heat storage; thus, good performance of the thermal

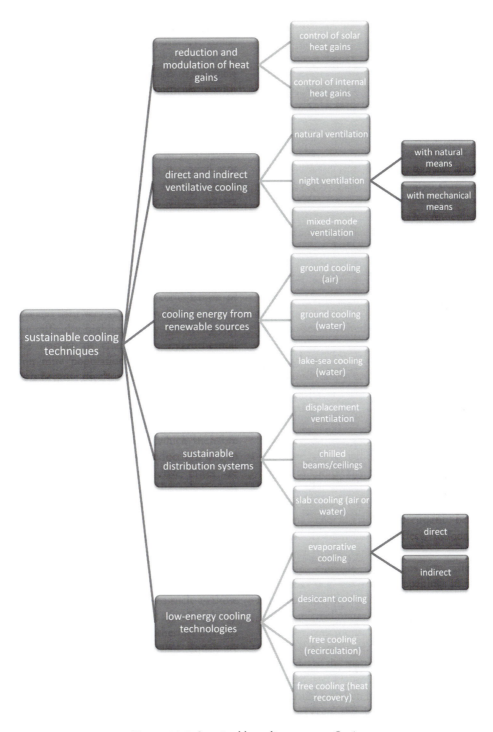

Figure 20.2 *Sustainable cooling strategy: Options*

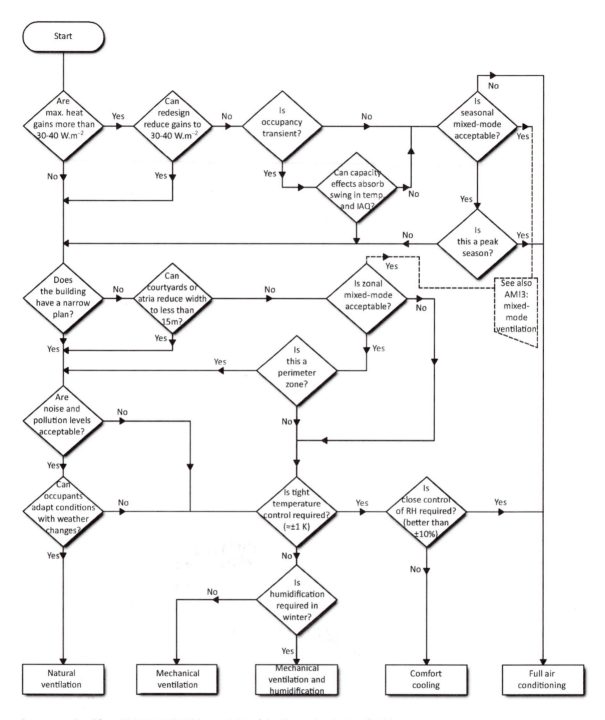

Source: reproduced from CIBSE AM10 (2005) by permission of the Chartered Institution of Building Services Engineers

Figure 20.3 *Selecting a ventilation strategy*

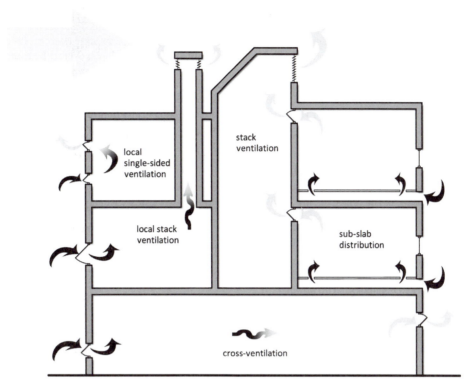

Figure 20.4 *Cooling by different types of natural ventilation*

mass is needed, together with a high correlation between it and ventilation air. However, night ventilation must be carefully controlled in order to avoid over-cooling of the building structure. More details concerning natural ventilation are given in Chapter 17.

Mixed-mode ventilation

Advanced mixed-mode ventilation is designed to achieve positive indoor environmental conditions while reducing the carbon emissions associated with mechanical cooling. In the design of mixed-mode systems, it is frequently important to separate the design of the indoor air-quality ventilation system from the design of the ventilation system for preventing summer overheating. It is of crucial importance that the predicted performance of buildings with mixed-mode ventilation systems at the design stage corresponds to the operational performance of the occupied buildings. Further research on the effect of occupant behaviour

(i.e. user interaction with ventilation system controls), internal heat loads and wind effects is needed in order to obtain an expected range of building performance. More details concerning mixed-mode ventilation are given in Chapter 17 and 18.

Cooling energy from renewable sources

Another way of cooling buildings is by using renewable energy sources such as the ground, lakes, the sea and rivers. These sources keep their ambient temperatures stable during the year and in this way can be used as a cooling or heating source.

Ground cooling (air)

This system uses a network of underground ducts, buried in the ground at approximately 2m to 4m in depth. The temperature of the ground at this depth is

Day time

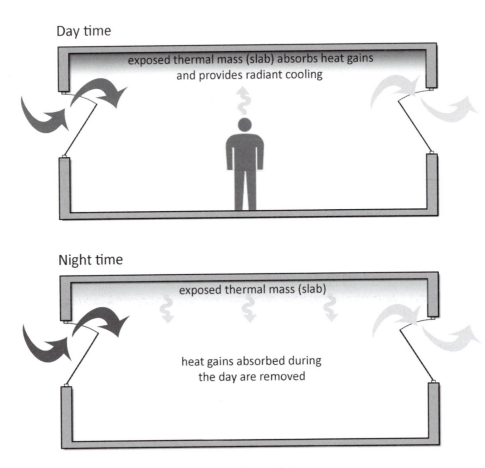

Night time

Figure 20.5 *Night ventilation strategy*

stable, usually around 10°C to 14°C in the UK. Air is supplied, as illustrated in Figure 20.6, and is cooled through thermal exchange with the ground. The cool air is then introduced to the building or used as pre-cooled air for the ventilation plant.

Ground cooling (water)

This system usually uses boreholes that are buried up to 150m deep into the ground. Heat transfer takes place either from the ground or from the aquifer. In this way, water is cooled in the cold borehole and is used for cooling via a heat exchanger that is usually a ground source heat pump. After this process, the warm water is re-injected back into the warm borehole and the procedure is resumed. More details concerning heat pumps for city centre buildings are given in Chapter 7.

Lake/sea cooling (water)

This system comprises an alternative borehole system described in the previous section. Cold water from a lake or sea is extracted and passed through the heat exchanger. In this system it is important that the depth from which water is extracted must be sufficient for the water to be cold enough to provide appropriate cooling.

Sustainable distribution systems

Sustainable distribution systems take advantage of the relatively high water temperatures (usually 14°C to 18°C chilled water temperature) to provide adequate cooling loads and more viable solutions to the low-energy cooling of buildings. There are three main systems:

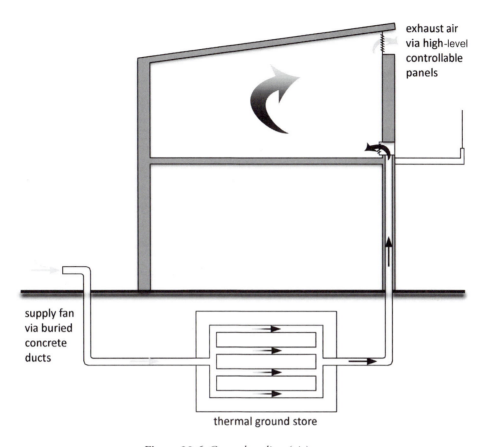

exhaust air
via high-level
controllable
panels

supply fan
via buried
concrete
ducts

thermal ground store

Figure 20.6 *Ground-cooling (air) system*

1 displacement ventilation;
2 chilled beams and ceilings;
3 slab cooling (air and water).

Displacement ventilation

Displacement ventilation is one of the most recent methods and is used most frequently in office buildings. The basic principle of this technique is illustrated in Figure 20.7. The air is supplied at low velocities and at a lower level, usually through a raised floor, and in this way creates a reservoir of cold air. This air is heated only when it comes into contact with an internal heat source, rises up and is extracted through upper-level outlets, usually mounted on the ceiling. The movement of the air is enhanced by the heat emitted by lighting fittings on the ceiling. More details concerning displacement ventilation are given in Chapter 8.

Chilled beams and chilled ceilings

Static cooling devices such as long rectangular beams (called chilled beams) and rectangular panels (named chilled ceilings) are used to provide cooling loads within occupied spaces: chilled water is passed through these devices. They both commonly supplement other systems, such as displacement ventilation. Figure 20.8 illustrates the combination of the three different systems. Chilled ceilings provide radiant cooling, while chilled beams mainly provide convective cooling. One major advantage is that the temperature of the used chilled water is high – between 15°C and 16°C – compared to conventional systems such as fan coils, which use temperatures in the range of 6°C to 8°C. More details concerning displacement ventilation are given in Chapter 8.

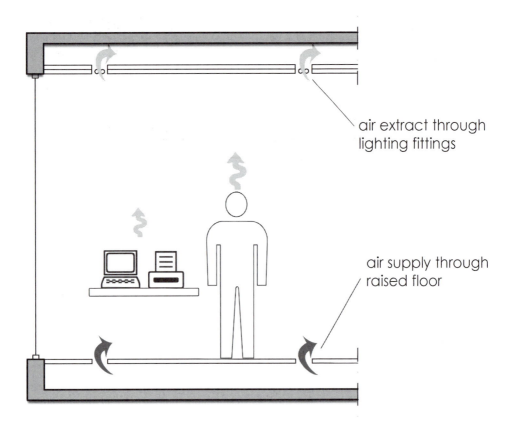

air extract through lighting fittings

air supply through raised floor

Figure 20.7 *Displacement ventilation system*

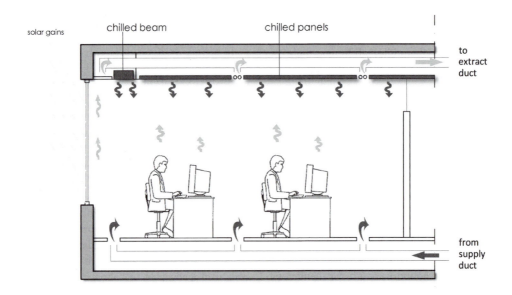

solar gains

chilled beam

chilled panels

to extract duct

from supply duct

Figure 20.8 *Chilled beams and chilled ceilings with displacement ventilation*

Slab cooling (air or water)

This technique is usually used with night ventilation in order to maximize the potential of cooling. Slab is constructed in a way that allows air to be passed in embedded channels (see Figure 20.9). During the night, air is passed through the slab to enhance its cooling. Inversely, daytime warm air is injected through the cool slab in order to be pre-cooled before being used to condition a space or sent to the ventilation plant. The slab-cooling technique can also be implemented by using embedded water pipes. Chilled water circulates through the pipes at temperatures of between 14°C and 20°C, providing cooling. Attention is needed to avoid condensation on concrete surfaces – this usually happens with lower water temperatures.

Low-energy cooling technologies

Low-energy cooling technologies include the incorporation of free cooling in an air-conditioning system that can take advantage of the weather conditions to reduce energy consumption by shutting down the cooling plant (CIBSE Knowledge Series, 2005).

Desiccant cooling

In this system, the extract air is used to cool fresh incoming air. The introduced air passes through a desiccant wheel, which uses specifically selected materials to achieve dehumidification, and this moisture is removed by the heated extract air (see Figure 20.10). After the desiccant wheel, the incoming air is cooled by a heat recovery device (thermal wheel);

this cooling load stems from the extract air. The cooled supply air can be cooled again by passing through an evaporative humidifier. The degree of cooling can reach 8°C to 9°C. This system works well in humid climates but not so efficiently in dry ones. Additionally, the desiccant material requires heat to dehumidify the air, which can be waste heat from another system or solar energy.

Free cooling (recirculation)

When the extract air is clean enough to be reused, recirculation of extract air can take place and save energy. The fresh supply air is mixed with the extracted air, conditioned and introduced into the occupied space (see Figure 20.11). This system is implemented in cases where the total volume of air needed to cool a space is greater than the amount of air needed to provide indoor air quality (minimum ventilation). In this way, the system can use minimum amounts of supply air and extract waste air equal to the amounts of air needed to provide sufficient ventilation to the occupants.

Free cooling with heat recovery

In cases where the previous method cannot be used because of contamination in extracted air, a heat recovery device can be used to transfer the heat from the fresh supply air to the extracted waste air (see Figure 20.12). This device can be a fan coil, plate heat exchanger or thermal wheel. A requirement of this system is that the temperature of the introduced air must be greater than that of the waste air; for this reason, the extract air is usually cooled by an evaporative humidifier.

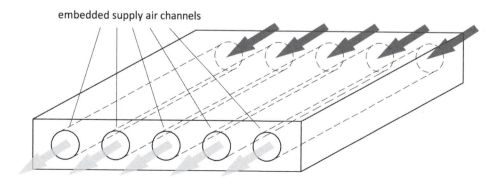

Figure 20.9 *Slab cooling with the use of air*

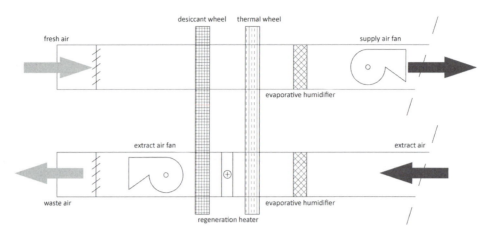

Source: reproduced from CIBSE Knowledge Series (2005) by permission of the Chartered Institution of Building Services Engineers

Figure 20.10 *Desiccant cooling system*

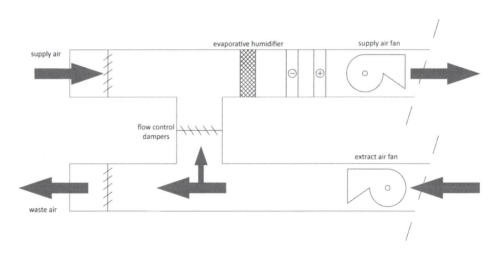

Source: reproduced from CIBSE Knowledge Series (2005) by permission of the Chartered Institution of Building Services Engineers

Figure 20.11 *Recirculation of the air system*

Evaporative cooling (direct and indirect)

Figure 20.13 illustrates that evaporative cooling can occur directly, where the incoming air is blown along a spray of cold water that cools the air before it is used to condition a space. However, in this scenario, the water content of the cooled air increases. To avoid this increase in moisture, indirect evaporative cooling can be utilized, where the cool air produced by the direct evaporative cooling process is passed through a heat exchanger, which cools the air supply. In practice, because of the limited cooling capacity of an indirect evaporative cycle, the primary air is often cooled again by direct evaporation or by a mechanical cooling system. This two-stage system is known as an indirect–direct system. In the UK, this technique is used as a supplementary cooling technique or in combination with desiccant cooling.

Cooling potential of sustainable cooling techniques

The cooling potential of each of the sustainable cooling techniques (IEA, 2000) is presented in Figure 20.14.

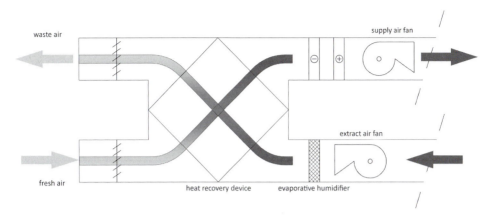

Source: reproduced from CIBSE Knowledge Series (2005) by permission of the Chartered Institution of Building Services Engineers

Figure 20.12 *Heat recovery system*

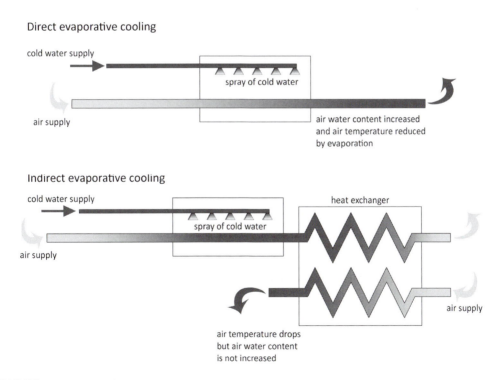

Source: IEA (2000)

Figure 20.13 *Direct and indirect evaporative cooling*

	W/m^2
direct and indirect ventilative cooling	
natural ventilation	30-40
night ventilation	20-30
mixed-mode	*
cooling energy from renewables	
ground (air)	~45
ground (water)	50-100
lake-sea (water)	-80
sustainable distribution systems	
displacement ventilation	30-65
chilled beams and ceilings	70-100
slab (water)	30-50
slab (air)	40-60

* depends on the energy consumed for generation and distribution

Figure 20.14 *Cooling potential of the sustainable cooling techniques*

Case study: School of Slavonic and East European Studies (SSEES) building

The building in this case study is located within a university campus at the heart of London. It is a five-storey construction, designed by Short and Associates, which accommodates the School of Slavonic and East European Studies (SSEES) at University College London (UCL). The building consists of a library with reading spaces and several offices. The general concept was to build a large naturally ventilated building – the first one within the urban heat island of London that uses passive downdraught evaporative cooling. The key component of the environmental strategy is the seasonal operation modes, which provides the opportunity of acquiring different ventilation modes dependent upon the external weather profiles (Lomas et al, 2004).

Ventilation strategy

The ventilation strategy, which deals with the site and the adjacent buildings, faced many restrictions: traffic and pollution from a nearby street and propinquity with a chemistry building at the back of the site. There were also acoustic restrictions within the interior spaces because of the need for the privacy of academic and research staff, as well as security limits regarding library stock. As a consequence, the building was sealed with no opening windows at the perimeter, and the central lightwell was placed at the centre of the building (see Figure 20.16).

The central well is the key feature for the ventilation strategy and is used to distribute the air within the building spaces (see Figure 20.17). It is attached to a plenum that connects the basement with the ground floor, which is also used for ventilation purposes.

The front façade is a heavyweight brickwork wall that is used as thermal mass. A ventilation void is created behind it which isolates the internal spaces and also acts as a buffer to reduce noise and pollution from the street. It is also used as a stack for the first three storeys of the front internal spaces. At the same time, roof-mounted chimneys at the front façade act as exhaust stacks for the last two storeys, while perimeter stacks at the rear ventilate the spaces that are located at the back of the building. The lower ground floor is isolated with its own stack, placed outside the building.

Cooling strategy

A good low-energy solution for cooling was sought: a way of distributing the air without mechanical support led to passive downdraught evaporative cooling. Basically, the air is inserted at the head of the lightwell and passes through the cooling coils, where its temperature drops (see Figure 20.17). This process creates a reservoir of fresh cool air that moves physically downwards and is distributed within the spaces through bottom-hung windows (see Figure 20.16). As the air is introduced at a low level in the occupied spaces, it is warmed by the internal heat gains and rises to the ceiling before being exhausted through the stacks. The whole strategy relies on

Figure 20.15 *Front façade of School of Slavonic and East European Studies*

Figure 20.16 *The central light well at the heart of the building with the bottom-hung windows*

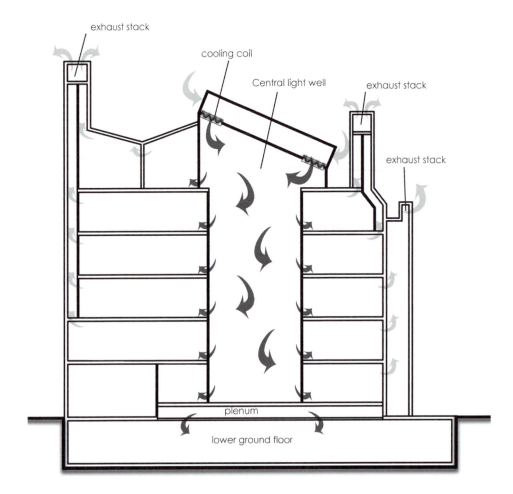

Figure 20.17 *Ventilation strategy during the summer period for the SSEES building*

the driving force created by the temperature difference of air. This physical movement of air is enhanced by two design features, which are implemented to optimize the buoyancy of air during summer:

1   opening windows at the base of each stack to exhaust cool air;
2   injection of waste heat from the cooling coils below the head of each stack.

Case Study: Portcullis House

Portcullis house is the new UK Parliamentary building, located opposite the Houses of Parliament and Big Ben at Westminster, London, designed by Sir Michael Hopkin's architects and partners. It is a seven-storey building that houses UK's 650 members of parliament in several offices, conference and committee rooms. The whole concept was to design a low-energy building that mostly takes advantage of the building fabric rather than the active mechanical and engineering services to provide good internal thermal comfort (Dix, 2000).

Building fabric and façade

Portcullis House relies on the integration of building services in the design of the building. The façade is a highly active construction that consists of triple-pane glazing with argon fill and low emissivity coating, and it also features a ventilative cavity, which serves for the

distribution ducts (see Figure 20.19). Louvres are used to block the lower sun angles during winter, while higher sun angles during summer are blocked by a light shelf; glass prism surfaces on the shelf reflect daylight upon the interior space. This results in doubling the daylight, especially in north-facing offices, where adjacent buildings obstruct a sky view. The façade has a high U value, which results in blocking the heat from outside to inside and vice versa; in this way, the interior heat is kept indoors. Thermal mass materials with high thermal resistance are used in the interior finishes and also in the ceiling to absorb the heat.

Ventilation strategy

The building uses a low-velocity state-of-the-art displacement ventilation system, instead of an air-conditioning system, which saves energy because it is assisted by buoyancy. The plan is organized around a central courtyard. Along the building perimeter, 14 chimney stacks ventilate the building; air is drawn in at

Figure 20.18 *General aspect of Portcullis House, Westminster*

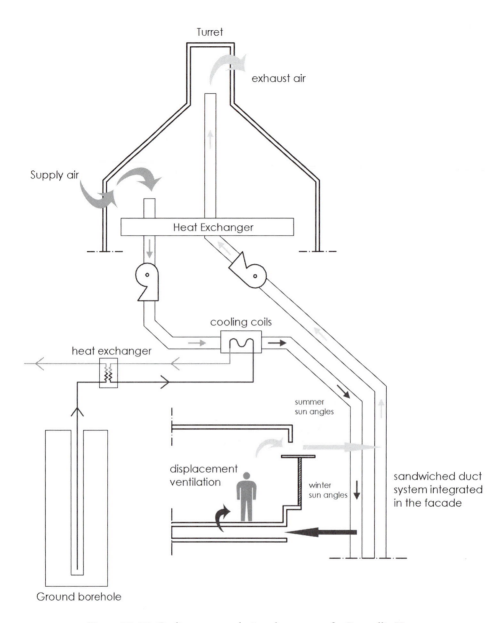

Figure 20.19 *Cooling strategy during the summer for Portcullis House*

the base of the chimneys and is distributed through the sandwiched duct system, integrated at the façade (see Figure 20.19). Each floor has a ventilation plenum at the floor level where air circulates before being introduced to the occupied spaces. Air is exhausted at ceiling level and distributed through the duct system at the façade to the chimneys. No recirculation of exhaust air takes place; but the system supports heat recovery through a roof-mounted rotary hygroscopic 'thermal wheel'; the recovered heat comprises solar heat captured at the façade, internal heat from occupants and electric devices, as well as heat emitted by radiators.

Cooling strategy

Two main strategies are being used to cool the building. Ground cooling takes place with two boreholes used to pump water from a ground depth of 120m to 150m. When the outside temperature goes above 19°C, groundwater of around 14°C is pumped and used via a heat exchanger to cool the ventilation air (see Figure 20.19). In this way, a 19°C temperature of fresh air is achieved; this air is used to ventilate and condition the occupied spaces through the displacement ventilation system. Night ventilation is also used, when needed, to enhance the cooling strategy of the building and to avoid overheating. In this way, internal heat gains absorbed by thermal mass materials during the day are removed. The ventilation rate during night ventilation is half of that used during the day, reducing the overall energy consumption of the building.

Case Study: Swiss Re Tower

The Swiss Re Tower is a 40-storey office, 180m tall, designed by Foster and Partners. It is located at 30 St Mary Axe in the centre of London. It is the first environmental skyscraper in the heart of the city, whose cone-like shape makes it a landmark. The concept was to design a building that takes advantage of integrating structure and building services within the architectural design. As a result, the basic element in the environmental strategy of the Swiss Re Tower was its façade, which is an active ventilative one. The building is equipped with mixed-mode ventilation; natural ventilation assists the mechanical air-conditioning system and reduces energy demand. Construction started in 2001 and occupation took place in 2004 (Powell, 2006a, 2006b).

From building design to ventilation strategy

The tower's standing shape is aerodynamic due to the different diameters of each floor plate, with the 17th level featuring the largest diameter. The plan is organized through a central core, where the staircases and elevators are located, while the offices are spread at the perimeter. Each floor plate has six triangular atriums at the perimeter, which feature a spiral stripe made of darker glass at the elevation (see Figure 20.21); this is achieved because each floor plate is twisted 5 degrees relative to

the floor below it. The atriums act as the lungs of the building, naturally ventilating the whole building. The circular plan is the key feature of the ventilation strategy. This shape, because of its smaller surface – approximately 25 per cent less than a rectangular one – copes with less heat losses and has fewer solar gains. The most significant advantage of this shape is that it deals well with the wind, preventing turbulence. Air flowing around the building creates positive pressure on the windward side and negative pressure on the sides of the building; this creates the perfect driving force for cross-flow ventilation. This pressure variation enhances natural ventilation; air enters through monitored opening windows in the atriums, which also act as buffers preventing draughts in offices. However, the overall ventilation strategy of the building is mixed mode, where air conditioning cannot be avoided because of the building height and the site location.

Façade design

The façade is the most important element of the environmental strategy of the building. It comprises of a triple-skin façade with a double-glazed outer skin, followed by a 1.0m to 1.5m gap (see Figure 20.22). The inner skin consists of a single glazing pane, a ventilative gap and a layer of aluminium louvres. The exhaust air circulates through the façade's gap and removes the heat coming from the inner glazed skin of the offices, as well as the heat absorbed by the blinds; in this way, the percentage of solar transmission is a mere 15 per cent, while the U value of the façade is reduced to $0.8W/m^2K$ when the air circulates through the gap. Therefore, the overall cooling load needed for the office space is reduced significantly.

Cooling strategy

Apart from the ventilative façade, which plays a major role in cooling the building, air conditioning is also installed. A mixed-mode system, which also uses natural ventilation for cooling reasons, is used for 40 per cent of the year. The whole concept of the air-conditioning installation is based on a decentralized system that serves each floor separately. Air is introduced through grilles at the façade at ceiling level (see Figure 20.22) and is passed through the air handling unit (AHU) before being introduced into the

Figure 20.20 *Swiss Re Tower, London*

Figure 20.21 *Atriums creating spirals of darker glass at the elevation*

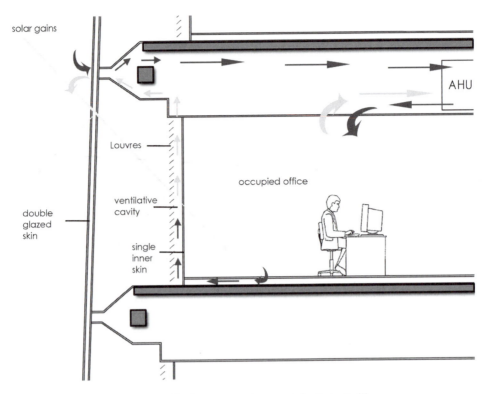

Figure 20.22 *Cooling strategy (summer) for Swiss Re Tower*

occupied space at high-ceiling level; fan coil units are used to cool the air. Part of this cool air is then extracted through floor outlets and passes through the ventilative façade duct, cooling the glass and the blinds before being extracted outside. Most of the heavy plant, such as chillers and tanks, are located in the basement of the building, while the cooling towers are located at 35th level. Energy efficiency is achieved through the use of the waste heat from condenser water. Waste heat is also used from the ventilated façade and is provided to the thermal wheels mounted at the AHU.

Case Study: National Assembly for Wales – the Senedd

The Senedd is a three-storey building, located on a prominent waterfront site in Cardiff Bay, Wales; it is designed by Richard Rogers and Partners. Architects and engineers worked together from the earliest stages of the building design. The design relies on the natural ventilation mode; the key environmental features are

the roof cowl, which is used for ventilation purposes and for maximizing daylight penetration within the building via the lantern. The main entrance area, the café and seating areas are open to the public, while there are three committee rooms as well as a debating chamber (Siambr) for the 60 assembly members (Smith, 2001).

Natural ventilation

The predominant mode operating in the building is natural ventilation. Public spaces are entirely naturally ventilated with the use of windows on the glazed façades of the building. A comprise feature is the use of thermal mass materials, such as concrete and slate, which help to temper internal conditions. The debating chamber and the committee rooms have an air-conditioning backup system, which is used when there are higher internal heat gains or when stricter internal conditions are needed. The air enters through inlets in the floor and is exhausted through windows in the committee rooms or through the roof funnel in the

Figure 20.23 *General aspect of the National Assembly for Wales - the Senedd*

Siambr (see Figures 20.24 and 20.25). The wind cowl located at the top of the Siambr is 6m high and has the possibility of rotating according to the prevailing wind; in this way, a negative pressure is created to the leeward side, where outlets are located to exhaust the warm air from the building and thus reduce the energy requirements for air conditioning.

Daylight

One of the most important elements of sustainability is daylight entering the Senedd. During the design stage, there was extensive modelling of solar penetration and natural light in order to provide the maximum amounts for both low winter and high summer sun angles, as well as at different times of the day. There is a combination of artificial and natural light. Natural light enters the building through the lantern at the rooftop funnel; this comprises a conical mirror that reflects the light within the building. Daylight penetration is also optimized by the glass façades on all four elevations of the building, as well as by the glazed roof light in the committee rooms.

Cooling strategy

There is a great deal of diversity in the Senedd in terms of environmental control. Minimum ventilation control occurs in the public spaces, while the committee rooms and the debating chamber at the heart of the building are highly controlled. It is here that the backup air-conditioning system is found. Ground earth heat exchangers are used for cooling; 27 boreholes are buried in the ground and are supplied with cool water via ground source heat pumps (GSHPs). Water circulates through a matrix of small pipes underneath the slate floor and absorbs the heat from the building. The heat is then deposited to the ground and the process resumes, resulting in a lowering of cooling-load demand. The system is also used as under-floor heating during winter. The whole system reduces the size of conventional boilers and chillers; GSHPs operate two to three times more efficiently than conventional systems. As a result, significant energy savings are achieved. The engineers believe that the building will use no more than 50 per cent of the energy that a conventional building demands in the same location.

Figure 20.24 *The funnel acting as the stack effect for the Siambr viewed from the public space*

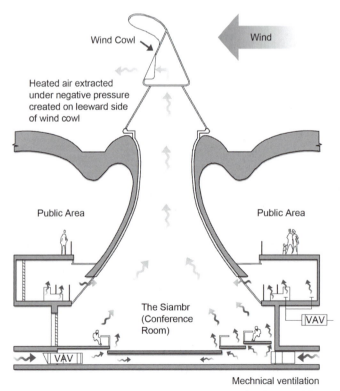

Figure 20.25 *Summer ventilation strategy for the Senedd*

Case Study: National Trust Headquarters – Heelis Building

Heelis Building is the new National Trust headquarters, located on the site of the Great Western Railway Works in Swindon. It is a two-storey construction of 7000m^2 that primarily accommodates offices, together with a shop, a public café restaurant and a membership recruitment area. The architects' (Fielden Clegg Bradley) key design feature was sustainability; in order to achieve this goal, high-quality benchmarks were essential. This is one of the few deep-plan office buildings in existence that almost exclusively uses natural ventilation to keep it cool, while also relying on natural daylight (Randall, 2006). The building has been fully occupied for two years.

Natural ventilation

The whole design of the building relies on a natural ventilation strategy. The plan is organized so that the main façade is due south and the double-pitched roof faces south–north. In this way, an east–west axis organizes the building plan with two main courtyards located in the middle; they act as lungs to provide natural ventilation even in the most central areas of the building. Air is introduced at the perimeter by high-level automatically controlled windows and large door-sized ventilation panels at the main south façade (see Figure 20.26). However, all windows have the ability to open manually; this gives the occupants the satisfaction of controlling indoor conditions. Air is exhausted via roof ventilators called 'snouts' (see Figure 20.27). Some of the exhaust outlets have a mechanical support, which is used in very hot, still internal conditions. The whole ventilation strategy is illustrated in two sections, presented in Figure 20.28. Natural ventilation is achieved by a stack effect, but is also enhanced by external wind pressure.

Daylight

Almost two-thirds of the Heelis Building relies on natural daylight. The roof's north-facing slopes accommodate glazed units; from here, daylight penetrates the building and reaches the ground floor. These units are shaded by south-facing photovoltaic installations, which provide nearly 15 per cent of the total electricity consumption of the building. Voids on the first floor allow natural daylight to reach the ground floor. The daylight factor is more than 5 per cent in most of the interior spaces; on the first floor, lights are rarely used, while on the ground floor there are only a few 'dark' spaces below the mezzanines that usually have their lights on. Daylight penetration is also enhanced by the two courtyards.

Figure 20.26 *Main south façade of Heelis Building, Swindon, UK*

Cooling strategy

The entire strategy for cooling relies on night ventilation. The 442mm thick walls, made of concrete block work and external brickwork, together with the roof, which is made of 80mm thick exposed precast concrete panels, have very high insulation values and high thermal resistances. In this way, they comprise the thermal mass of the building, which absorbs the internal heat gains during the day and purges them during the night. However, in spaces with high internal heat gains and stricter internal conditions, such as board rooms and computer rooms, mechanical cooling is needed. A mixed-mode system of local fan coils is being implemented; water is cooled by a zero-ozone depleting refrigerant.

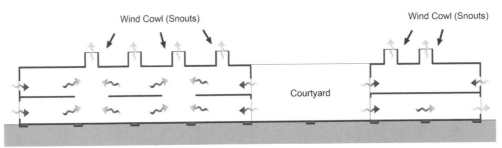

Figure 20.27 *The snouts at the roof of Heelis Building*

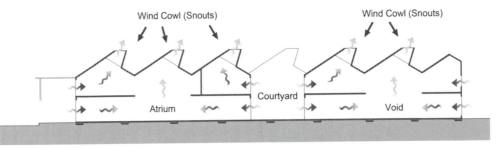

Figure 20.28 *Ventilation strategy for Heelis Building*

Acknowledgements

This chapter is based on a postgraduate dissertation entitled *Sustainable Cooling Strategies: State of the Art* (Lakkas, 2008), submitted in partial fulfilment of the requirements for the degree of MSc in Environmental Design and Engineering at The Bartlett, University College London.

References

CIBSE AM10 (2005) *CIBSE Application Manual 10: Natural Ventilation in Non-Domestic Buildings*, Chartered Institution of Building Services Engineers, London

CIBSE TM29 (2005) *HVAC Strategies for Well-Insulated Airtight Buildings*, Chartered Institution of Building Services Engineers, London

CIBSE TM36 (2005) *Climate Change and the Indoor Environment: Impacts and Adaptation*, Chartered Institution of Building Services Engineers, London

CIBSE Knowledge Series: KS3 (2005) *Sustainable Low Energy Cooling: An Overview*, Chartered Institution of Building Services Engineers, London

Correnza, J., Hyde, G., Kerr, G., Lake, R., Newman-Sanders, E. and Skuse, M. (2006) 'The National Assembly for Wales', *Arup Journal*, vol 41, no 2, pp3–14

Dix, T. R. (2000) 'An engineering approach to ventilation system design', *Indoor Built Environment*, vol 9, pp75–86

IEA (International Energy Agency) (2000) *Low Energy Cooling*, Technical Synthesis Report IEA ECBCS, Annex 28, ESSU (ExCo Support Services Unit), Coventry, UK

Keep Cool Project (2005) www.energyagency.at/publ/pdf/keepcool_freport.pdf, accessed 10 May 2008

Lakkas, T. (2008) *Sustainable Cooling Strategies: State of the Art*, MSc thesis, The Bartlett, University College London, UK

Lomas, K. J., Short, C. A. and Woods, A. (2004) 'Design strategy for low-energy ventilation and cooling within an urban heat island', *Building Research and Information*, vol 32, no 3, pp187–206

Ortiz, J. (2006) 'Go Figure', *Building Service Journal*, pp38–40

Powell, K. (2006a) *30 St Mary Axe: A Tower for London*, Merrell Publishers Limited, London

Powell, K. (2006b) *Richard Rogers: Complete Works*, vol 3, Phaidom Press Limited, London

Randall, T. (2006) 'Heelis: Central Office for the National Trust', in *Environmental Design*, Taylor and Francis, Oxon, Chapter 18

Smith, P. F. (2001) *Architecture in a Climate of Change: A Guide to Sustainable Design*, Architectural Press, Oxford

Smith, P. F. (2003) *Sustainability at the Cutting Edge: Emerging Technologies for Low Energy Building*, Architectural Press, Oxford

21

Indoor Air Quality in City Centre Buildings

Katerina Niachou, Mat Santamouris and Iro Livada

Introduction

The aim of ventilation is to maintain a comfortable and healthy indoor environment or even to cool buildings with minimum energy consumption. However, the consequences of ventilation might not be always beneficial, especially when fresh air is supplied from the urban environment. Because of specific urban characteristics, the potential of natural ventilation can be seriously diminished, mainly due to reduced wind speeds, variation in wind directions, high ambient temperatures and increased external pollutant and noise levels. Besides, the impact of ventilation on indoor air quality is a topic of major concern. Especially in urban buildings, indoor air quality is characterized with considerable interest since heavily polluted outdoor air penetrates the building shell and influences indoor air. Except for outdoor pollution, indoor sources and anthropogenic activities such as tobacco smoking may have a greater impact on personal exposure.

This chapter focuses on the experimental investigation of the impact of the urban environment on the effectiveness of natural and hybrid ventilation since the efficient design of these ventilation systems is a determinant for thermal comfort, indoor air quality and energy savings.

Airflow in the urban environment

Oke (1987) characterized wind variation with height over cities by defining two specific sub-layers: the so-called 'obstructed sub-layer', or urban canopy sub-layer, which extends from the ground surface up to the height of the buildings; and the so-called 'free surface layer', which exists above the rooftops. The obstructed or urban canopy sub-layer has its own flow field, driven and determined by the interaction with local features. The urban wind field is complicated. Small differences in topography may cause irregular airflows. A very detailed discussion of the problem in the urban canopy layer is given by Landsberg (1981). In general, the wind speed in the canopy layer decreases substantially compared to undisturbed wind speed, and its direction may be altered (Santamouris, 2001).

The airflow patterns in common urban structural forms such as urban canyons have also received much attention during the last years. Different airflow regimes can be observed in urban canyons (see Figure 21.1), determined by building (L/H) and canyon (H/W) geometry, as well as by the prevailing wind direction with respect to canyon long axis – namely, perpendicular, parallel and oblique flow (Oke, 1988).

The knowledge of airflow characteristics in the urban canopy layer is of high significance for pedestrian comfort, air quality, pollutant dispersion and ventilation studies.

Hybrid ventilation systems

Ventilation can be achieved through natural or mechanical forces or a combination – namely, in a hybrid or mixed mode – and it is considered one of the most important parameters for building design.

Hybrid ventilation is:

> … a new ventilation concept that combines the best features of natural and mechanical ventilation at different

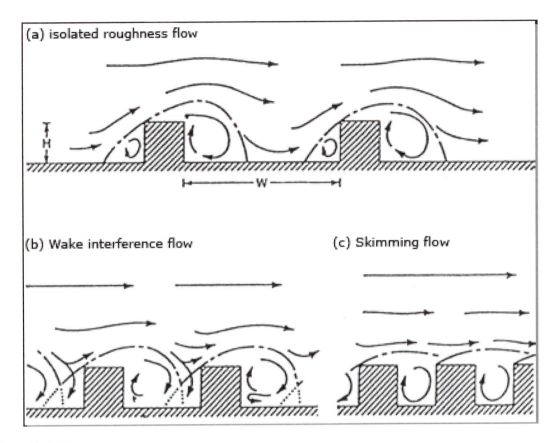

Source: Oke (1987)

Figure 21.1 *Airflow regimes associated with perpendicular incident flow over building arrays of increasing height and width*

times of the day or season of the year. It is a ventilation system where mechanical and natural forces are combined in a two mode system. The operating mode varies according to the season and within individual days; thus, the current mode reflects the external environment and takes maximum advantage of ambient conditions at any point in time. (Heiselberg, 2002)

Hybrid ventilation systems can be classified into three major categories:

1   natural and mechanical ventilation;
2   mechanically assisted natural ventilation; and
3   naturally assisted mechanical ventilation.

This chapter focuses on mechanically assisted natural ventilation where mechanical inlet/exhaust fans are used to enhance pressure differences when natural driving forces (wind effect and buoyancy forces) are insufficient.

Experimental indoor/outdoor air quality and ventilation studies in urban buildings

Despite the great number of experimental and theoretical studies on ventilation and indoor air quality, only a small number have reported on real buildings in the urban environment. Measurements of indoor pollutants in urban buildings have been performed in offices (Bernhard et al, 1995; Lagoudi et al, 1996a, 1996b), dwellings (Ilgen et al, 2001; Baya et al, 2004; Edwards et al, 2005; Lai et al, 2006; Gadkari and

Pervez, 2007), schools (Lee and Chang, 2000; Chaloulakou and Mavroidis, 2002), hospitals (Santamouris et al, 1994) and other public places (Lee et al, 1999; Li et al, 2001). Furthermore, only a few experimental studies of indoor air quality have been conducted together with ventilation and outdoor air pollution measurements. The latest experimental indoor and outdoor air quality with simultaneous ventilation studies in urban buildings are summarized in Table 21.1.

The experimental procedures that will be described in this chapter were undertaken under the European research programme RESHYVENT (2004) and consisted of field and indoor measurements in three residential apartments in Athens, Greece, during July to September 2002. Field experiments included air and surface temperature, wind speed and wind direction measurements, which were carried out inside two street canyons and above building roofs. Understanding and interpreting the complex mechanisms of airflow around buildings are crucial in terms of the exact description of the boundary conditions that constitute a prerequisite for further investigation of the performance of natural and hybrid ventilation systems in the urban environment. As a result, an emphasis was placed on the analysis of thermal and airflow characteristics inside the two urban canyons, and very interesting observations resulted (Niachou et al, 2007a, 2007b). At the same time, air temperature, ventilation and indoor air quality measurements (CO_2; ACH; total volatile organic compounds, TVOC) were measured in building interiors.

A full comparison analysis will be presented, taking into account ventilation and indoor air quality

Table 21.1 *Experimental indoor and outdoor air quality with simultaneous ventilation studies in urban buildings*

Type of buildings	Region	Period	Pollutants	Ventilation system	References
Three offices	London, UK	February and March 1990	CO_2, CO and NO_x	Natural	Phillips et al (1993)
Two offices	Birmingham, UK	February 1996 (one week)	CO_2, CO, SO_2 and NO_x	Natural, mechanical	Kukadia and Palmer (1998)
Seven residences	Birmingham, UK	August 1997 to July 1998	PM_1, $PM_{2.5}$ and PM_{10}	Natural	Jones et al (2000)
Ten offices and ten public places	Hong Kong	June 1998 to August 2000	VOCs	Mechanical	Chao and Chan (2001)
Ten residences	Hong Kong	Summer 1997	NO, NO_2, SO_2 and O_3	Natural, mechanical	Chao (2001)
Office	Helsinki, Finland	January 1999	SO_2, NO_2, NO_x, O_3 and particle size distribution	Mechanical	Koponen et al (2001)
Residence	Paris, France	Winter and summer 2000	CO, SO_2, NO, NO_2, O_3, VOCs, $PM_{2.5}$, black smoke	Natural, mechanical	Collignan et al (2001)
Student office	Hong Kong	March to December 2001	Respirable suspended particulates (RSPs) and NO_x	Mechanical	Chan (2002)
234 residences	United States	1999 to 2001	Carbonyls (aldehydes and ketones)	Natural, mechanical	Turpin et al (2004); Weisel et al (2005a, 2005b)
Residence	Athens, Greece	24 and 30 June 2002 (2 days)	CO_2, NO_x, O_3, SO_2 and TVOC	Infiltration	Halios et al (2005)
Eight schools	La Rochelle, France	Winter (one week) and spring or summer (one week)	NO, NO_2 and PM (0.3μm to 20μm)	Natural, mechanical	Blondeau et al (2005); Poupard et al (2005)
Three offices, one residence	Denmark, Sweden	2002 (2–6 days in each building)	Ultra-fine particles (UFPs)	Mechanical	Matson (2005)

measurements in naturally, mechanically and hybrid ventilation systems. Indoor air quality is examined in relation to a number of decisive parameters such as

- air exchange rates;
- outdoor pollutant concentrations; and
- indoor pollutant sources, mainly as a result of human activities.

Measurements and instrumentation

Indoor experimental procedures were carried out on a 24-hour basis during three measurement periods, consisting of five consecutive days in each apartment. The two street canyons were characterized by different geometry and orientation and they were adjacent to high-circulation roads. The major characteristics of the studied apartments and street canyons are summarized in Table 21.2.

The first apartment (A_1) was situated on the south façade of the first canyon, while the other two apartments (A_2 and A_3) were on the opposite building façades of the second canyon. Natural ventilation was provided through open windows from canyon or rear-canyon façades. The main difference between the third apartment (A_3) and the other two (A_1 and A_2) is that external openings were on the same side of the street and there was practically no natural cross-ventilation. In addition, windless conditions or calms were measured during the third experimental period outside apartment A_3. During the measurement periods, all apartments were occupied and the total number of occupants ranged from two to six, including smokers.

A total number of 114 ventilation – consisting of infiltration, natural, mechanical and hybrid ventilation – and indoor air-quality experiments were conducted. The single tracer gas (N_2O) decay method was applied at the first apartment (A_1) and the multi-tracer gas decay method with two tracer gases, N_2O and SF_6, was performed in other two apartments (A_2 and A_3). The Bruel and Kjaer multi-tracer gas acquisition system was

used and consisted of a photo-acoustic multi-gas monitor, a multipoint sampler and doser unit, and a controlling computer. The multi-gas monitor measurement principle is based on the photo-acoustic infrared detection method. Except for the two tracer gases (N_2O and SF_6), the multi-tracer gas acquisition system also measured CO_2 and TVOC (ref. toluene) concentrations inside and outside the ventilated spaces adjacent to external openings. Mixing fans were used to establish a uniform tracer gas concentration during the injection phase within the ventilated spaces. In all experiments, the minimum sampling period from one channel to the next one was one minute, while a total number of five measuring nozzles were appended inside each building apartment with one outside, adjacent to external openings. The ventilation instrumentation, furthermore, consisted of two T-series window fans appended vertically on wooden buttens attached at the position of external openings adjacent to canyon façades. The mechanical fans were reversible, operating either in inlet or exhaust mode, and they were characterized by a maximum performance of $730m^3/h$ with a reduction of $15.8m^3/h$ for 1Pa pressure loss.

Natural ventilation consisted of single-sided and cross-ventilation experiments. In single-sided ventilation, one or two external openings were considered from the same building façade. Cross-ventilation experiments were performed within two or more external openings placed on canyon and rear-canyon walls. Mechanical ventilation was studied with one or two inlet/exhaust fans. In the case of hybrid ventilation, 16 fan-assisted natural ventilation configurations were investigated (see Figure 21.2), where mechanical fan assistance was applied to enhance pressure differences across building façades.

Results and discussion

Ventilation experiments

The theoretical analysis focused on the estimation of air exchange rates based on multi-zone methods with one

Table 21.2 *Characteristics of studied apartments and street canyons*

Apartment	Area (m²)	Effective volume (m³)	Canyon	Orientation from north	H/W	L/W
A_1	65	112	Ragavi	100°	1.7	3.8
A_2	78	130				
A_3	50	120	Ag. Fanouriou	137°	2.6	9.5

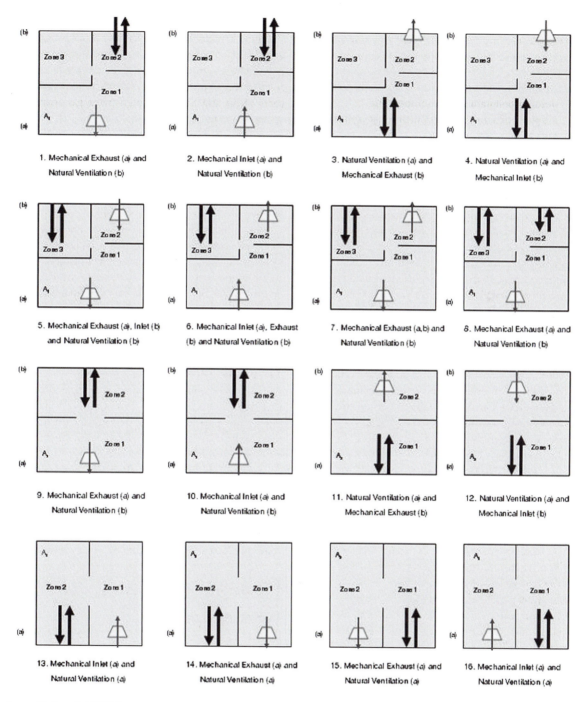

1. Mechanical Exhaust (a) and Natural Ventilation (b)

2. Mechanical Inlet (a) and Natural Ventilation (b)

3. Natural Ventilation (a) and Mechanical Exhaust (b)

4. Natural Ventilation (a) and Mechanical Inlet (b)

5. Mechanical Exhaust (a), Inlet (b) and Natural Ventilation (b)

6. Mechanical Inlet (a), Exhaust (b) and Natural Ventilation (b)

7. Mechanical Exhaust (a,b) and Natural Ventilation (b)

8. Mechanical Exhaust (a) and Natural Ventilation (b)

9. Mechanical Exhaust (a) and Natural Ventilation (b)

10. Mechanical Inlet (a) and Natural Ventilation (b)

11. Natural Ventilation (a) and Mechanical Exhaust (b)

12. Natural Ventilation (a) and Mechanical Inlet (b)

13. Mechanical Inlet (a) and Natural Ventilation (a)

14. Mechanical Exhaust (a) and Natural Ventilation (a)

15. Mechanical Exhaust (a) and Natural Ventilation (a)

16. Mechanical Inlet (a) and Natural Ventilation (a)

Source: Niachou et al (2007c)

Figure 21.2 *Hybrid ventilation systems measured in the three building apartments (A_1, A_2, A_3), where (a) refers to canyon façade and (b) to rear canyon façade*

and two tracer gases (Niachou et al, 2005). The estimated air exchange rates under different ambient weather conditions are illustrated in the form of box plots in Figure 21.3. In addition, the mean air exchange rates for each ventilation system in the three studied apartments are summarized in Table 21.3.

Natural cross-ventilation was proven to be very effective even for low wind speeds inside the two urban canyons. It was found that 95 per cent of the total measured wind speeds adjacent to external openings were lower than 1.5m/s and the corresponding air temperature differences inside and outside buildings were lower than 6° C. In the case of natural cross-ventilation with two or more windows, the estimated air exchange rates have a mean value ranging from 11h⁻¹ to 15h⁻¹ (see Table 21.3). Even under calm conditions (wind speed lower than 0.2m/s), natural cross- or single-sided ventilation was not eliminated since the air temperature differences between inside and outside the ventilated spaces compensated for the reduced wind effect.

In natural ventilation, a wider range of airflow rates exist because of the variability of natural driving forces. However, the existing variability of natural ventilation rates is greater in apartment A_1 (see Figure 21.3) in

comparison with the other two (A_2 and A_3) due to the variation of outdoor conditions and the implementation of cross-ventilation experiments between more than two windows.

In contrast to natural ventilation, mechanical ventilation was characterized by almost constant airflow rates, irrespective of ambient weather conditions. Higher ventilation rates were measured in apartment A_1 probably because the volume of the apartment was smaller. The observed variability in mechanical ventilation experiments (see Figure 21.3) is mainly attributed to different combinations of one or two inlet/exhaust fans.

Hybrid ventilation has been shown to be associated with rather lower air exchange rates than natural cross-ventilation (see Figure 21.4), but relatively higher values in comparison with single-sided ventilation (see Figure 21.5), especially under calm conditions. In general, air exchanges in the hybrid ventilation system presented a lower variability than in the natural ventilation system, but greater than in mechanical ventilation. The mean air exchange rates range from 6h⁻¹ to 15h⁻¹ according to the position of inlet/exhaust fans and external openings (see Table 21.3).

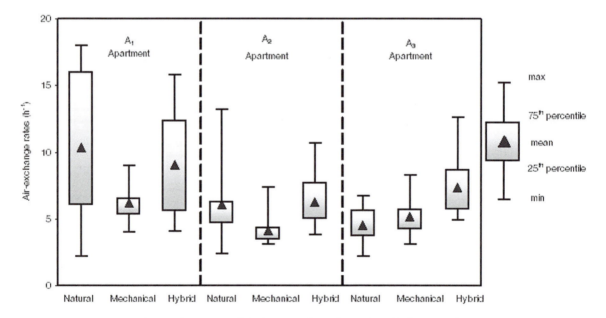

Figure 21.3 *Estimated air exchange rates (h⁻¹) for natural, mechanical and hybrid ventilation systems in the three residential apartments (A_1, A_2 and A_3) under different ambient conditions*

Table 21.3 *Estimated mean air exchange rates ($N_1(h^{-1})$, $N_2(h^{-1})$ and $N_3(h^{-1})$) for the total number of ventilation experiments (No) in the three residential apartments (A_1, A_2 and A_3)*

Ventilation	Description	No	N_1 (h^{-1})	N_2 (h^{-1})	N_3 (h^{-1})
Natural	Infiltration	3	0.3	0.3	0.5
	Single-sided with one window	14	3.1	4.5	4.2
	Single-sided with two windows	5	–	–	5.2
	Cross-ventilation with two windows	7	15.2	9.8	–
	Cross-ventilation with more than two windows	4	11.0	–	–
Mechanical	One supply/exhaust fan	15	5.7	3.8	4.9
	Two supply/exhaust fans	19	6.6	4.5	5.4
Hybrid	One supply/exhaust fan and natural ventilation with one window	31	7.4	5.6	7.4
	One supply/exhaust fan and natural ventilation with more than one window	8	13.2	5.9	–
	Two supply/exhaust fans and natural ventilation with one window	6	–	6.3	–
	Two supply/exhaust fans and natural ventilation with more than one window	2	15.4	–	–

The main result is that under the conditions in which the ventilation experiments were performed, where all internal doors were open, there is little advantage to be gained in using hybrid instead of natural ventilation.

It should also be stated that apart from the comparison of the estimated air exchange rates, there was a qualitative difference between natural and hybrid ventilation. The thermal comfort was completely different and the feel when someone was exposed to airflow during natural ventilation was much better than in rooms where airflow was assisted by mechanical fans.

Of course, this is not to say that hybrid ventilation has little use. There is definitely an advantage of hybrid ventilation when one is forced to have doors closed in

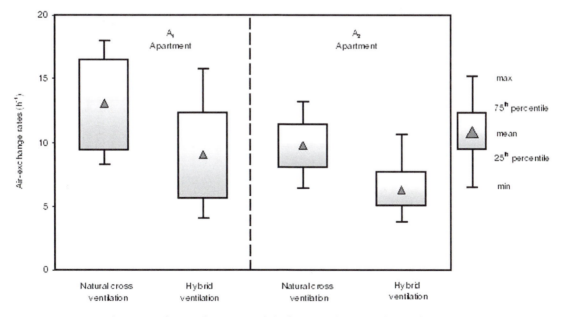

Figure 21.4 *Estimated air exchange rates (h^{-1}) for natural cross- and hybrid ventilation systems in apartments A_1 and A_2*

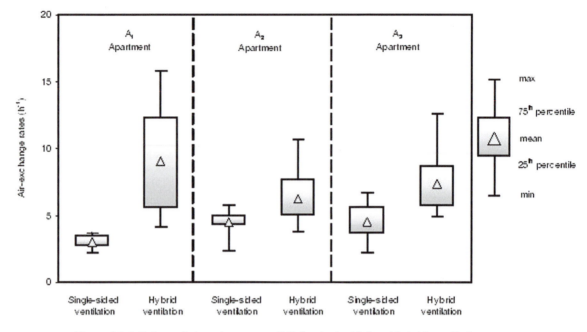

Figure 21.5 *Estimated air exchange rates (h^{-1}) for single-sided and hybrid ventilation systems in the three apartments (A_1, A_2 and A_3)*

an apartment, making natural ventilation much less effective. Besides, there is also an advantage when one needs hybrid ventilation to vent a closed space (kitchen or bathroom) where natural ventilation may be insufficient or when there are flows in the wrong direction.

Indoor air-quality experiments

For the study of indoor air quality, the mean weighted average pollutant concentrations $C_{in}(t)$ were estimated inside the ventilated spaces based on the mean zone concentrations, $C_i(t)$, where weighting functions are determined by the effective volume of each zone:

$$C_{in}(t) = \frac{\sum_{i=1}^{i=\kappa} V_i C_i(t)}{V_{tot}} \quad (1)$$

where:

- $C_i(t)$ = mean pollutant concentration in zone i (ppm);

- V_i = effective volume of zone i (m³);
- V_{tot} = total effective volume of each ventilated space (m³); and
- κ = number of zones in each ventilated space.

Then, the mean instant concentrations $C_{in}(t)$ were averaged for the time period from $t_0 = 0$ to $t_1 = e$, which corresponds to the tracer gas decay period during the ventilation experiments:

$$C_{in} = \frac{\int_0^e C_{in}(t)dt}{e - 0} \quad (2)$$

In addition, for the same time period the mean outdoor concentrations, C_{out}, were estimated outside the ventilated spaces:

$$C_{out} = \frac{\int_0^e C_{out}(t)dt}{e - 0} \quad (3)$$

where:

- $C_{out}(t)$ = pollutant concentration (ppm) outside each ventilated space at time t.

CO_2 measurements

CO_2 can be considered as a surrogate for other occupant-generated pollutants, particularly bio-effluents, and for ventilation rate per occupant, but not as a causal factor in human health responses (Apte and Erdmann, 2002). The primary source of CO_2 in buildings is the respiration of building occupants. The threshold limit value for eight-hour time-weighted average exposure to CO_2 is 5000ppm (ACGIH, 1991). ANSI/ASHRAE Standard 62.1-2004 states that CO_2 monitoring is a method of determining occupant variability. In case no national regulation is available, the European Standard prENrev 15251:2006 (CEN, 2006) indicates recommended CO_2 concentrations for different categories of indoor environments in residential and non-residential buildings. These values vary from 350ppm up to 800ppm above outdoor concentrations accordingly for high and acceptable or moderate levels of expectation in new and existing buildings.

Figure 21.6 depicts the cumulative frequency distributions of the absolute maximum indoor CO_2 concentrations in the three residential apartments (A_1, A_2 and A_3) during the ventilation experiments.

As shown, the absolute maximum CO_2 concentrations did not exceed 1600ppm, while the existence of concentrations above 800ppm was observed locally in rooms with more than two occupants, including smokers, and where fresh air was not efficiently distributed. The threshold value of 800ppm was defined as an indicator of a high level of expectation indoors since it was 350ppm above maximum ambient CO_2 concentrations, which were always lower than 450ppm.

TVOC measurements

TVOC may be used for a number of applications – namely, testing of materials, indication of insufficient or poorly designed ventilation in a building, and identification of high-polluting activities (ECA-IAQ, 1997b). Although there are no standards for indoor TVOC upper limits, Molhave (1990) has suggested four exposure ranges of TVOC (ref. toluene): a comfort

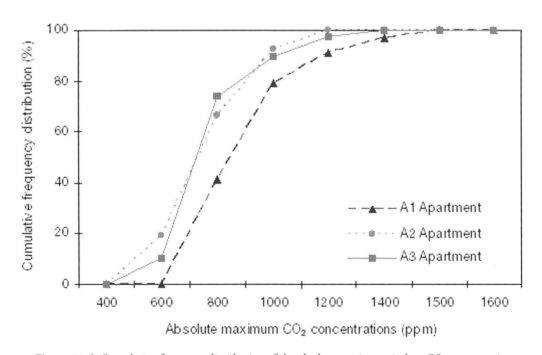

Figure 21.6 *Cumulative frequency distribution of the absolute maximum indoor CO_2 concentrations in the three residential apartments*

range ($<0.2mg/m^3$), a multi-factorial exposure range (0.2–$3mg/m^3$), a discomfort range (3–$25mg/m^3$) and a toxic range ($>25mg/m^3$).

Figure 21.7 shows the cumulative frequency distributions of the absolute maximum indoor TVOC concentrations measured during ventilation experiments inside the ventilated spaces.

Maximum indoor TVOC concentrations exceeding 0.8ppm (or $3mg/m^3$), where discomfort may arise, resulted from human activities related to tobacco smoking and the use of paints since the corresponding outdoor TVOC concentrations did not exceed 0.3ppm. In particular, in apartment A_2 during some hybrid ventilation experiments where an area-way was open, the maximum TVOC indoor concentrations were 12 times higher in comparison to ambient concentrations due to the renovation of an apartment inside the building (paints, glues, coatings).

With regard to TVOC emission rates, the mass balance equation was applied considering a steady-state analysis for periods of relatively constant TVOC concentrations when the only active sources were those associated with building materials and furnishings, based on the methodology described by Persily et al

(2003). The estimated mean emission rates in the three ventilated spaces ranged from 1.7 to $3.8mg·m^{-2}h^{-1}$ as a result of different furniture and environmental conditions. These values are in agreement with emission rates reported by Gustafsson and Jonsson (1993) and ECA-IAQ (1997a). However, a statistically significant variation of TVOC emission rates with air temperature was observed in each ventilated space. The extended analysis and the corresponding results were presented in detail by Niachou (2007).

Indoor–outdoor air-quality relationships

In order to investigate the effect of outdoor pollutant levels on indoor air quality, the correlation between the mean indoor and outdoor CO_2 and TVOC concentrations was studied in the three apartments (A_1, A_2 and A_3).

As shown in Figure 21.8, a statistically significant correlation described by an exponential formula was observed between the mean indoor and outdoor TVOC concentrations. However, the lowest correlation coefficient R was observed in the A_2 apartment due to the strong impact of indoor emission sources related to human activities. TVOC concentrations above

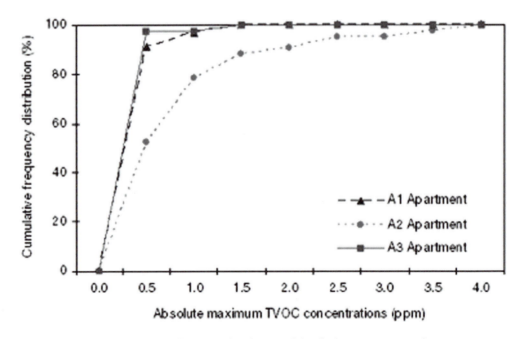

Figure 21.7 *Cumulative frequency distribution of the absolute maximum indoor TVOC concentrations in the three residential apartments*

0.3ppm were observed during tobacco smoking, while concentrations exceeding 0.8ppm were associated with the use of paints.

As expected, no correlation was found between the mean CO_2 concentrations inside and outside the ventilated spaces since indoor CO_2 levels are substantially affected by the presence of people.

Influence of ventilation on indoor/outdoor pollutant ratios

From the study of the impact of the measured air exchange rates on indoor/outdoor mean CO_2 concentration ratios, it was found that when air exchange rates increased, the mean values of CO_2 ratios decreased. This is depicted in Figure 21.9, where the

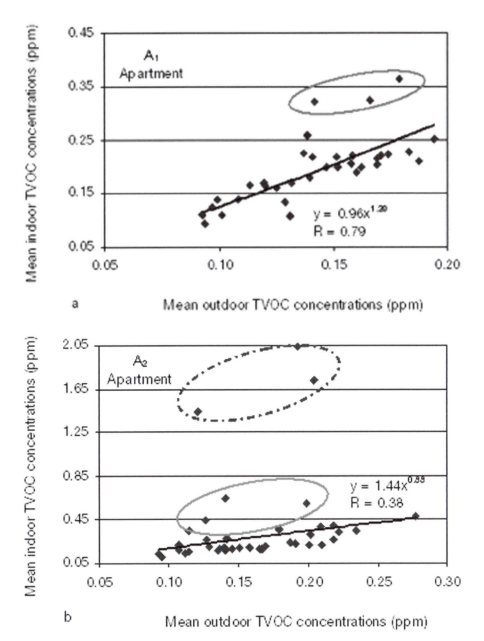

Figure 21.8 *Correlation between the mean indoor and outdoor TVOC concentrations during ventilation experiments in the three studied apartments (A_1, A_2 and A_3)*

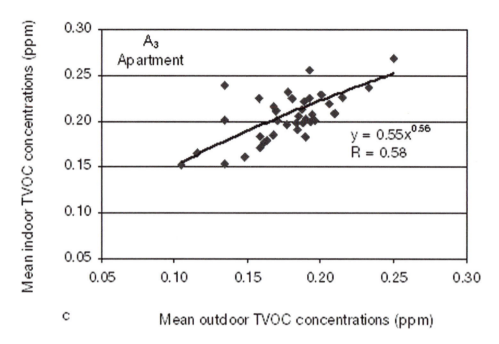

Figure 21.8 *Correlation between the mean indoor and outdoor TVOC concentrations during ventilation experiments in the three studied apartments (A_1, A_2 and A_3) (Cont'd)*

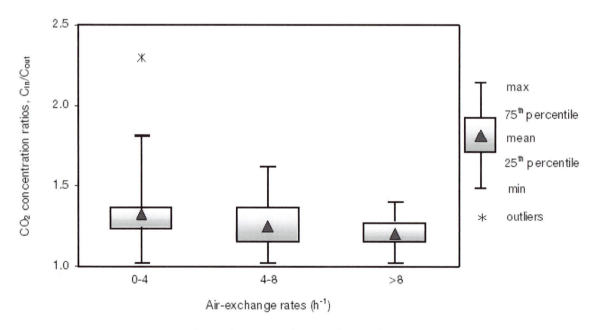

Figure 21.9 *Impact of air exchange rates (h^{-1}) on indoor/outdoor CO_2 concentration ratios (C_{in}/C_{out}) during ventilation experiments in the three residential apartments*

measured CO_2 concentration ratios (C_{in}/C_{out}) are illustrated in the form of box plots. The total number of air exchange rates in natural, hybrid and mechanical experiments under different outdoor conditions have been classified in three categories (0–$4h^{-1}$; 4–$8h^{-1}$; $>8h^{-1}$). Outliers are extreme values out of the confidence interval of 95 per cent (Zar, 1999).

However, when the impact of indoor emission sources on pollutant concentrations became significant, then the influence of ventilation was weaker. This was mainly observed with TVOCs and, as demonstrated in Figure 21.10, the increase of air exchange rates did not always result in lower indoor/outdoor concentration ratios (C_{in}/C_{out}). As mentioned above, maximum indoor TVOC concentrations were up to 12 times higher than the outdoor concentrations; but they are not depicted, so as not to diminish the distinctiveness of the box plots.

Thus, the control and minimization of indoor sources is essential in order to achieve the optimum indoor air-quality conditions with the minimum design airflow rates.

Table 21.4 presents the mean indoor/outdoor CO_2 and TVOC concentration ratios (C_{in}/C_{out}) in the three studied apartments for each ventilation system. In general, when human activities related to smoking and the use of paints were absent (unlike those values marked in bold typeface in Table 21.4), then the highest concentration ratios were observed during infiltration and single-sided ventilation, and the lowest in hybrid and cross-ventilation experiments. This is attributed, on the one hand, to the higher measured air exchange rates during cross-ventilation and hybrid ventilation experiments and, on the other hand, to the better mixing of air between the different zones inside the ventilated spaces (Niachou et al, 2007d).

Conclusions

A comparative monitoring analysis of different ventilation systems was carried out in three residential building apartments located in two urban street canyons. The ventilation performance of natural, mechanical and hybrid or fan-assisted natural ventilation systems was investigated, together with indoor air quality under different ambient weather conditions.

The ventilation experiments pointed out that, in spite of the reduced wind speeds in urban canyons, appreciable ventilation rates can be obtained with natural cross-ventilation. Even under low wind speeds

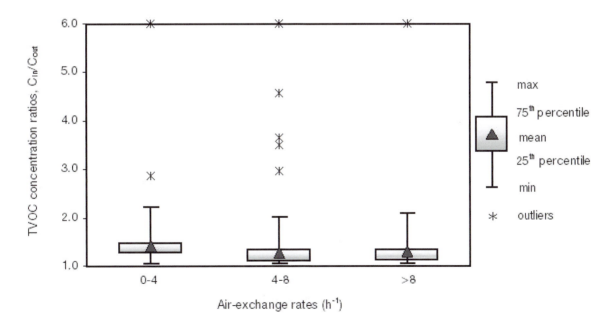

Figure 21.10 *Impact of air exchange rates (h^{-1}) on indoor/outdoor TVOC concentration ratios (C_{in}/C_{out}) during ventilation experiments in the three residential apartments*

Table 21.4 *Estimated mean indoor/outdoor CO_2 and TVOC concentration ratios $((C_{in}/C_{out})_1, (C_{in}/C_{out})_2$ and $(C_{in}/C_{out})_3)$ during ventilation experiments (No) in the three studied apartments $(A_1, A_2$ and $A_3)$*

Ventilation	Description	No	CO_2			TVOC		
			$(C_{in}/C_{out})_1$	$(C_{in}/C_{out})_2$	$(C_{in}/C_{out})_3$	$(C_{in}/C_{out})_1$	$(C_{in}/C_{out})_2$	$(C_{in}/C_{out})_3$
Natural	Infiltration	3	2.3	1.3	1.2	2.0	1.5	1.5
	Single-sided with one window	14	1.8	1.3	1.4	1.6	1.5	1.1
	Single-sided with two windows	5	–	–	1.3	–	–	1.2
	Cross-ventilation with two windows	7	1.3	1.2	–	1.3	1.1	–
	Cross-ventilation with more than two windows	4	1.2	–	–	1.3	–	–
Mechanical	One supply/exhaust fan	15	1.5	1.5	1.2	1.5	1.4	1.2
	Two supply/exhaust fans	19	1.3	1.1	1.1	1.3	4.8	1.2
Hybrid	One supply/exhaust fan and natural ventilation with one window	31	1.4	1.3	1.1	1.4	1.5	1.2
	One supply/exhaust fan and natural ventilation with more than one window	8	1.2	1.1	–	1.0	2.5	–
	Two supply/exhaust fans and natural ventilation with one window	6	1.4	1.2	–	1.5	5.6	–
	Two supply/exhaust fans and natural ventilation with more than one window	2	1.2	–	–	1.3	–	–

or calms, natural cross- or single-sided ventilation was not eliminated since the temperature differences inside and outside the ventilated spaces compensated for the reduced wind effect. This could be an advantage for night ventilation during summer periods or for natural ventilation during transient periods. Hybrid ventilation has been shown to be associated with rather lower air exchange rates than natural cross-ventilation, but higher air exchange rates than single-sided ventilation, especially in windless conditions.

Indoor air quality has been studied in relation to air exchange rates, outdoor pollutant concentrations and indoor pollutant emissions mainly due to human activities. A statistically significant correlation was found between the mean indoor and outdoor TVOC concentrations. However, the maximum indoor TVOC concentrations (greater than 0.8ppm) were associated with tobacco smoking and the use of paints. In addition, the presence of maximum CO_2 values (more than 800ppm) was related to increased occupancy and smoking.

As a result, source control to diminish pollution load in indoor environments will improve health and comfort. Furthermore, since indoor pollution unambiguously comprises a major problem, before thinking of increasing ventilation rates, it is a prerequisite to reduce indoor emission sources and, thus, to improve energy efficiency.

The knowledge and understanding of mass transfer mechanisms in urban buildings is of great importance for the appropriate design of natural and hybrid ventilation systems in order to accomplish optimum indoor air quality and thermal comfort conditions, as well as to succeed in energy savings, primarily for cooling.

Acknowledgements

The research for this chapter was performed under the framework of the RESHYVENT research project, which was financed by the Fifth Framework Programme of the European Commission, Directorate General for Science, Research and Technology under the contract ENK6-CT2001-00533.

References

ACGIH (1991) *Documentation of the Threshold Limit Values and Biological Exposure Indices*, sixth edition, American Conference of Governmental Industrial Hygienists, Inc, Cincinnati, OH

Apte, M. G. and Erdmann, C. A. (2002) 'Indoor carbon dioxide concentrations, VOCS, environmental sensitivity association with mucous membrane and lower respiratory sick building syndrome symptoms in the base study: Analyses of the 100 building dataset', *LBNL-51570*, Lawrence Berkeley National Laboratory, Berkeley, CA

ASHRAE 62.1-2004 (2004) *Ventilation for Acceptable Indoor Air Quality*, American Society of Heating, Refrigerating and Air-Conditioning Engineers, US

Baya, M. P., Bakeas, E. B. and Siskos, P. A. (2004) 'Volatile organic compounds in the air of 25 Greek homes', *Indoor and Built Environment*, vol 13, pp53–61

Bernhard, C. A., Kirshner, S., Knutti, R. and Lagoudi, A. (1995) 'Volatile organic compounds in 56 European office buildings', *Healthy Buildings 95*, vol 3, pp1347–1352

Blondeau, P., Iordache, V., Poupard, O., Genin, D. and Allard, F. (2005) 'Relationship between outdoor and indoor air quality in 8 French schools', *Indoor Air*, vol 15, no 1, pp2–12

CEN, prEN 15251:2006 (2006) 'Indoor environmental input parameters for design and assessment of energy performance of buildings addressing indoor air quality, thermal environment, lighting and acoustics', *CEN/TC 156*

Chaloulakou, A. and Mavroidis, I. (2002) 'Comparison of indoor and outdoor concentrations of CO at a public school: Evaluation of an indoor air quality model', *Atmospheric Environment*, vol 36, pp1769–1781

Chan, A. T. (2002) 'Indoor–outdoor relationships of particulate matter and nitrogen oxides under different outdoor meteorological conditions', *Atmospheric Environment*, vol 36, pp1543–1551

Chao, C. Y. H. (2001) 'Comparison between indoor and outdoor air contaminant levels in residential buildings from passive sampler study', *Building and Environment*, vol 36, pp999–1007

Chao, C. Y. H. and Chan, G. Y. (2001) 'Quantification of indoor VOCs in twenty mechanically ventilated buildings in Hong Kong', *Atmospheric Environment*, vol 35, no 34, pp5895–5913

Collignan, B., Flori, J.-P., Kirchner, S., Laurent, A.-M., Moullec, Y. L., Ramalho, O. and Villenave, J. G. (2001) 'Experimental study on the impact of ventilation parameters on pollutants transfer from outdoor air into a dwelling', in *Proceedings of 22nd Annual AIVC Conference*, Bath, UK

ECA-IAQ (1997a) *Evaluation of VOC Emissions from Building Products, Solid Flooring Materials: European Collaborative Action, Indoor Air Quality and its Impact on Man*, Report no 18, Office for Official Publications of the European Communities, Luxembourg

ECA-IAQ (1997b) *Total Volatile Organic Compounds (TVOC) in Indoor Air Quality Investigations: European Collaborative Action, Indoor Air Quality and its Impact on Man*, Report no 19, EUR 17675EN, Office for Official Publications of the European Communities, Luxembourg

Edwards, R. D., Schweizer, C., Jantunen, M., Lai, H. K., Bayer-Oglesby, L., Katsouyanni, K., Nieuwenhuijsen, M., Saarela, K., Sram, R. and Kunzli, N. (2005) 'Personal exposures to VOC in the upper end of the distribution: Relationships to indoor, outdoor and workplace concentrations', *Atmospheric Environment*, vol 39, pp2299–2307

Gadkari, N. M. and Pervez, S. (2007) 'Source investigation of personal particulates in relation to identify major routes of exposure among urban residentials', *Atmospheric Environment*, vol 41, pp7951–7963

Gupta, S. C. (1995) *An Introduction to Statistical Methods*, Vikas Publ. House, PVT Ltd, New Delhi

Gustafsson, H. and Jonsson, B. (1993) 'Trade standards for testing chemical emissions from building materials, Part I: Measurements of flooring materials', in *Proceedings of Indoor Air '93*, vol 2, pp437–443

Halios, C. H., Assimakopoulos, V. D. Helmis, C. G. and Flocas, H. A. (2005) 'Investigating cigarette-smoke indoor pollution in a controlled environment', *Science of the Total Environment*, vol 337, pp183–190

Heiselberg, P. (2002) *Principles of Hybrid Ventilation*, IEA, Annex 35, Hybrid Ventilation Centre, Aalborg University, http://hybvent.civil.aau.dk

Ilgen, E., Karfich, N., Levsen, K., Angerer, J., Schneider, P., Heinrich, J., Wichmann, H.-E., Dunemann, L. and Begerow, J. (2001) 'Aromatic hydrocarbons in the atmospheric environment: Part I. Indoor versus outdoor sources, the influence of traffic', *Atmospheric Environment*, vol 35, pp1235–1252

Jones, N. C., Thornton, C. A., Mark, D. and Harrison, R. M. (2000) 'Indoor/outdoor relationships of particulate matter in domestic homes with roadside, urban and rural locations', *Atmospheric Environment*, vol 34, no 16, pp2603–2612

Koponen, I. K., Asmi, A., Keronen, P., Puhto, K. and Kulmala, M. (2001) 'Indoor air measurement campaign in Helsinki, Finland 1999: The effect of outdoor air pollution on indoor air', *Atmospheric Environment*, vol 35, pp1465–1477

Kukadia, V. and Palmer, J. (1998) 'The effect of external atmospheric pollution on indoor air quality: A pilot study', *Energy and Buildings*, vol 27, pp223–230

Lagoudi, A., Loizidou, M., Santamouris, M. and Asimakopoulos, D. N. (1996a) 'Symptoms experienced and environmental factors and energy consumption in office buildings', *Energy and Buildings*, vol 24, pp237–243

Lagoudi, A., Loizidou, M. and Asimakopoulos, D. (1996b) 'Volatile organic compounds in office buildings: 2. Identification of pollution sources in indoor air', *Indoor and Built Environment* , vol 5, no 6, pp348–354

Lai, H. K., Bayer-Oglesby, L., Colvile, R., Gotschi, T., Jantunen, M. J., Kunzli, N., Kulinskaya, E., Schweizer, C. and Nieuwenhuijsen, M. J. (2006) 'Determinants of indoor air concentrations of $PM_{2.5}$, black smoke and NO_2 in six European cities (EXPOLIS study)', *Atmospheric Environment*, vol 40, pp1299–1313

Landsberg, H. (1981) *The Urban Climate*, Academic Press, New York and London

Lee, S. C. and Chang, M. (2000) 'Indoor and outdoor air quality investigation at schools in Hong Kong', *Chemosphere*, vol 41, pp109–113

Lee, S. C., Chan, L. Y. and Chiu, M. Y. (1999) 'Indoor and outdoor air quality investigation at 14 public places in Hong Kong', *Environment International*, vol 25, pp443–450

Li, W. M., Lee, S. C. and Chan, L. Y. (2001) 'Indoor air quality at nine shopping malls in Hong Kong', *Science of the Total Environment*, vol 273, pp27–40

Matson, U. (2005) 'Indoor and outdoor concentrations of ultrafine particles in some Scandinavian rural and urban areas', *Science of the Total Environment*, vol 343, pp169–176

Molhave, L. (1990) 'Volatile organic compounds, indoor air quality and health', in *Indoor Air '90: Proceedings of the 5th International Conference on Indoor Air Quality and Climate*, Toronto, Canada, 29 July–3 August, vol 5, pp15–33

Niachou, K. (2007) *A Study of Natural and Hybrid Ventilation in the Urban Environment: Experimental and Theoretical Investigation in Urban Canyons*, PhD thesis, University of Athens, Greece

Niachou, K., Hassid, S., Santamouris, M. and Livada, I. (2005) 'Comparative monitoring of natural, hybrid and mechanical ventilation systems in urban canyons', *Energy and Buildings*, vol 37, no 5, pp503–513

Niachou, K., Livada, I. and Santamouris, M. (2007a) 'Experimental study of temperature and airflow distribution inside an urban street canyon during hot summer weather conditions – Part I: Air and surface temperatures', *Building and Environment*, 30 March

Niachou, K., Livada, I. and Santamouris, M. (2007b) 'Experimental study of temperature and airflow distribution inside an urban street canyon during hot summer weather conditions – Part II: Airflow analysis', *Building and Environment*, 2 April

Niachou, K., Santamouris, M. and Georgakis, C. (2007c) *Natural and Hybrid Ventilation in the Urban Environment*, AIVC Technical Note 61

Niachou, K., Hassid, S., Santamouris, M. and Livada, I. (2007d) 'Experimental performance investigation of natural, mechanical and hybrid ventilation in urban environment', *Building and Environment*, 5 April

Oke, T. R. (1987) *Boundary Layer Climates*, Cambridge University Press, Cambridge

Oke, T. R. (1988) 'Street design and urban canopy layer climate', *Energy and Buildings*, vol 11, pp103–113

Persily, A., Howard-Reed, C. and Nabinger, S. J. (2003) 'Transient analysis of volatile organic compound concentrations for estimating emission rates', *Atmospheric Environment*, vol 37, pp5505–5516

Phillips, J. L., Field, R., Goldstone, M., Reynolds, G. L., Lester, J. N. and Perry, R. (1993) 'Relationships between indoor and outdoor air quality in four naturally ventilated offices in the United Kingdom', *Atmospheric Environment*, vol 27A, no 11, pp1743–1753

Poupard, O., Blondeau, P., Iordache, V. and Allard, F. (2005) 'Statistical analysis of parameters influencing the relationship between outdoor and indoor air quality in schools', *Atmospheric Environment*, vol 39, pp2071–2080

RESHYVENT (2004) *Cluster Project on Demand Controlled Hybrid Ventilation in Residential Buildings with Specific Emphasis of the Integration of Renewables*, Final report, European Commission, Directorate General for Research, Brussels, Belgium

Santamouris, M. (2001) *Energy and Climate in the Urban Environment*, James and James, Ltd, London

Santamouris, M., Argiriou, A., Daskalaki, E., Balaras, C. and Gaglia, A. (1994) 'Energy performance and energy conservation in health care buildings in Hellas', *Energy Conversion and Management*, vol 35, no 4, pp293–305

Turpin, B. J., Weisel, C. P., Morandi, M. T., Colome, S., Stock, T. H., Eisenreich, S. and Buckley, B. (2004) *Contributions of Outdoor PM Sources to Indoor Concentrations and Personal Exposures: Analysis of RIOPA PM Species Concentrations*, HEI report, Health Effects Institute and Mickey Leland National Urban Air Toxics Research Center, US

Weisel, C. P., Zhang, J., Turpin, B. J., Morandi, M. T., Colome, S., Stock, T. H. and Spekt, D. M. (2005a) *Relationship of Indoor, Outdoor, and Personal Air (RIOPA)*, HEI report, Health Effects Institute and Mickey Leland National Urban Air Toxics Research Center, US

Weisel, C. P., Zhang, J., Turpin, B. J., Morandi, M. T., Colome, S., Stock, T. H., Spektor, D. M., Korn, L., Winer, A., Alimokhtari, S., Kwon, J., Mohan, K., Harrington, R., Giovanetti, R., Cui, W., Afshar, M., Maberti, S. and Shendell, D. (2005b) 'Relationship of indoor, outdoor and personal air (RIOPA) study: Study design, methods and quality assurance/control results', *Journal of Exposure Analysis and Environmental Epidemiology*, vol 15, pp123–137

Zar, J. H. (1999) *Biostatistical Analysis*, Prentice Hall, New Jersey

22

Indoor Air Quality and Health

Marcella Ucci, David Crowther, Steve Pretlove, Phillip Biddulph, Tadj Oreszczyn, Toby Wilkinson, Glenis Scadding, Barbara Hart and Dejan Mumovic

Introduction: House dust mites, housing and health

House dust mites (HDM) can be found in beds, carpets and soft furnishings. They primarily feed on human skin scales and are normally invisible to the naked eye due to their size (less than 1mm) and their translucency. Since HDM thrive in warm and humid environments, their infestations are linked to climatic characteristics and indoor conditions. Exposure to HDM allergens can lead to allergic sensitization and to exacerbation of rhinitis, eczema and asthma symptoms. Noticeable differences have been found in the prevalence of allergic sensitization and asthma symptoms worldwide, with the UK having some of the highest values (ISAAC Steering Committee, 1998). Several epidemiological studies have reported an increase in the occurrence of allergies and asthma over the past 30 to 40 years, particularly in affluent countries. Some authors even refer to an 'epidemic' of allergy and asthma (Holgate, 2004), although there is some evidence that this 'epidemic' may have reached a plateau in certain countries, including the UK (Anderson et al, 2004). Other authors have also stated that the rise in asthma levels in Westernized countries may be due to recent changes in the building stock, where energy efficiency concerns may have contributed to excessively low ventilation rates in housing, resulting in favourable conditions for HDM infestations because of high moisture levels (Howieson et al, 2003). However, most existing data is inadequate for definitive conclusions to be drawn on whether low ventilation rates directly cause ill health (Davies et al, 2004).

Although it is unlikely that increased exposure to perennial allergens (such as dust mite allergens) is the *sole* cause of the allergy and asthma 'epidemic', these allergens do play a role in explaining, for example, the worldwide variations in allergies and asthma – which partly reflect differences in exposure to HDM allergens due to geographic variations in climatic conditions.

The term house dust mite refers to the mite family *Pyroglyphidae*, of which the three species most commonly found in house dust are *Dermatophagoides pteronyssinus* (DP), *Dermatophagoides farinae* (DF) and *Euroglyphus maynei* (EM). Two major groups of HDM allergens from the genus *Dermatophagoides* have been identified, referred to as group I allergens (called Der p1 for the species DP and Der f1 for the species DF), and group II allergens (called Der p2 for the species DP and Der f2 for the species DF). Both allergens are digestive enzymes excreted in mite faecal pellets that easily become airborne and are the right size to be inhaled deep into the lungs.

House dust mites rarely encounter water in liquid form but are able to absorb moisture from the air. If the ambient relative humidity (RH) is too low, mites dehydrate and eventually die. The critical RH low below which mites die is often referred to as the *critical equilibrium humidity* (CEH). For DF, the most common species in the US, CEH is temperature dependent (Arlian and Veselica, 1981). Some evidence exists that a similar temperature dependence of CEH also occurs for DP, the most common species in the UK (Crowther et al, 2006). Temperature also affects HDM egg-to-adult development times (i.e. lower temperatures giving rise to longer development times).

Thus, by adequately controlling the hygrothermal conditions of mite microclimates, it should be possible to reduce mite populations (i.e. psychrometric control). Because of the dependency of mite populations upon hygrothermal conditions, their growth in temperate climates is usually greater in late summer/early autumn, and winter months are crucial for reducing mite populations (Crowther et al, 2006). If outdoor winter air – with its low moisture content – is sufficiently heated in housing, the resultant indoor RH will be too low for mite population growth, which will thus decline. If these dry conditions can be maintained over winter, the mite population will be reduced to such an extent that it will not recover significantly during the more favourable late summer to autumn months.

HDM can survive when exposed to brief spells of high RH, even when the daily average RH is below critical levels. Nonetheless, the reduction of indoor RH is still a viable control method as mite development rates are much slower when HDM are only exposed briefly to favourable RHs (Arlian et al, 1999). For typical indoor temperatures, maintaining the average daily indoor RH below 50 per cent is often recommended to reduce mite levels and their allergens. However, feasible threshold levels for temperature and RH in housing are still being discussed. Taking into account the temperature dependency of CEH, Cunningham (1996) suggested that relative humidity should be kept under 40 per cent at 16°C; 45 per cent at 21°C; and 50 per cent at 26°C. Using Cunningham's figures, Lowe (2000) pointed out the important role of ventilation rates and also demonstrated that in UK dwellings – which are often under-heated – HDM psychrometric control can only be achieved if internal temperatures are raised significantly.

Most studies on the psychrometric control of house dust mites in housing have focused on mechanical ventilation. However, there is some scope for modifying residential hygrothermal conditions by changing the occupants' heating and ventilation habits. For example, a well-designed extractor fan can remove up to 70 per cent of moisture generated during cooking (Liddament, 2001). A UK study also found that the presence of an extractor fan in the kitchen was associated with lower HDM allergen concentrations (Luczynska et al, 1998). Furthermore, a large-scale study concluded that mite allergen exposure may be reduced by increasing the ventilation of the bedroom, particularly in winter (Zock et al, 2006). Nevertheless,

very few intervention studies have been carried out attempting to reduce HDM levels through the modification of occupant behaviour alone. Compared with methods acting on the building fabric or on heating and ventilation systems, behavioural changes can be inexpensive and implemented in shorter timescales.

Many strategies other than the psychrometric method are available for the control of HDM populations and/or allergens, including high-efficiency vacuuming, steam cleaning, mite-proof barriers and acaricides. However, most of these strategies can be time consuming, while the psychrometric approach could be 'built into' housing design or refurbishment, potentially reducing asthma symptoms and even preventing allergic sensitization. But it should be emphasized that psychrometric measures for the control of house dust mites do not remove any existing allergen reservoirs, which can be long-lasting. Therefore, in any study aiming to reduce adverse health impacts, any pre-existing HDM allergens have to be removed. On the other hand, most allergen removal strategies (e.g. steam-cleaning) are time consuming, cannot be applied to all possible dust reservoirs and need to be repeated over time. This is because if hygrothermal conditions continue to be favourable to mite growth, allergen levels will be replenished after some time. Psychrometric control methods should therefore accompany allergen removal measures (and vice versa) since they potentially strengthen and extend their effects.

There is still conflicting evidence as to whether any mite-control strategies can permanently reduce mite infestation to a level sufficient for health benefits (Gøtzsche et al, 2006). However, many studies on the clinical efficacy of HDM allergen avoidance measures have focused on the impact of one intervention type at a time; nevertheless, there is growing consensus that a *combination* of strategies is probably the most effective approach.

This chapter describes a pilot intervention study on house dust mite allergen avoidance for 12 asthmatic children (two being controls). The study adopted a holistic approach, with a number of measures for allergen (pet and mite) removal and avoidance, including tailored advice aimed at reducing mite population growth via changes in moisture production, heating and ventilation habits. The study addressed four issues:

1   the effect of allergen removal on the children's health;
2   the effect of tailored advice on occupant behaviour and the resultant hygrothermal conditions;
3   the effect of the hygrothermal changes on mite populations;
4   the efficacy of monitoring/modelling techniques.

The study was filmed by Twenty Twenty Television and resulted in two 50-minute episodes of the UK TV series *Dispatches* on Channel 4 (April 2006). Due to its short time scale and small sample size, the study did not aim to establish the clinical efficacy of allergen avoidance, but to illustrate its potential benefits and to give researchers the opportunity to test a protocol for a larger future study. In this chapter, the study is described with a view to demonstrating the complexities associated with housing, indoor air quality and health.

Study design and methodology

In October 2005, 12 asthmatic mite-sensitive children aged 6 to 14 were selected in the London area; 11 dwellings were examined overall, since two of the children were siblings living in one dwelling (here termed bedroom/child 12a and 12b). The properties included four flats, one detached house and six terrace houses. A pre-intervention analysis was carried out, where baseline measurements were taken of:

•   the children's health status;
•   HDM numbers and allergen levels in each dwelling (child bedroom: mattress, pillow, one soft toy and floor; living room: sofa and floor – all using a standard protocol);
•   hygrothermal conditions (monitored for two weeks, logging every 15 minutes);
•   building characteristics (including airtightness via a fan-pressurization test);
•   heating and ventilation habits.

The fan pressurization results at 50Pa were converted to an estimated air-infiltration rate in air changes per hour (ACH) under average external conditions. Prior to the interventions, the children's health status, including history of asthma, eczema and rhinitis, skin-prick testing and airway measurements were assessed by Dr Glenis Scadding, consultant physician at the Royal National Throat Nose and Ear Hospital. After the

pre-intervention study, a number of interventions were carried out, followed by a post-intervention study, where the children's health and the dwellings' hygrothermal conditions were monitored for six weeks. The interventions carried out after the baseline measurements were:

•   professional steam-cleaning of the child's bedroom and thorough cleaning of the dwelling (followed by further dust sampling);
•   replacement of carpets in the child's bedroom with laminate flooring;
•   covering mattresses, pillows and duvets with micro-porous mite-proof barriers;
•   removing pets and cuddly toys, and avoiding exposure to environmental tobacco smoke;
•   participants were also advised to implement a thorough cleaning regime throughout the post-intervention period.

Following the analysis of the pre-intervention study results, tailored advice was also provided on moisture production, heating and ventilation. Outdoor hygrothermal conditions were also monitored throughout the study. For the two households acting as controls, the interventions were carried out *at the end* of the post-intervention period; but their dwelling's hygrothermal conditions were monitored throughout the study. At the end of the study, further dust samples were taken and a final medical examination was carried out.

Study results

Table 22.1 shows the baseline results from the pre-intervention study, including the dust sampling findings. Since little dust was found in toys and pillows, the allergen results were not only expressed as allergen concentrations, but also as 'allergen loads' (i.e. total allergen weight collected for a given vacuumed area), corresponding to µg Der p1/m^2 (µg Der p1/total object area, for pillows and toys). The pre-intervention results included baseline indoor and outdoor hygrothermal conditions, from which the vapour pressure excess (VPX) (kPa) was calculated as the difference between indoor and outdoor vapour pressures. A dwelling's VPX is the result of the combination of ventilation rates and of the moisture produced by the occupants. The baseline hygrothermal conditions were also utilized to calculate the percentage of time the bedroom RH was above the

Table 22.1 Baseline measurements for building characteristics, hygrothermal conditions and mite infestation levels

Dwelling	θMoisture production (kg/day)	Volume (m³)	ΔAir Infiltration (ACH⁻¹)	*Mites (mites/m²)	*Der p1 concentration (µg/g)	*Der p1 load (µg/m²)	#Pre, VPX (kPa)	#Pre, percentage time CEH>RH (%)	#Pre, temperature (°C)	#Pre, RH (%)
1	7.2	163.1	0.2	20.3	23.0	1.16	0.6	92.1	20.9	68.7
2	4.2	198.6	0.4	0.0	1.7	0.10	0.2	18.1	20.7	52.3
3	3.4	127.2	0.5	0.0	0.3	0.13	0.4	66.8	20.8	57.3
5	6.5	484.5	0.9	0.0	0.4	0.01	0.2	0.0	20.9	40.4
6ᶜ	11.9	286.2	1.1	21.7	0.3	0.11	0.3	36.3	20.6	54.1
7	13.7	189.8	0.6	17.7	21.4	2.30	0.2	73.4	18.7	57.5
8ᶜ	6.4	137.4	0.5	0.0	3.3	0.24	0.4	37.4	22.3	55.8
9	7.9	215.9	1.4	0.0	(–)	0.02	0.2	47.2	20.2	54.5
10	6.3	141.3	0.6	0.0	0.9	0.11	0.4	20.2	22.1	54.6
11	10.1	396.1	1.3	5.3	1.8	0.31	0.2	99.2	17.4	61.8
12a	5.3	263.0	0.6	1.3	2.2	0.26	0.3	90.3	(17.6)	57.4
12b	5.3	263.0	0.6	0.0	0.8	0.12	0.3	100.0	(17.4)	60.5
Average	7.7	227.3	0.7	5.1	1.4α	0.16α	0.3	56.8	20.5	55.8
Outdoor conditions									11.4	76.8

Notes: c = control dwelling; * = bedroom, average of: mattress, floor, pillow; # = child bedroom; θ = whole dwelling, estimated; α = geometric mean; Δ = (air infiltration measured at 50 Pa)/20; (–) = missing data.

Central heating in dwelling 12 was malfunctioning in the pre-intervention study.

critical equilibrium humidity, with the latter being a function taking account of the effect of temperature (Arlian and Veselica, 1981).

The pre-intervention study results were analysed so that tailored advice could be provided to each household on the most appropriate heating, ventilation and moisture-production patterns, which could reduce HDM population growth. For example, in a leaky (and, thus, well-ventilated) dwelling inhabited by a household with average moisture production, it is not advisable to increase ventilation rates further since this might excessively reduce temperature levels. Although low indoor temperatures increase mite egg-to-adult development times, they also result in higher relative humidity, which is favourable for mite growth. The tailored advice was formulated by considering the baseline hygrothermal results, as well as the dwelling's measured infiltration rates and the household's predicted moisture production rates. The predicted daily moisture production (kg/day) was estimated by the moisture algorithm of condensation targeter II (Oreszczyn and Pretlove, 1999), which requires information on moisture-production items, such as number of occupants, frequency of cooking, bathing, etc.

Based on the pre-intervention results and depending upon the dwelling and occupant behaviour characteristics, each household was advised to

implement one, or a combination of, the following measures:

- reducing moisture production;
- increasing ventilation levels; and
- increasing temperature levels.

For example, household 1 – with low air infiltration rates, and highest RH and VPX levels – was advised to:

- only dry clothes indoors in a well-ventilated room, which is closed to the rest of the home;
- use the extract fans in the kitchen and the bathroom during use, and for at least 15 minutes afterwards;
- keep the trickle vents always open; and
- leave the windows slightly open for as long as possible.

On the other hand, household 11 – with low temperatures and high infiltration rates – was advised to increase indoor temperatures. Control households (6 and 8) did not receive the advice until the end of the study.

After the tailored advice was provided and implemented for six to eight weeks (post-intervention), the monitored hygrothermal conditions were analysed

Table 22.2 *Post-intervention hygrothermal results and difference with pre-intervention conditions for a child's bedroom*

Bedroom number	Post: VPX (kPa)	Pre–post [#] VPX (kPa)	Post: temperature (°C)	Pre–post [#] temperature (°C)	Post: RH (%)	Pre–post [#] RH (%)	Post: percentage time CEH > RH	Pre–post [#] percentage time CEH > RH (%)
1	0.6	0.0	19.4	1.5	59.8	8.9	76.3	15.8
2	0.1	0.1	19.5	1.2	40.7	11.6	0.0	18.1
3	0.2	0.2	19.6	1.2	41.9	15.4	0.0	66.8
5	0.0	0.2	19.2	1.7	37.6	2.8	0.0	0.0
6	0.1	0.2	18.0	2.6	41.6	12.5	1.8	34.5
7	0.2	0.0	17.4	1.3	47.4	10.1	9.5	63.8
8	0.5	−0.1	21.9	0.4	48.4	7.4	0.1	37.3
9	0.2	0	21.3	−1.1	38.4	16.1	0.0	47.2
10	0.3	0.1	20.4	1.7	43.5	11.1	1.2	19.0
11	0.2	0	17.8	−0.4	47.8	14.0	12.1	87.1
12a	0.0	0.3	17.3	0.3	40.3	17.1	5.6	84.7
12b	0.2	0.1	17.2	0.2	47.1	13.4	2.8	97.2
Average*	0.2	0.1	18.9	0.8	44.5	12.1	10.8	50.0
Outdoor	(n.a.)	(n.a.)	6.6	4.8	80.2	−3.4	(n.a.)	(n.a.)

Notes: # = pre–post difference; * = excluding controls (bedroom 6 and 8); (n.a.) = not available.

in order to assess whether a change had occurred in indoor conditions as a results of such advice. It was found that in all dwellings, the bedroom RH decreased from pre- to post-intervention periods, and the percentage of time the bedroom RH was greater than CEH ('percentage time RH > CEH') also decreased (see Table 22.2). In some dwellings, the monitored post-intervention bedroom RH was never above CEH.

It should be highlighted that the measured reduction in indoor RH levels was partly due to changes in outdoor conditions: although the average outdoor RH increased during the post-intervention period, it was colder and the outdoor absolute humidity was lower. In order to disentangle the weather effect from the implementation of advice, the pre- and post-intervention RHs were adjusted for each bedroom following a procedure described in another paper (Ucci et al, 2007) in order to be theoretically equivalent to a situation where outdoor conditions stayed the same throughout the whole study. Once the impact of changes in outdoor conditions was taken into account, it was found that the reduction in bedroom RHs was smaller than suggested by the measured results (see Figure 22.1) – particularly for some bedrooms (12.1 per cent measured pre-post average RH difference versus 5.1 per cent adjusted pre–post average RH difference, excluding control bedrooms).

A paired t-test showed that there was a statistically significant difference (p<0.01) between pre and post bedroom RHs for both the *measured* and the *adjusted* RH results. The importance of the adjustment procedure is illustrated by the case of the control

dwelling 8, where the measured bedroom RH decreased from the pre- to the post-intervention period. However, its adjusted RH *increased* (by a small amount; see Figure 22.1). This was due to an increase in the measured post-intervention vapour pressure excess (see Table 22.2), probably because of a reduction in the window opening for the colder outdoor temperatures. It should also be pointed out that the other control dwelling (dwelling 6) experienced an above average reduction in adjusted RH levels. However, it is possible that household 6 learned about the advice provided to other families. It is also possible that the RH adjustment method utilized in this study may underestimate reductions in relative humidity (see Ucci et al, 2007).

At the end of the intervention study, tailored interviews were carried out in order to further establish the extent to which households had implemented the advice. Based on the interview results, each household was given an 'implementation score'. No correlation was found between the measured pre–post RH reduction and the 'implementation score'. Therefore, for those dwellings which experienced small reductions in RH, it is difficult to establish whether this was due to:

- a lack of participants' action;
- adverse building characteristics hindering changes;
- limitations of the advice itself.

However, during the interviews it also became apparent that participants experienced some difficulties in reporting their ventilation habits coherently.

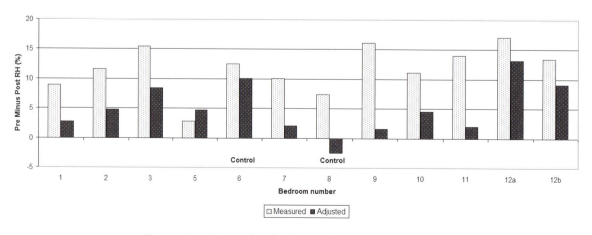

Figure 22.1 *Measured and adjusted reduction in bedroom RHs*

At the beginning of the intervention period, all soft furnishings were steam-cleaned. As a result, a statistically significant reduction was found for Der p1 load levels (p<0.01). At the end of the post-intervention period, the initial medical examination was repeated, and an improvement score involving symptoms, medication use and airway measurements was determined for each child by Glenis Scadding, who was blinded as to the HDM data. Figure 22.2 shows the child's improvement score plotted against the reduction in bedroom allergen load. The graph suggests that a (weak) correlation exists between health improvement and allergen reduction (r = 0.55; R^2 = 0.30). Some children experienced an improvement that did not correspond to a dramatic reduction in Der p1 levels. This may be due to confounding variables, such as concomitant allergies to pets which were removed from the homes or the placebo effect.

Modelling techniques

The HDM population model Mite Population Index (MPI) (Crowther et al, 2006) was utilized in this study in order to:

- help identify those dwellings most at risk from mite growth;
- assess the effect of changes in hygrothermal conditions on mite populations.

The MPI model predicts the likely effect of steady-state average hygrothermal conditions on HDM population growth. The output is the MPI index, where, for example, 1.1 indicates 10 per cent population growth and 0.9 indicates 10 per cent population decline. The results obtained by utilizing measured pre-intervention average conditions indicated that the mite populations were rather stable at an average MPI value of $\cong$ 1. This suggests that even small hygrothermal changes could determine whether the population grows or declines (threshold effect). Dwelling 1 had the highest predicted pre-intervention population growth for both bedroom and bed (MPI = 1.03).

Since the interventions included the removal of mites and their allergens, it was not possible to assess the *direct* effect of RH reductions on mite levels in the dwelling. Modelling was therefore utilized in order to assess the likely impact of hygrothermal changes on mite populations. In order to exclude the effect of

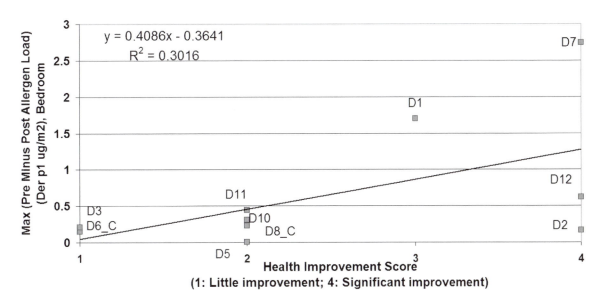

Note: * = difference in average Der p1 levels between pre- and post-intervention.

Figure 22.2 *Respiratory symptoms 'improvement score' and reduction* of Der p1 levels in child's bedroom*

changes in outdoor conditions, the monitored post-intervention temperatures and the *adjusted* post-intervention bedroom RHs were used as inputs in the MPI model. As indicated earlier, the use of adjusted hygrothermal conditions makes it easier to assess the likely impact of advice implementation on mite populations. Figure 22.3 shows a plot of the adjusted average hygrothermal conditions, with the pre- and post-conditions joined by an arrow for each bedroom (numbers near data points correspond to the bedrooms' code). The plot includes a curve – corresponding to an MPI value of 1 – above which mite populations grow and below which they decline.

The results show that in all but dwelling 8, conditions improved – independently from weather changes. Because of a threshold effect (linked to the CEH), even small reductions in RHs can lead to a reduction in mite populations (e.g. bedroom 1 in

Figure 22.3). Therefore, although the RH reductions obtained via changes in occupant behaviour may appear small, they could be sufficient to reduce mite infestations – particularly during wintertime.

Discussion

This chapter describes the methods and findings of a pilot intervention study on HDM allergen avoidance for asthmatic children, with a view to highlighting the complexities of such studies due to a number of confounding factors. First, the study shows that, depending upon the time of the year, changes in outdoor conditions may result in short-term improved hygrothermal conditions (i.e. less favourable for mite growth), thus confounding the effect of hygrothermal changes due to long-term interventions such as implementation of tailored hygrothermal advice.

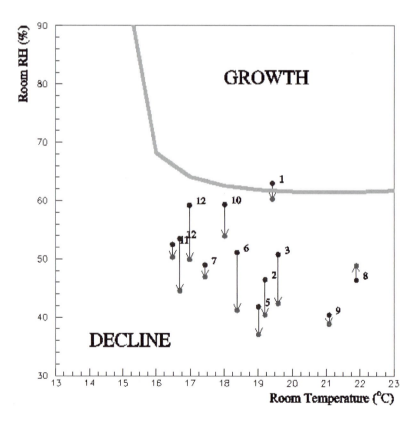

Note: The solid curve represents conditions where HDM populations are stable (MPI = 1).

Figure 22.3 *Predicted bedroom mite growth risk, using adjusted hygrothermal conditions:*
Pre- versus post-intervention

Furthermore, occupant behaviour can change in relation to outdoor conditions. It is therefore important to adjust for changes in outdoor conditions in any similar future study. Second, the study shows that changes in occupant behaviour can be difficult to assess – particularly with regard to ventilation habits. It is therefore vital that ventilation rates – not only air leakage – are measured in future studies, and a closer monitoring is carried out of occupant habits (e.g. through the use of participants diaries). As demonstrated in this study, it is vital that *tailored* advice is provided, ensuring that the most effective intervention is carried out, since greater ventilation rates are not always desirable (e.g. in a leaky building). Changes in occupant behaviours can also be hindered by adverse dwelling characteristics. For example, in this study household 1 was advised to increase ventilation rates; but their VPX did not decrease, most probably because of a combination of existing habits and their very airtight dwelling.

A further difficulty highlighted by this study was assessing the impact of changes in hygrothermal conditions on mite populations (and, indirectly, on health). This is because psychrometric control does not immediately affect HDM allergen reservoirs, which have to be removed in order to obtain any health improvement. However, allergen removal also results in killing the existing mite population, which therefore cannot be monitored for subsequent reductions due to hygrothermal changes. In any case, live mites are notoriously difficult to sample and mite populations would also be affected by changes in outdoor conditions. On the other hand, high allergen levels cannot be taken as a marker of favourable hygrothermal conditions since a reservoir effect can be observed – e.g. due to the age of the substrate (e.g. mattress) and to the ineffectiveness of some cleaning regimes. Therefore, the use of population modelling techniques such as those utilized in this pilot are recommended as a useful tool for assessing the likely impact of hygrothermal changes on mite populations. Although the current models are based on steady-state data, transient models for mite microclimates are being developed by the authors, which will allow for more accurate predictions of mite populations. Furthermore, the authors have also developed an innovative technique for monitoring the impact of a dwelling's hygrothermal conditions on mite populations – using encapsulated populations of mites, as described in a future paper. The development of models predicting the effect of hygrothermal

conditions on allergen levels (as opposed to mite population only) is also recommended since this would allow for a better understanding of the impacts of hygrothermal changes on respiratory health.

The study in this chapter shows some promising results with regard to its health impact. However, it should also be highlighted that due to practical constraints, it was not possible to adequately control for the placebo effect and for the role of other confounding health variables (e.g. sensitivity to other allergens) in this study. Above all, this study demonstrates the complexities associated with attempting to establish a direct link between changes in hygrothermal conditions in housing (e.g. due to changes in ventilation) and health (e.g. asthma). This is because any study attempting to do so is faced with a large number of variables whose direct measurement is often very expensive (e.g. ventilation rates) and/or challenging (e.g. meaningful mite levels). Furthermore, a number of the mechanisms involved in the links between housing and atopic asthma are not yet fully understood. For example, although much is known about asthma, there is still some uncertainty on the causes of asthma onset, and even on the definition of asthma itself. Similarly, the mechanisms that determine HDM sensitization following exposure to HDM allergens are not fully understood, nor are there clear threshold levels of exposure above which sensitization occurs. Another source of complexity of any such study is linked to the mechanisms which determine indoor hygrothermal conditions, upon which house dust mites are dependent. Building characteristics, occupant behaviour and climatic conditions all affect indoor conditions. However, these variables are not independent: for example, climatic conditions can affect occupant behaviour (e.g. less window openings in cold weather). Furthermore, it should be emphasized that although HDM microclimates (e.g. beds) are strongly influenced by room conditions, they nevertheless can differ from them as a result of, for example, the hygrothermal properties of the mattress, the amount of time the bed is occupied, etc. Figure 22.4 highlights the main variables that should be taken into account when considering the links between the building stock, house dust mite infestations (e.g. in a mattress) and health outcomes – with a focus on psychrometric control.

Despite the complexities discussed above, this study showed that there was a statistically significant ($p < 0.01$) decrease of measured bedroom RHs, which

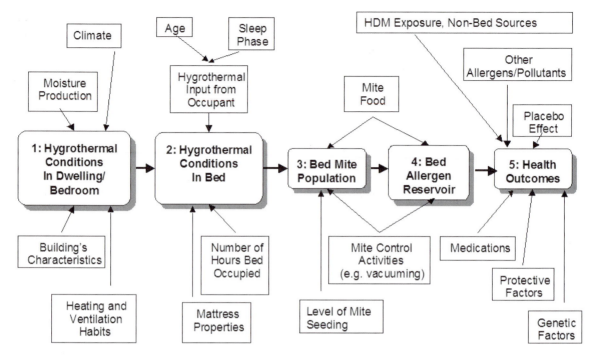

Figure 22.4 *Complexity of the links between hygrothermal conditions in dwellings, HDM levels in beds and adverse health outcomes*

remained statistically significant, although smaller, once the effect of changes in outdoor conditions was taken into account. The population modelling results indicated that during the pre-intervention period, mite populations were rather stable at an average MPI value of $\cong 1$, suggesting that even *small* hygrothermal changes could determine whether mite populations grow or decline.

Conclusions

This study suggests that in temperate climates, even small changes in hygrothermal conditions can be crucial in reducing house dust mite infestations, particularly during winter. Tailored advice on heating and ventilation habits can lead to valuable changes in hygrothermal conditions. In some cases, however, these improvements may be hindered by occupants' reluctance to change and/or by pre-existing adverse building conditions. Due to the complexities associated with these types of studies, formulaic interventions should be avoided, while careful consideration should be given to the study design and to appropriate monitoring and modelling techniques.

Acknowledgements

The authors wish to acknowledge: the TV production company Twenty Twenty Television for liaising with the study participants, collaborating with the research team and providing a contribution to the monitoring costs. Thanks are also due to Paul Meighan from Acaris for the mite allergen analysis of dust samples. This study was funded by the Engineering and Physical Sciences Research Council (EPSRC) (research grant: GR/S70678/01; PPE grant: EP/D064090/1 and Platform Grant EP/D506859/1).

References

Anderson, H., Ruggles, R., Strachan, D., Austin, J., Burr, M., Jeffs, D., Standring, P., Steriu, A. and Goulding, R. (2004) 'Trends in prevalence of symptoms of asthma, hay fever, and eczema in 12–14 year olds in the British Isles, 1995–2002: Questionnaire survey', *BMJ*, vol 328, no 7447, pp1052–1053

Arlian, L. G and Veselica, M. M. (1981) 'Effect of temperature on the equilibrium body water mass in the mite *Dermatophagoides farinae*', *Physiology Zoology*, vol 54, no 4, pp393–399

Arlian, L. G., Neal, J. and Vyszenski-Moher, D. L. (1999) 'Fluctuating hydrating and dehydrating relative humidities effects on the life cycle of *Dermatophagoides farinae* (Acari: Pyroglyphidae)', *Journal of Medical Entomology*, vol 36, no 4, pp457–461

Crowther, D., Wilkinson, T., Biddulph, P., Oreszczyn, T., Pretlove, S. and Ridley, I. (2006) 'A simple model for predicting the effect of hygrothermal conditions on populations of house dust mite *Dermatophagoides pteronyssinus* (Acari: Pyroglyphidae)', *Experimental and Applied Acarology*, vol 39, pp 127–148

Cunningham, M. J. (1996) 'Controlling dust mites psychrometrically: A review for building scientists and engineers', *Indoor Air*, vol 6, pp249–258

Davies, M., Ucci, M., McCarthy, M., Oreszczyn, T., Ridley, I., Mumovic, D., Singh, J. and Pretlove, S. (2004) 'A review of evidence linking ventilation rates in dwellings and respiratory health: A focus on house dust mites and mould', *International Journal of Ventilation*, vol 3, no 2, pp155–168

Gøtzsche, P.C., Johansen, H. K., Schmidt, L. M. and Burr, M. L. (2006) 'House dust mite control measures for asthma', *The Cochrane Library*, vol 3, pp1–38

Holgate, S. (2004) 'The epidemic of asthma and allergy', *Journal of the Royal Society of Medicine*, vol 97, no 3, pp103–110

Howieson, S. G., Lawson, A., McSharry, C., Morris, G., McKenzie, E. and Jackson, J. (2003) 'Domestic ventilation rates, indoor humidity and dust mite allergens: Are our homes causing the asthma pandemic?', *Building Services Engineering Research and Technology (BSERT)*, vol 23, no 3, pp137–147

ISAAC Steering Committee (1998) 'Worldwide variations in the prevalence of symptoms of asthma, allergic rhinoconjunctivitis and atopic eczema: ISAAC', *The Lancet*, vol 368, no 9537, pp733–743

Liddament, M. (2001) *AIVC Technical Note 53: Occupant Impact on Ventilation*, AIVC, Brussels, Belgium

Lowe, R. (2000), 'Psychrometric control of dust mites in UK housing', *Building Services Engineering Research and Technology (BSERT)*, vol 21, no 4, pp274–276

Luczynska, C. Sterne, J., Bond, J., Azima, H. and Burney, P. (1998) 'Indoor factors associated with concentrations of house dust mite allergen, Der p 1, in a random sample of houses in Norwich, UK', *Clinical and Experimental Allergy*, vol 28, no 10, pp1201–1209

Oreszczyn, T. and Pretlove, S. E. C. (1999) 'Condensation targeter II: Modelling surface relative humidity to predict mould growth in dwellings', *Building Services Engineering Research and Technology (BSERT)*, vol 20, no 3, pp143–153

Ucci, M., Pretlove, S., Biddulph, P., Oreszczyn, T., Wilkinson, T., Crowther, D., Scadding, G., Hart, B. and Mumovic, D. (2007) 'The psychrometric control of house dust mites: A pilot study', *Building Services Engineering Research and Technology (BSERT)*, vol 28, no 4, pp347–356

Zock, J., Heinrich, J., Jarvis, D., Verlato, G., Norbäck, D., Plana, E., Sunyer, J., Chinn, S., Olivieri, M., Soon, A., Villani, S., Ponzio, M., Dahlman-Hoglund, A., Svanes, C., Luczynska, C. and the Indoor Working Group of the European Community Respiratory Health Survey II (2006) 'Distribution and determinants of house dust mite allergens in Europe: The European Community Respiratory Health Survey II', *Journal of Allergy and Clinical Immunology*, vol 118, no 3, pp628–690

23

Indoor Air Quality and Ventilation Modelling

Zarko Stevanovic, Dejan Mumovic and Miroslava Kavgic

Introduction

Modelling is a very important activity in built environment engineering. The need for modelling arises from the complex systems and processes that must be addressed and which we cannot always afford to measure (monitor). We are frequently challenged to explain why an environmental system behaves as it does, to predict how it will evolve if left undisturbed, or to discern how a system will respond to a change (to predict the effects of future scenarios).

In practice, there are two classes of frequently used models based on material balance:

1 reactor (box) models;
2 general heat, mass and momentum balance models.

Despite the simplicity of reactor models, in many cases more detailed aspects of pollution phenomena must be considered in order to accurately model an environmental issue or process. General heat, mass and momentum balance models can be used to study more complex problems. Analytical solutions for these models are possible for only a small fraction of the cases of interest. Usually, one must either make major simplifying approximations about the system, as in reactor models, or use numerical methods to solve the governing differential equations of heat, mass and momentum conservation, as well as introduced turbulence model. The general heat, mass and momentum balance models that are numerically solved are known collectively as the computational fluid dynamics (CFD) technique.

CFD is now widely used for assessing thermal comfort and air quality in and around buildings. CFD can simulate airflow, the dispersion characteristics of air pollutants, and their temporal and spatial variations. When used carefully, optimizing input and output requirements, it can offer useful insights into the physical processes that govern the dispersion of atmospheric pollutants. This chapter provides a general guide to the use of CFD for assessing thermal comfort and air quality in and around buildings. Within this framework, relevant experimental and theoretical problems are also briefly discussed.

Airflow and pollution distribution around buildings

This section provides a step-by-step guide to the use of CFD for assessing pedestrian comfort and air quality around buildings. Furthermore, it highlights the fundamental problems of the micro-scale CFD models, which lie in the physical difficulties of modelling the effect of turbulence, as well as the accuracy of the spatial discretization of complex urban geometries, the numerical procedures applied, the boundary conditions and the physical property selected. This section presents the results of two case studies aimed at assessing:

- the suitability of a general CFD code for use in integrated urban air-quality modelling for regulatory purposes in Glasgow (Scotland);
- the impact of a new building on airflow and pollution distribution in a district of Copenhagen (Denmark).

Although, at this stage, the accuracy of developed urban air-quality models highly depends upon experience of its users, it is believed that use of a CFD in urban air-quality modelling could be to the benefit of urban planners, architects, heating, ventilating and air-conditioning (HVAC) engineers and all other professionals interested in public health.

Defining the geometry

Domain size

The choice of size of computational domain strongly depends upon at least two factors:

1 the size of the modelled built environment area; and
2 the wind direction.

No definitive studies have been conducted to identify the specific limits to which a computational domain of a built environment should be extended. However, the basic guideline of computational domain size is connected to the nature of conservation partial differential equations of heat, mass and momentum transport. These equations are elliptic ones; therefore, in order to obtain a solution, one must specify the boundary conditions on all domain faces. There is no difficulty in specifying boundary conditions at the inlet faces and the walls since they are known; however, the problem arises at the outlets and open surfaces where the boundary conditions are unknown. The common practice to overcome this problem is to extend the domain size to the level where we expect no change of fluid flow parameters (e.g. assuming zero gradients). Therefore, this depends upon the modeller's experiences. There are no general guidelines; but an analysis of the published literature suggests that the computational domain for buildings of height H should be extended upstream, downstream and vertically by H to 6H, 5H to 16H and 0.5H to 16H, respectively.

For a single building, or a simple group of buildings, where the size of each building in the lateral direction is comparable with their heights, the upstream, the cross-stream and the top boundary conditions should be extended to 5H, where H is the height of the tallest building (Hall, 1997). Downstream, the computational domain has to be extended to include the reattachment point beyond the latest building column, meaning that the outlet should be positioned at 15H behind the building.

However, in the case of a complex configuration of buildings, such as in the Glasgow case study, the situation is more complex. Knowing that one is constrained by present-day computer power, as a starting point, the upstream, cross-stream and downstream boundaries should be positioned at least at 5H, 7H and 12H, respectively. Assuming the same heights of buildings, the top boundary could be extended to 3H.

Object geometry

As can be seen in Figure 23.1, much of central Glasgow is divided into rectangular blocks by orthogonal streets. A block surrounded by streets usually consists of several almost regularly positioned buildings with small courtyards, or one large building. The older Victorian building style and height restrictions of approximately 20m have given rise to an almost regular array of streets with buildings all of a very similar height. This is very convenient for applying the following refinements:

• Linearization of minor irregularities in the street direction: as a consequence of this minor geometrical simplification, a significant reduction in the number of the cut cells may be achieved.
• Rotation of the supportive plate of the solid model: this simple technical solution enables the alignment of the solid model of an urban area with the direction of the non-uniform Cartesian grid and, hence, allows the use of very limited computer power without causing numerical diffusion (i.e. an artefact).

On the contrary, object geometry of the Copenhagen district area is characterized by a highly irregular street network that is shown in Figure 23.2.

Generally speaking, the level of detail required for each building is determined by both its distance from the point of interest, such as an air-quality monitoring station in an urban area; and the application of the CFD model. While the general wind flow pattern characteristics are determined by the distribution of buildings in the modelled built environment as a whole, the micro-environment is critical when assessing surface pressure on

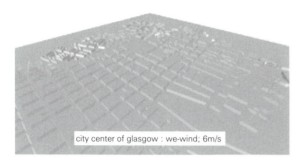

Figure 23.1 *Object geometry of central Glasgow area*

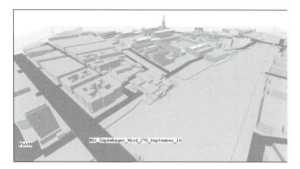

Figure 23.2 *Details of object geometry of Copenhagen district area*

the façade of specific buildings or, for example, dispersion of air pollutants from large boiler flues.

Numerical grid

Arguably, the most important step in CFD is the generation of a grid, which defines cells at which flow variables are calculated throughout the computational domain. As a general rule, if the configuration of buildings is not suitable for alignment of the grid with the local flow direction, body-fitted coordinates (hexahedral shapes) should be used. However, in the case of Glasgow and probably other Victorian cities across the UK, where cities are divided into rectangular blocks, a non-uniform orthogonal coordinate system may be used. In that case at least ten cells should be used between two buildings for rapid and accurate convergence. However, in the Copenhagen study, the authors opted for a dense uniform horizontal grid resolution as the highly irregular street network did not allow for the grid refinement.

Figure 23.3 *Details of horizontal numerical grid of central Glasgow case study*

Figure 23.4 *Horizontal numerical grid of Copenhagen district case study*

A well-designed grid is critical for an accurate CFD solution of airflow in a built environment, and time spent generating the grid is usually well spent. The numerical grids of central Glasgow and Copenhagen district areas are shown in Figures 23.3 and 23.4, respectively.

Defining the physical model

Governing equations

In urban air-quality modelling, a computational domain is set up within the atmospheric boundary layer assuming incompressibility of the air. Generally, the airflow-governing equations represent the

Table 23.1 *Summarized governing equations of the urban pollution model*

Governing equation	Φ	Γ_Φ	S_Φ
Continuity	1	0	0
Momentum	U_i	v_{ef}	$-\partial P/\partial x_i$
Energy	T	a_{ef}	0
Species concentration	C	D_{ef}	0

conservation of mass (continuity), momentum (Navier-Stokes equations), heat (energy equation) and species concentration (CO_2, CO, NO_x, SO_x, H_2O, etc.). All of these equations can be presented by means of the general conservation equation for property Φ:

$$\frac{\partial}{\partial \tau}(\rho\Phi) + \frac{\partial}{\partial x_j}(\rho U_j \Phi) = \frac{\partial}{\partial x_j}\left(\Gamma_\Phi \frac{\partial \Phi}{\partial x_j}\right) + S_\Phi \quad (1)$$

where Φ denotes the general airflow physical property (velocity, temperature, concentration, etc.), ρ denotes the air density, U_j denotes the component of time-averaged velocity vector ($j = 1,2,3$), and Γ_Φ and S_Φ denote the transport coefficient and source term aligned to the general variable Φ, respectively. It is common practice to represent the governing equations as in Table 23.1.

In Table 23.1, P denotes averaged atmospheric pressure, T denotes averaged atmospheric temperature, C is averaged species concentration, v_{ef} denotes effective molecular viscosity, and a_{ef}, D_{ef} denote effective thermal and mass diffusivity, respectively. In the case of isothermal airflow, the energy equation is omitted. However, as the airflow is turbulent, additional equations representing a turbulence model must be solved as well.

Turbulence modelling

In recent years, modelling of micro- and meso-scales of atmospheric boundary layer phenomena has received growing interest. One of the basic phenomena associated with air motion is its turbulence nature; therefore, many attempts have been made to produce sufficiently accurate turbulence models.

When asked about the applicability of individual turbulence models to specific situations, Professor Spalding, one of the founders of CFD, once replied:

'Nobody knows for sure'. This answer has become the well-known NOKFOS principle. Therefore, the suggestions made in this section on the use of CFD for similar built environment applications should be understood as a good starting point only, and the reader is strongly advised to keep up to date with progress in this rapidly developing research area.

In engineering practice, the most popular and frequently used two-equation turbulence model is the well-known k-ε model. However, the popularity of the k-ε turbulence model in engineering applications raises the question of whether it could be used for micro- and meso-scale modelling in the atmospheric boundary layer. Applying the standard k-ε turbulence model used in engineering applications to atmospheric boundary layer flows yields unrealistic results, since it is unable to reproduce the right level of turbulence in the weak shear layer away from the ground, where the turbulent viscosity is over-predicted (Detering and Etling, 1985). In order to overcome these misleading results, some modifications of the standard k-ε turbulence model have been proposed, modifying the set of the model's coefficients based on experimental evidence of the urban boundary layer (Rotach, 1995).

As noted previously, the additional modelled transport equations of the turbulence model have to be added to a set of governing equations. Fortunately, the structure of these equations has the same form as the general conservation Equation 1; therefore, the general variable Φ can be assigned to turbulence kinetic energy (k) and its dissipation rate (ε). Using these turbulence properties, it is possible to calculate turbulent parts of effective viscosity and diffusivity. Details of the modified two-equation turbulence model of urban boundary layer are presented in Table 23.2.

Boundary conditions

In order to solve the system of partial differential equations given above, the boundary conditions have to be applied to solid walls, inlets, outlets and open surfaces.

Solid walls. In urban areas, the airflow is highly turbulent, dominated by modifications of the atmospheric flow caused by the buildings, and the velocity of the airflow varies rapidly near walls. In order to solve this problem, avoiding the introduction of extremely fine grids, the conditions at building walls have to be connected to the dependent variables at the

Table 23.2 *Summarized two-equation k-ε turbulence model*

Turbulence model equations	Φ	Γ_Φ	S_Φ
Turbulence kinetic energy	k	$\nu + \nu_t/\sigma_k$	$2 + \nu_t\, S_{ij} S_{ij} - \varepsilon$
Turbulence dissipation rate	ε	$\nu + \nu_t/\sigma_\varepsilon$	$(\varepsilon/k)\,(C_{\varepsilon 1}\, 2\, \nu_t\, S_{ij} S_{ij} - C_{\varepsilon 2}\varepsilon)$

$\nu_t = C_\mu\ k^2/\varepsilon;\ S_{ij} = \tfrac{1}{2}\ (\partial U_i/\partial x_j + \partial U_j/\partial x_i)$

$C_\mu = 0.0324,\ \sigma_k = 1.0,\ \sigma_\varepsilon = 1.85,\ C_{\varepsilon 1} = 1.44,\ C_{\varepsilon 2} = 1.92$

$\nu_{ef} = \nu + \nu_t;\ D_{ef} = D + D_t;\ D_t = \nu_t/\sigma_Y;\ \sigma_y = 0.9$

near-wall grid cell. Therefore, the near-wall integration is bridged by empirical logarithmic wall functions. This technique is applied only to the first cell slab on the wall. As a result, the question relates to the heights of the first cells on the wall. The recommendation can be connected with the near-wall turbulence Reynolds number ($y^+ = C_\mu^{1/4} k^{1/2}\delta/\nu$), which should be less than 150. Here, δ is the normal distance of the central node of the first cell to the wall. If the suggested equilibrium logarithmic law wall function for smooth walls in the region of interest is selected, the numerical probe should not be placed in the first two cells (minimum) next to the wall due to the inherent inaccuracy of wall functions.

Inlets. At the inlet, the airflow entering the computational domain is usually defined as:

$$U(z_1) = U(z_2)\left(\frac{z_1}{z_2}\right)^\alpha \qquad (2)$$

where $U(z_1)$ is the wind speed calculated at height z_1, and $U(z_2)$ is the wind speed measured at height z_2. The power law exponent, α, depends upon the roughness of the surrounding built environment; but, in general, a value of 0.22 may be used for an urban area when the atmosphere is neutrally stratified. The turbulence intensity should be set to between 10 and 15 per cent.

Outlets and open surfaces. The outflow zero-gradients boundary conditions should be set up for all other boundaries of the computational domain (top, two side boundaries and the boundary behind the obstacles) in order to allow more natural outflow at all boundaries (all three components of velocity are calculated).

Defining the numerics

Discretization scheme

As we have seen, the equations governing the motion of airflow and concentration distribution in a built environment are partial differential equations. These equations have to be transformed into their algebraic analogues in the process called numerical discretization. There are three common discrete approximations – namely, finite difference, finite element and finite volume. The finite volume method is well established and used by major commercially available CFD codes (PHOENICS, Fluent, STAR-CD, etc.) and will be discussed in this section.

The most attractive feature of the control volume formulation is that it ensures global conservation of mass, momentum, heat and concentration independent of the grid size. This method divides the physical domain into discrete three-dimensional control volumes, so called cells, and then formally integrates the governing equations over them. While the diffusion process affects the distribution of a transported quantity, Φ, along its gradients in all directions, convection influences the transported property, Φ, only in the flow direction. This suggests that the same numerical solutions cannot be applied to solving both diffusion and convection problems. As the airflow in a complex built environment is convection dominated, care must be taken when discretizing the convection terms of the governing Equation 1.

Different linear and non-linear numerical schemes could be used for the discretization of convection terms. Linear methods, like the upwind method, tend to be highly diffusive, whereas non-linear methods tend to produce numerical oscillations near sharp gradients. Despite the diffusive behaviour of linear methods, some of them, such as the hybrid discretization scheme (Rosten and Spalding, 1987), can still be used in large-scale urban airflow calculations due to their bounded nature, stability and feasible convergence rates. However, this scheme (or any other first-order scheme) is recommended for initial calculations only. The modelling results would then be refined (if possible) using the higher-order discretization schemes.

Convergence criteria

The solution algorithm of the algebraic equations derived from the partial differential equations is iterative in its nature, meaning that successful progress towards a converged solution has to be measured using residual errors. As the solution progresses, the residuals should reduce. In urban airflow/quality applications, a limit on the residual error of 10^{-5} is recommended. Once all of the residuals fall below this limiting value, the calculations will be stopped.

Progress towards a converged solution can be additionally assessed by monitoring different variables, such as wind velocity and/or pollutant concentration, at specified locations within a computational domain. These so-called 'numerical probes' should be positioned in the area of interest (e.g. corresponding to the position of a monitoring probe in a real built environment). If values recorded by the numerical probe are constant for a number of consecutive iterations, and in agreement with experimental results, then the obtained solution has converged.

However, this might not always be the case (i.e. the solution shows poor convergence or no convergence at all). Progress towards a converged solution, in this case, could be assisted using various relaxation factors. As this step depends upon the experience of the user, it is very difficult to give specific recommendations and the user must learn by experience.

Grid independence

Flow calculations can be carried out using either a non-uniform orthogonal grid or body-fitted coordinates. In both cases, routine refinement tests have to confirm satisfactory grid independence. A grid has to provide the highest possible resolution near the ground and the roofs, and in the regions next to the windward and leeward sides of the street canyons. The grid spacing has to be varied gradually in order to avoid an increase in the truncation error and is limited by the maximum processing power of the available hardware. The change in any successive cell dimension should be kept at less than 30 per cent.

Visualizing airflow and pollutant dispersion

The two standard means of depicting airflow are velocity vectors and streamlines. Velocity vectors are arrows that point in the direction of airflow. They are also scaled and coloured so that the length and colour of the vector is proportional to the magnitude of the velocity. The vectors are usually drawn at each node. However, they can be thinned if needed or extra vectors interpolated if the nodes are too far apart to achieve good visualization; or – the opposite – they can be restricted to every second or third node. Streamlines are essentially a form of contour plot. They show lines of airflow; a fluid particle that is flowing through the computational domain will follow one of the streamlines. Generally speaking, streamlines are better than velocity vectors at representing the direction of fluid flow; but they tell little about how fast the fluid is moving. Details of airflow visualizing in both case studies are presented in Figures 23.5 and 23.6 for Glasgow and Copenhagen, respectively.

The two standard means of depicting air pollutant concentration are also contour lines and filled sub-areas within a specified range of values. The complexity of visualizing by this technique arises in the three-dimensional computational domain. One of the ways to overcome this problem is to present air pollutant concentration distribution separately by one specified plane, as is shown in Figures 23.7 and 23.8 for Glasgow and Copenhagen, respectively.

Model validation

As we have seen, CFD must be used cautiously to set up the model of airflow and/or pollutant (gaseous, passive) dispersion in a more complex built environment. When analysing the results of a simulation, the obtained airflow/pollutant distribution patterns have to appear qualitatively correct, and the paramount criterion is that the mass of fluid entering the domain should equal the mass leaving the domain (this is often calculated by software itself). If the airflow patterns obtained seem to be satisfactory, the next step is to compare modelling results against reduced-scale

Figure 23.5 *Glasgow case study: Airflow visualizing*

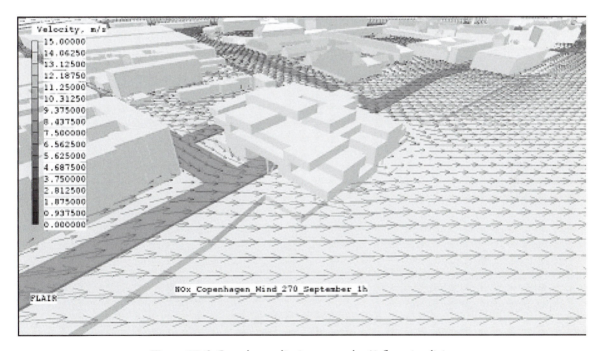

Figure 23.6 *Copenhagen district case study: Airflow visualizing*

(wind tunnel, water channel) or full-scale (field) experimental measurements. It is not always appropriate to simply compare CFD results with the measured data, obtained either from a wind tunnel or a real built environment (MacDonald et al, 1998; Liedtke et al, 1999; Schatzmann and Leitl, 2002) because they are physically different. Generally speaking, if all major similarity parameters were properly determined in the wind tunnel experiments, the measured results should be similar to that of the field test. However, they are not. The wind tunnel data are usually less intermittent because low-frequency

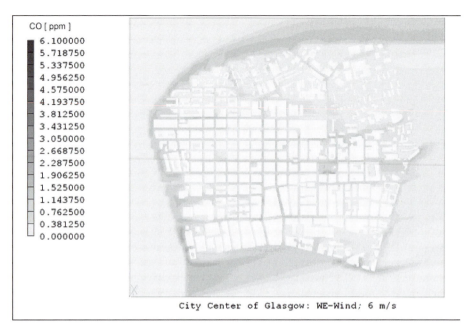

Figure 23.7 *Details of CO concentration distribution of central Glasgow case study*

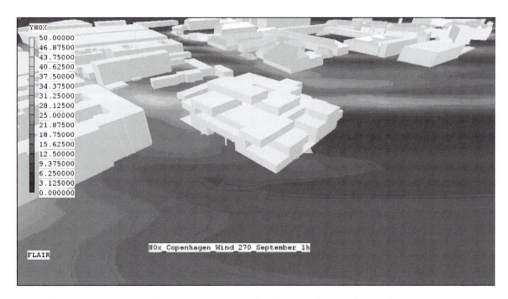

Figure 23.8 *Details of NO$_x$ concentration distribution of Copenhagen district case study*

wind direction variations present in the field are usually reduced in a ducted (wind tunnel) flow of finite width (Leitl and Schatzmann, 1998). As a consequence, the maximum averaged concentrations determined in the wind tunnel may be larger than those obtained in the field. Note, however, that other factors may also influence the degree of overestimation, such as the turbulence structure of the ambient flow or the source/receptor distance. As a result of the high intermittency, long averaging times are required in order to produce a meaningful mean value, and the most favourable averaging time of measurement periods is very difficult to determine since the atmospheric boundary conditions change frequently during a day. Usually, averaging times of 10, 15, 30 or 60 minutes are used. It is strongly recommended that the standard deviations should be attached to time-averaged concentrations determined in field situations, as this would be very valuable in validating the CFD model. Finally, the CFD model delivers a constant concentration value if stationary boundary conditions (wind speed, wind direction, wind profile and turbulence intensity) are used. Note that this value is not just time averaged, but also spatially averaged over the whole volume of a grid cell. Thus, model validation is certainly not straightforward, and it is essential that the fundamental differences be properly taken into account.

In conclusion, the physical nature of all wind tunnel experiments, field measurements and CFD modelling is significantly different and certain discrepancies in results may be expected. Furthermore, it is more important for a CFD model to be consistently accurate, to a certain level, across the whole of the computational domain rather than fit the measured data for certain specific locations only.

Airflow and pollution in buildings

The airflow pattern in a ventilated enclosure space such as rooms, offices, halls, theatres, etc. is mainly divided into two different concepts: mixing (dilution) ventilation and displacement. Mixing ventilation is characterized by the heating, ventilating and air-conditioning (HVAC) system, which provides fully mixed air in the whole enclosure space. In displacement ventilation, a stratified flow occurs through buoyancy-driven flow. The displacement ventilation concept may be perceived as an opportunity to improve both temperature and ventilation effectiveness. A typical displacement ventilation system for cooling supplies conditioned air from a low side (or floor) diffuser to the occupant's zone. The supply air temperature is lower than the operating temperature, causing vertical air movement through buoyancy force as the air is heated by the different heat sources (e.g. people, lighting, electrical machines, etc.). Heat sources create upward convective flows as thermal plumes. These plumes bring heat and contaminants from the surrounding occupied zone to the upper space of the enclosure space. Diffusers of return air are mainly located on the ceiling. A

stratification level exists where the airflow rate in the plumes equals the supply airflow rate. However, it is very difficult to obtain an ideal airflow pattern from the displacement ventilation concept when the interior geometry of different objects is complex.

Indoor air quality (IAQ) and thermal comfort (TC) are important factors in the design of high-quality buildings. Although there have been innovations in air conditioning and other forms of cooling or ventilation, which can be viewed as technological solutions to the problem of producing and maintaining energy efficient environmental conditions that are beneficial for human health, comfort and productivity, there is often a conflict between reducing energy consumption and creating comfortable and healthy buildings.

Theatres are the most complex of all auditorium structures environmentally. They usually have high heat loads, which are of a transient nature as audiences come and go, and which are also a result of lighting that changes from scene to scene, and they generally have full or nearly full occupancy. All of these factors place constraints on ventilation design, and if this is poor, it can lead to the deterioration of indoor air quality and thermal comfort. To analyse the level of indoor air quality and thermal comfort, as well as to identify where improvements could typically be made, a comprehensive post-occupancy evaluation study was carried out on a typical medium-sized mechanically ventilated theatre.

In this case study, the issues concerning the numerical aspects of the governing equations are the same as those given in the previous section and therefore have been omitted. The following sections highlight specifics related to CFD modelling in buildings.

Defining the geometry

Domain size

The theatre is roughly a rectangular box with a gallery over the rear and sides of the ground floor (or stalls), bounded by theatre hall external walls. The domain size is therefore constrained by the dimensions of the theatre hall. Around half of the ground floor area is given over to the stage. The auditorium is served by a displacement-type ventilation system. Fresh air is introduced via vortex diffusers, mounted at ground and gallery floor level directly under the seats, and boosted by a few circular diffusers in the ceiling of the gallery. Air is also supplied at low level from the side walls of the stage. Extract air is removed by rectangular outlet grilles set into the ceiling over the stalls and gallery level.

Object geometry

Basically, the geometric model of the building interior consists of three groups of objects:

1 the objects of the building interior;
2 HVAC objects; and
3 internal source objects.

Objects of the building interior

The objects of the building interior include internal walls, perforated plates, furniture, utility equipment, etc. Most of these objects are already defined in the building-oriented CFD codes. Apart from the geometric specifications of these objects, frequently there are options to specify object materials (metal, bricks, concrete, wood, plastics, etc.), plate roughness, heat release rate, etc. However, if there are highly irregular objects, such as the shape of the theatre gallery in this case study, a solid model of such an object can be created in any computer-assisted design (CAD) software and imported into CFD codes. An example is provided in Figure 23.9.

HVAC objects

Generally speaking, there are two groups of HVAC objects:

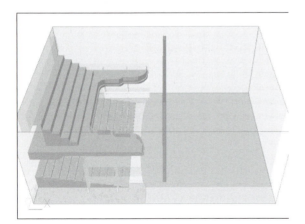

Figure 23.9 *Building interior objects of theatre case study*

1 those which belong to the HVAC system, such as HVAC casing assembly, rack-units, jet fans, etc.; and
2 HVAC air supply and exhaust units, such as different types of diffusers (round, vortex, quadric-rectangular, quadric-directional, displacement, etc.), grilles and nozzles.

Besides the shape and size of these objects, it is necessary to specify the air supply pressure, density, temperature, humidity and pollutant concentration, as well as to supply the volume flow rate. In the case of exhausting units, effective flow area and pressure drops have to be defined. The values of these parameters can be specified in two ways by using:

1 the design values; or
2 the measured values.

HVAC objects are actually specific inlet and outlet boundary conditions. In the case of the theatre, these specific boundary conditions are summarized in Tables 23.3 and 23.4, respectively, and are shown in Figure 23.10.

Internal source objects

Internal heat and mass sources are related to occupants and equipment. Occupants can be specified as shaped single seating or standing individuals, or by a rectangular box of a group of people. People are a source of heat (sensitive and latent) and mass (water vapour and CO_2 emissions). These parameters depend upon metabolic rates, external work activities, clothing, age, sex, etc., which can be found in various thermal comfort and indoor air-quality standards and guides (Tennekes and Lumley, 1972; CEN, 1998; ASHRAE, 2002). Equipment is also a source of heat (lighting, computers, domestic utilities, etc.). These internal sources can be specified as fixed values or time and space dependent as prescribed by manufacturers. In the case of the theatre, the internal sources are summarized in Table 23.5 and shown in Figure 23.11.

Numerical grid

The main dilemma in selecting grid generators is between structured or unstructured grids, and orthogonal or non-orthogonal grids. Each of these grids has its advantages and disadvantages related to

Table 23.3 *HVAC inlet boundary conditions of the theatre*

HVAC air supply system					
Supply diffusers	Number of units	Air temperature (°C)	Air humidity (kg/kg)	Volume airflow rate (m³/h)	CO_2 volume fraction (ppm)
Ground level					
Vortex	312	20	0.008654	15,650	350
Round	8	20	0.008654	1600	350
Gallery level					
Vortex	120	20	0.008654	6450	350
Mean stage level					
Grille	6	20	0.008654	6000	350

Table 23.4 *HVAC outlet boundary conditions of the theatre*

HVAC return air system				
Return diffusers	Dimension (mm)	Number of elements	Effective area (m²)	Pressure drop (Pa)
Gallery ceiling				
Grille	1025 × 525	10	0.269	2
Mean stage ceiling				
Grille	825 × 425	4	0.175	2

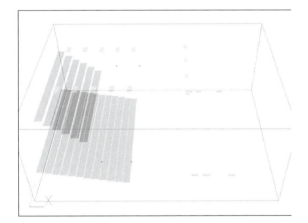

Figure 23.10 *HVAC objects of theatre case study*

grid complexity, solution convergence and time required computer modelling. Non-orthogonal and unstructured grids are very complex and sensitive to solution convergence; however, the complex shapes of internal objects, as well as complex building envelope walls, can be introduced without significant geometry approximation. On the other hand, orthogonal and structured grids are simpler; nevertheless, there is a need for some geometry approximation. In any case, the accuracy of the final solution should not depend upon the selected grid generator.

Computer resources should be used in a balanced manner, with care taken not to squander time by using excessively fine computational grids when the models of the physical processes are comparatively crude.

The opposite extreme should be equally avoided. Some turbulence models are rather elaborate and time consuming; these are sometimes (ill-advisedly) employed in circumstances in which (because many small solid objects are immersed within the fluid) the number of grid nodes between two adjacent solids is far too small for the velocity gradients to be computed with adequate accuracy. Therefore, there is a need for 'balanced accuracy' models and grid resolution, which, by avoiding extremes, make optimal use of limited computer resources. For example, one possible method is to generate an effective and simple grid using an orthogonal structured grid with the option to increase grid resolution in specific parcels through the technique of fine-grid embedding, because this provides sufficient ability to fit small-scale flow features without the computational overhead of fully unstructured grids.

Table 23.5 *Internal sources in the theatre*

| Occupants | | | | | Equipment |
Sensitive heat (W/person)	Latent heat (W/person)	Total number of individuals	Water vapour source (g/h/person)	CO_2 source above outdoor air (ppm_v)	Lighting (W)
Ground occupants					
60.5	55	332	55	450	0
Gallery occupants					
60.5	55	132	55	450	0
Mean stage					
60.5	55	4	55	450	19,600

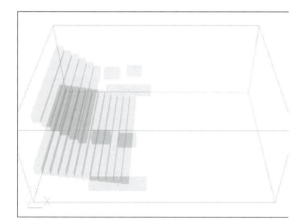

Figure 23.11 *Internal source objects of theatre case study*

Based on the previous discussion and a need for 'balanced accuracy' models, in the theatre case study, 140 × 153 × 75 cells were set up in the x, y and z directions, respectively.

Defining the physical model

Governing equations

A three-dimensional flow model should be set up using the incompressible steady-state Navier-Stokes equations, coupled with the continuity equation, and the energy, mass fraction of water vapour and mass fraction of carbon dioxide conservation equations (see Table 23.6). It should be noted that the additional source terms of buoyancy forces are added in momentum equations. The production of heat and mass from water vapour and carbon dioxide are specified as the boundary conditions.

Turbulence modelling

Apart from geometric complexity, the central physical phenomenon responsible for mixing processes is turbulence. Air motion and heat and mass transfer of related species such as water vapour and pollutant (e.g. CO_2) are turbulent in nature. The turbulence diffusivity, which causes rapid mixing and increased rates of

Table 23.6 *Summarized thermal comfort and indoor air-quality model of the theatre*

Governing equation	Φ	Γ_Φ	S_Φ
Continuity	1	0	0
Momentum	U_i	v_{ef}	$-\partial P/\partial x_i + \beta \varrho g_i (T - T_{ref})$
Energy	T	a_{ef}	0
Mass fraction of water vapour	X_{H_2O}	D_{ef, H_2O}	0
Mass fraction of carbon dioxide	X_{CO_2}	D_{ef, CO_2}	0

Table 23.7 *Summarized turbulence model used to determine thermal comfort and indoor air quality in the theatre*

Turbulence model equations	Φ	Γ_Φ	S_Φ
Turbulence kinetic energy	k	$v + v_t/\sigma_k$	$2\,v_t\,S_{ij}\,S_{ij} + B - \varepsilon$
Turbulence dissipation rate	ε	$v + v_t/\sigma_\varepsilon$	$(\varepsilon/k)\,(C_{\varepsilon 1}\,G - C_{\varepsilon 2}\,\varepsilon + C_{\varepsilon 3}\,B) + C_{\varepsilon 4}\,G^2/k$

$$v_t = C_\mu\,k^2/\varepsilon;\; G = 2\,v_t\,S_{ij}S_{ij};\; B = \left(v_t\,\beta\,g_i\,/\,\sigma_T\right)(\partial T\,/\,\partial x_i);\; S_{ij} = \tfrac{1}{2}\,(\partial U_i\,/\,\partial x_j + \partial U_j\,/\,\partial x_i)$$

$$C_\mu = 0.09,\; \sigma_k = 0.75,\; \sigma_\varepsilon = 1.15,\; C_{\varepsilon 1} = 1.15,\; C_{\varepsilon 2} = 1.9,\; C_{\varepsilon 3} = 1.44,\; C_{\varepsilon 4} = 0.25$$

$$v_{ef} = v + v_t;\; a_{ef} = a + a_T;\; D_{ef} = D + D_t;\; D_{t,H_2O} = v_t\,/\,\sigma_{H_2O};\; D_{t,CO_2} = v_t\,/\,\sigma_{CO_2}$$

$$\sigma_T = \sigma_{H_2O} = \sigma_{CO_2} = 0.9;\; \beta = 1\,/\,T_{ref}$$

momentum, heat and mass transfer are the single most important features as far as HVAC applications are concerned. In fact, the outstanding characteristic of turbulent motion is its ability to transport or mix momentum, kinetic energy and contaminants such as heat, moisture, pollutants and particles. The rates of transfer and mixing are several orders of magnitude greater than the rates due to molecular diffusion.

In this case, it is much better to apply one of the appropriately modified k-ε models since the extra sources due to buoyancy force fluctuations have to be added into k and ε equations. For example, the Chen-Kim modification of the standard two-equation k-ε turbulence model is frequently recommended. The modified k-ε model is summarized in Table 23.7.

Thermal comfort indices

One of the primary purposes of every environment is to provide a sensation of thermal comfort for its occupants. Thermal comfort is related to environmental parameters, such as air temperature, mean radiant temperature, air velocity and humidity, as well as personal factors, such as metabolic heat production, clothing, etc. Balancing the body's heat production with the body's heat loss at a comfortable skin and body core temperature defines a set of environmental and personal parameters that result in a neutral thermal sensation.

In practice, indoor environmental indices are rarely optimal for achieving thermal neutrality. In such cases, the thermal environment puts a strain on the thermo regulatory mechanisms of the body. The measure of this strain is provided by the PMV index, which is the predicted mean vote of a large group of people subjected to certain combinations of environmental parameters. The

Table 23.8 *Recommended categories for the design of mechanically heated and cooled buildings*

Category	Thermal state of the body as a whole	
	PPD (%)	PMV
I	< 6	$-0.2 < PMV < +0.2$
II	< 10	$-0.5 < PMV < +0.5$
III	< 15	$-0.7 < PMV < +0.7$
IV	> 15	$PMV < -0.7$, or $PMV > +0.7$

vote is represented on the seven-point thermal sensation scale, which ranges from –3 (cold) to +3 (hot). Dissatisfaction with thermal sensation is estimated using the predicted percentage of dissatisfied (PPD) index, which is calculated as a function of the PMV index. This is known as the PMV–PPD approach of thermal comfort quantification (ISO, 1994; ASHRAE, 2004, CIBSE, 2005). Recommended criteria for the thermal environment can be found in EN (2007). Examples of recommended categories for designing mechanically heated and cooled buildings are presented in Table 23.8.

Indoor air quality and ventilation rates

The most clearly defined area of indoor environmental health is occupational health, particularly since it pertains to workplace air contaminants. In general, in non-industrial environments there are many more contaminants that may contribute to problems; they are more difficult to identify; and they are usually present in much smaller concentrations. Different categories of indoor air quality exist that will influence the required ventilation rates. These categories can be expressed in different approaches as follows (EN, 2007):

- a combination of ventilation for people and building components;
- ventilation per square metre of floor area; and
- ventilation per person or according to required CO_2 level.

Through CFD simulations it is possible to obtain local distributions as well as averaged indoor levels of CO_2. The third approach is therefore the most appropriate to quantify indoor air-quality levels. Recommended CO_2 concentrations for the energy performance of building calculations and demand control are summarized in Table 23.9 (EN, 2007); the basic required ventilation rates for diluting emissions of bio-effluents arising from people EN (2004) are summarized in Table 23.10.

Table 23.9 *Recommended CO_2 concentrations above outdoor concentration*

Category	Corresponding CO_2 concentration above outdoor concentration (ppm)
I	350
II	500
III	800
IV	> 800

Table 23.10 *Basic required ventilation rates*

Category	Basic required ventilation rates	
	Expected percentage dissatisfied	Airflow per person (L/s/person)
I	15	10
II	20	7
III	30	
IV	> 30	< 4

Local air diluted through local ventilation rates can be assessed by the following simple formula:

$$\dot{V} = \frac{\dot{m}_{PROD}}{C_{IDA} - C_{SUP}} \qquad (3)$$

where:

- $\dot{V}$ = local volume flow rate of supply air (m³/s);
- $\dot{m}_{PROD}$ = local mass flow rate of bio-effluents production (mg/s);

- C_{IDA} = the allowed CO_2 mass concentration in the occupied space (mg/m³);
- C_{LOC} = the local CO_2 mass concentration in the occupied space (mg/m³).

In addition, when assessing local indoor air quality, the parameter known as the mean age of air (τ_{MAA}) is very useful. This quantity represents the time since air particle entry (e.g. related diffuser) at each point in the domain; it therefore provides a measure of air freshness, lower values being more favourable. It can be derived from its own transport equation, which is solved numerically, simultaneously with the set of governing equations (see Table 23.6) and turbulence transport equations (see Table 23.7):

$$U_j \frac{\partial \tau_{MAA}}{\partial x_j} - \frac{\partial}{\partial x_j}\left(\Gamma_{MAA} \frac{\partial \tau_{MAA}}{\partial x_j}\right) = 0 \qquad (4)$$

where Γ_{MAA} (m²/s) is the transport coefficient of τ_{MAA}.

In 'dead' zones, such as in recirculation areas, the time since entry will tend to be a large value as the air will be trapped there. These values should be treated as indicative rather than as exact. In regions where there is a reasonable exchange of air, the values will be correct.

Boundary conditions

The unique solution for the coupled partial differential equations of the set of governing equations (see Table 23.6) and turbulence transport equations (see Table 23.7) and Equation 4 can be obtained by specifying boundary conditions and related sources. Different classes of boundary conditions and related sources exist:

- inlet and outlet boundary conditions;
- internal heat and mass sources;
- wall boundary conditions.

Inlet and outlet boundary conditions, as well as internal heat and mass sources, are related to HVAC and internal objects. Details of these kind of boundary conditions were presented in the previous section.

Wall boundary conditions are specified by well-known logarithmic wall functions. However, the internal wall temperature has to be identified. Essentially, there are two possibilities in determining these temperatures: by calculation or by direct measurements. Calculations can be based on indoor and outdoor heat flux balances. It should be noted that radiation heat transfer must be taken into account.

For the theatre case study specifically, the surface temperatures of the ceiling, floor and internal walls were measured: 23.8°C, 22.8°C and 24.8°C, respectively, at the beginning of the monitoring period, staying almost constant during the performance.

Model validation

Rigorous CFD simulation requires implementing a sequence of stages: an object (a model); a discrete model and computational algorithm (computation); analysis of results; and comparison with practice. Two phases may be distinguished in mathematical modelling: choosing and validating a model. Therefore, any model that is used for future scenarios has to be validated by existing well-tested experimental or numerical cases. Obviously, the validation phase raises the question of which level of CFD accuracy has to be achieved. CFD accuracy is strongly dependent upon the designer's skill, experience and knowledge.

Accordingly, the increasing number and quality of numerical calculations of flow fields require more adequate and reliable data for examining CFD validation in order to decide whether the physics of the problem has been modelled correctly.

Generally speaking, there are no specific recommendations on acceptable CFD accuracy for built-environment CFD applications; however, Professor Spalding commented once that 'it is much better to be approximately right then absolutely wrong'. With this principle in mind, Figures 23.12 to 23.15 provide the distribution of a few parameters, such as airflow, air temperature, PMV and age, in the central vertical cross-section plane, clearly showing the basic principles of displacement ventilation.

In the theatre case study, indoor physical parameters were monitored before, during and after performance. These measured data have been used to validate CFD predictions. The numerical probe is located approximately at the same position as the location of measurement. It is the centre of the first exhaust diffuser, located on the theatre hall ceiling. The most appropriate way of comparing the experimental and numerical results is through the distribution of

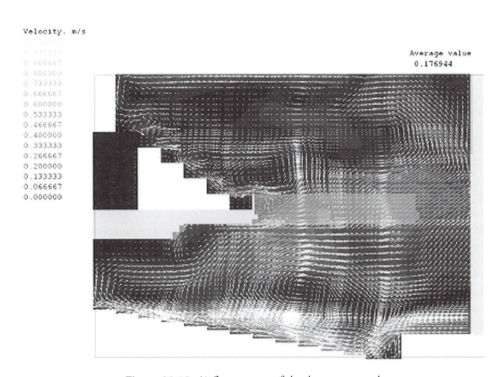

Figure 23.12 *Airflow pattern of the theatre case study*

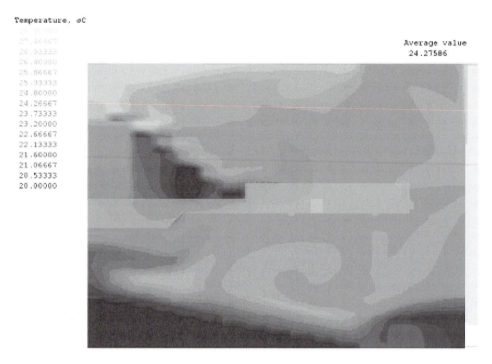

Figure 23.13 *Air temperature distribution of the theatre case study*

Figure 23.14 *PMV indices distribution of the theatre case study*

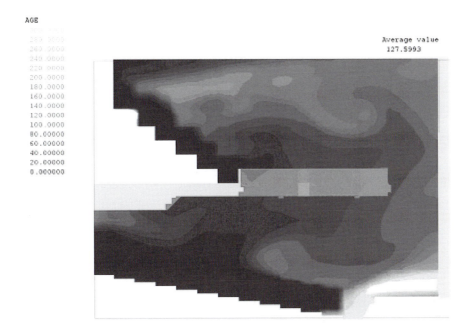

Figure 23.15 *Age distribution of the theatre case study*

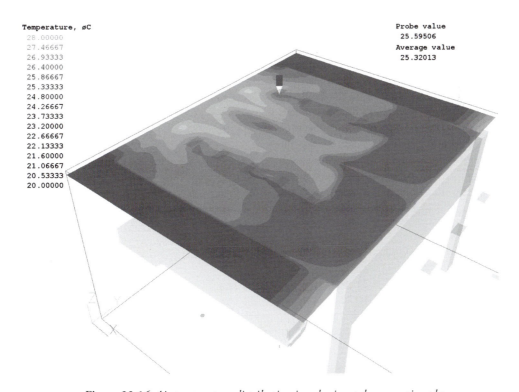

Figure 23.16 *Air temperature distribution in a horizontal cross-section plane*

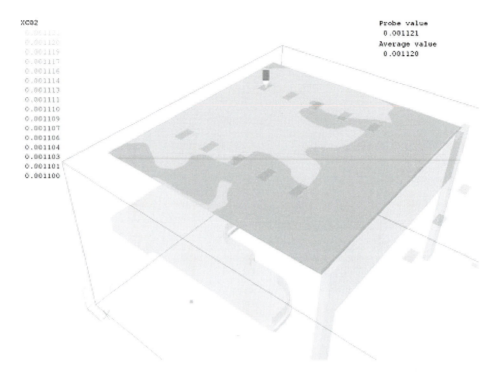

Figure 23.17 *CO$_2$ volume fraction distribution in a horizontal cross-section plane*

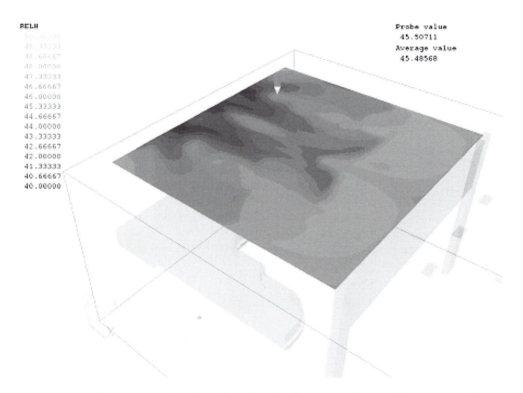

Figure 23.18 *Air relative humidity distribution in a horizontal cross-section plane*

Table 23.11 *Comparison of measured and numerical data*

Probe location (first exhaust diffuser)	Air temperature (°C)	CO_2 volume fraction (ppm)	Relative humidity (%)
Measured data	25.40	795.0	61.0
Numerical data	25.65	738.8	45.4
Relative error	1% over-predicted	7% under-predicted	25.6% under-predicted

related variables in the horizontal plane, located near the theatre ceiling. For example, the air temperature, CO_2 volume fraction and relative humidity distribution in the horizontal cross-section plane where measurement has been performed are shown in Figures 23.16 to 23.18, respectively. To the upper right of the figures, the probe value of the related variable is specified, as well as the average value in the shown plane. A comparison of measured and numerical data is summarized in Table 23.11.

Based on relative errors, it can be concluded that the air temperature and volume fraction of carbon dioxide are at the acceptable predicted level; however, the under-predicted level of relative humidity is too high. This should be expected since the partial pressure of water vapour and saturation pressure, as well as the mass fraction of water vapour are very sensitive to air pressure and density. Since the mixture of air, water vapour and carbon dioxide is assumed to be an ideal gas related to the air ideal gas law, it is reasonable to conclude that this is the main reason for the high level of under-predicted relative humidity.

Acknowledgements

This chapter is partially based on a postgraduate dissertation entitled *Comparison of the Thermal Comfort and Air Quality in Two Theatres with Different Mechanical Ventilation Systems*, submitted by Miroslava Kavgic (2006) in partial fulfilment of the requirements for the degree of MSc in Environmental Design and Engineering at The Bartlett, University College London.

References

ASHRAE (American Society of Heating, Refrigerating and Air-Conditioning Engineers) (2002) *ASHRAE Handbook*, ASHRAE, Atlanta, GA

ASHRAE (2004) *ASHRAE Standard 55-2004*, ASHRAE, Atlanta, GA

CEN (1998) *CEN CR 1752:1998 – Ventilation for Buildings: Design Criteria for the Indoor Environment*, CEN

CIBSE (Chartered Institution of Building Services Engineers) (2005) *CIBSE Guide A*, CIBSE, London

Detering, H. W. and Etling, D. (1985) 'Atmospheric boundary layer', *Boundary Layer Meteorology*, vol 33, pp113–133

EN (2004) *EN 13779:2004 – Ventilation for Non-Residential Buildings: Performance Requirements for Ventilation and Room-Conditioning Systems*, EN

EN (2007) *EN 15251:2007 – Indoor Environment Input Parameters for Design and Assessment of Energy Performance of Buildings Addressing Indoor Air Quality, Thermal Environment, Lighting and Acoustics*, EN

Hall, R. C. (1997) *Evaluation of Modelling Uncertainty (EMU Project Report): CFD Modelling of a Near Field Atmospheric Dispersion*, W. S. Atkins Consultants Ltd, UK

ISO (International Organization for Standardization) (1994) *ISO 7730-1994 – Moderate Thermal Environments: Determination of the PMV and PPD Indices and Specification of the Conditions for Thermal Comfort*, ISO

Kavgic, M. (2006) *Comparison of the Thermal Comfort and Air Quality in Two Theatres with Different Mechanical Ventilation Systems*, MSc thesis, The Bartlett, University College London, UK

Leitl, B. and Schatzmann, M. (1998) *Compilation of Experimental Data for Validation Purposes*, CEDVAL, Meteorology Institute, Hamburg University, Germany, www.mi-uni-hamburg.de/cedval

Liedtke, P., Leitl, B. and Schatzmann, M. (1999) 'Dispersion in a street canyon: Comparison of wind tunnel experiments with field measurements', in Borrel, P. M. (ed) *Proceedings of the EUROTRAC Symposium '98*, Southampton, 1999, pp806–810

MacDonald, R., Griffiths, R. and Hall, D. (1998) 'A comparison of results from scaled field and wind tunnel modelling of dispersion in arrays of obstacle', *Atmospheric Environment*, vol 32, pp3845–3862

Rosten, I. H. and Spalding B. D. (1987) *Phoenics Equations*, Cham, London

Rotach, M. W. (1995) 'Profiles of turbulence statistics in and above an urban street canyon', *Atmospheric Environment*, vol 29, no 13, pp1473–1486

Schatzmann, M. and Leitl, B. (2002) 'Validation and application of obstacle-resolving urban dispersion models', *Atmospheric Environment*, vol 36, pp4811–4821

Tennekes, H. and Lumley, J. L. (1972) *A First Course in Turbulence*, Massachusetts Institute of Technology, MA

OPERATIONAL PERFORMANCE OF BUILDINGS

Introduction: The Post-Occupancy Evaluation

Dejan Mumovic and Mat Santamouris

The post-occupancy evaluation (POE) of buildings is a vital component in the construction of complex built environments. In Part IV, Chapter 24 states that it is only from a sound understanding of how a building works, based on robust evidence, that the design process can be developed to produce the built environment that satisfies the needs of the occupants, owners and the larger environment in terms of reduced carbon emissions. The use of POE in benchmarking, appraising a building design and investigating a problem is discussed. In addition to energy use, sound technical methodologies for assessing internal environmental performance, such as thermal comfort, ventilation, lighting and noise, are proposed.

The key to predicted energy consumption lies in the way in which models are used to account for socio-technical factors (i.e. the interactions between the occupants and building and its services). In the process of evaluating various technical options, it is often the case that occupant behaviour is assumed to remain essentially constant (i.e. independent of the scenarios being tested). Alternatively, it may be implicitly understood that occupants will automatically shift from their existing patterns to a new behaviour appropriate to the proposed building specifications, such as ventilating buildings at the 'suitable' times. Chapter 25 explains that unexpected behaviour by occupants can degrade whole system performance and potentially overturn the savings expected by designers or policy-makers. Therefore, the aim of the chapter is to explore the socio-technical factors that operate in the built environment, specifically the relationship of occupant behaviour to energy use in the domestic sector, using three examples from the UK.

Last but not least, at the end of Part IV we have included three case studies:

1   *Chapter 26, Natural Ventilation of Auditoria: Three Case Studies.* This chapter presents guidance distilled from POE and experiences gained by the design teams involved to provide architects and engineers with some insight into the design of naturally ventilated auditoria. The selected case studies include the Queens Building at De Montfort University, the Contact Theatre in Manchester, which comprises two auditoria, and the Lichfield Garrick, also incorporating two auditoria.

2   *Chapter 27, A Naturally Ventilated Building in a City Centre.* The Frederick Lanchester Library in Coventry University is a deep-plan naturally ventilated building close to the city centre of Coventry. This chapter describes the design and operating strategies that are employed in the building and presents user comments, as well as results from monitoring studies, which include assessments of the building's thermal and energy-use performance. The building's likely performance in other UK cities is also discussed.

3   *Chapter 28, Impact of an Energy Refurbishment Programme in Chile: More than Energy Savings.* The analysis of housing energy performance in Chile has revealed how poorly designed dwellings could negatively feed the poverty cycle and how vulnerable to energy dependence such dwellings can be. This complex study highlights a number of issues of importance to the success of an energy refurbishment programme, including:

- the characterization of type, form, materials and heating systems of the housing stock;
- estimation of the current energy intensity of the housing stock;
- proposal of refurbishment goals;
- regional adjustment and optimized priorities;
- expected energy-intensity improvement, cost analysis and payback;

- expected social and private benefits;
- institutional requirements, human resources and financing schemes.

This chapter clearly highlights that sustainable building design and engineering requires an integrated approach to energy, health and the operational performance of buildings.

24

Post-Occupancy Evaluation of Buildings

John Palmer

Introduction

The post-occupancy evaluation (POE) of buildings is a vital component in the construction of complex built environments. It is only from a sound understanding, based on robust evidence, of how a building works in use that the design process can be developed to produce the built environment that satisfies the needs of the occupants, owners and the larger environment in terms of reduced carbon emissions. The history of POE goes back to the 1960s in the UK and was even designated as Part M of the Royal Institute of British Architects (RIBA) Plan of Work (Cooper, 2001).

A strict interpretation of POE requires that the building has been completed and occupied for a significant period – usually more than one year – and the evaluation relates directly to performance aspects of the building. However, a wider definition to include the design and construction process has been used (HEFCE, 2006).

Given that modern buildings are asked to respond to a wide range of performance demands – for example, optimized space provision, productivity, costs and energy – the designs have become more challenging for the architect. Hence, for more advanced and complex buildings, it is important to return to the building as constructed and used, as only by this method can we assess the success or failure of the design.

POEs can vary from a simple 'walk round' of the building through to detailed monitoring of minute-by-minute performance of a specific feature over a year of operation. This chapter will outline some of the issues that POE must address, as well as measurement and monitoring techniques that have been developed. It provides guidance on methods to adopt for the variety of issues that POEs can be used to appraise and shows the breadth of methods available. Pointers are given on how they can be used rather than the fine detail of any particular POE method, as these can be found elsewhere in the referenced material.

Post-occupancy evaluation tends to be used in the following situations:

* benchmarking;
* appraising a building design approach;
* investigating a problem.

The focus of a POE can be either on the physical aspects of the building and its performance, such as the energy or internal environmental conditions, or the responses of the occupants in relation to matters of productivity, health or amenity.

It is not particularly important which of these two possible motives is responsible for conducting the POE. The first question to be asked when considering a POE is 'why is this investigation being made?' Answering this question will set the scene for the choice and development of the appropriate approach. The methods used may be similar in these two cases; but the aims may be quite different. It is necessary to bear in mind that the occupant's satisfaction can be appraised as a result of some physical design feature of the building that is either working correctly or not; and the physical performance of the building may be a result of occupant usage. POEs have been used in all of these permutations. The following sections consider the main range of interests for POEs.

Benchmarking

Placing the performance of the building in the context of other similar buildings provides a useful pointer to how it is performing. This method has been widely employed in assessing energy performance, and a range of key performance indicators (KPIs) can be used to judge the performance. These may be absolute values of energy consumption; but most often they are based on a normalization procedure that makes for more reliable comparisons. For example, the energy use of a school may be expressed as the energy use per unit area of the school (kWh/m^2) or based on the number of pupils ($kWh/pupil$).

The KPIs tend to be based on the global performance of the building using the type of information which would be available from the utility meters used for billing. In some cases, it may be desirable to disaggregate the energy by end use. In the UK, Part L of the Building Regulations now require that this is possible in larger non-domestic buildings (BRECSU, undated). This benchmarking exercise is becoming more prevalent with the introduction of the Energy Performance of Buildings Directive (EPBD) (European Parliament and Council, 2003). This requires the energy performance of buildings to be measured and compared with benchmark figures.

Benchmarking can also be used for other aspects of the building such as the space allocation, productivity and costs of construction, which may be expressed, for example, as square metres per occupant or $£/m^2$. For the more subjective parameters, such as occupant satisfaction and amenity, it is more difficult to benchmark unless a consistent methodology and technique have been used.

Design approach

If the POE is being carried out to investigate the extent to which a design solution has been successful, it is necessary to have a clear definition of the design intention. There can be a range of design intentions and each of these can be expressed at different levels of design. The normal overarching design intentions relate to one or more of the following:

- low carbon/energy use;
- sustainability;

- high productivity;
- healthy occupants;
- low cost.

These overarching design intentions are typical of the aspirations of modern designs. However, which of these is relevant (and how these design intentions have been realized) needs to be specified before the POE begins.

Low-energy or sustainable designs may incorporate passive design features such as night-time cooling by natural ventilation or daylighting to displace electric lighting. It may be the purpose of the POE to evaluate the benefit of this design solution, precisely commission it or remedy a malfunctioning system. This is largely an exercise in building physics and, as such, will require a systematic measurement approach based on firm physical properties.

However, it is not only energy performance that may be the driving force behind the design. For example, a building may have been designed to produce a highly productive office facility. The actual design may have intended for this to come about by any of a number of solutions. It may be attention to the layout of the internal space in line with current ideas about working styles or it may be by narrow plan design giving good daylight and occupant control over natural ventilation. In this context we may use the term 'human factors' to address all of the variables that have an impact on the occupants and their experience of, and interaction with, the building – including 'occupant satisfaction'.

The term 'occupant satisfaction' as used here is taken to represent, in the broadest sense, the satisfaction of the people who inhabit the building. It can be the response of the day-to-day users of the building to how it affects their working experience and health; but it may also be the owner's expectation of productivity, cost, or the facility manager's ability to control building performance. Many of the recent approaches to POE have been directed towards the productivity and occupant satisfaction aspects of building performance (Jaunzens et al, 2002; BCO, 2007).

Productivity can be a function of a wide range of factors in the building. The physical aspects of the internal environment, such as thermal comfort, lighting and ventilation, can all have an impact on the energy performance as discussed above; but occupant satisfaction is also highly dependent upon these parameters. In addition to this, there are many other factors in the building that can affect productivity and occupant satisfaction.

It is the POE on the design aspect of the building that serves to provide the feedback to the design profession as to the success or failure of specific design solutions. Since POEs are not required as part of the normal duties of constructing a building, they are rarely carried out. Typically, in the UK, the POEs that have been conducted to establish the performance of a building, based on an interest in the design solution, have been funded as research projects (Post-Occupancy Review of Buildings and their Engineering, or PROBE, 1995–2002; Energy Performance Assessment, 1987–1992).

Investigating a problem

The most common POE is the evaluation that is carried out to determine why a building is not performing to the standard required. This can emanate either from energy or environmental requirements – too much energy or occupant dissatisfaction with internal conditions – or low productivity.

When productivity is the focus of the POE, the benefits to an organization can be great if the solution means less absence due to sickness or lower turnover of staff. The costs of a POE can be small compared with the long-term benefits of reducing these staff-related problems. The British Council for Offices' *Guide to Post-Occupancy Evaluation* (BCO, 2007) gives a number of case studies highlighting the benefits of POEs in offices.

Key issues that influence productivity, but are not related directly to environmental conditions, include personal control, responsiveness, building depth and work groups (Leaman and Bordass, 1998). However, factors such as layout of the space, aesthetics and privacy can also have an influence and confounding effect. Simply measuring the 'productivity' of the occupants of the office may not necessarily provide the answer to the underlying causes of the problem.

Physical performance evaluation

Providing the optimum internal environment for the occupants is one of the main purposes of the design of the building and its services. The combination of the building and its services should also do this with the least use of energy. This is a key area for POE as failure to achieve the design conditions will most likely affect the overall performance of the building and its occupants. For example, a novel daylighting scheme may well cause a problem for the occupants with regard to glare or gloom, and thus have consequences for energy consumption.

The key physical parameters of internal environmental performance that require study are normally:

- thermal comfort;
- ventilation;
- lighting;
- noise.

Thermal comfort

The thermal comfort of an occupant is dependent upon many variables (BSEN 7730, 1995). The most important parameters of the environment – other than the level of dress of the occupant – are temperature and the air movement. For most POEs, the key parameters to measure are either the dry air temperature or the mean radiant temperature and some aspect of air movement.

The most precise measure of thermal comfort is to use a 'thermal mannequin' (Tsuzuki et al, 1999). This simulates the human form and takes account of its own internal heat source and clothing levels. It is also fitted with the full range of sensors to determine thermal comfort. This is more of a specialist research method and is therefore not used in routine POE assessments.

Most commonly, the temperature of the environment is measured by a temperature sensor (platinum resistance) covered by a small (approximately 2.5cm diameter) black sphere. This will give a reasonable measure of the thermal experience of an occupant if the environment is reasonably uniform. If large radiant surfaces are near the occupants, then this asymmetric radiant field will distort the perception of thermal comfort. Placed in direct sunlight, this will give a very high reading.

The time interval for recording the temperature measured by this method does not need to be very short; a time interval of 15 minutes is quite adequate. Any requirement for a shorter interval probably implies that the issue is to do with draughts or transient radiation, rather than normal environmental temperature control.

Draughts are the second most important aspect of thermal comfort and this can be measured by a suitable anemometer. Air velocities over the range of 0.05m/s to 5m/s may be of interest; but these are at the lower end of the resolution for many anemometers as used in dealing with ventilation systems. The variability of draughts can also be an issue; therefore, in some cases, the 'turbulent intensity' of the air stream is also measured.

Ventilation

Measuring the ventilation rate in buildings is challenging. Unlike energy or occupant satisfaction, the rate of air exchange is difficult to measure directly. Even in mechanically ventilated buildings where the airflows in the ventilation system can be measured directly, the actual supply of external air will still depend upon other factors such as the air leakage of the building envelope and the ventilation system ductwork.

The most accurate methods of measuring fresh air rates involve some means of measuring a constituent of the internal air and noting its change with time. Ventilation studies in the past have used a range of tracer gases that are introduced into the building in a known way, and their concentration measured over time to provide the ventilation rate of external air not containing the tracer gas. AIVC (1988) describes in detail the alternative methods that may be used.

Unfortunately, many of the methods use gases such as sulphur hexafluoride or perfluorocarbons that may be unacceptable to occupants and are now even less tolerable as they have a high global warming potential. The simplest method is to use the carbon dioxide that is emitted into the building by the occupants. Using carbon dioxide from the occupants is safe and non-intrusive. If the building is empty, it can easily and safely be dosed with carbon dioxide, which provides even more control when determining ventilation rate.

A study in secondary schools in England used this technique extensively (Mumovic et al, in press), and in doing so carried out intervention studies to determine how changes in window use would influence the ventilation rate in the classrooms. Under normal circumstances in buildings, a carbon dioxide analyser measuring over the range of 0ppm to 5000ppm is required. The analyser should preferably have a sampling interval of approximately 5 minutes and an internal memory to store the results for later analysis.

The normal analysis is to determine the decay of the carbon dioxide under the ventilation conditions of interest. The rate of decay is then a function of the rate at which external air enters the space. It is possible to infer the ventilation rates of occupied spaces by the concentration of carbon dioxide measured directly; but this requires stable occupancy over a longer period of time to ensure that steady-state conditions have been reached.

Lighting

The way in which a building is lit can have significance for both energy use and occupant satisfaction and productivity. Large deep-plan offices must rely on electric lighting, and this has implications for energy use (not only for the lighting, but potentially for the air conditioning required to remove the heat it generates) and the visual comfort of the occupants. Providing daylight to the space can replace the electric lighting energy use; but in doing so, it must not produce glare or excessive solar gains.

A simple measure of the daylighting potential is to determine the 'daylight factor' in the building. The daylight factor is the ratio between the external global illuminance and the internal illuminance under a particular type of sky condition known as 'standard overcast'. Making a measurement of this is not difficult, but does require the simultaneous measurement of internal and external illuminance under a completely overcast sky – a condition that is less common than imagined. Measurements of illuminance over the range 100 to 20,000 lux would normally be adequate for determining the daylight factor. The measurement of the performance of a daylighting strategy is given in Heap et al (1988).

The most likely concerns from a POE of lighting will either be glare from incorrect provision of daylight or electric light, or excessive energy consumption of lights that are not sufficiently well controlled – either by the occupants or a lighting control system. Although glare is a subjective experience, measurements of the luminance environment may show if this is a likely cause.

Noise

The acoustic environment in a building can be a crucial factor in its success or failure. At the extreme end of the spectrum of performance requirements are spaces such as concert halls and recording studios that both have exacting standards. However, noise (simply defined here as an unwanted level of sound) is important in all building types. Schools are a particularly interesting case as they incorporate a wide range of activities within a single building. Teaching spaces, that have strict requirements of acoustic performance, can be in close proximity to gymnasia occupied with noisy activities. In the UK this has led to the publication of *Building Bulletin 93: Acoustic Design of Schools* (DES, 2003), which deals with the prevention and control of noise. It also deals with the fundamentals of acoustics and how it is measured in buildings, and provides a series of case studies.

If noise is considered a problem, it may be a consequence of a number of factors; but most likely it will be too much sound or a problem with reverberation time. The intensity of the noise is a function of the sound pressure level most commonly expressed as dBA, which is used to indicate the human response to a noise. The instruments for measuring sound are normally able to report a range of measures of the noise source, including the minimum and maximum and on a time-averaged basis.

The reverberation time in the space has an effect on the auditory experience, but is not easily measured without specialist equipment. In general, it may be that for acoustic problems it is advisable to take advice from an expert acoustician.

Energy performance

The energy performance of buildings is increasingly important as measures are taken to reduce their carbon footprint. The determination of the energy use of buildings has a long history and is, of course, used in billing for the energy utility. However, in terms of the POE of the performance, there are still a large number of variables to consider if a low-energy design intention is to be accurately assessed. The PROBE series of studies (Bordass and Leaman, 1995) adopted the *Energy Analysis and Reporting Method* (CIBSE, 1999).

Whichever method is used, it is clear that at least the occupancy of the building and the weather need to be taken into account. These are the two major determinants of the energy use of a building. The occupants need the building to be heated, ventilated and lit for their needs. If these are not fully measured, then the energy performance will not be fully appreciated. Likewise, if the weather prevailing at the time of the monitoring is not monitored in parallel, then the energy data may not reveal the answers that are required.

Simple analysis by means of degree days can go some way to describe the building performance; but it needs to be decided at the outset of the POE if this level of accuracy is adequate or if some specific design intention is being investigated. Measurement of energy use on a daily basis is a reasonable recording interval as it can be used to distinguish between weekdays and weekends. If some aspect of performance that changes during a day or night requires at least hourly measurements, it is better, in general, to measure at a shorter interval than to follow the minimum for analysis.

Disaggregating the energy into the end uses is often essential so that the performance of mechanical and electrical services can be determined. It may also be important to take account of incidental heat gains from lights and appliances: ignoring these can provide a significant underestimate of the heating energy required.

In larger buildings, there is usually a building or energy management system. It may be possible to use this for monitoring; but it is best to carry out a pilot study prior to committing to this in order to establish that it is possible to collect, store and allow for the retrieval of the necessary data.

In some cases, a very detailed evaluation of energy performance can be used to understand some of the underlying physical processes that are taking place. An example of this is the passive solar heating of dwellings in which a complex set of interactions exists between the available solar radiation and the way in which it replaces the need for heating energy. The Energy Performance Assessment Project (Hildon, 1986) and the 'Pstar: short-term energy monitoring methodology' (Palmer, et al, 1994) are examples of the techniques developed to investigate this aspect of building performance.

Human factors

'Human factors' may be the general term to describe all of the occupant-related issues that should be investigated in a POE. POEs can establish the performance of the building's productivity, health and amenity. It can highlight the perceptions of occupants regarding buildings performance, their understanding of control and the social interaction aspects of the building.

In response to this, a wide range of techniques has been developed to provide the correct level of information. The key to this is that the study should be rigorous and evidence based. Simple anecdotal information can be misleading and dangerous if due regard is not given to subjectivity or bias.

The BCO guide (BCO, 2007) gives as very good account of how to carry out a POE of occupant issues. It identifies the various techniques, such as questionnaires, structured interviews and focus groups, and how to deal with sampling and analysis.

Monitoring plan

Before beginning a POE, it is always advisable to have a clear and written aim so that the POE will be focused and effective. If there is no known and well-defined purpose to the POE, then it can become overly complex, ill defined and, finally, inconclusive. Each data point collected costs time, resources and money to acquire, and if the POE is not needed, it becomes a waste of time during the investigation, resulting in an excessive amount of data to process and analyse. In addition, it may not provide the correct answers.

The ideal approach is to prepare a monitoring plan that defines the purpose of the POE (i.e. what questions do we want to answer and what data will provide the answer?). The monitoring plan that comes from these direct questions will make the investigator consider how to answer them and what data are needed to provide a robust answer.

For example, if a new building has been designed to avoid overheating through the use of phase-change materials to provide thermal mass, the obvious question to answer would be: 'Does the thermal mass of the phase-change material reduce the level of overheating?' In asking this question, a POE can be developed in the form of a testable hypothesis; but, it

can be seen that even this simple question raises key methodological issues. For example, is the building to be compared with an identical building without the thermal mass; or, in the case of a single building, is the overheating to be measured before and after installing the material. If is it only possible to make measurements with the material already in place, then how do we determine the effect of the phase-change material on the overheating in isolation from other influences within the building? Detailed consideration of the analysis route will also help with deciding what factors should be measured.

An issue allied to this is the state that the building is in for the period of the POE. For example, is the POE carried out on the building 'as found' – possibly malfunctioning – or is it to be recommissioned to ensure that it is working at the optimum 'as-designed' condition. This is a key decision if the POE is studying the success of a design solution that may be condemned on the basis of a malfunctioning system. For very complex situations, this may warrant some modelling of the design to establish what factors are significant. The monitoring plan should also deal with the need for intervention studies.

Decisions will need to be made on the type of data collection method to be used and if it is to be locally based or remotely accessible by interrogation over the internet. The cost and scale of the project will determine some of these options; but data integrity and security are issues and the danger of data loss is important. Regular checking of data is required to ensure that the full data set needed for analysis is available at the end of the project. To this end, it is worthwhile retaining, and frequently updating, a 'data map' showing data availability over the monitoring period.

This applies to occupant issues as well as physical parameters. Changes in occupancy during a monitoring period can have a major effect on the performance that is being evaluated, and if this is not monitored during the project, the conclusions may be in error.

Example: Energy performance assessments

The Energy Performance Assessment (EPA) Project was a POE project that developed a rigorous methodology for monitoring and evaluating the performance of passive solar buildings, taking account of all physical aspects of building performance, such as energy consumption, solar performance, daylighting, natural ventilation, occupancy issues, thermal comfort, amenity, satisfaction, control and building cost (Hildon, 1986). For houses, pilot trials of possible methods for determining solar performance were backed up with dynamic thermal modelling of proposed methods.

The EPA Project used the standardized methodological approach in both domestic and non-domestic buildings to assess more than 30 buildings in the UK. The starting point comprised interviews with the designers to learn the design intent, and from this followed the monitoring plan in order to test the efficacy of the design.

The main aim regarding houses was to determine the 'passive solar-displaced space heating', a term

defined during the development of the project to judge the solar performance of a house. The analysis route for this can be seen in Figures 24.1 and 24.2, which show the need to measure variables at hourly intervals in order to provide the resolution required for the analysis, and how these were taken forward to provide an annual estimate of performance. Monitoring for a full year was seen as the minimum required in this case because of the whole-year response of a passive solar design in terms of displaced space heating in the heating season, and overheating in the summer and mid-season.

For non-domestic buildings, the design intention was less to do with solar-displaced space heating; instead, it was more frequently to do with a combination of daylighting and natural ventilation, with some element of solar heating. For these

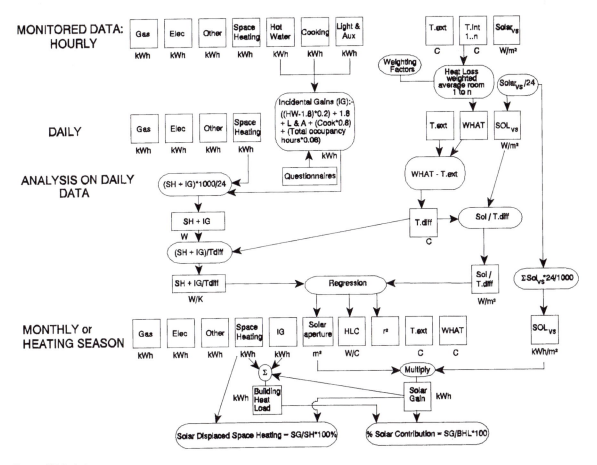

Source: EPA Project

Figure 24.1 *EPA analysis of hourly data*

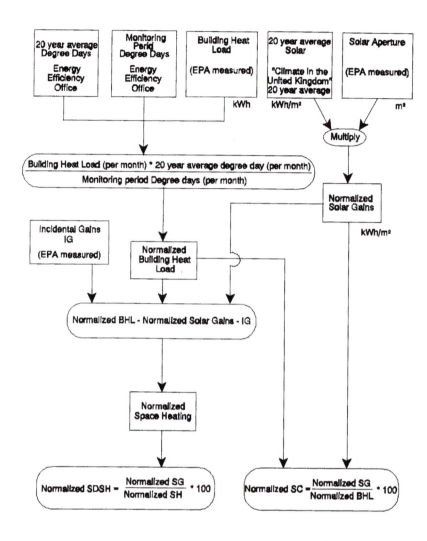

NORMALIZATION OF MONTHLY DATA

Figure 24.2 *EPA normalization of monthly data*

buildings, it was even more important to learn how the designer intended the building to operate.

However, it was acknowledged that passive solar design may cost more and possibly provide less thermal comfort (due to overheating) than a conventional house. Therefore, the POE evaluation also developed a series of questionnaires and occupant interviews to determine the occupants' satisfaction with the environment and their ability to control it.

Questionnaires were devised for both housing and the non-domestic buildings, to be administered on a monthly basis in order to understand the dynamics of

the occupants' response to the solar radiation and internal conditions. A least one interview was carried out with the occupants. The information from these questionnaires and interviews was collated with the physical measurements to establish a high level of understanding of the occupants' satisfaction and the conditions provided by the design.

For the dwellings, the costing of the house was carried out by the consultant QSs, who also worked out the over-costs due to the solar design. For the non-domestic buildings, the costs were based on tenders, but were normalized for location and time.

References

AIVC (1988) *Technical Note 24: Measurement Techniques Workshop Proceedings and Bibliography*, June 1988, AIVC, Coventry

BCO (British Council for Offices) (2007) *Guide to Post-Occupancy Evaluation*, BCO, London

Bordass, W. and Leaman, A. (1995) 'Probe 1 Tanfield House', *Building Services Journal*, September, pp38–41

BRECSU (undated) *General Information Leaflet 65: Metering Energy Use in Non-Domestic Buildings*, BRECSU

BSEN 7730 (1995) *Moderate Thermal Environments: Determination of the PMV and PPD Indices and Specification of the Conditions for Thermal Comfort*, BSEN

CIBSE (Chartered Institution of Building Services Engineers) (1991) *Application Manual 5: Energy Audits and Surveys*, CIBSE London

CIBSE (1999) *CIBSE Technical Manual 22: Energy Analysis and Reporting Method*, CIBSE, London

Cooper, I. (2001) 'Post-occupancy evaluation: Where are you?', *Building Research and Information*, vol 29, no 2, pp158–163

DES (Department for Education and Skills) (2003) *Building Bulletin 93: Acoustic Design of Schools*, TSO, London

Energy Performance Assessment Project (1987–1993), Sponsored by the Energy Technology Support Unit on behalf of the UK Department of Energy

European Parliament and Council Directive 2002/91/EC (2003) *Energy Performance of Buildings: Official Journal*, 4 January 2003

Heap, L. J., Palmer, J. and Hildon, A. (1988) 'Redistributed daylight: A performance assessment', CIBSE National Lighting Conference, Cambridge

HEFCE (2006) *Guide to Post Occupancy Evaluation*, www.aude.ac.uk

Hildon, A. (1986) 'Energy performance assessments', The Efficient Use of Energy in Buildings: Second UK ISES Conference, Cranfield

Jaunzens, D., Bordass, W. and Davies, H. (2002) 'More POE means better buildings', *Building Services Journal*, February, p48

Leaman, A. and Bordass, B. (1998) 'Probe 15: Productivity the killer variables', *Building Services Journal*, June

Mumovic, D., Palmer, J., Davies, O. M., Ridley, I., Oreszczyn, T., Judd, C., Medina, H. A., Pilmoor, G., Pearson, C., Critchlow, R. and Way, P. (in press) 'Winter indoor air quality, thermal comfort and acoustic performance of newly built schools in England', *Building and Environment*

Palmer, J., Pane, W., Shaw, P. and Burch, J. (1994) 'Energy prediction from short term monitoring: The PStar Method', Building Environmental Performance Conference, York

Tsuzuki, K., Arens, E., Bauman, F. and Wyon, D. (1999) 'Individual thermal comfort control with desk-mounted and floor-mounted task/ambient conditioning (TAC) systems', in *Proceedings of the Indoor Air Conference 1999*, Edinburgh, Scotland

25

Occupant Behaviour and Energy Use

Alex Summerfield, Tadj Oreszczyn, Ayub Pathan and Sung Hong

Introduction

Over recent years governments have refocused on energy efficiency in the built environment as a having an important role in meeting their commitments to avoid serious climate change, with the UK aiming to reduce its overall carbon emissions by 60 per cent from their 1990 levels by 2050 (DTI, 2007). There is also heightened interest both in ensuring that such policy measures work and that the predictions of resultant energy saving are accurate. An implicit assumption exists that improved efficiency, such as in appliances or heating systems, will lead to lower overall energy consumption. However, it has also long been recognized that a 'rebound effect' occurs, where some of the expected energy savings do not eventuate due to benefits being mitigated by changes in occupant behaviour. It may even lead to an overall increase in energy consumption by stimulating new demands (Saunders, 1992). However, the extent and full implications of this phenomenon remain a matter of ongoing debate (Herring and Roy, 2007).

The rebound effect has been delineated in terms of three categories (Dimitropoulos and Sorrell, 2006), normally framed in economic terms, but here interpreted in terms of occupant behaviour:

1 *Direct effects.* Occupants take the savings from energy efficiency improvements as an opportunity to use the system more. In dwellings, this can occur when occupants 'take back' the benefits of energy savings in a home due to a more efficient heating system as improved thermal comfort (say, higher room temperatures), rather than as lower heating costs.

- *Indirect effects.* If occupants find that energy costs associated with operating their home are lower, then more income is available to them to spend on other products and services, each of which involves energy in their production and delivery, such as new appliances or overseas holidays.
- *Economy-wide effects.* These reflect broad technological innovations or social changes that lead to long-term changes in the economy – for instance, broadband communications that enable occupants to work from home (and imply reduced energy required for commuting), but alter dwelling occupancy patterns and heating demands, or where innovation and efficiency lead to greater affordability of appliances that substitute energy for occupant labour, such as washing machines and dishwashers.

From an historical perspective, one of the best illustrations is given in the study by Fouquet and Pearson (2006), who examined the per capita usage of lighting in the UK spanning several centuries. Each shift in lighting technology from candles, to oil and gas lamps, and then to modern electrical lighting, represents a significant improvement in efficiency. But each has also been accompanied by a dramatic rise in lighting usage. So while the lighting efficacy – that is, the lumens per watt – of modern lighting is more than 700 times that of 18th-century oil lamps, consumption in lumens per capita has increased more than 6000 fold. Such demand is driven not only by the reduced cost of lighting as the efficiency improves and our relative wealth increases over time, but also highlights the great value that humans place on the amenity and aesthetics of lighting.

These effects are embodied in what has been termed the *Khazzoom-Brookes postulate* (Saunders, 1992), which takes a top-down approach (and the opposite of the conventional 'bottom-up' approach of researchers in the built environment) to suggest that while energy efficiency improvements might be justified at the micro-level, they lead to higher levels of energy consumption at the macro-level than in the absence of such improvements. While this is discussed elsewhere, there is ongoing debate as to the extent that this holds and its implications. In spite of manifold efficiency improvements, nations generally have struggled to reduce in absolute terms their overall energy usage alongside economic growth (Herring and Roy, 2007). Moreover, it has been argued that people have an apparently innate ability to find new ways of consuming energy (Oreszczyn, 2004).

Yet, this does not undermine the worthwhile objective of greater energy efficiency since it is also important to be mindful that the motivation behind all of this is not energy *per se*, but the environmental costs and carbon emissions associated with energy generation and distribution. Occupants can choose to take the benefits of using lower heating costs: they may further their consumption in carbon-intensive activities (such as a flight for a weekend holiday overseas), or they may shift to activities that have low or even negative carbon emissions, such as investing in renewable or low-carbon energy supplies. Such choices by households are, in turn, framed by wider government policies and priorities, and efficient dwellings support such policies. The main point is that energy efficiency in buildings and energy use by occupants is not an isolated relationship, but is set in a much broader social and economic context.

The issues are highlighted for building researchers and designers when using technical models to predict energy consumption for an individual building, or at the level of how the entire domestic building stock performs. These types of analysis have become an everyday part of professional activity, particularly with sophisticated computer simulations that provide a convenient and efficient tool for comparing the alternatives. These generate abundant quantitative data on building performance and even seductive graphics that convey confidence, whereas outcomes are uncertain and predictions seldom, if ever, verified over the long term. Indeed, the closer one examines how energy performance of the built environment is predicted, the more it seems entirely contingent upon occupant behaviour remaining as expected.

The key lies in the way in which models are used to account for these socio-technical factors – that is, the interactions between the occupants and building and its services. In the process of evaluating various options, it is often the case that occupant behaviour is assumed to remain essentially constant (i.e. independent of the scenarios being tested). Alternatively, it may be implicitly understood that occupants will automatically shift from their existing patterns to a new behaviour appropriate to the proposed building specifications, such as ventilating buildings at the 'suitable' times. For instance, with the installation of a new central heating system, it might reasonably be expected that occupants will operate this rather than the less efficient heating methods that they previously used. It will be seen that just such unexpected behaviour by occupants can degrade whole system performance and potentially overturn the savings expected by designers or policy-makers.

The aim of this chapter is to explore the socio-technical factors that operate in the built environment, specifically the relationship of occupant behaviour to energy use in the domestic sector, using three examples from the UK. The first is the Warm Front project, a government-funded energy efficiency scheme for vulnerable households that involved building improvements, such as cavity wall and loft insulation and, in some cases, gas central heating systems. Second, we examine the impact of conservatories – the typically prefabricated and highly glazed addition to existing homes – that was originally conceived of as a passive solar design retrofit. Last, we return to the 'low-energy' homes of Milton Keynes, previously described in Part II, Chapter 9 on environmental monitoring, to examine the impact of some of the many social and technological changes in the domestic setting that have occurred over time. This by no means provides an exhaustive list of behavioural effects, but aims to create an appreciation of the range of complex interactions that can occur in the real built environment, and beyond the often optimistic and overly simplified assumptions that underlie simulation models. The discussion section encapsulates the socio-technical factors at work in a schematic form to assist designers and researchers with their analysis and prediction of energy performance.

Examples from the UK domestic sector

Warm Front

The main aim of the Warm Front scheme is to alleviate fuel poverty by providing grants for the installation of cavity wall insulation, loft insulation, draught proofing and, for some particularly vulnerable households, the option of gas wall convector heaters or a gas central heating system (Hong et al, 2006; Wilkinson et al, 2006). In the UK a household is deemed to be 'fuel poor' if more than 10 per cent of total household income needs to be spent on fuel use to heat the home to an adequate standard of warmth, defined as 21°C in the main living room and 18°C in other occupied rooms during daytime hours (DTI, 2001). This is not the same as the amount that the household spends on fuel since many will reduce heating costs to a lower fraction by keeping their homes at a temperature much lower than is typical in the UK. This is precisely the behaviour that the scheme aims to address, since occupants are at increased risks of mortality and morbidity in dwellings with inadequate heating (Wilkinson et al, 2001).

Analysis of more than 1300 dwellings in the Warm Front scheme indicated that energy efficiency improvements led to an increase of both living room and bedroom temperatures, which was likely to have substantial benefits for the occupants in terms of thermal comfort and well-being. Under standardized external conditions of 5°C, the daytime living room temperatures were 1.6°C higher (19.1°C) and night-time bedroom temperatures were 2.8°C higher (17.1°C) in dwellings that received both heating and insulation measures compared with temperatures in dwellings prior to this intervention. Using the benefit of efficiency measures for improved comfort rather than lower fuel costs is known as the 'take-back' factor (Wilkinson et al, 2006). Temperatures were influenced by property characteristics, including age, construction and thermal efficiency, and also by the number of occupants and the age of the head of household. An improved thermal performance of the dwelling due to insulation and draught-stripping will itself reduce the decline in temperature when the heating system is off, which will tend to produce higher average temperatures. The choice of a warmer home, therefore, is far easier for occupants in such dwellings, especially

if the capacity of the heating system and its control also facilitate this, and, hence, is likely to lead to a significant increase in average temperatures. For Warm Front, the 'take-back' factor was both an expected and desired outcome, with subsequent results also showing a 'take-off' factor in some cases, where occupants were wearing less clothing in response to the higher internal temperatures (Hong et al, in press). This is an example of the interaction or bidirectional relationship between internal conditions and occupant behaviour.

In terms of energy savings, the findings indicated that cavity wall and loft insulation reduced space heating fuel consumption by 10 per cent in centrally heated properties and by 17 per cent in non-centrally heated properties. As a result, occupants were making use of a combination of energy savings and comfort benefits. The gas central heating system, although theoretically more efficient than the systems that it replaced, was not found to reduce fuel consumption even after adjusting for increased internal temperature. Again, there are a number of possible mechanisms at work to explain this. Analysis of pressure-testing data showed that the installation of the central heating system increased air infiltration rates, probably due to pipework penetrating the building fabric (Hong et al, 2004). But from a socio-technical perspective, having central heating was also associated with higher rates of window opening by occupants (3.3 days/week compared with 2.9 days/week for those without central heating). Thus, overheating or stuffiness that resulted from the central heating operation may have prompted occupants to increase the ventilation rate (Hong et al, 2006). Once a window is open in one room, it may easily be forgotten and left open while the occupant is in another, and the central heating – according to how the controls are set – will continue to heat the whole dwelling.

Another issue is when the expected behavioural change does not occur. Figure 25.1 compares performance based on predictions from technical modelling with monitored fuel consumption, and shows that the combination of insulation and central heating should have produced a decline of more the 60 per cent, whereas no significant difference due to central heating was identified in the data. One of the reasons for this was that there may not have been the expected efficiency gains from central heating (e.g. via the use of condensing boilers), perhaps due to the continued use of fixed-gas fires that remained in some

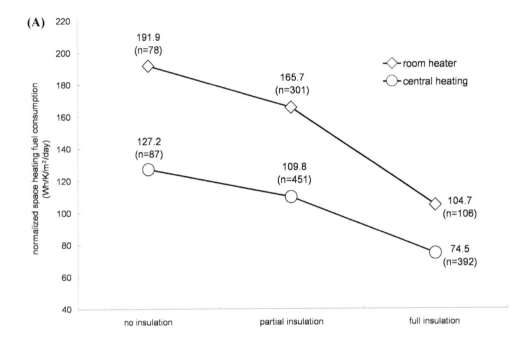

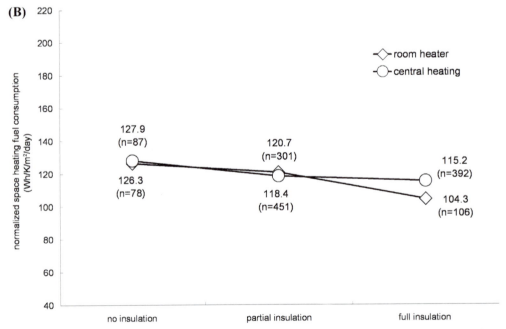

Figure 25.1 *Normalized space heating fuel consumption (Wh/K/m²/day) in Warm Front dwellings disaggregated by primary heating system and insulation level, according to (a) modelled results and (b) results from monitoring*

dwellings after the central heating refurbishment. In other words, although there is no direct data, some occupants, perhaps the more elderly, may have preferred to carry on heating their home in the way in which they were accustomed. Results from another study illustrates how the interaction between this behaviour and a central heating system may lead to a greater decline in overall system performance than might be anticipated (Bell and Lowe, 2000). By operating the gas fire in the same room as the thermostat control, the high temperatures would prevent the central heating system from operating. Thus, the much lower efficiencies from operating the gas fire will tend to prevail in the overall system performance, compared with the contribution from the more efficient gas boiler of the central heating system. This serves to illustrate how large variations in behaviour may occur in specific types of occupants, possibly according to their socio-demographic background (age, income, health, family structure) and lifestyle factors.

Trends in conservatory use

Historically, conservatories in the UK were the preserve of wealthy households and were used as a highly glazed space to protect plants over the winter months; but by the 1920s, they had become unpopular. Interest was reawakened during the 1970 to 1980s, when conservatories were considered from the perspective of being buffer spaces and one of the main options for passive solar retrofit. For the UK, research at that time estimated that each installation would provide 900 to 1000kWh/year of annual energy savings, with an additional 150kWh/year if the conservatories were double glazed (NBA Tectonics, 1992; ETSU, 1998). The identified potential energy savings were initially seen as due to the conservatory having the effect of additional insulation for the enclosed walls and windows, and also occurred as a result of supplying pre-heated ventilation air to the house via a fanned or natural convective loop (though subsequent analysis indicated that there were few occasions when this was worthwhile).

Although it was recognized that these savings would be heavily influenced by occupant behaviour, little research was conducted on exactly how conservatories were being utilized until a questionnaire survey of more than 1800 conservatory owners was conducted in 1991 (Oreszczyn, 1993). This revealed that two out of three conservatories were heated directly, and of the remainder, 72 per cent were heated indirectly by not having a door (open plan) or leaving the door open to the rest of the house. Thus, over 90 per cent of conservatories were heated by some means, with over one third of these heated regularly. Over half (51 per cent) of the directly heated conservatories had thermostats, with one quarter (27 per cent) of these set at 10°C or below – probably for frost protection of plants. Although there was uncertainty about the timing in which doors were left open relative to the timing for heating, it was clear that most conservatories were regarded as either an extension (by leaving the doors open) or integral (by not having doors) to the house.

Over the intervening years, this comparatively easy way of use a prefabricated unit to add floor area to a dwelling has proven to be immensely popular. By 2003, more than 200,000 new conservatories were being built annually in the UK, with an estimated 15 per cent of dwellings having a conservatory (*The Economist*, 2004). So, in 2004 to 2005, parts of the 1991 survey were repeated for more than 300 conservatory owners in London in order to see what changes in occupant usage had occurred (Pathan et al, in press).

It was found that more than 90 per cent of respondents now reported using their conservatory all year (up by almost 20 per cent on the 1991 figure). More than one third (38 per cent, up from 5 per cent in 1991) had no door between the conservatory and the rest of the house (see Figure 25.2). Nearly three out of four occupants heated their conservatory on a daily basis, with the majority of respondents heating it more than seven hours a day in winter (see Figure 25.3) and there has been a related shift to the use of central heating (69 per cent in 2004). When the analysis was repeated and the 1991 survey limited to those from a comparable region (southern England), these results remained essentially the same.

The issue lies in the potential impact that this occupant behaviour has on the overall energy performance of the dwelling by, for instance, using central heating to heat conservatories. This is due to the relatively poor thermal performance of the conservatory compared to other external walls – hence, greatly increasing the proportion of exposed area with relatively

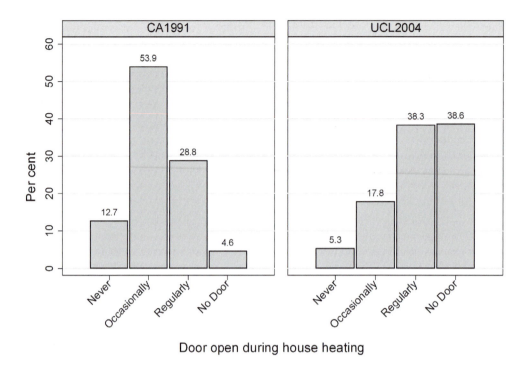

Figure 25.2 *A comparison of door openings (and the prevalence of conservatories without a door) across the two surveys*

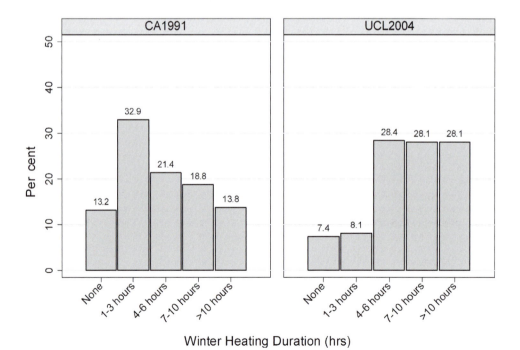

Figure 25.3 *A comparison of winter heating duration across the two surveys*

high U values. The policy fix, as suggested by technical models, might be to require conservatories to be double glazed with about a 30 per cent lower specific heat loss. Unfortunately, this again does not allow for adaptations in occupant behaviour: as further results from the 1991 survey show, double-glazed conservatories were heated for almost double the length of time compared to the single-glazed counterparts. It may be that while single-glazed conservatories tended to be too cold to heat in winter, the double-glazed conservatories provided the considerable amenity value of a habitable space all through the heating season that justified the increase in heating costs. By 2004, almost all conservatories were double glazed and used in winter. Since conservatories are perceived as integral to the rest of the house, so their function has changed and shifted from being just a passive solar space – even in the initial survey, almost two-thirds (64 per cent) used it after dark.

While building regulations in the UK have been amended so that open-plan conservatories must meet the general thermal performance standards that apply to normal building extensions, it is still the case in 2008 that conservatories with doors to the house and a floor area of less than 30m² are exempt. Doors may simply be left open or even removed after the final inspection. In the end, this must be taken as a cautionary tale of how an initial intention of improving the energy performance of the domestic sector with passive solar design has not only failed to provide the expected benefits from passive solar retrofit, but for many dwellings may have proven to be completely counterproductive in terms of energy efficiency.

Milton Keynes low-energy homes

A key objective with energy efficient design is not just the performance obtained at construction, but the enduring gains in efficiency that last over the life of the building. As was described in Part II, Chapter 9, the MK0 study of 'low-energy' dwellings in Milton Keynes has provided an invaluable opportunity to investigate changes in energy usage over 16 years. Out of a project that involved more than 120 dwellings, a sub-sample of 29 dwellings was monitored for both hourly energy and temperature from 1989 to 1991. By current standards, these homes may not be considered as being particularly efficient; but they are referred to as being 'low energy' since they were constructed to higher standards of energy performance than required by building regulations at that time. They incorporated features, such as increased floor and wall insulation, double-glazing and condensing boilers, to the extent that they broadly complied with building standards of a decade later (Edwards, 1990). In the follow-up study of 2005 to 2006, referred to as MK1, temperature monitoring and energy meter readings were undertaken in 14 of the gas centrally heated homes from the original sub-sample (Summerfield et al, 2007).

The socio-demographic changes that have occurred over the 15 years are shown in Table 25.1. One of the most striking changes has been the decline in the number of children (reflective of broader changes that have taken place in the demographics of the UK population), which is likely to have resulted in large differences in the lifestyle of the occupants. Second, there has been a marked increase in the number of appliances (of which we have only limited information

Table 25.1 *Household characteristics of the MK0 (1990) and MK1 (2005)*

Household characteristics (per dwelling)	MK0 (SD)	MK1 (SD)
Number of occupants	2.7 (0.1)	2.5 (0.1)
Number of children (<16yrs)	1.0 (0.1)	0.30 (0.05)
Annual household income (in thousand UK£)	–	53 (25)
Floor area (m²)	104 (3)	109 (4)
Bedrooms	3.1	3.2
Tumble dryers	0.1	0.5
Dishwashers	0.1	0.5
Televisions	1.2	1.5
Computers (including laptops)	–	1.6

from 1990), particularly the labour-saving devices of dishwashers and tumble dryers, which have increased fourfold. Although not included in the 1990 list, it is likely that computer ownership has also greatly increased and some appliances that are now relatively commonplace, such as game consoles or large flat-screen TVs, would have been non-existent in 1990.

However from Figures 9.3 and 9.4 in Part II Chapter 9, it was seen that the overall increase in daily gas consumption of 10 per cent to 71kWh/day (under standardized external conditions of 5°C) was primarily due to the increase in high-energy usage households, and this corresponded to the 9 per cent increase in floor area that occurred in these dwellings (Summerfield et al, 2007). The increase in electricity consumption of 30 per cent at 15kWh/day was even more skewed towards increases in high energy-using households, which also – as expected – were the larger dwellings. Some caution is required since the numbers in this sample are too small to ascribe changes to energy usage to specific household characteristics in a statistically significant way. However, research currently being undertaken with a total sample size of more than 40 dwellings confirms a similar pattern of results where changes are skewed towards higher energy users.

Underlying this phenomenon is the inherent asymmetry in the potential for occupants to alter energy usage, since there is a certain limit for a given building construction and external conditions below which energy usage cannot fall and still maintain thermal comfort and inside air quality. While even in a highly insulated building, no such inherent limit exists in the potential for increased energy usage as a result of occupant behaviour – except in the capacity of systems to supply energy and the occupant to pay for it! Moreover, conventional design can facilitate disadvantageous behaviours – for instance, simply in the consequences of forgetting to close a window or door. In MK1, 9 of the 14 households reported leaving their bedroom window open on winter mornings, usually to help ventilate the adjoining bathroom. If energy efficiency measures are in place, it is difficult to ensure that the system maintains optimal operation. A few of the Milton Keynes dwellings had relatively sophisticated heat-recovery systems, which the original owners may have been proficient in operating; but in the transfer of dwelling ownership over time, this knowledge had not been passed on so that the new owners were unaware of its existence.

Based on some of the general observations during fieldwork on the follow-up study, it was also clear that major changes had occurred in the way in which some occupants lived, and these were likely to be substantially different from the original design intentions. One was the number of occupants working from home. In many cases, spare bedrooms or extensions were used as studies and had large amounts of office and related computer equipment that were more typical of non-domestic environments. Since they are located in part of the dwelling that would have previously had minimal heating, indirect gains from this additional equipment may not contribute to reducing the usage of central heating. These indirect gains may even lead to greater energy usage, as in one case where the bedroom/office had five computers and suffered from localized overheating even in winter, with the result that windows were kept open in that room (inferring increased ventilation rates for the whole house).

As a result, part of this asymmetry in energy demand may also be related to the greater scope that larger dwellings provide for occupant lifestyles to have an impact – for instance, by having enough outdoor space to enable an extension to be added to the dwelling, this necessitates more heating and provides space to accommodate more appliances. If the space is highly glazed, then it will also increase heat loss. By contrast, occupants in smaller dwellings who do not have the land to provide this opportunity and accommodate such lifestyle choices may simply choose to move away instead. Hence, there is potentially a differential impact of occupant behaviour, increasing energy usage both at the level of day-to-day operation and in terms of more fundamental changes to lifestyle and building design.

Discussion

The three case studies have illustrated not only the important role of occupant behaviour in energy usage, but the diverse ways in which this influence can be manifested and disrupt predictions of energy savings from technical models. They may be summarized as follows:

•   Change or the extent of change in occupant behaviour may be very difficult to predict.

- In some cases, the issue is that occupant behaviour does not change precisely when some modification in behaviour is expected.
- Occupant behaviour is likely to vary across distinct occupant groups, such as the use of heating systems by the elderly, the poor, the wealthy and those in ill health,
- Occupant behaviour is an ongoing factor, not just an issue concerning initial occupation. Control systems, therefore, must be supported through the provision of information.
- Broader social changes over time, such as those related to lifestyle or technological innovation, may introduce unanticipated occupant behaviour, such as changes in different social groups and different designs.
- Occupant behaviour may result in energy efficiency measures performing less effectively than expected, even to the point of being counter-productive.

In the face of so many potential options for occupant behaviour to influence the energy performance of a dwelling, it is worthwhile reframing the issues into a schematic diagram that can delineate the various interrelationships at work. While Figure 25.4 uses generic descriptions (e.g. there are more aspects to building design than those listed), it delineates the various pathways leading to resultant energy usage and carbon emissions. First, there are the intrinsic properties of the building, such as infiltration rates, which affect the internal conditions, such as temperature and ventilations rates. These are also affected by the external conditions. An additional pathway may be traced from the building (and any extensions) to the occupant behaviour and their actions to influence the internal conditions – for instance, by setting the thermostat temperature or by opening windows. Thus, the relationship between the building and final energy use is also mediated by occupant behaviour.

External environmental conditions, primarily weather conditions but also pollution and noise, affect internal conditions and therefore can also prompt a change in occupant behaviour (e.g. shutting a window). Thus, relationships between occupants and the internal conditions are bidirectional, as each influences the other. The socio-demographic and lifestyle characteristics of the household, such as family size, education and income, have an influence on a

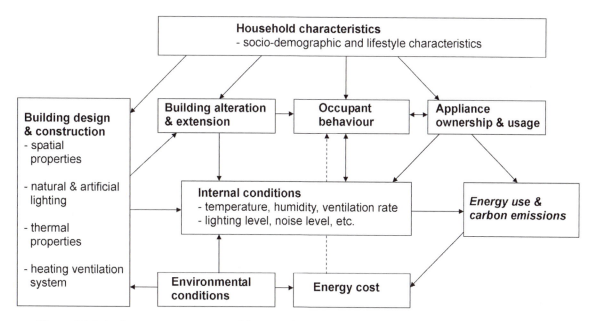

Figure 25.4 *A schematic representation of the interrelationships between occupant behaviour and other factors in influencing energy use in domestic buildings*

range of factors, including the scope of any building alterations, occupant behaviour, and appliance ownership and usage. This last factor can affect energy usage both directly and via indirect effects to the internal conditions. For instance, consider a tumble dryer that both consumes energy and contributes to moisture production in the house: since this may cause occupants to open windows, it also has a bidirectional connection with occupant behaviour (e.g. ownership of a smart energy meter may lead to occupants altering their thermostat setting).

In practice, when considering a specific scenario or energy efficiency measure, these pathways can be specified more precisely as mechanisms that alter the strength of the connections between each factor. Thus, it might be hypothesized that buildings constructed with lower infiltration rates will mean that external environmental conditions will have a reduced influence on internal conditions and, hence, energy usage. But it can also be seen that the same measure may result in a greater likelihood of occupants increasing ventilation rates by opening windows.

It is not feasible to eliminate pathways, particularly in the domestic sector where the occupants have control over their home environment. Rather, both researchers and designers should undertake sensitivity analysis by varying the level of interactions in order to find the most robust energy-efficient measures available. While energy costs are relatively low and occupants have poor feedback regarding their energy usage, there are limits to what designers can do; but generally it is worthwhile aiming for simplicity and minimizing the need for occupants to be specifically aware of the building operation. In other words, we should design so that the 'default' mode of building operation is one of the most efficient, and make the choice the easiest for occupants to attain. As Oreszczyn, one of this chapter's authors, is fond of reminding colleagues: 'It is not buildings that use energy, it's people in buildings!'

Acknowledgements

The Warm Front study was undertaken as part of the national evaluation of the Warm Front Scheme (England's home energy efficiency scheme). It was supported by the Department for Environment, Food and Rural Affairs (Defra) and the Welsh Assembly government under contract with the Energy Saving Trust (EST) (Contract Number M47). The views expressed in this chapter are those of the authors and not necessarily those of the funding departments. We would also like to acknowledge the support provided by Les Shorrock at the Building Research Establishment (BRE), who provided access to the original 1990 data set from Milton Keynes Energy Park, and to the residents who participated in the follow-up study.

References

Bell, M. and Lowe, R. (2000) 'Energy efficient modernisation of housing: A UK case study', *Energy and Buildings*, vol 32, pp267–280

Dimitropoulos, J. and Sorrell, S. (2006) 'The rebound effect: Theoretical basis, extensions and limitations', in *Proceedings of the 29th IAEE International Conference*, Potsdam, Germany, 7–10 June

DTI (Department of Trade and Industry) (2001) *UK Fuel Poverty Strategy*, DTI, London, www.berr.gov.uk/energy/fuel-poverty/index.html, accessed July 2008

DTI (2007) *Meeting the Energy Challenge: A White Paper on Energy*, DTI, Government Stationery Office, London

Edwards, J. (1990) 'Low energy dwellings in the Milton Keynes Energy Park', *Energy Management*, vol 26, pp32–33

ETSU (Energy Technology Support Unit) (1998) *House Design Studies Phase II*, ETSU

Fouquet, R. and Pearson, P. J. G. (2006) 'Seven centuries of energy services: The price and use of lighting in the United Kingdom (1300–2000), *The Energy Journal*, vol 27, no 1

Herring, H. (1999) 'Does energy efficiency save energy? The debate and its consequences', *Applied Energy*, vol 63, pp209–226

Herring, H. and Roy, R. (2007) 'Technological innovation, energy efficient design and the rebound effect', *Technovation*, vol 27, pp194–203

Hong, S. H., Ridley, I., Oreszczyn, T. and The Warm Front Study Group (2004) 'The impact of energy efficient refurbishment on the airtightness in English dwellings', in *Proceedings of the 25th AIVC Conference: Ventilation and Retrofitting*, Air Infiltration and Ventilation Centre, pp7–12

Hong, S. H., Oreszczyn, T., Ridley, I. and The Warm Front Team (2006) 'The impact of energy efficient refurbishment on the space heating fuel consumption in English dwellings', *Energy and Buildings*, vol 38, pp1171–1181

Hong, S. H., Oreszczyn, T., Green, G., Ridley, I. and the Warm Front Study Group (in press) 'Field study of thermal comfort in low-income dwellings in England before and after energy efficient refurbishment', *Building and Environment*

NBA Tectonics (1992) *Evaluation of Passive Solar Potential Multi-Residential Dwellings and Retrofit Measures*, Report to the Energy Technology Support Unit

ODPM (Office of the Deputy Prime Minister) (2006) *The Building Regulations, Approved Document L1a – Conservation of Fuel and Power in New Dwellings: 2006 Edition*, ODPM, NBS, UK

Oreszczyn, T. (1993) 'The energy duality of conservatory use', in *Proceedings of the 3rd European Conference of Architecture: Solar Energy in Architecture and Planning*, Florence, Italy, pp522–525

Oreszczyn, T. (2004) 'Our innate ability to think of new ways to use energy', *Energy and Environment*, vol 15, pp1011–1014

Pathan, A., Summerfield, A. J., Young, A., Lowe, R. and Oreszczyn, T. (in press) 'Trends in domestic conservatory use in the UK: Comparison between the 1992 conservatory association survey and the UCL 2004 survey', *Energy and Buildings*

Saunders, H. (1992) 'The Khazzoom-Brookes Postulate and neoclassical growth', *Energy Journal*, vol 13, pp131–148

Summerfield, A. J., Lowe, R. J., Bruhns H. R., Caeiro J. A., Steadman, J. P. and Oreszczyn, T. (2007) 'Milton Keynes Energy Park revisited: Changes in internal temperatures and energy usage', *Energy and Buildings*, vol 39, pp783–791

The Economist (2004) 'Britain in bloom', *The Economist*, 3 June

Wilkinson, P., Landon, M., Armstrong, B., Stevenson, S. and McKee, M. (2001) *Cold Comfort: The Social and Environmental Determinants of Excess Winter Death in England, 1986–1996*, The Policy Press for the Joseph Rowntree Foundation, Bristol, UK

Wilkinson, P., Oreszczyn, T. and Hong, S. H. (2006) 'Determinants of winter indoor temperatures in low income households in England', *Energy and Building*, vol 38, no 3, pp245–252

26

Natural Ventilation of Auditoria: Three Case Studies

Malcolm Cook and Alan Short

Introduction

The recovery of natural ventilation as a viable means of cooling and ventilation for large non-domestic buildings in temperate climates is now well established. More recently, the use of natural ventilation has been extended to the design of auditoria. The successful natural ventilation of auditoria is particularly challenging. Some of these challenges are highlighted here.

In natural displacement ventilation, layers of warm air at high level drive a flow of air out through high-level ventilation openings. This flow draws in fresh air at low level. Large inlet and outlet areas are required to ensure that the horizontal interface separating the fresh cooler air from the warmer stale air above remains above the breathing zone. For this reason, in an auditorium with raked seating, the height difference between the lowest and the highest audience seat, as a proportion of the overall internal height, is critical. The decision to introduce galleries or balconies in performing arts venues in order to increase capacity or to reduce the furthest distance to the stage has profound consequences for the design of the natural ventilation scheme.

Air inlets and damper controls need to be carefully considered to avoid wind-induced pressure imbalances where negative pressures at the inlet location prevent ambient air from being drawn into the building. Even when air is successfully drawn into a plenum below raked seating, care is needed in the design to prevent air from being driven directly through the plenum and out

of the building without being drawn into the occupied space.

Auditoria, whether for the performing arts or lectures, are occupied intermittently. The Building Management Systems (BMS) must be able to respond to these dynamics and have an operating resolution able to cater for a wide range of occupancy density, from full houses down to just a few people during rehearsals.

This chapter looks at how these and other technical challenges have been tackled in the design of three auditoria: the Queens Building at De Montfort University; the Contact Theatre in Manchester, which comprises two auditoria; and the Lichfield Garrick, also incorporating two auditoria. The chapter presents guidance distilled from the experiences gained by the design teams involved to provide architects and engineers with some insight into the design of naturally ventilated auditoria.

The Queens Building, De Montfort University

The Queens Building at De Montfort University in Leicester was completed in 1993 and contains two wholly naturally ventilated 180-seat wide-fan lecture theatres (see Figures 26.1 and 26.2). It represents the first attempt by architects Short and Associates to make a naturally ventilated auditorium. The natural ventilation strategy is buoyancy-driven displacement ventilation assisted by tall stacks (two per auditorium).

Fresh air is drawn in at low level beneath the seating rake. The orientations of the two theatres lie at 180 degrees to one another, which reverses the sense of the seating rake and the inlet and outlet positions. In terms of buoyancy-driven displacement ventilation, this should be irrelevant; in practice, anecdotal evidence suggests that the 'reversed' auditorium is less successful than the other in terms of acoustic performance and draught risk. This is thought to be because the air entering the 'reversed' auditorium air can bypass the plenum below the raked seating and enter directly into the space via 2.5m high heating elements. This results in less opportunity for acoustic attenuation and higher air speeds over the heating elements.

For the more successful auditorium, air is introduced from the north side via dampers behind belfry louvres 4m above street level (see Figure 26.3) into triangular plena subdivided by acoustic splitters before entering a full plenum above a 300mm *in-situ* concrete slab, below a timber- and steel-framed seating rake. Air enters the occupied space through continuous grilles in the risers to the stepped rakes, passing through finned tube heat exchanges. Warm stratified air then passes through large rectangular openings in the

vertical plane below soffit level into the parallelogram-shaped stacks. The stack terminations comprise four top-hung conventional steel-framed windows opening out, achieving an effective stack height of 17.6m. The envelope of each auditorium is in very heavy construction, using concrete and calcium silicate brick masonry.

Being one of the first of the new generation of large-scale naturally ventilated buildings in the UK, the design team was keen to test the likely performance of the system. Both physical and numerical techniques were used by the design team in developing the natural ventilation strategy. Dynamic thermal simulations were carried out to investigate the likely thermal performance of the auditoria over a typical year. This modelling work included looking at the effects on thermal performance of adding acoustic lining (i.e. reducing the exposed thermal mass), reducing internal heat gains, and increasing ventilation opening sizes (Eppel and Lomas, 1991). For the cases investigated, the number of occupied hours for which the dry resultant temperature was above 27°C was in the range of three to nine, using 1967 weather data for Kew, London; none of these hours fell in the term-time period.

Source: MJ Cook, De Montfort University

Figure 26.1 *View from the south of the Queens Building at De Montfort University*

Source: MJ Cook, De Montfort University

Figure 26.2 *150-seat auditorium at the Queens Building*

While dynamic thermal simulation models are ideal for predicting thermal performance over an entire year, they are not well suited for investigating detailed temperature and airflow distributions in individual spaces. This meant that for analysing the thermal stratification expected in the auditoria, a different technique was needed. Perspex scale models using brine in water to represent the flows driven by heat in air were used for this purpose (Lane-Serff et al, 1991). The models gave confidence that the basic design principles were sound in terms of whether adequate ventilation flow rates could be generated and whether warm air stratified above head height. Under some operating conditions, the models showed that over-ventilation could occur. Experiments with and without ventilation

stacks were undertaken and the decision was made to use two stacks for each of the auditoria in order to ensure stratification above head height.

Post-occupancy monitoring has been carried out by Clancy and Howarth (2000). More recently, researchers at the Institute of Energy and Sustainable Development, De Montfort University, have monitored temperature and CO_2 levels in the auditorium. Figure 26.4 shows a typical hot summer day when the auditorium was occupied for a two-hour period in the afternoon. Temperature and CO_2 readings are measured at the base of each ventilation stack. The intention is that the readings at these locations represent the conditions of the air leaving the space and are, thus, the worst case scenario. The occupied period is clearly

Figure 26.3 *Inlet louvres leading to plenum
below seating rake*

identifiable by the CO_2 readings, which rise to a peak of 1682ppm. Guidance on air quality standards for teaching spaces given in *Building Bulletin BB101* (DfES, 2006) recommends that the average and maximum CO_2 concentrations should not exceed 1500ppm and 5000ppm, respectively. The temperatures do not rise significantly above their night-time set-point temperatures of 20°C, illustrating the damping effect of the thermal mass exposed around the walls and ceiling of the auditorium. More interesting is the capacity of the thermal mass effect to hold internal temperatures below the external (ambient) temperature throughout the occupied period.

The design process and post-occupancy monitoring of the Queens Building led the design team to the following important findings, which were used in the development of subsequent projects incorporating natural ventilation:

- The minimum required ventilation rate of 5 air changes per hour (ACH) for fresh air was almost always achieved with ease in both summer and winter (Howarth, 1997).
- In heating mode, with a high buoyancy force, the stack effect was found to be too great (Clancy and Howarth, 2000) and finer control was required to provide smaller opening sizes to prevent cold draughts. Damper settings were designed to vary in 25 per cent increments, giving only five positions.
- The single-stage preheat strategy was too crude and air could bypass the finned tube units, particularly directly above the inlet openings into the base of the plenum. The conventional proprietary dampers appeared to leak in their fully closed mode (Asbridge and Cohen, 1996). These findings influenced the designers' approach to the natural ventilation strategy for the later Coventry University Library (Field, 2000), incorporating two-stage preheating and high performance dampers, developed by the manufacturers specifically for the project.
- The beneficial effect of the thermal mass is noticeable, especially when coupled with night-time ventilation, achieving a 1 degree fabric temperature rise (ceiling) over five days during daytime periods of 26°C ambient temperature and high occupancy. Typically, 5 degree internal fluctuations in temperatures are recorded against 13 to 14 degree external fluctuations. Howarth (1997) has suggested that the concrete-lined plenum is effective in damping the temperature of incoming air during the day, particularly after it has been subjected to night-time ventilation.

The Contact Theatre, Manchester

The original Contact Theatre was built in 1963 for the University of Manchester's drama department. In 1993, work began on consolidating the company's activities onto one site by adding new foyers and a 120 seat flexible studio performance space to the side of the original brick masonry auditorium, which remains within the enlarged building. The rebuilding and adaptation was completed in 1999.

Main auditorium

Air is introduced from an enclosed courtyard to the west, through a bank of acoustic splitters and directly

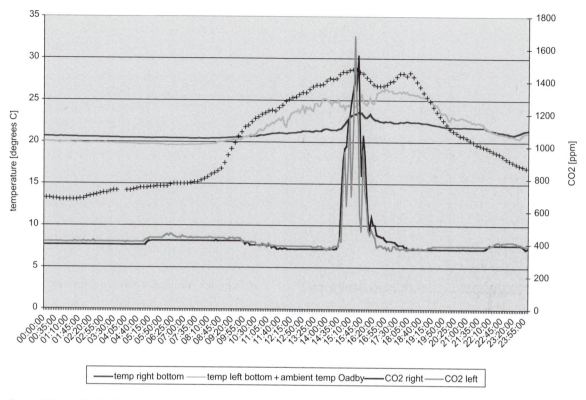

legend: temp right bottom — temp left bottom + ambient temp Oadby — CO2 right — CO2 left

Source: B. Painter, De Montfort University

Figure 26.4 *Monitoring data from the Queens Building auditorium during a hot summer day (30 August 2005)*

into a plenum below the raked seating. This is the only orientation available for locating inlets because the new foyers are arranged along the west side of the auditorium, blocking potential intake routes. Airflow paths of the cross-sectional area required, acoustically protected from foyer noise, would have necessitated so many separate high-level ducts to maintain workable head room as to be uneconomical and intrusive.

Incoming air enters into four compartments of the plenum below the raked seating in the auditorium. Each compartment is individually controlled by dampers operated by the Building Management System (BMS) in order to balance the distribution of air entering the auditorium. Thermal mass inside a concrete-lined labyrinth with block-work subdivisions helps to cool the air during peak summer conditions. Before entering the auditorium, the air path turns through 90 degrees. This helps to diminish the effect of sudden gusts of wind and helps to reduce external noise ingress. Heating elements are hung below each seating

platform in the airflow paths. Air then enters the auditorium beneath each seating row through continuous openings in the risers, providing a free area of about 20m^2 (equivalent to 3.2 per cent of the gross floor area).

Computational fluid dynamics (CFD) modelling revealed the possibility of warm air stagnating below the cantilevered control room, such that the occupants of the three rows of seats at the top of the rake below could penetrate the warm displaced layer. This was addressed in the design by adding extra air intake grilles in the floor of the rear gangway, providing 1.25m^2 of free area fed from a dedicated plenum (see Figure 26.5). In addition, the control room is detached from the rear wall to allow warm buoyant air to flow upwards into the roof cavity.

Air is exhausted through a new 5m high chamber cut into the existing roof profile (see Figure 26.5). Five stacks, each with a free area of 4m^2, sit above the void, with dampers and low speed fans located at the

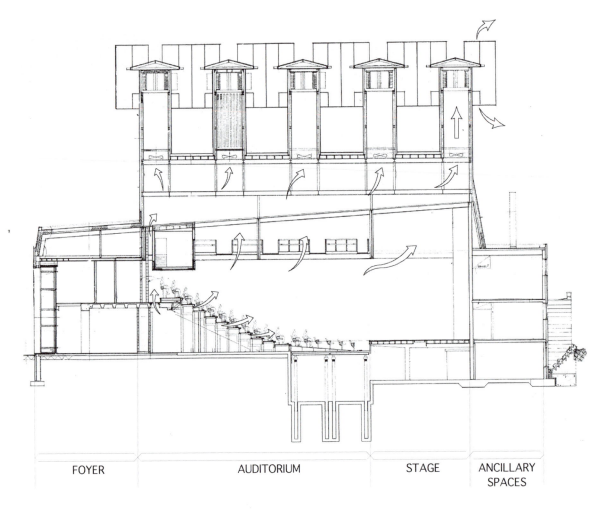

FOYER   AUDITORIUM   STAGE   ANCILLARY
                                            SPACES

Source: Short and Associates Architects

Figure 26.5 *Section showing ventilation strategy for the Contact Theatre, Manchester*

junction between the void and the auditorium. The large zone above the theatre lighting grid holds warm stale air before it flows into the roof void. The stacks contain arrays of vertically mounted splitters that help to minimize noise ingress from the nearby roadway and adjacent student's union concert venue. The stack terminations comprise two integrated orthogonal H-pots, which minimize flow reversal induced by wind pressures and generate negative pressure for all wind directions. Trays are suspended below the stack openings to intercept rain drops should they breach the geometry of the termination.

During commissioning, a heat load test was carried out in which 60kW of theatre lighting and 40kW of simulated occupants were used. During the test, no pre-cooling by the thermal mass in the intake ducts was available and about 50 per cent of the design airflow was achieved. The test operated for longer and with higher heat gains than were expected to be the case in reality. The results (see Figure 26.6) showed that the design temperature differential of about 3 degrees was achieved in most of the seating locations except in the top seating rows, which were slightly warmer; a revision to the controls has been implemented to improve this. Lowering the set point after the matinée simulation caused the fans to operate in the exhaust stacks; prior to this time, the fans were not needed for maintaining environmental conditions.

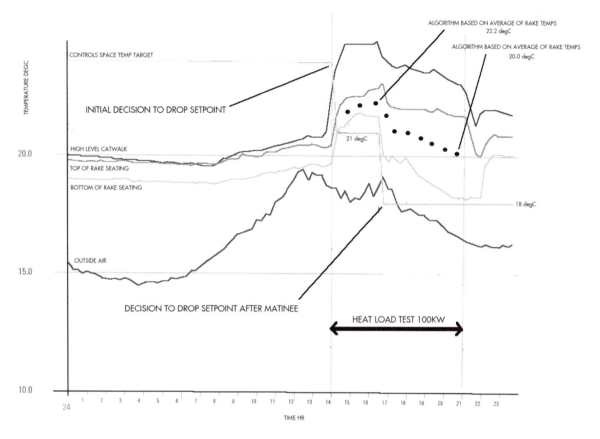

Source: internal project report by Richard Quincey, formerly of Max Fordham and Associates

Figure 26.6 *Results of heat load test conducted at the Contact Theatre*

Studio theatre

The studio is a flat-floored space elevated two storeys above the main auditorium scene assembly area and workshop. Air is introduced from the north side only at a height of 6m above street level. This flows into a 600mm high plenum below the entire floor. The plenum comprises a high thermal mass labyrinth and splits symmetrically into two paths via banks of acoustic splitters before dividing again into chambers beneath the studio floor. Air passes through heating elements suspended below grilles in the plane of the floor on all four sides of the studio. It is intended that open frame bleacher seating can be located over the grilles. The studio theatre is 6m high with acoustic absorbent panels partially covering all four walls.

Air is exhausted via four vertical openings at soffit level connecting to an exhaust plenum above the perimeter corridor on all four sides. A shelf is formed to intercept rainwater drops. Four tapering splitter chambers connect to masonry stacks above, teminating in cross H-pots at the same level as those venting the main auditorium. Three small half-bladed short-cased axial fans are placed at the base of each stack above the attenuators. This is more desirable, acoustically, than the position of the auditorium fans, which are located below the acoustic splitters for ease of maintenance. The studio stacks have accessible inspection panels at roof level. The fans have aerofoil blades and bellmouths, with speed controllers that enable slow-speed quiet start-up.

A simple wall-mounted dial in the studio enables staff to input the expected level of occupancy. Their prognosis informs the BMS, which makes a decision regarding the opening extent of the dampers in the inlet and outlet stacks. Anecdotally, the studio is a very successful and heavily used space.

Post-occupancy monitoring work (Woods and Fitzgerald, 2007) has suggested that, under certain conditions, inflow can occur through some of the high-level openings intended for outflow. It may be possible to avoid this by close control of inlet and outlet dampers to ensure high-level openings remain similar, or smaller, in size to low-level openings. Small-scale water bath models can be used to investigate such flow scenarios with multiple steady-state solutions (Chenvidyakarn and Woods, 2005).

The Lichfield Garrick

The Lichfield Garrick is a performing and static arts centre. This building was a rebuild project, albeit with significant reconstruction. It is exposed on three sides and butts up against a shopping centre along the north-east side (see Figure 26.7). In addition to the foyer and bar areas along two sides, the building comprises two key spaces: a 500-seat auditorium and a more flexible 180-seat studio space. Full details about the building are described by Gorst (2003).

Both auditoria employ buoyancy-driven displacement ventilation in which naturally occurring heat gains drive airflow out of the spaces through high-level openings, making way for cooler, fresher air to enter at low level. This was reasonably straightforward to develop for the studio space, which is rectangular in plan with moveable seating positioned to suit the performance style. In this zone, low-level air inlets were located along each of the long sides of the space. These are fed by a 'ventilated wall' on the south-east side of the building, which leads into a plenum below the floor. The inlets to the ventilated wall are shown in Figure 26.7. These provide a high-level intake position 3m above street level that reduce the ingress of pollutants and street noise. The outlet path is provided by a single stack. The stack contains a low-power fan, positioned above acoustic splitters, for use during peak load conditions. Above the fan the air flows through BMS-controlled dampers and out of the stacks through top-hung opaque panels. CFD simulations verified that warm air stratified safely above the occupants' breathing zone and drove a sufficient flow through the space.

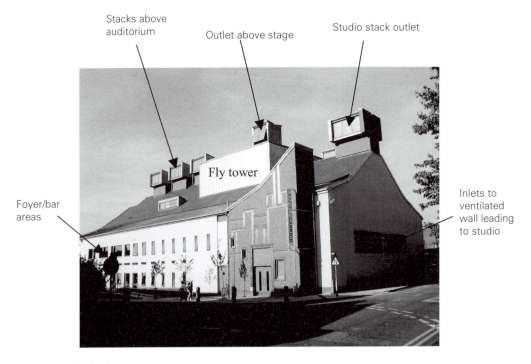

Source: M. J. Cook, De Montfort University

Figure 26.7 *Lichfield Garrick viewed from the south (shopping centre behind)*

The main auditorium, with its raked seating and high heat gains, posed greater design challenges. Seating is provided in two zones: stalls extending from the stage to the rear of the auditorium and a circle located above the rear stalls (see Figure 26.8). Heat gains from occupants and lighting could be as high as 110kW. The main challenge was how to provide the required 36m² of free opening area for incoming fresh air necessary to ensure warm air stratified above the occupied zone.

The final design uses a plenum below each of the seating rakes, supplied along sheet metal ducts from three sides of the building. On the north-east side, where the building abuts a shopping centre, openings below the eaves of the sloping roof lead into an acoustically lined vertical duct that guides air downwards and into the plenum below the rear stalls. This is supplemented by a duct passing through the lower ground floor from the south-west side and by ducts from the north-west passing at high level through the foyers on the ground and first floors. A duct, leading from above the rear stalls up to the ceiling above the circle, mitigates the build-up of warm air below the circle. Outflow paths for the main auditorium are provided by six stacks mounted along two ridge lines on the roof.

Fresh air supply to the stage is via a second ventilated wall at the rear of the stage, which is fed by openings in the south-east façade of the fly tower. The ducts lead to heating elements below the stage from where the air is drawn into the space through horizontal openings in the floor at both sides of the stage. Two stacks, located above the stage, provide the exhaust path.

CFD simulations were undertaken to predict the position of the interface between the fresh air and the stale warmer air above (see Figure 26.9). This led to recommendations for larger effective opening areas, which were realized through a combination of larger structural openings and lower pressure drops. Also, due to the light-weight nature of the internal surface finishes and the close proximity of the warm air stratification to the uppermost seating, low-power fans were installed in all of the outlet stacks for use under peak conditions.

During the July 2003 heat wave when external temperatures exceeded design conditions, internal temperatures remained comfortable for most of the time and for longer periods than anticipated. This illustrates the ability of the thermal mass in the intake ducts and plena, albeit modest, and the BMS-controlled dampers to prevent internal temperatures

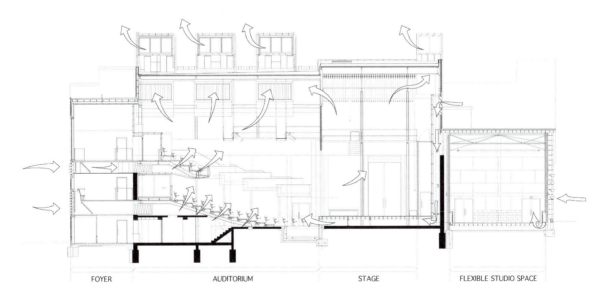

Source: Short and Associates Architects

Figure 26.8 *Section showing ventilation strategy for the Lichfield Garrick*

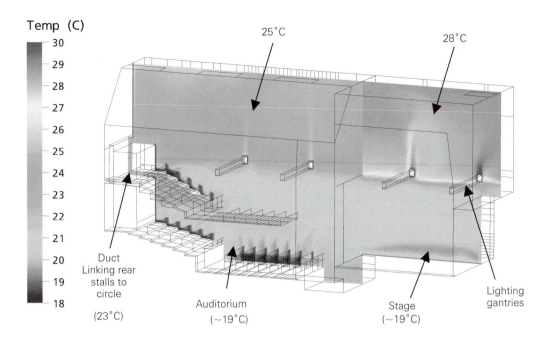

Source: M. J .Cook, De Montfort University

Figure 26.9 *CFD simulation of main auditorium showing stratification and duct linking rear stalls with circle (ambient temperature = 18°C)*

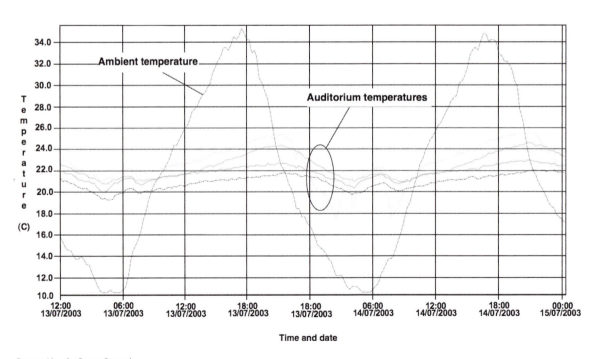

Source: Lincoln Green Control

Figure 26.10 *BMS data for the main auditorium at the Lichfield Garrick*

from rising to unacceptable levels (see Figure 26.10). In a similar way to the Contact Theatre, post-occupancy monitoring has suggested that, under certain conditions, inflow through the high-level outlet stacks can occur (Woods and Fitzgerald, 2007).

Design guidance

Experience gained during the design, commissioning and post-occupancy periods of the buildings described in this chapter has led to a substantial body of knowledge regarding the technical design issues surrounding naturally ventilation auditoria. A summary of this knowledge is given here; further details can be found in Short and Cook (2005).

Air inlets and supply ducts

Low-level air inlets need to provide large, secure free areas configured to exclude birds, rodents and large insects. Typically, open areas that total 1 to 2 per cent of floor area are required; but these should be calculated accurately based on the required air change rates and anticipated internal heat gains. Fly screens, grilles, dampers, acoustic attenuators and insulation will induce pressure losses along inlet paths. Cross-sectional areas need to be checked on construction drawings to ensure that the total *effective* area equates to what was identified as being required at the design stage. Computer simulations or analytical techniques are useful for investigating the effect of pressure drops due to devices such as grilles, dampers, etc.

Ideally, inlets should be located away from obvious sources of noise. This may not always be possible in dense city centres and a design strategy needs to be evolved to reduce, in particular, low frequency noise ingress at the building envelope or as close to it as possible. Inlet locations should avoid obvious localized sources of pollution, such as traffic junctions, car parks and loading bay areas. The performance of inlets should be robust to changing wind direction and the potential occurrence of negative wind pressures. Ideally, air should be drawn from several orientations; but the particular circulation requirements within the building may prevent this. Multiple inlet locations also helps with the challenge of realizing the large free inlet area required.

Well-sealed dampers are essential to prevent cold draughts and air leakage in winter (building regulations now require all new buildings to adhere to stringent pressure testing; DCLG, 2006). It is also necessary that such dampers have full modulatory control. This is to enable control of a wide range of airflow rates, from winter fresh air requirements (typically 10L/s per person) to summertime cooling requirements (possibly up to 10ACH).

Acoustic attenuation is required in the supply path to exclude urban background noise. The splitters will need to be accessible for maintenance and will reduce the effective duct area (typically by about 50 per cent). Care is needed to preserve the effective free area by increasing the overall duct size. Inlet ducts should be regarded as external spaces until the first dampers and heating elements are encountered. Therefore, they must be insulated from internal (heated) spaces – for example, the supply ducts traversing the foyer spaces at the Lichfield Garrick.

Plena

Heating elements behind grilles leading into the auditorium need to be configured to ensure that winter air at ambient temperature cannot bypass the elements. Plena should be compartmented as necessary in order to provide even distribution of supply air across the whole auditorium and to avoid incoming air flowing straight through the plenum without being drawn into the occupied space. Care is needed to ensure that adequate flow paths are maintained after compartmentalization (i.e. plenum compartments should be large enough to accommodate the air flowing into them from the ducts). Where possible, plena also need to be configured (and compartmentalized, if necessary) so that differential pressures at the inlet locations can be equalized by feeding chambers from different orientations.

The opportunity of using plena for locating thermal mass should be taken advantage of, where possible, to assist the thermal performance of the occupied space as acoustic requirements are likely to limit the use of exposed mass in the occupied space. The mass should be exposed to the airflow and be regenerated (cooled) by night-time ventilation.

High-level intakes

In certain circumstances, it is necessary or advisable to provide high-level air intakes on the outside of the building – for example, where adjacency to other buildings prevents intakes on the building façade – and to diminish noise and pollution levels. These must be designed and controlled so that they do not behave as air outlet routes under particular wind conditions. This risk can be minimized by positioning such intakes away from zones where there is known to be negative wind pressure (normally identifiable through wind-tunnel testing) and positioning heating elements such that they encourage air to rise into the occupied space rather than upwards through the stack.

Auditorium

The vertical distance between the lowest and highest members of the audience and between the head height of the highest audience members and the ceiling is critical. Numerical modelling, such as computational fluid dynamics modelling, is recommended to ensure that the interface between the warm stale air that collects in a layer beneath the ceiling and the cooler fresher air below remains above head height. The position of this interface depends upon the effective inlet and outlet areas and the height of the auditorium. The height required to ensure that the displaced warm layer remains above head height will affect the overall height of the building. Local planning officials and planning consultees will need to understand the natural ventilation strategy when determining their overall recommendations. The infrastructure related to ventilation cannot be considered in purely formal terms, the natural physics embodied in the proposal must be acknowledged.

The auditorium volume required for natural ventilation purposes may be in excess of the ideal volume to give the required reverberation time. Additional acoustic attenuation material is therefore likely to be needed; but its performance should be traded off against the usefulness of exposing adequate thermal mass to the occupants. Dynamic thermal simulation models can be used to assess the performance of exposed thermal mass.

Outflow paths

Ventilation outlets should be configured to achieve similar levels of acoustic attenuation as intakes. They are likely to be large (same order of size as air intakes), and will need to be accessible for maintenance, possibly from lighting gantries in performing arts venues. In some cases, such as the Lichfield Garrick, the exhaust

structures present an opportunity for incorporating acoustic absorption on surfaces facing the auditorium.

Low-power fan assistance provides a means of increasing flow rates in cases where it has proved difficult to realize the total opening areas required. It should be noted that fan assistance is intended for use under peak load conditions, rather than continuous use (i.e. the success of the natural ventilation strategy ought not to rely on such assistance during a typical day). If included, fans should be incorporated beyond acoustic splitters to attenuate any noise generated from being discernible in the auditorium.

Outlets should remove air at the highest soffit level to prevent pockets of trapped warm air from developing that could jeopardize the thermal performance of the space by increasing the temperature of any exposed thermal mass.

Outlet terminations

The termination design should be robust to changing wind direction and avoid the development of a positive pressure with respect to the inlet. This is possible using devices such as H-pots, as exemplified at the Contact Theatre, and/or a BMS algorithm that closes windward outlets. In many cases, it is beneficial to undertake wind tunnel tests in order to investigate the pressure distribution around the proposed termination device and differentials between inlet and outlet locations. Raising the terminations above the roof line using stacks helps to increase the buoyancy driving force. However, issues of wind control and maintenance become more critical.

Wind effects

Various points have been made in this section regarding the effects of wind on natural ventilation design. Indeed, it is often useful to commission wind tunnel tests in order to avoid placing intakes in low pressure regions or air recirculation zones that could fight against the upward buoyancy force inside the building. The urban context may also affect the performance of terminations, leading to a need for localized design solutions or, potentially, a fundamental reconfiguration. Note that the natural ventilation strategies described in this chapter use buoyancy-driven displacement ventilation and are designed to be independent of wind direction and speed. Although the authors do not deprecate the use of wind-assisted systems, they envisage such solutions to be less robust and more complex.

Conclusions

These three case studies illustrate many of the design constraints of naturally ventilated auditoria and demonstrate how natural ventilation and cooling can be achieved without the need for conventional air conditioning or mechanical ventilation. Each case study has built on the experiences of the preceding studies.

Much of the environmental design has been based on the use of physical modelling and computer simulation. These design tools proved to be very useful in predicting thermal performance and ventilation effectiveness, and are widely used today, especially in more complex or innovative design proposals.

Anecdotal evidence and monitoring data suggest that the case studies presented perform well, but do point to the need for good controls, high-quality components (e.g. dampers with airtight seals) and an understanding on the part of the building owners of how the Building Management System should be implemented, operated and maintained through the full life of the building. In parallel a sound understanding of the control strategy should enter the long-term culture of the building occupants.

Acknowledgements

The authors are grateful to Professor Martin Liddament (Veetech Ltd.) for permission to use material from the *International Journal of Ventilation* (Cook and Short, 2005) and to the Chartered Institution of Building Services Engineers for permission to base this chapter on work reported in Short and Cook (2005).

References

Asbridge, R. and Cohen, R. (1996) 'Probe 4: Queens Building', *Building Services Journal,* April, pp35–38

Chenvidyakarn, T. and Woods, A. W. (2005) 'Multiple steady states in stack ventilation', *Building and Environment*, vol 40, no 3, pp399–410

Clancy, E. M. and Howarth, A. T. (2000) 'An analysis of parameters affecting the internal environment of a naturally ventilated auditorium', *Building Services Engineering Research and Technology*, vol 21, no 1, pp1–7

Cook, M. J. and Short, C. A. (2005) 'Natural ventilation and low energy cooling of large, non-domestic buildings – four case studies', *International Journal of Ventilation,* vol 3, no, 4, pp283–294

DCLG (Department of Communities and Local Government) (2006) *Approved Document L2A: Conservation of Fuel and Power in New Buildings other than Dwellings*, DCLG

DfES (Department for Education and Skills) (2006) *Ventilation of School Buildings: Building Bulletin BB101*, version 1.4, Crown copyright

Eppel, H. and Lomas, K. J. (1991) 'Simulating the thermal performance of naturally ventilation spaces: A case study', in *Proceedings of Passive and Low Energy Architecture '91 Conference*, Seville, Spain, pp749–754

Field, J. (2000) 'Breeze blocks', *Building Services Journal,* December, pp18–22

Gorst, T. (2003) 'Civic life styles', *Architecture Today*, vol 143, November, pp34–46

Howarth, A. T. (1997) 'Stack ventilation in architecture', *Building Services Journal*, September, pp53–54

Lane-Serff, D. F., Linden, P. F., Parker, D. J. and Smeed, D. A. (1991) 'Laboratory modelling of natural ventilation via chimneys', in *Proceedings of Passive and Low Energy Architecture '91 Conference,* Seville, Spain, pp505–510

Short, C. A. and Cook, M. J. (2005) 'Design guidance for naturally ventilated theatres', *Building Services Engineering Research and Technology*, vol 26, no 3, pp259–270

Woods, A. and Fitzgerald, S. (2007) 'Dramatic ventilation', *Building Services Journal*, January, pp54–58

27

A Naturally Ventilated Building in a City Centre

Birgit Painter and Malcolm Cook

Introduction

The Frederick Lanchester Library at Coventry University, UK, (see Figure 27.1) opened in September 2000 and is one of the largest naturally ventilated buildings in the world. The deep-plan layout and its urban location, close to the city centre of Coventry, made the design of a low-energy building without air conditioning and with maximum daylight provision particularly challenging. Computer simulation techniques were used to assess the likely performance of the proposed design in order to ensure that the passive methods employed would be adequate to meet the cooling demands of such a large-scale building. The final design has proven to be very successful, both in terms of its thermal and energy-use performance, as well as its user satisfaction.

This case study describes the design and operating strategies that are employed in the building and presents user comments as well as results from monitoring studies, which include assessments of the building's thermal and energy-use performance. The building's likely performance in other UK cities is also discussed.

Description of the building

Much has been written about the design and operating strategies of the building by members of the design team (Cook et al, 1999a, 1999b; Short et al, 2004; Cook and Short, 2005; Lomas and Cook, 2005; Lomas, 2007; Krausse et al, 2007) and others (Field,

2000; Pidwell, 2001; McDonald, 2002). This section provides an overview of the design process, the environmental features and the intended ventilation strategy for the building.

Client brief

Coventry University required a large building (net floor area approximately 12,000m²) to accommodate the university library. In order to provide the required floor area and meet the local authority height restriction of four storeys, a deep-plan floor layout became unavoidable. It was important that the layout should be simple and, thus, easy to understand by its users. In order to allow for changes in study methods, the building was required to be able to accommodate the anticipated increase in the use of computers by the library users.

The client requested a sealed façade for security reasons. It was further specified that the new building should be environmentally friendly and as energy efficient as possible. For that reason, the potential for the use of sustainable building features such as daylighting, natural ventilation and the use of combined heat and power was to be investigated by the design team. The client was also particularly interested in assessing the likely environmental conditions prevailing in the building and the anticipated energy running costs. Computer models were therefore used to evaluate design options in the initial stages of the development.

The university also wanted the new library to be a distinctive building with an innovative design, which would receive national and international acclaim, and

Figure 27.1 *View of Lanchester Library from the west*

could be used as a teaching vehicle by its School of the Built Environment.

Site constraints

A number of further constraints were imposed by the location of the site. As the aerial view in Figure 27.2 shows, surrounding buildings, including a grade 2 listed hospital, limited the area available for the new building. Due to its city centre position and close proximity to a raised ring road, there were potential noise and air quality issues to be considered. Although located in the UK midlands, with its temperate summer and winter conditions, the site suffers from gusty and unpredictable wind conditions, which are

Figure 27.2 *Aerial view of the site, showing the proximity of the ring road and surrounding buildings*

typical for built-up city centre locations. Furthermore, the site is surrounded by a number of buildings of different height, which could affect airflows around the new building.

Environmental design features

The final design (see Figures 27.3 and 27.4) has a gross floor area of 9103m² and includes three deep-plan library floors, a smaller cruciform-shaped top floor and a basement, which comprises the book archive and a 24-hour computing lab. Apart from the basement, the building is fully naturally ventilated.

The four deep-plan library floors are penetrated by four 6m² corner lightwells and a central lightwell, which is tapered (6m² at the ground level to 9m² at the third-floor level) and only partly penetrates the ground floor (see Figures 27.5 and 27.8). Together with the large floor-to-ceiling height (3.9m), an under-floor plenum and 201.8m² perimeter stacks, these lightwells form an integral part of the natural ventilation strategy, as described below. The cross-sectional area of the stacks and the central lightwell increase with height in order to compensate for the reduced stack effect and to accommodate the larger volumes of exhausted air. The perimeter stacks, which extend 6m above roof level in order to achieve the required driving force for the stack ventilation, give the building its characteristic look (see Figures 27.1 and 27.6).

Another distinctive feature is the exposed thermal mass of the walls and ceilings (see Figures 27.5 and 27.7), which is fundamental to the passive cooling strategy. When required, air is allowed to enter the building at night, where it cools down the exposed building fabric. During the following day, the cool surfaces provide a radiant heat sink that offsets high air temperatures and helps to maintain the indoor environment at a comfortable resultant temperature.

In order to reduce heating demands, the building is very well insulated and comprises double glazing with an argon-fill cavity to all external windows. The U values of the materials used are significantly lower than the guideline values in force at the time and even exceed current guidelines (see Table 27.1).

The library has been designed to maximize daylight provision while keeping solar heat gains to a minimum. Small windows around the perimeter are enclosed by deep reveals and overhangs, and shading fins were placed on the façade in order to reduce direct sunlight entering the space (see Figure 27.6). However, the library is still perceived to have a bright feel due to the five lightwells that penetrate the space. The central lightwell is tapered, which assists daylight penetration. Workspaces are clustered around the lightwells, while the book stacks occupy the deeper parts of the building. At the top of each lightwell, an automatically controlled translucent blind can be closed to prevent direct solar gain during the summer months.

Since the library is used for a variety of purposes, from book storage to study areas for PC users and group work, the basic square open-plan floor layout has been adapted on each floor to provide a range of suitable spaces (see Figure 27.4). Offices and seminar rooms are located adjacent to lightwells and ventilation stacks in order to provide dedicated ventilation and daylight control.

Design study

During the design process the architects, Short and Associates, carried out a concept study that resulted in an initial design proposal (RIBA stage D design). Based on this proposal, detailed dynamic thermal and computational fluid dynamics (CFD) simulations were conducted in order to develop a design that would meet all heating and cooling requirements, while at the same time providing a comfortable indoor environment for building users and remaining energy efficient. The simulation studies are described in Cook et al (1999a) and only a summary is given here.

In order to model the time-varying interaction of internal temperatures and airflows as closely as possible, a combined airflow and thermal simulation study was carried out. For this purpose, an airflow network and a

(a)

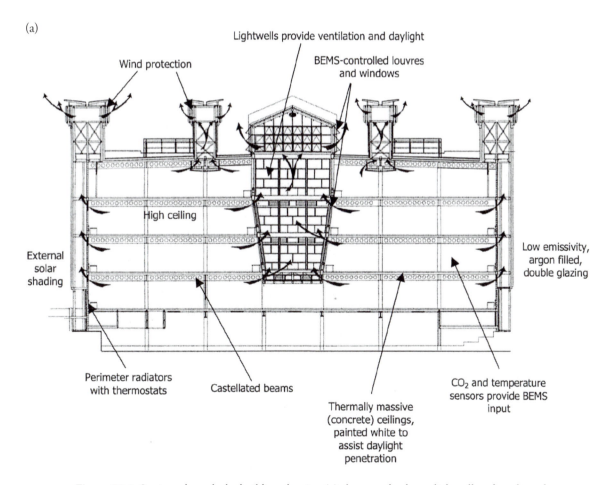

Labels in figure: Lightwells provide ventilation and daylight; Wind protection; BEMS-controlled louvres and windows; High ceiling; External solar shading; Low emissivity, argon filled, double glazing; Perimeter radiators with thermostats; Castellated beams; Thermally massive (concrete) ceilings, painted white to assist daylight penetration; CO$_2$ and temperature sensors provide BEMS input

Figure 27.3 *Sections through the building showing (a) the central exhaust lightwell and stacks and (b) the supply lightwells*

(b)

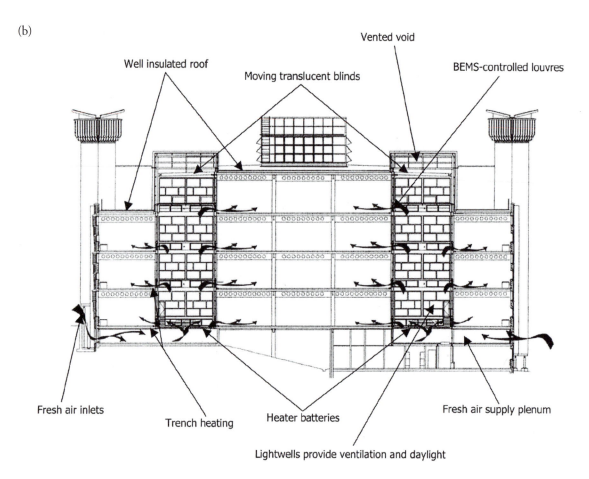

Figure 27.3 *Sections through the building showing (a) the central exhaust lightwell and stacks and (b) the supply lightwells* (cont'd)

thermal network of the proposed building were generated.

Table 27.1 *Comparison of the U values (W/m²K) of the building construction with old and current building regulation guidelines*

	Library (completed 2000)	Building regulations (1995)	Building regulations (2006: area-weighted average)
Wall	0.26	0.45	0.35
Roof	0.18	0.25	0.25
Windows	2.0	3.3	2.2

Source: Cook et al (1999b): building construction; DoE (1995) and ODPM (2006): building regulation guidelines

CFD simulations were carried out for a typical warm summer day using an ambient temperature of 24.5°C. Two occupancy scenarios were investigated, one for the expected occupancy (heat gains of 28W/m² core and 48W/m² perimeter, which included solar gain) and one for heavier use (42/m² core and 60W/m² perimeter). The CFD simulations did not take into account the effects of night cooling and exposed thermal mass, and assumed calm ambient conditions (i.e. no wind).

Dynamic thermal simulations were carried out to predict the building's internal temperatures throughout the year, taking into account solar shading, thermal mass and anticipated heat gains. Heating set points of 18°C (occupied) and 14°C (unoccupied) were imposed and a climate file for Kew 1967 was used (Holmes and Hitchin, 1978).

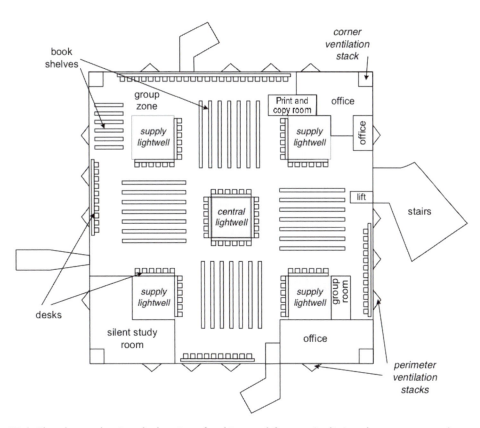

Figure 27.4 *Floor layout showing the location of architectural features (italics) and usage zones on the second floor*

The results of the CFD simulations showed that air change rates for the lower three floors were fairly well balanced, resulting in uniform temperatures across the floor plates. However, it was observed that under some conditions, warm air rising up the central lightwell, which had been exhausted from the lower floors, could flow out into the top floor rather than continue upwards to the outlet due to the lack of stack height. This resulted in reduced fresh air intake and a rise in temperatures on the third floor. To prevent this, the design was modified by sealing the central lightwell and the perimeter stacks at the top floor level, and providing dedicated exhaust stacks solely for this floor (see Figure 27.7).

The internal air temperatures predicted by the CFD simulations for the expected occupancy were 2.5°C to 3.5°C above ambient, increasing only by 1°C for the heavy occupancy scenario. Taking into account that the effects of night-time cooling and exposed thermal mass were not considered in the simulations and that dry resultant temperatures can be expected to be lower than the CFD-predicted air temperatures, these simulation results indicated that the library should easily be able to maintain comfortable internal conditions on warm summer days.

Figure 27.5 *Central lightwell, tapered to account for increased airflows higher up the building and to maximize daylight provision across the deep-plan floors*

Figure 27.6 *View of south façade showing perimeter stacks, shading fins, deep window reveals and overhangs*

Figure 27.7 *View of the third floor showing the central lightwell, exposed thermal mass, castellated beams and dedicated ventilation stacks*

This was supported by the results of the dynamic thermal simulations, which indicated that the building would be able to maintain internal dry resultant temperatures below 28°C at all times and only exceed 27°C for 11 hours of the year. It was further expected that with refined airflow control, using a sophisticated Building Energy Management System (BEMS), the building would perform better than these results indicated (i.e. lower maximum temperatures were expected).

Natural ventilation strategy

The building relies fully on buoyancy-driven displacement ventilation. Heat gains from the occupants and equipment cause the air in the spaces to warm up and rise. The large floor-to-ceiling height allows stale air to collect above head height and castellated beams (see Figures 27.5 and 27.7) enables it to flow across the ceiling toward the air exhaust openings around the central lightwell and the perimeter stacks (see Figures 27.3a and 27.5) from where it can flow up and out of the building. This stack effect causes fresh air to be drawn into the building at low level through a plenum beneath the ground floor, which supplies the four corner lightwells. From these lightwells the fresh air enters each floor at a low level (see Figures 27.3b and 27.8).

Airflow rates are controlled by dampers located at the entry level to the under-floor plenum and in the exhaust outlet in each perimeter stack. Airflow control to the individual zones on each floor is provided by

Figure 27.8 *Supply lightwell with low-level air inlet dampers and trench heating*

low-level dampers in each corner lightwell and high-level dampers in the central exhaust lightwell.

Heating is provided by preheating coils at the base of each supply lightwell and by trench heating at the point where the air enters onto each floor. Cooling occurs entirely by passive means using a combination of controlled natural ventilation and night-cooled thermal mass.

Building control

On each floor a number of zones with different occupancy and usage characteristics can be identified.

For example, on the second floor (see Figure 27.4) these include an open-plan area with book shelves; a silent study room; two differently sized group study rooms; study desks with PCs (open plan); study desks without PCs (open plan); a print and photocopy room; and two offices.

Conditions in each of the zones, both temperature and air quality (CO_2), are constantly monitored by the Building Energy Management System, which controls air inlet and outlet dampers, as well as heating settings, in order to provide a comfortable environment. To control these processes, the BEMS relies on data from a large number of sensors, which are distributed throughout the building. In the open plan areas, the sensors are positioned near the perimeter stacks, typically four pairs of temperature and CO_2 sensors along each wall. Additional sensor pairs are located in the enclosed study spaces and offices. Based on readings from these sensors, individually controllable dampers are adjusted to provide ventilation for thermal comfort and air quality in each of the zones.

The BEMS also regulates the night-venting behaviour of the building. The BEMS uses a self-learning algorithm to predict the likely ambient temperature for the following day and can thus initiate night-time cooling appropriately.

The following gives a brief overview of the intended operation in summer and in winter mode.

Summer operation

To ensure daytime thermal comfort, night venting is used to cool the exposed thermal mass of the building at night time. Based on prevailing weather conditions and estimated temperatures for the following day, the BEMS controls the air inlet dampers to the plenum and the outlets on the top of the central lightwell. If appropriate, they are opened to allow cool night air to enter the space. Over-cooling is prevented by fully closing all dampers to any floor on which the slab temperature falls below a set point of 18°C.

At the beginning of the occupied period, all dampers open in response to fresh air demand. As occupancy of the individual zones increases, heat gains from occupants and equipment result in buoyancy-driven airflow. The BEMS controls these flows by adjusting opening sizes based on both the air temperature and CO_2 measured in each zone. During

the day, the translucent blinds at the top of the lightwells may be closed to reduce solar gain and, thus, unnecessary heat gain to occupied spaces. The voids at the top of the supply lightwells can be cross-ventilated to avoid unnecessary heating of the supply air.

In order to prevent overheating of the building by ventilation air when the supply air temperature is above the internal space temperature, the inlet dampers are set to their minimum for fresh air provision. Comfortable conditions are then maintained by means of the pre-cooled building fabric and the reservoir of air inside the large building volume. When the supply air temperature falls below this set point and internal temperature readings dictate, the air inlets are opened again to maximize ventilation cooling.

Winter operation

In order to avoid heat loss during unoccupied periods, and particularly at night time, all ventilation openings are closed. The translucent blinds at the top of the lightwells are closed to prevent heat loss by radiation to the night sky. At about two hours prior to occupancy, the heating coils in the plena warm the air in the supply lightwells in order to avoid cold draughts when the supply dampers open into the occupied zones, and to reduce heat loss from the main library into a cold lightwell. When occupancy begins, readings from CO_2 sensors determine when the dampers need to be opened to supply fresh air. When supply air then begins to move from the lightwells onto the main library floors, it can be heated by the trench heaters at the point where it enters at low level onto each floor, if necessary.

Daylight provision is maximized by opening the blinds at the top of the lightwells during daytime.

Performance evaluation

Operation and use of the building

The Lanchester Library opened in September 2000 and now provides a range of library and computing facilities. Coventry University views the building as a landmark building and uses it as a prestigious feature for advertising its campus. The building has received national and international acclaim and won a number of awards, including the Brick Award Building of the

Year 2001; the SCONUL Library Design Award 2002; the Coventry City Council Design Award 2001; and The Institution of Civil Engineers Environmental Award 2001.

The library offers 1100 study places, 350 of which are equipped with PCs. With a daily average of 4500 visitors and average seat occupancy of 65 per cent, the library is significantly more popular than initially anticipated; it was designed for 2500 entries a day. The opening hours have been extended significantly from the originally anticipated period of occupancy of 8.00 am to 8.00 pm. The library is now open from 8.30 am to 12.00 pm during term time and 8.45 am to 9.00 pm during vacation time.

Since the building opened, some changes were made to the layout and operation of the building. During the first few months of operation, users and library staff found that strong draughts occurred on the ground floor as a result of air entering through the main entrance (a covered walkway between the library and the adjacent bookshop). An entrance lobby was added to overcome this problem. The number of PC workstations was increased according to requirements for more computer-based coursework, as anticipated in the client brief.

Both, the library and the estates staff are well aware that naturally ventilated buildings require different maintenance procedures than traditional mechanically ventilated buildings. They are dedicated to making the building work in order to maximize its energy efficiency potential, while maintaining occupant comfort, and therefore pay particular attention to addressing any concerns (e.g. local discomfort reported by staff in certain zones), keeping in mind the intended passive ventilation and cooling strategies.

For example, it was realized that the potential risk of cold air draughts around the supply lightwells in winter could be avoided by simply modifying the damper operating parameters. Rather than changing heating set points or blocking individual air inlets, which would have compromised the intended airflow paths, the risk of draughts was prevented by reducing the maximum opening range of the dampers to 20 per cent during winter operation: for summer operation, the setting is changed back to the default (100 per cent).

According to anecdotal feedback (Rock, 2007), the building has become a popular study location, partly due to its bright and airy feel, which is unusual for such a deep-plan building. The high number of library users

and visitors indicates that the building is well liked, and it has been reported that it functions as an informal meeting place, with the ground floor serving as a focal point for this.

In a world of increasing awareness of the implications of excessive energy consumption, the staff value the building's 'green' credentials and its pleasant working environment, which results from the provision of daylight and fresh air, avoiding all of the drawbacks of air conditioning.

The building's distinctive look makes it a feature of the campus and helps it to be a truly 'landmark' building.

Thermal performance

Using temperature and energy data for the years 2004 and 2005, the performance of the building has been evaluated in terms of its ability to maintain comfortable internal conditions throughout the year. Since overheating in summer is one of the potential problems associated with naturally ventilated buildings, particular attention was given to the effect of the night-time cooling on internal temperatures during periods with high ambient temperatures. The results from the 2004 to 2005 monitoring period were presented by Krausse et al (2007) and are summarized below.

Internal temperatures

Average temperatures inside the building remained relatively stable throughout the year (see Figure 27.9). During the heating season, the daytime indoor temperature remained below 24°C and decreased to approximately 21°C during the night, as set by the heating schedule and heating set points. Temperatures below the 21°C set point can be observed for non-occupied periods during weekends and the Christmas and Easter breaks when the building was not heated. Apart from the daily variability, the temperatures during the heating season also follow a regular weekly pattern, with lowest temperatures recorded on Sunday nights and peak daily temperatures rising throughout the week.

During the warmer periods of the year, internal temperatures are strongly influenced by ambient conditions but remain relatively stable due to the high thermal mass of the building and the night-venting strategy. Even during the two periods of prolonged

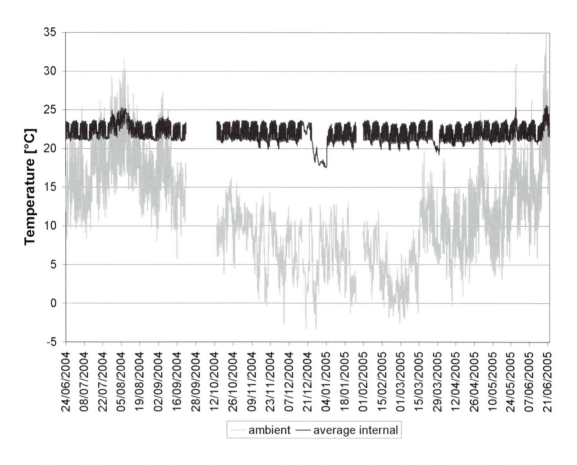

Figure 27.9 *Internal and external temperatures during the monitoring period (June 2004–June 2005)*

high ambient temperatures during the monitoring period, internal temperatures only occasionally exceeded 25°C, while ambient temperatures of up to 35°C were recorded.

During a prolonged hot spell in August 2004, a diurnal temperature swing in excess of 9°C was observed, indicating a substantial night-time cooling potential (see Figure 27.10). The data show that this potential was utilized well: temperatures generally remained in the range of 21°C to 22.5°C during the first four days of the hot spell and then gradually increased, with peak temperatures, however, remaining below 26°C at all times. This represents a temperature depression of over 5°C.

Although temperatures during this hot spell generally stayed within the desired parameters, there was some variation in the behaviour of the individual floors. The ground floor, which has the greatest stack height available and, thus, the greatest potential buoyancy-driving force, had the highest night-time temperature reductions. The third floor tended to be warmer than the second, which was warmer than the first. Considering the relative stack heights on each of these floors, and their similar occupancy characteristics, this is to be expected. It reinforces the notion that it is the top floors of naturally ventilated buildings that are the most susceptible to overheating.

Comparison with overheating criteria and simulation predictions

As outlined above, the computer simulations carried out during the design phase indicated that the building should be able to maintain comfortable internal temperatures throughout the year. In order to assess the building's actual performance, internal temperature

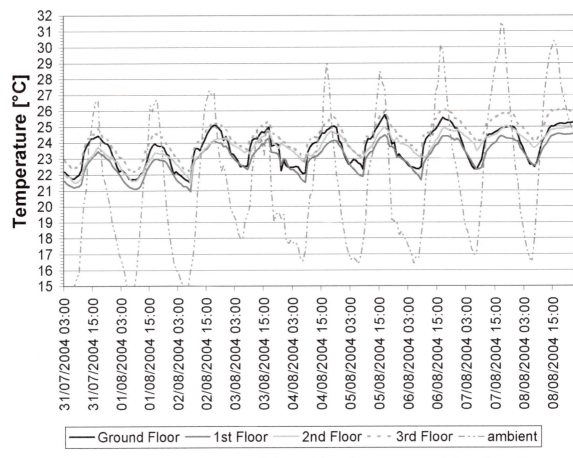

Figure 27.10 *Average temperatures on each floor and the ambient temperature during a 'hot spell'*

data from the monitoring study were compared with predictions from the simulation stage, as well as commonly used overheating criteria, published by the Chartered Institution of Building Services Engineers (CIBSE). The two criteria were:

1   *CIBSE Guide A* (CIBSE, 2006): 'dry resultant temperature should not exceed 28°C for more than 1 per cent of the occupied hours'.
2   *CIBSE Guide J* (CIBSE, 2002): 'dry resultant temperature should not exceed 25°C for more than 5 per cent of the occupied year'.

As shown in Table 27.2, temperatures remained below 25°C on the first floor throughout the monitoring period and only occasionally exceeded 25°C on the other floors. However, all floors of the building met the

CIBSE Guide A thermal comfort criterion, as well as the stricter criterion of the *CIBSE Guide J*. The building's performance also exceeded design stage expectations since internal temperatures never exceeded 27°C, which is better than the 11 hours predicted by the original simulations (Cook et al, 1999a).

Estimated performance in other UK cities

By comparing weather data recorded in Coventry during the monitoring period with that for other UK locations, it is possible to infer how the building would perform at these other locations.

An analysis was presented by Krausse et al (2007), who used CIBSE weather data from 14 UK cities (CIBSE, 2003), ranging in latitude from Plymouth and Southampton in the south to Edinburgh and

Table 27.2 *Number of hours during which various temperature thresholds were exceeded between 26 June 2004 and 24 June 2005 during the occupied period*

Guideline temperature	Number of hours over stated temperature (h)/percentage of occupied hours over stated temperature (%)				
	Ambient	Ground floor	1st floor	2nd floor	3rd floor
25°C	149h/4.1%	78h/1.95%	0/0	32h/0.8%	152h/3.8%
27°C	73h/2.0%	0/0	0/0	0/0	0/0
28°C	48h/1.3%	0/0	0/0	0/0	0/0

Glasgow in the north, to assess whether comfortable conditions would be maintained in the building if it was located in these cities (see Figures 27.11 and 27.12). For each city, both the test reference year (TRY), which typifies conditions experienced at the site, and the design summer year (DSY), which is intended for use in analyses to assess the risk of summertime overheating in naturally ventilated buildings, were used. The TRY is composed of 12 individual months chained together, where each month is the most typical of that experienced during a 20-year period, and the DSY is the third hottest year in the 20-year period (i.e. there is only one year in ten that is likely to be hotter).

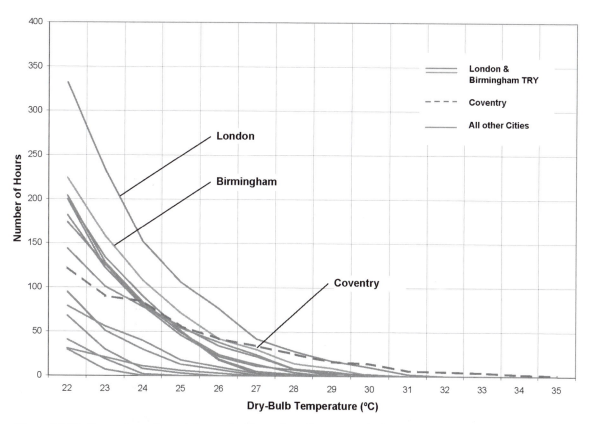

Figure 27.11 *Comparison of recorded exceeding hours from Coventry with the CIBSE's test reference year (TRY) data from 14 UK cities*

The total number of hours for which the ambient temperatures recorded in Coventry exceed certain values is compared with the corresponding values for the TRY and DSY data from 14 other UK locations. As Figure 27.11 demonstrates, the Coventry data show a similar trend to the TRY data of the other cities, but the number of hours with temperatures over 30°C is greater than in any other of the 14 cities. The comparison with DSY data in Figure 27.12 shows that the Coventry temperatures exceeded 26°C to 29°C more frequently than all but three of the other cities, indicating that the monitored year was a comparatively hot year.

Considering that the building met all three of the overheating criteria considered (see Table 27.2), it is reasonable to expect that the building would have met the *CIBSE Guide J* criterion (CIBSE, 2002) (i.e. less than 5 per cent of hours over 25°C, in 12 out of the 14

cities in a typical year; see Figure 27.11). It may also have remained comfortable, as defined by hours over 28°C, in the London environs. However, in the middle of the city comfort may have been compromised due to the substantial urban heat island effect. The results further indicate that the building could be expected to have remained comfortable during hot years (i.e. those that are only exceeded in one year in ten) at all locations, except perhaps Birmingham, Leeds and London (see Figure 27.12).

Energy consumption

The building consumed $0.049\text{kWh}/(\text{m}^2\text{h})$ of gas and electricity in 2004 (see Table 27.3). This includes the heating, lighting and power consumption of the 24-hour computer suite in the basement (air conditioned), as well as the four naturally ventilated

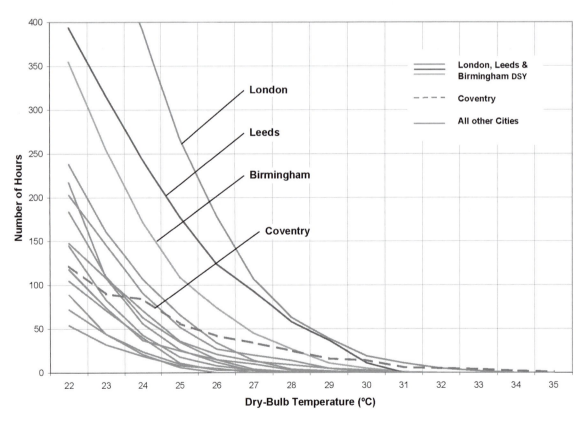

DSY (whole day)

Figure 27.12 *Comparison of recorded exceeding hours from Coventry with the CIBSE's design summer year (DSY) data from 14 UK cities*

Table 27.3 *Energy consumption of library in 2004*

	End Use		
	Heating	Electricity	Cooling
Total annual consumption (MWh)	1117	1012	205
Consumption per m² (kWh/m²)	95	86	17
Consumption per m² and per occupied hour (kWh/m²/h)	0.024	0.021	0.004

library floors. Since the library's energy consumption cannot be disaggregated from the total, a comparison can only be made by including the computer suite's consumption, leading to a rather conservative estimate.

However, even with this included, the building performs significantly better than the ECON19 typical benchmark for office buildings (BRECSU, 2000). As shown in Figure 27.13, the building uses 51 per cent less energy than the typical air-conditioned building and 35 per cent less energy than the typical naturally ventilated open-plan building. In fact, the Lanchester

Library also performs better than the office building built to the good practice standard for naturally ventilated open-plan office buildings.

Conclusions

The Lanchester Library at Coventry University uses a number of features that are typical for low-energy naturally ventilated buildings: exposed thermal mass; night-time ventilation; solar shading; high levels of insulation; good glazing specification; and daylight provision. By using these features, the design team was able to create a deep-plan city centre building that remains comfortable throughout the year without having the high energy demands associated with air conditioning and artificial lighting.

Performance monitoring has shown that temperatures within the library remain relatively stable and meet the overheating criteria recommended by CIBSE. The building would be expected to perform equally well in a range of other urban locations in the UK. Data has further shown that in terms of its energy-use statistics, the library compares favourably with good practice guidelines for similar buildings.

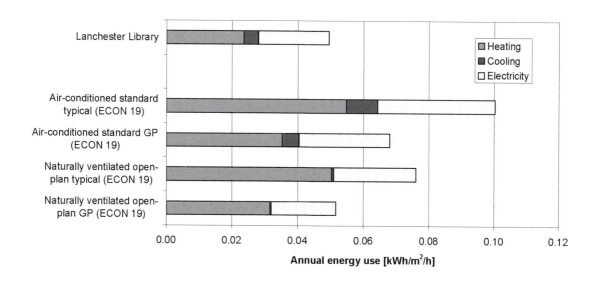

Source: BRECSU (2000)

Figure 27.13 *Comparison of the library's annual energy consumption during 2004 with ECON19 benchmark values for typical and good practice offices*

The successful measured performance is supplemented by positive perception. The library is considered a comfortable and stimulating place in which to work and study and is also used as a popular meeting place.

The success of the Lanchester Library shows that the perceived barriers to natural ventilation techniques, such as the need for deep-plan built forms, sealed façades to maintain indoor air quality and low noise levels and high internal heat gains due to computers with long periods of occupancy, can be overcome by applying an intelligently designed advanced natural ventilation approach.

It is, however, important that such innovative design is supported by the client, who needs to be actively involved throughout the design process in order to ensure that the building fulfils all their needs and to appreciate how the building is intended to function. This knowledge transfer ensures that after commissioning, the building is operated in a way that fully utilizes its low energy-use potential.

In the case of the Lanchester Library, the close involvement of the energy manager has revealed that adapting the operating strategy to seasonal variations in ambient conditions can result in improved performance. For example, summertime performance can be improved by closing the air inlet dampers when external temperatures rise above internal temperatures (controlling ventilation based on fresh air demand only), and the risk of over-ventilation in winter can be reduced by limiting the ventilation openings compared to summer operation, resulting in reduced heating energy consumption and draught risk.

Client involvement is also likely to result in a stronger feeling of ownership, which in turn helps to promote the building as a desirable space in which to work and as an asset that is cared for. It may also help users to view unusual characteristics of such a building as positive, rather than negative, features ('it has character').

The library has also demonstrated that it is possible to co-locate areas within a naturally ventilated building that are to be occupied for longer periods of time, especially into the evenings and night, by keeping them separately accessed and controlled. This approach ensures comfortable working conditions for night-time occupants without compromising the night-time cooling procedures and, thus, the thermal performance of the building's naturally ventilated areas.

Acknowledgements

The building was designed by Short and Associates Architects with staff from the Institute of Energy and Sustainable Development at De Montfort University serving as the environmental design consultants. The mechanical and electrical services consultants were Environmental Design Partnership. We gratefully acknowledge the continuing support from Pat Noon (head librarian), Caroline Rock (deputy librarian) and their colleagues, and from the Estates Department at Coventry University, particularly Jim Skelhon.

References

BRECSU (Building Research Energy Conservation Support Unit) (2000) *Energy Use in Offices, Energy Consumption Guide 19*, BRECSU, Energy Efficiency Best Practice Programme, www.cibse.org/pdfs/ECG019.pdf, accessed April 2008

CIBSE (Chartered Institution of Building Services Engineers) (2002) *CIBSE Guide J: Weather, Solar and Illuminance Data*, CIBSE, London

CIBSE (2003) *CIBSE/Met Office TRY/DSY Hourly Weather Data Set (CD-ROM) – 14 Sites*, CIBSE, London

CIBSE (2006) *CIBSE Guide A: Environmental Design*, CIBSE, London

Cook, M. J. and Short, C. A. (2005) 'Natural ventilation and low energy cooling of large, non-domestic buildings – four case studies', *International Journal of Ventilation*, vol 3, no 4, pp283–294

Cook, M. J., Lomas, K. J. and Eppel, H. (1999a) 'Use of computer simulation in the design of a naturally ventilated library', in *Proceedings of the PLEA99 Conference*, Brisbane, Australia, September 1999

Cook, M. J., Lomas, K. J. and Eppel, H. (1999b) 'Design and operating concept for an innovative naturally ventilated library', in *Proceedings of CIBSE National Conference*, Harrogate, UK, October 1999

DoE (UK Department of the Environment) (1995) *Approved Document L: Conservation of Fuel and Power, 1995 edition*, Building Regulations 1991, DoE, HMSO, London

Field, J. (2000) 'Breeze blocks', *Building Services Journal*, December, pp18–22

Holmes, M. J. and Hitchin, E. R. (1978) 'An example year for the calculation of energy demands in buildings', *Building Services Engineering*, vol 45, pp186–190

Krausse, B., Cook, M. J. and Lomas, K. J. (2007) 'Environmental performance of a naturally ventilated city centre library', *Energy and Buildings*, vol 39, no 7, pp792–801

Lomas, K. J. (2007) 'Architectural design of an advanced naturally ventilated building form', *Energy and Buildings*, vol 39, no 2, pp166–181

Lomas, K. J. and Cook, M. J. (2005) 'Sustainable buildings for a warmer world', in *Proceedings of the World Renewable Energy Congress*, Aberdeen, 22–27 May 2005

McDonald, A. (2002) 'Celebrating outstanding new library buildings', *Newsletter of the Society of College, National and University Libraries*, no 27, www.sconul.ac.uk/publications/newsletter/27/ARTICL27.PDF, accessed March 2008

ODPM (Office of the Deputy Prime Minister) (2006) *Approved Document L2A: Conservation of Fuel and Power in New Buildings other than Dwellings, 2006 edition*, Building Regulations 2000, ODPM, RIBA, London

Pidwell, S. (2001) 'Lanchester Library by Short and Associates', *Architecture Today*, vol 115, February, pp38–49

Rock, C. (2007) Deputy university librarian at Coventry University, Pers comm

Short, C. A., Lomas, K. J. and Woods, A. (2004) 'Design strategy for low-energy ventilation and cooling within an urban heat island', *Building Research and Information*, vol 32, no 3, pp187–206

28

Impact of an Energy Refurbishment Programme in Chile: More than Energy Savings

Eugenio Collados and Gabriela Armijo

Introduction

The energy crisis derived from increasing oil prices is striking low-income housing in Chile by aggravating the chronic problems of the poverty circle that links income, housing and health. The prevalent model of urban and architectural design reliant on plentiful energy, long-distance transportation and access to global markets is showing its weakness and vulnerability. Primary energy sources in Chile are increasingly dependent upon imported fuels, precisely when natural gas availability has plummeted and oil prices keep climbing. Inexpensive local wood fuel could be an alternative for domestic heating; but current technology is not environmentally compatible with urban population density. Thus, an urgent strategic change is required at all decision-making levels, recognizing the need to become energy independent. This change points to energy efficiency, less foreign dependence and major improvements in construction and heating technologies.

The lack of reaction in Chile after the 1970s world energy crisis, mostly due to the local availability of inexpensive fuels and a policy in favour of unregulated markets, has revealed a costly outcome in economic, social and environmental terms. In addition, the effects of a technological gap of two decades are such that fewer solutions are currently being offered, little knowledge has been integrated within architectural training and few engineering firms are prepared to take up the coming task.

Box 28.1 Fuel poverty concept

A first definition of the 'fuel poverty' concept was given by Lewis (1982) as 'the inability to afford adequate warmth in the home', in the National Right to Fuel Campaign in Bradford, UK. It refers to households that would need to spend more than 10 per cent of their annual income on fuels in order to achieve satisfactory indoor heating. The concept is what people would need to spend, not what they actually spend. In other terms, a fuel-poor household spends too much and/or suffers poor heating.

A definition more closely related to housing design is given by Healy (2004): 'The inability to heat one's home to an adequate (safe and comfortable) temperature owing to low income and poor (energy inefficient) housing'.

The British definition assumes as satisfactory heating where the main living area is at 21°C, with 18°C in other occupied rooms. It is assumed that heating is available for 16 hours per day for households likely to have occupants home all day, and nine hours per day for households in work or full-time education (Defra, 2003).

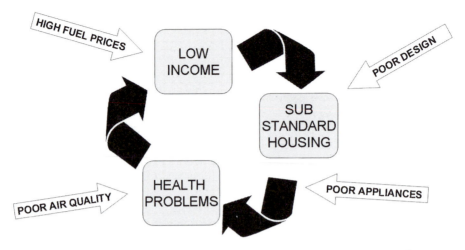

Figure 28.1 *Energy poverty aggravates chronic problems of the poverty cycle*

To face these problems, several initiatives are in place. The housing ministry started to enforce an energy building code in 2000 for all new housing. However, the replacement of the stock is very slow, given the lifetime of buildings. Widespread awareness of the profits of energy efficiency has not been enough to encourage investment mechanisms due to market failure (see Box 28.2). Since it is becoming more difficult to keep the existing stock operating at a sustainable level, the government advocates a policy aimed at improving the energy performance of this stock by attempting to break these market barriers. Consequently, a study was commissioned during 2006 to:

• identify and assess the potential measures and resources required for an energy refurbishment of residential buildings;
• estimate the impacts on energy demand from such measures;
• propose management models in order to channel private investment and promote private investment; and
• estimate the expected benefits, both private and social (Ambiente Consultores, 2007).

On the other hand, the National Commission of the Environment (CONAMA – the future ministry of the environment) promotes several programmes to control emissions from wood combustion appliances for heating and cooking. Since wood is by far the least expensive energy source for these purposes, just restricting its use as fuel is not practicable since it would necessarily increase health and inequality problems. As a result, the method of reducing emissions aims to lessen heating demand by means of improving the thermal performance of buildings and appliances, as well as encouraging the use of low-moisture firewood.

This chapter presents some results of these and other related studies and presents a pilot case study.

Box 28.2 Market failure: A barrier to improvements in energy efficiency

Energy-saving opportunities are immense with current technology; but new product standard mandates will be needed. Electricity consumption in residential buildings in the US in 2020 could be reduced by more than one third. The energy saving would result in a significant reduction in the amounts of fossil fuel burned and carbon dioxide, the main greenhouse gas, spewed into the atmosphere. Yet, market forces alone (even considerably higher energy prices) will not be enough to cause wholesale adoption of the most energy efficient technology.

This study emphasizes the need for correcting market distortions. Such distortions result from individuals lacking adequate information to make the best decisions or the market's failure to encourage individuals to make energy efficient investments.

'Everyone would be better off if the capital investments were made; but the individual parties do not have the incentives to make the needed investments.'

Source: McKinsey Global Institute (2007)

Background information

Energy and residential sector

The residential sector has not played a relevant role in the making of strategic decisions about energy-secure supply and efficient use in Chile. Access to electricity has been the only aspect of concern in national energy policies. A single fact clarifies the irrelevance of residential energy use: new buildings receive the approval certificate with no need to have a heating system or even a design of a heating system. Most buyers or tenants have to manage by themselves in order to provide some form of heating, choosing from the retail market without much technical or financial support.

Heating represents about 11 per cent of the country's energy consumption, although typical warmth and health conditions in residential buildings are far from being considered satisfactory. This historical failure to achieve effective, efficient and clean heating operation in residential buildings represents an enormous opportunity for energy efficient initiatives.

For this reason, this sector has been included in the recently initiated series of Energy Efficiency Programmes.

Social housing and energy policy

A social housing policy aimed at building the highest possible number of dwellings has prevailed in Chile for a long time, in spite of compromising quality standards. The model has been based on the state financing low-cost dwellings (under 10,000 Euros per unit, including land value). This model involves large building companies producing vast housing developments settled on low-priced suburban areas. Little care for urban design, architectural quality or technological innovation has resulted (Rodríguez and Sugranyes, 2005). The recent emphasis on the energy factor has dramatically exposed the unsustainability of such models. Programmes for enhancing the design standards of social housing have recently begun to provide a better living environment, acceptable size of dwellings and basic habitability. The poor quality of the existing stock and urban decay are also matters of growing concern.

The housing stock in Chile comprises approximately 4.4 million dwellings, of which only 0.8 million were built after the year 2000, when basic thermal insulation goals began to be enforced.

From those 3.6 million earlier dwellings, very few could be considered adequately insulated or sited in places that require little heating, meaning that there is an urgent need and significant opportunity for energy refurbishing. Otherwise, the burden of energy expenses on households would exacerbate low income, health problems, fabric decay and environmental problems.

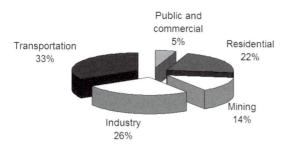
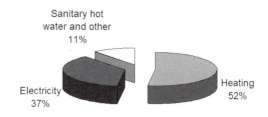

Source: CNE (2007)

Figure 28.2 *Energy share by sector (left) and by final use (right) for the residential sector in Chile*

Finally, it could end in a depreciation of scarce family assets, averting any hope of breaking the poverty cycle.

Facing the question of where to start in implementing an energy refurbishment programme, the first approach should be to arrange priorities simply according to climatic loads, starting from colder regions. However, heating deficiencies and energy poverty are not concentrated in higher latitudes since they are dependent on and biased by other social factors, particularly the source of available energy. In the far south regions (latitude 53° S), natural gas is still available, meaning low-cost supply in urban areas and energy poverty in rural areas. Population density is also scarce. Farther north (between latitudes 36° S and 45° S), climate is rainy, forests abundant and firewood is readily available in the countryside. In towns, however, fuel demand and prices have been rising continuously, becoming a heavy load for most families since the heating season may be nine to ten months long.

For many years there had been a shift from traditional solid fuels (coal, firewood and charcoal) to bottled propane and, in large cities, piped natural gas. A rise in propane price has meant that some families have had to return to their old firewood cookers, putting even more pressure on increasing fuel demand and atmospheric emissions. Northern towns, with milder winter seasons, are still relying on propane as a main source of heating, but gradually have started to shift to firewood stoves for heating.

In some southern urban areas, over 80 per cent of households rely on firewood while remaining energy poor; worst of all, air pollutants have deteriorated air quality to such an extent that health problems have become a major threat, in addition to diseases related to cold exposure and unflued heating. This fact has made it imperative to seek improvements in the energy performance of the housing stock in order to reduce the incidence of burning wood.

Box 28.3 Climates in Chile

Extreme latitudes in Chile are 18° S and 54° S, with urban areas at altitudes from sea level up to 2400m, involving all sort of climates except hot humid.

Biomes in Chile range from arid deserts in the north to cold steppes to the far south, with a strong contrast between coastal and inland valleys. Excluding high mountains, the lowest temperatures are found at latitudes 50° S and more than 100 km away from the sea.

This diversity of climates is both a challenge and an opportunity for smart design. In particular, in any location of the country, overheating control in summer can be achieved exclusively by passive means, either through solar control, roof reflectance, night ventilation, radiation cooling, evaporative cooling or other design options. Thus, there is no reason at all for air conditioning in residential buildings in Chile.

In most inland regions, wide day–night temperature fluctuations and moderate average temperatures allow for passive strategies based on thermal mass in order to reduce energy loads.

Current strategies to face the energy crisis in buildings

The current thermal quality regulations for new residential construction began to be enforced in 2000 for all new dwellings in Chile, according to seven thermal zones depending upon location and altitude. At its first stage, it covered only loft insulation. Since 2007, regulations were extended to windows, external walls and exposed floors, but only considered the main fabric of each envelope element, with no correction for thermal bridges. This regulation specifies mandatory maximum U values in W/m²K. No requirements are set yet for ground heat transfer, air infiltration, ventilation or heating. Table 28.1 shows a summary of requirements.

This regulation states the bottom line for design; but in most cases a much higher standard would be justified by a simple cost-benefit analysis, even with current fuel prices. However, both the lack of information by new owners in making their choice and the neglectful cover-up by the construction industry put pressure against reaching higher standards.

Regarding existing dwellings, the recent governmental response to face the fuel price increase was to subsidize the demand by compensating for its impact on low-income household budgets during winter. In reality, this policy would only sustain wastefulness and dependency upon imported fossil

Table 28.1 *Minimum requirements for new residential buildings according to thermal zones*

Thermal zone	Degree days (reference: 15°C)	Minimum U value for loft insulation	Minimum U value for walls	Minimum U value for exposed floors
		W/m² K	W/m² K	W/m² K
1	< 500	0.84	4.0	3.60
2	500–750	0.60	3.0	0.87
3	750–1000	0.47	1.9	0.70
4	1000–1250	0.38	1.7	0.60
5	1250 to 1500	0.33	1.6	0.50
6	1500–2000	0.28	1.1	0.39
7	>2000	0.25	0.9	0.32

fuels. In contrast, a subsidy aimed at reducing energy demand would result in permanent relief for household budgets, while also stimulating local markets with emerging insulation technologies and skilled labour. Ironically, running inefficient buildings with no refurbishment is the most expensive alternative by far.

Recent trends and energy crisis

Energy supply at the national level appeared to be secure and cost effective after gas pipes were built in the 1990s to bring natural gas from Argentina. Improvements in air pollution, wider access to utility gas and less expensive electricity were all positive results for over a decade. During this period, most new developments in energy technology were based on natural gas creating a lock-in. At the same time, renewable energies and biomass fuels were neglected as 'non-competitive' technologies, despite social awareness

and interest. However, imported gas shortages began in 2003 and prices have since kept increasing.

Heavy pressure is now being put on firewood, raising air pollution to unacceptable levels. Old firewood cookers are becoming valuable appliances for winter heating and many central heating gas boilers have been left redundant (Collados and Cifuentes, 2007). The effect of using wood combustion appliances for heating and cooking is directly related to PM_{10} concentrations – as is the case, for example, in the city of Temuco (see Figure 28.4).

On the other hand, architectural design is not prepared for changing to other heating systems such as solar thermal or geothermal, either centralized or individual, so propane portable heaters are the only alternative left to many urban households, particularly in blocks of apartments. Again, rising prices reveal how poor design could make a huge stock of buildings unsustainable under future conditions.

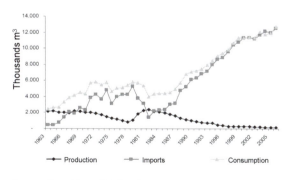 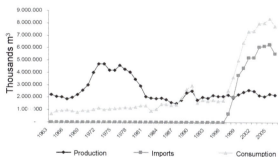

Source: adapted from CNE (2007)

Figure 28.3 *Historic evolution of dependence upon foreign fuels and the short-lived conversion to natural gas during the 1990s: Oil (left) and natural gas (right)*

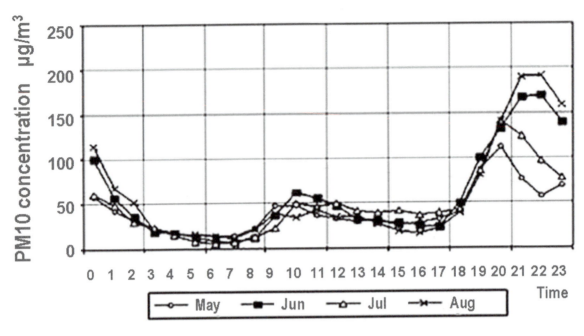

Source: Sanhueza et al (2006)

Figure 28.4 *Hourly PM$_{10}$ concentrations in Temuco*

Box 28.4 Barriers in technology uptake

In the residential sector, where energy makes up only a relatively small portion of total expenditure, the gap between the optimal and current level of energy efficiency is particularly large as a result of numerous market barriers. These barriers include lack of information and technical understanding, lack of disposable income for upfront capital investment, and split incentives between purchasers of equipment and consumers of energy.

Technology lock-in arises when a competitive advantage results in the mass uptake of a particular technology or fuel upon which the economy becomes reliant. Technological lock-in can prevent new technologies from entering the market given the significant costs associated with developing new supporting infrastructure and industries.

Source: Ford et al (2007)

Box 28.5 Health impacts from air pollution

Some of the main parameters to measure the impacts of air pollution on health are the daily number of healthcare deliveries under acute respiratory diseases (ARD) and the infant mortality form of ARD.

A strong correlation between the time series of deliveries has been found with the following variables (Barrios et al 2004):

- environmental: particulate matter under 2.5 micrometres in size (PM$_{2.5}$);
- meteorological: seasonal cycles and cold spells;
- epidemiological: outbreaks of contagious diseases;
- demographic groups: children under the age of five; pregnant women; older people;
- social vulnerability: overcrowding, substandard housing and poor combustion heating.

A recent study (Sanhueza et al, 2006) has identified the group of adults over the age of 65 as a high risk in Temuco. Several of these factors are directly related to the poor quality and/or the poor design of dwellings and their heating systems.

Figure 28.5 *Winter atmosphere in Temuco*

Fuel costs for heating

The cost of energy for heating may represent up to 20 per cent of household income for the lowest quintile. These most vulnerable population groups include those with less access to energy sources, the socially excluded and indigenous segments, mostly in southern regions (Márquez and Miranda, 2007). Even with such an impact on household budgets, heating needs cannot be fully afforded and average effective temperatures of around 13°C are far from satisfactory (see also Table 28.4)

The distribution of household income and energy expenditures is shown in Table 28.2.

Table 28.2 *Energy expenses per household per income quintile, excluding firewood*

	Quintile 1	Quintile 2	Quintile 3	Quintile 4	Quintile 5
Per capita annual income	477 Euros	928 Euros	1429 Euros	2208 Euros	7678 Euros
Percentage of household budget spent on energy, 1996	7.9%	5.8%	5.2%	4.2%	2.9%
Percentage of household budget spent on energy, 2006	10.8%	8.1%	7.3%	5.8%	3.9%

The above percentages could rise by 2% to 8% when firewood is included.

Source: Moreno and Rosenblüth (2006) and Márquez and Miranda (2007)

Box 28.6 Population in Chile, income distribution and housing quality

The population in Chile is 14.4 million urban and 2.2 million rural individuals (2002), growing at 1.3 per cent per year. Mortality rate is 5.4 per 1000 inhabitants, with an average life expectancy of 74.8 years. The average number of residents per dwelling is 4.2.

The quality assessment of dwellings shows a strong inequality, measured by the percentage of units with some deficit disaggregated by income quintile.

Table 28.3 *Percentage of dwellings with deficit per income quintile*

Type of deficit	Quintile 1	Quintile 2	Quintile 3	Quintile 4	Quintile 5
Overcrowding	27.9	15.5	8.5	4.7	1.4
Poor fabric quality	37.7	23.7	18.6	11.6	5.7
Poor access to utilities	31.8	19.0	12.7	6.5	3.7
Any type of deficit	61.8	42.2	31.0	18.9	9.4

Source: Moreno and Rosenblüth (2006)

About 79 per cent of dwellings have a quality mark 'acceptable'; 17 per cent are 'unacceptable but recoverable'; about 4 per cent are qualified 'unrecoverable'; and 11 per cent need enlargement to become 'acceptable'.

Appliances

The share of residential energy consumption by source is 14 per cent electricity; 8 per cent natural gas; 19 per cent liquefied propane gas (LPG), kerosene and oil derivatives; and 59 per cent wood and wood derivatives (Márquez and Miranda, 2007). The vast majority of kerosene and LPG heaters have open-flame unflued burners, generating significant amounts of water vapour and indoor pollution. A high percentage of wood consumption is concentrated in southern regions between 36° S and 45° S, and the wood is mostly used in burners that have efficiencies typically below 50 per cent.

If rural areas are included, only 63.2 per cent of households in Chile have a hot water heater or boiler – that is, about 1.6 million have no access to hot water. However, installed solar heaters reach only 6000m², or about 3000 dwellings in Chile, despite plentiful solar radiation availability reaching annual insolation values of between 1500 and 2000 kWh/m² for most cities.

Field assessment

A survey study carried out during winter 2007 (July and August) (IC, 2007) showed the actual temperatures

Table 28.4 *Percentage of urban households using appliances by energy source*

	Cooking	Heating	Hot water
Electricity	3%	11%	1%
LPG	88%	36%	70%
Natural gas	13%	3%	14%
Kerosene	0%	22%	0%
Wood	24%	67%	0%

(May include more than one source per household and use.)

Source: Baytelman (2005)

in 392 households located in four cities at different latitudes. All dwellings were built after 2002, meaning that they included loft insulation according to regulations. Some results of the survey are summarized in Table 28.5.

The survey also asked about the thermal perception of the residents, assessing it through a 1- to 7-point scale: 1 being 'fully unsatisfactory' and 7 'fully satisfactory'. The curve in Figure 28.6 shows that the population sample voted 'fully satisfied' when heating provided was, on average, 16.8°C.

Table 28.5 *Results from a survey on a sample of 400 dwellings built after 2002*

Town, latitude	Heating hours per day	Time of the day	Outdoor temperature (°C)	Indoor dry bulb temperature (DBT) temperature (°C)	Walls radiant temperature (°C)	Effective temperature (°C)
La Serena 29.9 S	1.18	Morning	15.4	15.6	10.7	13.1
		Afternoon	17.8	17.9	15.6	16.8
		Evening	15.8	18.0	16.9	17.4
Santiago 33.4 S	7.18	Morning	11.4	13.0	5.8	9.4
		Afternoon	15.5	15.6	11.3	13.4
		Evening	13.0	14.9	10.8	12.8
Concepción 36.5 S	7.02	Morning	11.1	11.8	2.7	7.2
		Evening	15.7	15.7	6.6	11.2
		Evening	12.9	14.7	7.6	11.2
Puerto Montt 41.5 S	13.88	Morning	9.3	13.6	10.8	12.2
		Afternoon	14.3	16.6	16.1	16.7
		Evening	12.5	16.1	16.9	17.2

Source: IC (2007)

It can be concluded that despite the growing incidence of energy expenses on household budgets, satisfactory levels of comfort and healthiness are not achieved. Again, reckless design and market failure are to blame.

Box 28.7 Effective temperature

The energy balance between the human body and its environment involves exchanges, through contact with the surrounding air and non-contact infrared radiation with surrounding surfaces. About 75 per cent of the subjectively perceived temperature is explained by air dry bulb temperature (DBT) and surfaces temperature. Other factors include air speed and humidity. Since radiation from different surfaces may vary, uneven radiation may also affect thermal comfort. In addition, body activity has a strong influence on comfort, given that all other variables are fixed.

Some definitions of effective temperature consider all factors; but in the cited field study, only DBT and radiant temperature were measured, assuming negligible air movement and calculating the effective temperature as the average between radiant and DBT values. Radiant temperature is measured with a non-contact infrared thermometer, with adjustment of the emissivity coefficient.

Design of a prioritized refurbishment programme

How to assess priorities

The method that was used for devising the energy refurbishment programme is presented here (Ambiente Consultores, 2007). It includes the following stages:

- characterization of type, form, materials and heating systems of the housing stock;
- estimation of the current energy intensity of the housing stock;
- proposal of refurbishment goals, regional adjustment and optimized priorities;
- expected energy intensity improvement, cost analysis and payback;
- expected social and private benefits;
- institutional requirements, human resources and financing schemes.

The output of the method is a prioritized programme that put a figure on costs and benefits for different refurbishing options applied to different building types and different locations.

Existing residential building types

In order to define the baseline (i.e. to estimate the thermal performance of existing housing stock), assumptions should be made about the buildings types

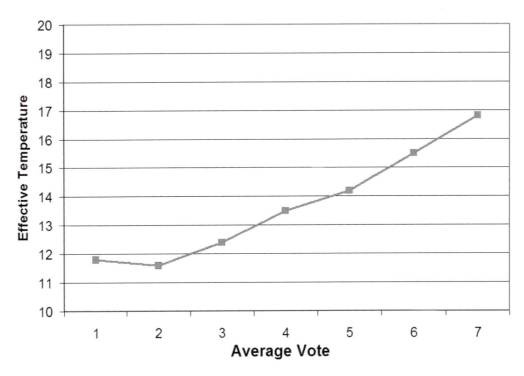

Source: IC (2007)

Figure 28.6 *Vote on subjective thermal perception in relation to effective indoor temperature*

that best represent the diversity of designs. Fifteen types had been already identified in an earlier study by DECON (2003). From those 15, the 10 most widespread types (see Figure 28.8) have been considered representative of all the existing stock built before 2000 for the purpose of this simulation, as detailed in Table 28.6.

Eight of the ten types have no insulation at all. Two types have loft insulation but no wall insulation. Most houses rely on a single heating appliance, and a small fraction of apartment buildings have central heating systems. Usually, hot water is provided by an independent gas heater (a tank-less type).

An example of a semi-detached type 2 house in La Pintana (thermal zone 3) is shown in Figure 28.9. The brick is exposed, with no insulation. Lofts are insulated with 80mm of glass wool.

An example of type 4 three-storey apartments in La Florida (thermal zone 3) is shown in Figure 28.10.

Examples of detached type 3 houses in Coyhaique (thermal zone 7) and type 6 and 8 houses in Valparaíso (thermal zone 2) are shown in Figure 28.11. Full cladding and insulation is standard in zone 7. There is no insulation in the walls, although 60mm of glass wool is required in lofts in zone 2.

Baseline energy intensity

Once defining the 'universe' of existing dwellings, it is necessary to estimate their thermal performance. Energy intensity measures the annual amount in kWh/m²/yr of effective thermal energy to be supplemented in order to ensure a 15°C minimum temperature throughout the winter, not including other gains from occupation, cooking or lighting.

Firstly, for each type of dwelling, a detailed analysis was carried out to calculate the rate of heat loss according to a temperature difference of 1°C as follows:

$$\text{Rate of heat loss} = \text{envelope heat loss} + \text{air change heat loss} \qquad (1)$$
$$\text{Rate of heat loss (Wh}^{-1}) = \Sigma\, U_i\, A_i \times 3600 + \text{ACH } V_h\, \rho_o\, c_p$$

BASELINE

REFURBISHMENT

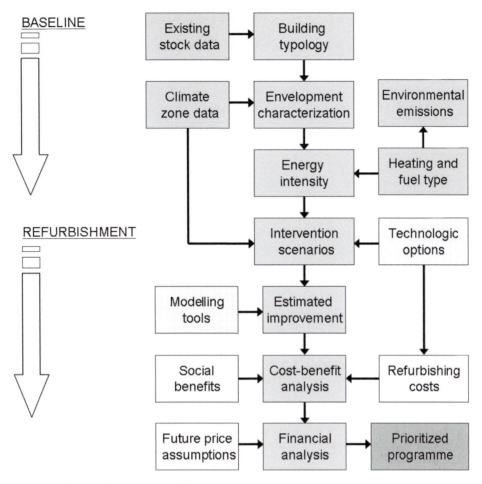

Figure 28.7 *Method of design of the prioritized refurbishment programme*

where:

- ρ_o = air density = 1.225kg/m³, at p_o = 101325Pa and T_o = 15°C;
- c_p = air heat capacity = 1.006kJ/kg K = 2.79 10⁻⁴ kWh/kg K;
- V_h (m³) = heated indoor volume;
- ACH (h⁻¹) = air change rate in air changes per hour;
- U_i (W/m² K) = air-to-air transmittance (U value) of envelope element i;
- A_i (m²) = exposed area of envelope element i.

Air changes were estimated as 2 (h⁻¹).

Then, for each combination of type and climate, the heating demand was estimated by:

Annual heating demand (kWh) = rate of heat loss × annual degree hours   (2)

Annual heating demand (kWh) = (Σ U_i A_i × 3600 + ACH V_h ρ_o c_p) × degree hours.

The degree hours were obtained from the monthly average data. A rather low reference temperature of 15°C was measured, considering that neither solar nor internal gains were taken into account. Values range from 10,000 to 77,000 heating degree hours. Solar

Table 28.6 *Characteristics of dwellings for ten representative types used in the baseline study*

	Prevalence (percentage)	Storeys	Size (m²)	Main material	Attachment
Type 1	13.9	1	32.5	Hand-made brick	Semi-detached
Type 2	12.3	2	40.0	Concrete reinforced brick	Semi-detached
Type 3	8.8	1	39.8	Wood	Detached, above ground
Type 4	7.8	3	42.8	Concrete reinforced brick	Apartments
Type 5	7.4	1	72.0	Hand-made brick	Detached
Type 6	5.7	2	81.1	Concrete reinforced brick	Semi-detached
Type 7	3.4	2	39.9	Wood	Semi-detached
Type 8	3.1	2	74.3	Brick ground floor Wooden first floor	Detached
Type 9	2.1	12	67.7	Concrete	Apartments
Type 10	2.0	6	68.3	Concrete	Apartments

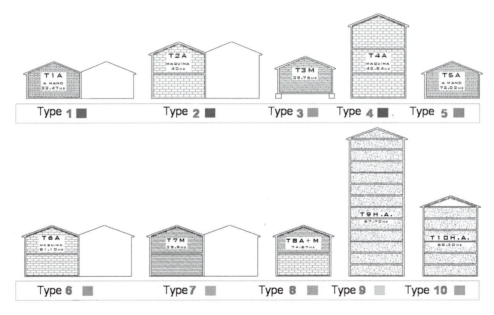

Source: adapted from DECON (2003)

Figure 28.8 *Building types (schematic) used in the baseline study*

gains could represent a significant gain in some locations, even in winter; but these calculations were not considered since orientation of type buildings is not a defined variable.

The resulting average energy intensity for the existing stock is 208kWh/m²/yr, spread in a wide range from 60 to 600kWh/m²/yr.

Potential scenarios of refurbishment

The best possible allocation of financial resources requires defining the number, type and places of dwellings to be refurbished, as well as the amount of investment in each one. Even assuming that any improvement of the thermal performance would be

Table 28.7 *Combinations of building type and geographic location for the 56 cases of the baseline that would represent existing dwellings built before 2000*

City	Calama	Valparaíso	Santiago	Concepción	Temuco	Pto. Montt	Pta. Arenas
Latitude	22.5 S	32.5 S	33.4 S	36.5 S	38.7 S	41.5 S	53.0 S
Altitude (m)	2320	9	475	12	114	85	37
Thermal zone	2	2	3	4	5	6	7
Degree hours	40,810	10,442	17,393	18,186	33,789	30,648	76,900
Type 1	x	x	x	x	x		
Type 2	x	x	x	x	x		x
Type 3		x		x	x	x	x
Type 4	x	x	x	x	x	x	
Type 5	x	x	x	x	x	x	x
Type 6		x	x	x	x	x	
Type 7		x	x	x	x	x	x
Type 8	x	x	x	x	x	x	x
Type 9		x	x	x	x		
Type 10		x	x	x	x	x	
Total	5	10	9	10	10	7	5

Source: Ambiente Consultores (2007)

Source: Oficina de Vivienda

Figure 28.9 *Example of social housing project under construction in La Pintana*

profitable in the long term, it is essential to make clear the priorities in assigning the right type of intervention and the right degree of improvement. The optimization process should consider the dwelling baseline, local climate, local fuel type and fuel price, as well as environmental, social or other factors, in order to allow fair comparisons between the simulated scenarios.

The first step was to define four scenarios for gradual steps of intervention:

- Scenario 1, or the baseline, involves only the maintenance of the existing stock with no improvement of energy performance.
- Scenario 2 involves reaching the energy standard according to mandatory regulation for new housing, including loft and wall insulation.
- Scenario 3 involves the same goals as scenario 2, but with extra wall insulation to match loft insulation.

Source: G. Armijo

Figure 28.10 *Example of social housing in La Florida*

- Scenario 4 involves the same goals as scenario 3, but with higher-quality windows of U value 2.4W/m²K.

For all interventions, the air change rate was assumed to be reduced to 1 air changes per hour (ACH); as a result, no mechanical ventilation is required to satisfy indoor air quality standards. Scenarios with higher airtightness would be desirable, but were beyond the scope of this simulation.

The baseline simulation model was then modified for each scenario, replacing the calculation parameters in order to assess the changes in energy performance. Each refurbishment scenario is then assessed by the energy intensity per square metre for any particular combination of dwelling type and climate. Results are expressed as a frequency distribution of dwellings according to its energy intensity value. Figure 28.12 shows the lightest grey curve for the baseline (no intervention) and darker shades of grey for scenarios 2, 3 and 4, representing growing degrees of intervention. The majority of the current stock of dwellings exhibit intensities above 100kWh/m²/yr, even some above 500kWh/m²/yr. For scenario 4, almost all intensities fall below 120kWh/m²/yr.

Average intensities for intervention scenarios 2, 3 and 4 would be 96, 75 and 66kWh/m²/yr, respectively, implying savings from 54 up to 68 per cent relative to current intensities.

Costs per refurbished dwelling

An inventory analysis was carried out in order to quantify materials usage and labour for each one of the 280 possible interventions. From a market analysis of the existing options to comply with transmittance values, the less expensive options were selected. Unit cost calculations included locally adjusted transportation and installation labour costs.

Source: JAVE

Figure 28.11 *Examples of house type 3 in thermal zone 7 and types 6 and 8 in thermal zone 2*

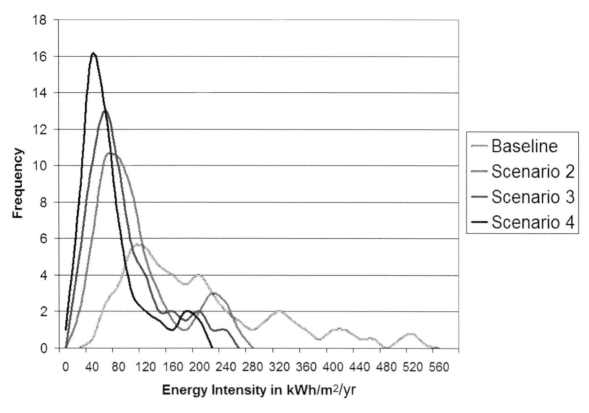

Figure 28.12 *Distribution of energy intensity for different scenarios versus the baseline*

Interventions to reach scenario 2 (compliance with new construction regulation) would cost up to 52 Euros per square metre. In some cases, the only cost would be sealing air infiltrations.

Interventions under scenarios 3 and 4 would cost between 27 Euros to 90 Euros per square metre (floor area of the dwelling). Compared to new building costs of around 250 Euros per square metre, refurbishment costs represent 11 to 36 per cent of the cost of new construction of social housing.

As expected, energy intensity reductions for the more substantial interventions are less significant in relation to additional cost. Considering all cases, the reduction in energy intensity could be up to 400kWh/m²/yr with an investment of 61 Euros per square metre. However, for some cases, a reduction of 230kWh/m²/yr could be achieved with an investment of only 10 Euros per square metre.

The total costs of refurbishment per dwelling range from 1000 Euros to 4800 Euros, including all types described in Table 28.6, all locations described in Table 28.7 and all scenarios of intervention.

Cost-benefit analysis

Having simulated the reduction of energy intensities after refurbishment, the monetary return of such improvement during a lifetime could be estimated. The method applied by Ambiente Consultores (2007) is aimed at estimating the net present value (NPV) of all future costs and benefits for each single refurbishment alternative. For the costs calculation, the following input data were considered:

- initial investment in materials, transportation and installation of all refurbishment elements;
- energy consumption costs at current prices, considering that for each location a different mix of fuels is used, from which the equivalent cost of 1kWh was estimated;

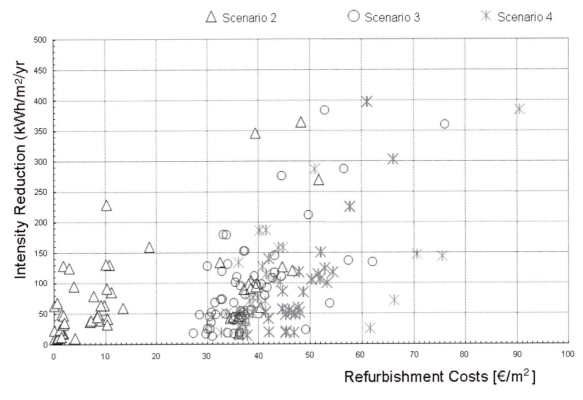

Figure 28.13 *Energy intensity reduction versus refurbishment costs for all cases*

- maintenance costs, estimating cost of labour and parts, including repairs from moisture damage;
- initial value, useful lifetime and residual value (the evaluation was made assuming a 20-year horizon).

The following assumptions were also considered:

- *Escalation rate (ER) of future prices of oil-derivative fuels.* Two rates were considered: a conservative one at 4 per cent increase per year, equivalent to the average from 1995 to 2005, and a realistic one, estimated at a 10 per cent yearly increase.
- *Discount rate.* Two options were considered: a social rate at 8 per cent for public investments and a private rate at 12 per cent for the private sector.

For estimating benefits, the following factors were considered:

- *Avoided costs in health services.* Only the costs for the health system related to a reduction in

environmental pollution (and not including patient valuation or labour time loss) were included.

- *Avoided costs in fuel.* These costs were obtained from the energy intensity differences with the baseline and the estimated fuel prices.
- *Reduction in maintenance frequency.*
- *Increase in residual value.* A growing residual value was assigned to progressive intervention scenarios.

Results were that for the highest degree of intervention (scenario 4), all cases but one showed positive NPV at an oil price ER of 10 per cent per year, evaluated at ten years. At the same scenario 4, but with an ER of 4 per cent, only 24 cases showed positive NPV, pointing to those types and cities where refurbishment is still profitable in less than ten years. NPVs are very sensitive to price escalation rate. Differences between building types are significant. Regional differences are mainly due to climate, with some exceptional results:

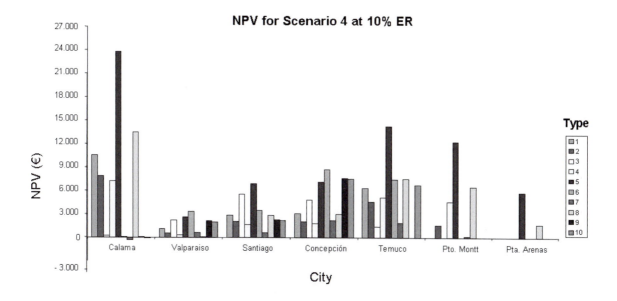

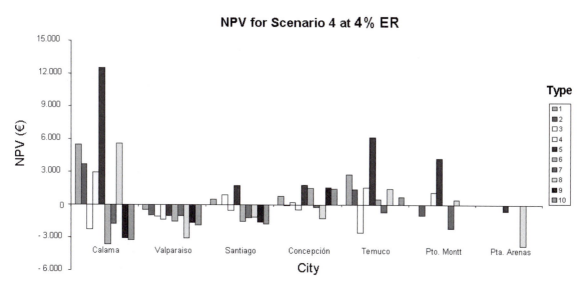

Figure 28.14 *Net present value after ten years of maximum refurbishment (scenario 4) for all types and cities at oil price escalation rates of 10 per cent (above) and 4 per cent (below)*

- Punta Arenas has the coldest climate, but an inexpensive natural gas supply; and
- Calama has cold nights every day of the year, but daily maximum temperatures above 20°C, which would allow for passive energy savings by means of thermal mass (not included in this simulation).

For scenario 3, results were similar to those of scenario 4.

For scenario 2, in all cases, NPVs at ten years were positive for both high and low ER. This result confirms

that a goal at least equivalent to the thermal regulation is justified under any future price condition.

Higher goals such as those of scenarios 3 and 4 are fully justified in certain places and with certain types.

Other expected benefits

A number of expected benefits were also identified, both social and private.

Expected social impacts include:

- *Energy security.* Less dependence upon imported fossil fuels would partially alleviate the impact of price increase. Lower demand would allow a shift towards local renewable sources based on biomass without exhausting natural resources.
- *Higher efficiency.* Lower burdens on budget would release financial resources after payback of investment is completed. Private savings could be redirected towards other investment sectors, improving capital mobility.
- *Higher comfort levels.* Higher and more uniform temperatures would be achieved. There would be less discomfort from cold walls, draughts and excess humidity.
- *Improved air quality.* Less fuel combustion in heating appliances would reduce emissions and lower concentrations of air pollutants, both indoors and outdoors, particularly in urban neighbourhoods.
- *Avoided health costs.* Reduction in diseases related to cold, mould and air pollution would mitigate loads on health services, particularly those for children, old people, people with chronic respiratory diseases and other sensitive population groups.
- *Lower carbon emissions.* Lowering the demand for heating would necessarily reduce the aggregated greenhouse gas emissions from fuels or electricity.
- *Employment.* Qualified staff would be required for proper installation of windows, wall cladding or loft insulation. Suppliers of parts and materials would also increase local employment.
- *Research, development and innovation.* Technology transfer, new solutions and optimization tools would increase research and development (R&D) activity. Experimental research and certification results would provide valuable information on successful solutions.
- *Native forest conservation.* Unlawful extraction of wood from native forests would be reduced because of the lower demand for heating.
- *Improved visibility.* Reduced atmospheric turbidity would improve visibility and mitigate the negative effects on safety.
- *Resilience against natural disasters.* Self-sustainment, local energy supply and less vulnerability to extreme weather, would mitigate the effect of hazards, particularly in a country with high seismic activity.

Expected private impacts include:

- *Energy savings.* Reduction in fuel and electricity expenses would directly benefit household budget. The cost of fuel storage and seasonal stock financing would also be reduced.
- *Lower depreciation.* The commercial value of properties would rise due to better performance, particularly if an energy performance certificate is provided. The market value of such certificates could immediately compensate for refurbishment costs.
- *Investment security.* The life cycle is extended. Capital assets are less vulnerable to future energy price fluctuations or energy shortage. The risk of vacancy due to high running costs is reduced.
- *Maintenance savings.* Maintenance frequency would be reduced, particularly on paints and wooden parts. Damage from condensation and freezing would also be diminished. Extended life would result in less frequent replacement of parts.
- *Comfort improvement.* More uniform temperatures throughout the house or flat, particularly for direct heating appliances, results in a larger useful area. Better windows would reduce cold spots and draughts. Higher temperatures of inner surfaces would improve the balance between radiant temperature and air temperature.
- *Health.* Better control of temperature and moisture would reduce the impacts on health due to damp walls, insufficient heating or cold spells.

Potential programmes

Box 28.8 Energy and sustainability

Chile has an immeasurable opportunity for progress towards a more sustainable energy policy. Even if more than 30 years have been lost in this subject because of inaction and ideological biasing, we are prepared to take advantage of the international experience, avoiding the mistakes made in the past and taking in the successful achievements in institutional and technical issues, as well as regulatory and promotion mechanisms.

The essential bases of energetic sustainability are:

- safe and timely supply, with reasonable quality and cost;
- energy and equality in terms of access to energy use, including local and economic issues;
- energy and environmental sustainability (most large energy projects have cast doubt about their environmental impacts not being fairly assessed or mitigated);
- energetic dependence (this topic has been long mentioned, but only recently has awareness been raised in Chile after gas shortages began in 2004);
- energy, community involvement and democracy (strengthening democracy is no doubt a foundation of sustainable development and this means creating channels for active citizenship to discuss issues such as the setting and technology of energy projects or property concentration in the energy sector).

Source: adapted from Maldonado (2006)

Proposed refurbishment programme

A progressive investment programme is structured by three objectives:

1 investment in substandard housing and low-income households located in polluted urban areas, maximizing social benefits;
2 investment in medium-income households, promoting massive refurbishment and maximizing both social and private benefits;
3 investment in promoting private investment and breaking market failures, maximizing private benefits and reducing the country's energy dependence.

Financing schemes

A programme for refurbishment of 20 per cent of dwellings built before 2000, to be implemented in 18 years, was proposed. This involves an average of 50,000 refurbishments per year, and a total public investment of about 1000 million Euros. Private investment would follow according to oil price evolution; but it is expected to be at least a similar amount. Some barriers limiting the feasibility of this programme are the lack of human resources to implement it and the uncertainty about the remaining lifetime of buildings.

The proposed programme includes three basic financing schemes. The first one, oriented towards low-income residents, is a full subsidy for refurbishment of up to 1400 Euros, provided the household is already registered as belonging to one of the two lower-income quintiles, the dwelling is located in a polluted area and the dwelling qualifies as 'unacceptable but recoverable'. This is a very favourable alternative to cash compensations for fuel price increase and also an alternative to extending health services.

The second proposed scheme is a matching grant for households that refurbish their dwelling to achieve the thermal standard of a new construction. The matching grant would benefit individual households or communities with non-returnable help of up to 1400 Euros per unit, not exceeding 50 per cent of total refurbishment cost.

The third proposed scheme would benefit larger energy consumers and only provides a mechanism for access to low-interest loans. The mechanism could be based on a situation where, after a given period of repayments on a loan, by which the capital is partially amortized, the guarantee provided to the bank by the total value of the property would also suffice to guarantee a further loan for refurbishment without the requirement on the part of the bank for a further guarantee. This could result in an increase in payments, which is typically less than the savings in energy expenses. The advantage of this scheme is that due to the low interest of mortgage loans, there would be no extra cash flow compared to previous loans if the remaining loan period is long enough. In case the debtor has not enough income to afford the increase in payments, the number of payments could be extended.

This scheme could break the barrier of initial investment without affecting the household budget. In addition, it is likely that the property would increase its commercial value, particularly if it achieves some certification, with benefit for both the owner and the lender.

A pilot programme under way

A more detailed analysis is focused on two districts of the Araucanía region: Temuco and Padre Las Casas, an example of the critical role of past housing design on users' welfare and long-term sustainability. The

Table 28.8 *Probability of use of appliances, by income group*

Appliance	Low income	Medium income	High income
Cooker	0.59	0.28	0.08
Foundry stove	0.10	0.04	0.03
Single-stage stove	0.11	0.39	0.30
Two-stage stove	0.00	0.08	0.09
Fireplace	0.00	0.04	0.07

Source: CENMA (2007)

Araucanía region has 930,000 inhabitants, of which 350,000 are in the main conurbation that includes the districts of Temuco and Padre Las Casas, with about 90,000 dwellings. Fast urbanization has meant more dependence upon energy supply and, thus, a higher number of pollution sources that eventually exceeded the natural capacity of atmospheric ventilation.

These two districts were declared 'environmentally saturated' in 2005 due to particulate matter (PM) concentrations exceeding $150\mu g/m^3$. About 87 per cent of PM pollution comes from residential wood burners for heating and cooking (PDA, 2007) (see Table 28.8).

A mitigation plan is under implementation and expects to reduce current concentration levels by 31 per cent by 2018. It includes improvements in fuel quality, combustion appliance quality and housing envelope quality. The total investment would be 18.7 million Euros and total benefits would amount to 55.3 million Euros (PDA, 2007).

A pilot project aimed at social housing has recently been implemented. At least 1000 dwellings would be refurbished during 2008, with up to 1400 Euros in subsidy, financed by the Housing and Urban Planning Ministry. Basic insulation treatments aimed at achieving compliance with the thermal regulations for new construction are being considered.

The effect of adding insulation to 1000 dwellings will be a reduction of 19 tonnes per year of particulate matter emitted by firewood heaters. The impact of such a measure may seem a small improvement of only 1.1 per cent of dwellings avoiding 0.5 per cent of emissions, adding up to 3737 tonnes per year of PM from all sources. However, since the programme has proven profitable in economic terms, it should be replicated as long as there are inefficient households willing to undertake it and capital resources are available. All estimations for pilot programmes have been made under extremely conservative assumptions.

The annual public benefits per dwelling are estimated at 119 Euros in terms of avoided costs in health services, in addition to 158 Euros of private savings (i.e. 142 Euros in terms of fuel and 16 Euros in terms of maintenance).

The cost of refurbishment will be 1332 Euros per dwelling (CENMA, 2007). At a discount rate of 8 per cent, the NPV of the avoided costs would amount to 1859 Euros for the first ten years and 2720 Euros for the first 20 years (authors' own calculation assuming fixed price for firewood). These last values would be the amount spent if nothing is done. In addition, enhanced quality of living would be a free benefit for households, as well as all other social benefits for the community.

Other subsidy programmes

Other potential subsidy programmes include the following:

- Subsidizing households that are currently using LPG for heating in order to compensate for price increases relative to 2007 prices, assuming an annual escalation rate of 4 per cent. No private or environmental impact is expected.
- Refurbishing households that are currently using LPG for heating. In this case there is a benefit for the household in terms of lower fuel consumption and higher levels of comfort. Assuming zero emissions from gas heaters, there is no environmental impact. In cases where the current heater has no flue, a flue type should be installed to compensate for less air infiltration in order to keep a healthy air quality.
- Refurbishing households that are currently using firewood for heating, and adapting to LPG. In this case there is a public benefit for eliminating a pollution source. A negative impact on the household is expected in terms of fuel budget and a positive impact in terms of higher levels of comfort.
- Refurbishing households that are currently using firewood for heating. Here there is a benefit for the household in terms of less fuel consumption and higher levels of comfort. In addition, there should be a positive impact on PM emissions because of less fuel burned.
- Appliance exchange in households that are currently using firewood for heating. In this case there is a benefit for the household in terms of lower fuel consumption and a public benefit for fewer emissions. An improvement of 50 to 75 per cent in thermal efficiency is expected, as well as emission reductions of 70 per cent.

Table 28.9 shows in monetary terms the impacts expected from different subsidy programmes for firewood users and LPG users, as well as firewood appliance exchange, all simulated for the current Temuco scenario under conservative assumptions.

Table 28.9 *Summary of costs and benefits of different subsidy programmes per household (own estimate)*

	Current LPG user		Current firewood user		
	Subsidy to LPG users	Housing refurbishment only	Housing refurbishment shift to LPG	Housing refurbishment only	Appliance exchange only
Cost of fuel price rise compensation (10 years)	−€1121	0	0	0	0
Cost of refurbishment (20-year lifetime)	0	−€1332	−€1332	−€1332	0
Cost of appliance exchange (10-year lifetime)	0	0	−€150	0	−€578
Annual savings in health services (public)	0	0	€170	€119	€131
Annual savings in fuel (private)	0	€855	−€150	€142	€27
Annual maintenance savings (private)	0	0	€32	€16	€16
NPV of public costs and benefits in 10 years	−€1121	−€1332	−€341	−€534	€301
NPV of private costs and benefits in 10 years	0	€5629	−€991	€1061	€288
NPV of all future benefits in the first 10 years	0	€5629	€349	€1859	€1167
NPV of costs and benefits after 10 years	−€1121	€4297	−€1133	€527	€589
NPV of costs and benefits over the next 10 years	−€4248	€2607	€1471	€861	€550
NPV of the costs and benefits after 20 years	−€5369	€6904	€338	€1388	€1139

Note: € = Euros.

It can be concluded from the figures in Table 28.9 that:

- The highest public return would be for a refurbishment and shift to LPG, but with a high private cost.
- The highest private return would be refurbishing a gas-user household, but with no public (environmental) benefits.
- Both refurbishment only and exchange only options would produce positive benefits in less than ten years.
- The worst option would be subsidizing the increase in fuel price (calculated at 4 per cent price escalation rate).

Conclusions

This analysis of housing energy performance in Chile has revealed how poorly designed dwellings can negatively feed the poverty cycle and how vulnerable to energy dependence such dwellings are. It has also demonstrated that there is no economic reason for not correcting the current deficiencies, thus avoiding future aggravation of energy supply or pricing. Responsible design, careful planning, interdisciplinary knowledge and accurate information are the tools needed to reach energy independence.

References

Ambiente Consultores (2007) *Programa de Inversión Pública para Fomentar el Reacondicionamiento Térmico del Parque Construido de Viviendas*, Urban Planning and Housing Ministry, Chile

Barrios, S., Peña-Cortés, F. and Osses, S. (2004) 'Effects for particulate material in atmospheric pollution on acute respiratory diseases in under 5 years of age', *Cienc. Enferm*, vol 10, no 2, Concepción, Chile

Baytelman, Y. (2005) *Comportamiento del consumidor residencial y su disposición a incorporar aspectos de eficiencia energética en sus decisiones y hábitos*, Department of Economics, University of Chile, Chile, www.cne.cl

CENMA (Centro Nacional del Medio Ambiente) (2007) *Análisis del impacto económico y social del Plan de Descontaminación Atmosférica de Temuco y Padre Las Casas*, University of Chile, CONAMA Araucanía, Chile

CNE (Comisión Nacional de Energía) (2007) *Balance Energético Anual*, CNE, www.cne.cl, Chile.

Collados, E. and Cifuentes, L. (2007) *Análisis del impacto económico y social de la norma de emisión de artefactos que combustionan leña*, Ambiente Consultores, Comisión Nacional del Medio Ambiente, Chile

DECON (2003) *Determinación de Modelos Tipológicos Base*, Instituto de la Construcción, Santiago, Chile

Defra (UK Department of Environment, Food and Rural Affairs) (2003) *The United Kingdom Fuel Poverty Strategy: First Annual Progress Report*, Defra, London

Ford, M., Gurney, A., Heyhoe, E. and Gunasekera, D. (2007) *Energy Security, Clean Technology Development and Climate Change: Addressing the Future Challenges in APEC*, ABARE Australian Bureau of Agricultural and Resource Economics Research Report 07.14, Canberra, Australia

Healy, J. D. (2004) *Housing, Fuel Poverty, and Health: A Pan-European Analysis*, Ashgate Publishing, Ltd, UK

IC (Instituto de la Construcción) (2007) *Determinación de la línea de base para la evaluación de la inversión en eficiencia energética en el sector residencial*, Deutsche Gesellschaft für Technische Zusammenarbeit (GTZ), Santiago, Chile

Lewis, P. (1982) *Fuel Poverty Can Be Stopped*, National Right to Fuel Campaign, Bradford, UK

Maldonado, P. (2006) 'Desarrollo energético sustentable: Un desafío pendiente', Paper presented to the seminar *Seguridad energética, América Latina: Reflejo de las contradicciones de la globalización*, French Embassy and Universidad La República, June 2006, Chile

Márquez, M. and Miranda, R. (2007) *Una estimación de los impactos en los presupuestos familiares derivados del sostenido aumento en los precios de la energía*, Programa de Energía de la Universidad Austral (UACH) and ASERTA Consultores, MINSEGPRES, Chile

McKinsey Global Institute (2007) 'Residential sector', in *Curbing Global Energy Demand Growth: The Energy Productivity Opportunity*, Chapter 3, www.mckinsey.com/mgi/

Moreno, L. and Rosenblüth, M. (eds) (2006) 'Brechas socioeconómicas de la población chilena', in *Umbrales Sociales 2006*, Fundación para la Superación de la Pobreza, Santiago de Chile, Chapter 1

PDA (2007) *Anteproyecto del Plan de Descontaminación Atmosférica de Temuco y Padre Las Casas*, Resolución Exenta no 1190 de 2007, Comisión Nacional del Medio Ambiente, Chile, www.pdatemucopadrelascasas.cl

Rodríguez, A. and Sugranyes, A. (2005) *Los con techo*, Ediciones SUR, Santiago, Chile

Sanhueza, P., Vargas, R. and Mellado, P. (2006) 'Impacto de la contaminación del aire por PM_{10} sobre la mortalidad diaria en Temuco', *Rev. Méd. Chile*, vol 134, no 6, June, Santiago

Speiser, R. M., (2008) *Energy Security and Chile: Policy Options for Sustainable Growth*, United States Association for Energy Economics, Working Paper 08-006, US

Index